Critical Acclaim for Gavan Daws's Books

"superb" *(BBC Radio World Series)*

"vivid" *(New York Times Book Review)*

"engrossing" *(Times Literary Supplement)*

"absolutely fascinating" *(Washington Post)*

"beautifully written, deeply perceptive" *(Los Angeles Times)*

"wonderfully diverse, intriguing" *(San Francisco Chronicle)*

"absorbing" *(Los Angeles Examiner)*

"colorful" *(Kirkus Reviews)*

"excellent" *(Sunday Times, London)*

"eloquent" *(Toronto Globe & Mail)*

"rich in insights" *(National Times, Sydney)*

"marvelously detailed, human and colorful" *(Publishers Weekly)*

"unforgettable" *(London Daily Telegraph)*

Other books by the author

Shoal of Time

The Hawaiians
(with Robert B. Goodman and Ed Sheehan)

Holy Man

A Dream of Islands

Night of the Dolphins

Land and Power in Hawaii
(with George Cooper)

Hawaii: The Islands of Life

Hawaii 1959-1989

Prisoners of the Japanese

Follow The Music
(with Jac Holzman)

Archipelago
(with Marty Fujita)

Bite The Hand: A Play

Documentary Films

Angels of War

Man Without Pigs

Honolulu
The First Century

Honolulu
The First Century

The Story of the Town to 1876

GAVAN DAWS

MUTUAL PUBLISHING

Library of Congress Cataloging-in-Publication Data

Daws, Gavan.

  Honolulu : the first century / Gavan Daws.

    p. cm.

  Includes bibliographical references and index.

  ISBN-13: 978-1-56647-779-6 (hardcover : alk. paper)

  ISBN-10: 1-56647-779-4 (hardcover)

  1. Honolulu (Hawaii)--History--18th century. 2. Honolulu (Hawaii)--History--19th century. I. Title.

  DU629.H7D39 2006

  996.9'31--dc22

                          2006019095

First Printing, September 2006

1 2 3 4 5 6 7 8 9

ISBN-10: 1-56647-779-4

ISBN-13: 978-156647-779-6

Design by Mardee Domingo Melton

Mutual Publishing, LLC

1215 Center Street, Suite 210

Honolulu, Hawai'i 96816

Ph: (808) 732-1709

Fax: (808) 734-4094

email: info@mutualpublishing.com

www.mutualpublishing.com

Printed in Taiwan

Table of Contents

Author's Note

Before the Hawaiian Islands were first set down on Western maps in 1778-1779, Honolulu was an unremarkable little village, a scattering of grass huts on a hot, dusty plain. Over the next half century, it became *the* community of Hawai'i, and it has remained so.

What transformed Honolulu was its harbor, opened up to the West by trading vessels in the 1790s–the only protected harbor in the islands that would admit deep-draught ships.

Honolulu's harbor was where the great world could come in– and come in it did. By the middle of the nineteenth century, Honolulu was the biggest and busiest island port town in the Pacific Ocean–in fact a port of world significance. It was the center of trade for Hawai'i, and the center of population, both native and foreign. It was also the capital of the Hawaiian kingdom, the seat of royalty, the focus of Hawaiian tradition. And at the same time, the town was the great breeding ground of social change and disruption.

This book takes the story of Honolulu to 1876, when a commercial treaty was signed with the United States that put the Hawaiian monarchy on the path to dispossession, and Hawai'i on the path to annexation by the US in 1898.

That is history. And the book is itself a historical document. It was written four decades ago, as my doctoral dissertation–the first PhD in Pacific History done at the University of Hawai'i, completed in 1966. (A sidebar about the passage of time: Those were the days before copying machines, let alone computers and the Web. All my notes were taken by hand, written or typed on half-sheets of 8 ½x 11-inch paper. How long ago that seems.)

I had no impulse to see my dissertation published. I have never been much of a fan of dissertations put into print in full (in fact they are almost always overfull–overstuffed). While I was drafting chapters, I did lift a couple of sections from the text for articles. And then, about halfway through, I got a contract with Macmillan in New York to write a general history of Hawai'i. That turned into *Shoal of Time*. Because Honolulu was the national capital, a lot of the history of the Hawaiian kingdom was made on the streets of the town. So some quite sizeable parts of the dissertation turned up in *Shoal*, which was published in 1968. Now, all these years later, the dissertation is going into print–borrowings for *Shoal* and all. I have to hope that the statute of limitations on self-copying has run…

The suggestion that the dissertation could be brought out as a book of local interest came from Bennett Hymer of Mutual Publishing. His thought was that the timing was suitable. The first decade of the 21st century is the centennial decade of Honolulu as a legally constituted and organized American city. Why not publish the prequel, so to speak–the story of the first generations of contact with the outside world?

Certainly early Honolulu had its own colorful story, about how its particular identity was shaped in those decades–a town like no other in the islands, and like no other for thousands of miles in any direction across the Pacific. So, indeed, why not?

I had not looked at the dissertation for more than half my life. It was typed by my wife on a manual machine–the amazing new IBM Selectric of the 1960s, with its whiteout function and its interchangeable fonts, being financially quite out of the question for us. The paper was showing signs of ageing; the ink of the ribbon typescript was graying. I read it through, slowly, putting it down, picking it up again, in alternating phases of partial recognition and total non-recall–what? whose voice was that?–and decided that if it was going to go into print, best that it should be published just as it was written then, no rethinking or recasting or spiffing up of phrases, to be read now as what the passage of time has turned it into–a historical document.

The only alteration in the text has been to put diacritical markings in Hawaiian words. This was not the practice in the 1960s; it is now; and on balance it made sense to have someone knowledgeable make the change. Currently, there are other questions about rendering Hawaiian words in an English-language text–whether to italicize, whether to add an *s* for a plural, and so on. Discussion continues, tilting this way and that. Bennett and I decided to leave those things the way I wrote them then.

So, except for diacriticals, the text is as it was. It has been digitally scanned for publication–footnotes, bibliography and all, with the addition of a computer-generated index. And some illustrations.

G.D.
Honolulu, June, 2006.

CHAPTER 1

The Early Years

High in the mountains behind Honolulu, the valley of Nuʻuanu takes on the shape of a great amphitheater; and there, where the northeast trades blow in off the Pacific and heap rain clouds upon the Koʻolau range, several small streams have their headwaters. To windward is the sheer thousand-foot drop of the Nuʻuanu Pali; on the leeward side, sloping valleys guide the streams in a southerly direction toward the coast of Oʻahu. Within a mile of their source, the waters fall about a thousand feet, hurrying through a country of dank forest and weathered rock. Farther down the valley, where winds and mists give way to calm sunlight, a single major stream (Nuʻuanu) emerges; then, when it has come close to the shore, it is joined by new tributaries from east and west (Pauoa and Waolani), and these waters mingle, flowing on to the sea by warm, dry coastal flats, until they are released in Honolulu harbor through a common mouth.

On either side of Nuʻuanu, this pattern of ridges and valleys and watercourses is repeated. Many streams drain the uplands of south-eastern Oʻahu, their paths to the sea set long ago by volcanic eruptions which shaped the island's mountain ranges and raised smaller eminences close to Honolulu such as Lēʻahi (Diamond Head) and Puʻuowaina (Punchbowl).[1]

Off the southern coast, fresh water meets salt in protected shallows, for much of Oʻahu is reef-bound. Indeed parts of the island itself are made up of stranded coral reefs. There have been several changes in the level of the ocean around the Hawaiian archipelago, and on Oʻahu it is possible to find great deposits of coral as high as ninety feet above sea level and as far down as eight hundred feet below the ground. In the course of the current period of surface stability, coral colonies have once again ringed the coast. Growth on the leeward side of Oʻahu has always been less extravagant than to windward; but even so the coral, in life very delicate, at the mercy of tide, temperature and predatory organisms, has in death confined the mouths of many streams to narrow channels and shallow waters.[2]

This process, the work of scores of thousands of years, was so far advanced when the Hawaiian islands were discovered by white men that only one place existed along the southern coast of O'ahu where deep-draught ships might find a way through the reef to protected moorings. From Wailupe to Waikīkī there was nothing but offshore anchorage; and at Pu'uloa a maze of reefs blocked access to the great harbor within. But at Honolulu, the ceaseless flow of Nu'uanu stream had produced in the harbor a conformation of raised coral reefs and mudflats, with a narrow navigable channel between, and deep water close to the shore at one point. Nowhere else in all the Hawaiian chain was such a set of conditions duplicated; and in this singular circumstance the city of Honolulu found the reason for its origin.

Honolulu had not been of great importance to the Hawaiians. Like many places in the archipelago, it was hot and dry, with a sparsely-covered hinterland stretching back toward cooler, richer valleys. Its beaches were indifferent, and the natives had no need of a deep-water harbor. With the spread of population in the centuries before the islands were discovered by white men, its valleys and reefs were worked systematically, but it never became a favored place of residence for the peripatetic great chiefs.[3]

When, at the end of the eighteenth century, white men brought O'ahu and the other Hawaiian islands into contact with a greater world, Waikīkī rather than Honolulu displayed the traditional life of Hawai'i in full flower. There, only a few miles down the coast from Honolulu, native chiefs and their subjects could enjoy constant sun and surf and gentle winds, fine sand and cool coconut groves, rich reefs and a well-watered hinterland.[4]

At Waikīkī, in orthodox Hawaiian fashion, the lines of production and consumption flowed, like water, from the mountains to the sea. There, as elsewhere, social groups had grown up within the land divisions natural to an island of valleys—the ahupua'a, wedges of land including mountain, valley, plain, seashore, and reef. The people of Waikīkī, like all Hawaiians, were able to associate their life, land and law with a great flow of dynamism, partly-felt, partly-realized, the source of all creation. Their universe was one in which the great positive force of mana and the regulatory and prohibitory force of kapu played directly upon the physical world. The most commonplace daily acts of building, planting, and fishing were invested with ritual significance and accompanied by ceremonial; and of all ceremonies, none were more important to the Oahuans than those performed by the ranking ali'i (chiefs) and kahuna (priests) at the Waikīkī heiau of 'Āpuakēhau and Papa'ena'ena.

The first foreigners who visited the southern shores of O'ahu were able to see Waikīkī at its best, before the harbor at Honolulu was discovered and the main currents of life shifted and began to flow toward the white man's world that developed there.

> The verge of the shore at [Waikīkī] was planted with a large grove of cocoanut palms, affording a delightful shade to the scattered habitations of the natives. Some of those near the beach were raised a few feet from the ground upon a kind of stage, so as to admit the surf to wash underneath them. We pursued a pleasing path back into the plantation, which was nearly level and very extensive, and laid out with great neatness into little fields planted with taro, yams, sweet potatoes and the cloth plant. These in many cases, were divided by little banks on which grew the sugar cane and a species of Draecena without the aid of much cultivation, and the whole was watered in a most ingenious manner by dividing the general stream into little aqueducts leading in various directions so as to be able to supply the most distant fields at pleasure, and the soil seemed to repay the labor and industry of these people by the luxuriancy of its productions.
>
> Here and there we met with ponds of considerable size, and besides being well stocked with fish, they swarmed with water fowl of various kinds such as ducks, coots, water hens, bitterns, plovers and curlews.[5]

At the turn of the nineteenth century, Honolulu began to displace Waikīkī as the natural center of life on O'ahu. The village on the harbor flourished greatly, becoming in two generations the overweening metropolis of the islands. In its speedy growth was implicit the transformation of a society several centuries old.

According to legend, the island of O'ahu was born of Papa, wife of Wākea. All Hawaiian rulers traced their descent from these progenitors, who appear in cosmogonic genealogies linking O'ahu with the other Hawaiian islands and with Polynesia at large. The name generally associated with the beginning of history on O'ahu is that of Newalani, a chief from "Kahiki" who came to O'ahu about thirty generations, or 750 years, before 1900.[6]

Traditional accounts of the early period of settlement record constant miraculous and supernatural interpositions in the affairs of men. Nonetheless, it is possible to view in human terms the lives of the chiefs who succeeded Newalani. By the time of Maweke (twelfth century?), the major political divisions of Oʻahu had been differentiated by inheritance—Koʻolau; ʻEwa-Waiʻanae-Waialua; and Kona, which included the area around Honolulu. In succeeding centuries, there appeared good rulers and bad, prudent men and reckless gamblers. The island passed through times of feast and famine, invasion and civil war. There were treaties and betrayals, parleys and massacres, courtships and abductions among the chiefs; and through all these Hawaiian society on Oʻahu moved toward the high level of elaboration and sophistication at which it was discovered by white men.

In the time of Pāʻao (23–25 generations before 1900), a new and more complex form of worship was introduced to the islands, in which a multitude of gods was served by an entrenched class of priests. Concurrently there emerged an elevated class of chiefs ruling within an intensified kapu system which protected them and at the same time pressed heavily upon the commoners. Ultimately there appeared kings who controlled entire islands, and thenceforth their decrees directed the dividing of lands, the taxing of produce, and the fighting of wars.[7]

In this evolution Oʻahu shared, as successive aliʻi exercised dominion over provinces united or fragmented, and as the island was subjected to attack from outside. The commoners for their part worked the land more intensively century by century, taking timber from the forest, thatch from the kula lands, bark for kapa cloth from their plantations, water for irrigated kalo gardens from valley streams, and fish from the sea.[8] Every skill, every craft, every accomplishment, every product remained at the disposal of the king, in whose hands the well-being of society rested, and who, being above all men, merited nothing less than total obedience. Born, as the legends claimed, to the roar of thunder and the flash of lightning, he grew up handsome and strong, a conqueror of man and nature, touched by an aura of danger and devastation.[9]

By the time of Peleiōhōlani, king of Oʻahu in mid-eighteenth century, the predatory great chiefs had outgrown their island kingdoms, and were engaging in interisland raids. Such campaigns, calling for heavy concentrations of men and materials, could be waged only by warrior kings controlling large populations. The fruits of royal rites of fertility and husbandry were now devoted not merely to the display of kingly magnificence, but also to the service of the god of war. The building of luakini heiau (war temples), consecrated with human sacrifice, absorbed increasingly the attention of the ruling chiefs; and the war god's demands pushed them to explore the furthest possibilities of their right to rule, leading them to invoke continued divine support by inflicting death and offering sacrificial victims in great numbers. In all this, the initiative lay with the windward kings, who controlled the two largest islands—Hawai'i and Maui. Peleiōhōlani was the last king of O'ahu able to stand against them. After his death, the blasts of aggression blew ever more strongly from windward to leeward. For a time, the dominant figure was Kahekili of Maui, who annexed O'ahu while on Hawai'i other contesting chiefs tried their strength. Out of that contest emerged Kamehameha, the great tiger-shark, who swallowed all.

Neither Peleiōhōlani nor any other chief of his time could have foreseen this course of events, for its catalyst—the white man—had not yet appeared. Then, toward the end of Peleiōhōlani's reign, the islands were discovered by Captain James Cook, R.N. At daybreak on January 18, 1778, his ships, sailing from the South Pacific for the northwest coast of America, raised two islands, one to their northeast, the other to their north. Light airs and calms held the vessels eight or nine leagues from land till sunset, and overnight they drifted some distance westward. At sunrise on January 19, the first island lay several leagues to the east. To reach it, Cook would have had to sail directly into the wind, and accordingly he made for the second island. So Kaua'i, not O'ahu, first received the impress of the foreigner.[10]

Cook landed on Kaua'i and Ni'ihau, and then stood away to the north, returning early in the next year to the windward islands, where he met his death, at Kealakekua Bay, Hawai'i, on February 14, 1779. About two weeks later, his ships, making their way up the chain to leeward, put in for water on the west coast of O'ahu, and for the first time white men set foot on the island. Peleiōhōlani was not there to greet them. He was at the east end of O'ahu, preparing to fight a war on Moloka'i. He had perhaps seen the British ships pass; but before he came home from his campaigns they had left the archipelago.[11]

Two more kings ruled on O'ahu before white men reappeared. Upon Peleiōhōlani's death, the island passed to his son Kūmahana. His reign was short; after three years the O'ahu chiefs conspired to depose him. "So thoroughly had he succeeded, during his short incumbency of office, to make himself disliked, that, in an age so peculiarly prone to factions, not a voice was heard nor a spear raised in his defence."[12] The O'ahu chiefs selected Kahahana as their new king. He was to be the last independent sovereign of O'ahu.[13]

Kahahana, born on O'ahu, was brought up on Maui as the foster son of the great chief Kahekili. Kahekili approved the ascension of Kahahana to the kingship of O'ahu, and the new ruler sailed with his retinue to be welcomed by his subjects at Waikīkī. Kahekili, however, was hungry for land and power, and he began to intrigue against Kahahana, hoping to weaken the younger king's authority. Successful in this, Kahekili massed his fighting men on Maui and invaded O'ahu.

He beached his war canoes at Waikīkī, surprising Kahahana, who was then living in Nu'uanu valley. While Kahahana was rallying his troops, eight of his warriors confronted Kahekili's armies at 'Āpuakēhau in Waikīkī. They killed many of the Maui men, but were themselves untouched by the spears that fell around them like rain. Makaioulu, one of the eight, a great fighter but slow and clumsy, was captured by the muscular Maui chief Kauhiko'ako'a, and was saved only when his friend Pupuka managed to strike Kauhiko'ako'a in the stomach with a spear; Makaioulu grasped the haft and pushed the point through the chief's body. All eight escaped, but they were unable to take with them the body of the dead chief, and because they failed thus to provide a sacrifice for the war god, their bravery counted for nothing, and Kahahana faced defeat in the campaigns that followed.

Disaster came soon enough, in spite of Kahahana's best efforts. Three times the Oahuans threw themselves against the armies of Kahekili, and as the battle raged behind Honolulu the corpses piled up, damming the stream of Kaheiki. Then Kahahana' s troops broke, and he and his beautiful wife Kekuapo'i fled to the forests. Kahekili took O'ahu, and for two and a half years the dispossessed king and his wife wandered miserably in the uplands, succored only by compassionate commoners. Finally, Kekuapo'i asked her brother for assistance—ill-advisedly, for he betrayed her husband to Kahekili, and Kahahana was tracked down and killed with his friend Alapa'i. Their bodies were taken on a double canoe to Waikīkī, where the new king waited. There Kahahana's corpse was sacrificed to the war god of Kahekili.

The rule of O'ahu, achieved with so much bloodshed, was maintained by further violence. After Kahahana's death, some of the remaining O'ahu chiefs plotted to strike down in one night the Maui suzerains who now controlled their lands. The plan aborted, and the vengeful Kahekili slaughtered most of the Kona and 'Ewa chiefs and tortured the chiefesses. In gruesome memorial, a Maui chief named Kalaikoa, living at Maunaloa, near Honolulu, built a great house called Kā'uwālua whose walls were made of the stripped and bound bones of the dead, and whose portals bore grinning skulls.[14]

Kahekili's rule was well established when once again foreign ships appeared. For several years after Cook no voyagers had come to O'ahu, or indeed to any of the Hawaiian islands. Then in June, 1786, the *King George* (Captain Nathaniel Portlock) and the *Queen Charlotte* (Captain George Dixon), British ships on a trip between the northwest coast of America and Canton, ranged along the southern coast of O'ahu and put in, ready to bargain for water.

With time to spare, and with the trader's incentive to find good harbors, the Britishers' coastal reconnaissances and inland walks still did not bring the anchorage at Honolulu into view. On this call, and on return visits made during the next twelve months, they watered first at Wai'alae ("King George's Bay") and then close to Kahekili's royal residence at Waikīkī ("Queen Charlotte's Bay"). With the king's permission, natives took supplies to the ships anchored beyond the reef; and the "chearful Woahoo damsels" arranged their own commerce with Portlock's sailors, inaugurating a long and vigorous tradition on O'ahu.[15]

While Portlock and Dixon were at Waikīkī in December, 1786, Kahekili built a house on a hill, sealed it with a kapu and used it as a place from which to tax his people's trade with the ships. He also toyed, apparently, with the idea of an outright attack on the white men. An old priest, who became something of a confidant of Portlock, pointed out a building which, he said, was to house Kahekili's akuas (gods). According to him, the chiefs were preparing to fight. Portlock readied his ships for defense, but the visit ended without unhappy incident.[16]

Kahekili's ambivalent attitude appeared again when James Colnett of the *Prince of Wales* put in at Waikīkī in December, 1787. Colnett's stay was very disturbed. Hawaiian thieves troubled him greatly; Kahekili came on board with a crowd of attendants, and there was a misunderstanding when he and Colnett jostled each other; a ship's dog chased some of the "Indians" around the binnacle. Later, there were fires and drumbeats in the village, and Colnett, convinced he could sense hostility looming, quickly set sail.[17]

In the first days of 1789, Captain William Douglas of the *Iphigenia* came up to Waikīkī bay, and, after some difficulty with fresh winds and heavy seas, anchored outside the reef. He was visited by Kahekili, who arranged to have hogs, kalo root, sweet potatoes and fish sent out. Kahekili cordially showed Douglas his village with its plantations and fishponds, but quite soon the friendly atmosphere was dissipated when Kahekili's people stole both of Douglas' anchors. The condition for their return was that Douglas should leave two armorers ashore. The bargain was finally closed with a musket, a pistol, and some ammunition, and a threat from Douglas that the village of Waikīkī would be burned if the anchors were not forthcoming. On return visits later in 1789, Douglas was made to pay very high prices for supplies, and to offer powder and shot as well.[18]

In all this opportunism directed at increasing his armed strength, Kahekili may have been doing nothing more than acting on general principle; but at the beginning of the seventeen-nineties there came a portentous challenge to O'ahu from Kamehameha of Hawai'i. On his home island, where no chief was dominant outside his own province, Kamehameha was still involved in local contests; but even so he believed himself strong enough by 1790 to confront Kahekili. He had been using a short period of peace on Hawai'i to build up arms. The times were favorable for this. As the fur trade developed in the northern Pacific, foreign ships began to put in at the islands in increasing numbers. Kamehameha acquired from them considerable weaponry, a small western ship, and two British sailors (John Young and Isaac Davis). He also concluded an alliance with the prestigious chief Ka'iana, recently returned from extensive foreign travels.[19]

Kamehameha struck first at Kahekili's island of Maui, which was under the government of Kahekili's son, Kalanikūpule. A few years before in an earlier clash, Kalanikūpule had been able to stand off the forces of the upstart Kamehameha; but now things were different. Kamehameha landed his army on Maui, paraded his sharp-toothed and glaring war god at Hāmākua Loa, found the auguries good, and defeated the forces sent to meet him, killing their leader in personal combat. He then marched his armies to Wailuku and drove the remaining warriors of Kalanikūpule back into 'Īao valley, steep and narrow. Women, children and old men watched from the heights as the foreign gunners Young and. Davis cannonaded into flight the traditionally armed and led Mauians. When all was silent but for the wailing of the women, Kalanikūpule was found to have escaped over the mountains, to take the disastrous news to his father on O'ahu.

Kamehameha sent an envoy to Kahekili to announce his intention of invading O'ahu. At Waikīkī the messenger confronted Kahekili, throwing down two maika stones, one black and one white. Kahekili read the symbols correctly: the white stone stood for peace, the black stone for war. "Go," he said, "tell Kamehameha to return to Hawaii, and when he learns that the black kapa covers the body of Kahekili [in death]...then Hawaii shall be the Maika stone that will sweep the course from here to Tahiti; let him then come and possess the country."[20]

Kahekili, in spite of this mild pronouncement, had no intention of allowing his own death to close the issue. He meant to take more immediate steps. On hearing that Kamehameha had returned to Hawai'i to protect his lands against a challenge from a local chief, Kahekili concluded that no better time could be chosen for the harassment of the victor of 'Īao. With his half-brother Ka'eokulani, consort of the ruling chiefess of Kaua'i, he grouped a fleet of war canoes at O'ahu and sailed for Hawai'i. With him went Ka'eokulani's s foreign gunner (known only as "Mare Amara"), some ferocious trained dogs, and Kahekili's special fighting men, the pahupū. Kahekili was named for Kāne-kahekili (Kane of the thunder, a god), and as a token of honor he had tattooed one side of his body black from head to toe. The pahupū were similarly marked.[21]

The allies skirmished and looted along Kamehameha's coastal lands on Hawai'i until Kamehameha's navy encountered them off

Waimanu. Young and Davis had mounted cannon on canoes, and on the western ship *Fair American*. For the first time a Hawaiian sea battle was fought in which both sides had foreign gunners.[22]

The campaign, though bloody, was indecisive. Kahekili withdrew to Maui, then to O'ahu. Kamehameha remained on Hawai'i, furthering his fortunes by the nicely-matched policies of building an imposing luakini heiau and permitting the assassination of his most dangerous local enemy.

During the breathing space which followed the battle of Kepuwahaulaula, events of the greatest importance took place on O'ahu: the harbor of Honolulu was discovered by the English merchant captain William Brown, and he became the first foreigner to involve himself heavily in the political affairs of the island. Brown's vessels, the *Butterworth*, the *Jackall*, and the *Prince Lee Boo* were engaged in the northwest fur trade, and in one or the other he made several visits to the islands in the early seventeen-nineties. Possibly in 1792, almost certainly before March, 1793, Brown found what others had missed, and took his ships through a narrow channel into the safe waters of Honolulu harbor—"Fair Haven," as he called it.[23]

The harbor had been elusive enough. Cook's expedition was miles to the west in 1778. Portlock and Dixon landed too far east in 1786–1787. On their departure they may have sailed past the entrance without recognizing what it was. So with Colnett in 1788 and Douglas in 1789. Joseph Ingraham was at Waikīkī twice in 1791, in the brig *Hope*. This was the year of Kahekili's campaign against Kamehameha, and Ingraham, like previous voyagers, found the warrior king faintly menacing. On neither of his visits did Ingraham look closely at the coastline west of Waikīkī.[24]

The next important visitor to O'ahu, George Vancouver, scrutinized the leeward shores in 1792 and noted two possible harbor openings, but did not enter either one.[25] Vancouver returned in March, 1793, on a disciplinary mission, to demand the punishment of the Hawaiian murderers of the surgeon and naturalist of his store-ship *Daedalus*, who had been killed while ashore at Waimea on western O'ahu. Kahekili produced three men for execution at Waikīkī, and they were duly shot. Then Vancouver, pursuing information he had picked up on the northwest coast of America, made another search for a harbor along the leeward reefs of O'ahu, under the guidance of Kamohomoho, a chief who had been helpful to him as a navigator off Hawai'i and Moloka'i.[26]

Kamohomoho took Vancouver from Waikīkī past Honolulu, and down to "O-poo-ro-ah," the impressive harbor of Pu'uloa (Pearl

Harbor). Vancouver accepted without question the chief's description of "Honoonoono" harbor as being "very much more shallow, and a smaller place." Kamohomoho was right, and yet Honolulu was by far the better harbor for western shipping, as a century of experience was to show. Pu'uloa, although it offered unlimited anchorage, was all but impossible to enter. Honolulu, so Brown later told Vancouver, "is smaller, and of less depth of water,...yet admits of a passage from the sea fathoms deep between the reefs; and opens beyond them into a small but commodious bason [sic] with regular soundings from 7 to 3 fathoms, clear and good bottom, where a few vessels may ride with the greatest safety..."[27]

Brown capitalized on his discovery by making an agreement with Kahekili under which the king "ceded" O'ahu (and perhaps Kaua'i) in return for Brown's guarantees of military assistance. What Kahekili meant by "cession" is not at all clear, though no doubt he was prepared to offer Brown the use of land and supplies in exchange for help in building up his armed strength against the time when he and Kamehameha might clash again (Kamehameha was certainly thinking along these lines when he and Vancouver negotiated a similar "cession" in 1794). The battle of Kepuwahaulaula off Waimanu in 1791 had been inconclusive: more red-mouthed guns might decide matters.

The years 1790–1795 were pre-eminently a time of blood and iron in Hawaiian history. The "cessions" arranged by Kahekili and Kamehameha were nothing more than unceremonious pieces of *Realpolitik*, disclosing the Hawaiian ali'i in their trickster, vow-breaker aspect. The kings were readying themselves for large-scale war, and their preparations may possibly be traced back to 1789, when Kahekili bargained ominously over anchors and arms with William Douglas at Waikīkī. The seizure of the schooner *Fair American* off Hawai'i in 1790, the theft of a ship's anchor at Waikīkī just before Ingraham's first visit in 1791, and the theft of the arms of the murdered officers of the *Daedalus* in 1792 may all be interpreted as connected with the military situation, By March, 1792, in fact, Kahekili was looking forward to war.[28]

Kahekili never met Kamehameha again. He made only one call on Brown's naval strength, in 1793, when the two sailed to Kaua'i. Kahekili was able to quell an incipient rebellion there simply by the grandeur of his presence, made more striking by his dramatic arrival on Brown's thirty-gun frigate *Butterworth*, the biggest ship in Hawaiian waters. In mid-1794, Kahekili died at Waikīkī, leaving his son Kalanikūpule on O'ahu, and his brother-ally Ka'eokulani in control of Kaua'i, Maui, Lāna'i, and Moloka'i. Without an immediate need for a common front against Kamehameha, these two chiefs had a falling-out.

Ka'eokulani had been away from Kaua'i for some time, and he decided to make a voyage home. Kalanikūpule, unsure of Ka'eokulani's motives but suspecting the worst, went to windward Oʻahu where Kaʻeokulani's canoes would pass, and dug trenches and put up earthworks, ready for war. A fierce battle was fought on land while Kaʻeokulani's fleet lay offshore. Once more foreign weapons worked devastation on traditional methods of waging war: Kaʻeokulani's gunner Mare Amara picked off one of Kalanikūpule's war-leaders as he stood, feather-cloaked, directing his soldiers with sweeping gestures. In the end Kalanikūpule halted the fighting, and the two chiefs met for a day of "mingled joy and weeping—joy for the ending of the war, weeping for the dead in battle and also for the death of Kahekili."[29]

Kaʻeokulani set off again for Kauaʻi, but was given pause by his discovery of a conspiracy among his chiefs, some of whom planned to throw him overboard when the canoes left Oʻahu's west coast. Kaʻeokulani resolved not to die like a drowned dog. In an effort to turn aside the disaffection, he proposed war against Kalanikūpule, saying, "E aho hoi ka make ana i ke kaua, he nui na moepu—it is better to die in battle; many will be the companions in death."[30] His chiefs, diverted by the prospect of loot, were ready to follow him in this new venture, and they were joined by some Oʻahu warriors from Waiʻanae and Waialua. Kaʻeokulani ordered his canoe fleet hauled up on shore, and an overland march on Kalanikūpule began.

Kaʻeokulani may have been hoping for a repetition of the battle just fought on the windward side of Oʻahu, in which Mare Amara had shot and killed a war chief. Simply to raise his sights a little was to be rid of Kalanikūpule and be master of all that Kahekili had once controlled. But by the time the armies of the contesting chiefs met in final battle, the balance of terror was conclusively with the Oahuans. Kaʻeokulani, victorious in the first weeks of the campaign, pushed through the ʻEwa district, coming to ʻAiea in the early part of December, 1794. There he was confronted by Kalanikūpule, and by the men and muskets of the Englishman William Brown.

Kaʻeokulani was outnumbered and out-manoeuvred. Nevertheless he fought all day on December 12, 1794, until his forces scattered and fled. He and his party took to the uplands, and he might have escaped had not his feather cloak, mantle of chiefly dignity, stood out brightly. Brown's men fired at him, pinpointing him for Kalanikūpule's soldiers, who came down upon him from high ground. There he was killed, together with his wives and his warrior chiefs.[31]

Kalanikūpule's rule was once more secure. Back in Honolulu harbor, Brown celebrated the victory. His two ships, the *Prince Lee Boo* and the *Jackall,* lay at anchor close to a third foreign vessel, the *Lady Washington* of the American John Kendrick, another pioneer trader in the islands. Kendrick became a belated casualty of the campaign. He was having dinner when the cannon of Brown's ships were fired in salute. One gun was loaded; grape and round shot smashed into the *Lady Washington,* killing Kendrick and some of his crew.[32]

Kendrick was taken ashore and buried; that night, natives despoiled the grave and stole his winding sheet.[33] Had William Brown been a Hawaiian, he might have been alarmed by these omens of death and desecration afflicting foreigners at Honolulu. Lacking such insight, he could hardly have been aware of the impending treachery of Kalanikūpule. Victory on O'ahu had inspired the king to think of further conquests to windward; and on January 1, 1795, he and Kamohomoho put into execution a carefully-organized plot to take Brown's ships from him and use them to invade Kamehameha's domains. While Brown's men were dispersed, some inland, others at the harbor, the Hawaiians fell upon them, killing Brown, his second-in-command, and some sailors. Kalanikūpule then readied his war party, forcing the mates of the *Prince Lee Boo* and the *Jackall* to navigate for him. With several ship-mates dead, and Brown's body stripped and slung upon a pole ashore, the foreigners had little choice. The expedition made one false start, and, after re-organization, George Lamport took the *Jackall* out of the harbor, carrying Kalanikūpule and his wife and some forty warriors. The *Prince Lee Boo* and a fleet of canoes followed. Instead of sailing down the coast, Lamport steered abruptly out to sea; and in a few minutes crowded with violence, bravery and luck, he and his skeleton crew seized arms and drove the Hawaiians overboard. Kalanikūpule was sent ashore igno-miniously in a canoe. Lamport and the other mate, William Bonallack, took their ships to Hawai'i, where they wrote a laconic letter to John Young and Isaac Davis describing the plot and its outcome, and sailed for Canton.[34]

Kalanikūpule's military advantage was dissipated; Kamehameha knew it. Kamehameha himself was as strong as he would ever be.[35] No opposition remained on Hawai'i; he had a battle-tested army and a fleet to move his men from island to island.

In the early months of 1795, he invaded and took Maui and Moloka'i, which under Kahekili had been linked with O'ahu. In mid-year, he prepared to cross with his great fleet to O'ahu. At this point the, dashing chief Ka'iana deserted him. Fairly obviously there was bad blood between the two. Ka'iana, handsome, widely-traveled, with a large following and probably foreign arms of his own, may have been regarded by Kamehameha as a persistent threat. There was also a suspi-cion that Ka'iana had committed adultery with one of Kamehameha's wives. On Moloka'i Ka'iana was carefully excluded from the war coun-cils, and he came to believe Kamehameha's chiefs might be plotting his death. As the fleet crossed from Moloka'i to O'ahu, Ka'iana and a number of his men chose a separate course, landed on the windward side, and allied themselves with Kalanikūpule.

Kamehameha took his fleet around the coast to leeward and landed between Wai'alae and Waikīkī, where he drew his canoes up on the shore and advanced on foot across the plains. He drove Kalanikūpule's forces to Nu'uanu valley, and there the Oahuans made a stand on high ground, fighting with their faces to the sea and their backs to the Nu'uanu Pali.

Force of numbers, skill in generalship, the cannon of Young and Davis, and the muskets of other foreigners in the train of Kamehameha determined the result. Even with the advantage of high ground, Kalanikūpule could not halt the advance of Kamehameha. At the head of the valley, where the walls grew steep on either side and the precipitous pali at the rear prevented any orderly retreat and regrouping, the Oahuans broke, scattering along the windy mountains, some to make their way out of Nu'uanu by the highest ridges, some to find a way down a dangerous trail to windward, others to leap to bloody death on the rocks at the foot of the pali. For the second time Kalanikūpule had suffered defeat at the hands of Kamehameha. As he had done after the battle of 'Īao on Maui, he sought sanctuary in the mountains. For several months he remained hidden in the highlands of 'Ewa. But just as his own father Kahekili had hunted down Kahahana in those hills, so now Kamehameha brought Kalanikūpule to bay. He was found and killed near Waipi'o, in 'Ewa, and his body was brought to the king. In the sacrifice of Kalanikūpule to the war god Kūkā'ilimoku, the disappearance of O'ahu's independence was ratified. The union of all the islands except Kaua'i was confirmed, and the institution of Hawaiian kingship was raised to its highest level.

For years afterward, Hawaiians passing over the battleground of Nu'uanu could point out what they called the footprints of Ka'iana; they would plant their feet as he had done and stand as he had stood, where he halted to hurl his last spear into the smoke of the white man's guns. From that spot they could see the valley spread out below them, and all the landmarks of the victory of Kamehameha, who needed no single place to mark his conquests, but shared with other great men the right to say, simply: Look about you.[36]

CHAPTER 2

Honolulu Under Kamehameha I

From the time of Kamehameha's emergence as a formidable warrior until his death in 1819, great changes took place in the Hawaiian islands. Cook's expedition to the northwest coast of America in 1778–1779 produced, within a decade, a lucrative trade in furs which attracted the ships of several countries; and his discovery of Hawai'i provided merchantmen with an ideal place to recruit and rendezvous. At first, in the days of limited contact, Kamehameha, Kahekili, and even Kalanikūpule were able to exploit on their own terms the triangular trade of the Pacific (between the northwest coast, Hawai'i, and Canton), concentrating upon the accumulation of weapons of war, and attempting extensions of royal power.

Kamehameha's brilliant use of new techniques, indeed, was turned to profoundly conservative purposes. Throughout his life he was ready to make changes so that things might remain the same. His English gunners made him the greatest Hawaiian culture–hero of all. Later, as more and more ships came,, his control of the islands' resources remained so sound and shrewd that while he was king there persisted something like an even balance of exploitation, a measure of rough justice, in relations between Hawaiians and white men. Only at the most abraded points of contact, the ports—and especially those on O'ahu— was the social surface much scarred, and even at Honolulu and Waikīkī change did not become apparent for some time. O'ahu after the battle of Nu'uanu was a prize in traditional terms, a flourishing island with rich valleys planted in kalo and teeming fishponds on the watered plains and within the reefs.

Kamehameha, as O'ahu's new king, assumed as a matter of course the religious functions of royalty, but after his victory at Nu'uanu there was little time for him to become absorbed in the leisurely life of the aristocracy at Waikīkī. The last major island, Kaua'i, remained outside his reach, and, until it could be brought under control, O'ahu was nothing but a stepping-stone to windward. Still, it was not to be negligently held, especially as conspiracy was not unknown in the backwash of victory.

Soon after Nu'uanu, Kamehameha heard that some chiefs were plotting against him at Pu'uloa. He went there secretly at night and listened to their plans. His presence was unknown to the chiefs, and with a nice economy of effect he merely planted his dagger in the ground outside their house, leaving them to discover next morning the miscarriage of their treason.[1]

With this treachery disposed of, Kamehameha could turn in earnest to the unfinished business of Kaua'i. It had taken him four years to conquer the other islands: now he marshaled his resources for a last campaign. He readied his cannon-carrying canoes, and ordered his English carpenters at Honolulu to build him a forty-ton ship. The gathering army, including sixteen foreigners, engrossed surplus food; and, in the haste to prepare for war, cultivation of crops was neglected. William Broughton, at Honolulu twice in the first half of 1796, tried to dissuade Kamehameha from the attack, but the king rejected his advice and asked instead for rigging and equipment to finish his new ship.[2]

In mid-1796 the war fleet sailed along the south coast of O'ahu. There were offerings and human sacrifices at 'Ewa, on the heiau of the feathered war god Kūkā'ilimoku, whose staring eyes had witnessed all Kamehameha's victories. The invaders set off for Kaua'i at midnight; but in the rough channel strong winds and waves began to buffet the leading canoes, and many were swamped and capsized. The disorganized fleet returned to Wai'anae, to burden once again O'ahu's depleted food supply.[3]

Before Kamehameha could mount a second attack, news came from Hawai'i of a revolt led by Nāmakehā, brother of the slain chief Ka'iana. The king's presence was needed. Consulting his advisers, he decided to leave O'ahu in charge of his own trusted men rather than nī'aupi'o chiefs of senior rank who might take advantage of his absence to follow the example of the rebellious Nāmakehā. Kamehameha left for Hawai'i in September, 1796; within a few months the rising was crushed, its leader defeated and sacrificed.[4]

With no pressing reason of state to take him back to O'ahu, Kamehameha remained on Hawai'i for five years. All along the chain there was peace, and time for him to perfect an administration that would bridge the islands, maintain his security, and promote an orderly flow of wealth in his direction. Characteristically, his methods combined piety and pragmatism. He was a great votary of the old gods, a great builder of heiau; and he encouraged the yearly religious festivals which involved every district. Equally enthusiastically he built storehouses for the harvest of tax goods these festivals yielded, and used his riches in trade with foreigners. The great chiefs, possible competitors for power, were politely encouraged to dwell at court, under the king's surveillance;

and Kamehameha gathered about him in addition skilled and talented men and women of every kind. Over each island he set a governor, and between Hawai'i and O'ahu he dispatched canoe-loads of strong paddlers with master navigators and messengers to carry salutations and commands to his appointees.[5]

It was an impressive feat of government, drawing on the best of tradition and innovation to create an expanded and stabilized world of power for the king. And yet Kaua'i remained to mar the symmetry of the scheme. Upon this standing reminder of his one great failure Kamehameha turned all his warrior-king's rage. To the destruction of Kaua'i's independence he summoned the mana of his war god, the prowess of his fighting chiefs, and the concentrated energies of all the islands of his kingdom.

Even before the peacetime regime was well established, preparations for a conclusive strike against Kaua'i were begun. Kamehameha had returned to Hawai'i in 1796 dissatisfied with the war canoes that had sunk in the Kaua'i channel. Once the revolt of Nāmakehā was crushed, he set his chiefs to building peleleu canoes—twin-hulled, broad and deep, with a covered platform. The new fleet, eight hundred strong, was five years in the making; and during this time the king continued to add to his foreign complement. His shipwrights built him several schooners; and from his growing trade with merchant ships he acquired a large armory of muskets and cannon. Very little was left to chance, and if the effort was disproportionate to the possible reward, this did not matter to Kamehameha. His success was unprecedented, but not complete. He fiercely wanted total power. The extension of his wish, the peleleu fleet, was like nothing ever seen before in Hawaiian waters.[6]

In 1802 the great armada was ready. It left Hawai'i, led by Kamehameha and his designated heir, the small boy Liholiho. They put ashore at Lahaina on Maui, where the warriors remained for about a year, "feeding and clothing themselves with the wealth of Maui, Molokai, Lanai, and Kaho'olawe, and worshipping the gods." Kamehameha sent ultimata to the king of Kaua'i, Kaumuali'i, but received no response. Kaumuali'i was preparing to defend his island, and then, if defeated, to flee to the western Pacific in a ship being built for him by foreigners.[7]

The peleleu fleet moved on to O'ahu, arriving about the turn of the year 1804.[8] In the majesty of his departure from Hawai'i, Kamehameha had paid no heed to the warning of a prophet: "A man-made canoe you have to sail away from Hawaii, but a god-made canoe it will be that brings you back again, and there will be a great pestilence." In the spring or summer of 1804 an epidemic struck with dreadful effect. Kamehameha fought off the disease, but it killed many of his war leaders, chiefs and fighting men. Death came within twenty-four hours—men walking on the road might die before reaching home—and the corpses turned black.[9]

This was the first great western epidemic to afflict Hawai'i. Kamehameha resorted to traditional means to combat it. The gods were angry, and his priests advocated offerings—hundreds of hogs, coconuts and plantains; and human victims. Three men who had broken an eating kapu were seized and prepared for sacrifice. Their eyes were scooped out, their arms and legs broken, and at the appointed time they were placed upon the altar of Papa'ena'ena.[10]

Regardless of ritual, the epidemic ran its course, leaving the army decimated; and this disaster saved the king of Kaua'i. The peleleu fleet never sailed. The invasion was abandoned, the dead were buried, and at Waikīkī the war canoes lay beached and rotting.

Evidently, Kamehameha had planned to set up residence on O'ahu after the invasion of Kaua'i;[11] in any event, he remained there for several years after the epidemic. He did not mount a third campaign against Kaumuali'i. In realistic terms, both kings were likely to lose by war and gain by peace. War drained royal resources; peace might bring new wealth to the islands as trade grew in the Pacific. Kamehameha, perhaps considering this, perhaps discouraged by his double failure to invade Kaua'i, perhaps less obsessed with total power as he grew older, settled upon a compromise. He continued to add to his navy. In 1805 he bought the 175-ton *Lelia Byrd*, which became his flagship, and he kept carpenters, smiths and ropemakers busy in his naval workshops at Waikīkī. At the same time, however, he let it be known that he would be satisfied if Kaumuali'i merely acknowledged his sovereignty in person and paid him tribute.[12]

Kaumuali'i, willing to pay tribute, and ready even to bow to greater strength, was reluctant to make his obeisance on Kamehameha's soil, and for good reason: the last chief to meet Kamehameha in this situation had been Keōua of Hawai'i in 1791, who stepped ashore from his canoe at Kawaihae only to suffer sudden death by murder.[13] Delicate negotiations went on for some time, with canoe-loads of gifts passing. At last the chiefs were brought together by the mediation of an American sandalwood trader, Nathan Winship. Early in 1810 his vessel carried Kaumuali'i and his retinue to Honolulu harbor, and they came ashore, escorted by celebration. The diplomatic issue was settled—Kaumuali'i might continue to govern Kaua'i as a tributary of Kamehameha. So the conqueror rounded out his domains, and Kaumuali'i escaped with his domestic rule intact. Also with his life, though for a time this was threatened: a group of Kamehameha's chiefs had conspired to poison Kaumuali'i, but Isaac Davis warned him, and the thwarted chiefs turned instead upon Davis and poisoned him. [14]

It was at Honolulu, not at Waikīkī, that Kamehameha concluded his entente with Kaumuali'i. In 1809 he had moved down the coast from the royal houses at Helumoa by 'Āpuakēhau stream and established himself at Pākākā not far from the mouth of Nu'uanu stream, with his court around him. Honolulu had already increased in size many times by the year of Kamehameha's shift (from "not more than half a dozen" native huts in 1803, to "several hundred" by 1809–1810)[15] and certainly the addition of the court enlarged it further. Still, the reasons for the move are not altogether clear. It was surely not that the port had become over-whelmingly busy—in the first year of the king's residence, ships arrived at the rate of only one a month, and for some years Kamehameha had been well able to handle a comparable volume of Honolulu trade from his home at Waikīkī. Nor was Honolulu a more attractive place to live than Waikīkī. It was hotter and dustier. Nu'uanu stream was tidal, and fresh water had to be brought from the inland springs in gourds. The beach-front, though rich in fish, was marred by mudflats. Perhaps it was just another passage in the wanderings of the Hawaiian monarchy. Whatever the case, the Honolulu sojourn did not last long. In 1812 Kamehameha and his court departed for Hawai'i, and the king died in 1819 without ever returning to O'ahu. In the twenty-four years between the battle of Nu'uanu and his death, Kamehameha spent only eight years on O'ahu and only three of those at Honolulu.[16]

As concerned Kamehameha's control over his own people and his relations with foreign traders, it did not matter greatly where he lived. He was the king. Power flowed outward and downward from him. His word was binding at a distance; his policies were administered on other islands by subordinates closely responsible to him, and his presence was not needed in the details of bargaining with foreigners.

Trade was a royal monopoly. When Kamehameha lived on Hawai'i, incoming ships normally touched there first for permission to visit other islands, and Kamehameha sent with them a "confiden-tial man" to relay orders to his governors. In this way he could arrange simple provisioning, or the more complicated matters of ship-buying and salvage, and even the transport of tax goods on foreign ships.[17]

Wherever he was, however, Kamehameha involved himself in trade, and with great gusto. At Waikīkī or Honolulu ships would anchor outside and wait for clearance from the king's men—Kalanimoku (the prime minister), Isaac Davis (governor for a time), or others. Then, under the direction of John Harbottle, the English-born pilot at Honolulu, hawsers would be run from the ship to rows of canoes, and paddlers would warp the ship into the harbor. For both merchantmen and ships of war there would be cannon salutes, and then the king would come out in a canoe, sometimes alone except for interpreter and attendants, sometimes surrounded by feather-cloaked chiefs and court members, sometimes dressed in European magnificence, seated on a gun-chest, his hand upon a silver sword, sometimes wearing very little at all, but always with his tooth-edged calabash spittoon. While his queens lolled on deck or threw off their kapa dresses and swam beside the ship, he would bargain over quantities and terms with the merchant captains. Strongly-built, stern-faced, taciturn, he was in late middle age still a formidable presence. He was a shrewd, hard trader, a match for even the sharpest New Englander; and after arrangements had been completed he was not above using his prerogatives to help himself to small things that caught his eye—mirrors, handkerchiefs, penknives and so on.[18]

Kamehameha was well aware of the worth of the hogs, fruit, vegetables, salt, and water his people brought to the shore at his orders and of the miscellany of European goods they received in return. In practice a good deal of the trade was by barter, but values were often expressed in money terms. Whenever he could, Kamehameha took Spanish dollars or other specie in exchange for his goods, and he was most unwilling to let money go back into circulation. Before he left Honolulu he gave one visitor a guarded glimpse of a storehouse containing thousands of dollars. He was in fact a persistent, even selfish accumulator, a king whose feeling for largesse was stunted, a great consumer only of other people's goods, food and liquor. If he had one weakness as a businessman-monarch, it was his predilection for ships. His plans for the invasion of Kaua'i led him to buy and build foreign vessels far beyond the needs of his peacetime interisland trade and tax-gathering; but even so, he did not commit the spectacular follies of his successors in this respect.[19]

One other trade linked ships and shore. This was the intercourse of sailors and Hawaiian women, begun with the first vessels to touch at Waikīkī in 1786. It was a lively business, limited only by periodic kapu that halted all contact with ships, occasional prohibitions by martinet captains, and a tax levied by Kamehameha, who enriched himself from every form of commerce. Women would come out to ships in canoes, or would swim out, carefully holding their kapa clothes above the water in one hand, to prevent their dissolution. There was no particular unwillingness on the part of the Hawaiians to allow this. "The husbands and parents, not knowing that it would bring trouble," wrote John 'Ī' i, "permitted such association with foreign men because of a desire for clothing, mirrors, scissors, knives, iron hoops from which to fashion fish-hooks, and nails."[20]

Ships' captains might deplore the way women clustered on board, in the rigging, on deck, below decks; philosophic scientists might be led to wonder whether feminine shame was an inborn human attri-bute or merely a European trait. These questions did not greatly concern common sailors, who were happy enough to make the most of a few days at the islands after weeks and months on the womanless waste of the Pacific. Pleasant companionship was likely to make them forgetful of time, and evenly-marked watches on board tended to dissolve alco-holically into hazy days on shore. One liberty party (doubtless among dozens) which failed to return on schedule was sought by ship's officers, and was eventually discovered "descending a hill near the village, each with a lass under his arm, their hats decorated with flowers, ribbons, and handkerchiefs, and a fifer and fiddler at their head, playing away merrily. They were all nearly 'half-seas over,' and were on their way to the ship when they perceived us. They insisted in a humble good-natured manner on our taking the lead; and as we were anxious to get them on board, we accordingly joined them, and marched on at their head. We had not proceeded far when the Eeoranee [Liholiho, son and heir of Kamehameha] met us, and he appeared so much pleased with the procession, that he fell into the ranks."[21]

Many sailors from other vessels never came back at all, and no doubt Hawaiian women were among the several powerful persuaders leading them to jump ship at O'ahu. By the time Kamehameha took up residence at Honolulu in 1809, as many as sixty foreigners were living in the district.[22] About half of these were miserable loafers, Pacific drifters cast up on the shores of Hawai'i. Some, like the escapees from the British prison colony at Botany Bay, New South Wales, had no great love for the islands; rather, they had very strong reasons for not returning whence they came. Alcohol was the social bond of these low beachcombers. A Botany Bay man is supposed to have set up the first still on O'ahu; and "it was no uncommon sight to see a party of them broach a small cask... and sit drinking for days till they [saw] it out."[23]

Understandably, Kamehameha was eager to hurry this class of men off the island, and he encouraged ship-captains seeking crewmen to recruit among them. As for skilled tradesmen, the pressure was of another kind. The king was always ready to offer inducements to an expert navigator, sailmaker, blacksmith, armorer, or ship's carpenter to enter his service; and his foreign retainers increased in number year by year. Often they were given land and allowed to take native wives; not unnaturally, many were glad to forsake the harshly constrained life of the sea.

Those foreigners did best who were closest to Kamehameha. Isaac Davis, who had been with the king since 1790, apparently spent a good deal of time on O'ahu after the conquest. As early as 1796 he was "supreme" at Honolulu, handling the provisioning of ships. In spite of a quarrel of some sort with Kamehameha in 1808, he retained his lands and property, and, until his death, at the hands of the poisoning chiefs in 1810, was a man of great wealth. He lived simply, in a native-style house spread with mats; but nearby was a storehouse where he kept his European trade goods and his native cloth, mats, and feathers. On Oʻahu alone four or five hundred people worked his land and paid him rent.[24]

After Davis' death, Oliver Holmes, an American, appeared to visitors the most important man on Oʻahu, next to the king. Like Davis, Holmes worked for a time as governor, and was addressed by the natives as "Eree Homo" (Aliʻi or Chief Holmes). Since his arrival in the islands in 1793 he had acquired extensive lands on Oʻahu and Molokaʻi. At Honolulu, Holmes had 180 servants or tenants living around him, including some to wait on table, napkin over arm, malo at the loins, as he served roast pork and roast dog to his guests.[25]

The third notable foreigner at Honolulu in Kamehameha's time was Don Francisco de Paula Marin, whose adventurous life had led him from Spain through Europe to Mexico and California, and thence to the islands. He had a gift for languages, speaking Spanish, French and English. To these he quickly added Hawaiian, and for a time he served the king as interpreter. In his stone house near the water, northwest of Kamehameha's dwelling, he lived with one female chief and possibly her sister too, sired many children, entertained ships' captains with wine from his vineyard and highly-colored stories of his past, and directed the cultivation of his property, which included gardens in the rear of the village and a small island at Puʻuloa.[26]

Davis, Holmes, and Marin (and other lesser-known men) had accommodated themselves to native life at Honolulu. All spoke the language fluently. All accepted tenancy at will under Kamehameha as the condition of their residence and wealth. All had married one or more native women (William Davis, the king's Welsh gardener, had suffered the indignity of being cuckolded by a native, who took Davis' wife away to another part of Oʻahu). Isaac Davis was a convinced thatch-house dweller and poi-eater; and Marin, a curious Christian whose religious pictures, acquired in Canton, slid apart to reveal "subjects of a far different nature," entered at least part-way into the Hawaiian psychic world and within a few years began to see native-style apparitions.[27]

For the receptive Hawaiian, there was no better place than Honolulu at which to learn about foreigners. When John ʻIʻi was a small country boy he was badly frightened by two haoles (literally "foreigners," used of white men), who jokingly said they would take him away because he was crying; but after some time in the town he lost most of his fears, "for there were many who constantly passed through the town from visiting ships. As he learned to associate with them, he found them pleasant...Thus the boy began to lose his country ways...It was customary for the children to follow the haole men, who made friends with them and took them by the hand, in the daytime. But they avoided these men at night".[28] Sundown held no fears for native women, who readily spent evenings aboard ship. And as young 'I'i and his friends played around the harbor, sailing toy boats and drawing ships in the sand, full-grown Hawaiians were signing on for voyages to Canton and the northwest coast, returning to astonish their townsmen with acquired clothes, speech, and experience.[29]

Learning was clearly advancing well beyond the sometimes ludicrous imitation which added cartridge belts to kapa clothes, Windsor coats to bare legs, and beaver hats to women's heads. To use an interesting example, the Honolulu Hawaiians, great gamblers like the rest of their people, took up card games with avidity and quickly became very skillful. These pre-literate putatively non-sequential thinkers, well trained in their own kōnane game, could soon beat foreigners at draughts, as did Kamehameha's queens with the "scientific amateurs" of one ship bound for the northwest.[30]

More important, along the shore from Waikīkī to Honolulu Hawaiian craftsmen were working at foreign trades. The king's smithy was run entirely by natives, and other crafts were learned with great facility. This, together with the king's propensity for the purchase of foreign ships and his subjects' enthusiasm for Pacific voyaging, moved one or two of the king's privileged haoles to try to slow down the rate of change. When Kamehameha wanted Archibald Campbell to make him some new sails, Campbell asked the English carpenter Boyd to build a loom, and Boyd refused on the ground that if the natives found out how to do everything, there would be no place for the foreign trader and specialist at the islands. Campbell also noted that Isaac Davis did not want natives to learn English, for much the same reason.[31]

There was certainly no lack of industry in practicing either foreign or traditional crafts, as observers from Menzies in 1792 to Campbell in 1809–1810 remarked. Campbell, who lived in the Honolulu district for more than a year, thought Hawaiians worked harder than any people he had ever seen. They themselves thought so too, reasonably enough, since almost the only foreigners they saw were beachcombers and sailors on leave. One hardworking haole, the gardener William Davis, was so different from his fellows that the Hawaiians suspected he was really an islander whose spirit after death had gone to England and returned in a foreigner's body.[32]

The industry of the Honolulans was certainly stimulated by the expanding foreign trade in the harbor. Kamehameha had this in mind when he took the lead in planting and working large gardens behind the town.[33] But hard, productive labor had been the normal lot of the Hawaiian, and the port had not yet turned him into a client of the foreigner. The good health of agriculture was the good health of society.

Indeed, beyond the raffish and faintly disorganized life of the "beach" there was still a very sure touch about the handling of all traditional forms in Honolulu. Kamehameha's waterfront storehouse might impress visitors, but the great source of wealth on Oʻahu and the other islands was the soil, and this truth was reaffirmed every year in the makahiki festival. While Kamehameha resided on Oʻahu, the makahiki procession issued from the heiau of Papaʻenaʻena at Lēʻahi and made its way with its carved gods, the akua loa (long god) and akua pāʻani (god of play), from the ahupuaʻa of Waikīkī to Honolulu and Kapālama and thence around the island, collecting at the boundary of each district the tax goods of the season. Kamehameha himself annually guaranteed the validity of the tradition and its promise of good times to come by ceremonially standing his ground and fending off death as spearthrowers hurled their pahoa at him.[34]

The traditional arts—like spearthrowing and the other games that accompanied the makahiki celebrations—were still taught, and maintained their vitality in the face of innovation. By 1810 Kamehameha had a western-style corps of guards, less than precise in their manual of arms, over-elaborate with their "All's well" cries every ten minutes, confused about word and deed as they said "Fire" each time before pulling a trigger. People called them Kulaʻilua (knocked over, by the discharge of the musket). Their gestures and movements were curious: "One had to bring the hand around to ignite it. Like the pushing back, so was the igniting. Strange were the doings of those days." By comparison, the dexterous malo-clad warriors training each night with hau-wood spears, points unwrapped, on the throwing fields behind the royal houses, were very impressive. The various schools, especially the king's own, produced virtuoso spear-throwers and dodgers, recognized and admired by all; and children imitated them with spears made of bulrush stems.[35]

There were other odd juxtapositions about the town, producing a disconcerting iconography. Kamehameha lounged all but naked outside the European house being built for him. Natives had western names tattooed on their arms; in 1812 a visitor saw Billy Pitt (the king's prime minister Kalanimoku), William Cobbett, Charley Fox, Thomas Jefferson, James Madison, Bonaparte, and Tom Paine at Honolulu.[36] A lascar tended the king's ropeworks, which were superimposed on an old maika course. There were Fourth of July celebrations with fireworks in the king's pāuhi (yam patch). But all this was seen as superficial, curious and entertaining at most, to be put off easily like western clothes, not touching the heart of things, which was as carefully planted in the soil as the buried navel strings and bones of Oahuans of centuries past.

Any change might be regarded as extraneous as long as the kapu stood. Kapu defined the limits of every aspect of life—social rank, sex, food, work, play, and so on—and this brooding omnipresence was as much a part of life as shadow was of a sunlit day. Kamehameha observed rigorously the formal kapu days of each month,[37] and commerce with foreigners was interdicted until the kapu was lifted. As for the Hawaiians, neglect of serious rules might bring sacrificial death. The worst moments in the life of young John 'I'i came once when he almost dropped the cover of a chief's spittoon, and again when, at a heiau ceremony demanding silence, he was seized by a desperate need to cough.

He held his throat with his hands until his eyes and throat were red, but finally he could no longer bear it. He coughed two or three times, but, fortunately, was not heard by those who had imposed the kapu. Those who were in the house with him were distressed, and one person dug a hole for him to cough into while another supplied a basin of water. When the kapu-freeing prayer was uttered, and the need for discomfort was over, he was greatly relieved. Had he been heard coughing, he would have been snatched from this world.[38]

Kanihonui, a young relative of Kamehameha, was not so lucky. He brought death upon himself in 1809 by committing adultery with the king's willful wife Ka'ahumanu. Kamehameha had specifically reserved her to himself, saying "six islands are free, the seventh is mine" (Ka'ahumanu was the seventh 'island'), but the young man was a daring transgressor. He slept with her while Kamehameha was away worshipping at the god house. A guard informed the king. Kanihonui was killed and his body was taken to Lē'ahi, while Ka'ahumanu mourned and drank and surfed at Kapua in Waikīkī.[39]

In the face of such dreadfulness, the secular penalties of the western world—once the use of firearms was understood—must have appeared puny. Commodore justice had come to Waikīkī as early as 1793, when Vancouver demanded the execution of the murderers of the *Daedalus'* surgeon and naturalist. He wanted to make the "ceremony" as "solemn and awful as possible." Accordingly, he had the three victims publicly shot to death with a pistol by a chief. He then proposed to hang the bodies on a tree near the shore, but was told that this would be very improper, and would "greatly offend the whole of the priesthood."[40] Vancouver's stunted sense of ritual drama, besides being offensive, was rudimentary compared with that of the kahuna,

whose silent strangling and bloody clubbing and chanting and drum-
ming had about them nothing of the merely exemplary. Vancouver was
both before and after his time. Cook was long dead, and no later white
man shared his aura of divinity; and it would be another two generations before Honolulans could be brought to appreciate the spare style
of a western public hanging accompanied by Protestant prayers. In the
meantime the haole's general insistence on property before person, and
the daily round of ship-captains' kickings, cursings, beatings and whip-
pings in Honolulu harbor, no doubt seemed merely whimsical.

With society apparently still well-integrated, and traditional
sanctions impressive by comparison with anything imposed from
outside, there seemed no reason to suspect that the traditional order
was close to collapse. The king was growing old, but his son Liholiho
had already been declared heir. Still a young boy during Kamehameha's
Honolulu sojourn, Liholiho was being instructed painstakingly in his
royal duties, and was trying out his kingly immunities in various ways
such as banging together the heads of John 'I'i and his other small attendants. 'I'i himself was destined by birth and aptitude to take up a career
in the king's court, and, for all his daydreams of ships and horses, he
never imagined any other way of spending his life.[41]

By 1812, Kamehameha was ready to leave Honolulu. Again,
his reasons for returning to Hawai'i are obscure, except for inconclusive references to his old man's fear of conspiracies. Though he wished,
so some thought, to remain on O'ahu and end his days there, he had
"observed that the chiefs were increasing their households and culti-
vating large tracts in Ko'olau Poko, Ko'olau Loa, Waialua and 'Ewa to
feed their followers. They were also storing guns and powder bought
from the foreigners. This caused him great uneasiness..."[42] Preparations
for his return took several months. There was more than one false start,
but eventually he sailed with his court in the sandalwood ships *Albatross*,
O'Cain, and *Isabella*. With him went his wives, his son Liholiho and the
young 'I'i; and upon his departure a certain splendor left the life of
Honolulu. His rule continued to run there, no chiefs rose in rebellion, the
regular tax collections were made, the kapu days were observed; but the
king was gone, and his heir was learning to be king on Hawai'i.

In Kamehameha's absence, Honolulu continued to prosper as
the major port of the islands. Up to 1815, even with the development
of sandalwood trade, the pattern of ship movements in the Pacific
remained much as it had been earlier in the century. Vessels loaded
and wintered on the northwest coast of America or in California, and
made only brief stops at the islands on the way to and from Canton.

On the American coast the Spanish maritime hegemony had long been broken by ships of Great Britain, the United States, and Russia, all of which were represented in the ports of the islands in the early nineteenth century. Although Great Britain had begun to drop behind the United States in Hawaiian trade, there was still a great sense of royal fraternity in the mind of Kamehameha, dating from the time of Vancouver's visits in the seventeen-nineties. Until the end of his life, the Hawaiian king continued to alternate his requests for British ships with protestations of good will for the rulers of Great Britain. In 1812 the outbreak of war between Britain and the United States caused a mild flurry in the islands, where British privateers menaced American merchantmen, causing something of a pile-up of furs originally shipped for Canton; but peace left Americans once again in solid control of the Hawaiian trade, especially in sandalwood.[43]

Britain for brotherhood, then, and the United States for trade; and Kamehameha over all. With these relationships well established by the time the king left O'ahu, it was upsetting soon afterwards to find a Russian-employed adventurer working to engross the sandalwood trade and bring about a division of the kingdom. Since 1804 there had been Russian contact with the islands, and the possibility of a settlement there had been discussed. Nothing was done, however, and certainly nothing of the kind was officially planned when in 1815 Georg Anton Schäffer was sent to the islands on a simple salvage mission by Alexander Baranov, Chief Manager of the Russian-American Company in Alaska.[44] Schäffer's instructions had quite precise limits, but once in Hawai'i he was seized by that peculiar vision of realms and islands which was to animate a long line of political fantasts in the Pacific throughout the nineteenth century. For eighteen months Schäffer agitated the kingdom from Hawai'i to Kaua'i, and his activities left some permanent marks on Honolulu.

Schäffer arrived at Kamehameha's court on Hawai'i in November, 1815, carrying Baranov's instructions to present himself as a naturalist. Only after he had gained the king's confidence was he to raise the salvage question; having done so, he was also to arrange trading privileges and a sandalwood monopoly. In all this he succeeded for the moment. Kamehameha, disregarding the cautions of John Young and several American traders, gave the Company sizeable lands on windward and leeward O'ahu, and set aside one of his Honolulu storehouses as a factory. Encouraged by these grants, and sped on his way by rumblings from the king's advisers, Schäffer made a visit to Honolulu in May, 1816, and sailed shortly thereafter for Kaua'i, to transact his salvage business with Kaumuali'i.

Kaumuali'i, six years after his resignation of sovereignty to Kamehameha, was still an unwilling subordinate and a quiet irredentist.

Schäffer himself pretended to consider Kamehameha a dreadful tyrant, and the disaffected Kaumuali'i was more than ready to open the matter of a possible alliance. The two quickly disposed of the salvage case, and went on to conclude an agreement giving the Russian-American Company land and a sandalwood monopoly on Kaua'i. More was to come. By June, 1816, the king was telling Schäffer that "Maui, Oahu, Lāna'i and Molokai belonged to him [Kaumuali'i], and if Russia would help him to get them back, he would give her half the island of Oahu, and all of the sandalwood forever, and also whatever provinces I might want to select on the other islands."[45] This was heady talk for Schäffer. With the Russian flag already waving on Kaua'i and great gains in prospect on O'ahu, he sailed to Honolulu in August to buy an armed merchantman for Kaumuali'i, and to inspect the Russian factory there.

At once he came up sharply against the political and economic interests of Kamehameha's retainer John Young and the entrenched American traders. They insulted him and harassed his men. When he left once more for Kaua'i, they encouraged the natives to destroy his buildings at Honolulu. They themselves followed him to Kaua'i, and attempted to haul down the Russian flag, only to be turned back by Kaumuali'i's armed guard with fixed bayonets.[46]

Schäffer spent the last months of 1816 surveying his domains on Kaua'i, giving his lands Russian names (the beautiful valley of Hanalei, however, became Schäfferthal), calculating revenues from the cotton, kalo, maize, sandalwood, salt and tobacco he would one day harvest, and raising fortifications against the outside world. By the end of the year he was looking forward to confirmation of his proceedings from his superiors. It did not come. Baranov in Alaska disavowed his dealings; and when the Russian brig *Rurik* visited the islands late in 1816, its commander, Lieutenant Otto von Kotzebue, pointedly dissociated himself from Schäffer.

From his first landfall at Hawai'i in November, 1816, Kotzebue had been prejudiced against Schäffer. He was met by armed Hawaiians; and Kamehameha told him that Schäffer was encouraging Kaumuali'i to revolt, and had interfered with a Hawaiian sanctuary at Honolulu. Kotzebue took great pains to assure the king that Imperial Russia was not responsible for Schäffer's actions. At Honolulu, even with a king's messenger on board, the reception of the *Rurik* was hostile; and although relations improved after Kotzebue's meeting with the high chief Kalanimoku, there were still tense moments. The Hawaiians were building a fort at the waterfront, and when Kotzebue asked to inspect it he was told abruptly that it was kapu, especially to Europeans. An attempted survey of the harbor was resented by the natives, who saw Russians putting flags up and thought this marked a revival of

Schäfferism. Kotzebue willingly substituted brooms for flags. His own views were clear—the islands should remain a "free port;" and any attempt by a foreign power to take possession would no doubt fail in the face of American and British opposition. Having told every important Hawaiian he met that Schäffer was not a servant of the Russian government, Kotzebue confirmed this by sailing from Honolulu on December 14, 1816, bypassing Kaua'i altogether.[47]

Reality was beginning to close in on Schäffer. Kamehameha knew of his expansionist alliance with Kaumuali'i, and also knew that the scheme had no backing from the Russian government. Kaumuali'i must have been badly embarrassed to find that his partner's political credit was not good. On top of everything, the Americans at Honolulu were spreading rumors of difficulties, then of war, between the United States and Russia, and threatening that if Kaumuali'i "did not chase the Russians from the islands there were now eight ships at Oahu to come to Kauai and kill not only every Russian but even all the Indians [Hawaiians]."[48]

In the circumstances, it is surprising that Schäffer managed to hold an untenable position as long as he did. The end, when it came, was ignominious. Kaumuali'i forced him to leave Kaua'i in May, 1817, and, after a futile resistance, Schäffer set out for Honolulu in the leaking *Kad'iak*. He was not permitted to enter the harbor. George Beckley (Kamehameha's fort commandant) and a group of chiefs offered safe conduct for the Russians and Aleuts aboard if Schäffer himself would go as a prisoner to Hawai'i. When Schäffer refused, the Russians were told that anyone disembarking from the ship would be shot.[49]

Finally, on July 1, the *Kad'iak* was towed into the harbor by Hawaiians, who almost ran her on the reef. Three days later, the Americans prepared to celebrate July 4th. All ships in port were decorated with bunting; at noon Schäffer hoisted the Russian flag, upside down, the signal of distress. An American captain sent Beckley to order the flag turned around. Schäffer argued that his ship was still in jeopardy. "This caused a great commotion on the American ships," he wrote, "however, Captain Lewis, who declared the Russian position just, settled the dispute, which in the meantime cost several broken goblets and glasses."[50]

Isaiah Lewis of the ship *Panther* was Schäffer's only friend in Honolulu. He owed Schäffer a debt of gratitude for medical treatment the year before, and now he offered him an escape from danger—passage to Canton. With the agreement of his party, Schäffer left the *Kad'iak* in charge of a lieutenant, and on July 7 the *Panther* carried him down the coast from Honolulu, past the abandoned (indeed never occupied) land-grant at 'Ewa. Next day, the *Panther* anchored at Waimea on Kaua'i, and there, within sight of rivers and valleys he had explored and named for Russia, Schäffer knew the humiliation of being hidden in his cabin so that Kaumuali'i's natives would not see him.[51] On the way west to Canton, Schäffer amplified his casebook of American mercantile villainy; but this was after the event. Although there was desultory correspondence about the Hawaiian adventure for a few years more, Russian interest in the islands virtually returned to its normal low level as soon as Schäffer's ship dropped out of sight over the horizon. Kamehameha ruled still, Kaumuali'i remained confined to Kaua'i, and on July 4 every year the American sea-captains at Honolulu flew their flags and fired rockets.

When Schäffer sailed, Kamehameha had less than two years of life left to him. His royal power had survived unimpaired, belying his fears of conspiracy. He was to die as he had lived—the grand monarch. There was, however, one thing he could not control—the sheer volume of foreign traffic around the islands; and it was precisely at this point, where his royal mana and kapu powers approached an ill-defined boundary, that trouble developed. All through his reign a subtle subversion of Hawaiian life had been taking place, and in his last years the blows inflicted upon the material and moral order of his people assumed the seriousness of trauma. Soon after Kamehameha's death in May, 1819, change became revolution. The new king, Liholiho, at the urging of Ka'ahumanu and his mother Keōpūolani, assented to the overthrow of the kapu system, and ancient Hawai'i was dismembered and buried with Kamehameha's bones.

On O'ahu, from the time of the very first contact with foreigners, there had been problems associated with the kapu.[53] When Portlock and Dixon were at Waikīkī in December, 1786, they enjoyed two weeks of more or less unrestricted trade with Kahekili's people. During that time, too, women were allowed aboard the ships. Then, on December 1, the canoes left and did not return to trade again till December 17, at the completion of one of the four kapu periods of the month. From then to the end of Portlock's stay, no women came out. The captains were told that a woman had been discovered violating a kapu by eating pork on board ship, and had been put to death ashore.[54]

Peremptory handling of kapu-breakers was characteristic of the pre-white period. Had the woman broken an eating kapu on shore among her own people, discovery would have brought death. Subsequent visitors to O'ahu recorded instances of death for breaches of kapu. The only ritual killing at Honolulu when Campbell was there in 1809–1810 occurred when an intoxicated Hawaiian left the heiau during a kapu period and entered a house where women were segregated. He was seized and taken back to the heiau; his eyes were put out and he was left for two days, then strangled and laid before the wooden image of a god.[55] Several years later, when the *Rurik* was at Honolulu towards the end of 1816, the ship's artist Louis Choris saw the body of a woman floating in the harbor. She had been drinking, and had gone into a men's eating house. For this she was immediately strangled and thrown into the sea. During Choris' stay, too, a wife of the high chief Kalanimoku inadvertently remained longer than she should have on board an American ship one day, returning to shore only after the sun had set. By then a kapu period had begun. Women were not permitted on the water at such times. Ashore an angry crowd waited to punish her. She escaped the penalty, which was death, only through the intercession of Englishmen and Americans.[56]

This raises the question of the influence of foreigners upon the integrity of the kapu system. Clearly, there was confusion in this regard, although one or two reciprocal understandings, arranged quite soon after the discovery, continued to operate in a useful way as late as 1819. When foreign captains wanted to clear their vessels of natives (especially of women), they could declare a kapu and the chiefs would ensure that the prohibition was enforced.[57] Similarly, a general kapu announced by a chief would halt all contact with ships. Peter Corney, on one of his visits to Honolulu, arrived during the makahiki festival, when no canoes were allowed on the water, and his ship had to wait ten days before Kalanimoku and John Young came out to greet the visitors.[58]

Yet there were many instances in which ambiguities appeared. When Isaac Iselin was on Hawai'i in 1807, a sailor from his ship inadvertently stepped on kapu ground and was confined by Hawaiians until the kapu was lifted. Later, at O'ahu, Iselin's vessel had Hawaiian men and women aboard, and while the men dined with ship's officers, the women watched from a hiding-place and ate pork stealthily handed them by sailors—a double violation.[59] Campbell remarked, speaking of 1809–1810, that although kapu were "generally observed, the women very seldom scruple to break them, when it can be done in secret; they often swim off to ships at night during the taboo; and I have known them eat of the forbidden delicacies of pork and sharks' meat. What would be the consequence of a discovery I know not; but I once saw the queen transgressing in this respect, and was strictly enjoined to secrecy, as she said it was as much as her life was worth."[60] Without doubt Campbell was referring to Ka'ahumanu, who concurrently was taking advantage of Kamehameha's absences at the god house to sleep with Kanihonui, and to drink herself to intoxication with her favorite companions, two Aleutian women.[61]

Almost from the beginning, haoles and Hawaiians were treated differently with respect to their obligation to observe the kapu.[62] When

Colnett was at Waikīkī early in 1788, his ship was crowded with Hawaiians, including Kahekili and his attendants. At one point, wrote Colnett, "I took hold of the man they called their King he push'd me from him, which I laugh'd at, as a jest, the supercargo going on deck after dinner, the King was going to force himself into the Cabin, & on being told he should not, gave the Supercargo a shove, which he return'd & the King went off much displeas'd."[63] This insulting physical contact would have meant the end of a Hawaiian's life. Twenty years later, in Campbell's time, natives still had to noho, or squat, as the king's water gourds went by; but haoles were exempt from this observance. Kamehameha, however, once refrained from entering a house where Campbell was at work, because this would have placed the building under kapu.[64] Ross Cox, at Honolulu early in 1812, unthinkingly removed a western-style hat from the head of Liholiho, and was struck by the prince's attendant. The king's negro armorer Anderson, who happened to be passing, explained to Cox that any native who did that would suffer instant death.[65]

By the time of Kotzebue's visit in 1816 there was evidence of considerable disarray in the kapu system at Honolulu. A commoner's body floating in the harbor had greeted the Russians, but then male and female ali'i came on board ship to eat together—although some prohibitions still held within this irregular circumstance. Kotzebue had invited Kalanimoku, Ke'eaumoku (Ka'ahumanu's brother), John Young and others to mid-day dinner. They came well-dressed and well-mannered. Not much food was eaten, however. The pig served by the Russians had not been consecrated at the heiau, and it had contaminated all other food cooked at the same fire. So the Hawaiians watched while the Russians ate, and themselves merely nibbled at biscuits, cheese and fruit. Reciprocal toasts were drunk to the Emperor of Russia and Kamehameha, and all remained good friends. Women chiefs were at table (it was the Russians' impression that the kapu was less stringent on shipboard than ashore), and they drank heavily enough to become tipsy.[66]

Not long before the *Rurik* arrived at Honolulu, Schäffer's Russians apparently profaned a heiau, and a new one was built. Suspicion of Russians was still strong enough to bar Kotzebue from inspecting an incomplete fort; and yet, on the very night of the shipboard dinner just described, the naturalist Chamisso was permitted by Kalanimoku to enter a heiau, remain there throughout a kapu period, and watch religious ceremonies. These were familiar to Chamisso from the writings of early explorers. What surprised him was the attendant gaiety and merrymaking, which, he said, were so extreme as to make a European masked ball look like a funeral ceremony. There were entertainments during pauses in the rituals; Chamisso reclined on a mat and was served baked kalo and poi. At one point, he inspected a feathered basketwork god, and when, curious, he ran his fingers over its teeth, the young man carrying the idol moved it suddenly to make it appear as if it had swallowed Chamisso's hand, and exploded in laughter when Chamisso pulled his arm back.[67]

A little more than a year later, after Peter Corney's ship was admitted to Honolulu harbor at the end of the makahiki, normal trading and native life ashore were brought to a halt while the body of the recently-dead chief Ka'ōleiokū was prepared for burial. Natives, but not haoles, were forbidden to go on the water. Later,

> a crier went round the village, calling out, that if any man, woman or child, were seen out of their houses, or showed a light or fire, or even smoked a pipe, after 8 o'clock that evening, they would instantly be put to death. These restrictions extended not only to the white people, but even to the ships in the harbour; nay, hogs, dogs, fowls, etc., were not allowed to be out, lest they should make a noise, nor were the ships suffered to strike the bells in the morning.
>
> At sunrise the Taboo was taken off the ships, but still remained on shore. This day the priests were employed burning the flesh off the bones, and scraping them quite clean; the ashes were deposited in the sea; the bones were then carefully packed up, and a large double canoe despatched with them to Owhyhee. Six hours after the canoe sailed, the Taboo was taken off the bay, and the canoes were allowed to go on the water...

Corney was very much interested in the Hawaiians' religious observances, and he took the trouble to ask questions and record information about the chief's burial, the makahiki, and other ceremonies. One of his more interesting observations was that the common people appeared to know "nothing more about their religion than a stranger who never saw the islands," and he noted further that the chiefs told him they themselves went to the heiau "more to feast than pray, which I believe to be really the case." Chamisso, also an intelligent eyewitness of latterday religion, had remarked, independently of Corney, upon the strong element of play in proceedings at the heiau. Play, of itself, is not an unusual element in primitive religion.[68] But Corney went on to indicate that it was not play alone he saw—it was frivolous trifling: "Mr. Cox (the high chief Keeaumoku]...sets the wooden gods and priests at defiance; he says, that they are all liars, and that the white-men's God is the true and only God."[69]

There was apparently, then, some readiness for the overthrow of the kapu when it came in 1819. No steady, incremental progression had been visible; rather, a random and piecemeal erosion of values occurred in the course of some decades of confused and inconclusive dealings with foreigners. In time, the old certainties themselves were thrown into doubt. Prominent in this general picture was the monumental Ka'ahumanu, wife of Kamehameha, a woman of forceful personality and great political power, under disabilities as long as the kapu system prevailed, a close observer of the white man's ways, and possibly a cunning kapu-breaker herself as early as 1810. She was a frequent user of alcohol, the white man's solvent for guilt; and it is worth noting that liquor and kapu were antagonistic elements. Drunkenness led to the death of two commoners who blundered across prohibitive lines, one in Campbell's time, one in Choris'. Surely on O'ahu, between Portlock's first visit and the year 1819, there occurred many unobserved, unrecorded, unpunished, liquor-induced breaches of kapu. In the end, of course, the Hawaiians abandoned the kapu and kept hold of the bottle.

Not without loss: kapu had been the keystone of the arch supporting the traditional life of Hawai'i.[70] When it fell, the whole edifice fell with it. No wonder, then, that images of destruction entered the minds of Hawaiians as they faced a new era without the old gods. The same Ke'eaumoku who had trifled with his religion in 1818 later came to have terrifying dreams. Three years after the fall of the kapu he dreamed that he saw all the islands on fire, and was greatly alarmed, but was unable to find a way to escape or a place to hide from the dreadful conflagration.[71]

CHAPTER 3

Merchants and Missionaries in the Eighteen-Twenties

W hite men at Honolulu in the early years concerned themselves very little with the idea of community, and even less with western solutions to municipal problems. "White chiefs" such as Isaac Davis prospered within the Hawaiian polity; their special interests would not necessarily be better served by the growth of a western town at the port. Don Francisco de Paula Marin was a man of great practicality and considerable organizing ability; he governed his own estates very competently, but refused to put his skills at the service of the community at large. With few exceptions, the remaining white men at Honolulu before 1820 were sojourners. Their lives were centered about the port rather than the town. With the permission of the chiefs, haoles were able to exploit the resources of the islands and the ocean, but not until the eighteen-forties were they allowed to hold land in fee simple. The attitudes of most, therefore, remained strongly extraterritorial. For fifty years after the discovery of the harbor, white men took what they wanted from Honolulu and did not return loyalty in equal measure to the town.

This was the way of the merchants. As for the missionaries who came in the eighteen-twenties, Protestants and Catholics alike expected to live out their years in Honolulu. They shared with all Pacific evangelists certain unresolved conflicts in teaching and practice—should Christianity civilize the natives, or should civilization Christianize them? For many years, because of poverty and lack of technical resources, the missionaries were forced to live closer to the Hawaiian standard than they liked; and Protestant evangelists in particular rejoiced to see material progress among the natives. Understandably, however, their concern was not so much for the physical world about them as for the moral universe. Further, as it happened, no great missionary builder like John Williams of the South Seas or Father Laval of Mangareva was assigned to Honolulu; and so missionary influence upon the arrangement and appearance of the town was not especially striking.

The great chiefs were well placed to become "westernizers." Not all chose to do so, and those who did confined their efforts, for the most part, to their own property. Commoners sometimes attempted to follow the example of innovating ali'i, but such was their penury that few could afford anything more than a single item of foreign clothing or equipment.

Thus, some time passed before western buildings came into wide use among the natives. After the breaking of the kapu, the traditional "exploded house" living arrangement of the Hawaiians was abandoned. Once it was no longer necessary to segregate the sexes in their domestic activities, huts served indiscriminately, and at Honolulu, where the population was increasing rapidly, dwellings became crowded. Until about mid-century, Hawaiian commoners solved this problem simply by building more thatch houses.

The village that grew up on the harbor in the eighteen-twenties was hardly impressive. One major trail from the waterfront to Nu'uanu Valley gradually became a street, defined by encroaching buildings and leveled by traffic. Another trail, passing across the rear of the village and branching in several directions on both sides, marked a kind of inland limit to concentrated building and habitation as late as the eighteen-thirties.

Kamehameha's Honolulu had covered the same area and more in 1810, without however, including as large a population. The old king's style of living had dictated that his own complex of houses be built close to the water. Chiefs and specialists—kahuna, warriors, boatbuilders and fishermen—were clustered along a mile and a half of beachfront between Nu'uanu and Kaka'ako.

During the twenties and thirties, continued disturbances of the material and moral order brought about great changes in this traditional town plan. The soldiers of the kingdom withdrew from the drilling and spear-throwing fields to a fort on the waterfront. Kahunas ceased to practice publicly, and their heiau fell into disrepair or were torn down so that the stones might be used for other purposes. The lōkū (game-playing and entertainment areas) lost their leisure-hour primacy as missionaries urged the superiority of learning and prayer over mere play. A smattering of facilities appeared at the waterfront—hulks, wharves, small shipyards, markets and storehouses. Business premises were grouped at the principal landing place, and a tributary area of grog-shops and boarding houses developed on the Nu'uanu trail (later known as "Fid Street" for its brothels and bar-rooms). An increasingly congested community of natives dwelt in thatch huts along the beach. Interspersed, with no real attempt at segregation by race or class, stood the houses of white residents and chiefs—thatch, wood, adobe or coral stone.

The existence and growth of the town were conditioned at all times by the state of the harbor. Luckily, it was adequate in its natural form until mid-century. The bar, covered by more than twenty feet of water at high tide, would admit any whaler, merchant vessel or man-of-war. The channel between the reefs was narrow but safely navigable. Deep water lay close to shore. No expensive installations were needed. As for winds and tides, nothing much could be done about them, but if they were capricious or unfavorable at times, unlimited native labor was available to warp ships in and out of their anchorage.

The potentialities of the harbor had scarcely been explored, much less realized, by 1820. The village on the waterfront was insignificant, dwarfed by the inland mountains. Upon this minute stage, nonetheless, several themes were stated during the twenties which would take decades to play out. Such was their urgency that municipal considerations, for the most part, were set aside; such was their diversity that the growth of a sense of community in Honolulu was delayed until after mid-century. The sandalwood trade reached its height in the early twenties, fading away quickly thereafter and leaving the Honolulu chiefs heavily indebted to American traders. During the same period, whaling grew in importance, bringing with it grave problems of social order. Protestant missionaries from New England arrived in 1820, to offer chiefs and commoners a vision of life initially more difficult and forbidding than anything previously experienced in the islands. The small successes they achieved among the natives were counterbalanced by virulent opposition from their own countrymen and other foreigners at Honolulu. The planting of a French Catholic mission colony in 1827 further complicated the religious issue. Throughout all this, the kings of Hawai'i, resident in Honolulu, were victims of circumstance rather than initiators of policy. Liholiho (Kamehameha II) left the islands in 1823 and died in London in 1824. His successor was the adolescent Kauikeaouli (Kamehameha III). Under a regency which tended more and more to accept the view of government promulgated by the Protestant mission, Kauikeaouli moved toward personal rebellion. In this he was encouraged by an anti-mission faction which included Boki (governor of O'ahu) and his wife Liliha, the consular agents of the United States and Great Britain, and a sizeable group of resident foreigners. Visits by foreign men-of-war, riots, and threatened rebellions disturbed the town. The decade ended with the disappearance of Boki in the South Pacific, but without any solution to problems raised in the twenties, which were carried over in more complicated form to the thirties.

In the last years of Kamehameha I, Pacific traders began to realize the value of Hawaiian sandalwood in the market at Canton. The growing importance of this trade brought about changes in the business and social life of Honolulu. Sandalwood abounded in the hills of most of the islands. Attempts had been made to exploit it as early as the seventeen-nineties. The first shipments to Canton, however, were badly received—the quality was inferior—and not until a generation later was another effort made to add sandalwood to the stock of American goods in the China trade. After a promising start, in which Jonathan and Nathan Winship, together with William Heath Davis, made monopolistic arrangements first with Kamehameha and then with Kaumuali'i, trade was interrupted by the War of 1812. When normal business was resumed in 1815, it was not the Winships but others who commanded access to sandalwood in Hawai'i.[1]

Even then the trade developed relatively slowly. There were great stands of sandalwood in the islands, and an insatiable demand at Canton; the impediment was Kamehameha, who held a royal monopoly in this as in all other commerce. He refused to trade except in return for foreign ships, and not until 1816 were the first such bargains made. After that, however, business boomed. Kamehameha bought six vessels in three years, paying for all of them in sandalwood, and with this impetus the American-Hawaiian share of the Canton market rose.[2]

Honolulu, of course, shared in this increased activity; and when, in 1817, Kamehameha entered the trade directly by sending a shipment to Canton on his own account, the major Hawaiian port moved into a new stage of sophistication. Kamehameha's captain, Alexander Adams, took the *Kaahumanu* to China loaded with sandalwood, and returned to tell his master that harbor dues at Canton had consumed the profits. Kamehameha, always able to make good use of experience, set up a system of charges at Honolulu. Thenceforth, ships paid forty dollars to lie outside the reef, sixty dollars to anchor inside the harbor itself.[3]

Sandalwood was only the newest and most spectacular trade item affecting the port of Honolulu. Northwest furs had lost their dominant position in Pacific commerce but remained important in a more diversified trade. The coast of California was on the verge of being opened to commerce with the Hawaiian islands, and far to the north were the Russian settlements in Alaska, with which there was a limited contact. Honolulu was becoming the hub of a very widespread and complex trade system, and to all this was soon added the stimulus of the whaling business, as new grounds were discovered off Japan and ships touched regularly at the islands on their voyages to and from the Western Pacific.[4]

This commercial situation, already offering many possibilities, became even more fluid and speculative with the death of Kamehameha, the accession of Liholiho, the abolition of the kapu, and the relinquishment of the royal monopoly of trade. In the early eighteen-twenties, fortunes might be made in the islands, and the business world Honolulu changed with these new circumstances. Already the old practice of unloading goods in charge of a supercargo, who would depart after making his sales, was being modified by the arrival of resident agents of American business houses. As the twenties opened, the Boston firms of Bryant & Sturgis and Marshall & Wildes had men in the islands. A representative of the latter firm, John Coffin Jones, a New Englander in his early twenties, carried a commission from the United States government as agent for commerce and seamen.[5] In 1818 the young James Hunnewell of Boston became Honolulu's first resident trader. His connection with the town's business community survived his departure from the islands in 1830, and his establishment grew under later owners into the great firm of C. Brewer & Co., still a powerful mercantile house in mid-twentieth century.[6]

For haoles in the early eighteen-twenties, however, tenure was most precarious. Liholiho, uncertain of his strength and afflicted by rumors that some of the high chiefs were conspiring to rebel against him, was also suspicious of foreigners. His fears were fed by two of his retainers, the Scot Alexander Adams and the Englishman William Sumner, who seem to have wanted Americans removed from the islands. In August, 1820, Liholiho empowered Jean Rives (a dwarfish Frenchman resident in the islands since 1804 and a member of Liholiho's court since about 1810) to go to Honolulu and expel all propertyless foreigners unaffiliated with the king or his prime minister, Kalanimoku. The edict, announced at the house of Boki, governor of O'ahu, was not immediately enforced; but in November a number of Americans, apparently feeling threatened by Rives, took their native wives and some other Hawaiians and founded their own colony on Fanning's Island in the equatorial Pacific. Others remained at the pleasure of the king—their property, like that of the natives, subject to his whims and to the depredations of the chiefs.[7]

Into this shifting, uncertain situation, New England Protestant missionaries carried the certainties of the Christian gospel. Their arrival in the islands, early in 1820, was the culmination of a movement which had begun in 1809 when a young Hawaiian named 'Ōpūkaha'ia, left on the east coast of the United States by an American merchantman, attracted the attention of a clergyman at Yale College. 'Ōpūkaha'ia became, in that period of intense interest in missionary activity, the symbol of all suffering heathens in the Pacific. He died in 1818, a convinced Christian full of unrealized evangelistic hopes for his people. Within two years, the Sandwich Islands Mission of the American Board of Commissioners for Foreign Missions had been dispatched.[8]

It was only upon approaching the island of Hawai'i, in March, 1820, that the missionaries learned of the death of Kamehameha and the abolition of the kapu by Liholiho. To them, of course, the overthrow of the old religious system seemed an act of Providence, but many of the foreigners around Liholiho were not at all anxious to see new gods substituted for old. Arguments were advanced by John Young, Jean Rives and others against allowing the missionaries to remain—they would involve themselves in island politics, they would interfere in trade, their presence would alienate the British government. Four days passed before the king decided that the missionaries might stay—for a probational year.[9]

Then the question of location arose. Kailua, the king's residence, was unattractive to the eye of the New Englanders—lava-covered, hot and dry, without much cultivable land or fresh water. For many reasons, it would be good to have a station at Honolulu, centrally-located in the chain, with access to the world at large through the port. Liholiho was reluctant to allow stations to be set up beyond his immediate supervision, and again he hesitated. Finally he agreed to keep some missionaries around him and let the rest go to O'ahu, Then who should go? Of the fourteen mission members, only two were ordained ministers. By the vote of the mission, Rev. Asa Thurston was chosen to stay at Kailua, Rev. Hiram Bingham to establish the station at Honolulu.

Bingham, a granitic Vermonter just entering his thirties, had been drawn to mission work by the story of 'Ōpūkaha'ia. He was to stay at Honolulu for two decades. Already, during the outward voyage, he had begun to take a position of unofficial leadership; now he had been assigned the most important and most public place in the mission plan. He had a full measure of the energy, tough-mindedness, self-righteousness, and censoriousness that were the glory and the bane off New England Protestantism. For twenty-one years in Honolulu he exploited his strengths and was excoriated for his faults. He was a participant in every important mission development, as well as in many great events affecting the Hawaiian nation. After his departure in 1841 Honolulu was never the same, for mission or government, Hawaiian or haole.

Bingham and the rest of the Honolulu contingent sailed from Hawai'i to O'ahu in the *Thaddeus,* which had brought them from America. Early on April 14, 1820, they raised O'ahu and coasted as far as the Honolulu roadsteads, where they dropped anchor. Bingham and some of the others went ashore to find Governor Boki, only to be told by Marin, the government interpreter, that Boki was at another part of the island. The mission party spent the rest of the day sightseeing in Honolulu. They visited the fort on the waterfront, walked through the village as far as Pauoa valley, and climbed to the top of the extinct crater of Puʻuowaina (Punchbowl), where they stood and looked down over the southern coast of Oʻahu, from Lēʻahi to the Waiʻanae range in the west. Below in the sunshine lay the sleepy village, with its clusters of grass huts and its occasional stone buildings. Behind them, in the hinterland, the valley streams flowed into irrigated gardens where the kalo grew, its green leaves "beautifully embossed on the silvery water." Bingham looked down over this scene of "peculiar and thrilling interest," fore-seeing "toil and privation,...various conflicts, and probably...death, but... triumphs to the gospel, where heathenism was to be extirpated, and churches were to be planted, watered and made to flourish." He exulted, believing himself more blessed than Moses, who had been able to look upon but not enter the promised land.[10]

Before the struggle for possession of Honolulu could begin, Bingham had to wait two days for the return of Boki; and when the governor did come back he was, characteristically, drunk. Bingham was inclined to dismiss him as simply unfit for his post, and his experience with Boki during the next decade strengthened this opinion. But there was more to Boki than a mere fondness for drink. His administration of Oʻahu, begun in the last years of Kamehameha and continued under Liholiho, reflected, to be sure, a good deal of the looseness and disorganization of the new regime; and within himself, Boki was simultaneously repelled and attracted by the white man's world. During the twenties he experimented in turn with local and foreign trade, sugar-making, tavern-keeping and organized prostitution. Yet there was a barely-concealed nativism about him. In spite of a sojourn in Great Britain in 1824, he never became really literate in English, and carried out official business through interpreters. He was, of all the high chiefs of his generation, the most reluctant to give up native customs. His smile was a reminder of this—he lacked four front teeth, knocked out in a demonstration of grief at the death of Kamehameha. In his flirtations with the harsh disciplines of western trade, politics and religion, and in his concurrent yearnings for the allurements of the life of old Hawaiʻi, Boki was a remarkable and pathetic transitional figure in the history of Honolulu and of the islands at large. For the Hawaiians, the first of the nineteenth century was filled with intimations of doom. The fate of Boki, caught up as he was in alternating struggles, accommodations, withdrawals, and final collapse, prefigured that of a good many of his people. In the decade after his confrontation with Bingham, the questions life put to him became too complex for him to answer. He was pulled in many directions and could never commit himself to a consistent course of action. Quite early he began to resolve his problems in drink, and eventually, goaded by Bingham and others, he destroyed himself. One of his contemporaries put it very neatly, in the earthy Hawaiian idiom—

Boki was a calabash of poi which fermented, turned sour, pushed off its cover, and overflowed.[11]

Boki was finally ready to talk with Bingham on April 17. He gave permission for the *Thaddeus* to enter the harbor; and the next day the missionaries came ashore and walked through chattering crowds to inspect the three grass huts offered them by the Americans Isaiah Lewis, Joseph Navarro, and one of the Winship brothers who had made arrangements for this accommodation in Boston before they had sailed. By April 19 they were completely disembarked. That evening they prayed and then slept fitfully in their new dwellings while the guards at the fort nearby turned their hourglasses and struck bells and shouted their watchmen's reassurances throughout the night.[12]

Bingham, his wife, and his fellow-workers (the farmer Daniel Chamberlain and his family, the married printer Elisha Loomis, and a few American-educated Hawaiians), under instruction from the ABCFM, aimed at "nothing short of covering [the Sandwich Islands] with fruitful fields and pleasant dwellings and schools and churches; of raising up the whole people to an elevated state of Christian civilization." Granting that "except the Lord build the house they labor in vain that build it," they realized nonetheless that the Lord himself would not build the house, and that "the preacher and translator, the physician, the farmer, the printer, the catechist, and schoolmaster, the Christian wife and mother, the female teacher of heathen wives, mothers, and children, were indispensable."[13]

There was, in fact, plenty of work for all. The Lord would not build the house; neither, so it seemed, would Boki. He refused the missionaries' request for a permanent site at the rear of the village, and would not allow the foreign community to subsidize the building of the projected mission houses. While the mission waited for Boki to make up his mind, housekeeping went on under difficulty at the three grass huts, with no crockery (poorly packed in barrels, it had been reduced to dust in transit from America), practically no furniture, an outside stove fenced off to keep out the ubiquitous natives, wood and water brought at great expense from some distance away, and a laundry on the banks of a "heathen brook" in the valley behind Honolulu. Finally, Boki chose a somewhat arid location at Kawaiaha'o, about half a mile east of the landing place, and went to work in desultory fashion to arrange for houses to be built there.[14]

The missionaries were few. In Honolulu alone there were three or four thousand natives, on O'ahu an estimated twenty thousand.[15] Access to these "suffering souls" was not made easier by Boki, who showed profound indifference to the whole Christian enterprise. Bingham and his colleagues, impatient to begin useful work, turned instead to the foreign community for aid. Several residents had attended the first simple services held ashore, and old Oliver Holmes had been reduced to tears by the sound of hymns he had not heard for twenty years or more. Now the mission, with the help of the pious merchant James Hunnewell, memorialized residents and ship-captains, asking their cooperation in a "systematic effort to provide for the comfort and education of orphan children (of whom many may be found here) by donations... to be used by the mission for the benefit of such children, in training them up in knowledge and virtue, in the useful arts of civilized life, and in the principles of the Christian religion..."[16]

Among the hundred or more permanent white residents at Honolulu were many who had fathered "orphans." Marin, Oliver Holmes (former governor of O'ahu), George Beckley (one-time fort commandant), John Harbottle the old pilot, Joseph Woodland (an escaped convict from Botany Bay who had served as a gunner for the king), Joseph Navarro, a contentious American whose love-life later led to gunplay, and Anthony Allen, a New York negro who had become a substantial landowner and tavern keeper at Waikīkī, were among the first parent-patrons of the school. Poalinui, a Hawaiian, brought her two fatherless daughters; William Beals, a boy whose sailor father had died at Canton, enrolled himself. Less than a month after the school opened in May, 1820, there were twenty students; by September, forty or more. Mrs. Bingham began teaching them elementary English reading and composition with a heavy religious content. Most survived the first hō'ike (examination) in September, reciting in their own tongue such scriptural precepts as this: " I cannot see God but God can see me—Jehovah is in heaven and he is everywhere." The school entered its second quarter with pupils cheerfully making the half-mile walk to the mission buildings, and returning to spread their wisdom among their friends.[17]

In the midst of this first institutional growth came Liholiho's order for propertyless haoles to leave the islands. After some discussion it was agreed that missionaries were exempt from the edict. A month later—the day after the first school hō'ike—they were able to move into the buildings finally readied for them by native laborers working under Boki's direction. The Hawaiians had hand-carried timber fourteen miles and thatch three miles for the grass houses at Kawaiaha'o. Thenceforth it was from this headquarters that the mission operated: a scattering of huts connected by a covered lānai (verandah or walkway), a well nearby, a storehouse, and a building used as a school and church, all requiring a great deal of labor for upkeep.[18]

In June the missionaries opened a weekly singing school, "for the improvement of ourselves and others in sacred music." Several white residents joined, and harmony pervaded the relations of missionaries, merchants and sea captains until the end of the year 1820. Captain Pigot, a New Yorker, had asked the mission to tea immediately they arrived. In May, the English whaleman Valentine Starbuck invited them to dine with him; later he collected money for the orphan school (he raised $1,000 out of $1,300 subscribed by October), offered to deliver mail, allowed the missionaries to hold divine service aboard his ship, and gave them wash-tubs, crockery, and excellent butter. His gifts were matched by those of the Nantucket whaler Captain Allen (dried apples, oil, candles, butter, tea, and a book on the Lancastrian system of education), Captain Blanchard of the *Thaddeus* (a northwest hat and two tablecloths made at Kodiak), Woodland the ex-convict (milk and potatoes), and the friendly negro Anthony Allen (two bottles of goat's milk a day, a clothesline, squashes, chair timbers, and goat skins for chair bottoms). Up to that point, at least, Psalms 37:3 might safely be quoted: "Trust in the Lord and do good; so shalt thou dwell in the land, and verily thou shalt be led." Lines of communication, then, were open between the mission and a dozen or more residents and regular visitors.[19] There remained, however, the better part of a hundred white men who could not be reached (including the Botany Bay men, who actively resisted the gospel), not to mention the thousands of natives who did not attend school, and the hundreds who walked to Kawaiaha'o on Sunday not to enter the thatch building but merely to stand outside the fence and make noise. Unchurched haoles did not directly concern the Kawaiaha'o brethren, although as Christians they were ready to welcome anyone to divine service. Their mission was to the natives. But how to reach them?

In time the support of the chiefs was to open the way. For the moment, however, the most important ali'i in Honolulu, Boki, was of no help. He was pretending to learn English from a non-missionary, a stuttering Britisher, and was making fitful efforts to interest himself in Bible studies; all in all, though, he was less than useful. One of the American-educated Hawaiian Christians, Thomas Hopu, was teaching among his countrymen in the face of ridicule and hatred. Another, William Kanui, had begun to backslide soon after arriving home, and was drinking and breaking the sabbath. He was excommunicated from the months-old church in July. To offset this, there was always the example of the pious 'Ōpūkaha'ia; mission women were able to reduce their pupils to tears with the affecting tale of his life and death. One student, Sally, wife of the carpenter Edward Jackson, knew English and was used as an interpreter; another, Hannah, the striking daughter of Oliver Holmes, held regular prayer meetings in her house, for both natives and haoles. But when Elisha Loomis went out to preach extemporaneously in his imperfect Hawaiian he attracted few listeners, and the only response came from a native who wanted to learn to pray so that he might grow rich and have clothes like a missionary.[20]

For the most part, indeed, outside the tiny area the mission had claimed for Christ there was disregard where there was not misconception or outright suspicion. Many Honolulans had had themselves tattooed after the death of the previous ruler. On arms and chests were the words, "Our great and good chief Tamaahmaah died May 8, 1819," and although the kapu had died with the old king, and some natives treated kahuna and images with contempt, ancient habits lived still. Kahunas warned natives that in consequence of the breaking of the kapu everything would dry up for want of rain; the missionaries were pleased when heavy showers fell in mid-May. Soon after, there was a stir in the village when it was found that a kahuna and his wife had been attempting to pray a native to death. "Filthy songs" and rhythmic side-slapping in a house near the mission disturbed Daniel Chamberlain late at night. A hula for Boki in July drew a crowd of two thousand, and eager spectators were beaten back with an ox-goad to make room for the five "curiously dressed" young girl dancers and fourteen or fifteen "calabash musicians."[21] Toward the end of the year there was even a reminiscence of the makahiki festival, which had been abandoned formally with the kapu. The great days of the martial arts were gone, and when, in October, a boy was hurt in a boxing match, the games were stopped before they had really started; but there was drinking, feasting and dancing for more than a week in December.[22]

The outlook appeared somewhat bleak. For every small Hawaiian boy or girl who came to learn "civilization" as a domestic in the mission there was another who found the constraint unbearable and retreated to the village, sometimes taking his western clothes, sometimes leaving them. For every gift from a foreigner there was a theft by a native, and long after the gifts ceased, the thefts continued. Generally, the natives seemed indolent; their manner of life appeared to require little labor from them, so the missionaries believed, and the Hawaiian females "thought work a disgrace." There was even evidence of infanticide to appall the determinedly fecund mission ladies. Clearly, the Word of God was not sufficient in itself to change the Hawaiians, especially while it was being preached with poor facility in the native language and received with little comprehension of English.[23]

Mission strategy had called for the help of influential chiefs, but from Boki aid had not been forthcoming. Then, in September, 1820, the ali'i, meeting on Hawai'i, determined that Liholiho should take up residence in Honolulu. Perhaps the royal presence at the port, arranged for reasons of state, would incidentally improve matters for the mission.

The announcement of the king's coming had at least one immediate effect—it spurred the natives of Honolulu to great activity. A lavish hula was planned. Dancers practiced all day in a big yard next to Boki's house. Early in the morning they were called together, and then for hours, to the pounding of drums and gourds and the chanting of the singers, hundreds of dancers garlanded with green leaves and flowers and adorned with rattling dog-tooth anklets, moved to and fro in serried ranks, their bare brown flesh glistening in the hot sun. Several mission pupils were required to dance, and there was a tug-of-war between the school teachers and Boki, ending with the agreement that the girls should attend classes and also take part in the hula, but be exempt from dancing on the Sabbath. Hannah Holmes said she would dance in obedience to Boki, but would not sing or dress native-style or make offerings to the god of the hula.[24]

The king made an unexpectedly early appearance in 1821. On the night of February 3, cannon shots at Waikīkī announced the arrival of his newly-acquired and sumptuous ship, the American-built *Cleopatra's Barge*, bought on credit with the promise of more than $50,000 in sandalwood. The fort on the waterfront fired salutes, bells were rung, and the battery on Pu'uowaina joined in, splitting the night with sound. Natives flocked noisily to the landing place, bringing barking dogs, hogs and poi for a welcoming lū'au (feast). The king came ashore, royally drunk on Sunday morning; and when Bingham visited him to pay his respects (accompanied by Asa Thurston, who had left Kailua), Liholiho was not in a condition to talk to them. His favorite wife, Kamāmalu, demonstrating a sharp sense of social expediency, raised his nerveless hand so that the missionaries might touch it. With this less than faint salute the Christians perforce remained content.[25]

In the weeks after the king's arrival, the great hula went on apace, even though Liholiho was not yet ready to settle permanently, making instead more than one trip back and forth among the windward islands. Late in February another circumstance heightened the intensity of the celebrations—Likelike, wife of prime minister Kalanimoku, was approaching childbirth. On the night of February 25, cannon salutes and drunken toasts signalled the baby's birth, and the parents prepared to exhibit the infant to their people at a dollar a visit. But within forty-eight hours the child sickened and died; and a week later Likelike herself was dead, weakened by fever and dysentery, and by alternate immersions in warm and cold water. There was wailing all through the village. In the house of mourning where Kalanimoku sat with the corpse, people cut off each other's hair, burned faces, shoulders, and arms, and knocked out teeth.[26]

Bingham wanted to use the occasion of Likelike's death to preach a sermon. Kalanimoku was willing. March 11 was a Sunday; perhaps the hula might be stopped so that the natives could be instructed in the

Christian view of heathen death. Bingham found the king returning to the village from a bathing party with his train of noisy attendants, drunk, as he had been for weeks. Liholiho had been roaming erratically since his spectacular appearance early in February. Now, he said, he wanted to go back to Maui the next day; the hula could not be halted, he must see it that afternoon. Bingham preached his sermon from the lānai of Likelike's house, while not far away the hula drums played.[27]

Try as they might, the missionaries could not understand the king's perverse and passionate attachment to the dance. Invited to earlier hulas, they had been intrigued by the lavish scale of the performances, repelled by the open sensuality everywhere in evidence, and further alarmed, in their Protestant way, by the sight of the "court of Laka," goddess of the hula, set up on the dancing ground and decked with kapa and leaves. They asked about the image, and were given conflicting answers: it was a tutelary deity, it was to keep order, it was "for play," it was nothing. One day when rain spoiled the dance, a hula-master scolded and beat the idol for its delinquency, and yet many of the dancers prayed to it, called their ornaments by its name, threw their green leaves into its court, danced to it, ate to it, smoked to it, saying it would give them great skill. The king had forsworn the old gods, and yet he encouraged this mummery. It remained a mystery. None but Jehovah could know what was in the heart of the Hawaiians, but the missionaries rightly suspected a strong and lingering affection for the old ways, qualified only by remembrance of the harshness of the kapu system.[28]

Thus, with few achievements to celebrate, the missionaries the first anniversary of their coming to Honolulu. They held a day of thanksgiving and prayers together with a school examination. Soon afterwards, Liholiho's peregrinations ceased for a short time, and he remained at Honolulu during the middle months of 1821. It continued to be difficult, however, to pin him down to the quiet rectitude of Sabbath observance and church attendance. He would visit the missionaries, utter a few encouraging platitudes, and be off, drawn by running natives in the borrowed mission handcart, trailing shouts and dust down the Waikīkī road. Invited to Sunday meeting, he would say he was tipsy, and that it was not right to go drunk to church. Most chiefs took their cue from him, saying that when the king went, so would they go. Kalanimoku, at one time immersed in a gambling game, said his heart would be with the mission but his body must stay where it was. Among the commoners, Saturday reminders of the coming Sabbath elicited refusals or excuses more often than not. Nonetheless, there were minor gains. By mid-1821 a bigger church building was needed. In September it was ready, a thatched house partly financed by chiefs and residents, with pulpit, doors, windows, and lamps added by foreign workmen.[29]

Although this assistance from foreigners, including William Heath Davis, Eliab Grimes, William Ebbets and Marin, appeared to be willingly given in mid-1821, the missionaries were soon thwarted by them in another important venture. The mission had decided that a voyage to the Society Islands in the South Pacific would be very useful. There, English evangelists of the London Missionary Society had been at work since 1796, and without doubt the Sandwich Islands Mission could learn a great deal from them about Polynesian languages, the problems of printing and publishing for natives, and the needs of island missions in general. King Kaumuali'i of Kaua'i offered the use of one of his brigs, and Liholiho, Ka'ahumanu and Kalanimoku had no objections. But the Honolulu traders, led by United States Commercial Agent John Coffin Jones, raised strong opposition. Society Islands speculators might come to Hawai'i, injuring trade; American honor would be damaged by British assistance to the mission; the missionaries should not put themselves under such obligations to Kaumuali'i; the trip would be useless anyway, because the languages of the two archipelagoes were totally dissimilar.

These arguments were of course unfounded. The only solid reason, one not advanced by Jones, was that Kaumuali'i was deep in debt to the Americans, who may have wanted to keep his ship working for them. It is not clear how the merchants managed to convince the chiefs that the trip should be called off, but succeed they did. In the perspective of later events, this may be seen as the first in a long series of harassments of the mission by the mercantile community of Honolulu.[30]

It was not really surprising that antagonisms should have developed. New England was offering the islands a somewhat peculiar version of Protestantism and the rise of capitalism. The mission church, formed at least in part under the influence of the American frontier, was more emotional and febrile than that of classic Calvinism. Nonetheless, it preached the old virtues of thrift, frugality, and sobriety. The business community, an outrider of the boom-and-bust United States economy of 1819 and later, was not conservative and accumulative—but speculative in the extreme. The mission found it hard to penetrate the depths of the Hawaiian soul; merchants, by contrast, found it very easy to initiate chiefs into the mysteries of business on credit. Liholiho's ship, the *Cleopatra's Barge,* was only one of several floating follies for which the chiefs contracted to pay fabulous amounts of sandalwood. The great years of this bubble-trade were short—from the death of Kamehameha to the end of 1821; but by that time the ali'i owned "ten large & elegant brigs, besides a large number of Sloops & Schooners all of which they have purchased from the Americans." In 1821 alone 30,000 piculs of Hawaiian sandalwood were shipped to Canton.[31]

Purchases were not confined to sailing ships. The chiefs bought other things lavishly on credit—muskets, powder, wines and spirits, silks satins, brocades, and (the height of conspicuous consumption) cut glass, expensive dinner services, billiard tables, and frame houses shipped around the Horn in knocked-down form and erected in Honolulu. To pay for all this, commoners worked long hours in the mountains of O'ahu (and other islands) and carried their loads of sandalwood to the hot, dusty waterfront, where the logs were weighed out picul by picul and stored in warehouses. This was forced labor just as prolonged and exhausting as anything demanded by the traditional order—perhaps more so. Although a visitor remarked approvingly that "instead of a divided and lawless aristocracy, the King and his Chiefs compose a united corps of peaceable merchants, those principal object it to become rich by the pursuits of trade," these riches were accumulated at the cost of the vital energies of ordinary Hawaiians.[32] Men, women and children on all islands were forced to gather wood to pay the chiefs' promissory notes. Agricultural and other routines were neglected. Food was short in many places at many times, while silks and satins lay piled in sea-chests at the chiefs' houses.[33]

By the middle of 1821, several tendencies were apparent. The chiefs, whose last few ship purchases had been notoriously ill-advised, were becoming more careful of committing themselves heavily in that direction, although their appetite for other goods remained insatiable. Their credit was perilously overextended; the sandalwood stands were greatly diminished. It was becoming harder to arrange quick payments; but merchants, caught between the need to realize on previous contracts and the need to dispose of new shipments of goods arriving every month, had to continue taking promissory notes. Toward the end of the year, John C. Jones wrote home that there were price wars among the Honolulu merchants. Trade was very difficult; he advised his principals, Marshall & Wildes, not to send any more large cargoes. Sandalwood exports to Canton confirmed his estimate of the situation: 30,000 piculs of Hawaiian wood were sold there in 1821, but the figure fell to less than 8,500 piculs from all American sources in 1823–1824.[34]

All this trouble was very much between the traders and the ali'i, but merchants found a way to involve the mission. Jones, with that characteristic attribution of malicious motives and perfected schemes which was to become so much a part of mission–mercantile relations in the years ahead, claimed that the decline of trade was caused by Protestant meddling. The natives had come to know the value of things too well, "and if they do not there are plenty of canting, hypocritical missionaries to inform them." The mission's Hawaiian helpers alone had injured American trade in the islands more than $5,000,000 (it is worth noting that at current figures, this would have been about twenty-five years' trade). Bingham was a complete tyrant, a religious despot, trying to get all the trade of the islands into his own hands, so Jones claimed.[35]

The missionaries had regarded Jones as a "pleasant young man" when he arrived in the islands in May, 1821, to take up permanent residence.[36] Now they thought so no longer; and they found themselves forced to distinguish ever more sharply between friend and foe. Some New Bedford and Nantucket captains they liked very much; the Northwest traders they considered degraded, disgusting men who had sunk to the level of the heathen, indulging unblushingly in vice; and the resident merchants and beached captains they came to distrust increasingly.

There emerged many occasions for discord. It was difficult for a missionary to enter a Honolulu store without being engaged in violent argument by loungers. Jones, William Heath Davis and others took the part of the renegade missionary doctor Thomas Holman in a dispute that continued for months as Holman and his wife, in bad repute and finally suspended from the mission, traveled from island to island and at last came to Honolulu to embark on a ship bound for America. In time the missionaries acknowledged that their preaching style was "too plain and pointed to suit the latitudinarian ears and hearts of seamen." When Asa Thurston read a sermon of Rev. Dr. Porter on inebriation, a Captain Porter left the meeting-house in a fury, cursing and threatening to set fire to the church or blow it up. William Heath Davis marched drunkenly to Kawaiaha'o with a ragged military band, asking for brandy, and was refused. He went away calling upon God to damn him if he ever went there again. His later apologies did not carry conviction. He had been telling Liholiho the missionaries were not to be trusted; he insisted that they would become numerous and take over the islands. He proposed that the king set up another church in the village and listen to sermons by Davis and Jones alternately.[37]

In principle none of this should have worried the mission. The Lord would put honor on obedient people; others were contemptible, like the prophets of Baal.[38] Still, the town's troublemakers were capable of doing harm. The missionaries were dismayed to find that their promising pupil Hannah Holmes had learned some of her English from William Heath Davis, by whom she had had one child, and with whom she was still living. Bingham's attempts to get her away into a more respectable home alienated Davis; and when Davis died, rum-soaked , late in 1822, John Coffin Jones became Hannah's "protector." Thenceforth Jones' animus against the missions, already intense, took on a violent and bitter personal note as the strongest possible missionary suasion was brought to bear upon his mistress.[39]

All this was distressing enough. Perhaps worse was the fact that merchants and captains had easy access to Liholiho, making the missionaries' task the more difficult. While haole traders remained dissipated, laws against intoxication could not be enforced among natives. In turn, Liholiho's rampant drunkenness made it almost impossible to deal sensibly with him. Bingham did what he could by exhortation and precept. Once, he boldly took an uncorked bottle of spirits and upended it before the king, who, wrote Bingham, "was offended, and muttered indignation in terms which I did not fully comprehend."[40] The foreigners put the king's liquor to different purposes. One morning, Liholiho was supposed to go to the mission; but his barber, while cutting the king's hair, rubbed gin on his head "to stop him catching cold." Liholiho smelled the gin and drank it up, then went off to spend the day beating time with sticks at a hula where some of his wives were dancing.[41]

Almost any occasion would do for drink: New Year's Day, the anniversary of Kamehameha's death, a dinner given by John Coffin Jones, the arrival of an old acquaintance or the appearance of a congenial stranger. The king might limit himself to some *feux de joie* from the battery at the fort, or he might set off on long carouses, some of which rendered him irrational for weeks on end. One drinking bout almost killed him. At the beginning of March, 1822, the king was taken ill at his Waikīkī beach residence, and Bingham found him in dreadful condition—rigid, shaken by convulsions, bleeding from the mouth. There was no foreign doctor in town, and the efficacy of native medical treatment had been called in question to some extent by the abolition of the kapu. The chiefs turned to the missionaries. Bingham took medicine to the king, and stayed with him all night, amid the weeping ali'i. For days afterward the king was deranged, and amused himself by picking up straws and presenting them with a great deal of dignity to people around him.[42]

In this context, Liholiho's attentions to religion and literacy were not much more than perfunctory. From time to time, stricken by alcoholic remorse, he would tell the missionaries he intended to drink rum no longer, but would worship Jehovah and observe the Sabbath. His presence at services, however, was unpredictable. Occasionally he would come, to sit in a cluster of prone wives and fly-hunting attendants flourishing fans of peacock feathers; he might stay until the sermon was over, he might not. When Elisha Loomis finally got the mission press ready for work early in 1822, Liholiho joined the interested crowd and ran off some pages himself, spending a long time thereafter looking at his own name in print. Later in the same year he and his wife went through a stage of writing little personal notes to the mission; but though Liholiho assured the missionaries that he would eventually tell his people they must all know the good word, still he insisted that he himself should be the first to learn. And he seemed unteachable.[43]

So 1822 passed and 1823 came, and still the merchants' goods piled up in the king's grass palace, and still his excesses appeared unrelieved by any evidence of Christian grace. He continued to be despotic, inflicting punishments for crime which appalled the mission. A thief was flogged through the royal fleet, suffering 260 lashes, and was then taken out and drowned in the harbor; a young chief involved with one of Liholiho's queens was decapitated in his sleep with a western ax.

Sometimes the king gave a good impression. He could set a table for twenty with blue china, cut glass and spermaceti candles, for meals of turtle soup, meat and vegetables. On holidays he and his court turned out, dashingly dressed in clothes made for them by the foreign tailors of Honolulu or cut to their measurements in Canton: suits and waistcoats of satin or good broadcloth, silk stockings and elegant pumps, and, for the women, long dresses of velvet, satin, damask, or crepe. The apartments of his queens were filling up with chairs, writing-desks, bedsteads, and pier-glasses, in imitation of the things they found pleasant or useful about the mission buildings.

For the most part, however, life at the royal court was lived on the floor, in traditional Hawaiian style. Visitors brushed aside in the course of Liholiho's drunken dashes to and from Waikīkī might come upon him later in his Honolulu thatch house, snoring on a mat with a pet hog stretched out beside him, a naked queen stroking his brow, the inevitable attendants fanning away the flies and singing, and on the walls obscene pictures scrawled by white men. The king often seemed not to know what to do with himself, and his silk-draped, flower-decked six-foot queens were equally indolent, diverting themselves with arguments over cards, drinking great quantities of wine and spirits, fondling their pet hogs or inspecting their lapdogs for lice, or sleeping *en deshabille* upon their piled-up mats. Outside the commoners worked to gather sandalwood, and retired to their low, smoky, dirty huts along the beach. Season by season, the traditional tax goods flowed to the king, to be counted and stored by Kamāmalu. But within the court, cut loose as it was from the governance of the seasonal ceremonies, time passed either with the feckless speed of a wave across the beach at Waikīkī, or with the cloying sluggishness of poi being fed to a reclining, open-mouthed, overweight chief.[44]

Among some of the ali'i, however, a different spirit was at work. Cox (Ke'eaumoku, governor of Maui, then resident on O'ahu), who had dreamed of the islands ablaze, came to the mission for guidance, and was offered salvation through Christ. Already captivated by the printed word when Loomis allowed him to make the first impressions in early 1822, Cox set up a school in his own house at Honolulu. Kamāmalu, principal wife of Liholiho, found it fashionable for a short while to do the same. At one time in 1822, with events running temporarily in favor of the mission, there was a shortage of teachers, and a chief pressed into service a six-year-old mission pupil.

By far the most important of the ali'i to come under mission By influence was Ka'ahumanu. On first acquaintance with the evangelists she had been cold, offering them no more than Liholiho had—a little finger at arms' length. But two years' experience had changed her. In August, 1821, she had followed Liholiho to Kaua'i on an unpremeditated trip during which the king finally settled the question of Kaumuali'i's relation to the monarchy. Ka'ahumanu had been very much attracted to the dignified though aging king of Kaua'i, and she was party to a plan which led to his being brought back to Honolulu. She married him almost immediately, native-style, at a ceremony in which a piece of black kapa was thrown over the couple as they lay on bed-mats. Taking Kaua'i further into her keeping, she married as well Kaumuali'i's handsome son Keali'iahonui, who towered almost seven feet. Within a few days of this triumph of political sexuality, Ka'ahumanu fell seriously ill. During her convalescence she was nursed and instructed by Hiram Bingham and his wife Sybil, and she emerged much more receptive to Christian teaching. Thenceforth she turned to study of the scriptures, with only occasional backslidings (as when she ordered sacrifices of hogs and dogs for Cox during his last illness in 1824). In August, 1822, she made a tour of the windward islands, tearing down heathen idols which still stood there. Back in Honolulu, she resumed her lessons, took part in the school examinations (where she wrote of her repentance of sin), and rode to church in a carriage bought from Captain Dixey Wildes, with a dozen men harnessed to the shafts, Kaumuali'i beside her, and Keali'iahonui as postilion.[46]

In the course of 1822 and 1823, missionary influence began to affect many male and female ali'i. Besides Ka'ahumanu, Kaumuali'i, Keali'iahonui and Ke'eaumoku, those who attended service included Kalanimoku (prime minister), Kuakini (John Adams, governor of Hawai'i, at times resident on O'ahu), Nāihe (the national orator), La'anui, a minor chief, and the women Kapi'olani and Nāmāhana, as well as the little prince and princess, Kauikeaouli and Nāhi'ena'ena, son and daughter of Kamehameha.

A prolonged visit to Hawai'i in 1823 by William Ellis of the London Missionary Society's South Seas Mission, accompanied by some Tahitian helpers, made a useful substitute for the voyage thwarted in 1821 by the Honolulu traders. In 1823, too, the second contingent of American Protestants arrived in the islands, and the day-to-day work of the Honolulu station—indeed, of the whole mission—was immeasurably strengthened by the labor of the painstaking, calm, sensible secular agent Levi Chamberlain, who took charge of a depository for all mission goods. With new workers new stations could be set up: now there were missionaries on Hawai'i, Maui, O'ahu, and Kaua'i. In spite of Liholiho's wish that he should lead the way in learning, it was evident by mid-1823 that he was far behind most of his ali'i, and many commoners too, for the school system, though limited, was beginning to produce results. Almost all of this, of course, was in the nature of mere outward profession. There was no suggestion that any semi-literate Hawaiian knew enough Calvinist theology to be sure that he was approaching the state of grace. Still, a religious and cultural gap was clearly opening up between several of the powerful chiefs on the one hand, and Liholiho on the other (and Boki, too, second only to his king in general swinishness, as the mission saw it).

There remained times, however, when the entire Hawaiian community, ali'i and commoners alike, could join in reminiscences of the old days. Even though many of the ceremonies which had united the living and the dead had vanished, and a different social and ritual calendar was developing (involving the Sabbath, the monthly concert of prayer, New Years Day, Christmas, July 4, and so on), an occasion such as the anniversary of Kamehameha's death could call forth a deep response. The 1823 celebration was one of unparalleled pageantry. Just as early contact with westerners had produced unheard-of royal power before bringing down the kapu system, so now it gave material splendor to a ceremony which had largely lost meaning and which seemed on the point of disappearing altogether. Bradford Smith has compared the parade of 1823 with the high leap of a mortally-wounded animal.[47]

All Honolulu was absorbed in the weeks of preparation; and the fortnight of celebration began with nightly hulas and a European-style feast for some hundreds of guests, presided over by the king. The climax came on the last day. The best description of events is that of Rev. Charles Stewart, one of the recently-arrived Protestant evangelists, whose writings, almost alone in the Hawaiian missionary corpus, added to routine condemnations of heathenism an involved, half-infatuated sense of physical presence, of display, of theater:

> Tameha-maru [Kamamalu], on this day, as usual, a conspicuous object. The *car of state* in which she joined the processions, passing in different directions, consisted of an elegantly modelled, *whale boat*, fastened firmly to a platform of wicker work thirty feet long, by twelve wide; and borne on the heads of seventy men. The boat was lined, and the whole platform covered, first with fine imported broadcloth, and then, with beautiful patterns of tapa or native

cloth, of a variety of figures and rich colours. The men supporting the whole, were formed into a solid body, so that the outer rows only, at the sides and ends, were seen; and all forming these, wore the splendid scarlet and yellow feather cloaks and helmets than which, scarce anything, can appear more superb. The only dress of the queen, was a scarlet silk pāʻū, or native petticoat, and a coronet of feathers. She was seated in the middle of the boat and screened from the sun, by an immense Chinese umbrella of scarlet damask, richly ornamented with gilding, fringe and tassels, and supported, by a chief standing behind her, in a scarlet maro or girdle, and feather helmet. On one quarter of the boat, stood Karaimoku, the prime minister,—and on the other, Naihi, the national orator, both, also, in maros of scarlet silk and helmets of feathers, and each bearing a kahile or feathered staff of state, near thirty feet in he height. The upper parts of these kahiles were of scarlet feathers, so ingeniously and beautifully arranged...as to form cylinders fifteen or eighteen inches in diameter, and twelve or fourteen feet long; the lower parts, or handles, were covered, with alternate rings of tortoise shell and ivory of the neatest workmanship and highest polish. The queens Kīnaʻu and Kekaunuohi presented themselves much in the same manner, as Tamehamaru; But, instead of whale boats, had for their seats *double canoes.* Pau-ahi, another of the wives of Riho-riho, after passing in procession with her retinue, alighted from the couch on which she had been borne—set fire to it, and all its expensive trappings—and then threw into the flames, the whole of her dress, except a single handkerchief to cast around her. In this she was immediately imitated by all her attendants: and many valuable articles—a large quantity of tapa—and entire pieces of broadcloth, were thus consumed...it was to commem- orate, a narrow escape from death by fire, while an infant... The dresses, of some of the queens dowager, were expensive and immense in quantity. One wore *seventy-two* yards of kerseymere of double fold: one half being scarlet and the other orange. It was wrapped around her figure, till her arms were supported hori- zontally by the bulk; and the remainder was formed into a train, supported by persons appointed for the purpose.

The young prince and princess [Kauikeaouli and Nahienaena] wore the native dress—maro and pāʻū—of scarlet silk. Their vehicle consisted of four *field*-bedsteads, of Chinese wood and workmanship, lashed together side by side, covered with hand- some native cloth, and ornamented with canopies and drapery of yellow figured moreen. Two chiefs of rank bore their kahiles:

and Hoapiri and Kaikio'ewa, their stepfather and guardian, in scarlet maros, followed them as servants: the one, bearing a cala-bash of *poe* and the other, a *dish of baked dog* for the refreshment of the young favorites...

The king and his suite made, but a sorry exhibition. They were nearly naked—mounted on horses without saddles, and so much intoxicated, as scarce to be able to retain their seats, as they scampered from place to place in all the disorder of a troop of bacchanalians. A body-guard of fifty or sixty men in shabby uniform, attempted by a running march, to keep near the person of the sovereign, while hundreds of ragged natives, filling the air with their hootings and shoutings, followed in the royal chase.

Companies of singing and dancing girls and men, consisting of many hundreds, met the procession in different places—encir-cling the highest chiefs—and shouting their praise in enthusiastic adulation. The dull and monotonous sounds of the native drum and calabash—the wild notes of their songs in the loud choruses and responses of the various parties,—and the pulsations on the ground, of the tread of thousands in the dance, —reached us, even, at the Missionary enclosure.[48]

The question remained: how to bring the capering king within the mission enclosure, and, through him, shut out the pulsations of heathenism? In 1823, Lilioliho, urged by the mission to make a firm commitment to the gospel, said that in five years he would put aside sin.[49] That might have marked the year 1828 as the starting-point for unimpeded evangelization had not other circumstances made for an earlier beginning.

Late in 1823, Liholiho's chronic restlessness drove him to plan his greatest voyage, a trip to England—to see his "friend" King George IV, to discuss British-Hawaiian relations, but mostly just to look at the world. The mission thought such a journey, properly supervised, would be very good for the king. They suggested that the English missionary William Ellis should accompany him, and that Liholiho should add New England to his itinerary. Bingham wrote to the ABCFM that he would rather see Liholiho exposed to the bracing morality of New England than allow him to be debauched and swindled in Great Britain. Several chiefs supported Bingham, but Liholiho, a convinced anglophile, was not enthusiastic about these new proposals. Other ali'i opposed the voyage altogether, on traditional grounds. The anti-mission group in Honolulu and at Lahaina (where some discussions took place) worked to loosen the Christians' hold on the venture. In the end, Liholiho, Kamāmalu, Boki, and others of his suite departed for England on a British whaler, *L'Aigle*, whose captain, Valentine Starbuck—in 1820 one of the mission's best friends—had become so antagonistic toward mission Protestantism that he refused to find a place on board for William Ellis, who wanted to go home to England and had considered that Liholiho's trip offered a chance to do good on the way.[50]

For the Hawaiians, who could elicit tears and wails to dramatize a parting of just a few days, the sailing of *L'Aigle* was a harrowing experience. On November 23, the king asked for the prayers of the mission, and the chiefs heard the stranded William Ellis preach from psalms 107, 23-24: "They that go down to the sea in ships..." Four days later, the king went on board *L'Aigle* Kamāmalu stayed ashore a little longer, wailing, throwing up her bands, and chanting:

> O Heavens O earth!
> O mountains and seas!
> O commoners and people!
> Farewell to you all.
> O soil farewell.
> O land for which my father suffered,
> Farewell,
> O burden that my father strived for.
> We two are leaving your labors.
> I go in obedience to your command,
> I will not desert your voice.
> I go in accordance with the words you spoke to me.[51]

The departure of the king and queen plunged the commoners into a paroxysm of license. As in ancient times, a crisis in the life of a great aliʻi released sympathetic disruptions among his people. Despite the fact that dozens of ordinary Hawaiians each year made long cruises in the Pacific on foreign vessels, an ocean voyage seemed a venture fraught with danger for Liholiho. The exploits of the great navigators of the Polynesian past were now only legend. Many Hawaiians, watching the masts of *L'Aigle* sink below the horizon, believed they were seeing the king lowered into his grave. In Honolulu, during the next few days, "guns were fired, drunken men wept and rioted, prostitution was rife."[52]

The aliʻi who had assembled at Honolulu to take leave of their king remained for a time, meeting in council on December 1 to discuss the course of government under their accepted leaders, Kaʻahumanu and Kalanimoku. Later that month the institutional beginnings of a new morality appeared. On Saturday, December 21, a crier passed through the village at the order of Kalanimoku, prohibiting travel and work on the Sabbath, and ordering the people to cook their food on Saturdays, since fires must not be lit on Sundays. At the beginning of 1824, these injunctions were repeated on most of the other islands. In April, 1824, another meeting of important chiefs was held at Honolulu, in a schoolhouse built by Kamāmalu before her departure for England. The broad question of national reform was raised. Ka'ahumanu and Kalanimoku reaffirmed their attachment to the mission, and recommended that other chiefs and head-men should encourage their people to observe the Sabbath, attend school and church, and in general obey God's word, paying particular attention to the problem of reckless gambling which pervaded every Hawaiian sport and amusement. Thenceforth the missionaries, supported by the chiefs, were able to extend their sabbatarianism to the hinterland of Honolulu. They held services at Waikīkī, in Mānoa valley, in Nu'uanu, and at Moanalua, and as they rode to and from these rural areas, they remonstrated with natives discovered working or gaming with maika stones on the Sabbath.[53]

Results, as always in the early years, were mixed. Black looks and evasions were encountered, and in Honolulu the crier was forced to traverse the village once more, after two girls in competition over the same lover disturbed the waterfront with a week of hula dancing and noisy argument. Nonetheless, the mission could point to increased church and school attendance, a steady demand for mission publications and an enthusiasm for instruction among the chiefs. Early in 1825, groups of men and women were formed, pledged to abstain from immorality. They met weekly, for hymn-singing, "social prayer," and exhortation. A dozen or more chiefs joined, together with serious-minded commoners. From among these inquirers came the first Hawaiians admitted to communion at Kawaiaha'o Church late in 1825.[54]

Without much doubt, the absence of Liholiho from the Honolulu scene helped the mission greatly. In March, 1825, the shocking news came that the king would never return. He and his wife Kamāmalu were dead. Less than two months after arriving in London they had been taken fatally ill with measles. On his deathbed Liholiho dictated a will which confirmed a verbal arrangement made before he left the islands. The throne was to go to his younger brother under the protection of Ka'ahumanu and Kalanimoku. Boki took command of the royal entourage, and, after an audience with George IV, brought the bodies of the king and queen back to Hawai'i on the British ship *Blonde*, commanded by Lord George Byron.

On O'ahu, where news of the deaths preceded the arrival of the *Blonde* by two weeks, the chiefs reacted in a way which demonstrated

their new Christian seriousness. There was no trace of the ancient predis-
position to fight over the spoils of the kingdom, not even a reminiscence
of the instability that had attended Liholiho's accession six years earlier.[55]
Instead, a two-week season of prayer was ordered by Kalanimoku. It
even seemed that world travel and the assumption of responsibility had
made a better man of Boki. When the *Blonde* touched at Lahaina on Maui,
its first Hawaiian port of call, Boki maintained enlightened dignity in the
face of the traditional wailing and self-abasement with which the common
people greeted him when he stepped ashore. He went with missionary
William Richards to pray, and later wrote to his brother Kalanimoku in
Honolulu, asking him to forbid in advance all old-style irregularities. As
Boki left Maui, he exhorted the natives of Lahaina to "regard the word
of God and cast off all their heathenish practices." The next day, May 6,
1825, the *Blonde* anchored in the Honolulu roads and fired a fourteen-
gun salute which was answered from the town. The chiefs assembled at
Ka'ahumanu's beachside house, and as Boki's party came ashore there
was great, although seemingly Christian, grief. After an emotional progress to Ka'ahumanu's house and thence to the missionary chapel, Boki
spoke, "very earnestly commending the religion of the Bible, and manifesting a serious desire to observe it himself."[56]

An audience was held, at which Lord Byron met King Kauikeaouli
and the Princess Nāhi'ena'ena and presented than with gifts from George
IV (among other things, a royal Windsor uniform with sword and epau-
lets for the eleven-year-old monarch). Later, while minute guns boomed,
the bodies of the dead king and queen were brought ashore in their triple
coffins of lead, oak and mahogany, to be set down upon the spot from
which the king's entourage had departed in 1823. They were taken to
funeral services at Kawaiaha'o behind a procession composed of twenty
kāhili-bearers, the marine band of the *Blonde* and a crowd of mourners
and dignitaries; then the coffins were placed in Kalanimoku's house to
await the construction of a suitable mausoleum.[57]

Sermons preached at Kawaiaha'o made special mention of
Boki's safe return. The natives had been astonished at his metamor-
phosis, affecting to believe after listening to his virtuous speeches that
someone else was in Boki's skin. All the same, he had not completely
abandoned his past mode of life under the stress personal grief and
new political responsibility. He invited a party from the *Blonde* to visit
Wai'anae, where he owned land, and there twenty-five girls danced a
hula for him, celebrating his fortunate homecoming. In all, however, the
missionaries were very satisfied with the new, sobered Boki. The officers
of the *Blonde* shared this good opinion. They had come to like Boki, and
were touched by his sadness at their departure from Honolulu early in
June. They looked forward to a substantial future for him.

This chief has brought from Europe ideas that will be most useful to his country. Convinced of the advantages and necessity of industry, he has resolved to set the example of it on his own estate and in his own person. Instead of the indolent repose and enjoyment, in which, like the greater number of chiefs, he formerly indulged, he now rises early, and goes to his fields, where he superintends his workmen, instructing them in new and better methods of cultivation. He is active and constant in his duties, as governor of Oahu; and by his mildness and kindness to his dependents he has acquired the love of all the common people. His superior information and his good temper make him equally a favorite with the chiefs...[58]

The lesson of the king's disastrous voyage was not lost on Honolulu's Hawaiians. Although he had been buried by the mission, he had died outside the church. On the first Sabbath in June several ali'i (Ka'ahumanu, Kalaninoku, Keali'iahonui, Kalakua, Kapi'olani, La'anui, and Nāmāhana) stood at Kawaiaha'o and requested full membership. This moment of humility and submission was something the missionaries had waited five years to see. Eager as they were to have the most prestigious chiefs of the kingdom as members of their Honolulu congregation, they were not quick to admit the applicants. The ali'i were placed on six months' probation. Following their example, commoners flocked to church, and soon there were a hundred candidates for baptism at Kawaiaha'o. The schools became crowded. Honolulu alone had almost two thousand pupils by September, 1825. Congregations increased: Bingham preached to as many as three thousand each Sunday. The mission press worked overtime—from March to October, 1825, sixteen thousand spelling books and several thousand catechisms were printed and sold to natives for many times their cost, where just a few years before no one would take the books on any terms.[59] With the Hawaiians of Honolulu united in a common grief, articulated for them at least in part by the mission, it began to appear that the future might belong to the Protestants.

There remained the problem of the foreign community. Early in August, 1825, old Oliver Holmes, father of the spirited Hannah and her sisters, died in the midst of a drinking bout. Most of the town's foreigners and natives attended his funeral. The missionaries had been invited also. Charles Stewart made a prayer at Holmes' house; and Levi Chamberlain and Elisha Loomis prepared to walk in the procession. But when they saw their fellow mourners, they turned aside. Holmes' daughters were squired by their lovers and other foreigners were arm-in-arm with "notorious prostitutes." The missionaries found themselves unable to condone such a breach of Christian decorum. As they hastened home, they noticed the flags of the town's grogshops at half-mast for Holmes, a steady customer.[60]

Holmes' funeral exemplified very neatly a schism—incipient in 1821, well-developed by 1825—between the Americans of the mission and the foreigners of downtown Honolulu. Many of the latter had taken mistresses among the native girls. Some, indeed, showed a preference for the half-caste girls of the mission schools. Hannah Holmes continued to vacillate between the mission and the house of J.C. Jones; her sister Polly was away on the northwest coast with a ship-captain; Charlotte shortly gave birth to a child by a haole; only Mary married her white man.[61]

For the rest, as Captain Dixey Wildes put it, life was divided into three parts—drinking, gambling, and sleeping. Business was seasonal and sporadic; it did not absorb a great deal of time. Foreigners at leisure amused themselves with horserides to the valleys and boating excursions along the coast. They spent days rolling tenpins at Anthony Allen's tavern in Waikīkī or betting on horse races, foot races and whaleboat races. After sundown they might repair to the card table or the billiard saloon, or stand at the bar of one of the dozen or more grogshops in Honolulu. Or they might casually seduce a native girl. The most jaded indulged in a great deal of aimless wandering about town at all hours of the clock, which opened the way for some typical products of boredom—practical joking, property damage, and brawling. In 1825, three foreigners requested Bingham to marry them to their native women. This merely pointed up the moral delinquency of scores of others. Perhaps a dozen foreign residents, more recently arrived than the old guard like Marin and Holmes, claimed respectability. They were well-connected, or had money, or were deacons of the church at home in America (though none felt inhibited from appearing publicly with prostitutes in Honolulu). Perhaps a hundred others in the floating world of the village were little more than miserable squaw-men.[62]

In addition to, and related to this constant local irritation, there was the fact that the whaling trade had begun to alter the nature of downtown Honolulu. As the sandalwood business passed its peak, leaving the merchants of Honolulu with a great many promissory notes of doubtful value signed by Liholiho and other chiefs, the whaling grounds of Japan were opened, creating a succession of economic interest which produced change and expansion at the waterfront.

Every year after 1819, whalers going to and from the northern Pacific made seasonal stops in the spring and fall to refit and refresh at Honolulu (and at Lahaina, Maui, and one or two places on Hawai'i). This meant, to begin with, an increase in the number of vessels arriving each year, sufficient by 1822 to support a shipyard at Honolulu harbor. Liholiho made a short-term gain from the traffic when he raised port charges during the early twenties. His experiments inadvertently but quickly established the point at which the advantages of the safe harbor and developed commercial community of Honolulu ceased to be attractive in the face of high fees for pilotage and anchorage. A sharp drop in patronage at Honolulu in 1824 brought an answering reduction in charges the next year.

For the chiefs, the business of supplying whalers and other trading vessels was lucrative. At times of heavy traffic in 1822 and 1823 they kapu'd potatoes, hogs and kalo to themselves. No commoner could sell directly to foreigners, either on board ship or ashore. All business passed through the hands of the chiefs, who either established a market or designated a trusted man to handle the trade, and then levied taxes on the cash received. The commoners responded by neglecting agriculture, and this in turn made provisions scarce and prices high. The missionaries at Honolulu, dependent like others upon native sources of food supply, suffered a double discomfort. They had to pay outrageous prices for food, and, at the same time, foreigners accused them of encouraging the chiefs to corner the market, thus setting artificial levels of exchange.[63]

The sale of foreign trade goods was also profitable. By 1823, four American firms had outlets in Honolulu, doing an estimated total business of $100,000, with supercargoes and agents on the scene throughout the year. Several other small grass-hut stores of obscure origin supplied natives and foreigners with a miscellany of goods. Prices were high. Levi Chamberlain, the mission's secular agent, thought some items cost as much as a hundred percent more than they would have on the American mainland. Cash was scarce, especially at the mission, and coins from many parts of the world were current at arbitrary rates. Bills of exchange, when they could be arranged, often carried discounts of up to twenty-five percent.[64]

Within this increasingly westernized ambience lived growing numbers of Hawaiians: two or three thousand in 1822, four or five thousand in 1823, an estimated six thousand in 1825, dwelling eight or ten to a hut in a square mile of land at the harbor and on the plains. To these were added permanent foreign residents and seasonal waves of whalers, and an off-season group of beached, disabled or delinquent seamen. By 1826, the westernization of the town was physically evident in the "number of wooden houses, the regularity of the town laid out in squares, intersected by streets properly fenced in and the many notices which appeared right and left, on pieces of board, on which we read 'An Ordinary at one o'clock, Billiards, the Britannia, the Jolly Tar, the Good Woman.' &c."[65]

Any regularity was nothing more than physical. Within the changing society of the port, a distinct lack of satisfactory social control was evident. Native chiefs were still prestigious. Their influence over commoners meant that relations between native and native remained more or less patterned and orderly. But, predictably enough in the crowded, heterogeneous, loosely-administered town, incidents occurred between foreigner and foreigner, foreigner and native, foreigner and native government, and foreigner and missionary, which in time burst the bounds of the institutions of local and national government, making it impossible even for uneasy co-existence to survive at Honolulu.

Strife assumed many forms. The first published laws of the Hawaiian kingdom, promulgated in 1822, had attempted to regulate the conduct of sailors, but desertion continued to pose a problem for ships' captains. Sometimes commanders were able to get help from the chiefs and people of the port; at other times there seemed to be a native conspiracy against the return of fugitive seamen. Lazy, disputatious, or mutinous sailors could be incarcerated at the fort on the request of captains; but seamen locked up by the chiefs for offenses committed on land could not always be freed at a captain's word. There were brawls between sailors ashore, a few of which ended in murder; and once, when a negro sailor molested a native woman, a large mob of Hawaiians formed in the streets and pursued the man as far as the mission at Kawaiaha'o, where he took refuge. The chiefs' trade kapu greatly incensed ships' captains, to the point where one engaged the fort commander in violent argument, and others stockpiled gunpowder on board their ships against possible violence. In 1825, an American named Sistare lured away the native woman of Joseph Navarro (Navarro had been a patron of the orphan school, and the woman in the case was Poalinui, who in 1820 had brought her children by previous liaisons to the school). Enraged, Navarro confronted Sistare with two pistols and shot him in the leg. The chiefs, in consultation with several foreign residents, ordered Navarro to leave the islands. He departed for Fanning's Island, where he had gone once before, a victim of Liholiho's 1820 banishment.[66]

Over the question of foreigners' access to native women major trouble eventually developed, within a context of increased general concern for morality on the part of the chiefs and mounting pressure from the seaports. As late as 1822 it had still been possible to see the traffic in women at Honolulu as mere picturesque hedonism. Economics and morals were secondary issues, or even non-existent considerations. When Gilbert Mathison's ship left Honolulu in August, 1822, "between twenty and thirty females, who had been living on board with the sailors, according to immemorial usage, still remained, and seemed unwilling to quit the ship. At length, when we had advanced about a mile out of the harbour, they took a most tender leave of their respective sweethearts, and with loud laughter and cries, and huzzas from the crews, leaped overboard in one instant into the sea, here they remained swimming and diving, and playing about the ship, like so many mermaids in their native element, until a breeze sprang up; and as we bounded merrily before it, women and canoes, and houses and the land itself, gradually disappeared from our view."[67]

The moral issue did not arise with great force till 1825-1826; but, toward the end of 1823, as part of a general trade kapu, females were forbidden to board ships unless a dollar a head was paid at the fort. Late in 1824, by which time Ka'ahumanu and other chiefs were fairly well committed to mission ways, some ship captains themselves initiated a move to keep women off vessels in the harbor. Elisha Loomis printed handbills for them, but few masters could be induced to sign. They refused on the practical ground that many sailors would desert if women were not allowed on board ship.[68]

At the end of June, 1825, in the wake of general advice from Lord Byron and specific counseling by the missionaries, a meeting of chiefs resolved to outlaw vice, drunkenness, theft, and non-observance of the Sabbath. In August, the chiefs announced that all Hawaiians must observe the Sabbath, attend worship, and go to school. Gambling and adultery were also prohibited. Soon, chiefs at the busy ports of Honolulu and Lahaina extended the ban on adultery to include the activities of women going off to ships. Levi Chamberlain predicted trouble: as soon as this became a criminal act, and as soon as native girls were prevented from living with foreign residents unless they were lawfully married, the mission could expect the kindling indignation of dissolute foreigners to burst into flame.[69]

Chamberlain was right. By October, the laws were in effect at Honolulu and Lahaina. Guards were posted nightly to watch the harbors. At Honolulu, one woman attempted to swim off; she was pursued, caught, put in irons, and exhibited in town. According to Elisha Loomis, twenty or thirty Honolulu girls took this occasion to forsake their foreign lovers, refusing to live with them outside marriage, and applying instead to enter native schools. The stir this caused was outdone by the outraged reaction of whalermen, returning from long cruises in the northern Pacific for the fall layover in Honolulu. On October 4, twenty sailors came to "King" Bingham's house, wanting to know why women were not allowed on ships as before. Bingham directed them to Ka'ahumanu, saying that the ruling came from the chiefs, not the missionaries. Ka'ahumanu told them that she and the other ali'i had been guided by the word of God. The sailors said their captains and officers would support them in getting women, whether peacefully or by force, and they dispersed only when Kalanimoku threatened to put them in the fort.[70]

A few days later, news came from Lahaina that the Englishman William Buckle and the crew of his ship *Daniel* had encountered the kapu on women at Maui, and had blamed the missionary William Richards. Sailors had come ashore under a black flag, armed with knives and out for Richards' blood, but had retreated when opposed by a large group of Hawaiian supporters of the mission carrying clubs and stones. Soon afterward, the Honolulu chiefs in council moved to take sterner measures against women going off to the ships. On October 20, some offenders had their heads shaved. At the end of the month, Buckle's *Daniel* arrived at Honolulu. Three boat crews landed and marched toward the mission house at Kawaiaha'o. The chiefs, forewarned, had posted guards in the streets. Five sailors were arrested and put in irons at the fort, not to be released until the *Daniel* was ready to sail. The others went back to their boats; the guards, several hundred of them, with loaded muskets, remained on the streets. This did not prevent insults to the missionaries and a few half-hearted drunken forays against Kawaiaha'o, but in time the *Daniel* departed, the guard was lifted, and December opened quietly.

On December 4, several of the chiefs, having completed their religious probation with a successful defense of morality at a difficult period, were received as members of Kawaiaha'o Church. The following Sunday, Kalanimoku, one of the new communicants, stood up at the close of divine service and asked all chiefs and teachers to assemble next morning to discuss the adoption of the Ten Commandments as fundamental moral law. Elisha Loomis wrote at the time that the missionaries had not been consulted about this move. Attending the meeting, by invitation, they found the king present, accompanied by armed guards. Around him were ranged most of the resident foreigners and several ship captains, American and English.

Ka'ahumanu and Kalanimoku spoke in favor of the moral laws. The foreigners, led by the Americans William Ebbets, Stephen Reynolds and John Meek, unanimously attacked the scheme, blaming Bingham as its instigator. Bingham denied this; the chiefs, he said, were the lawmakers, and the missionaries did not wish to interfere. The foreigners turned to Boki: he had been to England, they said, and knew how things were done there. Boki told the king that if the laws were promulgated they would not have his support. Kauikeaouli, not yet in his teens, obviously did not know what to say or do. Finally, he announced that he was afraid, and that it would be best to defer the laws.

The foreigners had carried their point by sheer vehemence. The missionaries were saddened, but convinced nonetheless that it was God's purpose to establish His laws in the land despite the malice and rage of the enemy. Next day, Loomis of the mission press issued the Ten Commandments in Hawaiian, together with fourteen rules which readily identified Christians; and natives crowded around to take the sheets from the press, "joyful" that they had obtained the commandments of God.[71]

The imbroglio over the question of morals did not have a chance to untangle itself. In December, 1825, and January, 1626, several female offenders were taken, and some were set to carrying stones for a new church building. In January, 1826, too, the first American man-of-war to visit the islands arrived—USS *Dolphin* commanded by Lieutenant John "Mad Jack" Percival. Under orders to arrest a party of mutineers encamped on the Mulgrave Islands, Percival was also directed to investigate, while in the Pacific, the matter of the Hawaiian chiefs' sandalwood debts, which were long overdue for payment. He distinguished himself most at Honolulu by his vigorous advocacy of free trade in women.

Percival's stay got off to an uncertain start when the missionaries did not come down to the waterfront to welcome his ship. Further, Percival fired courtesy salutes on a Sunday, even though the chiefs had asked him to postpone the observance. Ashore, he entertained the chiefs, to put them in a receptive frame of mind for discussions of the sandalwood debts, and he mollified the sabbatarians by attending church services. Then he asked the chiefs to remove the kapu on women in favor of the *Dolphin's* men. The chiefs consulted the missionaries, and the missionaries quoted from the Bible.

One Sunday toward the end of January, Percival took some of his officers and several Honolulu foreigners on an excursion to Pearl River. Natives there, on Ka'ahumanu's instructions, stopped them from fishing and lighting fires. Ka'ahumanu had also ordered that no women be permitted to visit them. Percival returned to Honolulu very angry. Through the first weeks of February he tried rational argument: Lord Byron, so Percival claimed, had been allowed women (false, said Elisha Loomis). Then Percival used bluster: he told Boki he would tear down the missionaries' houses. On Washington's birthday, February 22, he conferred again with the chiefs, saying that America and England both sanctioned prostitutes at Waikīkī to keep them away from the *Dolphin;* they refused to release them.

On Sunday, February 26, as Bingham was preparing for services in Kalanimoku's stone house, a group of men from the *Dolphin* burst in demanding women. Outside more than a hundred sailors began to smash the windows with clubs. Then they left to descend upon Bingham's house at Kawaiaha'o. Bingham, afraid for his wife and children, ran to his home. He found that his wife had locked the door. The sailors caught him in his yard and surrounded him, flourishing clubs and knives. Some natives, including the Christian female chief, Lydia Nāmāhana, were there. As Bingham raised his umbrella to ward off a blow from a club, Nāmāhana put up her arm to help him and was struck. At this, the Hawaiians threw themselves upon the sailors, and in a few seconds knocked out several and seized and bound others. Loomis and Chamberlain arrived as a native was raising a rock to brain a prostrate sailor; they were just in time to save the seaman's life. Bingham managed to get inside his house as another wave of sailors flung themselves against the door. Before the rioters could do more than break a window or two, Percival and his officers appeared and caned their men into quiet.

That night Percival, having imprisoned a few of the ringleaders and advised other commanders to keep their liberty parties small, made some muted apologies for the attack on the missionaries, but followed this with another demand that the kapu be lifted. Governor Boki yielded, with the acquiescence of his fort commander Manuia. The missionaries could do very little. Their stated position was that the law and its enforcement were in the hands of the chiefs. As boatloads of women passed back and forth in the harbor, the Christians set aside a day to fast and pray that the judgment of God might be averted from Hawai'i, and that Percival might see the light. The churchgoing chiefs for their part had not known what kinds of resistance were lawful. They had put hundreds of men in arms on the night following the riot, and guards were placed on the streets thenceforth. By April 1, the chiefs felt ready, to override Boki and reimpose the kapu. A crier carried the word through the town; and from then on a gun was fired at nine o clock each night to warn natives and sailors to clear the streets.

There was no more rioting. Percival, at a dinner for the chiefs, read from the Bible a passage concerning Solomon, who was a wise man with a thousand wives; in private he tried to induce one of the Holmes girls to live with him. Finally, to the unbounded relief of the missionaries, the *Dolphin* sailed on May 11. Assessing their losses, which included the disbandment of two schools for native girls, the Protestants reaffirmed what they had been convinced of for some time: that there was nothing but hostility all about them in the foreign community, and that it was vain to hope for aid from anyone outside the small mission circle.[72]

That circle had soon to be drawn even tighter than before. In 1825–1826, the mission acquired another formidable enemy to stand beside John C. Jones. Richard Charlton, a trader who had visited the islands earlier in the eighteen-twenties, was commissioned as British consul for the Sandwich, Society, and Friendly Islands. He had arrived in Honolulu just before the *Blonde*. Consular affairs had taken him to the South Pacific at the time of the *Dolphin* riots, but on his return he continued a policy he had put into action almost on his first day ashore: that of reviling the mission.

From the American Protestant point of view Britain could hardly have made a worse choice. Rough, obtuse, foul-mouthed, choleric, Charlton matched and even exceeded J.C. Jones in fantasies about the purpose of the mission, and he suffered in addition from an ingrained suspicion and hostility about the larger motives of the United States in the Pacific. He faced Honolulu with a mixture of contempt and unselective rage. He drank to excess; he fornicated; he was chronically litigious; he menaced white men with duelling pistols or had his bully boys beat them; he threatened natives with flogging or decapitation; he spoke wildly of killing Ka'ahumanu and tearing down the Honolulu fort; in 1829 he lassoed a Hawaiian and dragged him a mile behind his horse; he assaulted a newspaper editor; he accused a British merchant of sodomy; he slaughtered trespassing cows and chickens without mercy. For two decades he laid about him savagely and clumsily: and from the debris of his personal dealings in the village he constructed great diplomatic causes. When, after twenty years, the efforts of the Hawaiian government and the Honolulu mission to have him removed were at last successful, he departed leaving his archives in shambles, his illegitimate offspring unprovided for, and in the courts of Honolulu (and the chancelleries of Hawai'i and Britain) the most involved and painful case of land litigation in the history of nineteenth-century Hawai'i.

There was no love lost between Charlton and J.C. Jones, nor between Charlton and other Americans, notably Stephen Reynolds, himself a man of no little irascibility. But these eccentrics, of whom Honolulu was acquiring perhaps more than a fair share, could find common cause in attacking the mission (for its part not entirely devoid of originals). Charlton's wedge to split open the mission-government united front was Boki, whose temperament was more volatile than that of his brother Kalanimoku and the other Christian chiefs. Boki, from about the time of the *Dolphin* riots, had begun to find more gratification in downtown Honolulu than at Kawaiaha'o, and his foreign experience and attachments were, after all, British.

Boki continued to be a churchgoer until about September, 1826. He had been baptized by a Catholic priest on board Louis de Freycinet's *Uranie* at Honolulu in 1819, and had attended communion with the officers of the *Blonde* on his way home from England in 1825. Accordingly, he was permitted to partake of the Lord's Supper at Kawaiaha'o. Then not long after the *Dolphin* riots, a rumor reached Elisha Loomis that someone was once again allowing women to board ships and was taxing the traffic in prostitution. Loomis questioned the young king, who denied any part in the business, saying that if it were anyone, it must be Boki. A little later, Loomis learned that Boki owned a billiard room in town, and this discovery filled Loomis with indignation.

Levi Chamberlain spoke against gambling at Sabbath service, but reports persisted of Boki's gaming—and drinking. Loomis asked the Christian chiefs to speak to Boki about this scandalous conduct. A tremendous storm broke. Boki attacked the missionaries for presuming to dictate law in the islands. He refused to allow them any competence in this; the authority, he said, was all with the king. As for gambling, King George of England gambled, so did Prime Minister Canning, and so would he. Boki and the young king did not appear at church for two weeks, but the missionaries were convinced that the course of true morality had the, support of most of the chiefs, including Boki's brother Kalanimoku. At least the missionaries knew where Boki stood. With characteristic Calvinist satisfaction at having identified a black sheep, Loomis wrote: "We have long suspected Boki's professions of piety had little solid foundation. We are glad be has now come cut boldly for it is best men should be ranged under their proper colors...We are glad Boki no longer labors in disguise."[73]

Boki was an influential enemy. He occupied a high post in Honolulu as governor of O'ahu, and in addition his visit to England had endowed him with immense prestige. For some time after his return, chiefs and commoners alike listened avidly and respectfully to his accounts of high life in London. On formal occasions, he shone in the full-dress uniform of a British major-general, and he saw to it that his retainers were colorfully clothed. He was generous with patronage, and with land, to the point of giving away tracts to which he had no title. He and his free-living wife Liliha commanded a considerable following among the non-Christian natives of Honolulu. Most significant of all, Boki enjoyed the confidence and friendship of the king. They went everywhere together—to church when they felt like it, on sandalwood-cutting expeditions, on sailing jaunts between islands, up to the quiet retreat of Mānoa valley, down to the grogshops and billiard saloons at the waterfront.

Boki's open hostility was a sharp reminder to the missionaries that their accomplishment in Honolulu, though promising, remained limited. It was all the more galling, therefore, when foreigners savaged them as if evangelization had been a total success. John C. Jones rose to new heights of abusiveness as the missionaries attempted to lead natives to habits of work and habits of grace. Jones claimed Hawaiians had been seduced from one to the other: "the religion that has been taught these people inculcates no honesty, no work, by grace they are to be saved." Honolulu was a doomed place, where nothing but the "sound of the church going bell is heard from the rising to the setting sun and religion is cramm'd down the throats of these poor simple mortals whilst certain famine and destruction are staring them in the face." Work and grace were obsessive themes with Jones: the chiefs' sandalwood debts remained unpaid, and Hannah Holmes alternately shared Jones' bed and deserted him for Christ. It was all Bingham's fault, so Jones reasoned. The Honolulu traders organized a petition against Bingham, and Jones went to the king more than once to demand that the "meddling, overbearing, dogmatical preacher" be removed.[74]

In town, when missionary encountered merchant, prolonged and vituperative theological disputes took place. Stephen Reynolds gratuitously labelled the bachelor missionary Levi Chamberlain a fornicator. At Kawaiaha'o, when the mission scheduled mid-week prayer meetings, the foreigners staged horse races outside the church and urged the king to attend. When a Tahitian mission helper began to hold prayer meetings at the Honolulu market, Jones threatened to shoot him.

Even formal contact was almost non-existent. Jones read funeral services over deceased Americans rather then invite missionaries to preach, and he and a naturalist left at Honolulu by a British man-of-war conducted English-language church services in the town so that foreigners need not suffer at Kawaiaha'o. Invitations to dinners celebrating July the Fourth only grudgingly included missionaries, or excluded them altogether. Union defeated factionalism just once, in the second half of 1826. On December 21, the Americans of Honolulu assembled to pay tribute to Thomas Jefferson and John Adams, after news of the great men's deaths reached the islands. A procession left Jones' house, and, while minute guns were fired, the participants marched to an open place set aside for religious exercises. There a hymn was sung, and Bingham preached.[75]

Opposition from residents was by now to be expected; aggravatingly enough, their critical remarks were seconded by some important visitors, like the naval commanders Otto von Kotzebue and Frederick William Beechey. Kotzebue had been at Honolulu before the missionaries came; be returned in 1824, and found not progress but decline in every aspect of native life. His was a philosophical stance as much as anything else. He was a late adherent of eighteenth-century thinking of the "Noble Savage" school, who had seen Hawaiian society before the breakdown of the kapu. The missionaries, Romantic constructionists of Calvinism, heavily committed to the idea of the native as suffering heathen, could hardly have formulated a program to suit Beechey, a Britisher whose perceptions of the Honolulu scene were mediated by Charlton. He was predisposed to find what he did—a hang-dog native population, demoralized rather than inspirited by the American mission, condemned to endless pious labor, without the rewards they would have won had they developed business competence of the own, without the leisure they would have enjoyed had the mission never come.[76]

Percival's obstructionist attitude was worst of all. He was a representative of the United States who, unaccountably, did not support his nation's religious envoys. The mission was much more pleased with the next American naval commander to visit Honolulu: Thomas ap Catesby Jones of USS *Peacock*. Jones' instructions empowered him to clean up the rat's nest of beached sailors lodged at Honolulu. Whaling interests were worried that the wild and lawless life of the deserters might lead to piracy and murder. In addition, Jones conducted negotiations at Honolulu which placed the sandalwood debts of the Hawaiian chiefs on a regularized basis, with provisions for periodic payments. Removal of the deserters would improve the climate in which the mission worked; liquidation of the debts would benefit the merchants.

Jones arrived at Honolulu on October 10, 1826. He began immediately to round up American deserters. After a large group was screened on November 1, thirty men were dispersed on board the *Peacock* and the several American whalers in port. Others were set to hard labor, loading ships or pulling heavy carts about town. A system of liberty passes for all sailors was arranged; those ashore without a ticket might be fined. $50. Jones put other suggestions before the chiefs to help them with the problem of desertion; but as long as life at sea and life in the islands exerted their various pressures, sailors would continue to leave their ships.

At the beginning of November, Jones submitted to the chiefs the sandalwood claims of the American merchants. Six weeks passed. The traders, at first willing to leave the matter in Jones' hands, were calling by December for an early issue, and talking about the necessity for the use of force On December 27, an agreement was signed. The chiefs acknowledged debts amounting to 15,000 piculs, or $120,000–160,000. Under a tax law proclaimed that day, each able-bodied Hawaiian was given nine months to bring to the chiefs half a picul of good sandalwood or its equivalent in Spanish dollars or commodities. At the same time, he could cut for himself another half-picul. Each woman was to bring a woven mat or a length of kapa worth one Spanish dollar. The year 1827 saw great activity, but when another American man-of-war made a stop at Honolulu in 1829 the debts were by no means paid, and the whole agreement had to be re-negotiated. Not until 1843 were the notes of 1829 redeemed.[77]

Jones performed two other functions while at Honolulu. On behalf of the United States, he signed an informal treaty of commerce and friendship with the chiefs; and he presided over a hearing to consider the mission-merchant feud. Within three months of the departure of John Percival, Ka'ahumanu and Bingham had toured O'ahu advocating the acceptance of the Ten Commandments as a basis for public policy. In September, 1826, the mission's general meeting at Honolulu heard a committee recommend that the evangelists, while abstaining from political interference, should not cease to lift up their voices against the vices of Hawaiians. This "lifting up of voices" might properly include advice and information about Christian laws and political institutions.

Late in October, when the *Peacock* had been in town more than two weeks, the missionaries distributed to all residents and ship-masters a printed circular, making unmistakably clear the commitment of the Protestants to morality in government, together with definitions of the rights of Hawaiian rulers and the duties of their subjects. Furthermore, they invited investigation of their course.

The mercantile-consular opposition, including Stephen Reynolds, Dixey Wildes, John Meek, Eliab Grimes, John Dominis, John C. Jones and Richard Charlton, proposed a confrontation before the commander of the *Peacock*. The mission urged them to put charges in writing; the residents announced that they wanted merely a candid hearing of the mission's self-defense.

The stage seemed set for a decisive meeting; but when the two parties came together at Boki's house on December 8 very little was resolved. Charlton acted as spokesman for the anti-mission group. His criticisms were wide-ranging: he found fault with the chiefs, the people, and the schools, as well as with the missionaries themselves.

Other foreigners spoke, but none was willing to put his objections on paper as the mission wanted. Boki took no part; Charlton said this was because no chief dared speak against a missionary. The churchmen produced a written endorsement from John Young (now reconciled to the presence of the mission) and relied on the tacit support of the Honolulu chiefs. Inconclusive discussion took place; then ap Catesby Jones adjourned the meeting, saying that he found the mission circular "full and fair." There had been a chance for its incorrectness to be demonstrated; no one had made use of that opportunity. Jones reiterated his general approval of the mission venture both before and after he left the islands, and the missionaries made the most of this, but the departure of the *Peacock* left things very much as they had been. No short-term intervention could provide solutions for the strife that beset Honolulu.[78]

If the mission had the backing of Captain Jones, the foreign residents had the king in pawn. Boki, and through him Charlton, influenced the young Kauikeaouli far more than the mission or the Christian chiefs could. In the continuing battle over morals, the king emerged as a friend of men stigmatized by the church. Ka'ahumanu could not make Kauikeaouli listen to her; Kalanimoku, the king's other official protector, was old and mortally ill. Kauikeaouli began to disregard his studies in favor of the ancient sports, and his people followed him. In February, 1827, when Frederick Beechey of the *Blossom* was in Honolulu once more, a three-day hula was given, and the king went to all the performances, the first two of which were held at Boki's sugar plantation in Mānoa valley. Beechey observed that the frilly dresses of the dancers suggested an indecency he had not remarked before, when they were unclad. Levi Chamberlain regretted a combination of evils: "the amusement, he wrote, "was connected with intemperance. Just at evening we saw a company returning on horseback—some of than apparently the worse for liquor. In the company were several foreigners."[79]

This particular aspect of the situation in Honolulu was complicated by the ill-health of prime minister Kalanimoku, who had become an exemplary Christian. The days were long gone since he, with chiefly insouciance, had burned part of the village of Honolulu to smoke out an errant wife, or, with heathen carelessness some years later, had taken his brother Boki's wife (Boki in turn had acquired Liliha from his nephew to supply the deficiency). It was Kalanimoku's captured wife, Likelike, who in 1821 had borne him the child whose birth was celebrated by the detonation of two hundred pounds of gunpowder, and whose death was the occasion of the disputed hula of Liholiho and the funeral sermon of Bingham. Since 1821, Kalanimoku's riotousness had changed to piety. He had been the first chief in Honolulu to be married in a Christian ceremony and among the first to receive baptism from the mission (this cancelled a Catholic baptism in 1819, performed by the same priest who had baptized Boki). Now, early in 1827, Kalanimoku was readying himself for a Christian death, and Boki was drifting farther and farther from the church. Once, there had been great affection between the brothers, but the new order of things had driven them apart; and when after several tappings by foreign doctors, it became clear to Kalanimoku that his dropsy was incurable, he went to Lahaina to die, telling the missionary William Richards he could no longer suffer Honolulu because of Boki's iniquity.

I was one day very low and all the chiefs came to see me, After I revived a little, I perceived my brother was not there—I enquired for bin when I was told that he was at his house in a fit of intoxication, feeble as I was I ordered my waggon brought to the door, and being removed into it I proceeded immediately to his house—I entered the door and looked—he saw me and said "I am wicked." I answered, I have often heard of your intemperance but now I have seen—When I was supposed to be dying all the chiefs came to see me; but my only brother was not there. He said again, "I am wicked." I answered, it is ended, I am about to leave you.[80]

Kalanimoku died in February, 1827, and the news of his death reached Honolulu on the weekend of Boki's hula for Beechey and the king. The loss of Kalanimoku certainly debilitated the mission and strengthened Boki. Some expected the prime minister's death to touch off a crisis, not only for the mission in Honolulu, but for the nation at large: Boki might try to dislodge Ka'ahumanu from her regency, turning his personal control over the king and the town into control over the kingdom. Up to this point Boki had not tested his following among the faction-ridden native and foreign communities of Honolulu. In December, 1826, Levi Chamberlain had heard whispers of possible rebellion; and Beechey, close to Boki and Chariton during his 1827 visit, wrote that Boki was assembling men at the Honolulu fort. A week after Kalanimoku's death the issue came into the open, and in a simple verbal trial of strength the supremacy of Ka'ahumanu was reaffirmed. A question arose at a chiefs' meeting concerning a state visit to Hawai'i. Boki wanted to go; Ka'ahumanu challenged him, and Boki replied, "It is with you—if you wish to go—go, and take along the king and his sister; it is with you to exercise authority. Kamehameha at his death committed his son to your charge and the kingdom to your care—and it was the wish of Kalanimoku that you should still have the charge. The mana is yours."[81] Ka'ahumanu exercised this mana in defense of morality when in May, 1827, she charged Boki, Liliha, and several members of the king's train with misconduct, intemperance, fornication, and adultery, and had them fined—just a few days after the facile Boki had told Levi Chamberlain that he wanted to turn to the pono (the good) and that the king had acquired a Christian instructor.[82]

In July, 1827, French Catholic missionaries arrived in Honolulu, introducing another disturbing element to the volatile local scene. The idea for a French mission dated from Liholiho's voyage to Great Britain in 1823–1824. One of the king's traveling companions was Jean Rives, the Frenchman who had been tutor to Liholiho and who later became a "white chief" with several wives and large landholdings. Rives left the royal party in London and went to Paris to advocate a French settlement in the islands, where, Rives claimed, he was a person of great importance. As the plan developed, it provided for a commercial colony to be established with the support of the Ministry of Foreign Affairs and the Bureau of Commerce and Colonies. Missionary priests from the Society of Piepus accompanied the colonists. The ship *Comète* brought to Honolulu on July 7, 1827, several agriculturists led by a young Frenchman, Auguste de Morineau, a lawyer who hoped to become French consul; and six missionaries, three of them priests, under Father Alexis Bachelot, apostolic prefect.[83]

Rives was not there to greet them. Returning from Europe on another ship, he had reached the California coast, where he learned that the death of Liholiho had cost him his privileged position in the islands. He never came back to Honolulu; thus the French were in a very uncertain situation. They landed without permission from Ka'ahumanu, who, in fact, tried to get rid of them immediately. She summoned them to her; they disregarded the call. She sent for Boki to carry out a re-embarkation order, but Boki was away in the country, and by the time he returned the *Comète* had sailed, leaving the Frenchmen ashore.

Alone among the chiefs Boki was friendly to the French. There is no reason to believe that he felt himself bound by his Catholic baptism of 1819. There is, however, every reason to think that he saw the Catholic mission as an instrument for disrupting the relations of the American Protestants with the Hawaiian government and thus advancing his own ends. He arranged the use of houses for the newcomers and later granted them land (in the possession of the Catholic church to this day), attended Mass, and stood in the way of a systematic persecution projected by Ka'ahumanu and tacitly countenanced by the Protestant mission.

Even with Boki's help, there was little the Catholics could do. Their workers cultivated land; the priests baptized children brought to them by foreigners (John C. Jones, Stephen Reynolds, and John Ebbets had refused to have the sacrament performed at Kawaiaha'o). In January, 1828, a small Catholic chapel was opened, and the priests began to preach and teach. In 1828 they baptized seventeen natives, twelve of them children. In 1829, up to July, they baptized more than eighty. These were modest beginnings, especially since Morineau and two of workers had left Honolulu less than two in months after arrival, and in 1829 one priest and on lay brother had departed. Still, the mere presence of Catholics in the islands was sufficient to alarm the Protestants. Even before the *Comète* anchored at Honolulu, Bingham had received news of the French mission, and had written for advice to his superiors at the American Board in Boston. In the interim the Protestant missionaries preached against idolatry and began work on a geography text for use in native schools, which pointed out the relative progress made in different parts of the world under Protestantism and Catholicism.

Catholicism in its first few years remained a side issue. In the meantime the controversy over morals returned to the center of the stage. At Lahaina, Governor Hoapili of Maui had been trying to prevent native women going aboard ship. This course of action had the support of the resident missionary William Richards. In October, 1827, the crew of the English whaler *John Palmer* had gone so far as to fire cannon-shot into the village of Lahaina after unsuccessful forays ashore for women. News of this came to Honolulu toward the end of the month. The sympathies of foreigners were very much on the side of the sailors. In the midst of discussion, Captain Buckle of the *Daniel* returned to Honolulu, to find that his conduct at Lahaina in 1825, when he allegedly bought a native girl from a female chief, had found its way into print in the New York *Observer*, copies of which had ready reached Honolulu. Enraged, he was about to go to Lahaina and confront his enemy Richards; instead, Ka'ahumanu called a chiefs' council in Honolulu and asked Richards to attend. She had in mind general considerations as well as a hearing of the difficulty between Buckle and Richards. Some Honolulu natives believed Richards might be banished or put to death. Buckle threatened to kill Richards and bombard Lahaina. Richard Charlton said the missionaries should be prosecuted for libeling Buckle, and the publishers of the libel should be pilloried or chained to a block for ten years. Charlton went on to talk of taking Richards and Levi Chamberlain to England. Stephen Reynolds hoped that, at the very least, Richards would be tried before a jury of Americans. All were disappointed. The chiefs merely heard partisans of both sides and dismissed the charges against Richards. They went on, in the first week of December, 1827, to take up once again the question of a fundamental moral law for Hawai'i.[84]

The rebuff to the foreigners over the Richards case was followed by concern over the laws drafted by Ka'ahumanu and scrutinized for Christian propriety by Bingham. Six crimes were proscribed: murder, theft, adultery, prostitution, gambling, and selling of alcoholic spirits. Boki opposed actively the passage of any such laws. It was suggested that Governor Kuakini of Hawai'i (John Adams) should take the code to England for approval by King George; Boki said the king would not see Adams, and that, in any event, King George had left lawmaking to the chiefs. Adams said that if Hawai'i needed British permission to make laws, then Britain would send men-of-war to enforce them and Hawaiians would lose their freedom.

Boki's non-cooperation may be traced to the fact that he had something of a vested interest in all but the first two of the six prohibited activities. Charlton, too, was in general opposition, and in the end, after more consultations, a crowd gathered on December 14 in a coconut grove by the waterfront to hear a prayer by Bingham, the singing of a Hawaiian hymn, addresses by Boki and Ka'ahumanu and the proclamation of only three laws—against murder, theft and adultery. These were to go into effect three months later, over the king's signature. The remaining laws were to be subjected to more study, with the aid of handbills printed at the mission press.[85]

The year 1828 was the most peaceful of the decade. There were no sailor riots and no serious contretemps between missionaries and foreign residents. This was so partly because the moral laws of 1827 were ignored by Boki. Then too, the projected additions to the laws were delayed until 1829. The third contingent of Protestant missionaries arrived in March, 1828, bringing to Honolulu a doctor, Gerrit Parmele Judd of New York state, who resigned from the mission in the eighteen-forties to enter the Hawaiian government and became, after Bingham's departure, the lightning rod for all anti-Protestant and anti-government storms.[86] In mid-1828, there was a brief flurry of excitement when it was reported that Richard Charlton was fomenting revolt among O'ahu's foreigners, who would back him in killing Ka'ahumanu, but this was evidently nothing more then a fantasy on Charlton's part. Stephen Reynolds wrote sensibly that although Charlton might be ready to take up arms against the chiefs, no one would join him.[87]

There was, however, renewed tension as 1829 opened. The disaffection of Boki and the king persisted. There was talk that Ka'ahumanu intended to poison Boki, unseat the king, and place either the king's half-sister Kīna'u or Kīna'u's son upon the throne. Boki went about telling foreigners that the mission chiefs were plotting a massacre of haoles. In April, 1829, it appeared as if Boki might be about to make another attempt to overthrow Ka'ahumanu's regency. Bingham heard from a "respectable trader" that John C. Jones, Charlton, and others were talking of war, and that Boki planned to attack Ka'ahumanu when she came back from a trip to windward. Boki was, in fact, assembling his men at Waikīkī, against the strong urgings of Kekūanaō'a (father of Kamehameha IV and V, and later governor of O'ahu). Ka'ahumanu returned to Honolulu on April 8, 1829. With war seemingly imminent, Bingham stretched the missionary injunction against political interference (not for the first time), and met with Boki and the king at Boki's Blonde Hotel, a two-story wooden building named after the vessel which had brought Boki back from England in 1825 and later turned by him into a tavern, "where noisy swine gathered...drunkenness and licentious indulgence became common, and people gathered...for hulas and filthy dances. Foreigners came [there] to find women and Kaahumanu and the missionaries were discussed there."[88]

In these uncongenial surroundings, Bingham undertook to propitiate Boki—with great success. Once again Boki found himself unable to translate his inchoate ambitions into action, and Bingham left him willing enough to put aside the sword he had never really unsheathed. Boki promised to attend to Christian instruction, and the king, too, offered to take up his books again. That evening Bingham served tea to the subdued insurgents. The king requested that Ka'ahumanu join them. They sang hymns together; and a few days later Boki became a member of the Monday evening class for inquiry into the meaning of scripture.[89]

After a mere ten days Boki fell into a severe dispute with his wife Liliha. With some difficulty, a native teacher brought them together once more. Boki reaffirmed his good intentions late in May. At the close of a Saturday service, he went home with Bingham, saying he would call frequently to ask about his Christian duties.[90] A fortnight later, Boki abandoned his piety, and outraged Christian virtue by getting drunk and urging traditional incestuous royal marriage between the king and his sister, Princess Nāhi'ena'ena. Evidently, Ka'ahumanu had arrogated to herself the privilege of making a match for Kauikeaouli, and this infuriated Boki, whose blurred vision of the good life focused at times on the lost institutions of ancient Hawai'i. Levi Chamberlain describes Boki's outburst:

> Three native schooners arrived from Lahaina this morning The Princess [Nahienaena], Hoapiri wahine [wife of the governor of Maui], Kekaunohi [a female chief] and Keali'iahonui [the young husband of Kaahumanu] came with her. They were met by Boki who had been drinking; and he said to the Princess do you kill Kaahumanu & all her family & take your brother for a husband, or you will not be king of these islands Kaahumanu will set up Kamehameha. If you and your brother marry and have a child he will be the rightful heir to the kingdom. The princess replied, What you say is foolish.—Boki took her by the ear to pull her along saying what did you come down here for; did you come as a god to be worshipped?—He endeavored to separate her from her attendants in order to retain her into the house alone with the King; but Kekaunuohi & Keali'iahonui remained

with her while some of her attendants run off to inform Hoapili
wahine.—She however got out of the hands of the governor and
went to the house of some of the other chiefs.[91]

The king and the princess were, in fact, sleeping with each other,
had been ever since 1824, when Kauikeaouli was ten years old and
Nāhiʻenaʻena seven. The question of the royal marriage had been raised
time to time, and an incestuous union apparently had the approval of
the chiefs in 1828 and 1829. The Protestant mission, confusing what
was with what ought to have been, publicly defended Nāhiʻenaʻena's
"character" from the aspersions of Honolulu traders. The missionaries
preferred to think of Nāhiʻenaʻena as she appeared at the dedication
of a new church at Kawaiahaʻo, which took place in July, 1829.[92] At the
inaugural service in the huge thatch meeting-house, the king and the
princess offered spontaneous prayers and joined in the chanting of the
Hundredth Psalm in Hawaiian, to the gratification of the mission. Boki
was there, very uncomfortable. He was in charge of public works on
Oʻahu, and the building of the church must have been ungrateful task.
He assisted in carrying Kauikeaouli and Nāhiʻenaʻena to the ceremonies
on a litter, but during the service he and his wife Liliha sat apart from the
other chiefs, restless and ill at ease.[93]

Boki was by now veering from pole to pole of Honolulu society.
In April the frustrated rebel, in mid-year the drunken nativist, in July a
surly celebrant at Kawaiahaʻo (and also at the July 4 dinner, where he
refused to drink a toast to Kaʻahumanu), he was in September once more
a true seeker after immortality. He applied for admission to the pōʻaha, a
group of earnest native hopefuls, required to abstain from every kind of
vice and professing to seek as their greatest concern the salvation of the
soul. Still, he did not give himself completely to the mission: he gathered
at his house a group of skilled kahuna and began to practice traditional
medicine, with its undertones of the black arts.

In August, Kaʻahumanu, unquestionably supreme in politics,
had instructed Boki that the Catholic Mass was forbidden to Hawaiians.
It was Boki's work as governor to enforce the prohibition, but he did
not; and for another few months his passive support of the French was
just sufficient to deter Kaʻahumanu from taking matters entirely into her
own hands. Kaʻahumanu, however, pushed her moral authority a step
farther in September when she issued an edict ordering all unmarried
couples—whether native and native or native and foreigner—to dissolve
their alliances.[94]

There was no immediate reaction, though it would have involved
(among many others) John C. Jones, who at that time presided over a
three-cornered menage with Hannah Holmes and Lahilahi, a daughter

of Marin. Jones' attention, and that of all Honolulu, was diverted by the first major public explosion of British Consul Richard Charlton. Charlton was a great legalist on matters of his own (if not of others') property rights He shot cattle straying on his Honolulu lands, while his own livestock wandered everywhere. At last, in October 1829, an exasperated native took a gun, chased a trespassing cow of Charlton's onto a common, and killed it.

Charlton wanted to punish the Hawaiian personally. The chiefs offered to assess damages if the native proved to be at fault, but this was too dilatory a course for Chariton.. He and John C. Jones sought out the killer of the cow, put a noose round his neck, and dragged him behind a horse to the village. The man fell, exhausted, but Chariton continued to pull him along the ground. The native was saved from serious injury by the intervention of Samuel Mills (an American-educated mission Hawaiian named for a pioneer evangelist), who cut the rope and freed him.

Charlton called a meeting of Britishers. They used the death of the cow as a basis for complaints to the chiefs that foreign property and foreign lives were constantly endangered in Honolulu. Threats were made that the matter would be referred to the British government unless the chiefs arranged quick redress. Charlton was able to collect 45 signatures supporting this statement, and a further 16 illiterates made their marks. The government's response came quite soon, in the form of an edict printed on the mission press, and worded, so Stephen Reynolds thought, by Bingham (though the prose was more Hawaiian than missionary in tone). The edict allowed Chariton no latitude at all. He had shot cattle for trespassing, without having made his boundaries known; his own cow had trespassed on well-defined private ground. His angry handling of the Hawaiian was rash and criminal; the wounding of a beast was by no means equal to the wounding of a man. The laws of the islands, previously published, held for both natives and foreigners.[95]

Charlton was intransigent. He opened a correspondence with the British Foreign Office; but the Hawaiian government had scored a victory for its power to promulgate and enforce its own laws, including the moral laws held over from 1827. The chiefs' general course was approved (and the moral influence of the Protestant mission lauded) by the commander of an American man-of-war which anchored at Honolulu on October 14, just a week after the government edict was issued. Captain W. C. B. Finch of USS *Vincennes* came to the islands with a letter: from Samuel Southard, Secretary of the Navy, praising the Hawaiians' progress toward civilization through Christianity, and authorizing Finch to inquire into breaches of island law by Americans. This happily-timed visit was very much appreciated by the Hawaiian chiefs, and the officers of the *Vincennes* were duly feasted in various places about Honolulu—the king's thatched residence for one, and Nu'uanu valley for another, where, at the urging of Boki's wife Liliha, Finch and his men sampled live shrimp.[96]

In the course of his visit, Finch re-opened the sandalwood question. Payment of debts had languished somewhat after the burst of activity which followed the visit of the *Peacock* in 1826, At that time, fifteen thousand piculs had been acknowledged as due the Honolulu Americans. By September, 1827, about four thousand piculs had been distributed among the creditors; by January, 1828, almost seven thousand. This left more than half the debt still on the books; and when Finch arrived in October, 1829, nearly two more years had passed and the figure had risen above ten thousand piculs. According to the merchants, a great deal of wood had been harvested in the hills—about twenty-five thousand piculs altogether. But the chiefs neglected their old debts, preferring instead to squander their new wealth on new possessions. The merchants presented their claims to Finch at the end of October. He conferred with the chiefs, and at the beginning of November, the king, Boki, and four others signed two notes, one for 4,700 piculs, representing the remainder of the debt owed from 1826, the other for 2,165 piculs, an amount they owed for the purchase of a ship early in 1828.[97]

The *Vincennes* agreements tied Boki, in particular, very tightly. In 1826 he had taken personal responsibility for payment of part of the debt assessed by Thomas ap Catesby Jones of the *Peacock*. For a year thereafter he had worked diligently to discharge his obligation, without much support iron his fellow chiefs. The debts had not been liquidated, and now a new schedule of payments committed him heavily once more in his official capacity as governor of O'ahu.

Boki's difficulties over sandalwood were compounded by his other financial troubles. In fact, a luxurious style of living coupled with commercial failure meant that he was fairly trapped. In the mid-twenties he had planted some sugar cane in Mānoa valley, with the aid of an Englishman, John Wilkinson. After Wilkinson died in 1826, Boki took charge himself, running a road into the valley and setting a hundred natives to work on the plantation at $2 a week. A mill was built, apparently with the idea that processed sugar might be sold in California, but by the end of 1827 nothing had come of the plan. In 1828 Boki made an arrangement with a group of foreigners, including John C. Jones, William Ebbets, and the sometime business partners Stephen Reynolds and William French. These men were convinced enemies of the mission. They set up a still and began to make rum from the plantation's molasses.

Ka'ahumanu imposed a kapu upon its manufacture. The Protestant mission would not lend its ox-carts—the only ones in Honolulu—for the carrying of cane. Finally, Ka'ahumanu ordered the cane torn up. The still passed into the hands of a Dr. Serriere. He was incompetent, and lost money. In 1830, the distillery continued to operate under the direction of a French agriculturist, who had come to the islands with the mission-colony in 1827. He used kī-root instead of molasses, but even this circumvention of Ka'ahumanu's kapu did not make the venture a success. William French claimed that it cost him $7,000; Boki must have suffered too.[98]

Boki had other business interests as well, but it is doubtful that he profited from any of them. From 1827 on, he speculated in trade at Canton, Manila, Tahiti, and the Russian settlements in Alaska. With return cargoes, he traded in Honolulu. Boki's small dry goods stores competed unsuccessfully with those of foreigners, and soon his shops were known among the natives as 'ai'ē nui—deep in debt. His biggest enterprise was the Blonde Hotel, scene of his confrontation with Bingham in 1829. Nothing is known of its finances, although in general, grogshops and houses of assignation enjoyed better prospects of survival than most businesses in Honolulu, the moral law notwithstanding.[99]

By the end of 1829, then, Boki might well have found the islands insufferable. He was bound to the uncongenial labor of the sandalwood debts; his trading voyages netted him nothing; his sugar plantation was finished; Ka'ahumanu was too powerful for him in politics; the mission chiefs, coached by Bingham, were implacably opposed to him; the Hawaiian past was slipping away; his marriage plans for the royal brother and sister would probably come to nothing. He was beaten at every turn.

By a stroke of seemingly happy coincidence, Boki found a way to free himself from his heavy constrictions. In the month of November, 1829, the same month in which he signed the *Vincennes* notes, a ship arrived from Port Jackson, New South Wales, bringing news of a rich sandalwood island far to the southwest—Erromanga, in the New Hebrides. Boki wasted no time. He signed contracts with foreigners to direct and navigate an expedition. Within a few weeks, he recruited more than four hundred men. The *Kamehameha* carried about 250, most of them armed with muskets; the *Becket*, under Manuia, Boki's fort commander at Honolulu, carried about 180, among them a hundred soldiers from Boki's following at Honolulu and Wai'anae, where he owned lands. Not stopping even for the Sabbath, Boki's men worked hard to get the ships ready. They loaded all kinds of supplies, including gunpowder for the armed force. A few days before he sailed, Boki went to a church meeting and spoke: "Chiefs, teachers, relatives, and all those who have offered me help, listen to my thought. My sins are known to you, my stink has gone out from Hawaii to Kauai. My sins are many; I myself am responsible for them. I am going on account of the king's debt, not for idle pleasure. Pray God to guard me."[100]

Boki went aboard the *Kamehameha* but did not sail immediately, because the *Becket* was not ready. The king, Liliha, and Boki's friends in Honolulu were perturbed and grief-stricken. Kekūanaōʻa and others made last-minute efforts to dissuade Boki from going, but to no avail. On December 3 the *Becket*, commanded by Boki's friend Manuia, finished loading and joined the *Kamehameha*. The ships fired cannon shot in salute, and stood away to the south.

Six months went by. Early in June, 1830, the brigantine *Dhaulle* came to Honolulu from the sandalwood islands via Canton, bringing news that the *Kamehameha* had not reached Erromanga. The *Dhaulle* had heard reports while in the New Hebrides that a severe gale had been blowing when the *Kamehameha* sailed from Rotuma to Erromango, and that a small ship in the area had sighted pieces of wreckage on the open sea. In July, a schooner in port from the south confirmed this ominous information, adding that the *Becket* was returning alone via the Society Islands.

On the afternoon of August 3, 1830, the *Becket* dropped anchor at Honolulu. Horrifyingly, there were only twenty people on board—twelve natives and eight foreigners. All the rest were dead of a disease which had struck on Erromanga. The *Becket* had arrived there from Rotuma, and Manuia had settled down to wait for the *Kamehameha*. Boki's ship did not appear. Instead, word reached Erromango of the sighting of charred flotsam at sea. Manuia dispatched a boat to circle the island for signs of survivors. Nothing was found. The *Becket* stayed five weeks at Erromanga, but the sandalwood searchers, assisted by Rotuman natives, met with no success. The Erromangans were hostile, and there was bloodshed. Then sickness descended upon the ship. One hundred and eighty were dead before the *Becket* reached Rotuma again. Another twenty sick men were landed there. Manuia was among those who died, and his body, stitched into a tarpaulin, was brought home on the *Becket* for burial in Hawaiʻi. Boki was heard of no more.

His disappearance was regarded by the Protestant missionaries as, God's judgment upon a hardened sinner. Boki's expedition, formed for unworthy ends, had profaned the Sabbath in the course of its hasty loading. Without any doubt, it was the further sin of smoking in the gunpowder-filled hold that had brought about Boki's violent end. For the missionaries, the account was closed. The response of the common people of Honolulu was different. They wailed day and night for some time.

The affair had a strange aftermath. In 1831, a native from Wai'anae, Boki's old territory, hurried into Honolulu, shouting, "Boki is at Waianae! Boki is at Waianae with a warship!" The man was taken before the governor until the truth of his story could be tested. "The people were in an uproar, some frightened, some pleased," wrote the native historian Kamakau. "The red dust rose in clouds from the plain of Kaiwi'ula as natives and foreigners started out on horseback for Waianae. The church party who had declared Boki a stinking spirit became like a blunted needle." But it was all hallucination. The man had dreamed it, and he was publicly whipped for the disturbance he had caused. Reality had dealt Boki false to the last.[101]

The Eighteen-Thirties

In the eighteen-thirties, Honolulu experienced continued moral upheaval. For two years after Boki's departure, his wife Liliha attempted to perpetuate the administration he had bequeathed her, and in this relaxed atmosphere Catholics as well as immoralists were tolerated. The Protestant chiefs removed Liliha from office and expelled the Papists in 1831, whereupon a new effort was made to erect a Calvinistic godly community in Honolulu. The pious labors of the chiefs ware nullified when, in 1833, the young King Kauikeaouli rebelled against his mentors. Not until 1835 did the town return to sabbatarian normality, and a further three years passed before the temperance movement regained its former strength.

Catholic priests appeared in the islands once again in 1837. This time the chiefs drove them out forcibly, over the protests of foreign consuls and naval commanders. Persecution of native Catholics followed, reaching its height during a remarkable Protestant religious revival which swept the islands from 1837 until the end of the decade. Most powerful on the island of Hawai'i, the awakening was strong enough at Honolulu to lift the missionary church to unprecedented spiritual influence.

The spell of charismatic preaching and communal conversion was broken in 1839 by the arrival of a French man-of-war. At cannon's point the Hawaiian government was compelled to establish toleration for Catholics at Honolulu and throughout the islands. By the end of the decade, the great days of Protestant evangelism were over. The notable men of the first contingent were aging. Many of the converted ali'i were dead. Catholicism enjoyed parity of opportunity. The schools were no longer controlled by the Protestant church, but by the government. During the next fifteen years—up to the mid-fifties—Protestantism assumed a position as one among many elements in the increasingly complex life of Honolulu.

When Boki sailed for the New Hebrides, he left his wife Liliha in charge of Oʻahu, and she assumed in addition Boki's especially privileged relation with the king. By mid-1830, it was evident that Boki would not return. It was clear also that Liliha proposed to continue her husband's lax moral and administrative policy at Honolulu. To the mission-affiliated chiefs this was offensive in the extreme, and they made ready to remove Liliha from the governorship of Oʻahu. The aliʻi came to this decision while accompanying the king on a tour of the windward islands. When the news reached Honolulu, Liliha prepared to rebel rather than relinquish her post. Her quarrel was with the Christian chiefs, not the king: only with great reluctance did Kauikeaouli agree that Liliha should be stripped of office, and he remained her close friend throughout.

Liliha called together her followers, the majority of them men— from Boki's lands at Waiʻanae. Her lover of the moment, the chief Pākī, bought muskets, powder and shot in large quantities. Toward the end of February, 1831, Levi Chamberlain heard that five hundred men, then a thousand, were under arms at the Honolulu fort and the Punchbowl battery. The Christian chiefs, assembled at Lahaina, dispatched Liliha's father Hoapili, governor of Maui, to reason with his daughter. Hoapili, a friend of the mission, was able to repeat the moral victory achieved by Bingham over Boki in 1829. He simply dissolved Liliha's rebellion in words. Meekly, she resigned the government of Oʻahu, surrendered the muskets at the fort, and went with her father to Lahaina.

Very few of Liliha's followers were Christians. As long as the fort was in their hands, no prayer meetings were held there—the missionaries, disapproving of Liliha's course, suspended work among the soldiery. After Hoapili broke up the insurrection in March, he dismissed Liliha's supporters from the fort and placed Christian natives in charge, upon which the mission resumed its meetings.

A more difficult issue arose when the foreigners of Honolulu complained that someone had written to the chiefs on Maui saying that the haoles were plotting against the king. They absolutely disavowed any such intention, saying they were completely loyal to Kauikeaouli, and that in fact they were organizing a great welcome for the king when he should return from windward. Nonetheless rumors persisted that the king might be in danger. Levi Chamberlain thought the foreigners simply wanted Kauikeaouli in their hands so that they might have him dictate policy free from the heavy moral pressure exerted by chiefs and missionaries. Gerrit Judd, however, heard that the foreigners hoped to lead the king into the fort and persuade him to sanction the murder of Kaʻahumanu and the older aliʻi. The high chief Kekūanaōʻa was supposedly ready to thwart this conspiracy by force—he would keep the king under armed protection until the chiefs were established once again in

Honolulu. Whatever the real truth of the foreigners' schemes, nothing happened. Hoapili took the precaution of placing a kapu upon the waters of Honolulu harbor on the day of the king's arrival; and Kauikeaouli came ashore on March 15, 1831, without the escort of twenty boats planned by the foreigners.[1]

At a public meeting on April 1, Kauikeaouli announced that he had sequestered the lands, forts and laws of Honolulu, and had given them to Ka'ahumanu. She in turn decreed that governmental policy in future would be based upon the Ten Commandments, and that the law would be enforced at Honolulu by a new governor of O'ahu—her brother Kuakini (who was governor of Hawai'i as well).[2]

Kuakini was an enormous chief, almost four hundred pounds in weight, a man of considerable intelligence and great authority, a pharisaical Christian who combined strict observance of the new religious forms with a traditionally arbitrary view of the prerogatives of a chief. He used Christianity primarily to dragoon his people after the failure of the kapu. At the meeting of April 1, he forbade gambling, the retailing of liquor, and the sale of liquor licenses in Honolulu. During the weeks that followed, he instituted a regime which the foreigners came to regard as a moral reign of terror. His police, led by a native called "Big Ben," patrolled the town with Genevan scrupulosity, taking wine from private dinner tables, breaking up the foreigners' billiards and bowling games, and putting a stop to Sunday riding, fiddling, dancing, and carousing.

Bingham was approached by the Englishman Dr. T.C.B. Rooke, who asked him to use his influence with the chiefs to have the regulations relaxed. Bingham, back in his role as non-interventionist missionary now that Honolulu was in the hands of the moralists, made the debater's point that if Rooke allowed him the power to relax regulations, he also allowed him the power to tighten them. The foreigners then met to frame their own protests to the king,[3] and quite soon they were able once more to buy liquor in Honolulu, although Kuakini continued to refuse legal permits for the traffic. Major progress toward New England morality was made in Sabbath observance, but in achieving "universal silence" on Sundays the mission and the government condemned themselves to noisy argument with foreigners during the rest of the week.

Once again, Bingham was the storm-center, At the height of the sabbatarian conflict, when crowds of natives gathered in the streets each Sunday to watch club-wielding policemen topple foreigners from horseback, Bingham came to believe that his own life was jeopardy at the hands of a cabal of Honolulu residents. Written charges and denials flew back and forth between Kawaiaha'o and the village. So impossible were relations that it required the establishment of citizens' committees and, ultimately, the mediation of United States Commercial Agent Jones to bring the matter to a stage where it no longer aroused publicly expressed wrath on either side.[4]

The chiefs who had determined that Liliha must be removed from office took a decision at the same time to eject the French Catholic missionaries from Honolulu. Ka'ahumanu's implacable hostility toward the Papists had been somewhat mitigated by Boki's friendliness, but even before Boki left the islands at the end of 1829 there were indications that the queen regent's political dominance would be used to suppress Catholicism. On August 8, 1829, she ordered the priests to halt their public services. Next day, guards were posted around the Catholic mission buildings and at the home of Marin, who had himself been performing services and baptisms. Boki countermanded Ka'ahumanu's instructions, but his departure from Honolulu soon afterward left the French mission very vulnerable. The high chief Kekūanaō'a told the priests on Christmas Day, 1829, that they must quit the islands. This was premature, for the ali'i were divided on tactics, but in January 1830, Ka'ahumanu reiterated her order forbidding the holding of services for natives. Stubbornly, however, a small group of Hawaiian converts continued secretly to attend Mass, to visit the priests for spiritual guidance, and to resist all attempts to force them to recant.

The chiefs' disapproval turned to persecution: as early as January, 1830, a woman was imprisoned, and soldiers went to the Catholic buildings and drove natives out. Interrogation by the king and other chiefs led some to give up their religion, but others persisted. In mid-year, about a dozen Catholic converts who scorned apostasy were confined in the fort at hard labor. Later, as many as fourteen inmates, men and women, were set to cutting and carrying stone or making mats pending their renunciation of Catholicism. The priests managed to baptize only two adults and twelve children in 1830.

By the end of that year the Protestant chiefs were beginning to talk of expelling the French Catholics, who had remained quiet in the face of the persecution of their adherents. The chiefs, as mentioned, met to windward, and, in the absence of Liliha (whose connections the Catholics through Boki made her suspect), made up their minds. Liliha's projected rebellion delayed the issue until April, 1831, but then, with Liliha dislodged and Kuakini's moral program at its height, the chiefs sent for the priests. At the fort, an order of expulsion was read. Stephen Reynolds heard that the chiefs warned the priests to be gone in three months on pain of losing their property, in four months on pain of being put in irons at the fort. The priests would not promise to go, but took the precaution of burying their church ornaments and concealing the rest of their belongings.

In June, Kuakini tried to arrange passage for the priests on a ship bound for Europe, without success. Their three-month stay was up, and, although the church's property was not confiscated, in July more natives were jailed for their religion. Twelve, including some minor chiefs, labored on a stone wall at Waikīkī. By September, the Protestant chiefs were ready to take the step. The priests were unwilling to leave voluntarily, and one chief therefore placed a government-owned vessel, the *Waverly*, under the command of a longtime Honolulu resident named William Sumner, with instructions to disembark the priests on the California coast, where Catholic communities might receive them. The two ordained priests, Alexis Bachelot and Patrick Short, were drummed to the waterfront and taken on board the *Waverly* on December 21, 1831, while salutes were fired from the fort at the harbor and the battery on Punchbowl. The *Waverly* sailed that afternoon. There remained at Honolulu two lay arti-sans (a carpenter and a mason), and fewer than two hundred baptized natives, all but thirty-five of whom were children.[5]

Throughout the years from 1827 to 1831, the chiefs justified their anti-Catholicism by arguing that idolatry had been outlawed in 1819 with the overthrow of the kapu. The word ki'i was used to describe heathen and Catholic images alike. In this view, it was not Catholicism per se that caused trouble, but idolatry, and idolatry was also insubordination. The Protestant missionaries, for their part, were sufficiently ambivalent. They distrusted the "Jesuits" deeply. As early as July, 1828, Bingham prophesied that the presence of Catholics in Honolulu would be disas-trous to the islands. He and his fellow Congregationalists believed that Hawai'i simply was not big enough for the two religions—the Protestant truth and the religion of the beast—and they wished the Papists would go. The Protestants made their dislike clear in sermons and in other ways, yet they were dismayed when physical violence followed their verbal attacks. Levi Chamberlain, for one, believed that coercion was not warranted by Scripture and would not achieve any good purpose. Ephraim Clark, a more recent arrival, agreed. Still, the missionaries concluded, it was for the chiefs to decide, and without any doubt the government had the sole right to grant or deny·residence to outsiders.

Honolulu's foreigners thought all this mere sophistry. They saw the persecutions as stemming from Protestant instruction, or even from missionary inspiration. A case might be made in this direction. Although the General Meeting of the Sandwich Island Mission in 1831 cautioned the chiefs against persecution for conscience's sake, still a resolution recom-mended that the government be "decided and energetic" in its policies. On the very day Kauikeaouli signed William Sumner's commission as commander of the *Waverly*, the Protestant mission fasted and prayed that divine guidance might aid the chiefs. In January, 1831, the month in which expulsion was planned, Bingham was accompanying the chiefs on their state tour. In December, the month in which the expulsion was carried out, he was in daily contact with Ka'ahumanu and others.

The foreign community was willing enough to beat the Protestant mission with the stick of Catholic persecution (partly in return for unfounded statements by the Protestants that residents had helped to organize the Catholic mission). Aside from this, however, the foreigners were divided over the departure of the priests. Charlton intervened on behalf of the priest Patrick Short (who was not a Frenchman but an Irishman, a British subject). Charlton and John C. Jones both lodged letters with the chiefs to the effect that the priests had not once interfered with Hawaiian politics. Stephen Reynolds joined Jones in worrying that the expulsions might be broadened in scope to include other residents. Marin, the only foreigner of importance with true Catholic origins, assisted the French mission in many ways, but his influence with the chiefs was a thing of the past, and he remained quiet at the time of the expulsion. William Sumner, chosen by the chiefs to take the priests away, thought it an ungrateful task, one that would earn him the hatred of the rest of the foreign community. He told Bingham the residents had threatened to hang him and steal his ship, but that he would do the job to stave off rebellion in the country.

This fevered estimate of the situation, characteristically Honoluluan, was hardly reflected in the actions of the foreigners on the day Bachelot and Short went aboard the *Waverly*. A group came down to the water to wish the priests well and express regret at their departure. Not even the faintest vestige of violence appeared.[6]

By the beginning of 1832, then, Catholicism at Honolulu was in disarray—the priests gone, the artisans powerless, the most ardent natives in prison. Resident foreigners were submitting with bad grace to silent Sundays and were confining their drinking to private parties, where they could salute the American flag in whiskey or break crockery or encourage the Holmes girls to take some good "fids of wine" undisturbed by the moral police of Kuakini.

Ka'ahumanu and Bingham, architects of the victory of Protestant morality, could be well pleased with the natives. Following a mission decision to make abstinence from liquor an official church policy, a call to form a temperance society in April, 1831, drew a response from about a thousand Hawaiians (as compared with only six of the three hundred or more foreigners on O'ahu). Bingham's congregations each Sunday were numbered in the thousands, even though the reward of church membership at Kawaiaha'o was withheld from all but a few hundred.

The schools of Honolulu and O'ahu were flourishing, working almost at the fullest extent possible under the imperfect system of instruction by natives and periodic missionary examination on the basis of limited printed material. As the new decade opened, the mission and the chiefs inaugurated a plan of district organization aimed at providing more immediate supervision of native schools.[7]

Meanwhile, O'ahu's Hawaiians approached the quarterly hō'ike so enthusiastically that at examination time rural O'ahu was deserted and agriculture was suspended, as thousands crowded into town for a week or ten days, waiting their turn to put pencil to slate at the crier's command or to recite selected sentences in unison. The Hawaiians managed somehow to infuse these occasions with their genius for display, for decoration, for jollity, for public performance, for communal experience. Within the confines of literacy and piety, there might be discerned echoes of the great hula gatherings of the early twenties:

> The shell horn has been blowing early for examination of the schools in the meeting house. About 2000 scholars present, some in large quantities of native cloth, with wreaths of evergreen about their heads, and hanging down toward their feet,—others dressed in calico and silk with large necklaces of braided hair and wreaths of red and yellow and green feathers very beautiful and expensive.
>
> It was a pleasant occasion, in which they seemed interested and happy, and it was for them in place of our N.E. commencements and cattle shows and elections, & c., with less exposure of health and morals, for the men drank no rum, and the ladies were not severely clad. The King and chiefs were present and examined among the rest. They read in various books, and 450 in 4 rows wrote the same sentence at the same time on slates. They perform this with some ceremony. In this exercise, one of the teachers cried out with as much importance as an orderly sergeant would in your trainings, and immediately the whole company began to sit up straight. At the next order, they stood on their feet, at the next they "handled slates" or "presented", i. e. they held them resting on the left arm as a musician would place his fiddle. At the next order, they brought their pencils to bear upon the broadsides of their slates ready for action. Mr. Bingham then put into the crier's ear the sentence to be written, which he proclaimed with all his might, and a movement of the 450 pencils commenced which from their creaking was like the music of machinery lacking oil. Their sentences were then examined and found generally correct.[8]

Ka'ahumanu, by this time, was growing old; she entered her seventh decade and her seventh year of Christian life in 1832. In September, 1831, she had made the last of her many tours on behalf of the Gospel, travelling about rural O'ahu with the young king, exhorting the natives not to return to idolatry and commending to them the worship of the true God. Later in the year she spent some time on Hawai'i, returning to Honolulu in 1832 to greet with tears of gratification a new contingent of Protestant missionaries—the fifth since 1820, including in its number Richard Armstrong, a future cabinet minister of the Hawaiian kingdom.

This was almost the last public act of Ka'ahumanu. She had been ill and weak for some time, and in the spring of 1832 she withdrew from Honolulu to the cool green valley of Mānoa, where she had maintained a country cottage for several years. Her servants carried her there on a bed, and she never went back to the town. Her sickness became final in June, 1832. She lived just long enough to receive from the mission press a morocco-bound copy of the recently completed New Testament in Hawaiian. On June 4, with a great crowd gathered in silence about her house, she sent for the missionaries, and they came to stand at her bedside among the chiefs—her brother Kuakini, her sister Hoapili-wahine, the children of Kamehameha (Kīna'u, Kauikeaouli, and Nāhi'ena'ena) and others. Ka'ahumanu sank rapidly. Before dawn on June 5 she died, calling for Bingham, and whispering the words of a Hawaiian hymn: "Lo, here I am, O Jesus, Grant me thy gracious smile."

Her body was taken back to her Honolulu house. The mission, then in general meeting, voted to halt business until after her funeral. On June 7, amid the lamentations of the people, the new church bell at Kawaiaha'o tolled the measure of her procession. Bingham preached from the text, "I have fought a good fight," and afterwards Ka'ahumanu's coffin was taken to the royal mausoleum where Liholiho and Kamāmalu lay. The foreigners had wanted to fire muskets and play martial music, and they were present with fiddles, fifes, and clarionets; but the mission decreed that only minute guns and bells were proper, and the king and Kuakini quieted the band after it had played a few bars.[9]

Honolulu and the kingdom were still young enough to have matters of importance decided by persons, not institutions. The loss of Ka'ahumanu might jeopardize the moral gains of the past year. Within a month of her death, the town was told that the young Kauikeaouli would now rule, not merely reign, and that his sovereignty would be conditioned by the revival of the old office of kuhina nui, to be filled by Kīna'u (daughter of Kamehameha, widow of Liholiho, half-sister of Kauikeaouli). The office of kuhina nui had been created by Kamehameha I before his death, to provide a balance for the expected instability of Liholiho. There had been no incumbent since 1823, and the revival of the office in 1832 was fairly clearly the result of an attempt on the part of the chiefs to maintain a moral equilibrium in high places. Kīna'u was closely connected with the Protestant mission; the king was, by this time, a willful young man of eighteen.[10]

Kauikeaouli, since the late eighteen-twenties, had shown signs of becoming another Liholiho. Under the influence of Boki and Charlton he had spent much of his childhood with foreigners, and by 1829 was a tavern owner and billiard room keeper. His incestuous union with Nāhi'ena'ena was deplored, then temporarily forgotten by the missionaries in the sobriety of his conduct at the dedication of the new Kawaiaha'o church in July, 1829. The missionaries, however, did not follow the king to downtown Honolulu, where his activities took him into strange places. In 1829 Stephen Reynolds, whose native mistress had died in May, seduced and then married a sixteen-year-old part-Hawaiian girl named Susan Jackson, daughter of a foreign carpenter. Just before their wedding, Susan told Reynolds he was not her only lover: she had been meeting the king almost every day for some months, including the month of July, in which the Kawaiaha'o dedication took place. Even after Reynolds married Susan, she visited Kauikeaouli at the royal command, saying she must and should go to the king's house whenever he might summon her. Under pretense of walking to the bath-house in Nu'uanu or to prayer-meeting at Kawaiaha'o, she continued to bedevil Reynolds with these assignations.[11]

Kauikeaouli did not confine his attentions to Susan Jackson. Indeed, his involvement with her was the least public of his affairs. Apart from his ineradicable attachment to Nāhi'ena'ena, he became enamored of a girl named Ka'amanaeile in 1831, saying he wanted to marry her. He did not, however, pause in his pursuit of the wife of the chief Kahekili. A few months later Kekūanaō'awas forced to beat his wife Kīna'u, the ostensibly pious kuhina nui, for intimacy with the king. At the end of the year Kauikeaouli fixed upon Kalama, daughter of a minor chief, for his mistress, and announced at the start of 1832 that she would be his wife. From the chiefs' point of view, this match was not all that could be desired. For the mission, it was a dangerous liaison. Church members held a fast day in January, 1832, prayers for the salvation of the king. All things considered, the mission felt it prudent to keep Nāhi'ena'ena (herself showing great waywardness) out of Honolulu, but in May, 1832, she came down from Maui—under the protection of the Lahaina missionary William Richards, her special mentor.[12]

The king had been encouraged in his errant course by a visit from the American man-of- war *Potomac* in mid-1832. Some of the officers and men had contributed a bell to Kawaiaha'o, but others, including Commodore John Downes, were less pious. In public, Downes was polite to the missionaries while condemning their moral legal proclivities and speaking against the Ten Commandments as laws. Privately, he and other officers from the *Potomac* sampled the delights of the town in company with the king's retinue.[13]

Kauikeaouli's particular punahele, or favorite, among the natives was Kaomi, son of a Hawaiian woman and a Tahitian mission helper. Kaomi had been an interested Christian in his youth, but upon being denied baptism he turned against the church. He had learned something of native healing from Boki, and was a notable raconteur. This combination of skills quickly made him a close friend of the king. Kaomi was, in addition, a protégé of Liliha, whose forced retirement from the governorship in 1831 left her free to indulge in a boisterous personal life at her home in the western part of Honolulu, far away from Kawaiaha'o.

As 1833 opened, the king was spending more time with Kaomi and a rowdy group of attendants called the Hulumanu than with the major chiefs. His restlessness became outright disaffection when Kīna'u, on behalf of the ali'i, refused to allow him to buy an expensive ship, the *Bolivar*. This rebuff marked the beginning of a moral counter-revolution in Honolulu, and by extension the whole kingdom.[14] With Liliha's support and the enthusiastic participation of Kaomi, Kauikeaouli revived the hula in Honolulu. Eruptions of drunken singing and dancing broke out at the homes of the king and the ex-governess. Kauikeaouli was transformed into a monarch of misrule. He and the Hulumanu consumed thirty-two barrels of spirits in the first week of their deliberate overturn of temperance; and they mocked Christian burial by interring in a coffin (with prayers in Hawaiian) the body of a baboon, which had died after being left with the king by Commodore Downes of the *Potomac*.

This was bad enough. Worse still, the king and Kaomi began actively to carry the fight to their new enemy, the old Establishment. They compelled church members to drink in a sardonic reversal of the scene at the breaking of the kapu in 1819, when 'ai noa—free eating—had symbolized freedom from old restrictions. Now, free drinking meant liberty from the church. Kaomi took swords, horses and lands away from Christians and gave than to his own men. There were rumors that Kīna'u was to be seized and the fort occupied by the king's party. Kīna'u continued to oppose Kauikeaouli, and declared a public fast day for Christians on March 3. Before dawn, a messenger came secretly to Bingham to tell him that the king planned to break the Sabbath with amusements, then to take the life of Kīna'u. The assassination, like all others bruited in Honolulu since the poisoning of Isaac Davis in 1810, did not occur. The king, however, did tell Stephen Reynolds that church-going was not mandatory.

In the second week of March, disorder spread. The hula, until then confined for the most part to the king's yard, was seen at many places in the village, and traditional games like 'ulu maika reappeared. Then, on March 9, the king sent a crier through the streets to announce the abrogation of the moekolohe (adultery) laws, and of all other laws except those respecting theft and murder. Misrule reached new heights on March 12, when the king directed the prostitutes of Honolulu to pay court—and pay taxes—to his mistress.

The remonstrances of Kuakini, and the presence of Hoapili, recently arrived from Maui, accomplished nothing. On the evening of March 14, about midnight, a crier ordered the Honolulu people to assemble at the king's house the next day. Before morning Kauikeaouli sent Kaomi, clad in the uniform of a government officer, to deliver a document to Kīna'u, proclaiming that the king was taking control of all lands conquered by Kamehameha; dispensation, the adjudgment of life and death, and the determination of right and wrong, now rested solely with him.

By noon on March l, several thousand natives had gathered. Also present were the foreigners, who had especially been asked to attend. Kauikeaouli repeated to the crowd the edict he had sent Kīna'u the night before. He was assuming total sovereignty over his kingdom. He would rule with justice, he said; but neither chiefs nor foreigners had any voice in the law. Then, surprisingly for those who thought he was quite under the influence of Liliha and Kaomi, he confirmed Kīna'u as kuhina nui. Kīna'u, Hoapili, and the female chief Kekāuluohi made short speeches, acknowledging his overlordship.[15]

This arrogation of sovereignty by Kauikeaouii ushered in a two-year period of shifting relationships between the king, Kīna'u, and the council of chiefs. The issue was eventually resolved in 1835, by the king's more or less permanent surrender of legislative power to Kīna'u.[16] For Honolulu in mid-March, 1833, the immediate result was a brief truce. The king and his Hulumanu, uniformed and epauletted, went to church on March 17. There was less gaming in the streets, although it continued outside the village. By April, Hoapili was reassured sufficiently to return to Maui.

Some things could not be put together again. Congregations at Kawaiaha'o declined. The schools in the Honolulu district lost about two out of every five pupils. Accordingly, the mission was compelled to reappraise its educational system, the more so since the lull of March and April proved merely transitory. Kaomi soon led the king to try once again to dismiss Kekūanaō'a as fort commandant and head of the king's guard, urging his replacement by the half-caste John Stevens, a Hulumanu. Kekūanaō'a threatened to tear down Kaomi's house, and guards were deployed. The Honolulu chiefs feared bloodshed, and the Maui ali'i were called to another council. In June, they made a concerted effort to remove the king from the corruptions of Honolulu and guide him to the more salutary environment of Lahaina, at that time relatively free of grog-shops and hula-masters. Curiously, in view of their moral purpose, they used Nāhi'ena'ena to persuade the king. Kauikeaouli followed her partway to the waterfront, but there he was halted by a group of foreigners who induced him to stay.

From then until the end of the year, the chiefs worked hard to revive the moral law, but the king and his Hulumanu resisted with all their force. Incursions on propriety were resumed. One Hulumanu's wife ran away to sleep with a native church member, and his cronies ordered the guns at the fort and on Punchbowl fired in mocking salute. The hula rose again, and the drumbeats were heard nightly in Kaomi's yard. In mid-July, the king opened the fort and liberated all the imprisoned deserters, who took up residence happily at Alexander Smith's grog-shop-cum-boarding house. Kīna'u then assumed command of the fort and would not surrender it to the king. Kauikeaouli left Honolulu to roam about O'ahu for several weeks. In his absence, the town criers promulgated the moral laws once more, but in the country districts of Ko'olau, Waialua and Pu'uloa the king's retinue passed through quiet villages like a plague of locusts.

All this time, the star of Kaomi was in the ascendant. He had been active soliciting Kauikeaouli to dispossess "undeserving" Christians and transfer their lands to those loyal to the king. In April, Kaomi had been encouraged by the king to take over the Honolulu market with its lucrative tax revenues; and in November, after Kauikeaouli returned from his rural rides. Kaomi sent out a crier announcing a tax on all laboring men and another on people who washed clothes in Nu'uanu stream. Levi Chamberlain heard that the revenues would be used to pay Kaomi's debts.

The upstart leader of the Hulumanu became so obnoxious to the council of chiefs that in March, 1834, the ali'i Kaikio'ewa had him arrested while he was asleep, bound, and locked in the fort. The king sent word to have Kaomi released; no action was taken, and the king himself had to go to the fort and free his friend, under the eyes of a great crowd of natives. This was on March 15, the anniversary of Kauikeaouli's assumption of sovereignty. Four days later, the foreigners formed a procession and rode from a tavern called the O'ahu Folly to present the king with a gorgeous uniform bought for him in Lima, Peru—worth about $850 in Honolulu. The king donned the outfit and rode back to the Folly with the foreigners, applauded by hundreds.

In June, 1834, after more carousing, Kauikeaouli retired to Pearl River. On June 9, Dr. T.C.B. Rooke was called to treat the king.

The rumor in Honolulu was that Kauikeaouli had attempted suicide. All the chiefs went; so did Hiram Bingham and Gerrit Judd, the mission doctor. Stephen Reynolds heard that the king had tried to drown himself and cut his throat. The visitors found the king totally uncommunicative. Judd thought Kauikeaouli had been deranged for some time, probably from drink.

This crisis had come just a day after the king had urged his sister Nāhiʻenaʻena to go to Maui with him. Afraid of Hoapili, she had declined. Six weeks later, shocking news reached the Honolulu mission. The king, on July 21, had publicly slept with Nāhiʻenaʻena at ʻEwa in the presence of the chiefs, and was planning to take her to Waiʻanae, Bokiʻs old land, as far away from teachers as possible. He could not accomplish this. The chiefs parted the royal brother and sister and sent Nāhiʻenaʻena to Maui, where heavy church discipline was laid upon her.[17] A marriage was then arranged for her with William Pitt Leleiōhoku, son of the late prime minister Kalanimoku, but her incestuous affection for the king lingered. Nāhiʻenaʻena lived only a more years. She died late in 1836, obese, debauched, diseased and guilt-stricken, one of the most tragic figures of the period of mission dominance.

After almost two years of waywardness, a suicide attempt, forcible separation from his sister, and the birth of a child to his mistress (whom he refused to marry until after Nāhiʻenaʻenaʻs death), the king was ready by the beginning of 1835 to make his peace with the chiefs. They met in council at Honolulu and the king approved a short code of laws. Its tone was very much that of earlier codes. Kauikeaouli put his signature to five chapters dealing with murder., theft, adultery, perjury, drunkenness, and other crimes. At the public proclamation, the king placed law enforcement in Kīnaʻuʻs hands. She was also formally named governor of Oʻahu, though in fact her husband Kekūanaōʻa did the daily work of the office, remaining in charge of the island and the fort at Honolulu until his death in the eighteen-sixties.

The king, from that time forward, virtually abandoned affairs of state. Kīnaʻu, through her influence as kuhina nui, and through her husband Kekūanaōʻa, controlled the government of Honolulu, Oʻahu, and the kingdom. Kauikeaouli, freed of the cares of monarchy, pursued his pleasure in the foreign community. There, he might be seen riding or sailing, bowling or playing billiards with residents and transient seamen, or sharing with Kaomi periodic reminiscences of the riotous days of 1833.[18]

With Honolulu back in the hands of the Protestant chiefs, the missionaries at their general meeting in 1835 turned again to the question of temperance. Since the organizational meetings of 1831 and 1832, little had been done, and of course the king's example had been disastrous throughout 1833 and 1834. Licensed and unlicensed grog-shops flourished in Honolulu.[19] Now the missionaries resolved to set up a system of quarterly meetings on all islands, to try to convert the chiefs to total abstinence, and with their help to prevent the making, selling, and drinking of liquor.[20] Late in 1835, more than 2,700 Honolulu natives, including Kīna'u, Kekūanāo'a and the female chief Kekāuluohi, petitioned the king to outlaw the liquor traffic. This had not much effect. The king himself owned three distilleries and at least one tavern in Honolulu. In the summer of 1836, after their general meeting, the missionaries urged the closing of the saloons, again to no avail. The king continued to grant liquor licenses in 1837.

The missionaries persisted, encouraged by temperance captains and a handful of residents. In 1838, with the king taking a less and less prominent part in the direction of policy and the native population at a high pitch of religious enthusiasm, they made great headway. In March the king, at Lahaina, agreed to limit the number of liquor licenses for Honolulu to two. He also signed decrees providing for ten o'clock closing of grog-shops, with penalties against publicans who permitted drunkenness on their premises. The chiefs achieved almost total prohibition in August, when they announced that from January 1, 1839, it would be forbidden to make, sell, or import spirits, and that wines would be subject to a duty of fifty cents per gallon. Over the protests of many foreigners, these "wholesome" regulations were widely published and rigorously enforced.[21]

The problem of Catholicism became public once again in the mid-thirties. Bachelot and Short had been expelled in 1831. The two artisans still at Honolulu were unfitted for evangelistic work, and any case Ka'ahumanu had interdicted all Catholics from public activity. Her death eased the situation somewhat: Kauikeaouli showed profound indifference to theology from whatever source. Commodore Downes of USS *Potomac* spoke to the king in August, 1832, about the natives still confined in the fort or at hard labor on the walls and swamps of Waikīkī, and when British Consul Charlton added his voice, the prisoners were released. From 1832 to 1835, there was no molestation of Catholics. The case of the recreant king sufficiently occupied the attention of the Protestant mission and the Christian chiefs.

Bachelot and Short had remained on the California coast, hoping that an opportunity would arise for them to return to the islands. In 1833, the Vicariate Apostolic of Eastern Oceania was established, and Bachelot was made apostolic prefect of the area north of the equator. The Vicar Apostolic despatched Brother Columban Murphy from the South Pacific island of Mangareva to Honolulu in the fall of 1835 to appraise the situation there. Murphy was optimistic. He went to California to arrange passage back to the islands for Bachelot and Short. They were unable to make the voyage until 1837. In the meantime, Murphy sailed south to Valparaiso, and from that city Father Arsenius (Robert A.) Walsh was sent to Honolulu. He arrived at the end of September, 1836.

Kīna'u and the other chiefs at once told Walsh he must leave, and only the intervention of Chariton and the appearance of two men-of-war, one British and one French, prevented his expulsion (Walsh was a British citizen and a member of a French missionary order). Kauikeaouli warned Walsh in writing at the end of 1836 that he must not teach anyone, native or foreign, on pain of being sent from the islands as his predecessors had been.[22]

This prohibition against teaching still stood when in April, 1837, Bachelot and Short returned from California to Honolulu on the brig *Clementine,* owned by Jules Dudoit, a man of French extraction but a British subject. The priests did not make their presence known, but they were discovered and ordered to leave by Kekūanaō'a, acting as governor of O'ahu. Bachelot and Short chose to remain, despite repeated suggestions that they depart. The chiefs were determined to see them aboard the *Clementine* by her scheduled sailing date, May 22. On May 20, native constables took Bachelot and Short from the French mission buildings to the waterfront, where a boat awaited them. The priests insisted that the constables should "force" them to enter the boat by formally laying hands upon them, though no violence was employed.

Dudoit refused to have the priests aboard the *Clementine* unless they came voluntarily and unless he was paid for their passages. The boat returned to shore to pick up more native policemen. After a second unsuccessful attempt, the priests were finally set on deck. Dudoit, opposed to the expulsion and ready to obstruct it by any means, now alleged that his vessel had been seized by the government. He hauled down his colors, sent his officers and men ashore, and followed them. Charlton met Dudoit in the street, and the consul burned the British flag of the *Clementine* on the spot. Bachelot and Short were left aboard ship, quite alone. That evening, Walsh visited them, and Kīna'u had food sent out, but the waterfront and the beach were patrolled by native soldiers, and, according to Stephen Reynolds, the guns of the fort were loaded with grapeshot.

Dudoit protested to Governor Kekūanaō'a about the seizure of his ship. The American merchant William French, who had a consignment of goods aboard the *Clementine,* added a complaint relating to the confiscation of his cargo. Documents were sent to the king on Maui. When Kauikeaouli came to Honolulu he took the position that the government had not seized the *Clementine,* and that the priests were not prisoners. At least this was his public stand: Stephen Reynolds said that in private the king admitted the Hawaiian government's error, and wanted to see Dudoit and William French reimbursed. On one occasion, Reynolds wrote, agreement was almost reached, but Charlton interrupted in a rage and killed any chances of success. Later messages signed by the king were in language Reynolds described as "insolent," and reparations were refused. Reynolds blamed this stiffened attitude on coaching from the chiefs and missionaries; he thought he recognized Bingham's handwriting in some of the documents. On June 17, Kauikeaouli sailed again for Maui. He still disclaimed any intention of seizing the *Clementine* (which by this time had begun to settle into the water), but refused to allow the priests to come on shore, and repeated his demands that the *Clementine* should take them away.

Dudoit set out for Valparaiso on June 28 in the *Flibberty Gibbet,* with letters from the British and American consuls to the Pacific fleets of the two nations, asking for assistance in recovering the *Clementine.* The *Flibberty Gibbet* leaked, and had to turn back. She sailed again on July 1. Within two weeks (though not as a result of the *Flibberty Gibbet's* voyage) two men-of-war put in at Honolulu: the British ship *Sulphur,* Captain Edward Belcher, on July 8, and the French frigate *La Venus,* Captain Abel du Petit-Thouars, on July 10.

Informed by Charlton and J. C. Jones of the priests' predicament, Belcher asked Kīna'u to release them, without avail. When du Petit-Thouars came ashore, he went with Belcher, Charlton and Jones to talk once more to Kīna'u. Again the kuhina nui was adamant. Bingham had interpreted for Kīna'u at the first confrontation, and had spoken up on his own account against Belcher's expressed intention of seizing the *Clementine;* this would cause bloodshed, Bingham said. At the second meeting, Belcher and du Petit-Thovars wanted Bingham out of the room, but Kīna'u insisted that he stay. This he did, but only on sufferance. At all subsequent conferences he was under very sharp scrutiny by the ships' officers, and one French naval lieutenant boorishly bustled him with elbow and sword.

After the second conference, the commanders moved to blockade the harbor, recover the *Clementine,* and put the priests ashore. Belcher hoisted the British flag on the *Clementine,* and du Petit-Thouars disembarked three hundred men to protect Bachelot and Short in the town. As the priests walked to the Catholic mission buildings, natives crowded around, so Stephen Reynolds wrote, crying out: "Now we cut no more stones!"

The king and some of the chiefs from Lahaina returned to Honolulu on July 20, to consider the problem of the priests' residence on shore. At first the king remained firm that they should leave on the *Clementine;* but in further discussions with Belcher, du Petit-Thouars, Charlton, and Jones (mediated by Bingham after other interpreters had failed to make themselves understood) agreement was reached that the priests might stay at Honolulu until passage was available to some civilized part of the world. Belcher guaranteed in writing that Patrick Short would not break Hawaiian law; du Petit-Thouars agreed that Bachelot should not preach.

The men-of-war sailed without further incident. In September, Short left for South America. In November, Columban Murphy, who had visited Honolulu in 1835, returned as an ordained priest, and was allowed to land only because he did not disclose his new status to the authorities at Honolulu. His companion, the French priest Louis Maigret, was barred from residence, and sailed quite soon, accompanied by Bachelot. Only two priests now remained in Honolulu: Walsh and Murphy. Their activities were sharply circumscribed by a proclamation signed by Kauikeaouli on December 18, 1837, rejecting the Catholic religion and prohibiting its teaching anywhere in the islands.

Catholic teachers landing from ships might be imprisoned until they could be removed; shipmasters might forfeit their vessels and be fined for refusing to carry them away.[23]

From the time of the visit of Columban Murphy in 1835 to the expulsion of the priests at the end of 1837 and on to Kīnaʻu's death in 1839, there was continued persecution of Hawaiian Catholics. Natives were put in irons at the fort or consigned to hard labor around Honolulu, cutting and carrying stones for fences or, in the case of persistent recusants, disposing of excrement from the fort.[24] After the prohibition of December, 18, 1837, the Honolulu police sometimes searched native huts, hoping to surprise Catholics at prayer. Some converts left Honolulu for Waiʻanae, Boki's old district, where sympathy for Catholicism lingered on under the new head-man. In spite of the pro-Catholic, anti-Protestant, anti-government blasts of the newly-established *Sandwich Island Gazette* (to which Walsh was a frequent contributor), harsh punishment continued. Not even the intercession of Captain Russell Elliot of the British man-of-war *Fly* in the fall of 1838 could accomplish the liberation of prisoners.[25]

There was definite support for the chiefs' position among at least some of Honolulu's natives. Catholic prisoners were constantly taunted by idle watchers (it was as easy to raise a crowd for this sport in Honolulu as for anything else with spectator value). At least once, this activity exceeded even the loosest limits of decency. In January, 1839, a sailor died on a Russian-American Company ship anchored at Honolulu, and funeral services were conducted by a Greek Orthodox priest traveling aboard the vessel. Natives disturbed the priest by shouting and crossing themselves.

Later in the year, the chiefs denied Walsh permission to bury a Mexican who died in Honolulu; and when old Don Francisco de Paula Marin died, his funeral service was arranged by the Protestant mission.[26]

The death of Kīna'u in April, 1839, brought to prominence the female chief Kekāuluohi, guardian of the successor of Kīna'u (the infant princess Victoria Kamāmalu, daughter of Kīna'u and Kekūanaō'a). Kekāuluohi began her tenure as kuhina nui by ordering the arrest in mid-June of 67 Catholics living at Wai'anae. During their thirty-mile forced march to Honolulu, one man became exhausted, dropped out, and died. The rest were brought before the Honolulu chiefs for interrogation. All but thirteen were freed after promising to obey the laws.

The remainder were taken to the fort and tied up overnight, some of them with their arms raised and bound over a seven-foot partition. This cruelty was protested by two Congregationalists, Bingham and William Richards (the latter had left the mission to become an officer of the Hawaiian government). The thirteen were soon released.[27]

A week later, two native women were arrested for their religion. They were questioned by officers at the fort, and then shackled, one to a tree and the other to the eaves of a low thatched house, without food or water. Next morning they were found by Jules Dudoit (one of the principals in the *Clementine* episode and by now the informal French consular agent) and William Hooper, a partner in the Honolulu firm of Ladd & Co. Bingham was called. Artemas Bishop, another Protestant missionary, involved himself in the case, and soon there was a crowd of foreigners at the scene. They remonstrated with Governor Kekūanaō'a, who denied responsibility for the mode of punishment while affirming the reason for it. In the end, the two women were freed.[28]

Nine native Catholics remained in jail at Honolulu. Some had been at hard labor since 1836; the rest had joined them in 1837 and 1838. Although the *Sandwich Island Gazette* drew attention to their plight in July, 1839, the government made no move to release them.[29] Their liberation was effected in the course of the establishment of religious toleration in Hawai'i—under the guns of a French man-of-war.

The active anti-Catholicism of the late thirties and the concurrent strength of the temperance movement were part of a larger resurgence of Protestantism which followed the bad days of the king's outburst in 1833–1835. In fact, the persecutions of 1838 and the drive to institute total abstinence occurred in the midst of a Great Revival ranking in intensity, duration, and numbers of converts with the largest religious awakenings in modern evangelical history.

The Hawaiian churches generally, and especially that of Honolulu, had entered a depressed period with the death of Ka'ahumanu in 1832 and the moral revolt of Kauikeaouli which followed. The superficiality of the Protestant achievement was exposed as church congregations dwindled and the common school system fell into ruins. Missionaries at Honolulu and elsewhere wrote embarrassed letters to their patrons in Boston, explaining that their evangelical success had been exaggerated by distant observers, that the outward Christianity of the commoners was the result of influence exerted by the chiefs, and that very often the chiefs themselves favored Christianity for the wrong reasons. What was worse, an ex-missionary, Charles Stewart, whose visits to the islands produced two adulatory books, had been badly misled by appearances. His works were pious frauds and could do the mission no real good.[30]

This very dark period passed with the return to power of Kīna'u at the opening of 1835, and from then on the tone of missionary correspondence brightened. Congregations at Kawaiaha'o rose again, school attendance climbed slowly under the reorganized district system, the mission press printed scores of thousands of pages of religious prose, and the complete Bible in Hawaiian was published by the end of the decade. Between June, 1831, and April, 1837, five missionary companies arrived in the islands. By 1838, there were 17 stations, 27 ordained ministers, and a total of 87 workers in the archipelago. Honolulu had the largest number: Bingham, Reuben Tinker, and Lowell Smith, missionaries; Gerrit Judd, physician; Levi Chamberlain, secular agent; Samuel Castle, his assistant; Amos Cooke, teacher; Edwin Hall, printer, and Henry Dimond, bookbinder, with their wives and families.[31]

Together with this increase in manpower, there emerged some new doctrinal and practical emphases. Many of the younger missionaries were products of the period in American church history known as the Second Great Awakening, a time when the heat of American evangelism was most evident in the frontier churches of New York state. There, revivalism flamed and flickered so fiercely and so repeatedly that one area came to be called the "burned-over district." Several whose decision for Christ had led them into the Sandwich Island Mission were converts of Charles Grandison Finney, inheritor and developer of the skills of the great eighteenth-century revivalists and harbinger of the whole era of modern revivalism. Those who had not felt the Finney touch were at least familiar with his techniques. His revival sermons and lectures were passed from hand to hand on voyages to the Sandwich Islands and read from more than one Hawaiian pulpit during the eighteen-thirties and forties.[32]

As early as 1832, on remote Kaua'i, there had been a sudden and unexpected revival. Missionary Peter Gulick wrote asking for assistance, and Hiram Bingham went from Honolulu to work with Gulick, viewing with some astonishment and some reservations the trembling, falling, weeping, and convulsions which afflicted the Hawaiians. Three hundred Kaua'i natives offered themselves to God in the course of several weeks.[33]

Nothing comparable took place at missionary stations further down the chain; but beginning in 1834, protracted meetings were held on most islands at the new year. The annual general meeting of the mission at Honolulu in mid-1836 was followed by intensive evangelistic activity. The delegates recorded their concern about the state of Christianity throughout the world. They memorialized the ABCFM at length, urging more attention to mission work at large and greater resources for their own mission in particular. Back at their home stations, the missionaries began to hold special services and protracted meetings. These were repeated at the turn of 1836-1837. On O'ahu, preaching teams visited Honolulu and the rural stations of 'Ewa, Waialua, and Kāne'ohe successively for a series of six-day meetings, exhorting the natives and holding sessions of prayer and enquiry on the Finney model. Missionary station reports for the year ending May, 1837, spoke almost uniformly of a heightening of religious feeling.

Embryonic revivals were noticed at several stations in the middle months of 1837, and interest remained strong until November. Then, with startling suddenness, the east coast of the island of Hawai'i seemed to take fire. Titus Coan, an exemplar of the religious style of the Second Awakening, had been touring his parish for months, speaking at crowded gatherings. On November 6, 1837, he began a protracted meeting at Hilo before a congregation of several hundred, expounding vigorously in images of struggle and victory, pain and defeat, the choice between Heaven and Hell that lay before sinners. The next day, a tidal wave struck the village, causing great damage and taking thirteen lives. It was a "sign from God." Thenceforth, Coan's congregations were extraordinary in size and fervor. He left his center of enthusiasm to tour the neighboring district of Puna in January, 1838, and the contagion spread with him. Concurrently, Lorenzo Lyons had been working zealously with his congregations at Waimea, Hawai'i, and now he began to achieve results apparently as spectacular as Coan's. The mission station of Wailuku, on Maui, had also been hit by the tidal wave, and both there and at nearby Lahaina, mission meetings took on extreme revivalistic aspects within a matter of days.

No strict sequence of events is ascertainable for the passage of the revival to O'ahu and Honolulu. Judging by the language of missionary letters and station reports, it would seem that the violence of feeling which characterized the awakening on Hawai'i was present only in a modified form at Honolulu and surrounding stations. Nonetheless, outbursts did occur at Honolulu during the regular new-year protracted meetings of January, 1838, continuing thereafter on O'ahu and the other major islands (Kaua'i and Moloka'i). Congregations at Kawaiaha'o grew too great for Bingham to handle. Lowell Smith came in from 'Ewa to set up a second native church in Honolulu, at Kaumakapili, in a tangle of native huts and grog shops toward the rear of the village. Smith was soon attracting as many as two thousand listeners each Sunday, and Bingham's congregations remained between three and four thousand, indicating that about one out of every two natives in the Honolulu district was affected in some way or another by the revival.[34]

On Hawai'i, Coan and Lyons were baptizing by the thousand, Coan in the belief that converts inside the church had a better chance of surviving a cooling-off period, Lyons in a Millerite fear that earthly time was dreadfully short. Neither of these approaches pleased the Honolulu preachers. They were appalled by such mass admissions, which gave Coan and Lyons three-quarters of all church members in the islands and Coan the biggest Protestant congregation in the world for a time. Bingham, among many others, was convinced that the "juniors" were admitting too quickly. His own group baptism of 181 early in 1839 fell far short of Coan's epic ceremonies, the largest of which involved 1,075 converts, sprinkled from a basin as Coan walked among them.

Bingham preferred a long waiting period, and in this he was supported by the ABCFM. But even with inherent conservatism operating at Honolulu, natives in great numbers literally fell before the power of God. Meeting in mid-1839, the missionaries at Honolulu jointly recognized the possibility of mistakes in assessing the sincerity of native converts, together with the probability that a few mission members had erred on the side of liberality and naiveté. This meant nothing to Coan and Lyons, who found the dust and noise of revival meetings nothing less than proof of the presence of God. Reluctantly, for their part, Bingham and the other Honolulu preachers were caught up in a dramatic battle for souls, played out before their eyes each day by fainting Hawaiians.

It was, in fact, not conservative ecclesiastical policy which was perceived by the Honolulu natives, but basic evangelism in preaching. Almost despite themselves, Bingham and his fellows had opened the way for a revival by stressing "the cardinal points, the ruined condition the sinner and his exposure to everlasting death; the utter inexcusableness of his continuing his rebellion against God; his need of justification through the righteousness of Christ; the freeness and fullness of redemption through his blood; the duty of immediate repentance and faith as the condition of pardon; the necessity of the aid of the Spirit of God in the work of regeneration and sanctification; and the importance of immediate submission to his guidance, teaching, and commands." Perhaps the profoundest insight into revivals set down by the eighteenth-century

American master Jonathan Edwards was that which identified "imitation" as the most potent sustaining agent in an awakening. Observation had demonstrated this, be said; and certainly events in the Hawaiian islands a hundred years after he wrote seemed to bear him out, as the tidal wave of conversion from Hawai'i struck and spent itself on other islands.[35]

There was never to be another awakening in Honolulu (or Hawai'i generally) like that of the late thirties. Quite suddenly, the revival at Kawaiaha'o and Kaumakapili was virtually extinguished by the interruption of an outside agency—French naval strength, enlisted on behalf of the Catholic religion in Hawai'i.

On July 9, 1839, within a few weeks of the persecution of the Wai'anae Catholics by the new kuhina nui Kekāuluohi, the French frigate *L'Artemise,* commanded by Captain C.P.T. Laplace, arrived at Honolulu. Laplace had come from Tahiti, where he had secured redress for wrongs allegedly inflicted upon Frenchmen by the native government. Under orders to follow the same course at Honolulu, Laplace consulted only the French consular agent, Jules Dudoit, and, without coming ashore, issued a manifesto calling for the establishment of complete religious freedom for Catholics, a government bond of $20,000 to guarantee observance, and a salute for the French flag. Immediate compliance with every point was demanded on pain of the use of force.

Dudoit took this minatory document to the chiefs, and Laplace blockaded Honolulu harbor as an earnest of his intentions. Dudoit carried with him as well letters from Laplace to the British and American consuls, offering protection on board *L'Artemise* for those of their nationals who feared violence from the natives in the wake of the manifesto. From this asylum Laplace specifically excepted the Protestant clergy, authors, as he put it, of the insults suffered by France at the hands of the Hawaiian government. He regarded the missionaries as part of the native population, liable to undergo the unhappy consequences of a war they themselves had provoked. The Honolulu missionary Samuel Castle wrote that the mission ladies might be exposed as well to the lust of French sailors.

The new United States Consular Agent, Peter Brinsmade, a partner in the firm of Ladd. & Co. (and a man acceptable to the Protestant missionaries, who had lobbied for J.C. Jones' removal and Brinsmade's appointment), wrote to the mission informing them of Laplace's intentions. The mission asked, and was granted, protection under the American flag. Foreigners of all nationalities conferred with Brinsmade and the British acting consul (George Pelly of the Hudson's Bay Company agency) to discuss safety measures should Laplace bombard the town.

On July 10, a meeting named a committee of seven to direct residents in case the Honolulu natives attacked their property. They asked the chiefs for permission to arm themselves against thieves and looters. The response was favorable. On July 11, the foreigners' committee of vigilance met to distribute arms and arrange defense dispositions.

Laplace put a deadline on agreement to his terms. King Kauikeaouli was away at Lahaina, where he had been spending much of his time since the death of Nāhi'ena'ena in 1836. A ship was sent to Maui to bring him down, with hostages placed on *L'Artemise* to guarantee his arrival. John 'I'i, onetime playmate of Liholiho and now one of the most responsible Christian Hawaiians, alternated as hostage with Timothy Ha'alilio, another educated and trusted native very useful to the government.

While the town waited for the coming of Kauikeaouli, the chiefs, afraid of Laplace's guns, decided to pledge the king in advance to the terms of the manifesto, and the foreign community set to work to raise the $20,000 bond demanded by the Frenchman. The mercantile firm of Peirce & Brewer, successor to James Hunnewell, lent $6,000, $2,000 of which they got from shipbuilder James Robinson. Ladd & Co. lent $5,000, Stephen Reynolds $1,100, Henry Zupplien (an eccentric boarding-house keeper) $1,000. Other small loans made up the balance. By midday on July 13 the money was ready. Early in the afternoon Governor Kekūanaō'a, Timothy Ha'alilio, and William Richards (now a government minister) took the sealed chests out to *L'Artemise;* twenty-one guns were fired from the frigate and the fort.

The next morning, Kauikeaouli landed at Honolulu with fifty soldiers. Laplace came ashore with ten armed men and a band, and marched through the dusty streets to attend a military mass celebrated at one of the royal residences by Father Robert Walsh. That evening, many of the foreign residents dined with Laplace and Walsh aboard ship. Once these amenities were observed, Laplace and the king, together with the royal advisers, spent the next few days negotiating a short treaty of commerce and friendship (both of which hitherto had been noticeably absent in French-Hawaiian relations).

On the morning of July 17, the work was complete. One stipulation, Article VI, overturned the total abstinence laws of the kingdom, by providing that French merchandise, including wine and brandies, should be freely admitted to Hawaiian ports under duties limited to 5 per cent ad valorem. Article IV placed trials of French residents accused of "any crime whatever" in the hands of juries to be chosen by the French consul and approved by the Hawaiian government. These two articles were to remain as points of controversy in the islands, and especially at Honolulu, for more than a generation.

Laplace sailed on July 20. The aftermath of his visit was, of course, profound. While he was at Honolulu, drunken foreigners celebrating the end of total abstinence had surrounded the Protestant mission with shouts and musical bands, and one had said that if he could find Bingham he would take off his head. At the end of the month there appeared in the *Hawaiian Spectator* an article by a young American named James Jackson Jarves, who claimed that the king had been bullied by Jules Dudoit into signing the treaty, under threat of violence from Laplace. Dudoit was infuriated. He called the article a libel, and urged Kauikeaouli to punish Jarves. Arbitrators were appointed—Stephen Reynolds and William French for Dudoit; William Hooper (a Ladd & Co. partner) and Dr. R.W. Wood, a respectable American, for Jarves. The fifth man was George Pelly, acting consul for Great Britain. Testimony was taken in mid-August. William Richards' version of events enraged Dudoit so much that he followed Richards from the arbitrators' room with a horsewhip, saying that only Richards' black coat protected him. The referees' verdict was that Jarves had failed to prove the truth of his accusations.

The missionaries responded by sending a protest against Laplace's menaces to the American government, routed through the rooms of the ABCFM in Boston. They continued to oppose Catholicism in private, and they enlisted the written support of the commanders of American naval vessels which visited Honolulu towards the end of 1839.[36]

After a time, it became clear that the Laplace incident had not irrevocably harmed the Protestant mission. Rather, events had simply overtaken the Calvinists in their attempt to exclude the rest of the world and raise a holy city at Honolulu. After twenty years in the field, many of the figures so prominent in the early days had departed. Ka'ahumanu, Kīna'u, Kalanimoku, Kapi'olani, Boki, Liliha, Nāhi'ena'ena, Hoapili, Kaomi, and other friends and enemies were dead. Joseph Navarro was dead too. James Hunnewell had long ago returned to Boston. J.C. Jones was gone. Charlton was to remain just a few more years (though they were to be his most important ones). The revival had waxed and waned, but Laplace had come and gone too, and now Catholics were free to dwell on equal terms with Calvinists, drinkers with teetotallers. More significant still, outside the narrowly-defined moral universe of the mission, developments quite beyond Protestant control—increased trade, a vastly enlarged foreign community in the process of changing from sojourners to residents—were working further revolutions. No more than the Kamehamehas were the missionaries able to hold back the future.

The departure of Hiram Bingham, who returned to the United States in 1840 for the sake of his wife's health, marked the end of an era.

Since 1820, Bingham had been in the eyes of Honolulu's foreigners the archetype of the Protestant missionary, and they had focused all their resentments upon him, often unfairly. Bingham suffered this imposition acutely but willingly, to the point where he shouldered the burden unnecessarily. When Beechey and Kotzebue had criticized the general mission accomplishment in print, Bingham complained that their acerbity was unwarranted, since he himself had done nothing to offend them. Others called him "King," "Bishop," "Cardinal" or "Pope." He himself always publicly denied any formal leadership of the mission, though he took the unsolicited responsibility of writing quite strong letters of judgment on his fellow workers both to his colleagues and to the American Board.

His successor at Kawaiaha'o, Richard Armstrong, thought Bingham a good, somewhat "Jesuitical" manager, whose stratagems were vitiated by being too obvious. No wonder, then, that storms burst about Bingham's head and he sought private solace in sawing at his bass viol and singing. He affected, nevertheless, to hate strife. "When I was a boy of fourteen," he wrote in 1835, "my teacher told my mother, that 'Hiram was a peacemaker in the school.' After the test of a college life, I received a similar testimony from my reverend President. And I have lived long enough in Honolulu to know whether I can be insulted by friend or foe...and yet studiously seek to do good in meekness to those that oppose themselves: but I have not lived in strife long enough to *love* it. Yet 'when I am for peace, they are for war.' And I would fain know how I may in future avoid the stings of these thorns in my side? *When will they cease?"*

They "ceased" only with his sailing. Bingham left behind an impressive monument. He had brought the Honolulu congregation to the stage where it could raise at Kawaiaha'o a real New England church, complete in everything but a steeple, a building for which natives cut and hauled coral-stone and timber for the best part of six years. Construction had been carried on all through the difficult and splendid years of 1836 to 1839. The new Kawaiaha'o was not opened for worship until 1842. Under its cornerstone were buried a Hawaiian Bible, and mathematics and anatomy texts in the native language. A Hawaiian engraver prepared the brass plate which told the story of Kawaiaha'o. The building, designed by Bingham himself, has stood ever since. It was hardly his fault that, in the generation after he departed, other structures and their functions dominated the town.[37]

CHAPTER 5

The Growth of the Town to Mid-Century

Late in the eighteen-thirties, after almost sixty years of contact with white men and two decades of education at the hands of Protestant missionaries who were also American republicans, the ruling chiefs of Hawai'i began to consider in earnest a fundamental alteration in the government of the islands. From the beginning, the prerogatives of chiefs and the claims of foreigners had been chronically in conflict. By the late thirties, too, the commoners, though quite without means of translating discontent into political action, were not so complaisant under the rule of the ali'i as they once had been.

Opinion in favor of change was sufficiently strong to permit the framing of a Bill of Rights in 1839. This pioneering work was followed a year later by the writing of a constitution for the kingdom. Legislative authority was vested in a council of chiefs. There was in addition a small body of popular representatives, whose functions were little more than advisory. Ultimate judicial authority resided in a supreme court, of which the king and the kuhina nui were members. Executive authority was with the appointees of the king and the kuhina nui.[1]

For Honolulu the most important official was the Governor of O'ahu, who reported to the supreme executive. Generally speaking, he had charge of all governmental business within his jurisdiction not set aside by law to other officials. Thus his duties were manifold. He sat as judge in cases involving foreigners and natives; appointed inferior judges; supervised tax collection all over the island; controlled the town's fort, prison system, police force, markets, and public works; and allowed or disallowed marriages and divorces, paying close attention to those involving foreign men and native women.[2]

Most of these functions might be regarded simply as continuations or extensions of powers delegated to governors of islands by Kamehameha I. In fact, very few laws bearing directly upon local government were passed in the wake of the constitutional changes of the late thirties. The king and the chiefs, meeting in council at Lahaina in mid-1840, prepared a brief list of duties for the "officers of the city of

Honolulu," but the projected administration was never implemented. A few months later, in November, a law was enacted empowering any chief or governmental officer to call a meeting of "all the people" of a locality should the inhabitants request him to do so. Such meetings might frame local law concerning fences, roads, wandering animals, and the like. These laws might be enforced within a locality provided they did not conflict with the laws of the kingdom.[3]

Here, within the mixed governmental system of Hawai'i, there was one of many echoes of New England political practice—the town meeting. Prior to 1840, local initiative had rested solely with resident chiefs, who might or might not act at the request of natives and foreigners. Now a possibility existed that local government might develop a real identity. It remained only that in Honolulu—a possibility. Occasionally during the next fifteen years one place on O'ahu, the rural village of Waialua on the northern coast, took on the semblance of a community in its use of the 1840 statute on local laws;[4] but Honolulu never did. Much less did Honolulu proceed along New England lines and achieve self-government under a charter. Incorporation was suggested at various times in the forties, usually on the ground that local improvements ought to be the responsibility of some kind of local government. One of the white members of cabinet, Minister of Foreign Relations Robert Crichton Wyllie, had a somewhat broader vision of the benefits of municipal government. He saw decentralization not only as a sensible way of doing official business at the local level, but also as a means of reviving a feeling of community among the natives. Their ties to the soil (and to family and kinship groups) had been cut by mobility and drift. Hawaiians seemed easily seduced by the attractiveness of the white man's world growing up at the port towns. Perhaps a strong "parish" organization would help to reverse this unhealthy trend, by restoring a sense of participation and purpose to the lives of all natives, whether they chose to dwell at Honolulu or remain in a rural district.[5]

Wyllie's views never really took hold. When incorporation did come in 1850, it was of a merely formal sort. On August 29, 1850, Honolulu was elevated by decision of the king and council to the status of a city, and was named at the same time capital of the islands. Two weeks later, an act was written to render uniform the various districts of the islands for educational and taxation purposes. The districts thus created were to be subdivided into townships enjoying the right to make local regulations. For Honolulu, this was the effective limit of action. The kingdom's Cabinet Council proposed in December, 1850, the establishment of municipal government for Honolulu, and it was agreed that the Privy Council should be asked to direct Supreme Court Justice William Lee to prepare a charter. The Privy Council, however, concluded not to act, but rather to postpone discussion. In 1851 the government weekly, the *Polynesian,* reported "great diversity" of opinion among the residents of Honolulu on the question of a city charter. Certainly the national government would be relieved of the necessity to sustain Honolulu's administration. Authority would pass to local residents, and perhaps in this way public improvements might be made more quickly, helping to turn Honolulu into a real city. On the other hand, self-government might cost as much as $30–50,000 a year, about one-third of the total annual governmental budget. To pay for a mayor, councilmen, police, prisons, and so on would require a very high tax rate, especially as the city had no property from which revenue might be drawn, unless the kingdom should relinquish its markets and wharves.

Apparently the national government was unwilling to transfer responsibility to the city, and the city remained unwilling to assume it. A bill introduced in the 1852 legislature did not pass its third reading. A Privy Council resolution in mid-1853 produced nothing. Wylie's persistent advocacy later in the fifties was fruitless, even in a period when the national government was extremely short of funds and might have been expected to welcome a chance to cut expenses. Thus Honolulu was without a charter. It continued so until the beginning of the twentieth century, by which time, of course, the kingdom itself was a thing of the past and the islands had become a territory of the United States.[6]

Many functions normally carried out by local administrations were performed in Honolulu by the national government—for example, by the kingdom's Board of Health and its Public Works Bureau. In the discharge of municipal duties, the Governor of O'ahu was closely supervised by cabinet ministers. For the rest, voluntary associations of one sort or another haltingly supplied the deficiencies of governmental institutions. Honolulu in the forties and fifties lacked, in fact, any strong sense of community—even the Chamber of Commerce formed in 1850 quickly became moribund. Yet the city was the business center of the islands, the center of population, the focus of foreign contact; and Honolulu's people were witnesses, initiators, beneficiaries, and sometimes victims of almost every major movement and contest in the islands.

One of the principal questions confronting the kingdom as the forties opened was that of land. This issue took its shape and reached a resolution almost solely on the basis of Honolulu's experience. The critical years were those of the later eighteen-forties., but the history of the problem was as old as the kingdom itself.

Under Kamehameha I, sovereignty and land ownership were inextricably linked. Both were in the hands of the king. Chiefs, and through them commoners, held land at the royal pleasure. All paid heavily in taxes and services for the privilege. After the death of Kamehameha there occurred a devolution of power into the hands of the great ali'i, who quickly became the dominating political and economic force in the islands. By 1825 the chiefs had secured the right to pass on their lands by inheritance, which they had not been able to do under Kamehameha. Having thus consolidated their own position and ensured their affluence, they could be brought only with great reluctance to consider over the next two decades the possible rights of the disadvantaged groups who were their tenants—commoners and foreigners.

The commoners could do very little to initiate change, bound as they were by a tradition of subservience to the ali'i. The chiefs regarded them, even after the breaking of the kapu, as nothing but worms in the dust. Throughout the twenties and thirties, commoners continued to be liable for taxes on their persons and on their produce, taxes so heavy as to vitiate any attempt on their part to escape from mere subsistence. Production was their task; the inverted pyramid of consumption was also theirs to support.

As for the foreigners, their concept of property clashed with that of the ali'i almost from the beginning. Agitation for changes in the land system thus came almost exclusively from westerners, as did agitation for constitutional government. The two revolutions, each centering on Honolulu, were accomplished in the same decade.

In the early days it had been possible for a white man to attain a special position in relation to land, by attaching himself to Kamehameha and, through services or expertise, gaining the rank of ali'i with all its rewards. No matter how long his residence, however, the threat of dispossession remained, as Marin found in 1823 when he incurred the wrath of the Honolulu chiefs over his handling of their foreign trade goods. For short-term residents, tenure was even more precarious. In the twenties they might be sent out of the country at the chiefs' pleasure, whereupon any land they had occupied reverted to the chiefs, regardless of claims by the white men's women and children. Even for peaceful and sober foreigners there was no guarantee of uninterrupted tenure. Chiefs permitted haoles to occupy more or less well defined lots in the village. Upon these lots buildings might be erected. There were, however, no formal leases. The ali'i often reminded their foreign tenants that permanent occupancy was not a right but a privilege, and hence most buildings were none too lavish. No idea existed in the chiefs' minds that a foreigner's "right" to a lot or even to his improvements might survive the tenant himself. Foreigners might buy and sell the "right" of occupancy, and improvements might be transferred, but such transactions required the approval of the chiefs.[7]

The right of foreigners to hold land was closely connected, of course, with the question of their prior right to enter the country and do business there. No foreign government ever denied the ultimate discretion of the kingdom in this respect, though on occasion local representatives of the great powers called for very rigorous definition of the restrictions the Hawaiian monarchy sought to impose. Up to about 1830, with nothing but the informal "treaty" drafted by Thomas ap Catesby Jones in 1826 to regulate their foreign dealings, the ali'i managed to have their way; and the first really sharp contest between foreigners and natives over property of any sort—the Charlton cow case of 1829—resulted in a victory for the monarchy. In the next decade, however, Honolulu's foreign community grew rapidly, changing in character to include substantial businessmen as well as the beached sailors of previous decades. Property and business interests of Americans in Honolulu in 1829 had been worth an estimated $80–100,000. By the mid-thirties, the figure was about $400,000 for all islands. At the opening of the forties, estimates were much higher still—about $300,000 in real estate and $43,000 in shipping owned at Honolulu, largely devoted to servicing the whaling industry, which by then was bringing well over a million dollars worth of American shipping to the islands each year. There was a proportionate growth in business at the port. With about six hundred Americans in the islands, most of them at Honolulu, the issue of property and commercial rights inevitably became more acute.[8]

In 1836–1837, naval representatives of three great powers-the United States, Great Britain and France—attempted to improve the position of foreigners in regard to residence and landholding. In October, 1836, Commodore Edward Kennedy of USS *Peacock* conferred for four days with the king and the chiefs on matters of foreigners' land tenure, their right to transfer leased property, and their right (heretofore denied) to lease land for agriculture outside Honolulu itself. Kennedy was able to make very little impression on the fixed position of the government that royal sovereignty carried with it inalienable rights in the soil, and that all issues arising from the land question must remain at the discretion of the king.[9]

Just as Kennedy was about to leave Honolulu, the French warship *Bonité* (Captain A.N. Vaillant) and the British man-of-war *Actaeon* (Lord Edward Russell) arrived. Each commander in turn involved himself in the question of foreigners' rights (their immediate concern was to try to establish the tenure of Catholic missionaries in Honolulu). Lord Edward Russell, after scrutinizing the lengthy list of complaints brought to his attention by British Consul Charlton, proposed a treaty giving British subjects the right to bring vessels and property to the islands, to live there, build houses and stores, and dispose of their property with the knowledge and consent of the king. The most important phrase concerned the king's part in granting and manipulating these "rights." This was to be a fruitful source of trouble, especially in view of the fact that the king's signature on the treaty was obtained only after the "wholly dictatorial" Russell, supported by the blustering Charlton, made implied threats that if Kauikeaouli refused to cooperate, the *Actaeon* would fire on Honolulu.[10] The right of Frenchmen to most-favored-nation status was reluctantly granted in the next year, 1837, when Captain Abel du Petit-Thouars, in Honolulu at the time of the *Clementine* episode, induced King Kauikeaouli to sign a convention guaranteeing parity of treatment. The French interest in property and commerce at Honolulu—and the British interest too, for that matter-were, of course, insignificant by comparison with American investments.[11]

The king and the chiefs were determined to retain total sovereignty over land, especially in Honolulu and Lahaina. Early in 1838, they drafted an "Ordinance for the cities of the islands," forbidding the sale of house lots without the consent of the king, as "entangling the rights" of the kingdom; the sale of house lots in secret; the giving up of lots for debt; and the sale at suction of house lots belonging to deceased persons. All these were stigmatized as "evil acts." At the same time, the ali'i disclaimed control over chattels.[12]

This was the situation when, in 1839, the Bill of Rights was drawn up. The Bill itself, and the 1840 constitution which followed, did little to assure tenants' rights. An effort was made to prevent abuses of the old sort by the chiefs. This, naturally, was more to the advantage of commoners than of foreigners. Then too, the 1840 constitution contained the first formal statement of the idea that commoners had rights of ownership in the lands of the kingdom. But for foreigners, the problem persisted: there was no concession of their right to hold actual title to land. In 1841 the Hawaiian legislature, meeting at Lahaina, empowered island governors to lease land to foreigners for as long as fifty years. This arrangement was no less unsatisfactory than the old indeterminate leases of earlier decades had been. Indeed, trouble followed. The legislature directed foreigners to register their leases in writing at the governors' offices, so that rent payments might be regularized. The business community of Honolulu regarded this edict as an imposition serious enough to justify consular intervention. Richard Charlton, Jules Dudoit and Peter Brinsmade all made protests to the king and to Kekūanaō'a. The government attempted, inconclusively, to clarify its position in a way acceptable to the foreigners, but the issue remained open.[13]

After this flurry, the land question, in terms of constitutional change, was held in abeyance during the first years of the forties, while the ultimate question of Hawai'i's future was fought out on the diplomatic level. By 1844, royal sovereignty appeared at least temporarily secure, and the question of property rights for foreigners and commoners returned to pre-empt the attention of Hawaiian legislators and administrators.

Some quite strong reasons existed for major change. With the increase of Honolulu's foreign population, the question of foreign rights had grown more urgent. Late in the thirties, too, a kingdom-wide interest in Hawaiian agriculture and manufactures developed. The first stirrings of an upheaval in land, population and politics on the west coast of America were discernible as the United States prepared to involve, itself heavily in Oregon and later California, and the implications of all this for Honolulu's commerce and Hawai'i's agriculture were beginning to be considered. Tightly bound up with these issues was the question of the Hawaiian commoner upon the land. Should he continue to be essentially a feudal retainer, or should he be permitted, now that his right to own land was recognized in the constitution, to become an independent yeoman?

By 1844 the government was ready to authorize a full-scale investigation of the entire land question, and in the next year, as part of organic legislation setting up executive departments, a Board of Commissioners to Quiet Land Titles was created. So too was a land office, established within the new Department of the Interior. In general, Hawaiian subjects were to be allowed to purchase land in fee simple. Aliens and subjects alike might lease land for as long as fifty years. All claims dating from before the organic act, whether those of subjects or aliens, were to be reviewed by the Board of Commissioners, whose dispositions would give title in the form of a Land Commission Award. The successful claimant might pay a commutation fee, thus extinguishing the governments interest in his land. He would then possess a Royal Patent in fee simple.[14]

Guided by these general rules, the Board of Commissioners met at Honolulu. Its first members were the ex-missionary William Richards, now a cabinet minister; John Ricord, the king's American-born Attorney-General, who played a great part in framing the organic acts; J.Y. Kānehoa, a descendant of John Young; and two educated Hawaiians, Z. Ka'auwai and John 'I'i. From February to August, 1846, the Board worked to prepare a set of principles which would serve as permanent guidemarks. These were approved by the legislature. The major concern of the principles was the separation and definition of the property interests of government, landlord, and tenant. The great division of land which followed was based on their dicta.[15]

Meanwhile, the Board of Commissioners began to hear claims pertaining to lands, mostly house lots, already occupied by natives and foreigners in the Honolulu area. Day by day, month by month, the Board took testimony. Not until December, 1847, did attention pass to the kingdom at large; and even after that date, work continued sporadically on later Honolulu claims.

The Board held its first meetings in a building called Hale Kauwila, which, until then, had been used by the chiefs for councils and feasts. Every Wednesday after mid-February, 1846, it was crowded with claimants. Within the Honolulu area, those with foreign names hurried to register their claims. As events were to show, it would take time to convince even urban Hawaiians of the advantages of a secure title, whether at leasehold or in fee-simple. No such education was necessary for foreign businessmen; of course: they moved quickly to regularize their leases, and later, when conditions were relaxed, to buy land in fee-simple.[16]

Equally quickly, too, the beached foreigners of past decades appeared before the Board, claiming confirmation of rewards for services performed long ago. Alexander Adams, former pilot of Kamehameha I, more recently Honolulu's harbor pilot, and now the lusty old patriarch of a vastly-ramified family with widely-spread estates around Honolulu, claimed and was awarded several pieces of land: a town lot; about four acres of Waikīkī land over which he had been konohiki (agent or steward for a chief) since the days of his royal benefactor; nearly three hundred acres of kalo land and upland in Kalihi valley to the west of Honolulu proper; and an estate of almost twenty-five hundred acres, at Niu, a sunny valley a few miles east of Diamond Head.[17]

Adams was unusually long-lived. Most of his old cohorts were dead, especially those who, like Adams himself, had settled in the islands before the breaking of the kapu. Long ago they had submerged their nationality and their legal identity in the service of a primitive king. They had married native women, and had sired children of mixed blood. Now their heirs, many of whom bore Hawaiian first names and foreign last names, were able to trace the vicissitudes of their families through a quarter-century or more of caprice on the part of the aliʻi, and finally to establish their property rights under a westernized jurisdiction.

George Beckley, pilot and fort commandant at Honolulu for the first two Kamehamehas, had died in 1826, naming Alexander Adams as his executor and guardian of his heirs. Beckley was now judged entitled to have bequeathed to his part-Hawaiian descendants an acre of land in Honolulu, seventy acres at Kalihi, and thirty-six in Mānoa.[18] Other names from the past were heard—Blanchard, Davis, Ebbets, Harbottle, Holmes, Jones, Manini (once Marin), Rives, Sumner, Winship, Woodland—formerly western, now borne by part-Hawaiians married in most cases to other part-Hawaiians or full-blooded Hawaiians rather than to haoles. Here were the beginnings of an urban Hawaiian land-owning class, many of whose members were to prove unable, for various reasons, to hold their Honolulu property in the two generations ahead. From the beginning, they had relied on haole assistance to keep their lands and boundaries intact in the somewhat predatory world of Honolulu. Stephen Reynolds, for example, spent a great deal of time helping Hannah Holmes to administer her rental lots; and Gerrit Judd was useful in the same way to Robert G. Davis (Hannah's son by William Heath Davis).[19] Once it became possible for part-Hawaiians (and full-blooded Hawaiians) to alienate their own lands, they tended to lease or sell cheaply and somewhat improvidently, with the result that land ownership in Honolulu became more an index of rising foreign commercial interest than an expression of native rights of ownership.

Foreigners who had played even more humble roles in the making of Honolulu were also recalled, either in person or through their heirs—Peter Anderson, Kamehameha's negro armorer; Bob the Tailor Kilday, an Englishman who had stitched coats for Liholiho in the era of the first great Hawaiian dandies and had been rewarded with the gift of a lot in Nu'uanu, which he held stubbornly in the face of the chiefs' efforts to remove him; Louis Gravier, a French sailmaker who had outfitted the *Becket,* one of the ships Boki took on his sandalwood expedition; the illiterate Englishman Tom Hunt, one of Kalanimoku's sea captains, who had been given land by his patron and was then dispossessed for drunkenness; Dutch Harry Zupplien the tavern-keeper, who since 1810 had been burying his hard-earned money in his Honolulu backyard; Yankee Jem Vowles, the notorious barroom brawler; Lewis Rees, the Welsh herdsman and servant of Manuia who had sailed with Boki; Black George Hyatt, the negro who played his clarinet for the kings of Hawai'i and provided music for Honolulu's first cotillion; Long Tom Gandall, the chiefs' gunpowder expert, employed on Honolulu public works jobs; John Gowan, citizen of Boston, who had been Kaumuali'i's linguist on Kaua'i; Portuguese Jo; Charles the Lascar; and dozens of others about whom virtually nothing is known.[20]

Together with all these, the businessmen of the town and the representatives of the two missions, Protestant and Catholic, established their rights to land around Honolulu.[21] Finally, as Honolulu's chiefs and commoners came before the Board of Commissioners, the outlines of a town committed to western property practices became visible. Over fish-ponds, kalo patches, heiau sites, lōkū or game playing areas, and kapu places of bygone days, the surveyors and draftsmen laid their precise measurements. Valley boundaries which formerly had been defined by the direction in which a stone would roll were now fixed by triangulations. Traditional landmarks like streams, trees, prominent rocks, and stone-heaps gave way to markings on maps. The old konohiki system, under which a chief appointed an agent or steward to manage his lands, was replaced by a system in which each owner determined for himself the best use to which his land might be put, being free to cultivate, lease or sell at will.[22]

In the course of his testimony before the Board of Commissioners, Stephen Reynolds recalled how in 1823, when he had come to the islands to stay, not many house lots had been fenced and very few indeed enjoyed the privacy of adobe walls. There had been no streets, but only pathways leading to the main trails quartering Honolulu.[23] The city began at the waterfront and straggled to an end less than a mile inland, considerably short of a stone wall, built about 1830 part way across the entrances to Mānoa and Nu'uanu valleys with the idea of restraining grazing cattle.[24] Late in the eighteen-thirties, before the property issue in Honolulu was anywhere near resolution, the local chiefs were seized by a fit of energy for road and bridge building around the town, and for a few weeks crowds of natives labored, straightening and widening streets, and often clipping slips of land from lots which had encroached upon thoroughfares.[25]

Now, by 1850, the bulk of the Board's work was done in Honolulu. Titles were clear and most boundaries were settled. There was a sense of definition about the town that had never existed before. Promiscuous huddles of Hawaiian thatch huts, though still numerous, were interrupted more and more by individual houses of western design in adobe wood or stone on individual lots. The streets once again were cleared of obstructions. Finally the town was ready to be declared a city, the capital of the islands. Concurrently the streets were officially named—twenty-nine of them, from the big thoroughfares running up from the waterfront (Maunakea, Nu'uanu and Fort) and the principal streets crossing them (Merchant, King, Hotel and Beretania) down to lesser lanes and places. The old sailors' names, such as Fid Street, formally gave way to the new, such as Nu'uanu; though, interestingly enough, sailors' names for districts within Honolulu, like "Egypt," "Cow Bay," and the "Black Sea," lingered on for another twenty years, as did the complementary Hawaiian district names. Most of the street names decided upon in 1850 were western, though signposts carried Hawaiian renderings as well.[26] Like all major rearrangements, this reorientation of streets and boundaries in Honolulu created considerable discontent. For years afterward there were private quarrels and lawsuits over rights-of-way, trespass, and disputed claims. The fact was, however, that a great change had been accomplished. Honolulu's new outlines were those within which the land developments of the succeeding quarter-century were carried out.[27]

By the time the Board of Commissioners had roughly completed its work in Honolulu, it had awarded title to 325 lots, most of them covering less than one acre, on the seventeen most important streets and lanes in the town (excluding insignificant pathways). Of this number, foreigners or half-castes with western names held 119. Overlying and surrounding this quite well-recognized town center was a more amorphous area, later described (but never defined) as "Honolulu City." It consisted of 82 more or less distinct areas of varying size (from a few acres up to several score), all carrying Hawaiian names from the old days, some located in the interstices of the street blocks, others on the periphery of the commercial area stretching toward the valleys. In "Honolulu City," a total of just over seven hundred awards were made, some of them several acres in extent, most nothing more than house and garden lots. Of this total, 38 were held by people with western names— haoles or identifiable half-castes. Farther away from the harbor and the business quarter were land divisions incorporating valleys and other traditional sites, In these areas, which stretched from Moanalua in the west to Wailupe in the east, haole names disappeared almost entirely from the register of landowners. The largest single estate in the Kona district was at Moanalua, where William Sumner owned seven thousand acres. Nearer Honolulu, Kalihi and Kapālama had seven and six haole proprietors respectively (including Alexander Adams). To the east of the town proper, a very few haole names appeared in Makiki, Mānoa, Pālolo, Wai'alae-Iki, Wai'alae-Nui and Wailupe. Pāwa'a, between Honolulu and Waikīkī, included six foreigners among its 17 landowners. Waikīkī itself had only two (including Adams) out of more than 250 listed.[28]

The king and the chiefs held choice lots scattered about the district, in town and out. The Catholics were given title to a cathedral site in town and other lots elsewhere. The Protestant mission lots, including a sizeable estate at Punahou in Mānoa, were held at first in common and then distributed to individuals, except for church and school lots. Also defined were government lands, and a special category unique to Honolulu—fort lands, some fifty patches in Honolulu, Kalihi and Waikīkī, to be cultivated by soldiers and tenants of the Governor of O'ahu. Later, these and other government lands were used for school sites.[29]

Ownership of land was established by the Board of Commissioners. Occupancy and use, especially in the town proper, were determined to a great extent by the growth of the port. A close link existed between the land revolution and a business revolution which took place in the Pacific during the same period.

By 1830, the old Pacific trading complex based on fur and sandalwood had been superseded by whaling as the major interest of

Honolulu. In the ten years since whaling vessels first put in at Hawaiian ports, Honolulu had come to expect scores of such ships each fall and spring. The only other town in the islands equipped to supply whalers' needs was Lahaina, on Maui, and from 1820 to 1830 (according to the very sketchy figures available) arrivals at Honolulu more than doubled those at Lahaina, rising to more than a hundred three times in the decade. The "golden age" of American whaling began when rich grounds were discovered in the Arctic during the thirties.

In 1829 there had been about two hundred American ships in the business; by 1834 there were four hundred, by 1846 more than seven hundred. At one time or another in the course of their extended cruises, which often lasted more than two years, the whalers touched at the Hawaiian islands. Without Hawaiian ports, especially Honolulu, the trade would have been severely hampered. Without the whalers, business in the islands (and especially at Honolulu) would have been equally inhibited. There remained subsidiary commercial connections, of course. Trade with California and the northwest coast continued, for example. But throughout all the years of the whale trade, from the twenties to the sixties, there was only one short period (during the California gold rush) when merchant ships outnumbered whalers at island ports. In most years, whalers outnumbered merchantmen about two to one. It was certainly true, as the astute observer Robert Crichton Wyllie remarked in the mid-forties, that the prosperity of Hawai'i depended mainly upon the whalers. If that business should fall off, he wrote, the islands would relapse into primitive insignificance.[30]

In the twenties, Honolulu alone grossed between $71,000 and $134,000 a year from whaling; in the thirties between $69,200 and $129,750. On each visit, a typical whaler spent between $800 and $1,500 for provisions, equipment and repairs, $200 of this on local produce such as vegetables and meat, the rest on imported articles from stores. In terms of money left in the islands, the whaling trade was worth as much as all other businesses handling goods for export and re-export. Many of these businesses had come into being with the whaling trade and could not survive without it.[31] This circumstance remained true on an expanded scale throughout the golden years of the forties.

Somewhat surprisingly, Honolulu did not develop its own whaling industry with locally-owned ships and locally-based captains. An expedition was fitted out in 1831, and had moderate success. There were others later, designed either for offshore whaling around the islands or for longer voyages in the Pacific. In 1858, toward the end of the era, nineteen whalers were registered under the Hawaiian flag.[32] All in all, however, the local accomplishment was small. It is rather difficult to see why. There were many skillful sea-captains in Honolulu's permanent population. Scores passed through the islands each season and might have been engaged. Rarely was trouble experienced in making up a crew of white men and natives at Honolulu or Lahaina.

The situation has usually been explained in terms of lack of capital, and this may well have been the determining factor. Several Honolulu businessmen, it is true, made fortunes ashore. James Hunnewell, for example, having arrived in the islands virtually without funds, left for the American mainland in 1830 with seventy thousand dollars. His partner and successor Henry Peirce sailed from Honolulu in 1843 with a hundred thousand dollars.[33] Whaling was a very expensive trade, however. By the forties it cost more than $40,000 to outfit a ship. Then too, the Honolulu shipyards, able though they were to handle repair work, did not have the costly special equipment and skilled labor available in the old-established whaling harbors of New England. Henry Peirce had been a partner in the 1831 whaling venture; but he and Hunnewell (and others), prospering greatly as land-based servants of the whalers, in all probability were unwilling to lay out great sums of money to become competitors in a world market subject to wide fluctuations.

In the generation after the coming of the whalers, the Honolulu business community grew quickly. Just as the whaling trade was largely in the hands of Americans, so too was Honolulu's wholesale and retail trade. In the thirties, there were half a dozen or more substantial mercantile houses at the port, chief among which were the Hunnewell–Peirce firm (which later became C. Brewer); William French; Eliab Grimes & Co.; Stephen Reynolds; and the British-owned outlet of the Hudson's Bay Company (widely regarded as an interloper in American preserves in Honolulu, and the subject of commercial and psychological warfare from the time of its establishment in 1834 to its closure at the end of the fifties). By 1840 the services offered to residents and visitors were extremely diversified: twenty retail and four wholesale stores, two hotels, two taverns, twelve boarding-houses for seamen, seven bowling alleys, three vegetable markets, two provision stores, four blacksmith shops, one copper-foundry, fourteen ship carpenters (principal among them the shipbuilding firm of Robinson & Co. on the point in Honolulu harbor, dating from 1822), sailmakers, calkers, and a great many other tradesmen such as shoemakers, saddlemakers, butchers, bakers, engravers, and printers.[34]

One-man businesses or brief partnerships remained the rule, but several large firms were able to expand and open branch stores either elsewhere in Honolulu or at Lahaina on Maui, which became an independent commercial center drawing on a rich hinterland to supply whalers. Lahaina was small by comparison with Honolulu, with about half the total population and a somewhat smaller percentage of foreigners to natives throughout the whaling period. Nonetheless, the two ports became great rivals for the business brought to the islands by whalers.[35]

Honolulu harbor was enclosed and safe; once inside, a ship could ride out the most severe of storms. By contrast, Lahaina's roadstead was wide open. While trade winds blew from the north-east, this was not a disadvantage. But at the turn of each year the trades gave way to what was called kona weather, with drenching rains and southerly gales, which were greatly troublesome at Lahaina roads. To add to the problem, the kona winds frequently blew at their worst during the fall whaling season, which was busier than the spring season. Port charges were higher at Honolulu than at Lahaina, especially in the early years. Then too, supplies were generally cheaper at Lahaina. As traffic increased, Honolulu grew crowded at the peak of the fall season. Its very protectedness might then become a nuisance to a captain in a hurry. He could not simply weigh anchor and leave, as at Lahaina; it might take Honolulu's pilots several days to extricate one vessel from rows of ships so tightly packed that a man could walk from deck to deck across the harbor and never get his feet wet. Finally, the same kona storms which buffeted Lahaina often kept dozens of whalers huddled within the harbor at Honolulu, unable to go out against the wind. Sometimes ships were delayed in this way for as long as two or three weeks.

These constants and variables, combined with others of a different kind, produced changing relationships between the two ports. As the figures show, between 1820 and 1830 Honolulu attracted twice as many whale ships as did Lahaina. Throughout the thirties, arrivals were much more evenly distributed. In the forties, when total arrivals reached unprecedented heights, Lahaina began to draw twice as many ships as Honolulu. Lahaina did not lose this advantage until the early fifties when, with total arrivals still numerous, the two ports returned to rough parity, with Lahaina remaining slightly in advance of Honolulu. By the late fifties, total figures were down substantially, and Lahaina slipped behind Honolulu again as the whaling trade declined.

How might these differences be explained? Initially, Honolulu's harbor and shipyard would have been sufficient to attract the greater number of ships. Liholiho's early experimentation with high port charges at Honolulu sent more whalers to Lahaina in 1825. Reductions brought them back again the next year. In the thirties, and particularly the later years of the decade, the whaling industry was embarrassed (together with the entire United States economy) by uneasiness culminating in the crash of 1837. Increased patronage of Lahaina by a generally decreased fleet probably represented bargain hunting in supplies.

In 1840, conditions changed. Firstly, the white potato began to be grown in quantity at Kula, Maui, on the slopes of the great volcanic crater, Haleakalā. Among sailors, the white potatoes of Lahaina were far more popular than the sweet potatoes of Honolulu. The new trade was very profitable throughout the forties, especially toward the end of the decade when the California gold rush added an insatiable market on the west coast of the American mainland (so much so that the potato lands on Maui came to be called "Kaleponi" or California, because fortunes could be dug from the earth there).

Concurrently with the development of the white potato business, the island of Maui and its principal port, Lahaina, underwent a change of administration. Since the mid-twenties, Hoapili, most dedicated of mission chiefs, had been governor. He had spent his life attempting to extirpate grog shops and brothels from his jurisdiction, which included Maui, Molokaʻi, and Lānaʻi. The moral history of his port had been much more consistent than that of Honolulu. Lahaina would have attracted the minority group of "temperance captains" in the New England whaling fleet, as well as masters who had difficulty holding crews and wanted to offer their men as little reason as possible to go ashore and sample the delights of a Hawaiian port-of-call.

Hoapili died in 1840. He was followed in turn by Keoni Ana, Bennett Nāmakehā, and James Young Kānehoa, all of whom showed much stronger interest in money than in morality. As chiefs, they would automatically collect a large tax on goods passing through the market. The whaling fleet promised other sources of revenue as well. Accordingly, the governors of the forties allowed sailors free rein in Lahaina. Grog shops and brothels sprang into existence, in amazing numbers. For several years in the forties there were probably more grog shops and prostitutes per sailor in Lahaina than in Honolulu, if contemporary comment is to be trusted. Vice had flourished constantly in Honolulu; but now Lahaina sported the potato and the prostitute, and the combination was all but irresistible.

By the mid-forties, prostitution had become a matter for national concern. The moekolohe laws (against fornication and adultery) had been enforced rigorously by Hoapili on Maui, and energetically but without success at Honolulu during the several periods of religious fervor since 1820. With the rise of the whaling industry to great heights in the mid-forties, and the descent twice a year of crowds of sailors upon the ports of the islands, it became apparent that the issue of prostitution was not only moral but economic. In terms of the spiritual and physical health of the nation, prostitution could hardly be allowed to continue; in terms of the economic health of the islands, it could scarcely be permitted to cease.

The notable Hawaiian scholar David Malo, writing in 1847, bemoaned the fate of Lahaina in the period of moral laxity that characterized the regime of James Young Kānehoa: "Great is the prostitution at Lahaina, it is the great thing. All the women come to Lahaina for it. Some put to them the question, What brings you here? They reply, We came to sell.—What have you to sell? They reply, We sell ourselves."[36] The same was true on a larger scale at Honolulu. As the opposition paper, the *Sandwich Island News,* pointed out, not a native vessel came to either port in the whaling season that was not packed with women from the rural districts of the islands—thousands each year. Apothecaries probably did two-thirds of their business in medications for venereal disease among the native population, according to the *News.* Retail traders in the same way did nine-tenths of their business with native women, not even bothering to stock most items until the whaling season, since it was only in those months that women had money. On the average, seamen spent $10 a head in their three or four weeks ashore; with (conservatively) 12,000 in port in a flush season, $120,000 would be left in town. Of this, grog-shop keepers and prostitutes garnered nearly all, with about nine-tenths of the total going to prostitutes. Thus, women at the ports could put almost $100,000 a season into the hands of retailers, who would in turn pay wholesalers, who would in turn pay customs duties to the government. In addition, the government drew on the revenues of prostitution through police court fines, poll taxes, and passage money on government interisland vessels (fares were $1 each way to and from the port).[37]

In all the years from 1820 to 1860, there was rarely a time when Hawai'i's exports and domestic produce supplied to ships came at all close to matching imports in value.[38] The islands suffered chronically from an adverse balance of trade, and in such a situation prostitution was economically useful, however deplorable in terms of morals and national health. In 1846–1847, for example, the estimated earnings of native women through prostitution were approximately equal to all reported government revenues. It is possible that, had prostitution been abolished, sailors might have found other ways of leaving much of their pay in the islands, with the same effect of bolstering the economy. It should be noted, however, that in 1855, when a restraining law temporarily lessened the numbers of women at the sea ports in the fall season, retail storekeepers at Honolulu remarked upon dullness of trade and scarcity of money.[39]

Foreign Minister Wylie, a courtly bachelor, was a great champion of female virtue and a great worrier over its apparent absence among the women who flocked to Honolulu twice a year. He tried on several occasions to have preventive legislation enacted, without success for the most part. His plan, in general, called for strong local governments which would prohibit native women from traveling between ports without good reason; a licensing system for passengers; and fines for breaches of rules. Three legislatures rejected his bills, and a modified version enforced for a short time in 1855 accomplished little. As long as native women coveted gaudy clothes, as long as their husbands, fathers and families remained short of money to buy horses or pay taxes, and as long as sailors came to port rich with money accumulated during a season's cruise, there would be prostitution at Honolulu.[40]

Prostitution owed its existence primarily to the whaling trade, and the whaling trade at Honolulu was brought into being by the harbor. All through the early years of whaling, the harbor remained physically unchanged, its natural characteristics adequate even though traffic increased year by year. The golden age of whaling, however, made apparent its limitations.

From earliest times, it had been rather difficult for ships to enter the inner harbor. Large vessels had to be warped in by hawsers run along the eastern reef to the shore. Power was supplied by natives on foot or in canoes, and later by oxen and horses as well. As more and more ships came to the harbor, this clumsy method grew less and less satisfactory, but the next advance, steam power, did not come until 1855.[41]

The building of wharves also lagged behind demand in the golden age. The first facility, dating from the mid-twenties, was merely a sunken hulk at the shoreline. By 1850, there were several wharves, some government-owned, the rest in private hands; but even so, a general improvement was needed. The same conditions existed with regard to warehouses and storage space.[42]

Harbor works were first given serious consideration in the mid-forties, when it was discovered that silt from Nu'uanu stream was reducing the depth of water close to shore. Some visiting ship captains suggested that a diversionary wall be built at the mouth of the stream, so that the current would no longer take detritus out into the harbor but would spread it instead over an area of shallow reefs to the northwest. The wall was duly built, stretching westward from the foot of Maunakea Street.[43]

The wall did nothing to ease the problem of inadequate wharfage. In connection with this, as with so many things, the indefatigable Foreign Minister Robert Crichton Wyllie had an ambitious plan. His ideas had been published at Honolulu in 1844, before he took office, but not until 1850 were they given a sustained bearing. By that time, even the most insouciant local legislators were aware of developments taking place on the west coast of the United States which night conceivably put

Hawai'i at the center of an American-Asian commercial zone of considerable importance. Gold-rush California was booming. San Francisco had become a thriving port, a possible challenger to Honolulu as a whaling entrepot. Steam navigation was being discussed everywhere. Plans existed for lines along the American west coast, across the Pacific to Hawai'i, and on to Asia and the British colonies in the southern hemisphere.[44]

Against this large-scale background, Wylie's early schemes assumed realistic proportions. His project called for a deepened harbor, a widened channel, and greatly increased wharfage and storage apace at the water's edge. The waterfront area could be extended at the site of the old fort, by 1850 a dilapidated and useless wreck (ruined under circumstances which will be discussed in the next chapter), and at Waikahalulu reef southeast of the fort. If a retaining wall were built as far as the deep water mark, and the confined reef were filled in to ground level, then this would provide wharfage which would be adequate indefinitely. At the same time, the business district would be enlarged by some dozens of acres.[45]

On the opposite, or western, side of the harbor lay another large reef, owned by the Honolulu firm of Sea & Sumner. Improvements were planned there, to match those at Waikahalulu, but the government could not come to terms with Sea & Sumner. Finally, the legislature of 1854 authorized the building of a single retaining wall at Waikahalulu, the demolition of the fort, and the laying of rubble on the reef, to produce what came to be called the "water lots."[46]

Detailed plans for the works at Waikahalulu were drawn up under the supervision of the Scot William Webster, a trained engineer. Finances were arranged in a less systematic way. The legislature rejected Wyllie's proposal of a large bond issue. A plan to sell parts of Waikahalulu reef to pay for improvements was struck out of the 1854 bill. The legislature voted $40,000, and more money was appropriated in successive sessions—never as much as was needed for the speedy completion of improvements, but enough to keep the reef development at the head of a limited public works list, even in periods of financial trouble. As Wyllie said, this was one of the best possible investments that could be made by a city at Honolulu's stage of maturity.[47]

Meanwhile, the government faced a legal contest over its title to Waikahalulu reef. The counter-claimant was Queen Kalama, wife of Kamehameha III; the issue concerned ancient Hawaiian land customs. Water rights, including those pertaining to reefs, were extremely important in the traditional Hawaiian economy. Their disposition at the time of the land reforms of the late forties led to the institution of many lawsuits. Kalama had claimed and been awarded the 'ili of Waikahalulu (an 'ili was a well-defined subdivision of the larger tract called an ahupua'a). The award had been made with the tacit understanding, later made explicit in a Privy Council resolution, that the sovereign rights of the king (representing the government) extended from high water mark to a point a league out to sea, and that no private rights could be sustained within that area except for rights to fish and cut coral stones.

In 1852, Kalama challenged the government's claim to ownership of all territory beyond the high water mark, when the government leased part of Waikahalulu to an American steamship company then preparing to establish a line in the islands. A lengthy hearing before the land commissioners demonstrated beyond doubt the legality of the government's title. Kalama did not rest content. She pursued the matter closely during the early months of 1854. The legislature of that year named Princes Lot and Alexander a Privy Council Committee to negotiate with the queen (and with the king, who as a private person joined his wife in urging her claim). The royal couple insisted upon Kalama's legal right to Waikahalulu, and asked for $25,000 as the price of relinquishment. The Privy Council thought that one-eighth of the reef should be sufficient, or, in lieu of that, $15,000. It proved not to be. The king and queen held out for more, and finally the matter was compromised at a cost of $22,000.[48]

Equipment for dredging and pile-driving could not be manufactured in Honolulu. Supreme Court Justice William Lee, who went to the east coast of the United States on government business in 1855, was commissioned to employ experts and arrange purchases. Lee returned to Honolulu from Boston via Cape Horn in February, 1856, bringing with him a knocked-down steam-dredger and pile-driver, and also the frame and machinery of a steam tugboat, all to be assembled at the Honolulu waterfront.[49]

The tugboat, readied for work by the Scot James Munroe in yards at the foot of Maunakea Street, christened *Pele* after the Hawaiian volcano goddess, and launched early in August, 1856, was from the beginning a great asset. The dredger was less successful. Its purpose was to improve access to the harbor by deepening the bar at the entrance. An experienced engineer, Thomas Hughes, had been brought from the United States to run the machinery, but even under his expert command, it became clear that the dredger could not work at the bar on any day when there was a swell, and there was a swell almost every day. Hughes and his dredger, however, did good work inside the harbor, providing fill for Waikahalulu (and, in the process, bringing up from the harbor floor a number of stone adzes, and a war club). In 1857, after a new prison was built for Honolulu to the west of the harbor, the fort was demolished and its coral stones were used in the retaining wall along the filled reef.

The stone blocks were laid by Hawaiian divers, who were paid $2.50 a day for going fifteen feet to the bottom once every ten minutes during their two-hour work periods. On the reef itself, fill was spread by convict labor. Before the end of the fifties, the first of the "water lots" were ready for sale and lease. By 1870 an esplanade of about twenty-two acres had been created, with a sea frontage of 2,000 feet on water twenty to thirty feet deep, for a cost just less than a quarter of a million dollars.[50]

Harbor improvements were designed to meet the needs of shipping coming to the islands from outside. For interisland shipping before the advent of steam in the fifties, the undeveloped harbor was perfectly adequate. There remained in Honolulu harbor, even after the entry of steamships to the interisland trade, a motley fleet of sailing ships, from tiny, locally-built, erratically-navigated and often unseaworthy native boats (the "poi clippers"), to elegant schooners like the *Emma Rooke* and the *Nettie Merrill*, built to island specifications on the east coast of the United States.[51]

The most reliable interisland vessels were those which ran during the fifties on regular schedules (subject always to weather). Owned by Honolulu merchants, they brought to the metropolis sugar, molasses, wheat, firewood, and pulu (a fiber stripped from tree ferns common in the islands, that had a short but spectacular vogue in the United States as an anti-rheumatic mattress stuffing).[52]

At the other end of the scale were coasters owned and sailed by natives. A passion for boats was second only to a passion for horses among Hawaiians at mid-century, and interisland travel was endemic. The Hawaiian style of life was transferred intact to ship-deck, with all its overcrowded hilarity, its hogs and dogs and pipes and calabashes of poi, its singers and story-tellers. On all but the very best schooners, white cabin-class passengers were confronted with the choice of stifling below decks or joining the open-air "steerage" class of natives on deck. Only the hardiest of foreigners could make a journey between islands without succumbing to profound self-pity. The sights and sounds and smells of native life overwhelmed those of delicate sensibilities, the channels were rough, and wretched sea-sickness was all but inevitable.[53]

On the majority of the coasters, Polynesian self-confidence about navigation persisted long after the ancient voyagers' skills and intuitions were gone. Interisland sailing was marked by wild miscalculations and bizarre mishaps. Most Hawaiian captains held prayers twice every Sunday, but very few had compasses or other instruments. As a consequence, simple faith was open to subversion by negligence or bad weather, especially at the turn of the year when the kona winds blew, taking small craft far from the routes regularly followed in the trade wind season.

The experience of the hundred-ton schooner *Pan* may stand for that of dozens of others. In January, 1853, she took down to Hawai'i 270 passengers, and on her return to Honolulu brought back 190, together with 20 turkeys, 30 pigs, 7 chickens, 30 dogs, 1 pair of oxen, 1 mule, 14 cords of wood, 11 canoes, and other items. A few weeks later, having left Kaua'i for Honolulu carrying 300 barrels of potatoes, sugar, 75 hogs, and 16 passengers (including Supreme Court Justice William Lee), she encountered a severe storm. Fifteen miles from Honolulu, she was far to the leeward, with the mainsail blown from its ropes, all the other sails damaged, and twenty hogs drowned on deck by repeated drenchings. Eventually she made Wai'anae, many miles leeward of Honolulu, and the passengers came to town overland.[54]

A new era began to overtake the old when in May, 1846, the *Cormorant*, the first steamship ever seen in Hawai'i, came to anchor at Honolulu and everybody ran to visit it and to explore the marvels of its machinery.[55] The rise of steam in the Pacific was coincident with the height of the clipper-ship era, and though residents and newspaper editors were greatly impressed with the speed, utility and maneuverability of steamers coming to Honolulu harbor, still there was a poetry about the clippers that appealed to the beached mariners of the islands as they watched the big ships passing along the south coast of O'ahu., great clouds of canvas set, and bound for China.[56]

Pacific navigation was in flux at mid-century. The whaling industry had given rise to an increased mercantile traffic. Honolulu's principal business connections were with the United States. Lesser contacts linked the islands with Great Britain and Germany. In mid-century three ex-Honolulu men, James Hunnewell, Henry A. Peirce, and Charles Brewer, all by then returned to the east coast of the United States, established a line of sailing ships to run to San Francisco, Honolulu, Hong Kong and Manila. This line remained important even when Honolulu's trade pattern shifted to focus on California.[57]

Gold-rush San Francisco became Honolulu's opposite number late in the forties. Soon, too, there was a rail service across the Isthmus of Tehuantepec, making it unnecessary for passengers to go around Cape Horn, though freight generally followed the sea route until American transcontinental railroads were built at the end of the sixties. Packets sailed to the islands from San Francisco, and in 1855 the Regular Dispatch Line, organized by G. B. Post & Co. and other San Francisco businessmen, began operations with 300-ton clipper barks.[58]

The coming of steam had been heralded in the islands as early as 1848. During the next six years, a number of abortive attempts were made to link the islands and the American continent. The Hawaiian government was willing to grant privileges to any company offering reliable service, and there were numerous applicants. Some firms were nothing but paper enterprises. Two others—one a group trying to set up a San Francisco-China line, the other looking towards a San Francisco-Honolulu run—failed to meet time stipulations imposed by the government. A third proved to be a speculation connected with American hopes for annexation of Hawai'i in 1854; and a fourth fell foul of Hawaiian governmental suspicions on this point, and could not obtain the monopolistic privileges it requested. Oceanic steamship lines were still ten years away.[59]

When steam did come to the islands on an organized basis, it was not for trans-Pacific voyaging but for the interisland service.[60] As with the trans-Pacific schemes, there had been, in the period following the great California expansion, several proposals for Hawaiian interisland steamship lines, including one planned by Honolulu businessmen intrigued by the New York test runs of the sensational Ericsson caloric engine, which later proved to be a scientific bubble.[61] There seemed every reason for optimism about the success of interisland steamers. Wyllie had thought as early as 1844 that a 300-tonner might pay its way. No one doubted this by the end of the forties, and the establishment of a service that might eliminate annoyances caused by unreliable sailing vessels was eagerly awaited.[62]

Out of the welter of half-formed schemes laid before the Hawaiian government emerged the offer of Captain William Howard of San Francisco. He and his associates gained in July, 1851, the exclusive right to run steamers between islands for five years, with privileges of wharf age at Honolulu harbor. Howard contracted to put one steamer into operation within ninety days of September 1, 1851, and a second steamer within two years if traffic should warrant it.[63]

Howard's firm never produced an adequate first ship., much less a second. The 600-ton *Constitution,* brought to Honolulu for one experimental voyage, was greeted with enthusiasm. "The blowing off of her steam on Saturday, after she came to in our harbor,' wrote the *Polynesian's* reporter, "was music to our ears." But times were slack in the islands in the aftermath of the California boom, and the *Constitution* proved much too big and unwieldy for reef-dodging among the islands. After one run between Honolulu and Lahaina she returned to California, and that was the last of the Howard line.[64]

Howard's rights lapsed with time, and the Hawaiian government prepared to transfer them to any firm that could supply an interisland steamer of suitable size. A San Francisco group, headed by Garet W. Ryckman and represented in Honolulu by the American attorney Richard Bowlin, was successful over several competitors in obtaining governmental approval. The side-wheel steamer *S. B. Wheeler,* brought to the islands in the fall of 1853 and renamed *Akamai,* was put into regular service after a trial run to Lahaina. Ryckman's group had demonstrated its apparent capacity to fulfill the government's a requirements. It was incorporated as the Hawaiian Steam Navigation Company, with a ten-year monopoly of interisland steam transportation, as well as the steam tug business of Honolulu harbor. As additional encouragements, Ryckman's firm got free water, free wharfage at the government jetties when these were not otherwise occupied, and duty-free importation of machinery.[65]

Under the Hawaiian flag, the *Akamai* sailed several times between Honolulu and Lahaina. Occasional runs to other ports were made, and one or two pleasure jaunts were organized, as when the natives of a Maui sugar plantation hired the *Akamai,* or when she took more than two hundred Honolulu natives, fifty foreigners, and "most of the ladies of easy virtue" on a day-long cruise out to Diamond Head and along the south coast of O'ahu.

This was the high point of the *Akamai's* usefulness. In January, 1854, with the king and his suite aboard, bands playing and flags flying, she went aground while leaving Honolulu harbor on a holiday cruise. Boats from USS *Portsmouth* freed her. Soon afterward, the *Akamai* broke her rudder chains and tiller between Kaua'i and Honolulu. Early in January, 1854, she made a perilous return voyage from Lahaina, overloaded and barely able to cope with bad weather. She labored through high surf into Honolulu harbor, and remained there the rest of the month, trapped like a sailing ship by kona winds.[66] Obviously, steam was no panacea for the ills of interisland navigation.

The coastal trade should have been profitable, according to all indications. Some sailing vessels had recently been withdrawn; fresh produce was grown on all islands for sale at Honolulu, and passenger traffic was heavy.[67] Yet the *Akamai* never did well. In April, 1854, she ran out of coal and lay at Honolulu for two months before her owners managed to buy 1400 tons, about a year's supply. Then, late in August, she sailed for Lahaina, carrying four or five hundred passengers and nineteen horses. She left with her guardrails under water, and many people thought she might meet trouble. Two days later she was back. She had been overtaken by squalls, and had begun to leak. The captain brought the *Akamai* around with difficulty, and headed her toward Honolulu with all hands pumping and bailing and still unable to keep up with the inflow of water. Clearly the ship was in bad condition—

unseaworthy and ready for condemnation, the *Polynesian* thought. This was her final voyage as a coaster.[68]

Ryckman's a firm shortly acquired two more ships: the *Sea Bird* a 440-tonner in good condition, and the older *West Point,* 239 tons. The *Sea Bird,* renamed *Kamehameha,* lasted only six months; she was withdrawn on the ground that she was too expensive to operate in a business that required only one ship. The *West Point,* renamed *Kalama,* was a failure. Her hull and boilers constantly needed repair, and she made only sporadic trips before turn-of-the-year storms drove her ashore on Kaua'i, where she was totally wrecked, on January 5, 1856, In the meantime the *Akamai* was being used, with little success, as a tug in Honolulu harbor. No steamer remained in the interisland trade. Ryckman's group did nothing more to carry out the terms of its charter. In October, 1856, the Hawaiian Supreme Court stripped the company of its rights.[69]

The rise and fall of the Hawaiian Steam Navigation Company coincided closely with a strong American annexationist movement in the Hawaiian islands (to be discussed in the next chapter). The Hawaiian government had accepted Ryckman's proposition in good faith, but there is no doubt that the San Francisco promoters hoped to turn their speculation into a profitable item should the islands fall into American hands. An American diplomat in Honolulu came to the conclusion that Ryckman's group had not only predicted but had fomented annexationism among the Americans at Honolulu. "The old 'Hawaiian Steam Navigation Company,'" wrote United States Commissioner David Gregg, "is hopelessly broken down. It was originally a mere speculation, with reference to the chances of 'annexation.' Its boats were old and worthless...The excitement of 1854, as I now am fully aware, was created by its chief manager and his agents in order to drive the Hawaiian Government into a connexion with the United States."[70]

Repeatedly disappointed and even bilked by outsiders, the Hawaiian government turned to consider the establishment of a government-owned interisland line, or at least one in which the state might share control with private capitalists. A plan to have a steamer built in Boston and sent to Honolulu was developed by Henry A. Peirce, but negotiations were abandoned during the American commercial panic of 1857. Not until 1859 did a new Hawaiian Steam Navigation Company come into existence, organized by the Honolulu businessmen James N. Green, C.A. Williams, and A. Mitchell. Their 400-ton screw steamer *Kilauea,* Boston-built, arrived at Honolulu on June 28, 1860, to begin a seventeen-year career as Hawai'i's principal interisland freight and passenger carrier.[71]

The same forces which opened up the possibility, if not the actuality, of reliable steam transportation also gave rise to the hope of better mail services for the Hawaiian islands, A dislocation in time was one of the severest penalties attached to life in Honolulu for those who valued their ties with the outside world. From the period of the first permanent white settlements early in the nineteenth century, Honolulu had been mail-hungry. For years, the sight of a foreign sail could halt normal activity. Every advance on the world scene in the way of faster ships, new routes, or scientific discoveries making for speedier communications was fully reported and widely discussed in Honolulu. The completion of the Atlantic cable late in the fifties, for example, precipitated a day-long celebration in the town. Church bells were rung for hours, flags of all nations were flown, and a hundred-gun salute was fired by the government to mark the "eighth wonder of the world."[72] Thus, development on the west coast of America brought with it hopes of better letter-carrying service to Honolulu.

Until then, most mail from the United States had come around Cape Horn. Ships generally sailed in the fall and reached Honolulu in the spring. In the middle to late forties, voyages averaged five to five and a half months. Delays might be exacerbated further by transshipment of mails at Valparaiso to vessels bound for the islands of the Pacific. These might spend up to two years in the ocean before making port at Honolulu, and their vagaries were a source of complaint as late as the eighteen-sixties.[73]

A new route was opened up in the eighteen-thirties, much shorter, but more expensive and not much more reliable. Mail could now be sent overland across Mexico from Vera Cruz to Mazatlan and thence to the islands. It might suffer along the way the heavy exactions of merchants and consuls attending to delivery. Then too, the Mexican War caused disruptions in the forties. The Mexican route was used in addition to yet another route—from America or Europe around the Cape of Good Hope, across the Indian Ocean, and into the western Pacific. Both remained subsidiary to the Cape Horn route until mid-century.

By various means, then, and in various states of obsolescence, the mails made their way to Honolulu. There, until 1850, the Hawaiian government did not concern itself with the regulation of the mails. Incoming mail from ships

> was usually poured from the bags etc. onto the floor of the counting room of the consignee of the vessel, or of the Harbor Master's office, and those expecting letters gathered around the pile to assist in 'overhauling' or 'sorting,' picking out their own, and passing over their shoulders the letters &c of those standing

in the outer circles. Letters for Capts. and crew of ships on cruise addressed to care of Ship Chandlers went to their offices, the Seamen's Chaplain took those sent to his care, and the remainder for sailors went into the old tea chest in the Consulate. When the whalers came into port to recruit, their crews made the rounds of the Ship Chandleries, the Chaplaincy and the Consulate in search of news from home, and the old tea chest was upset and overhauled many times daily while the fleet was in port.[74]

Outgoing mails were collected at consulates, in business houses, or at the office of the *Polynesian* to be bagged for free transport on ships departing for California or the east coast of the United States. In neither direction was passage or handling regulated by international treaty. Nor did the emergence of western government in Hawai'i in the mid-forties lead immediately to an efficient postal system. Organic legislation included enabling acts, but not until 1850 was a post office created. By then, increased traffic to and from California, and the concentration of business connections in San Francisco, had led to a great improvement in mail times.[75]

In August, 1850, a Hawaiian-American mail treaty took effect. At the end of that year, a government-organized post office opened at Honolulu, in the charge of Henry N. Whitney, a missionary son who was in the stationery and bookstore business, and who later served as government printer for a time and then established the *Pacific Commercial Advertiser*, an important Honolulu newspaper. For $250 a year, Whitney supervised incoming and outgoing mail, both domestic and foreign, and began to issue postage stamps at two, five, and thirteen cents—the famous "Missionary" stamps whose rarity has made them worth scores of thousands of dollars in recent years.[76]

In an office on Merchant Street, Whitney and his successors handled increasing numbers of letters, newspapers, and other pieces of mail. By 1854, about fifteen thousand items arrived annually from the United States and Europe, eighteen thousand went out, and one thousand every month were carried each way between O'ahu and the other islands. The volume rose every year, to a total of about seventy-five thousand for 1855. After that year, the whaling fleet declined, but the mails did not.[77]

Difficulties continued with the trans-Pacific mails. Sealed bags were sent between Honolulu and San Francisco, and private express firms added their efforts to those of the government post offices. Nonetheless, mails sometimes were not transferred quickly from one ship to another. Occasionally, entire bags were lost; wax seals melted on letters sent by tropical routes; and so on. At Honolulu, where each whaling season brought bulging mails, Whitney set up a separate box for every ship, doing away at last with the old tea chest system. In the mid-fifties, there were often as many as ten thousand letters awaiting delivery to whalermen at Honolulu and Lahaina. The *Polynesian* printed huge lists of unclaimed letters, and names reappeared for as long as two or three years in the era of prolonged whaling cruises.[78]

Between islands, postage was free, on the supposition that any charge would discourage natives from using the mails. Volunteer postmasters and mailmen covered routes on the outer islands. As the quantity of mail became greater—about thirty thousand letters in 1851, most of them written by Hawaiians—it became clear that improvements were needed. Postage charges were introduced at the end of the fifties, payment for workers was arranged, and routes were regularized. There were hazards. For one thing, the erratic coasters of the day were also the mail-carriers. Then too, the values of postage stamps bore no close relation to the denominations of coins current in the islands, so that natives and postmasters often could not make correct change. This problem was solved by mutual agreement: sometimes a sender paid double, sometimes he paid nothing. By 1860 the interisland system was working well. Stamps were popular among the natives. Twenty-seven postmasters were needed to handle the mails on the principal islands, and receipts covered two-thirds of costs.[79]

In one way or another, the common sailor provided a great many Honolulans with a direct livelihood. In consequence, a number of institutions emerged either to serve or to exploit him.

The missionaries from the beginning had done their best to interest sailors in evangelical Protestantism. In the New England whaling fleet, some captains ran "temperance ships" and would not hunt on the Sabbath. Such men found the Honolulu mission congenial. They were, however, in the minority. Others had to be sought out actively by the missionaries, who spent as much time as possible distributing bibles and tracts to often ungrateful seamen.

In 1830, with a growing whaling fleet frequenting the harbor, Honolulu's Protestant missionaries wrote to the American Seamen's Friend Society of New York, asking them to appoint a chaplain to the islands. The Society chose John Diell. He and his family arrived in Honolulu in May, 1833. King Kauikeaouli and Kīna'u granted Diell two pieces of land, one near the waterfront where a two-story chapel was built, and the other a house lot nearer the center of town.[80]

Diell proved to be a militant evangelist, who did not hesitate to seek out seamen in grog-shops as well as on board ship. He also served the foreign community of Honolulu. His chapel became the home of the tiny Bethel Church, organized in 1837 with a membership of seven, which gave foreigners a place to worship until the non-missionary Protestant community grew large enough to need a separate church.[81]

Diell was consumptive. In 1838 his health became so bad that he had to withdraw from his work for a time. He died at sea on a voyage home to the United States in January, 1841. For a short while his pulpit was filled by Reuben Tinker, a missionary who had severed his connection with the ABCFM, and by lay preachers like Peter Brinsmade (United States Commercial Agent, a partner in the business firm of Ladd & Co., and a founding member of the Bethel Church). Diell's permanent successor was Samuel Chenery Damon of Holden, Massachusetts, a graduate of Andover Seminary. Hiram Bingham, by then back in the United States, interviewed Damon about the possibility of coming to Honolulu for the Seamen's Friend Society, and this was arranged. Damon arrived with his wife in October, 1842, to take up a ministry that ended only with his death in 1885.[82]

Damon was a remarkable man—dedicated, energetic, an epitome of the very best in generalized Puritanism, ideally suited to be a mediator between port and town. For four decades, he was a useful spokesman for common sense and moderation in a city greatly given to fanaticism of one sort or another. Damon spent between two and three thousand dollars a year at the height of the whaling era, distributed free a thousand copies of each issue of his monthly journal, *The Friend,* boarded every whaler and merchantman that came to town, maintained a continuous correspondence all over the Pacific, and guided about seventy-five seamen a year to the Honolulu Sailors' Home, thus keeping them away from the less savory boarding-houses of the port. One man's life for forty years, however, represented only a tiny portion of the time and energy expended by Honolulu on the accommodation of the seaman.

Damon's Bethel was near the center of the section of Honolulu devoted to serving the whaling trade. This district spread outward from the harbor in annular rings, as each season in the forties and early fifties brought new increments of growth. It was, in spite of the presence of the Bethel, preeminently an area catering to immorality, so much so that the Honolulu authorities, unable to extirpate vice, moved in legalistic fashion to contain it. In 1848, an ordinance was passed to prohibit the issuing of liquor licenses outside a few blocks around the waterfront.[83] Honolulu underwent many changes in the next three decades, but the principle survived that the natural limits of vice should be legally defined.

Within these bounds, sailors might encounter trouble in many forms. Some deserted from their ships, swimming ashore or floating in on boards and tea chests. Others mutinied, or set fire to their ships, or bored holes below the waterline with augers. The hope of these desperate men was that they could lose themselves in the jumble of native houses and grog shops along the waterfront, or pass through the town to the hills without being apprehended. Honolulu's native police, however, were very vigilant where sailors were concerned—unfairly so, as the seamen saw things. Deserters and liberty men alike were closely watched by the constables, who until 1859 were paid a percentage of fines. Seamen arrested for desertion, drunkenness, fornication, or "furious riding" were led to the fort in constant procession. This last crime was a specialty of Honolulu (and Lahaina on Maui). The Hawaiian's mania for speed was shared by the sailor, who would come ashore for sightseeing, hire a horse and saddle from one of the innumerable waterfront loafers, and set off at a gallop along Nu'uanu Street, only to be brought up short by fine-hungry policemen. So profitable was this sequence of events that the Honolulu fort became known to seamen as "The Mint."

These and other contretemps naturally produced arguments, which turned often enough to violence. In such cases, the police could usually count upon the enthusiastic assistance of native boat boys, water sellers, porters, and peddlers who crowded the waterfront at the height of the whaling season. More than once, riots assumed serious proportions, endangering the peace of the whole downtown section of Honolulu.[84]

Together with the attempt to confine sailors to a few city blocks near the harbor, there went an effort to clear them from the town altogether at night. Ever since the beginning of the commercial era, there had been curfew laws, with guns or bells signaling the end of the liberty men's hours on shore. Infringements were common. For a time, it was possible even for a pious sailor returning from prayers at the Bethel to be arrested. Theater-goers sometimes suffered the same fate. Not surprisingly, most of the offenders were sailors who did not want to leave the taverns, or those who stayed too long at houses of assignation.[85]

The local authorities, then, were sufficiently bothersome to seamen. In addition, the waterfront abounded with land-sharks who preyed upon sailors—confidence men, opportunistic boarding-house keepers, sellers of adulterated liquor, and procurers, all eager to separate the mariner from his money. The seaman's recourse in time of difficulty was his consulate. Because most sailors at Honolulu were Americans, the United States Consulate was the busiest office in town during the whaling season. Treaties and Hawaiian laws left obscure many jurisdictional questions. How far out to sea did Hawaiian law hold? Could Hawaiian officials board foreign ships? Who should pay consular shipping fees, masters or seamen? Should consuls be notified when sailors were arrested? Could foreign seamen be tried in Hawaiian courts? Should consuls have the right to aid in the selection of juries? What was the status of Hawaiian seamen on American ships? Who was finally responsible for seeing that they were correctly shipped, discharged, and paid off with their proper share of a whaling voyage's profits? All these questions were argued at length. Toward the end of the whaling era, the direct confrontation of consul and Hawaiian government was complicated by the appearance in Honolulu of a large class of native lawyers, who literally stood in the streets between the waterfront and the consuls' offices and exhorted seamen taking grievances to the consul to retain an attorney instead and seek a judgment in the courts.[86]

Of all ports in the world, Honolulu and Lahaina were most heavily frequented by American ships and seamen in the forties and fifties. Consular expenses were therefore very high, including as they did the care and repatriation of sick, disabled, and abandoned sailors. Concurrently with the growth of whaling, consuls at Honolulu and Lahaina became very sophisticated in the manipulation of their official accounts. Hawaiian posts became the most eagerly contested in the whole of the United States consular corps, for the simple reason that, at the islands, a man might make his fortune in the service of his country.

The easiest way to divert federal money was through the consular hospitals. From the eighteen-twenties onward, distressed seamen put ashore at Honolulu had been a problem. At first, they were boarded in the town's taverns, whose publicans charged the consulate a daily rate. Occasionally, when a man-of-war came in from a long cruise with cases of scurvy aboard (not uncommon in the United States Navy as late as the eighteen-fifties), the Hawaiian government would make available a public building, such as Mauna Kilika, close to the waterfront, as a temporary hospital. Eventually, the home governments assumed full responsibility for facilities. Under Consul-General William Miller, a British marine hospital was built in Pauoa valley behind Honolulu on the land of an English-born tavern-keeper, Joe Booth. With the name of "Little Greenwich" it served from 1845 to 1851, when a new hospital was opened on Miller's property, "Little Britain," east of the town on the way to Waikīkī.[87]

Given the small volume of British commerce with Hawai'i, there was never more than a handful of British sailors on the consulate's books. It was at the American consulate that peculation on a grand scale occurred. From the time of the first United States commercial agent, John Coffin Jones, legitimate requests had been made for reimbursement of money paid out on behalf of sick seamen. Jones' successor, Peter Brinsmade, was a man of reasonably high principles, but the consuls who followed Brinsmade at Honolulu in the middle and late forties appear to have been willing to inaugurate private spoils systems. One or two vice-consuls at Lahaina in the same period also left the islands as wealthy men.

Greatest of all predators was Benjamin Angel, consul at Honolulu in the early fifties, the record years of whaling. Angel perfected a system of competitive bids among physicians in the town. The medical profession was overcrowded, and doctors were eager to add the consulate's *per capita* and *per diem* fees to their uncertain income. Some paid Angel as much as $1,000 to secure their appointment. Once installed, they cooperated with Angel in filling the hospital, since profits were greatest when the number of patients was large. The United States government did not think it necessary to build a marine hospital at Honolulu in this period. Instead, purveyors were chosen by the consul to house, feed, and clothe patients. Angel made sure that this office too was filled by competitive bid. With Angel's connivance, a successful applicant might then charge as much as 200–300% above prices current in Honolulu for rent of premises, supply of food, and clothing (Honolulu prices were themselves often 100% above those in the United States). Angel and his physicians and purveyors recruited patients for the hospital in the streets of the town, paying little attention to the state of a man's health, his previous employment, or his citizenship. Thereafter, the "patient" might be kept on the hospital's books for an inordinate length of time, to the enrichment of Angel and his appointees.

Angel, as it happened, was personally unpopular among residents of Honolulu and among American seamen and ship-captains. His venal administration of the hospital, however, was apparently unknown outside the medical community until 1854, when he was sued in the Honolulu courts by the consulate physician B.F. Hardy. Hardy claimed that Angel had withheld from him $1,000 in fees.[88]

United States Commissioner David Gregg examined this case, turning up in the process another dispute concerning the sale of the purveyorship. Angel's criminality was clear. Gregg was amazed at its scope. Stories were told of "kickbacks" and "presents" of ten or twenty percent on fees collected by purveyors and physicians, bags full of currency left unattended where Angel might find them, "financial expressions of gratitude" on sentimental occasions, and so on.

Gregg forwarded his sensational findings to Washington, but despite his revelations, the Honolulu consulate (and the consular office and hospital at Lahaina as well) continued to be run corruptly. Angel's appointment was not renewed in 1854–1855. Representations had made against him at Washington by whaling interests, and his offer to David Gregg of $5,000 if Gregg would use his influence went unaccepted. But those who followed Angel in office tended to follow his principles, too. Consul Darius Ogden was judged by Gregg to be honest enough, but a "tool of others." Among these others was Dr. George Lathrop, at one time or another in the middle fifties both acting consul and consulate physician. Lathrop combined personal profit-taking with violent American nationalism (his part in Honolulu's politics will be discussed in the next chapter).

A major investigation was made at the end of the fifties. Calculations in Washington indicated that, in 1857–1858, disbursements from the fund for destitute seamen amounted to $70,392 at Honolulu, $71,206 at Lahaina, and $8,581 at Hilo, Hawai'i—a total of more than $150,000, or just over half the sum appropriated by Congress for the relief of sailors throughout the world. Special commissioners were dispatched to the islands aboard USS *Levant* to gather evidence. With the assistance of the Hawaiian authorities, hearings were held, and the *Levant* departed on her return voyage carrying a complete report. She was never heard of again. At the expense of scores of lives, consular corruption had gained a respite. Sharp practice was permitted to enter a natural decline with the entire whaling industry in the eighteen-sixties.[89]

Whalermen and native prostitutes between them accounted, directly or indirectly, for most of the prisoners in the Honolulu fort at any given time. Until 1851 there was no regulatory statute covering prisons, and the fort was run at discretion by Governor Kekūanaō'a, with a handful of white aides and squads of fort soldiers and constables. Like most nineteenth-century prisons, it was a noisome place. Filthy earth-floored cells each held as many as fifteen or twenty convicts. There was no real segregation of the sexes, so that fornication and adultery, which had led to imprisonment in the first place, might be repeated in jail. Police brutality went beyond whipping, which was a punishment approved by haole governmental officials like Gerrit Judd and practiced by foreign representatives like Richard Charlton. The other side of the coin was laxity. There were frequent escapes by sailors and male Hawaiians, and nocturnal excursions by Hawaiian women anxious to work off their fornicator's fine and be freed.

Investigations of complaints made by prisoners or consuls were carried out in the later forties, but comprehensive reform was begun only in 1850. In 1849 the fort reached the end of its useful life, when it was wrecked by French sailors. It continued, however, to house prisoners for another eight years, together with a separate lock-up, newly-built. In 1857, an architect-planned prison was built at Leleo, west of Honolulu proper, and the fort was demolished. A reconstruction of the police force was attempted in 1850 by the first Marshal of the Kingdom, William Parke. Under Parke, a special group of haole constables was recruited, not only to cope with local disturbances but also to strengthen the town against possible trouble emanating from the California goldfields. The new organizational chart was somewhat more satisfactory than the old, but, given the nature of the town and the quality of the constabulary upon which Parke might draw, abuses would be certain to recur. Curiously enough, there existed side by side with this indifferent administration one aspect of prison work which was carried out with formidable efficiency. Public executions by hanging were conducted by white men, most of whom happened to be British. Malefactors were despatched without bungling: time after time; observers reported "not a quiver."[90]

Problems of local government were approached casually in respectable Honolulu, away from the waterfront and the fort. Municipal need was counterbalanced by factional irritation, native apathy, and official poverty, creating a nice equilibrium of non-accomplishment. Streets and bridges were a case in point. As late as the forties, wheeled traffic was not especially heavy anywhere outside the downtown business district. Streets were maintained by natives, laboring under the direction of chiefs on work days set aside each month. This arrangement, a remnant of tradition, was sufficient to keep the streets of the town at a usable level. One by-product of constitutional government was the emergence of a new system in which road supervisors were elected by natives—a retrograde step. Natives naturally chose the easiest of taskmasters, men whose daily demands from laborers were negligible. Under this regime, developmental plans were subverted along the characteristic Hawaiian lines of sociability and sloth. In the late fifties, the position of road supervisor for Oʻahu became appointive, and some semblance of professionalism appeared, most notably under the leadership of T.G. Harding. Even so, Harding and his colleagues were hampered by governmental poverty on the one hand, and by unskilled foremen and laborers on the other.

Meanwhile, the condition of the streets elicited continuous complaints in the Honolulu press. Offal and garbage lay piled in the gutters. Dead dogs and cats were left decomposing for weeks. Horses' legs were cut and broken by iron hoops, smashed bottles and potholes. Inconvenience reached two seasonal peaks, the first in the summer, when hot, dry, weather raised dust on unpaved surfaces and the trade winds spread clouds of it everywhere, the second during the kona storms, when Nuʻuanu stream filled with incredible rapidity and discharged flash floods upon the town. In such instances, the legislature might be induced to make an appropriation or levy a special tax, but, for the most part, private initiative and voluntary association were required to supply the deficiencies of government.

Many problems of public safety and health were not well handled in Honolulu. Livestock driven through the streets to slaughterhouses on the harbor killed more than one person, injured many, and frightened scores. Unruly as the cattle were, they were only somewhat more dangerous than the "furious riders" of the town, native and haole. There were one or two favorite raceways in Honolulu—the top end of Nu'uanu Street, where barroom bets led to contests on a flat stretch of road; and the east end of town, where buildings gave way to the Waikīkī plains. Dozens of accidents occurred at these places. Monarchs of Hawai'i, cabinet ministers, and private citizens were tipped without distinction from their carriages or flung from horseback when they encountered reckless riders. Normal traffic had its hazards, too—there was no agreement about driving and riding on a given side of the street. Natives rode anywhere, and foreigners held stubbornly to the custom of the country of their origin, with the result that there were many head-on collisions.[91]

This picture of private interest at war with public interest to the benefit of neither was repeated in many other ways. A Board of Health created in 1850 struggled along with virtually no legislative appropriations, while offal lay in the streets, cesspools filled up, and the town in hot weather sweltered under a thick miasma. Citizens' committees and Commissioners of Private Ways met frequently to widen and straighten streets which, even after the land divisions of the forties, were progressively narrowed and obstructed by encroaching walls. Inflammable grass and wood houses were built close together in the indeterminate business and residential quarter near Nu'uanu stream, causing an ever-present fire risk about which government did very little until the fifties. In that decade, an inefficient water supply with limited reticulation was strained to the utmost by the addition of a system of hydrants and reservoirs, and volunteer fire companies were given tax exemptions and free land lots for their engine houses. Market regulations framed to confine vending to a few locations near the waterfront were disregarded. Sellers of produce set up stalls on the streets for shoppers coming in from the valleys, with the result that traffic was blocked and the most rudimentary sanitation was impossible. The government's market building with its own wharf was little better—effluvium drained from it into the harbor and washed along the wharf areas of the major business houses.

Only on questions of morality were regulations plentiful, and only in such matters was there a consistent attempt at enforcement. Just as the government wished to contain vice within a small area near the waterfront, so it wished to legislate morality for the kingdom at large.[92] Among the foreign advisers of government, there was a strong opinion that urban life, inherently vicious, was especially harmful to Hawaiians. The health of the nation, therefore, would best be sustained if natives were kept away from the ports, and out of the grog shops and brothels should they perchance come to town. The failure of this policy was profound. Efforts to prevent migration to Honolulu and Lahaina proved vain. Then too, sickness was often carried back to the countryside by girls who went to the ports for the whaling season, returning home gaudily dressed and infected with venereal disease. By mid-century, many rural areas were seriously depopulated.

It was the hope of the government that education might emerge as a countervailing force against social trends which threatened to destroy the Hawaiian people. The schools had ceased to be a monopoly of the Protestant mission in 1840, when, far in advance of many more civilized parts of the world, a governmental system of education was established. Religious toleration was also a policy of state. Accordingly, Catholic and Protestant schools for Hawaiians, offering instruction in the native language, were set up on all major islands and at Honolulu. Sectarian war, in this period, moved off the streets and into the schools. At the same time, a prolonged argument raged over the question of instruction in Hawaiian rather than in English for natives. What were the schools trying to produce? What was the educated native supposed to do in his own society? There was no consistent answer to these questions, but one thing seemed clear—it was widely believed a native could not best reap the benefits of instruction in Honolulu. Urban immorality meant educational blight. Most major efforts to create an educated elite among the native commoners were mounted away from the metropolis, principally on Maui and Hawai'i. Honolulu, of course, had common schools, financed by the government and taught in the Hawaiian language. These showed the usual faults and virtues of their kind, and suffered as well from the distractions of life at the port. More important than the common schools were a few special schools, unique to Honolulu. Opened in the thirties and forties, they influenced greatly the town and the nation.[93]

The first of these was Punahou School, founded by Protestant missionaries in 1841. Between 1820 and 1840, almost two hundred children were born to missionary families in the islands. Their educational prospects were dark. The overwhelming labor of evangelism among the Hawaiians left many missionaries with no time to teach their own children. The financial arrangements of the mission, which provided for families out of a common stock, allowed no surplus funds for education. Then too, Hawai'i in its partly-evangelized state was regarded as an unfit habitation for budding American Protestants. Missionary parents felt an urgent need to keep their children safe from the taint of association with unchurched haoles, and, even more, from the degradations of Hawaiian society. As for native servants, mothers could arrange to have them within earshot while children were in their care, or they could dispense with domestic help altogether. They could keep their children in enclosed or walled play areas kapu to natives. They could try to make sure that the children learned no Hawaiian words, since the word and the deed were closely linked in their minds and Hawaiian utterance was frightening in its frankness. But even this might not be enough. Clearly, the best solution was to send children home to New England for an education. More than thirty boys and girls made the long voyage before the Sandwich Island Mission, in the late thirties, began seriously to consider starting an academy at Honolulu.[94]

Punahou School was built in 1841–1842 on a stretch of land at the entrance of Mānoa valley a few miles from the town of Honolulu. A newly-arrived missionary, Daniel Dole, took charge of the first class, which met in mid-1842. Of the fifteen children, some were boys, some were girls, some boarders, some day-students. All were mission children. Over the years, enrollment grew, but Punahou maintained its exclusiveness.[95]

Within the limits of the staff's numbers and capacities, a good liberal education was attempted, along New England lines. Classical and modern languages, mathematics, geography, music, art, and composition were taught, among other subjects. There were recitations from scripture at breakfast, prayers morning and night, and church meetings on Sunday. No midday meal was eaten on the Sabbath, the better to concentrate the minds of the young scholars upon their Christian duties.[96]

Punahou's Christianity was not totally contemplative, The school developed quickly all the apparatus of New England in its "benevolent empire" period. There were aid and service clubs. Newspapers were published by the Philographic and Philomathian societies. A vigorous debating group throve in various incarnations for decades, discussing questions of moment (Does the reading of novels have a bad effect on the reader? Yes. Ought theaters to be abolished? Yes. Is there sufficient employment to support the mission children in the islands? No. Should children be allowed to learn the native language as soon as they choose? No).[97]

All this ratiocination was matched by muscular exertion, for the boys at least. They were up before sunrise every week-day to work in the Punahou fields, they swam in the pool at Punahou spring, and they hiked and rode as often as they could, with the encouragement of Principal Dole, who himself took part. For the girls, dancing of course was barred, but there were calisthenics ("Presbyterian dancing," as mission critics called it), and again swimming and hiking. Muscular Christianity, then, and minimal co-education. Boys sat opposite girls at meals, girls promenaded separately at recess, and all social contact occurred under the unwinking eye of an archetypal maiden-lady mission schoolmistress, Miss Marcia Smith.[98]

In the eighteen-fifties, Punahou graduates began to move on to New England colleges such as Williams and Yale, where they earned a good reputation. With this encouragement, Punahou added—very ambitiously—a higher level to the school at Honolulu, which became known as O'ahu College.[99]

The college's early history was checkered. At the time of its foundation, Punahou itself was in something of a slump. Many children had been withdrawn by their parents. Punahou was being slighted in favor of the Royal School in Honolulu, taught by a New Englander, E.G. Beckwith (affiliated with the mission by his marriage to Caroline Armstrong, daughter of the one-time Kawaiaha'o pastor and current head of the government's office of public instruction). A faction within the mission arranged to bring Beckwith to Punahou, upon which Daniel Dole resigned abruptly, after more than a decade of hard work.

Beckwith assumed the responsibility of raising Punahou's standards, commensurate with the name of O'ahu College. This took some time. The missionaries, comprising Hawai'i's intellectual elite, by no means formed a financial elite. Most parents could scarcely pay the cost of their children's tuition. They could not possibly endow professorial chairs. Soon after Beckwith became principal, the College had to be closed for a year while he toured the United States seeking money. His trip coincided with the business panic of 1857, and netted very little. The College was still on less than solid ground when Beckwith resigned in 1859, giving way to a missionary son, William DeWitt Alexander.[100]

With rare exceptions, Punahou and O'ahu College relied in their early years upon New Englanders and those of New England descent to recreate New England in Honolulu. The only "outsiders" on the staff were foreign-born teachers of languages and music. As for the students, not until seventeen years after the opening were a few children of Hawaiian blood admitted, together with a handful of children from respectable non-missionary families in Honolulu.[101] The offspring of missionaries went to school with each other; when they graduated, some remained to teach the younger ones. As they grew up, they indulged a tendency to marry each other. The Cousins' Society (descendants of missionary brothers and sisters) had a heavy Punahou component. The original plan of educational and social exclusiveness had worked as fully as might have been expected.[102]

At the end of a generation, Punahou had educated 290 pupils. About half this number had made public profession of religion. Eight had become ordained ministers. Of these, five were in the islands. About twenty had taken bachelors' degrees at American colleges, some of them with great distinction. There were three lawyers, two doctors, and several students destined for these professions. Many were teachers, including the principal himself, W.D. Alexander. Several had fought in the Civil War. Most notable was Samuel Chapman Armstrong, who rose to the rank of general and later founded the celebrated Hampton Institute for negroes in Virginia. Locally, a great many taught in native Sunday schools. Of the rest, most were in business at Honolulu or on plantations on the outer islands. Unquestionably, the elite was using its talents.[103]

During the first decade of Punahou's existence, an experiment quite similar in intent and quite different in result was carried out in a quadrangular adobe building toward the northeast end of Honolulu, about equidistant from the royal palace and Kawaiaha'o church. There, from 1839 to 1850, the missionary couple Amos and Juliette Cooke, assisted by John 'I'i and his wife Sarai, worked to prepare the children of the chiefs for their future role as leaders of the kingdom.

The Cookes were still in their twenties when they took charge of the Chiefs' Children's School in 1839. Amos had studied a year or two at Yale, and had also had some business experience before he became an assistant missionary. Juliette was among the first women permitted to attend lectures at Amherst, and she had taught for a time in a New England seminary. As they themselves were painfully aware, the Cookes were very much an average missionary teacher couple—it was their school that was remarkable.[104]

Cooke, together with some of his contemporaries, had been called to missionary work just as the anti-slavery crusade was gaining momentum on the American mainland. He himself was a convinced abolitionist, one of several who organized an anti-slavery society at Honolulu. Older men such as Bingham, Judd, Chamberlain, and Richards had more or less made their peace with the imperfections of the Hawaiian system of government. Cooke, newly-arrived, could not reconcile himself to the fact that despotism continued to flourish in the islands after two decades of evangelism. When the Chiefs' Children's School opened, the monarchy was, to be sure, on the brink of self-limitation in the interests of constitutional government, but this meant little or nothing to the young chiefs, who from the time of their birth had grown up like the ali'i of old, surrounded and venerated by kahus (guardians). Accordingly, Cooke's somewhat spartan Protestant republicanism was put to a severe test.

Cooke began by trying to sever, as completely as possible, the children's associations with their former status. An orthodox high missionary fence was built around the schoolyard. Even this, however, was not enough to deter the kahus, who "lurked about" and congregated in the yard of Kekāuluohi's house close by. Sometimes the children climbed the fence to go to their attendants; sometimes the kahus came inside at night and were discovered making the children's beds. Before the guardians were finally driven off, with many tears and lamentations, Alexander's kahu succeeded in taking him away to Maui for several months.[105]

Inside the fence, Hawaiian speech was discouraged and English was imparted at every opportunity. Language change was difficult. Worse, Hawaiian attitudes lingered. Ghost stories brought on nightmares. When the kuhina nui Kīna'u died, the children, including one of her sons, told Cooke she had been prayed to death by a kahuna. At other times of illness in the school, anxious parents called upon native doctors, who came secretly to treat the children, often contradicting the advice of the mission's physicians. Once, on a walk to town, Cooke and Moses saw a mark in the dirt, said to have been put there by a sorcerer. Cooke derided and defaced it, but Moses fell sick for some days. All in all, the Cookes found it harder than did the teachers at Punahou to supplant "feelings" with "principles."[106]

The aristocratic pretensions of the young chiefs were a continual source of chagrin to Cooke. Determined to bring his charges to heel, he had recourse to the standard persuaders of his time, practices acceptable not only to him but to the Punahou staff and to most other American teachers of the mid-nineteenth century—isolation, detention (sometimes under lock and key), withholding of food, corporal punishment, and so on. This pedagogical approach was considered sufficiently harsh by the Punahou children, who had been prepared for it in their own homes. To the young chiefs it seemed outrageous. Two generations previously, their bodies would have been sacred, and even an accidental contact might have meant death to the offender. Their kahus had always treated them tenderly, understanding that their bodies were the repositories of mana. Now, with the permission of the chiefs, the kahus had been banished, and the pupils were being manhandled by their new teachers, allegedly for their own good. Not long after the school opened, Cooke had occasion to chastise Alexander and Moses, and the latter, already the nominal governor of Kaua'i, told Cooke haughtily that he was "he keiki a ke ali'i" (a child of the chief). Cooke replied that *he* was king of the *school*.[107]

As long as his students were young, Cooke continued to be king. In general, the scholars responded satisfactorily to his demands in the classroom. By 1845, the lines of the curriculum were set—English grammar and composition, arithmetic, geography, natural history, morals, a verse of scripture daily, and extra reading such as Cook's voyages, Dibble's history of the Sandwich Islands, Sparks' life of Washington, the history of the Reformation, memoirs of the French Revolution, and lives of distin-

guished European princes and princesses.[108] Mrs. Cooke was a keen
and talented musician, and although she thought of music as a peripheral matter, not central to the kind of education the young chiefs should
have, still she endorsed it as a rational form of enjoyment to keep them
from idleness. One casual by-product of the school was thus a line of
royal musicians and composers. Kalākaua and Lili'uokalani, especially,
wrote in later years many very engaging Hawaiian songs.

In common with Punahou's teachers, the Cookes believed in
strenuous exercise for their charges. They built playgrounds at the school,
and Cooke often took the boys riding, hiking, and swimming. Together
they made trips to other islands, climbed mountains and observed the
volcanoes of Hawai'i.[109]

Part of the children's preparation for later rule was to visit and
be visited by naval commanders and other distinguished foreigners. The
impression left by the young chiefs was very good. By the mid-forties,
they could put on a fine show in the classroom, speaking fluently in unac-
cented English, doing mental multiplication of decimals at high speed,
playing musical instruments, and singing harmoniously.[110]

Cooke, however, found even the company of the most respectable
foreigners and visitors less than completely salutary for his pupils. The
problem was complicated—how to prepare the children for the world
and yet at the same time keep them from the world? Matters did not
become any simpler as the young chiefs approached precocious maturity. Cooke had encouraged them to sign pledges which committed them
to forgo licentious conduct and conversation, to abstain from impious
thoughts, and to promote moral purity. In addition, they had all signed
the temperance pledge in 1842. By the middle of the decade, however,
Moses, the oldest pupil, was quite restless under these restrictions.[111]

Moses, at age sixteen, had become in fact an anti-establishment
conspirator, organizing clandestine visits to the rooms of the female
students, and leading midnight excursions over the fence to the town,
where he and his younger brothers talked and drank with disreputable
companions, among them Binns the Barber, a negro, and the musician
St. John. By 1845, Moses was in total revolt, and Cooke was appalled to
stumble upon a fantastic scheme concocted by the young prince, who
hoped to disappear from the islands with the aid of Binns and others. An
assistant teacher brought Cooke a letter filled with bitterness, from "John
David Hammond, Commander in Chief of the Hawaiian Army" (Moses)
to "Governor B.F. Snibbs" (Binns), written at the "Hotel de Invalido"
(Chiefs' Children's School).

> My dear friends make haste & tell me what is the best
> way for us to clear out as fast as we can. I cannot stay

in the land of my birth...For they shamefully treated
us... It was the love of liberty that enticed us to leave
our native shores... Can you make a bargain with the
captain of the Brig *Euphemia* to take us down to Tahiki
[sic]... If we would leave these Island, then I shall bid
farewell to my native land. And see no more the face of
my parents
And leave my lovely Alrica [unidentified]
Far, Far behind me, and may that Crook [Cooke] would
search for us
But in vain. In vain he looked for us.

Prolonged interrogations and several applications of rawhide
forced the details of the plan from Moses and his brothers. The more
Cooke heard, the more he was convinced that the young chiefs were
corrupt, "like a wild ass's colt...degenerate plants of a strange vine...
deceitful above all things and desperately wicked." The matter was
taken to the Privy Council. King Kauikeaouli agreed that the boys' privileges should be curtailed. They were to be given spending money only
by Cooke, and their servants were not to see them for three months.

The prohibitions did not work well. Moses still managed to have
brandy and cigars brought to his room. When the visiting Danish naval
commander Steen Bille of the *Galathea* came to the school and distributed
medals for academic achievement, Moses stood up with the rest to sing
the rousing temperance song, "Nothing is so good for the youthful blood
as pure and sparkling water;" but when Steen Bille asked him privately
if he would not rather sing "sparkling champagne," Moses agreed, and
entreated the captain "for God's sake not to betray him."[112]

In talking with Moses about morality, Cooke found it increasingly
necessary to emphasize the seventh commandment. Soon it became clear
that Moses had not taken to heart his teacher's exhortations. In December,
1846, the young prince was discovered jumping from his window late
at night, on his way to visit Kalama, wife of King Kauikeaouli. Under
questioning, he admitted that he intended to sleep with the queen, but
exculpated her entirely. During the next two weeks, he was reported as
"breaking down lath and plaster" to get to the queen's house, and in a
perfect piece of Freudian acting-out he shot some arrows into her enclosed
yard. Kauikeaouli was quickly convinced of his wife's guilt.

At the same time, another discovery was made at the school—
the fifteen-year-old pupil Abigail Mahena was pregnant, and Moses was
the father of the child. Abigail was sent off to Kaua'i to be married to an
unsuccessful scholar from the Lahainaluna Seminary on Maui, Keaupuni
by name.

Moses made a long confession of his delinquencies to Minister of Public Instruction William Richards, a former missionary, and then repeated it before the king. The case went to the Privy Council. Richards testified that Moses was constantly falling into vice, disobeying his teachers, and leading other pupils astray. It was resolved that he should be dismissed from the school. The government stripped him of his real and personal property, and placed him under the special care of John ʻĪʻī. Dispossessed though he was, Moses continued to spend extravagantly, even after his father, Kekūanaōʻa, warned the people of Honolulu not to trust his son, whose debts Kekūanāoʻa would not pay.[113]

Faced with the need to counteract the disastrous examples of Moses and Abigail, the Cookes were more than ready to acquiesce in the marriage of Abigail's half-sister Jane Loeau, at eighteen a senior pupil in the school. Jane—part-white, pretty, a fine pianist, able to cut and sew her own dresses but not particularly fond of housework—was being courted by John H. Jasper, a Baltimore-born lawyer who had settled in the islands two years before. Jasper had established a reputation for "temperance and morality," and this far outweighed the sad physical fact of a disfigured nose, the result of wounds sustained in the Florida wars. His prospects were good—he was the government's registrar of conveyances at $2,000 a year. He was generally liked; he had written proper letters to Cooke asking permission to pay his attentions to Jane; his southern origins allowed him to think of monarchy and a hierarchical society as congenial; and he and Jane seemed very fond of each other. The Privy Council gave formal approval to the match, although one or two chiefs expressed doubts about the practice of marrying well-born Hawaiian girls to foreigners. Early in September, 1847, the wedding was performed at the school with great ceremony, before an audience including the king, the queen, the cabinet, the diplomatic corps, visiting naval commanders, and members of the Protestant mission. Jane played the piano at the reception, the guests enjoyed their cake and lemonade, and the Jaspers retired to take up residence in a well-furnished house not far from the school. It seemed to Mrs. Cooke a "heaven-made match."[114]

Even so, the Cookes were not sure that they could carry on much longer at the school. The depravity of the students seemed overwhelming. At times they appeared more like "hardened New England sinners" than like properly Christian children. It was becoming difficult to keep Moses' brothers, Lot and Alexander, from taking the path to ruin. They too indulged in midnight excursions, going to parties in the foreign community or to a dancing school downtown, where they loitered disguised but not incognito. And neither they nor any other pupil, young or old, had been converted. The question plagued Cooke, as it had ever since Moses began to slide in 1844—should he and his wife sacrifice their lives and the eternal good of their own children for those who had no heart to improve by it?[115]

Cooke was able quite soon to make a forceful appeal to Lot and Alexander. Late in 1848, a measles epidemic swept the islands and killed many Hawaiians in Honolulu and elsewhere. Among the dead was Moses, who had departed from life aged nineteen, debauched, in debt, and a disgrace (as Mrs. Cooke wrote) to his parents, the school, and the nation. Cooke used Moses' death as a text from which to lecture the two surviving princely brothers. He felt, so he said, great fears for Moses' soul. If Lot and Alexander grew up as Moses had, then the Cookes would leave the school and return to the United States. Cooke predicted that unless the brothers prepared themselves properly for public service, the monarchy would not outlive King Kauikeaouli. Without the aid of the Almighty, Cooke concluded, Alexander and Lot could not stand against the temptations that would confront them.[116]

Early in the new year, at the urging of Cooke, Gerrit Judd, and others, the Privy Council withdrew Lot and Alexander from the school. The princes went to live in Nu'uanu valley. Each was set to work at $300 a year—Lot with Chief Justice of the Supreme Court William Lee, and Alexander with the government's legal adviser, Asher Bates, brother-in-law of Gerrit Judd.[117]

By this time, the Cookes themselves had fairly made up their minds to quit the school. There remained, however, the problem of Bernice Pauahi, eighteen-year-old daughter of Pākī and Konia and last descendant of Kamehameha I. Some of the chiefs expected that either Lot or Alexander would marry her. Bernice had listened to her parents' importunities on the subject, and had opposed the idea firmly—if her parents wished to bury her in a coffin, she said, she would as soon have them do that as marry Lot. Much more interesting to her was the New Yorker Charles Reed Bishop, an official in the Hawaiian civil service. Their courtship—long conversations, moonlight walks, and seraphin serenades by Bernice—was approved by the Cookes, but for some time Bernice's parents were strongly against the match. Other opinion, however, favored the marriage, and the ceremony was held in mid-1850, despite the refusal of Konia and Pākī to attend.[118]

With this successful finale rounding out a decade of work, the Cookes felt free to retire from the school. Cooke joined his colleague Samuel N. Castle at the Honolulu missionary depository for a time before the two went into business as Castle & Cooke, a firm which quickly became a leader in the town's mercantile community.[119]

What had the Chiefs' Children's School accomplished? Every Hawaiian monarch from Kamehameha IV was at least competent in English, and this was important in their expanded world. Alexander

Liholiho and his wife Emma were sufficiently cultivated to charm the British visitor Lady Jane Franklin and other sophisticates. William Lunalilo became a renowned dinner-table wit, scoring at will off American, British, and French diplomats, and foreign-born cabinet ministers less facile than he. The fourth and fifth Kamehamehas, Alexander and Lot, were kings as vigorous as any in Hawai'i's history, with the exception of Kamehameha I. Familiarity with English and a sense of royal responsibility were certainly to be expected from pupils of the Chiefs' Children's School. So was a social conscience. This was perhaps best exemplified in the efforts of Alexander and Queen Emma to halt the ravages of depopulation among their people by establishing Queen's Hospital in Honolulu. Bernice Pauahi Bishop's great estate, inherited from the Kamehamehas, was bequeathed to the Hawaiian people at large for educational purposes. To carry out the terms of her will, the famous Kamehameha Schools were founded in Honolulu late in the nineteenth century.

All this night have been satisfactory enough to the Cookes and the rest of the Protestant mission. Yet Cooke, withdrawing from his work at the school in 1850 (before all the social returns were in), could find very little to praise in his products. The school, he said, had perhaps served a useful negative function. It had kept the viciousness of the aristocratic youths in check until the nation reached a point at which their influence was less deleterious than it would have been earlier. Any one of the students, at large in society, would have cost the nation more than did the entire school. This was a rather bitter verdict to hand down,[120] but time showed that there were elements of truth contained in it. Moses and Abigail, of course, led the list of delinquents. Alexander, brought up by the Cookes and bearing the marks of their sternness in his mind and across his back, reacted more subtly but equally sharply against American Protestantism the moment he was free. He grew up to be a very gay blade about town, often seen in the taverns and billiard rooms. On becoming king, one of his first acts was to subscribe to the *Times* of London. His marriage to Emma Rooke was celebrated according to the rites of the Church of England, and he was responsible for making Episcopalianism a state religion in everything but name. His successor, Lot, a taciturn, uncompromising man, abandoned the liberal constitution of 1852 in favor of a much stronger monarchy. Concurrently, he showed signs of approving and even leading a people's return to the hula, medical kahuna-ism, and other practices dating from before the arrival of the missionaries. The brilliant Lunalilo was a drunkard and a wastrel; he was in the care of financial trustees and doctors all his short adult life. At one time it was suggested that he should marry the Princess Victoria Kamāmalu, heiress of Ka'ahumanu and a contemporary of Lunalilo at the Chiefs' Children's School. She too was fond of wine, and Lunalilo said such a marriage would never work—if he happened to be sober she would be intoxicated, and their happiness could not be complete.[121] As for Kalākaua—a king extravagant in the use of royal prerogatives sexual, financial, and political, totally improvident, alternately a client and a racial enemy of America—his reign was the very negation of mission teaching.

Beyond all this, the great tragedy of the school was most evident in the lives of some of the girls. The boys had been able, however unlawfully, to go out and find the world; the girls had sedulously been kept from it. Within a few years of the Cookes' departure the seclusionist policy was in serious question. The Princess Victoria was seduced in the royal palace by Marcus Monsarrat, a Honolulu auctioneer, leading the urbane Hawaiian foreign minister Robert Crichton Wyllie to remark that if Victoria's education had been more elegant her taste at least would have been better.[122]

Most distressing of all was the story of the half-sisters Abigail and Jane, the one whose marriage had been a disgrace, the other whose marriage had been an example. Abigail lived on Kaua'i for a time with her dragooned husband. She bore Moses' child, then drifted back to Honolulu where, without the formality of a divorce, she became the mistress in turn of both partners of the business house of Porter & Ogden. Porter returned from a voyage to the Australian colonies to find himself supplanted by Ogden. They fought, blackening each others' eyes, without resolving the issue of the possession of Abigail. Finally Porter asked her to marry him. She refused; he took a pistol and shot at her, wounding her in the head, then shot and killed himself. Abigail recovered, and bore his posthumous child six weeks later.[123]

As for Jane, her "heaven-made match" with John Jasper failed for conspicuously earthly reasons. Jasper, a stereotypic ante-bellum, southerner in all ways (save that he had married a woman of color), began to drink heavily. By 1849, he was unable to carry on his work as government registrar. Jane strayed and contracted a venereal disease. Jasper died of it; Jane survived to become a glittering prostitute in Honolulu's floating world, "steeped in vice, but sprightly intelligent, and able to converse not only with propriety but elegance," according to United States Commissioner David Gregg, who met her in 1854. The world had taken Jane entirely, and yet the vestiges of her missionary education at the Chiefs' Children's School enabled her to maintain herself with a tarnished grace.[124]

The O'ahu Charity School, brought into existence to serve the young half-caste population of Honolulu, attempted a special solution to some perplexing educational problems. Was language a vehicle of culture? Would natives and half-castes be best suited by acquiring a western education in their own language? Or might English provide a better means for their acculturation? In the larger view, should boys and girls of mixed blood be expected or encouraged to become "white" in anything more than name?

Some foreign residents, parents of half-caste children, agreed from the beginning with the Protestant missionaries that Honolulu was an unsavory place in which to raise young people. Several men, among them Stephen Reynolds, sent their children home to the United States. Others, unwilling to go to such expense, depended at first upon Mrs. Bingham's makeshift school. Toward the end of the eighteen-twenties, the mission turned away from the education of half-castes, choosing instead to concentrate its efforts upon the undifferentiated native population. The residents then banded together to form the O'ahu Charity School.[125]

Actually, the school had its origins in a minor hiving-off from the mission. A missionary helper named Andrew Johnstone, assigned to the depository, showed an interest in work among sailors and foreigners. For a short time, Johnstone taught a small school in the town. When, in 1832, the foreigners appointed a committee to establish a permanent school, they invited Johnstone and his wife to take charge. This raised the problem of the Johnstones' connection with the Sandwich Island Mission. The foreigners' new enterprise, no matter how worthy, was outside the proper mandate of the mission. Should the Johnstones accept the salary offered by the foreigners, the mission tie would be broken. The issue was settled unhandily, as were so many matters which divided the members of the mission. For two years, the Johnstones taught at the Charity School with the official approbation of the Sandwich Island Mission. Then the ABCFM ruled against a continuance. Thereupon, the Johnstones withdrew angrily from the mission.[126]

There was a larger question involved, as far as the mission was concerned. The trustees of the OCS were selected for the most part from the Honolulu business community, and among them were several inveterate mission-baiters. Should the mission support such an institution, even tacitly? It seemed for a time as if the School might bring the town's factions together somewhat. The formative months and the inaugural ceremony passed with good will on both sides. The trustees, however, determined upon a strong secular policy for the school, stipulating that religious literature other than the Bible should be barred, and that the Bible should merely be read and not taught in a sectarian way. Nor did they give the question of Sabbath observance the attention Hiram Bingham thought it deserved. Within six months of the opening,

Bingham was prohibited from entering the building to preach or to conduct a singing school the residents had started there. Specifically, this was because he had published a letter in an American journal saying that a large percentage of foreigners at Honolulu were drunkards, not troubling to distinguish between sailors and merchants. In general, it was an extension of the merchants' battle with him. It is worth noting that other missionaries were permitted to enter the school. Reuben Tinker preached there from time to time, and Gerrit Judd led evening singing classes for adults.[127]

Some missionaries doubted that the OCS would prove useful. Gerrit Judd, for one, could envision no agent of social improvement in the islands except the mission. Judd acknowledged that educated half-caste boys might become clerks for traders. In his opinion, however, the very fact that they were taught in English would wean them away from helpful work such as teaching. As for the girls, they would, "if we may judge from past experience, become mistresses for 'Gentlemen.'" Bingham held similar views, thinking that a smattering of English might prove harmful rather than beneficial to children of native mothers "exposed to the influence of the profane man, & opposers of the truth." He himself, and most of his brethren too, preferred to make knowledge accessible to natives through the Hawaiian language. But, more liberal than Judd on one point, Bingham allowed parents the undisputed right to choose the language in which their children were to learn.[128]

The OCS trustees regarded these attitudes as cold water thrown upon their efforts. Work went on in a chilly atmosphere. The anti-missionary *Sandwich Island Gazette* remarked upon the mission's failure to assist the school. Judd, on his side, believed he could notice "an unusual clamor against the mission...whenever there was a subscription to be filled for the school." This was not altogether surprising. Many of the men elected trustees in the thirties were parents of half-caste children born out of holy wedlock—John Coffin Jones, Richard Charlton, Alex Adams, Eliab Grimes, Stephen Reynolds, among others—and this was just one moral score on which they proved unsatisfactory to the mission. Although some attended Christian services at the Bethel of the Seamen's Friend Society, others were churchless. The trustees and patrons of the OCS between them crossed some national and occupational lines (their grouping was in this way a rarity in Honolulu), but the moral gulf separating them from the mission remained unbridged, even in the cause of education.[129]

In its first decade, the OCS attracted pupils from places as distant as Kamchatka and California (Thomas O. Larkin, United States Consul in California, enrolled his son). The coral-stone, cupola-topped building accommodated between fifty and eighty pupils in the late thirties and early forties. In 1844, the Johnstones engaged in a brisk quarrel with the trustees, and withdrew to begin a private school. The OCS fell into a decline.[130]

Partly responsible for the waning interest of the town's businessmen was a broad social trend. At the time the school was established, half-castes and sea-orphans were subjected to evil influences in the town. Haole fathers, among them some of the leaders of the foreign community, could readily see and answer to the need for reclamation of their children. Since then, however, many of the old residents had left the scene. Some were dead, some had returned to their home countries. The foreign population at large had grown greatly. Newly-arrived businessmen were able to employ haole assistants, and were thus insulated to some extent from native and half-caste life. Among the wealthy of Honolulu, then, a direct interest in the OCS existed no longer. Those of philanthropic bent found an outlet for their charity among distressed foreigners.[131]

With this, the education of half-castes at Honolulu relapsed into an unsound condition. At the opening of the eighteen-fifties, the OCS was reorganized. Minister of Public Instruction Richard Armstrong recommended in 1851 that a special tax be imposed on the white population of Honolulu, to provide instruction for the "interesting and increasing numbers of white and half-caste children...neither white nor half-caste children any where attend the public schools taught by natives." A public meeting of residents approved the idea. As legislation took shape, it called for a supporting tax, to be disbursed by a controlling body of elected committee members chosen by those liable to the tax. The law survived an attack on its constitutionality (the argument was that the white population was being taxed twice for education— once for the public schools, and once again because they were white). The first committee consisted of Stephen Reynolds, Robert G. Davis (half-caste son of Hannah Holmes and William Heath Davis), Samuel Chenery Damon (Seamen's Chaplain), Supreme Court Justice William Lee, together with Minister of Public Instruction Armstrong, ex officio. Under the new name of the Honolulu Town School or Free School, and with a new teacher, G.B.C. Ingraham of Maine, the school flourished again, at least until Ingraham's death in 1865. At that point a decision was made to segregate the sexes. The immediate successor of the OCS took the name of Mililani Girls' School.[132]

Of all those connected with the O'ahu Charity School, the most active in its affairs was Stephen Reynolds. He had become, in late middle age, a considerably crabbed eccentric, his business faltering in the face of competition, his sour hatred of the Protestant mission burgeoning into irrationality, his autumnal marriage to the young half-caste Susan Jackson disintegrating as she fled domesticity for the wayward delights of Hawaiian society. Nonetheless, for more than fifteen years Reynolds was a school trustee or committee-man, unfailingly generous with time and money, devoted to the welfare of the OCS. Further than that, Reynolds concerned himself deeply with the upbringing of half-caste girls, in the hope that he might save them from becoming "mere kanakas." For more than a decade, while his own children were at school in the United States, Reynolds took into his home several girls of the town, who learned the ways of polite western society under his tutelage.[133]

One of the most interesting institutions of Honolulu at mid-century was Reynolds' dancing school. In April, 1841, Reynolds took a few girls from the Charity School to the house of Hannah Holmes for dancing lessons. For twenty years, Hannah had been the archetypal half-caste beauty of the town, pursued, fought over, and won by numerous white men. There was very little she would be unable to teach Reynolds' girls. The dancing lessons continued sporadically for a year at Hannah's, and then at Reynolds' house for more than a decade. Quite soon the evening classes began to attract the haole bachelors of the town, several of whom later married girls from the school. Foreigners already married to native women paid visits as well. By August, 1842, the school had the approval of Kekūanaō'a and other chiefs. Sea-captains and officers— but not common sailors—were admitted by invitation. In return, they frequently invited the girls to ride out into the countryside and picnic with them during their stays in town.[134]

British Consul-General Miller announced that he would willingly entertain at his house any girls from the OCS or the dancing school. Two other members of the consular group—Jules Dudoit and United States Commissioner Anthony Ten Eyck—occasionally made a more than formal friendly gesture toward the enterprise. Even United States Consular Agent Peter Brinsmade, a New Englander with some theological training, was impressed by the social grace of Reynolds' girls, and did not hesitate to dance with them.[135]

Recognition of this kind marked something of a high point in the acceptance of Reynolds' girls among people "of the better sort." Their opportunities were enlarged when, in 1846, Reynolds became Hawaiian consul for the German cities of Hamburg and Bremen. Thereafter, he made a habit of taking his girls to official functions, including receptions at the royal palace. The experience was unhappy. Although Reynolds had supplemented the girls' dancing lessons with careful instructions about dress, table manners, and polite talk, they were, for the most part, frozen out of conversational cliques and cotillion sets. As often as not, they finished an evening dancing with each other, sometimes in a separate room. One or two important men made sporadic attempts to cross these strongly-drawn lines, but white ladies almost never did. Instead, they warned new arrivals in town that association with half-whites meant automatic disqualification from proper society. They refused to accept invitations to gatherings where half-whites might be present. Once some ladies, having arrived at a party, walked home immediately in the rain rather than stay in a house where a half-white woman was already ensconced as a guest. Occasionally, a part-white girl gained entree to the home of an exclusivist lady (for example, on the arm of a business associate of the host). In such a case, the lady of the house might neglect to take the shawl of the unwelcome visitor, or to talk with her, or to form a cotillion set with her, preferring instead to overload other groups. For the half-caste wife of a successful haole businessman there might exist a kind of tolerance. For an unattached half-caste girl there was none. Throughout the forties, the victory of the white wives was all but complete. Not until the later fifties, when an elegant half-white (Emma Rooke) shared the Hawaiian throne, did social patterns re-form.[136]

In the meantime, Reynolds did the best he could for his girls. It was not always easy. He saw dangers everywhere, and agonized over their growing-up. His catalogue of proscribed activities was almost as long as that of some of the mission ladies (although it differed in content—for example, he forbade his girls to attend Kawaiaha'o Church or go to Sunday school). The girls could not go to parties or dances without Reynolds' permission. Any young man wishing to pay his attentions to a dancing school girl needed Reynolds' approval. These precautions he held to be necessary, because in the slanderous town of Honolulu there were always people ready to post anonymous placards in the streets traducing the girls' characters, or to remark that any one of them could be had for a dollar, and so on. Loiterers often lounged about the dancing school when it was in session—or, worse, about the girls' sleeping quarters when it was not; and Reynolds had to drive them away.[137]

Even those who proposed marriage were not always satisfactory to Reynolds—struggling printers, small businessmen, actors, carpenters—marginal men in their own group making alliances with marginal people on the Honolulu scene. There were not, in the end, a great number of happy results, even under Reynolds' careful supervision. His own married life with Susan Jackson had been disastrous. Susan had become an erratic drunkard and adultress, following the downward spiral so common among women of her age and time on O'ahu, and so deplored by Reynolds and the mission alike. Reynolds might not see Susan for months at a time. Then he would come upon her with her friend and partner in delinquency, Hannah Hooper, ex-wife of the educated Hawaiian Timothy Ha'alilio, drunkenly stripping off their dresses in a boat at the harbor and standing in their shifts before the gaze of sailors, or rioting about the town at night in the company of kanakas. So with some of his other girls—two had to be barred from a series of subscription balls in the town for bad morals, and one of these later married a white businessman who forged $50,000 worth of whaler's exchange bills and decamped for California. Several, so Reynolds heard, were responding to the seigniorial calls of King Kauikeaouli as Reynolds' own wife had done earlier. Reynolds' favorite, the young Harriet Blanchard, who was in his charge for seven years and whom he referred to as his adopted daughter, vacillated between his protective custody and that of a Hawaiian uncle who wanted to make her a prostitute. After almost falling victim to a young foreigner who taught for a time at the O'ahu Charity School, she married unsuitably. Her husband, the itinerant actor, J.S. Townsend, did little either for her or for the general respectability of interracial marriage.[138]

By mid-century, then, the city of Honolulu possessed a legal and territorial identity it had not enjoyed a generation earlier. Administration of municipal affairs, however, remained poor in the extreme. The whaling trade brought prosperity, and linked the port ever more closely with the outside world. Socially, the Honolulu scene was complex. The white population was growing rapidly; so was the town's native community. Time had taken the westernizing process from the hands of the missions, and had placed it in the rougher hands of the townspeople at large. None of the native social groups which emerged seemed to prefigure, with any certainty, the growth of a Hawaiian community that might sustain itself with dignity in the morally ambiguous setting of the port town.

CHAPTER 6

The National Capital

D uring the fifteen years that followed the punitive visit of Laplace in 1839, the world weighed heavily upon Honolulu. Long before the city was designated capital of the kingdom, it had become the center of national life—the place to which, as a matter of course, foreign powers assigned their senior diplomatic and consular representatives. Pre-eminence in political affairs entailed exposure to serious problems. While natives on the outer islands enjoyed a relatively untroubled existence in the eighteen-forties and fifties, Honolulu with its mixed population was racked by a succession of calamitous disturbances which pushed the monarchy to the verge of extinction. In this perilous circumstance, municipal considerations were subsumed in the larger issue of the nation's struggle for survival. For a decade and a half, the history of Honolulu and the destiny of Hawai'i were indistinguishable.

The locus of strife lay in the relationship of foreigners to the Hawaiian government. At Honolulu, the haole population increased from two hundred in the early thirties to almost a thousand at midcentury. The monarchy's best efforts proved inadequate to accommodate this giant cuckoo in the nest.

Seemingly, the eighteen-forties offered a fair chance that difficulties arising at Honolulu might be resolved peacefully. Constitutional innovations, religious toleration, and the land revolution—all these combined to remove old occasions of dispute and to create a society rather more open than that of the twenties and thirties. Nonetheless, factions arose in the forties whose feuds brought the city to a higher pitch of tension than ever before.

The new parties were based upon national divisions. Foreigners, to be sure, now tended to stay longer at Honolulu than their predecessors had done. Some even considered the city to be their permanent domicile, rather than a mere place of sojourn rich in exploitable resources. Among most haoles, however, there survived an irresistible impulse to refer problems to their home governments. Official representatives of foreign powers took the initiative in this respect, encouraging their nationals at Honolulu to turn trivial local happenings into diplomatic issues, and pressing to absurd lengths assertions of British superiority, windy French imperialism, or fanatic American insistence on inalienable rights. As often as not, personalities rather than substantive principles were at stake. Honolulu at mid-century, in one of its aspects, was little more than a stage upon which were acted out the public passions and private pains of expatriates.

Thus, the entire systems of foreign nations forced their way into the very streets of the city. Clashes of thought and practice led inevitably to trials at law. But whose law should prevail? At Honolulu, litigation involving foreigners was as inconclusive as it was recurrent. Consuls and commissioners roughly pushed aside local magistrates, and legal cases in endless procession—rapes, property disputes, business failures, sailor riots, newspaper wars—made their way remorselessly to the national, and then to the diplomatic, level.

Against this constant invasion of its sovereign powers, the defenses of the Hawaiian monarchy were feeble enough. Its treaty arrangements were generally unsatisfactory; more than once, Honolulu was threatened with violence by foreign warships. The establishment of western-style governmental departments, most of them headed by foreigners, marked the beginning of formal administration but not the end of procedural arguments. At the same time, a vain attempt was made to shield the person of the king in his palace at Honolulu from the unannounced incursions of foreign diplomats, through the adoption of the code of etiquette of the Congress of Vienna.

So signally did the government's strategies fail that the stability of the monarchy was endangered. As the scale of events grew larger, King Kauikeaouli shrank more and more from royal responsibility. His foreign cabinet ministers, burdened by affairs of state and simultaneously entangled in local transactions, could scarcely contain the whirl of crisis generated at Honolulu. Minister of Public Instruction William Richards almost literally worked himself to death. Foreign Minister Robert Crichton Wyllie, inundated by official documents, wrote and docketed and minuted his way into hallucinatory exhaustion. In the early eighteen-fifties, Finance Minister Gerrit Judd's personality began to unravel under the intolerable strain of office. His eventual political fall convulsed Honolulu for months.

The health of the nation was put in jeopardy in 1853, when smallpox struck at Honolulu. Even this catastrophe was turned to advantage by the city's foreigners. In the wake of the dreadful epidemic, cabals formed, urging either revolution and a filibuster republic, or annexation by the United States. By late 1854, the end of the monarchy seemed imminent. Only the death of King Kauikeaouli and the accession of the vigorous ruler Alexander Liholiho allowed Honolulu to emerge into the calm of a brief period of Victorian elegance.

The harbinger of trouble at Honolulu as the eighteen-forties opened was the contumacious British consul, Richard Charlton. The immediate matter at issue was land. Ever since 1826, Charlton had held possession of a sizeable plot of ground not far from the waterfront and a smaller plot in the rear of the village at a place called "Beretania" (a Hawaiian rendering of the word "Britain"). It was generally understood that Charlton did not occupy these lots as an individual but as the official representative of Great Britain.[1]

The legality of Charlton's tenure was never questioned. Nor was there any controversy about the boundary dividing Charlton's downtown lot from the lot next to it, a place named Pūlaholaho which covered more than an acre of beachfront land. Then, in the first months of 1840, Charlton presented to Governor Kekūanaō'a of O'ahu a document purporting to be a 299-year lease of Pūlaholaho, dated 1826, and signed by Boki as Governor of O'ahu and Kalanimoku as regent of the kingdom.[2] At the same time, Charlton laid claim to some land at Wailele in Mānoa valley. The government acknowledged without demur his title to Wailele, but asked for more time to consider his claim to Pūlaholaho. There were obvious complications. A 299-year lease dated 1826 was a uniquely formal instrument from a period in which most land matters had been handled verbally and boundaries had been defined by custom only. Then too, by 1840 the Hawaiian signatories were all dead. Furthermore, Pūlaholaho had been occupied since 1826 by people other than Charlton, Attendants of Ka'ahumanu, the original owner, lived there; chiefs beached and stored their canoes and boats; and foreign businessmen built stores, warehouses and living quarters. At times, as many as fifteen buildings stood on Pūlaholaho, Not once had Charlton protested or demanded rent payments. No living chief had ever heard of the Pūlaholaho lease. Neither had anyone in Honolulu, native or foreign, ever seen the document before Charlton, in April, 1840, produced it and asked peremptorily to be put in possession of the property for the remainder of the lease period.

The Hawaiian government developed two lines of thought. First, the lease itself might be a forgery. Second, even if it were granted that the signatures of Boki and Kalanimoku were genuine, the lease would still be invalid because neither chief was empowered to deed land. In 1826, Ka'ahumanu was sole regent, with the right to award titles and leaseholds. Kalanimoku and Boki were mere administrators.

By the end of June, 1840, Charlton had written several letters to the king urging his case.[3] On June 30, Kauikeaouli ruled that the lease was not good. Charlton added this enormous personal grievance to his always overflowing stock of consular complaints. He told Governor Kekūanaōʻa that if his land claims were not honored, the Hawaiian government would be in far worse trouble than at the time of the *Clementine* episode of 1837. Charlton went on, in the course of other business at the fort, to assert the superiority of British over Hawaiian law, to threaten a native officer with hanging and decapitation, and to brandish his horsewhip during discussions of foreigners' rights. In the meantime his cattle continued to trespass, and his dog bit a foreign lady, for which he was fined $5.[4]

Charlton's attention was distracted from the Pūlaholaho lease when, in March, 1841, the Hawaiian government ordered the natives of Honolulu to spend three days working on the roads, or to pay a commutation of twenty-five cents a day. Several British merchants affected to regard this as a dreadful infringement of their right to the labor of their native domestics. Accordingly, they memorialized Governor Kekūanaōʻa, who replied correctly that the king was well within his prerogatives in imposing a customary labor tax upon his subjects. The correspondence was printed in the Honolulu weekly newspaper, the *Polynesian*. As soon as the issue was published, Charlton went with the supercargo of an English ship to the home of the *Polynesian's* editor, James Jackson Jarves, and took a horsewhip to Jarves' shoulders. Jarves' friend, the young American merchant James Fowle Baldwin Marshall, who was on a social call, threw Charlton to the floor, bruising the consul's hip severely and breaking one of his fingers. Jarves meanwhile caned Charlton's accomplice briskly. Neighbors finally separated the combatants. Charlton left without his hat and whip, which were used in evidence against him when a charge was laid before Kekūanaōʻa. The consul and the supercargo paid fines of $6 each at the fort. Charlton threatened retribution. He wrote home to the British government, asking that a man-of-war be sent to Honolulu. Not surprisingly, the request was ignored.[5]

This episode did not endear Charlton any further to the Hawaiian government. No move was made during the next eighteen months to put him in possession of Pūlaholaho. His choler mounted. In September, 1842, without any announcement of intention beyond a single curt note to the king, Charlton left Honolulu, bound for England, avowedly to secure justice for British subjects in the islands and at the same time to prevent the rise of American influence. The personal insults he had suffered at the hands of the Hawaiian government, he said, would not go unredressed.[6]

Charlton's consulate was placed in the care of Alexander Simpson, a young relative of Sir George Simpson of the Hudson's Bay Company. Sir George had visited Honolulu earlier in 1842, and had become interested in Hawaiian independence. Alexander Simpson, however, was an ardent British imperialist. From the moment of his arrival at Honolulu, he had championed the cause of the town's "aggrieved" Britishers, and had begun to plot the annexation of the islands by Great Britain.

Simpson's views were common knowledge. The Hawaiian government refused to recognize him as consul. Simpson objected. Privately, he described the king and his native ministers as "cyphers," and Gerrit Judd as the author of his troubles—a man of bad character and strong anti-British prejudices. Despite his tenuous position, Simpson carried out minor consular functions, frequently drawing the attention of the Hawaiian government to problems of Britishers at Honolulu.[7]

Soon after his "appointment," Simpson found himself embroiled in the commercial difficulties of Charlton as well as the official business of the consulate. Charlton owed a considerable sum of money to the Valparaiso firm of Sewall Patrickson, whose directors commissioned George Pelly (the Hudson's Bay Company agent at Honolulu) to act for them in collecting the debt. A foreign jury tried the case in Charlton's absence, disregarding the protests of Mrs. Charlton, who had remained at Honolulu to supervise her husband's business affairs, and who now claimed that the courts of Honolulu were incompetent to hear such matters. Pelly obtained a judgment of almost ten thousand dollars against Charlton. Alexander Simpson, following the line of Mrs. Charlton's protest, called a meeting of Britishers. Resolutions were forwarded to the Hawaiian government, maintaining that the attachment of Charlton's property in favor of Sewall Patrickson was an insult, that the trial had no validity, and that Simpson enjoyed the confidence of the British community.

Simpson's attempts to halt the attachment were futile, but he took further steps that were to have profound consequences. He requested the commander of the British fleet in the Pacific to send a man-of-war to Honolulu as a matter of urgency, to exact full recompense for past injuries, and to stay as long as British interests were in need of protection. Admiral Richard Thomas received Simpson's correspondence at San Blas, Mexico. Thomas despatched the frigate *Carysfort,* commanded by Lord George Paulet, under instructions to guard British interests and to restore Charlton's attached property, forcefully if necessary, should the situation at Honolulu be as Simpson had described it.[8]

Just a week after Richard Charlton sailed from Honolulu, bound for London with his casebook of grievances, the British Foreign Office issued a long memorandum setting out its views respecting the Hawaiian islands. Britain was portrayed as seeking no more than parity of treatment in Hawai'i. Annexationist ambitions were disavowed. Naval officers in their encounters with native chiefs were ordered to act with forbearance and courtesy, avoiding harsh interference with the laws and customs of the country. Neither Charlton, nor Simpson, nor Admiral Thomas, nor Lord George Paulet knew of the existence of this statement of policy when, on February 10, 1843, the *Carysfort* anchored in Honolulu harbor.

Paulet was greeted by Alexander Simpson. William Hooper, acting consul of the United States, and Jules Dudoit, the French consular agent, were acknowledged in a "cool if not insulting manner," as were other residents. Gerrit Judd was told that no representatives of the Hawaiian government would be received until British grievances were redressed. King Kauikeaouli was at Lahaina, as usual. Until his arrival at Honolulu, Paulet could do nothing of importance. He contented himself with an inspection of the Protestant mission buildings, and with desultory visits to the homes of a few prominent merchants.

More than this would have been required to conciliate the Americans of Honolulu. American and French ships in the harbor had raised flags to welcome the *Carysfort*. After Paulet's stiff introduction, they lowered the flags, while sailors on board the English man-of-war shouted: "Now let those bloody Yankees look out—we have got a man of war here now—we will let the bloody Yankees know who we are now." Morale ashore improved when, on February 13, USS *Boston* docked at Honolulu. More than thirty foreigners, mostly Americans, took part in a cordial meeting with Commander John C. Long.

Like Paulet, Long could do nothing more than wait for King Kauikeaouli to appear.[9]

The Americans came out in force once more three days later, when the king arrived from Lahaina. Paulet did not greet him personally, but merely sent a short note requesting a private interview. The king refused to see Paulet, and suggested that the British commander should either submit a written document or see Gerrit Judd. Thereupon, Paulet sent the king a list of six British grievances, specific and general, adding an ultimatum that if these were not attended to by four o'clock the next afternoon, "immediate coercive steps" would be taken. Paulet was confident that one shot from the *Carysfort* would disperse any number of Hawaiian troops assembled to prevent a landing. Long was quite without instructions to cover a cannonade; he could do nothing but watch. He sent a note to Dudoit, promising him asylum should hostilities break out. Ashore, Consul Hooper offered help to the Americans, who had protested to Paulet that the threat of gunfire left them no time to provide for their own safety. On the morning of February 18, a brig was towed into the harbor to be used by British residents as a refuge during the attack. All over town, foreigners piled money, papers, clothes, and other property on carts and sent them down to the waterfront to be put on board. Early in the afternoon, news came that the king had capitulated. Salutes were fired at 2 p.m. to mark the agreement.[10]

The terms were those of Paulet's first memorandum. Simpson was to be recognized as consul, instantly and publicly. He was to be approached directly by the king, so that all British grievances against the Hawaiian government might be redressed. The attachment on Charlton's property, arising from his debt to Sewall Patrickson, was to be removed. In other disputed commercial cases, new and fair trials were to be held. In future, no Britisher was to be put in irons at the Honolulu fort except on a charge of felony, defined in British legal language. All arguments involving Britishers must be referred to juries approved by the British consul.

The king agreed to Paulet's demands with the greatest reluctance. Some residents advocated letting the *Carysfort* "fire and be damned;" others believed that submission under protest was the better course. Judd took the latter view. Together with the king's note of acquiescence to Paulet, Judd wrote a statement of protest and appeal addressed to Queen Victoria.

This was Alexander Simpson's finest hour. British honor had been vindicated by British naval strength. While sailors from the *Carysfort* brawled with natives along the waterfront, Simpson, capitalizing on the presence of Paulet, extorted more concessions from the government. Kauikeaouli was compelled to sign a clearance for Charlton's 299-year lease at Pūlaholaho. Legal decisions adverse to Britishers were listed for review, and claims were filed for indemnities amounting to more than $100,000.

Conferences took place from February 20 to February 23, with Simpson always at Paulet's shoulder. So severe were Lord George's demands that Kauikeaouli and his advisers became convinced Paulet was aiming at the annexation of the islands. Gloomily, the town's Americans arranged their annual observance of Washington's Birthday on February 22 (the committee was divided on the question of inviting British guests). On February 23, the king met privately with Dudoit, Hooper, Judd, and Commander Long, to discuss the possibility of ceding the islands jointly to France and the United States, thus avoiding a forced cession to Britain. Papers were readied, but on the morning of February 24 Judd changed his stand, and would not support the king's decision to sign. Kauikeaouli was desperate. He had made up his mind not to go on. The British were out to ruin him, he could see; he was ready to give up, so his advisers reported. Various abysmal alternatives were considered. The foreigners heard that Paulet once again was threatening gunfire. Judd appeared on the streets escorted by native guardsmen, but the day passed without serious incident. On February 25, Kauikeaouli relinquished the islands at last to Paulet, stipulating at the same time that the Hawaiian government would make every effort to regain its sovereignty.[11]

A town crier announced that cession ceremonies would be held at the Honolulu fort. By three o'clock, a large crowd had gathered. British marines and Hawaiian soldiers formed a hollow square within the walls of the fort. Paulet and his officers took up their places beside the king and the chiefs on the verandah of one of the fort houses. Kauikeaouli made a short speech in Hawaiian, and Judd translated it into English. "Hear ye! I make known to you that I am in perplexity by reason of difficulties into which I have been brought without cause; therefore, I have given away the life of our land, hear ye! But my rule over you, my people, and your privileges, will continue, for I have hope that the life of the land will be restored when my conduct is justified." The deed of cession was read, and at ten minutes past three the Hawaiian flag was hauled down and the British flag was raised, as the fort and Paulet's ship exchanged salutes. The *Carysfort's* band played "God Save The Queen," and then, with "refined cruelty," "Isle of Beauty, Fare Thee Well."[12]

Paulet described the basis of the new government. The king and his chiefs would continue to administer the affairs of the native population. For the affairs of foreigners, a commission would be created, consisting of the king or his deputy, Paulet, and two officers from the *Carysfort*. Hawai'i's laws and public finances would remain untouched, under the commission's supervision. All existing agreements made by the king and the kuhina nui would be honored. No grants of land would be awarded by the commission until the British government approved Paulet's actions.[13]

The reaction of the foreign community in general was one of outrage, especially among the Americans, who had never before been so considerate of Hawaiian independence. For the most part, utter disbelief was expressed when Paulet and Simpson claimed they had acted to forestall a French coup of the kind which had just taken place at the Marquesas Islands in the South Pacific. The natives of Honolulu were quiet enough, although one or two scuffles occurred in taverns downtown. At the Chiefs' Children's School, the young students removed the gold bands from their caps, saying that they were no longer ali'i. Throughout the term of the cession, they held the British in contempt. Prince Lot referred to Paulet's men as "lobster-backs," and the children staged indignation meetings, planning revenge against the usurpers.[14]

After some hesitation, Judd consented to serve as the Hawaiian representative on Paulet's commission. His first act, unknown to Paulet, was to send a protest to the British government. Lord George had admitted the right of the Hawaiians to do this, but had attempted to block the possibility in practice. Paulet's own account of the seizure was to be hand-carried by Alexander Simpson on the Hawaiian government schooner *Hooikaika*, confiscated in Honolulu harbor and renamed *Albert*. Judd was asked by the chiefs to select an envoy to deliver the government's version of events. At a dance aboard Commander Long's USS *Boston*, Judd talked in secret to the twenty-four-year-old American merchant J.P.B. Marshall, who agreed to undertake the mission.

Judd prepared Marshall's credentials and papers, working by night in the royal tomb on the palace grounds not far from his own house, and using as a desk the coffin of Ka'ahumanu. When the documents were ready, a native canoe brought the king from Maui to sign them. At a council held in darkness at Waikīkī, away from the *Carysfort*, Kauikeaouli penned his name and left again, while Paulet sat at dinner in Honolulu, The *Albert* sailed on March 11 with Simpson aboard, and also Marshall, who for public purposes was said to be travelling on business for Ladd & Co. Security had not been perfect—a handful of residents knew what was afoot—but Paulet suspected nothing.[15]

Even before the departure of the *Albert*, Paulet violated the terms of the cession by interfering with Hawaiian law as it affected Honolulu. On March 2, mobs of sailors and natives thronged the streets at night. Many Hawaiians, believing the town's old laws to be suspended, refused to obey native constables. Paulet went ashore with armed marines and subdued the unruly crowds, injuring several natives in the process. The same evening, an 8 p.m. curfew was instituted for both natives and seamen. Paulet affirmed that Hawaiian law still applied to Hawaiians; but this was the first and last time he went out of his way to make such a statement. Within a week, an order was published all over O'ahu repealing the laws against fornication. Constables need no longer arrest unmarried men and women for fornication, and women might now visit ships in the harbor without penalty. This policy was reiterated late in April, when Paulet discovered that women imprisoned in the fort were being let out at night to work off their fines either with the fort soldiers or with sailors from the *Carysfort*, and that some of the chiefs had been sharing in the revenues.

Not only in the matter of community morals did Paulet make changes. To pay the commission's clerical expenses, an impost of 1% was levied in addition to regular import duties, and the Sandwich Island Mission's exemption from duties was revoked. The liquor licensing system of Honolulu was liberalized, as were laws regarding auction sales. The tangled affairs of the foundering business partnership of Greenway & French were taken up, unhelpfully. Claims to land in Honolulu were registered by the commission on behalf of Englishmen and others. A new constabulary was recruited, whereupon the laws against "furious riding" fell into disuse and British sailors galloped at high speed all over town. A native regiment called the "Queen's Own" was organized (flouting the jurisdiction of Governor Kekūanāo'a at the fort), and Judd was ordered to use funds from the Hawaiian treasury to pay the wages of these turncoats.[16]

Paulet's commission did not supplant the Hawaiian national parliament, which held legislative sessions at Lahaina from April 4 to May 4. When Judd returned to Honolulu, he protested many of Paulet's innovations, particularly the new moral ordinances, whose patent looseness dismayed the missionary community. Paulet and his fellow commission-member, Lieutenant Frere of the *Carysfort*, refused to re-establish the old regulations. A complete rupture of civil relations between Paulet and Judd ensued. Paulet abused Judd, and Judd resigned from the commission on May 11.

The commission now lacked even formal acquiescence on the part of the Hawaiian government in framing ordinances. Paulet visited the king on Maui to try to make new arrangements. Kauikeaouli asked that Judd be reinstated, and that the laws revert to their previous state. Paulet refused, and so the commission was left to take sole responsibility for its own acts. Judd continued to hold office in the Hawaiian government. He used his post at the Treasury to harass Paulet. With the king's support, Judd declined to release funds to pay the Queen's Own regiment. Only when Lieutenant Frere appeared in full uniform with side arms did Judd hand over the money. Then Judd went even further: he withdrew from circulation all records and papers of the government, and conducted cabinet business alone at night in the royal tomb, leaving Paulet's commission fairly stranded.[17]

On May 24, with Judd ousted, new laws in force, and power unlimited, Paulet's government celebrated Queen Victoria's birthday with salutes from the decorated *Carysfort*, sky rockets, blue lights, and cannon-fire from the fort at the waterfront and the battery on Punchbowl. In the first week of July, with Judd's shadow government at work in the royal tomb and the commission's activities at a minimum, the Americans celebrated July 4. Three days later, an American man-of-war, the *Constellation*, arrived at Honolulu (replacing the *Boston*, which had sailed soon after the *Albert* in March, carrying documents directed to the United States government).

On July 11, the *Constellation's* commander, Captain Lawrence Kearny, protested publicly against acts of the commission which affected adversely the interests of Americans at Honolulu. Privately, forty of Kearny's men ashore on liberty prepared to haul down the British flag. They went to William Hooper at the American consulate, announcing that they lacked only a leader. Hooper, of course, dissuaded them, but then on July 11. Kearny himself indulged in flag-play. Kearny had a large Hawaiian flag made (Paulet had destroyed all he could find), following which he invited the chiefs to visit the *Constellation,* where he saluted them under their national colors. Paulet remonstrated with King Kauikeaouli, claiming that by taking salutes under a flag other than the British Kauikeaouli lost all right to consideration and protection.[18]

Meanwhile, news of the cession had reached Admiral Thomas of the British fleet at Valparaiso. Thomas had received on April 1, 1843, the policy statement of the British Foreign Office on Hawai'i. Paulet's actions were wildly outside the scope of these instructions. Thomas sailed at once for Honolulu aboard his flagship, the *Dublin,* and anchored there on July 26, to the salutes of Kearny's *Constellation* and another American warship, the recently-arrived *Hazard.* Paulet and Thomas conferred aboard the *Dublin.* Then Thomas sent a note to the king, asking for an audience. Within twenty-four hours, the news was abroad in the town that independence would be restored next day. Stephen Reynolds wrote that only a Hawaiian flag was lacking.[19]

The ceremony, in fact, was delayed while Thomas and King Kauikeaouli met to frame articles covering the future treatment of Britishers in the islands. Their agreement, subject to ratification by Thomas' home government, guaranteed British subjects parity with other foreigners.

On July 31, the whole town repaired to the eastern plains to watch the restoration ceremonies. The king appeared, escorted by his royal guard and cheered by the crowds. A Hawaiian flag was furled upon a staff, and, as the king drew closer, the colors were broken out as cannon were fired on the plains, at the fort, in the harbor, and on the summit of Punchbowl. British marines passed in review and then fought a mock battle, to the delight of the Hawaiians. About noon, the martial observances ended, and Kauikeaouli returned to his residence.

Later, he walked in procession with his chiefs to the stone church at Kawaiaha'o. In a short speech, he gave thanks that the life of the land had been restored, and exhorted his people to obey the laws. Gerrit Judd read in Hawaiian the declaration written by Admiral Thomas turning back sovereignty to the king. The Hawaiian motto is derived from the king's speech: "Ua mau ke ea o ka 'āina i ka pono" (the life of the land shall be preserved in righteousness). The site of the restoration ceremony was later designated Thomas Square.[20]

To mark the restoration, all prisoners in the fort were released. Labor taxes were remitted for ten days. The Queen's Own regiment was disbanded, and its members were pardoned for having sworn allegiance to a foreign ruler. All over town during the next ten days, there were official dinners, private dances—and drunken brawls. At a great temperance feast held in Nu'uanu valley on August 2, the newly-written Restoration Anthem was sung, to the tune of "God Save The Queen:"

> Hail! to our rightful king! We joyful honors bring,
> This day to thee!
> Long live your Majesty!
> Long reign this dynasty! And for posterity,
> The sceptre be.
> Hail! to the worthy name!
> Worthy his country's fame!
> Thomas, the brave!
> Long shall thy virtues be Shrined in our memory
> Who came to set us free
> Quick o'er the wave!...

Then the dignitaries, tightly-uniformed and bestrapped (and, in the case of the Admiral, corseted), lowered themselves to mats spread on the ground under a canopy of Hawaiian flags, and addressed themselves to great quantities of poi, hogs, fish, and turkeys, prepared for them by natives. Only Honolulu's Englishmen, supporters of Paulet, did not attend, preferring to nurse their humiliation in private.[21]

Life in Honolulu quickly returned to normal. The king departed once again for Lahaina; liquor laws reverted to their old form. Notices were posted in the town asking creditors of the officers of the *Carysfort* to submit their accounts. On August 23, the *Carysfort* hoisted sail. To everyone's disappointment, there was no wind. Two days later, with baffling breezes, she made her way out of the harbor. Admiral Thomas remained at Honolulu another six months, dispensing benevolence, and doing a great deal to salve the wounds inflicted by Paulet upon the life of the town and the kingdom. In September, news came that the British government had disavowed completely the seizure of the islands by Paulet. A few months later, the house formerly occupied by the commission caught fire and was burned to the ground. Thomas sailed early in March, 1844, carrying with him the good wishes of the entire community. Paulet came back to Honolulu aboard the *Carysfort* in August, 1844, in the course of a Pacific cruise. Salutes were exchanged between ship and shore, but Paulet's requests for a conciliatory audience with the king were refused, and in a fit of pique he ordered the *Carysfort's* gunners to fire random volleys of blanks in the middle of the night, waking the town and alarming the natives. A subtle revenge was inflicted upon Paulet, however. His final communication with the Hawaiian government, a letter written from Hilo, Hawai'i (his last port of call before leaving the islands for the northern Pacific), complained that a native laundryman had stolen some of his clothes.[22]

While these events were taking place at Honolulu, Richard Charlton was pursuing his official and private interests in England. Concurrently, William Richards was in Europe, commissioned by the Hawaiian government to gain from the great powers a recognition of the independence of the islands. During his sojourn at London, Richards also discussed the grievances of Charlton. After prolonged negotiations, it was agreed that the British government might make unilateral decisions on some matters. Several cases, including the commercial suit of Pelly vs. Charlton (over the Sewall Patrickson debts) were settled in favor of the Hawaiian government. In addition, rules were drafted for the regulation of the trial and imprisonment of Britishers in the islands.

One issue alone proved troublesome—Charlton's claim to land at Pūlaholaho, based upon the lease allegedly signed in 1826 by Boki and Kalanimoku. The original lease document had been left at Honolulu. It was thus impossible for either party in London to argue the genuineness of the signatures. Charlton, however, insisted that Kalanimoku was regent of the kingdom in 1826, and was therefore competent to sign the lease. The British government accepted this version of Hawaiian constitutional history. William Richards was informed that, provided the lease was shown to be genuine, Charlton must be put in possession of the disputed land. Under protest, Richards consented.

Richards then attempted to exact damages from Britain for injuries suffered by residents of Honolulu under the Paulet regime, whose activities had been disavowed by Britain following the restoration of Hawaiian sovereignty. The British ruled that the cession had been a voluntary act of King Kauikeaouli; hence, no indemnities could be justified.[23]

Even though the British government supported Charlton's claim to Pūlaholaho, it was recognized that whatever usefulness he had had as consul in the islands was at an end. General William Miller, a veteran of the Latin American Wars of Independence, was appointed British Consul-General to Hawai'i, succeeding Charlton. Miller's instructions directed him to see that Charlton was placed in possession of Pūlaholaho, with the stipulation that the lease of 1826 must be proved genuine.

Miller's interpretation of his powers became clear upon his arrival at Honolulu early in 1844. He confined his investigations to the single point of the authenticity of the signatures, and quickly decided that they were trustworthy. The Hawaiian government, for its part, amassed a great amount of evidence to the contrary. Doubt was cast upon the general literacy of Boki and Kalanimoku, and especially upon their ability to write. Dozens of witnesses were asked to think back twenty years in an effort to recall if Boki closed the dot over his "i" or left it open, or if Marin, who had witnessed the deed, used a figure-eight shape in making his flourishes. The conclusion, almost universally agreed in by King Kauikeaouli, the chiefs, Gerrit Judd, and responsible natives such as John 'Ī'i and the Lahainaluna scholar David Malo, was that the signatures were forged.

At the same time, the Hawaiian government pursued a second line of thought—that Boki and Kalanimoku were incompetent to sign the lease. This argument, developed in 1840 when Charlton first made his claim, was sustained thereafter in the face of British contentions that it was irrelevant. The evidence was strongly in favor of the Hawaiian government, but neither General Miller nor his superiors regarded it as sufficient to overturn Charlton's claim.

While the Hawaiians collected sworn testimony, Miller went ahead to have the lot at Pūlaholaho measured and readied for Charlton's occupancy. By 1844, the value of the land had risen to about $15,000. Miller, a narrow constructionist in terms of the genuineness of the lease, became a very broad constructionist when equipped with surveyor's poles and measuring tape. His original orders specified that Charlton should receive only those parts of the additional land at Pūlaholaho which had not been appropriated by other persons without protest or obstruction by Charlton. But as Miller defined the lot, it included 23 houses with 156 occupants, and the boundaries cut through a stone house belonging to the king and a residence of Stephen Reynolds.[24]

In the face of repeated attempts by the Hawaiian government to stay execution, Miller became peremptory. Upon receiving from London final confirmation of his orders, Miller prepared to give possession of Pūlaholaho to Charlton, who had returned to the islands with great expectations in May, 1844.[25]

Before this could happen, Charlton had to confront another adversary. In 1842, when George Pelly was dunning him for the debt owed to Sewall Patrickson, Charlton had refused to pay, and had added to his intransigence a public statement, repeated several times, that Pelly was a sodomite. As a result of this unfounded charge, Pelly was shunned in 1843 by his fellow-Englishmen, the officers of Paulet's *Carysfort* and Thomas' *Dublin*. When Charlton appeared once again at Honolulu in 1844, Pelly sued him for slander, rejecting an offer made by other Honolulu businessmen to settle the matter privately. The case was heard before Governor Kekūanāo'a and a foreign jury, with visiting ship-captains acting as talesmen. The slanderous charge of sodomy was clearly related to Pelly's demand for Sewall Patrickson's money. This was demonstrated without doubt. Although Charlton protested the composition of the jury, an award of $3,450 was made against him. Pelly paid his attorney $500, and gave the rest of the money to Mrs. Charlton.[26]

Charlton was now free to be put in "undisturbed" possession of Pūlaholaho. Undisturbed he remained, at least for a few months. Toward the close of 1845, he began to sell his Honolulu properties, realizing handsome prices. He left Honolulu for the last time early in 1846.[27]

This was not the end of difficulties over Pūlaholaho. The Hawaiian government continued its investigations. Correspondence and testimony were gathered and printed. Foreign Minister Wyllie discovered the journal of Don Francisco de Paula Marin, translated it from Spanish to English, and announced (without making the manuscript public) that it proved conclusively Ka'ahumanu's sole right to grant land in 1826. Consul-General Miller enlisted the aid of the British navy, and one commander made a minatory purchase of cannon-shot while at Honolulu. The Hawaiian Princess Victoria Kamāmalu, heiress of Ka'ahumanu, claimed for herself the entire waterfront, including Pūlaholaho, and the government was forced to pay off her father, Kekūanaō'a, in order to prevent a re-hearing of the entire sorry affair. Offshoots of litigation stemming from Charlton's disposition of lands and leases continued to pass through Honolulu's courts and up to the Hawaiian cabinet for the rest of the decade. The most irritating of these was a spectacularly trivial, bad-tempered, and prolonged argument between Minister of Finance Judd, Minister of Foreign Relations Wyllie, and Consul-General Miller, concerning the leasehold and rents of Charlton's former premises at Beretania, now occupied by Miller. The three dignitaries quibbled for months over the value of a few shade trees that Miller had chopped down. In 1851, Wyllie expressed a fervent wish that the grave might "close over Charlton and his mysteries forever, without any further question as to his motives or his doings." Charlton died in England at the end of 1852.[28]

Concurrently with Charlton's claim, another important legal case was making its way from the courts of Honolulu to the foreign offices of Hawai'i, Great Britain, and the United States. It concerned the finances of an ostensibly bankrupt mercantile firm at Honolulu. The principals were two; the money at stake was more than $100,000; the ramifications were great.

William French, a well-established American merchant who had been in the islands since the early eighteen-twenties, had formed a partnership at Honolulu in 1840 with an Englishman, Francis John Greenway.[29] Greenway was to manage French's business in Honolulu while French went to the outer islands to supervise his agricultural interests there. In April, 1842, Greenway declared himself unable to meet his financial obligations, called his creditors together, and appointed assignees to administer his property—Stephen Reynolds, Alexander Simpson, and Henry Skinner (a merchant, and a fanatic

British nationalist like Simpson). William French protested, rightly believing his firm not to be bankrupt. He too selected assignees to pay the partnership's debts—Stephen Reynolds and the American merchant William Ladd.

The assignees failed to reach agreement, either among themselves or with their opposite numbers. Stephen Reynolds, charging that Alexander Simpson lacked integrity, withdrew from Greenway's group, but continued to act as auctioneer in selling Greenway's assets. Reynolds also tried to obtain Greenway's books. Simpson and Henry Skinner would not relinquish them. They turned them over instead to British Consul Charlton for safekeeping, following this with a lengthy complaint to the British government about harassment by the Hawaiian authorities, whose aid Reynolds had enlisted. Late in 1842, Skinner and Simpson tried to repossess by force a building belonging to Greenway which had been sequestered by the government. The two assignees took with them fifty English seamen. Skinner broke open the door of the building and generally terrified the caretaker. Gerrit Judd remonstrated with him, but Simpson said it was no use making threats—he had only to raise his finger and the sailors would do his bidding.[30]

At the time of Paulet's seizure of the islands early in 1843, Alexander Simpson departed for England, leaving Greenway's papers with the commission government. When Hawaiian independence was restored, British Consul-General Miller took charge of the records. Early in 1844, it became clear that much of the alleged commercial disorder sprang from derangement on Greenway's part. He had been behaving peculiarly for some time; now he slipped into insanity. He had thrown a lighted lamp at William Ladd; he had threatened to set fire to a thatch house (the one occupied by the British Commission, which ultimately did burn down); he had jumped from an interisland schooner in mid-channel, and was saved only by great good luck.

Greenway's sanity was tested in May, 1844, before a jury of nine foreigners, including Stephen Reynolds, Gerrit Judd, Jules Dudoit, and Robert Crichton Wyllie. Witnesses all agreed that Greenway was flighty and disordered, often through inebriety; that he was given to vehement language and strange gesticulation; and that his conversation and correspondence were studded with inapposite quotations from Shakespeare. In his own testimony, Greenway described supernatural sights visible only to himself. The jury, after thirty minutes' retirement, pronounced him insane with lucid intervals, dated his insanity from May, 1842 (when he declared insolvency), and recommended some form of mild restraint or guardianship.[31]

By this time, the British government had ruled against protests in the Greenway case forwarded to them by Charlton and Alexander

Simpson. Thenceforth, the matter was handled by the Hawaiian government and the business community of Honolulu. William French took it upon himself to settle all debts. Greenway left Hawai'i for Australia, to live with relatives there (his brother was a Sydney convict who became a noted architect). With the aid of Attorney-General John Ricord, a rationalization of claims was achieved.[32]

More than $100,000 was involved, or several times the amount of Charlton's claim at Pūlaholaho. Legal complications were correspondingly severe, and dependent cases embroiled many merchants at Honolulu: Stephen Reynolds, Jules Dudoit, Henry Skinner, Starkey & Janion (an English firm), George Pelly, William Paty (later a business associate of Gerrit Judd), and Timothy Pitman.

All legal roads at Honolulu in the forties seemed to lead with a terrible fatedness to Richard Charlton. So, too, did the Greenway case. Charlton won a court decision against Greenway's claim to a part of the Pūlaholaho lot, which Charlton had deeded informally to Greenway years before, and which was repossessed for Charlton under the general Pūlaholaho decision. This verdict created great acrimony in the town, and was later modified by the law advisers of the British Crown (both Charlton and Greenway were British citizens).[33]

John Ricord's conscientious administration enabled the O'ahu Court of Chancery to rule in 1847 that William French was competent to manage his own affairs. By that time French, still burdened with debt and cumbered with a large family, was ill and losing his eyesight. He died in 1852, trying vainly until the last to restore his fortunes to the standing they had enjoyed before his partnership with Greenway united business success and mental failure.[34]

Neither the Pūlaholaho claim, with all its overtones of consular chicanery, nor the Greenway-French bankruptcy proceedings with their widespread repercussions in the business community, had the spectacular influence on local and national life of yet a third affair proceeding at the same time as the other two—the case of Ladd & Co. In this tangled matter, it was not alone the property of foreigners that was at stake, but the future of the entire Hawaiian population on the undeveloped lands of the archipelago. The cases of Charlton and Greenway & French, after all, involved nothing more than the application to Hawaiian situations of established foreign legal and diplomatic processes. The Ladd case raised much more profound questions.[35]

The three business partners were Peter Brinsmade, William Ladd, and William Hooper, all New Englanders under thirty years of age. They came to Honolulu in mid-1833 with good recommendations, although James Hunnewell of Boston had reservations about their probity. Brinsmade had spent some time as a theological student at

Andover and Yale before turning to business. His partners showed equal evidence of piety. They were welcomed by the missionaries, and this alone was sufficient to render them deeply suspect among the merchants of the town. Levi Chamberlain hoped that their presence would prove a blessing; Henry A. Peirce, who succeeded James Hunnewell in business without sharing his mission affiliation, wrote contemptuously of "pious traders," and extrapolated from the establishment of Ladd & Co. a Protestant scheme to dominate the islands' commerce.[36]

Brinsmade, Ladd, and Hooper moved from the beginning within the mission orbit. Despite harassment by profane Americans, their firm prospered. They secured large commissions from Princess Nāhi'ena'ena and from the Protestant mission itself, although Levi Chamberlain declined their offer to transact all mission business, finding their terms too steep. Good feeling survived longer acquaintanceship. Brinsmade was instrumental in establishing a foreign church in Honolulu. Support from the mission later helped him to obtain the United States Consular Agency at Honolulu after J.C. Jones was ousted. When Brinsmade was away from the islands, William Hooper served as his consular deputy.[37]

By the mid-thirties, Ladd & Co. were ready to extend their field of operations. They presented to the Hawaiian government a plan for a large leasehold on Kaua'i, where natives might raise sugar cane on shares, to the benefit of the nation's commerce and the encouragement of thrift and industry among the Hawaiians. The proposition was appealing. Among Americans concerned with the fate of the Hawaiian people, there was a persistent strain of thought in which the islands were viewed as virgin land, where a civilized and Christianized native race might transform itself into a sturdy yeomanry. The rise of the port towns of Honolulu and Lahaina, with their unholy fascination for young Hawaiians, was beginning to produce severe deracination among rural natives. This trend was clearly visible to visitors and to resident missionaries alike. The lengthy and impassioned memorial sent by the missionaries to the ABCFM in 1836 stemmed in part from an urgent belief that the process must be reversed if demoralization and depopulation were to be forestalled. With the backing of the influential missionary William Richards, Ladd & Co.'s project was approved, and a profit-sharing scheme in the cultivation and refining of sugar was inaugurated at Kōloa, Kaua'i, in 1835.[38]

Encouraging results after two years of operations at Kōloa led Hooper and his partners to set before the mission a much more ambitious plan. Ladd & Co. would lease an entire district. A chief would exercise authority there on behalf of the government. The company would invest $10,000 in a sugar community, and would also support Protestant teachers, physicians, and evangelists. The missionaries, doubtful that such an arrangement would work, offered to forward the details to the government, though without strong endorsement.[39]

Nothing came of this, but during the next two years the minds of Brinsmade, Ladd, and Hooper were active on an even more grandiose scale. Their connection with the mission, and the mission's connection with the government, brought into glittering existence in 1841 the largest of the many mercantile bubbles in Honolulu's history.

Ladd & Co. had always suffered from a lack of working capital. Because of this, they had been forced to pay high interest rates on short-term loans. About 1840, they determined to find a buyer for their properties in Honolulu and their leaseholds on Kaua'i. They may well have been seriously embarrassed. In 1837, Brinsmade had estimated his investment in Kōloa plantation to be $30,000, but he had said then that his money was on the point of bringing him 50% a year, and that he would hold on. Now, however, he became the prime mover in the search for a purchaser.[40]

Once again, William Richards was of great assistance. By now he was the principal counsellor of the king. With his help, a secret contract was negotiated in November, 1841, giving Ladd & Co. the right to begin agricultural operations on all unoccupied and unimproved land in the islands. Sugar mill sites were to be selected within one year, operations to begin within five. The agreement was to run for a century. A joint stock company was to be formed. The king was to have unlimited subscription rights and the remainder was to be thrown open to capitalists of any nationality.[41]

At the end of 1841, of course, the independence of the Hawaiian nation was in jeopardy. Unequal treaties with foreign powers impaired the sovereignty of the king; Laplace was only two years gone and more trouble loomed with the French; Charlton was amassing grievances.

Accordingly, Ladd & Co. added a stipulation in the secret contract —that unless Hawaiian independence were guaranteed, the terms should be null and void. The Hawaiian government thereupon requested Peter Brinsmade to go overseas as an informal agent, promoting independence at the same time as he disposed of the exclusive rights of Ladd & Co. under the terms of the November contract.

Brinsmade was not able to interest American capitalists in his developmental plan. Nor could he raise any money in England or France. There was, he heard, a possibility that surplus capital might be available in Belgium for speculation, and indeed his opening talks with the Belgian Company of Colonization proved fruitful. Brinsmade's account of prospects in Hawai'i earned him access to important people, including the King of Belgium.

With this much gained, Brinsmade was delighted to hear of the formal Hawaiian independence mission of William Richards, in Europe to negotiate equal treaties for Hawai'i and to obtain solid assurances from major powers on the subject of Hawaiian independence. Brinsmade had made representations for independence; now the independence mission could be set to work for Ladd & Co. Once more, William Richards was Brinsmade's instrument. Richards carried a power of attorney from the Hawaiian king; Brinsmade had the power of persuasiveness. Seduced by the promise of a directorship in the great colonization company to be formed, Richards signed on behalf of King Kauikeaouli the "Belgian Contract" of May 17, 1843, under whose terms Ladd & Co. transferred their Hawaiian lands and privileges to the Belgian Company of Colonization, which in turn agreed to set up a subsidiary called the Royal Community of the Sandwich Islands, with a capital of several hundred thousand dollars. For this transfer Ladd & Co. were to be paid $200,000. They were also to receive cash in lieu of part of their stock holding. The Royal Community was to begin agriculture, manufacturing, and commerce in Hawai'i as soon as possible after Hawaiian independence was secured.[42]

At this point in negotiations, news of the Paulet episode in Hawai'i reached Europe, and the entire question of Hawaiian independence was taken up once again, not to be settled until late in January, 1844. With this difficulty overcome, Brinsmade was able to go ahead in Brussels. On April 13, 1844, the "Statutes of the Royal Community of the Sandwich Islands" were made ready for signature by Richards, his fellow-envoy Timothy Ha'alilio, Brinsmade, and the directors of the parent group, the Belgian Company of Colonization.[43]

At Honolulu, meanwhile, the affairs of Ladd & Co. had not prospered. Kōloa plantation had not lived up to expectations; neither had the firm's Honolulu store. Paulet's commission government had disrupted business in the islands, particularly for Americans, just as it was to hold up negotiations for independence in Europe and delay the establishment of the Royal Community for almost a year. Ladd & Co. came very badly to need the $200,000 transfer fee and the cash in lieu of stock promised them under the Belgian Contract. By October, 1843, Brinsmade was receiving letters from his partners at Honolulu saying that they were ready to suspend operations. In the hope that the Belgian Contract would redeem them, however, they held on until 1844, borrowing money at ruinous rates—3% per month on a $5,000 note early in the year.[44]

News from Europe was awaited desperately. It could scarcely be good. In Brussels, less than a month after the signing of the Statutes, Brinsmade received a letter from Richards saying that Richards now regretted ever having been involved in the Belgian Contract. If there were any way out, Brinsmade should take it; for his own part, Richards wrote, he would give "no small sum" to have his name off the papers. Brinsmade of course had to stand—he could do no other; but weeks went

by, then months, and the Royal Community made no move to raise money
through sales of stock. Brinsmade's own resources began to dwindle. He
had to borrow money from Richards so that he could stay in Europe and
try to drum up capital from other investors. Nothing worked. Finally, the
penniless Brinsmade left for the United States and Hawai'i, arriving at
Honolulu early in 1846 on an unpaid ticket.[45]

He returned to a bankrupt firm. Money owed to the government and to private creditors had piled up; Ladd & Co. could not pay.
Choosing the lesser of two evils, the firm closed its doors on November
1, 1844, and the partners proceeded to allow the government to recover.
The government had been delaying collection of notes against Ladd &
Co., amounting to about $14,000. In the community, the firm owed well
over $100,000. It was a spectacular failure, just as the Belgian Contract in
its early weeks had promised spectacular success. When the bad news
became known, there was "great commotion" in the town. Stephen
Reynolds thought he and many others would certainly lose by the affair,
and that he might as well laugh as cry.[46]

Even after their failure was made public, Ladd & Co. were given
time to try to raise the $14,000 they owed the government. Ladd and
Hooper called upon Stephen Reynolds and others for help, but could
find none. Such a risk was too great for a Honolulu businessman.

Almost certainly, too, there existed a feeling of silent satisfaction
at the toppling of the "pious traders." By March, 1845, no doubt remained
that the Belgian Contract was worthless. In mid-year, the government
began to auction the properties of Ladd & Co. There had been a decent
enough period of waiting. Now Gerrit Judd and Robert Crichton Wyllie,
cabinet members and fierce Hawaiian nationalists, could take exemplary action against Ladd & Co., commercial and political interlopers
and monopolists to boot.

Once the case came before the courts, the familiar procession of attempted reference to higher authority was begun. William
Ladd protested a jury trial held to assess the real value of the government's promissory notes, on the grounds that the jury was incompetent
to decide such a substantial matter (though it was composed mainly
of successful Honolulu businessmen). He also claimed that both
parties had agreed to put Ladd & Co.'s affairs beyond the jurisdiction of Hawaiian courts. Toward the end of 1845, an American naval
commander expressed a wish to have the courts of Honolulu suspended
in cases where American citizens and the Hawaiian government were
joint parties. Thenceforth, Ladd & Co. protested every legal step taken
by the government.[48]

The scope of litigation was broadened after the return of Peter
Brinsmade to Honolulu early in 1846. Brinsmade launched a $50,000

suit against James Jackson Jarves, editor of the *Polynesian* (which by now was the organ of government), claiming that libels and slanders by Jarves had injured the prospects of the Belgian Contract. The government called many prominent residents for jury duty, leading Stephen Reynolds to remark cynically that Brinsmade was thus unable to have them testify on his behalf. The case was never heard. Attorney-General John Ricord managed to secure the withdrawal of the suit on a technicality. Judge Lorrin Andrews (another ex-missionary in government) presided over preliminary hearings in which Ricord's argument was upheld. Several Americans were asked to give evidence. Some refused, on the grounds that Andrews was incompetent. United States Consul Alexander Abell placed before Governor Kekūanaō'a a long statement of alleged irregularities in courtroom procedure; United States Commissioner George Brown protested Andrews' right to sit as a judge. Foreign Minister Wyllie in turn protested these protests to Washington. Before Brinsmade dropped his charges against Jarves, a wealthy and respectable American, Dr. R.H. Wood, had been fined for contempt of court, and three of his fellow-nationals—Stephen Reynolds, E.H. Boardman, and John G. Munn—had been committed to the fort for the same reason.[49]

The main business of Ladd & Co.'s debts still lay before the courts of Honolulu. The partners took the position that any sales of their property by the government were void, because under the Belgian Contract all their assets had been transferred to the Royal Community. They then attempted to regain the right to select lands under their first contract with the Hawaiian government, dated November, 1841. The government prohibited this, arguing that once Ladd & Co. transferred its assets to the Royal Community, the partners lost their contractual rights. In November, 1845, the contract of 1841 expired by limitation. Nothing now remained for Ladd & Co., except the possibility that a suit for damages against the Hawaiian government might succeed.

They mounted a suit after Peter Brinsmade failed in his libel action against James Jackson Jarves. Brinsmade, on his way from Europe to Hawai'i, had tried to induce the government of the United States to intervene in behalf of his firm, but Secretary of State James Buchanan had refused.[50] This circumstance did not prevent the newly-appointed United States Commissioner to Hawai'i, Anthony Ten Eyck, from declaring himself a supporter of Ladd & Co. (a course which later brought censure from Buchanan and contributed to Ten Eyck's removal from office). Ten Eyck became the firm's principal counsel, and was instrumental in having the suit for damages heard by arbitrators rather than by a jury.

He argued the case at great length and with great heat against the government's advocate, John Ricord. Factions had long since formed in the town. Brinsmade and his party established a newspaper, the *Sandwich Island News*, in opposition to the *Polynesian*, and week by week, torrents of invective and satire were poured over the heads of the officers of government. Gerrit Judd retaliated by setting native policemen to watch William Ladd's house day and night, and by giving Police Prefect Arthur Brickwood a Treasury Office spyglass to keep track of those who went in and out of Peter Brinsmade's home.[51] In the arbitration hearings, Ten Eyck's style of questioning and summation (that of the plain man, the frontier attorney) contrasted strongly with Ricord's elaborate, authority-studded formulations. The fight was construed by the *News* as a battle of right reason and humanity against the calloused and encrusted powers of the state monster; in the *Polynesian*, the contest appeared as one of order against anarchy.

Day by day before the arbitrators, linen was washed that had been dirtied as long ago as the eighteen-twenties. More than one man left the islands in the wake of disclosures about the handling of governmental and private contracts in Honolulu and Lahaina. Ten Eyck made William Richards look alternately venal, foolish, and incredibly naive (the last was without doubt closest to the truth); Ricord made Ladd & Co. seem like consummate villains, men who used political intrigue to cloak commercial ineptitude. Gerrit Judd emerged in testimony as the grey eminence of government, capable of reaching far beyond the statutory bounds of his office to raise up and pull down men of all sorts, Ladd & Co. included, on the basis of nothing more than an avowed hostility to incursions by foreigners upon the Hawaiian government.

Ladd & Co. claimed damages of $378,000 in all. Sitting in judgment were two reputable merchants: Stephen H. Williams for the government, J.F.B. Marshall for Ladd & Co. Should the arbitrators disagree, they were to submit claims and testimony to an American naval captain expected soon to arrive in the islands.

This proved unnecessary. After Ladd & Co. had presented evidence which covered more than five hundred printed pages, the firm withdrew from the arbitration, claiming that the government was using ruinous procrastination and allowing extravagant expenses in order to make it impossible for the partners to go on with the hearings. Judd in particular, so they said, had harassed them beyond endurance, obtaining judgments for claims in the courts, attaching property, and entering their homes to seize articles of the most trifling value (including family Bibles). All this, so Ladd & Co. alleged, was in pursuance of Judd's own private interest in rent money from a wharf lot leased by him to Ladd & Co. The partners depicted Judd's acts as a violation of the arbitration compact, under whose original terms they ought to have been protected from sacrifice and alienation of property. Rather than acquiesce any longer in governmental browbeating, they abandoned the arbitration and assigned their assets to individual creditors.[52]

Efforts were made to resolve the issue, by means either of a joint-stock company, a private administration, or partial payment in lieu of full recompense. After mid-1847, creditors had charge of the company's books and properties, but lawsuits continued as sales and dispositions were carried out."

Brinsmade journeyed to Washington at the turn of 1848 to set the company's case before his home government. He had no success. Meanwhile, Judd continued his periodic seizures of William Ladd's property. In 1851, the partners made an appeal to the Hawaiian government for relief on another matter. At the time of the French-Hawaiian commercial treaty negotiated by Laplace in 1839, Ladd & Co., "wrongly encouraged" by Hawaiian statesmen, had shipped cargoes of sugar to France. The French government failed to honor its obligations under the treaty, and Ladd & Co. lost heavily. The Hawaiian government declined to take responsibility for French delinquencies. In 1854, William Ladd approached the new United States Commissioner to Hawai'i, David Gregg, and asked if the company's claims might be made a diplomatic issue. Gregg interested himself in the case without achieving anything.[54]

The affair was a long time dying. Without doubt, it delayed the settlement of the disputed question of foreigners' rights at Honolulu and elsewhere. It exacerbated as well the troubled issues of the competence of Honolulu's courts and the good faith of the Hawaiian government in its dealings with Honolulu's foreign businessmen. The destructive course of litigation ruined in addition many personal friendships. Peter Brinsmade, in particular, felt betrayed and abandoned, after what he regarded as a heroic effort to bridge by honorable means the gulf between money and morals at Honolulu. In a long series of articles in his *Sandwich Island News*, Brinsmade ran the gamut from pain to rage and then to elegiac calm as he surveyed the wreckage of his commercial and personal life. At the end of it all, he owned nothing but a tiny plot of land on Kaua'i. To obtain title even for this, he had to petition the government, begging the cabinet's indulgence so that his dead wife might remain buried there, secure at last from legal storms.[55]

Charlton, French & Greenway, and Ladd & Co. were not the only ones to agitate Honolulu society and Hawaiian government in the forties. There was a multitude of lesser cases, many of which became major nuisances when reference to foreign governments or to visiting naval commanders was attempted. Two in this category were small land claims (the matters of James Ruddacks and Thomas Phillips, both British subjects); a third was a rape case.

John Wiley, a beached American, raped a Honolulu native girl in 1844. Out of this miserable circumstance developed an assertion by Acting United States Consul William Hooper (a Ladd partner on the brink of financial ruin) and United States Commissioner George Brown (a perennial enemy of the Hawaiian government) that Wiley's $50 fine was improperly levied—that the case should have been heard by an all-foreign jury. Wiley was jailed subsequently for concealing property which should have gone to the payment of debts he owed a business partner. Commissioner Brown came to his assistance with vituperative letters, and appealed in addition to the captain of an American man-of-war in town at the time. This case, as much as anything else, led to the interdiction of Brown from intercourse with the Hawaiian government and his removal from office. Nor was Wiley's life any better for the help of his country's official representative; he went to California in the gold rush period, and committed suicide there in 1849.[56]

In the middle years of the decade, 1845 and 1846, virtually all the cases mentioned thus far were before the courts of Honolulu (and the foreign offices of Great Britain and the United States) at the same time. For a few years, there had been no direct attacks on Hawaiian sovereignty by the French, but the matters of parity for Catholicism and liberal entry for French liquor lay athwart good relations between Hawai'i and France. Following the Laplace incident of 1839 and the Paulet seizure of 1843, visits to Honolulu by men-of-war were much more frequent, and in most months one or more national ships were riding at anchor in the harbor. Naval commanders, as has been noted, wore recruited as advisers and arbiters in the affairs of their fellow-nationals. By the mid-forties, their crews had begun to add to Honolulu's afflictions by becoming an independent force for disorder, fomenting violence in the streets, and creating further cases for diplomatic reference.

On one or two occasions, sailors dissatisfied with Honolulu's curfew law broke into taverns and drank the night away at the expense of publicans. At other times, they fell afoul of the native police, and armed themselves with clubs and stones against the night-sticks of the constabulary. Then, at the end of September, 1846, a major riot occurred when police clashed with the liberty men of the British warship *Juno*. There were conflicting stories about the start of the fight. One version had it that a policeman manhandled a sailor, another that a constable was called by a woman to remove a European from a grogshop, causing a scuffle. In any event, on the evening of September 28, about 7.30 p.m., at a tavern not far from the Seamen's Chapel in downtown Honolulu, there came the shrill whistling that was the usual call for police, and the shouts of "Haul in! Haul in!" that summoned sailors to the defense of their fellows. A full-scale riot was soon in progress. Several constables were bruised, three sailors from the *Juno* were hurt, one seriously, and a haole passerby, employed in the Honolulu firm of Makee and Anthon, was mistaken for a sailor and was badly mauled.

The commander of the *Juno* complained to the Honolulu authorities about the abuse of his men. Attorney-General John Ricord put the matter in the hands of Lorrin Andrews, who heard cases involving foreigners at Honolulu. Andrews reprimanded Police Prefect Arthur Brickwood for having been less than active in the suppression of the riot. Brickwood, a former petty officer in the British Navy who left Her Majesty's service after striking a superior, had stood under a verandah smoking a cigar while the Hawaiian police pummeled the *Juno's* men.

Andrews regarded his judgment as sufficient concession to the importunities of Captain Blake, who had spoken with unseemly heat in the courtroom, who had not bothered to acquaint himself with Honolulu's port regulations, and who had allowed his men to come ashore and parade through the town brandishing clubs on the nights after the riot. Blake went on to demand compensation, equal to a pension, for one of the sailors from the *Juno,* who was permanently incapacitated. This matter occupied the attention of the Hawaiian Foreign Office for more than a year. Minister Wyllie, in offering a token payment, recalled the many instances in which Britishers had damaged Hawaiian persons and property without making recompense—the cow case of 1829 when Charlton had dragged a native on the end of a rope; the $100,000 worth of damages to Honolulu under Paulet's regime, and the personal suffering of Hawaiians wounded by the bayonets of British marines; Charlton's fraudulent possession of Pūlaholaho; and so on.

Sailors' riots did not cease with the *Juno* affair. Later in the decade, British seamen repeated the grogshop invasions of the mid-forties; in 1850 an attempt was made to storm the fort at Honolulu and release seamen imprisoned for breaking the moekolohe (adultery) laws; and in 1852 the fort was almost breached and part of the town burned by rioting sailors.[57]

The Hawaiian chiefs, in all their dealings with foreigners during this period, relied heavily on the talents and strength of will of the former missionary doctor Gerrit Judd. Over the years, Judd took it upon himself to make good personally any deficiencies in the institutional arrangements of government. In him, policy and personality were inextricably linked, and, for a decade after his entry into government in 1842, a great part of the history of Honolulu and the Hawaiian kingdom revolved about him.

Judd's readiness to become embroiled in politics made him in some ways the heir of Bingham. As his directing hand became more and more decisive in the policies of the monarchy, so he became more and more subject to harassment by foreigners. Like Bingham, Judd contented himself with the thought that men of strong Protestant principles would serve the kingdom more worthily than could non-Christian foreigners.

Certainly the virulence of the businessmen's response to his acceptance of a post in the government led him to conclude, by reverse logic, that he had made the right choice.

Criticism was also levelled at Judd by his missionary brethren. Those who had thought Bingham too much of a politician were even more censorious of Judd, who severed altogether his formal connection with the Sandwich Island Mission, but was still unable to escape derogatory comments from Congregationalists who believed firmly in the complete separation of church and state.[58]

Nonetheless, Judd enjoyed the unrestrained confidence of the chiefs. He spoke their language perfectly, he tended their sick bodies, he translated their documents and mediated their disputes with white men, defending all the while with his considerable force the right of Hawai'i to exist as an independent native kingdom.

Within a very few years, Judd's power became almost complete. Appointed successively to several cabinet posts, he concerned himself, no matter what his title, with all sorts of governmental business, from the most involved diplomacy to the minutest matters of markets, wharves, roads, and rents at Honolulu. Governor Kekūanaō'a of O'ahu and Minister of the Interior Keoni Ana were more than willing to take Judd's advice on the administration of their departments, and they frequently turned over to him the execution as well as the formulation of policy.[59] Judd throve on backbreaking work. He wore the stars and ribbons of office proudly, despite the satirical remarks of the democratic dressers of Honolulu (both lay and clerical). In procession, he marched always closest to the king, impervious to the protocol-bound remonstrances of other foreign cabinet ministers. And he listened with dignity and gravity to the seventeen-gun ceremonial salutes which attended his journeys among the islands.

There is no doubt that Judd enjoyed power. Equally obviously, he knew its uses. Once he suppressed an issue of the government's official weekly, the *Polynesian*, because he disagreed with an editorial.[60] On another occasion, he fought to a standstill the mercantile company of C. Brewer. The firm's partners had taken offense at some statements in a pamphlet published by the government during a commercial court case.

They withdrew their paid advertisements from the *Polynesian* and placed them in the *Friend*, the monthly newspaper of the Honolulu Seamen's Friend Society. Judd set about to compel the editor of the *Friend*, Samuel Chenery Damon, to raise his advertising rates. He went on to say that the last great opponent of the government, Richard Charlton, had not prospered, and he urged C. Brewer & Co. not to "war with the government," threatening that if they did so, the government would war with them by every lawful means. Charles Brewer took his accumulated grievances to United States Commissioner George Brown, who demanded the impeachment of Judd on the grounds that he was an instrument of arbitrary and oppressive government. Judd survived the test triumphantly. The king appointed to the investigating committee three men—Attorney-General John Ricord, a close friend of Judd; Minister of the Interior Keoni Ana, who was indebted to Judd for whatever efficiency his department possessed; and John 'I'i, the reliable Christian Hawaiian. Testimony favorable to Judd was well received; very little of any other kind was heard. Commissioner Brown continued to be abusive. The government, for this and other reasons, interdicted him from further communication, and Brown remained officially helpless until his departure from the islands a year later. As a last step, Judd had Charles Brewer removed from his nominal post as Peruvian consul to the Hawaiian islands.[61] In the tangled affair of Ladd & Co., Judd, on behalf of the government, took a strong line against the company. At the same time, he pursued as a private individual the collection of wharf rents owed him by William Ladd, to the anger of the foreign community and the distress of the missionaries. Judd's ingrained suspicions of all foreigners seeking land privileges found expression when the Board of Commissioners to Quiet Land Titles was created in 1846. At the discretion of the Board, foreigners who swore allegiance to the Hawaiian king might be admitted to permanent residence in the islands. Judd was not a member of the Board, but many people accused him of using his control of the Treasury to manipulate petitions for allegiance and claims for land, so that only the applications of his friends and supporters succeeded.[62]

In 1848, Judd faced impeachment once again. This time George M. Robertson, a clerk in the Interior Department, brought against Judd sixteen charges broken down into one hundred and seventy-five specifications. Among other things, Robertson alleged that Judd as Minister of Finance interfered in the Interior Department and in the office of the Governor of O'ahu; traded (unlicensed) in foreign goods with his close friend William Paty, harbor master and customs commissioner at Honolulu; deprived residents of property by illegal methods; set spies among Honolulu's foreigners; appropriated public money and property to his own use; misdirected governmental funds, spending excessively on roads in Nu'uanu valley where he himself lived, and denying other valleys and roads; and was generally incompetent as Minister of Finance. Judd was to appear before the investigating commission early in December, 1848. With possible impeachment hanging over him, and his situation far more serious than it had been in 1845 when George Brown attempted to force him out of office, Judd took an extraordinary step, one which cost him some valuable friends.[63]

Ever since the Ladd & Co. affair, the *Sandwich Island News,* under successive editors and with successive backers, had been hammering away at governmental pretensions to dignity and probity. Most damaging of all the *News'* efforts was a series of well-written burlesques published under the title of the "Tongataboo Letters," purporting to be communications from a mythical archipelago, in which one of the most absurd of the characters was readily identifiable as Judd. Later, the *News* took up the question of Attorney-General John Ricord's abrupt departure from the islands, asserting that the cabinet had juggled truths to permit Ricord to relinquish his Hawaiian allegiance and resume American citizenship. Judd was anxious to find out who was responsible for these scurrilities. Toward the end of 1848, he persuaded William F. Rogers of the Honolulu customs house to investigate secretly. With Judd's approval, Rogers paid a *News* printer, James Peacock, $300 to steal the manuscripts of the offending articles. Judd's suspicions were confirmed. The handwriting on one set of sheets proved to be that of Anthony Ten Eyck, United States Commissioner to the Hawaiian Islands and an unrelenting opponent of the government ever since the Ladd & Co. arbitration.

The town burst into an uproar. Ten Eyck, without doubt, was pinned to the wall, a diplomat exposed as an anonymous subverter of the government to which he had presented his credentials. His claim that he was not the author but merely the transcriber of some of the manuscripts helped him not at all. King Kauikeaouli closed correspondence with Ten Eyck, and instituted proceedings to have him removed from office.[64]

The question remained of Judd's machiavellian methods. Keoni Ana, the Minister of Interior, was upset. Richard Armstrong, who had relinquished the pulpit at Kawaiaha'o in favor of the portfolio of Public Instruction, did not know what to think. Judd's brother-in-law Asher Bates, the government's legal adviser, informed Armstrong that in civilized countries spies were regarded as odious, but not those who paid spies. The larcenous Peacock, for his part, said he had done the deed as a patriotic duty (he was an allegiance man), and that the $300 was paid to enable him to leave the country ahead of retribution at the hands of foreigners (in fact he did not leave until 1850, and then just ahead of his creditors). Judd was unrepentant. He had suspected Ten Eyck for a long time. It was a dirty business, he agreed; but he added that when a man was hunting a fox and the animal ran into its hole, it had to be tracked. Wyllie, by this time aligned against Judd on many matters, fell into one of his characteristic fits of Highland-laird chivalry. As he saw it, the affair had placed Judd the man in conflict with Judd the minister. "I would wash my hands, at once, from such a Government," Wyllie wrote to Richard Armstrong, "were it not that the King is wholly blameless, & that on such trying emergencies, when danger & disgrace unjustly threaten the *Throne,* it becomes *trebly* the duty of every Minister, not to abandon it."[65]

In the end, the government supported Judd. The cabinet, after declaring that Judd's act had no official sanction, promulgated a decision by Asher Bates and Supreme Court Justice William Lee to the effect that the stolen papers were not property in the sense that they had any monetary worth, and that therefore the removal from the *News* office was not larceny. The Privy Council voted to reimburse Judd for the $300 he had spent in securing the papers.

With this out of the way, the attention of the town returned to Robertson's impeachment of Judd. The investigating commission met more than forty times, heard testimony that filled an entire volume of the Privy Council Record, reduced the number of charges from sixteen to six, and finally ruled in favor of Judd. As in the Ladd & Co. arbitration, a great many overgrown and quiet trails of commerce and politics were cleared for inspection, and the interpenetration of private and public life that so marked Honolulu was once again revealed; but at the end of it all, late in April, 1849, Judd remained Minister of Finance with the confidence of the king.[67]

No sooner had excitement subsided after the affair of the *Sandwich Island News* manuscripts and Judd's impeachment than Honolulu found itself in danger from foreign guns, this time those of the French. There were chronic questions unresolved between Hawai'i and France, dating from the visit of Laplace in 1839—parity in the educational field between Protestants and Catholics; the imposition of duties on French liquors at Honolulu; and the use of French as one of the official languages of the kingdom. There were, in addition, the usual minor consular complaints of the type specialized in by all of Honolulu's intransigent foreign representatives. A French-Hawaiian treaty, drafted in 1846, was being considered by both governments when in 1848 a new French consul, Guillaume Patrice Dillon, came to Honolulu.

From the beginning of his tenure, Dillon proved himself the equal of Richard Charlton in obnoxiousness. With the possible exception of the educational issue, his complaints were trivial, and eventually his own government disavowed almost all his work; but while in office he pressed absurd claims incessantly, harassed the king and the cabinet without pause, wrote voluminously for the opposition newspaper, the *Sandwich Island News,* intrigued to have Richard Armstrong, Gerrit Judd, and Robert Crichton Wyllie removed from office, and finally almost forced the Hawaiian government to demand his dismissal. James Jackson Jarves, former editor of the *Polynesian,* was commissioned in mid-1849 as a special envoy to set the matter of the objectionable Consul Dillon before the French government. For his own part, Dillon took direct action.[68]

Just as Jarves departed for the American mainland and the European continent, the commander of the French fleet in the Pacific, Rear-Admiral Legoarant de Tromelin, was approaching Honolulu in his flagship, *Poursuivante.* De Tromelin had visited the islands in 1848 and had made a good impression on Foreign Minister Wyllie. On his return visit in 1849, he put in at the island of Hawai'i. To King Kauikeaouli, Gerrit Judd, and the missionary Titus Coan, who were at Hilo, de Tromelin appeared the very soul of amiability. Immediately the *Poursuivante* anchored at Honolulu, the admiral was offered accommodations at Wyllie's pleasant home in Nu'uanu valley, "Rosebank." De Tromelin declined, and took up residence instead with the malign French consul, Patrice Dillon. Within a very short time, all hope vanished that the admiral's visit might ease difficulties between Frenchmen and Hawaiians.[69]

On August 22, de Tromelin issued an ultimatum that recalled the days of Laplace and Paulet. Unless the four major demands of Consul Dillon were met within three days, the admiral would use "all the means at his disposal" to obtain redress. He meant force. Wyllie played for time. There were no issues, he said, that could not be solved by Jarves, the Hawaiian commissioner currently on his way to France. De Tromelin reiterated his demands. Wyllie answered that if the French used violence, they would have it on their own consciences.[70]

De Tromelin posted a circular on August 24, threatening hostilities next day. Residents secured their property as best they could. At Kawaiaha'o, $45,000 in businessmen's gold and silver was stored in safes by the Protestant missionaries. As the sun rose on August 25, a crier was on the streets warning natives to stay indoors. Later in the morning, Gerrit Judd and William Lee conferred with de Tromelin on his flagship, but the French were beyond reason. Consul Dillon struck his flag and left his house, placing upon Hawai'i the responsibility for any damage done. Boatloads of French sailors came ashore early in the afternoon, and, in disregard of protests from British Consul-General Miller and United States Consul Joel Turrill, proceeded to wreck the Honolulu fort.

They freed all prisoners, spiked cannon, broke swords, muskets, and bayonets, and threw hundreds of kegs of gunpowder into the sea, blackening the water for days afterwards. They ransacked Governor Kekūanaō'a's house, smashing everything including his clock, and scrawled obscene epithets and self-congratulatory phrases ("Les Braves Poursuivantes") in charcoal. They broke calabashes and dropped them into a well; they removed camphor-wood chests containing kāhili feathers and other mementos of Kekūanaō'a's dead wife, Kīna'u. They placed guards at the fort, the gunpowder magazine, the government offices, and one or two other buildings, and then retired to the harbor where they seized the king's yacht, *Kamehameha III.* Later, the Hawaiian government reckoned damages at more than $100,000.

The natives of Honolulu, ordered by Governor Kekūanaō'a and the king not to resist, looked on with contemptuous amusement. Some American residents, drinking in a waterfront grog-shop, concocted a tipsy scheme to make the French think a foreign sally on the fort was imminent. Their efforts were rewarded on the night of August 30, when the gullible French commanders doubled the number of sentries and marched them about importantly with lights and drumbeats until a late hour. In the harbor, the small American man-of-war *Glyn,* returning from a voyage to the western Pacific, lay with springs on her cables, ready to turn broadside and engage the *Poursuivante* and its companion vessel, the steamer *Gassendi,* should the French open fire on the town. No diplomatic settlement was achieved. On September 5, the *Poursuivante* sailed, carrying Patrice Dillon, who was bound for France and (although he did not know it) for reprimand and removal. The royal yacht *Kamehameha III,* confiscated and manned by a French crew, had already sailed for Tahiti. She was never returned to the king.[71]

In the wake of these outrages perpetrated by the French, Gerrit Judd was commissioned to follow James Jackson Jarves to Europe, where Hawai'i's problems might be resolved, particularly those connected with the French treaty. Judd carried secret instructions empowering him, should Hawaiian independence not be reaffirmed unequivocally, to bargain away the sovereignty of the islands and the lands of the chiefs (his acts, of course, were subject to ratification by his home government). Such extreme measures proved unnecessary, but Judd was quite unable to bring the French government to terms. Not long after he reached the islands again in September, 1850, a new French consul, Emile Perrin, successor of Dillon, arrived at Honolulu aboard the warship *Sérieuse.*[72]

Quite soon the demands of Perrin, echoing those of Dillon and de Tromelin, pushed the Hawaiian government again to the brink of surrendering sovereignty. As the menacing *Sérieuse* lay in the harbor, and as Consul Perrin spoke mysteriously of his "extraordinary" official powers, Honolulu prepared once more to suffer violence. British Consul-General Miller had no orders covering such a situation; neither had Luther Severance, the recently-arrived United States Commissioner. Miller's private inquiries convinced him that Perrin would not use force: that, in fact, the distracted state of Honolulu was the product of machinations by American annexationists. Miller, therefore, elected to do nothing. The Hawaiian government, certain for its part that Perrin's threats were real, turned to Severance, who promised that, should the Hawaiian flag be lowered and the American flag be raised, lives and property would be protected by the guns of USS *Vandalia* (Captain William Gardner), then in port. Severance and Gardner made ready to move, and even to fire upon the *Sérieuse* should the French compel the Hawaiians to lower their flag.[73]

Hawaiian-American intentions leaked to Perrin, as surely they were meant to do. He retreated from his stated position, and a temporary rapprochement was accomplished before he returned to France in May, 1851, for further instructions. From then on, the French difficulty subsided to proportions which approached reality—that is to say, insignificance.

France's real interest in the Hawaiian islands, as distinguished from the doctrinaire imperialism of the July Monarchy of Louis Philippe and the Second Empire of Louis Napoleon, was minuscule. At the time of de Tromelin's depredations in 1849, a resident of Honolulu reviewed the status of Frenchmen in Honolulu. There were, he wrote, only twelve Frenchmen in the islands' foreign population of six hundred (aside from French priests). Honolulu had only one French merchant, who did one-thousandth part of the islands' business; so, also, with the town's one French tavern-keeper. In all of Honolulu's history, only one complete cargo of French goods had passed through the customhouse. During the last five years, not one French merchant vessel had arrived. A few small French schooners had come, carrying cargo from other countries consigned to British and American merchants at Honolulu. Between one hundred and fifty and five hundred American whalers visited the islands annually, compared with only five to nine French whalers. Virtually all liquor was imported by British and American wholesalers. It was drunk by Britishers and Americans. There were more Chinese than Frenchmen in the islands, doing six times the amount of business without complaining that they suffered because Chinese was not an official language of the Hawaiian government. Eight years later, Foreign Minister Wyllie estimated that French imports to the islands between 1845 and 1857 amounted to $72,000, of which $10,000 represented liquors. In the same period, British and American imports totalled $9,000,000.[74]

Relations between Hawai'i and America were much more complex. Since the eighteen-twenties, the United States had dominated

Hawai'i's commerce, and Americans outnumbered all other foreigners at Honolulu (and at most places in the islands, for that matter). National origins were of great moment to the Yankees, who affirmed their own background persistently and noisily. Surges of British influence at the time of Paulet's seizure, and French influence under de Tromelin, Dillon, and Perrin did nothing but sharpen American self-consciousness.

Some of America's consuls and diplomats during the forties carried overweening patriotism to the extreme, refusing to confine themselves to the official sphere and invading at every opportunity the local institutions of Honolulu, especially the courts. Then, toward the end of the forties, groups of mainland Americans began to consider Hawai'i in terms of annexation to the United States. At the same time as the Hawaiian government, in desperation, was contemplating the surrender of its sovereignty to America in 1851, filibusterers on the west coast were preparing to attempt the subversion or the overthrow of the monarchy.

Filibustering movements appeared in California. West-coast nationalism of the first period of Manifest Destiny, social disturbance on the goldfields, the vigilante approach to law—all contributed to the half-realized ebullitions of the era. Their natural target in the Hawaiian islands was Honolulu.

As early as the end of 1847, British Consul-General William Miller predicted danger from California. The tide of migration would soon reach the islands, he wrote, and western settlers were uncontrollable. Two years later, messages were received from San Francisco that shadowy groups there were plotting the downfall of the Hawaiian monarchy. Partly as a precautionary measure, but mainly because of de Tromelin's destruction of the Honolulu fort, the Hawaiian Privy Council began to plan improvements in the armed forces and defense works.[75]

Late in 1850, a gathering of foreigners at Honolulu discussed reports that the town and the islands were threatened by California "ruffians" and "cut-throats." Foreign Minister Wyllie saw no reason to think filibustering expeditions would be countenanced by American authorities in California. Unconvinced, the foreigners' committee passed resolutions, advocating, among other things, a stronger police force for Honolulu. Quite soon, the Privy Council endorsed their views and began to make necessary preparations. By mid-1851, Wyllie had come to believe that the repeated rumors had some substance. Thenceforth, he was the prime mover in readying Honolulu to meet any possible challenge.[76]

In mid-October, the San Francisco papers published reports that more than a hundred and fifty "restless young bloods" were about to sail for the islands with the avowed purpose of "revolutionizing the government of His Kanaka Majesty." This news reached Honolulu just in advance of the clipper *Game Cock,* which entered the harbor on November 15, carrying a party headed by the celebrated Californian Sam Brannan, former Mormon leader, San Francisco vigilante, and gold-fields capitalist. Letters brought by the *Game Cock,* and other stories of vessels sailing from California to the islands, caused the Privy Council to increase the number of foreign policemen in Honolulu. Wyllie was now certain the kingdom was in imminent danger. He drew up an elaborate (and unworkable) scheme for the defense of all the islands, calling for thousands of native "pikemen" and "cavalry," and foreign militiamen pledged to take the marauders without killing them, since for "every one dead 100 stout yankees would take his place."[77]

Brannan moved his two dozen followers into The Bungalow, a handsome but decaying coral-stone house at the east end of Honolulu. Quite soon, Marshal of the Kingdom William Parke discovered by bribing one of the filibusterers that Brannan's men had come to Honolulu under the impression that King Kauikeaouli, overborne by events of the past several years, would gladly relinquish his crown and retire on an annuity. Brannan was absurdly unrealistic about the kind of govern-mental changes the major powers would have permitted in Hawai'i; but, ignorant of this, he assigned posts in his future government to his *Game Cock* confederates—collector of the port, commander of military forces, governor of this or that island, and so on.

In typical Honolulu fashion, great schemes turned to nothing. Brannan and a handful of his men went to Lahaina to discuss matters with the king. Kauikeaouli, forewarned by Marshal Parke and Governor Kekūanaō'a, would not see them, even after they sent in their cards. No violence occurred. Rumored landings of shiploads of desperadoes on the outer islands did not take place. No pirate ship appeared to cut off the king's yacht on a trip to Honolulu. At the turn of 1852, after one or two clashes with the police over drinking and furious riding, the majority of the *Game Cock* men went back to San Francisco on the *Golden Rule.* Brannan had been the first to leave. A few who stayed were prose-cuted and convicted in the courts of Honolulu, on evidence supplied by a disgruntled filibusterer. During their voyage to the islands, Brannan's followers had rifled the *Game Cock's* mailbags. Finding letters addressed to Prince Alexander Liholiho, British Consul-General Miller, and other men of importance in the Hawaiian official community, they had opened and read them. Some contained descriptions of the attempted filibuster and of the men involved. Brannan's men destroyed these, allegedly without the knowledge of their leader.[78] Within a few months of the departure of the *Game Cock,* concern over filibusters died away almost completely. Wyllie remained convinced of the need for a strong Hawaiian standing army. Not many shared his opinions. Captain Gardner of USS *Vandalia* was thanked for his courtesy in detaching one of his marine officers to train native soldiers during the critical period, but soon after he sailed, "A Taxpayer" complained in the *Polynesian* that great numbers of troops at the ready were a drain on the treasury. At the end of March, 1852, the Privy Council moved to reduce Honolulu's permanent garrison from a hundred to sixty, and to fix the number of unpaid militiamen on O'ahu at one hundred instead of the eighteen hundred called for in Wyllie's plan for total preparedness.[79]

When the question of armed force was raised once more in Honolulu, it was not through fear of filibusters (though there had been a recurrence of ominous letters from San Francisco in mid-1852) but because of an old problem—sailors' riots. The fall of 1852 brought a record crowd of ships to Honolulu harbor after a successful season, and hundreds upon hundreds of seamen took their usual boisterous liberty in the town's waterfront grog-shops and the euphemistically-named "boarding-houses."[80]

Inevitably, some found themselves confined in the fort for infractions of the law. On the night of November 8, a seaman named Henry Burns, from the whaler *Emerald*, was imprisoned for drunkenness and disorderly conduct. Locked in a crowded cell with several other sailors, he began to tear up bricks from the floor and throw them at the door. Jailer George Sherman took his club into the pitch-black cell and flailed about. He hit Burns on the head, injuring him fatally.

The next morning, Marshal of the Kingdom William Parke convened a coroner's jury from among Honolulu's foreigners, but even before the cause of Burns' death had been legally established, sailors gathered about the fort, demanding that Sherman be given up to them. Parke armed all the fort's soldiers and police, then took seventy-five men to the gate with the intention of dispersing the mob. He was halted by a note from Governor Kekūanāo'a ordering him to remain within the fort, ready to defend it should the sailors attack.

Nothing happened for the rest of the day. On November 10, Burns was buried in Nu'uanu valley, and a great many seamen followed the cortege to the cemetery. That night, a group went to free some American sailors from the marine hospital, where, so it was said, sick men were being mistreated. The hospital purveyor, John Ladd, left just ahead of the crowd with his money and papers, to take refuge in the house of United States Commissioner Luther Severance.

There was no evidence of mistreatment at the hospital, but at the same time, other sailors downtown were beginning to show more dangerous tendencies, threatening to fire the city, flourishing firearms, and brandishing clubs. Commissioner Severance tried to quiet the angry sailors, and so did United States Consul Elisha Allen, by assuring them that Sherman would be tried by due process of law. This had no effect. The seamen returned to the fort to demand once more that Sherman be surrendered to them.

Others went to the police station, near the waterfront. They drove out the officers, broke up the furniture, piled it inside, and set it afire. They formed a ring outside, not allowing anyone through, and when fire companies arrived they cut their hoses. The station burned down, and with it some other government offices housed in the same building, together with two nearby butcher's shops.

The wind at the time was a light breeze from the south. Had the regular northeast trades been blowing—from the town to the sea— the fleet might have been set ablaze, densely packed in the harbor as it was and loaded with whale oil. One ship moored very close to the burning police station in fact caught fire, but the flames were put out by the rioting sailors. Part of the mob was sobered by this near-disaster; the rest went on to invade downtown taverns, drinking them dry in succession. By eleven at night many were very drunk, and the idea of doing personal violence upon members of the Hawaiian government entered their minds.

Gerrit Judd was chosen as the first victim. About fifty men left the taverns to make the long march to his home in Nu'uanu valley. The road was dark; only a few arrived at the gate. There, they were confronted by Judd, his son Charles, and the family friends Aaron Howe and Richard Coady—all carrying pistols. There was nothing for the sailors to do but return to town. Another group, headed at much the same time for the eastern part of Honolulu where Minister of Public Instruction Richard Armstrong lived, also turned back without harming anyone.

On the morning of November 11, Governor Kekūanaō'a had informed the consular corps that the government was powerless to protect foreigners. Volunteer militia companies were organized. Arms were issued to two hundred infantrymen and fifty cavalrymen. They drilled hurriedly, then went out to clear the streets of sailors under a writ of martial law (drawn up by Marshal Parke in lieu of the hesitant Kekūanaō'a). By the night of November 12, the foreign volunteers and the native constabulary controlled the town. No shots had been fired. Forty or fifty sailors were in jail, having suffered only blows from clubs and stones.

In the calm that followed, warning circulars prepared by Commissioner Severance and Consul Elisha Allen began to take effect. Orders requiring seamen to stay aboard ship were enforced by native policemen who imprisoned sailors found on the streets. The crisis was over.

It remained to try some of the riot's ringleaders. Several were jailed. A handful of these men provided a link between the riot of 1852 and the incomparably greater disaster of 1853—a terrible smallpox epidemic. Marshal Parke wrote: "...there were six out of the number convicted who had had smallpox, and in the great epidemic...they did a work for which no money could compensate them."[81]

On February 10, 1853, the American ship *Charles Mallory* out of San Francisco reached Honolulu harbor, flying a yellow flag from the foremast—the signal of serious disease aboard. One passenger was suffering from smallpox. He was isolated for two weeks on an islet at Kalihi, to the west of Honolulu harbor. Others who disembarked were vaccinated and quarantined at Waikīkī.[82]

This was by no means the first smallpox scare in Honolulu's history. Suspect ships had put in at Honolulu during the eighteen-thirties and forties, without, however, introducing disease. By way of response, the government had enacted quarantine laws in 1839, 1842, and 1845–1846, and there had been periodic interest (though little real accomplishment) in systematic vaccination for the islands' population. The *Charles Mallory* arrived in the islands at a time when smallpox was rampant on the west coast of America. Fresh vaccine, recently bought by some of Honolulu's doctors, was available. At the urging of the physicians, the Privy Council set up an inexpensive (and inefficient) program of vaccination administered by Richard Armstrong, Minister of Public Instruction (Armstrong was not a doctor). The Privy Council recommended as well the establishment of a quarantine ground and a pest hospital, sites for which were to be chosen by Minister of Finance Gerrit Judd, the former missionary doctor.[83] By the beginning of March, the quarantine period for the *Charles Mallory's* passengers had ended and no new cases had appeared. Armstrong's program of vaccination got under way about the same time. On March 31, the *Charles Mallory* sailed, with the convalescent smallpox victim aboard. Honolulu was left in the lull customary between whaling seasons.[84] Almost six weeks later, on May 11, 1853, a rumor was heard and then confirmed in Honolulu that smallpox had been discovered on Maunakea Street in the downtown business district. Marshal William Parke arranged to have the victims, two Hawaiian women, examined by George Lathrop, an American physician with a large practice among the town's natives, and Edward Hoffman, a genial German doctor who made a great part of his living from his drugstore. It developed that the victims had caught the disease from a third woman, then convalescent from a slight attack. She had been treated by Lathrop's Hawaiian assistant, Kinikake, who was unfamiliar with smallpox. Kinikake had prescribed purgatives and a gargle for the woman's symptoms, which she described as a sore throat and pains in the head and back. This third woman in turn had a sister living at Waikīkī who had been sick some time earlier of a skin disease which covered her from head to foot.

The Waikīkī girl made her money stringing flower leis for sale in Honolulu. She habitually saved a lei for her sister, and her sister had infected the two women ultimately diagnosed as smallpox cases on Maunakea Street. Thus, possibly, there had been smallpox at Waikīkī at least some weeks before it was identified three miles away in Honolulu. The Waikīkī natives, not recognizing the disease, had seen no need to inform white doctors or town officials. The infected lei-seller had been treated by her own father, who claimed to have cured her, and who also offered to attend the Maunakea Street women.[85]

Where the smallpox come from? Ultimately from California; but precisely how did it make its way to the yard on Maunakea Street? This was argued strenuously in 1853 and later. If the connections linking the Waikīkī lei-seller with the Maunakea Street victims formed a path along which the disease travelled, then its source might well have been the *Charles Mallory*, which did not leave Honolulu until March 31, and whose passengers had been quarantined at Waikīkī. Another possibility, brought forward then and later, was that the disease had come to Honolulu from San Francisco in a cargo of old clothing sold at auction off the ship *Zoe*. The *Zoe* was at Honolulu from March 23 to the end of the first week in April. More than one report identified the first victim as a native woman who had been employed to wash some of the clothes. Yet a third source was mentioned: a sailor from California was known to have slept with a Hawaiian woman who lived in the yard where the disease was discovered. Modern opinion regards the clothes as an unlikely source. Most probably a human carrier, not necessarily recognized as a case, spread the infection.[86]

Whatever the source, there was no time to lose once the presence of the disease was known. Within two hours, the Maunakea Street yard was under a governmental kapu, and adjoining lots were fenced off while contaminated grass houses and clothing were burned. On Monday, May 16, King Kauikeaouli approved a public health act hastily drafted and passed by the legislature. Three Royal Commissioners of Health were appointed—Gerrit Judd, Marshal William Parke, and the English physician T.C.B. Rooke. During the next few days, the commissioners, with Rooke as chairman, made rough plans calling for general vaccination, hospital accommodations, scrutiny and warning for ships entering the harbor, and the establishment of a network of sub-commissioners for the outer islands. Judd had thought it unnecessary thus far to prevent natives from travelling between islands, but, in the opening week of June, with almost twenty cases and three deaths reported in Honolulu, disease broke out on a native schooner sailing between Oʻahu and Maui, and the vessel returned to Honolulu. Thenceforth, the commissioners ruled, no unvaccinated person might leave the town.[87]

Crowds besieged Honolulu's drugstores for vaccine matter, but disease spread faster than did methods of prevention. Every early reported case was traceable to the source of infection on Maunakea Street, where prompt action had been taken to isolate and decontaminate the infected area. Even so, smallpox quickly appeared several miles outside Honolulu, in the rural district of 'Ewa. By June 11, almost every district of Honolulu was reporting cases; by June 18, the total of reported cases rose to 114 and reported deaths to 41; within the next week these figures doubled. In the terrible months of July and August, total reported cases for O'ahu reached almost four thousand and deaths more than fifteen hundred, mostly in Honolulu. From then on, incidence and mortality in the town itself declined quite sharply. Honolulu was virtually safe by the end of October, but the rest of the island—and the outer islands—continued to suffer as the disease spread farther and farther from its source. By the end of January, 1854, when for the first time no new cases or deaths were recorded, the islands had reported a total of 6,405 cases and 2,485 deaths.[88]

From the beginning in Honolulu, a great difference in the incidence of the disease became apparent between white men and natives. Only a handful of white men died, though virtually all in the town were exposed continually. But Hawaiian inattention or aversion to western medical treatment and elementary sanitation, which had angered white men since the time of the first missionaries, now assumed a fatal significance. Many of Honolulu's natives, to be sure, were vaccinated either by physicians or volunteers, but hundreds—probably thousands—refused or evaded help. Some simulated scars with self-inflicted scratches rather than submit to the white doctors or their deputies. Others retreated into traditionalism and sought help from medical kahuna. Within a few short weeks, the dreadful consequences were visible. Hawaiians were falling sick and dying everywhere. Some were abandoned, to die alone. Their bodies were left uninterred. Others were buried coffinless, in graves so shallow that wandering dogs and pigs could disturb them without difficulty. Many native families devotedly and uselessly nursed the sick at home, and carefully laid the dead under the earth floors of their thatch-huts or in their houseyards (following traditional Hawaiian burial practices), thus condemning themselves in many cases to follow the dead into the same grave.[89]

Early in June, Minister of Public Instruction Armstrong called for a day of humiliation, fasting and prayer to be observed on June 15. Throughout the epidemic, clergymen of all denominations worked to alleviate suffering. Protestant preachers urged the benefits of vaccina-

tion upon their flocks. Lowell Smith of Kaumakapili Church set up a
vaccination and food station; Catholic priests went among the sick
and baptized the dying whenever they could; and some newly-arrived
Mormon missionaries labored to expel the disease by anointing with oil
and laying on hands, advising natives at the same time to avoid orthodox
white physicians.[90]

Normal life in the town seemed about to disintegrate. Workmen
and domestic servants vanished. By the beginning of July, the produce
markets were deserted. Fresh beef could not be found anywhere, no
one would eat Hawaiian-raised pork or chicken, and fish and vegetables were served and eaten only with great trepidation. Hawaiians
fled the town by hundreds, the healthy to evade exposure to disease,
the sick to escape they knew not what. They went into the hills behind
Honolulu or the country districts to wait out their time (and involun-
tarily to spread infection), or they took to interisland boats and canoes
in defiance of the Health Commissioners' decrees. Within six weeks
of the discovery of the disease on Maunakea Street, more than a thousand had left Honolulu for other towns, most of them to be turned
away there by frightened natives. Many villagers simply stoned
anyone attempting to enter. The people of Waialua, in western Oʻahu,
organized a kind of vigilante association to prevent strangers from
crossing a bridge leading into the village. For those who remained in
Honolulu, death was all around. Yellow flags hung before doorways on
every street. The congregations of Kawaiahaʻo and Kaumakapili each
lost more than three hundred members; and the legal columns of the
Polynesian began to fill up with attorneys' announcements about the
disposition of estates of Hawaiians who had committed their property
but not their persons to western ways, who had secured their lands
and made their wills but had not been vaccinated.[91]

The government had done its best in impossible circumstances.
The commissioners appointed under the public health act of May 16 had
been authorized to provide medical attention, food, lodging, and clothes
at government expense, and to make and enforce regulations. Within a
very short time, every Honolulu physician was working. Schoolhouses
and other buildings were pressed into use as hospitals or food dispensaries
or relocation points. Even so, facilities and services were overwhelmed.
Several hospitals were opened in the district, of which four were the
biggest and most important: one at King and Alapaʻi Streets toward the
east end of Honolulu, beyond the Kawaiahaʻo mission of the Protestant
church; another at Waikīkī; a third at Kalihi on the western side of the
town; and the fourth and principal one at a place called Honuakaha in
the district of Kakaʻako just seaward of Kawaiahaʻo, where the dead
were buried.

To this last place were brought most of the cases—living and dead—picked up in the town by the wagon-drivers of Marshal William Parke. Quite soon, their work became impossibly arduous as the disease spread and the yellow flags proliferated. With some policemen refusing duty and others laboring to exhaustion, Parke was authorized by the Royal Health Commission to draft able-bodied men who had recovered from the disease, on pain of imprisonment or fine. At the same time he acquired, with the promise of pardon, the services of several white men in the fort (among these were six sailors jailed after the riot of 1852, all of them immune through previous exposure to smallpox). The wagon-drivers on their daily rounds perforce became hardened to their work. In time, they were able to achieve the domestication of horror and death and could stop for a drink at a tavern, leaving their corpse-laden wagons outside. But at Kaka'ako hospital one of the prisoner-workers, Peter Jordon, began to see ghosts; and as for the Hawaiians themselves, some were convinced that death was a certainty there. Autopsies were being performed, and the Hawaiians heard that a man had been killed, his throat cut open, and his corpse abused. This caused general panic, and many natives fled to lie concealed among their friends when first symptoms appeared.

Even though deliberate mistreatment was rare at Kaka'ako, the hospital was a frightful enough place. At the height of the epidemic, forty or fifty bodies each day were buried close by. Within a matter of weeks, the cemetery became dangerously overcrowded as rows of narrow, shallow graves were dug in the loose, sandy soil. Ultimately, more than a thousand corpses were packed together, many of them buried on their sides to conserve space, in graves just wide enough to admit a body and only three feet deep.[92]

Governmental employees were not the only ones who gave their time and risked their lives in the fight against smallpox. Doctors, and a great many white residents as well, worked without ceasing during the first two months of the epidemic. In mid-July, when disease and death were at their height, a letter signed by "A Physician" was printed in the *Polynesian*, criticizing "government apathy." Marshal Parke and his policemen had done good work, the writer acknowledged, but there should be fifty more like him. Why would not the government act more efficiently? Was it waiting for aid from the foreign residents? If so, they would help. With the whaling season close at hand, Honolulu's prosperity might be endangered if the town did not make itself ready to receive the fleet. The same issue of the *Polynesian* contained an announcement of a public meeting to be held on the evening of Monday, July 18, at the Honolulu courthouse. Among those endorsing the gathering were many important men representing the town's official, mercantile, and missionary groups: Gerrit Judd; Drs. George Lathrop, Edward Hoffman, Benjamin Hardy, and Seth Porter Ford; Charles Brewer II, Charles R. Bishop, and Joseph Booth (a prominent English tavern-keeper); Foreign Minister Wyllie, Prince Lot Kamehameha, Minister of Public Instruction Armstrong, among others.[93]

Dr. Wesley Newcomb was chosen to preside over the meeting of July 18. Opening discussions included remarks that "some members" of the government had been lax in failing to adopt a comprehensive program of vaccination at the first evidence of smallpox. Obviously, these criticisms were aimed at Gerrit Judd and Richard Armstrong. The meeting then invited the practicing physicians of the town to co-operate with a committee of twelve in drawing up plans to improve the handling of the epidemic. On the evening of July 19, seven resolutions were forwarded to the Privy Council. Their substance was that the city should be divided into districts under volunteer leaders, so that better preventive measures might be taken. Improved arrangements for vacci-nation were needed, and public hospitals should be set up outside the town. More rigorous sanitation was called for—grass houses and other contaminated matter should be burned, and "disease-carrying" dogs should be killed. Thereafter, the Privy Council used these resolutions as the basis of the government's attack on smallpox.

The meeting of July 19 did not end with this. George Lathrop, the physician who had confirmed the existence of smallpox on Maunakea Street in May, read a "pungent" series of resolutions attacking Gerrit Judd and Richard Armstrong for their negligent approach to the epidemic in its early stages. The *Polynesian* claimed that Lathrop's outburst came as a surprise to all but two or three of those at the meeting, and that majority opinion was firmly against him. The opposition *Weekly Argus*, however, reported that Lathrop's speech was greeted with loud applause.

Next evening, the anti-Judd and Armstrong forces met once more, to pursue the political implications of Lathrop's resolutions. Again, Dr. Wesley Newcomb was in the chair. D.P. Penhallow and John Meek were vice-presidents (both men were sea-captains and former harbor-masters and pilots at Honolulu); William Ladd, a partner in the ruined firm of Ladd & Co., was secretary; Christopher Lewers (an Englishman just establishing himself in business) was assistant secretary. Newcomb and Lathrop made speeches. So did the American dentist J. Mott Smith, the militia captain A. J. McDuffie, and the obscure American lawyer J. D. Blair. The meeting resolved to petition the king for the dismissal of Judd and Armstrong, and a Committee of Thirteen was authorized to obtain signatures.[94]

This move set off a round of huge, noisy, sometimes near-violent public meetings as factions formed about the issue of the removal of

Judd and Armstrong. The core of the opposition, which called itself the "Independent" party, claimed that Judd and Armstrong were great peddlers of influence and patronage in the government, who nonetheless had not employed their powers to stop the entry of smallpox in the first place and its spread thereafter. In later weeks, these charges were both made more specific and expanded to absurdity. Armstrong's plan for vaccination after the *Charles Mallory* scare had been useless (a harsh judgment). The Royal Commissioners for Health had allowed people other than doctors to vaccinate, and these ministrations had been worthless (quality of vaccine rather than profession of vaccinator seems to have been the operative factor). Honolulu's physicians at that time had suggested a districting scheme and vaccination by qualified people, but Judd had suppressed their report, which was never seen by the Privy Council (not proven by the evidence). Judd had been paid $2,000—by whom not specified—to permit the *Charles Mallory* to enter the harbor (vicious and false).

While these charges were being flung about, in fact before some of them reached print, the Committee of Thirteen was collecting signatures. Its petitions came before the Privy Council apparently supported by 258 white residents and 11,500 natives. The white signatories announced themselves as loyal citizens and denizens of the islands (inspection later showed that 189 were aliens); they identified themselves unhesitatingly with the fate of the kingdom. But, they warned, history showed that monarchs surrounded by "pernicious councillors" could never make their people happy. The king's confidential advisers were undeserving of his trust and should be dismissed. Judd and Armstrong must go. "Their inefficiency and misdeeds may be artfully conceal'd from your Majesty, but their selfish cupidity, political imbecility, and malfeasance in office are well known, and grievously felt by your people." All the living, and the dead too, clamored for their dismissal, the petition asserted.[95]

By the beginning of August, the Committee of Thirteen's foreign and native petitions against Judd and Armstrong had been answered by a number in favor of retaining the two ministers. A Privy Council committee appointed on August 8 to scrutinize the documents reported, a week later, that the names of more than two hundred and fifty white men and approximately eleven thousand, five hundred natives appeared on petitions demanding removal. About three thousand names, mostly native, were signed on petitions in favor of retaining the two men. Almost all native signatures, on both sides, were written in only three or four hands. About half had a mark in the form of a cross affixed, but by the same hand as the signature. Among the foreign signatures against the ministers, two appeared twice, and several seemed to have been done in the same handwriting. Many of the names were quite unknown to the Privy Council committee. A check in the records showed that of the more than two hundred and fifty petitioners, fewer than seventy were naturalized Hawaiian subjects. Even assuming all signatures to be genuine, the committee concluded, there seemed no reason to dismiss the ministers. Searching investigation had failed to elicit misdeeds or inefficiency on the part of Judd; and as for the other charges, they were vague and general, lacking specific allegations.[96]

On the evening of August 15, the implacable anti-ministerial faction held a mass meeting demanding once more the resignation of Judd and Armstrong. Asher Bates, Judd's brother-in-law, spoke emotionally on behalf of the ministers, but resolutions were passed calling for their removal. The tone was that of the Committee of Thirteen's petitions: "Could the voices be heard of those thousands of your Majesty's people who have recently been so suddenly swept from time into an awful eternity, through the criminal parsimony and neglect of these Ministers, they would cry night and day to reprove and in some measure avenge the wrong done your people, by dismissing such faithless Ministers..."[97]

Nine Privy Councillors discussed their own committee's report with the king on August 17. The remaining members were silent. Wyllie's view was that the issue of cabinet responsibility was at stake; he could take no part in a move which might lead to some members recommending the dismissal of others. Keoni Ana followed Wyllie.

Judd and Armstrong were obviously disqualified from voting on their own political future. Asher Bates had listened to some earlier deliberations without participating, but was absent on August 17. After a wide range of opinion was expressed, the nine members voted 5/4 in favor of asking Judd and Armstrong to resign. Prince Alexander Liholiho and seven other chiefs divided 4/4. Honorary Privy Councillor Charles Gordon Hopkins, an English-born, naturalized Hawaiian and a protégé of Wyllie, cast the decisive vote.

Judd resigned as a Royal Commissioner for Health on August 22, but did not surrender his documents of authorization as Minister of Finance. Two days later, the king sent Prince Alexander Liholiho to accept Judd's papers. Judd refused to relinquish them. For another week, in the face of mounting storms from the opposition, he clung to his cabinet post. Finally, the king directed all his ministers to resign. Judd was the last to return his commission, on September 3. On September 5, every minister was reappointed, except Judd. Armstrong retained the portfolio of Public Instruction, and Judd was succeeded as Minister of Finance by the former United States Consul to Hawai'i, Elisha Allen.[98]

At the Honolulu courthouse, where the first public meetings had been held, the Committee of Thirteen and its supporters gathered once more on September 8. Wesley Newcomb was in the chair. Under his guidance, the meeting approved resolutions composed by George Lathrop, J. D. Blair, and John Mott Smith, celebrating the end of the "malignant tyranny" of Judd, and calling for manifestations of public joy at the birth of the "delightful influences of liberty, free conscience and independent actions." Accordingly, on the night of Saturday, September 10, a torchlight procession with bands and banners made its way through the town to the king's residence, as all manner of guns were fired and street-corner orators declaimed before huge crowds. It was a moment to remember. In honor of the event, the opposition newspaper changed its name from the *Weekly Argus* to the *New Era*. Judd, thoroughly shaken and embittered, announced his return to private practice as a physician.[99]

The effects of the smallpox epidemic upon Honolulu and the islands generally were catastrophic. A tragic loss of morale was discernible everywhere among the natives. Schools and churches lost many members by death and desertion. The principal native congregations at Honolulu—Kawaiaha'o and Kaumakapili—were reduced by several hundreds; and at 'Ewa, to the west of Honolulu, the Protestant pastor Artemas Bishop estimated that of the twenty-eight hundred Hawaiians who had once lived in his district, twelve hundred were dead. His church never recovered from this blow, and the same was true of many other congregations. The great awakening of the eighteen-thirties had been followed first by a small but virulent epidemic of measles in 1848 and then by the smallpox of 1853. To surviving natives, God's goodness seemed at least questionable.

Economic life at Honolulu was more resilient. It had been feared that the smallpox epidemic would cause whaling captains to avoid Honolulu in the fall of 1853, to the ruination of commerce. The epidemic, however, had abated in the town by October, and Honolulu was safe when the crowds of whalers came back from their cruises in the North Pacific. A record number of whaleships anchored at Honolulu in 1853, and the total figure for all Hawaiian ports was the fourth highest in the history of the industry.

For a short time in Honolulu, city of feuds, disaster encouraged common cause among groups previously hostile to one another. Especially after the establishment of a districting system administered by volunteers, cooperation and sacrifice of self-interest emerged—a rarity in the town's history. The spirit of community enjoyed only a limited and fugitive existence. Sectarianism remained powerful. Protestant ministers in particular were indignant that other denominations gained death-bed converts. Within the lay population, new factions rose from the remnants of the old to dislodge Judd. Several of the "dedicated" doctors of mid-

1853 pushed forward to claim compensation in money for their services. Led by the tough-minded and disputatious Lathrop and Newcomb, they made their demands the business not only of the Hawaiian government, but also of American consular and diplomatic representatives. Four years after the last smallpox victims were buried in communal graves at Kaka'ako, wrangling was still going on.[100]

Attention devoted to these matters might have been turned more productively to the question of effective vaccination and quarantine. Twice within the next generation smallpox returned to Honolulu, carried aboard ships; twice, failures of diagnosis permitted the disease to reach the town and infect residents.

Judd had been a convenient scapegoat for the aroused passions of the foreign population of Honolulu during the epidemic of 1853, but it would be a mistake to regard his dismissal merely as a ritual sacrifice performed to achieve the purification of the town. His fall had its origins elsewhere than in the epidemic.[101]

Judd remained convinced that the tremendous hostility he encountered in 1853 was generated by a clique of dishonorable men, acting solely from personal spite. In his eyes, they were simply the last in a long line of enemies who had been attempting his destruction ever since he took office—Paulet, George Brown, Charles Brewer, William Ladd and his associates, Anthony Ten Eyck, George Robertson, and finally the Committee of Thirteen.[102]

On the surface, Judd's analysis was plausible. Preeminent in the dealings of the Committee of Thirteen were George Lathrop and Wesley Newcomb, with whom Judd had crossed swords many times. In 1851, Judd and two other referees ruled against Lathrop in a lawsuit concerning the lease of a sugar plantation. A few months later, Lathrop applied for a loan from the government, only to be refused by the same Privy Council that had just lent $3,000 to Judd's prospective son-in-law, Aaron Howe. In 1852, the tariff on liquors imported for medicinal purposes was reduced. Lathrop, being a physician, naturally expected to share in this benefit. Judd, however, debarred him, on the ground that Lathrop served liquor to customers in his drugstore. Lathrop appealed to the Privy Council, but figures were produced showing that Lathrop's use of "medicinal" liquor was greater by far than that of any other doctor, and his petition was denied. Nonetheless, Lathrop took his case before the legislature of 1853, complaining that Judd was victimizing him.[103]

As for Wesley Newcomb, Judd and he had been bickering ever since the *Charles Mallory* smallpox scare. They disagreed over the best way to prepare vaccine, then over quarantine measures, then over the right of doctors to enter infected areas. Finally, when the exasperated

Judd ordered Newcomb out of his office, Newcomb left, telling Judd he would *"kick his Ass* for him the next time he met him."[104]

Concurrently, Judd was fighting wars on many other fronts. Enmities incurred in the forties haunted him later. William Ladd appeared as a member of the Committee of Thirteen. George Robertson, who had become Speaker of the House of Representatives in 1852, engaged Judd in a running battle over Judd's refusal to honor House drafts on the treasury. Judd created a new storm in the community when he fired his auditor, William Jarrett, accused him of embezzlement, and pursued him remorselessly through the courts. Jarrett was finally acquitted and reinstated in government service after Judd's removal, at which time an investigating committee held Judd himself to be responsible for the alleged deficiency. Several years went by before it was agreed that the entire affair had been due to Judd's faulty bookkeeping, rather than to criminal intent on either side. Immediately, however, insult was added to injury when Judd employed his own son, the seventeen-year-old Charles, as Jarrett's successor. Charles Judd's short incumbency was marked by an uproar when he and his father auctioned a herd of government horses to themselves.[105]

In addition to these particular cases, there had always to be considered the enmity of the drinkers of Honolulu. Judd, although he smoked and chewed tobacco (scandalizing some of his former missionary brethren), was a vehement and aggressive advocate of total abstinence from liquor. His tenure as an officer of government was marked by frequent campaigns to extend and enforce punitive laws relating to the town's publicans and their patrons. Foreign Minister Wyllie, who liked his wine and brandy, maintained that most of Hawai'i's difficulties with France began when Judd, in disregard of a common diplomatic arrangement, refused to allow French Consul Patrice Dillon to land one or two barrels of liquor free of duty. Wyllie claimed, too, that Honolulu's rabid temperance movement had done much to lead French Commissioner Emile Perrin to threaten violence against the government in 1851. United States Commissioner Luther Severance, more sympathetic to Judd than was Wyllie, had the same problem in mind when he wrote that two-thirds of the foreigners who demanded Judd's dismissal in 1853 were simply looking for cheap liquor.[106]

No matter how many enemies Judd accumulated among the foreigners of Honolulu, he might still have survived had he enjoyed the confidence of the cabinet. But by 1853 this, too, had vanished. After Judd, the most powerful foreigner in government was Wyllie. The two men, in strenuous opposition since the late forties, cut off social intercourse in 1850, communicating thereafter only in writing. Wyllie, at odds with Judd over principles and methods of government, came in time to suspect his rival's motives and to impugn his honor—always the end of the road for Wyllie in personal relations. Major confrontations occurred during discussions of Judd's diplomatic mission to the United States and Europe in 1849, and during the constitutional debates of 1852. On the very brink of the smallpox upheaval in 1853, Judd, whose own competence and integrity as Minister of Finance were under attack, withheld a payment to Wyllie. The sum at issue was $9.6-1/2. Enraged, Wyllie dashed off a thirty-page letter accusing Judd of being an uncivil, wretched quibbler, and reminding him that Wyllie had honored unquestioningly Judd's diplomatic expenses in 1849, which amounted to thousands of dollars. Furthermore, Wyllie pointed out, Judd himself had been overdrawn by hundreds of dollars more than once in the past decade. Finally, Wyllie wrote, Judd's unforgivable rudeness in matters of finance had alienated in turn John Ricord, James Jackson Jarves, William Richards, and William Lee.[107] By this time, all except the last were dead or had left Honolulu. When the hour came, Lee sided with Wyllie, standing aloof as Judd was cut down by his enemies.

As Judd's biographer-descendant, Gerrit Judd IV, has observed, Judd's dismissal from the king's ministry might be regarded primarily as a product of his personality. "By temperament Dr. Judd was strong-willed, stubborn, and implacably hostile to all who disagreed with him...Upon occasion, especially in time of crisis when he drove himself to exhaustion, his manner was abrupt and unconciliatory. At such moments, often with the best of intentions, he goaded his opponents to fury."[108] This fury overflowed during the smallpox epidemic.

Far more important than the question of Judd's dismissal from the king's ministry was the issue of Hawai'i's continued existence as an independent kingdom. The warships of the French and the filibusterers of Sam Brannan had come and gone, leaving Hawaiian sovereignty intact for the time being. Nonetheless, discussion of the ultimate fate of the islands continued unabated. During the political upheaval which attended the smallpox epidemic of 1853, the possibility that the islands might be annexed by the United States became a topic of consuming interest in Honolulu. It divided the town into new groupings; it played a part in Judd's downfall. It was not quieted, even temporarily, until after the death of King Kauikeaouli at the end of 1854.

Many Americans at Honolulu favored annexation of the islands by their home country. Some were Manifest Destiny men, rabid nationalists, their minds inflamed by the election to the American presidency of the expansionist Democrat Franklin Pierce, who took office in 1853.

Others, less extreme, saw American annexation as an alternative to engulfment either by France or by Great Britain. Ideology and expediency came together in economic terms in the minds of yet others, who could see great benefits should Hawai'i fall within the tariff structure of America. This last argument took on particular force in the early fifties, when Hawai'i's market in California diminished and the economy of the islands suffered. Especially at Honolulu, real estate prices dropped sharply, goods moved sluggishly, and investments of all sorts declined in value. On the outer islands, several sugar planters went bankrupt, pulling Honolulu's mercantile houses into difficulties. To many observers, annexation by the United States seemed to offer an escape from ruin.

By the opening of the eighteen-fifties, annexationism had made its way even into the cabinet of the Hawaiian kingdom. Curiously, in view of the annexationist taint of much of the opposition to Gerrit Judd, Judd himself was an annexationist during the last few years of his ministerial tenure. The fierce protectiveness he had once shown toward the monarchy changed, amazingly rapidly, to a willingness to bargain away the throne of the Kamehamehas. Like everything else about Judd, this conversion was complex. Judd left Hawai'i on a diplomatic mission in 1849. At his departure, he was the undisputed master of policy. In his absence, however, parts of a new liberal policy were enacted. Foreigners were permitted to acquire land in fee simple without signing naturalization papers. Under Wyllie's influence, a great relaxation occurred in all matters pertaining to liquor. Judd found, upon his return to the islands, that his personal dominance was challenged in ways previously unthinkable. Within the cabinet itself, new groups formed against him. In the city at large, his prodigal alienation of former friends and colleagues had left him dangerously isolated. Then too, he was losing control of the powers of patronage which had once been his exclusively, especially in matters of land. In sum, he was less and less able to withstand political attacks. By the early fifties, apparently, he was ready to bring the temple down around him.

In the course of his travels abroad in 1849, Judd became acquainted with Alfred G. Benson, a New York shipping millionaire, who expressed interest in making investments in the Hawaiian islands. With Judd's help, Benson was awarded the franchise for a drydock and marine railway in Honolulu harbor, to serve the expected steam traffic of the future. In 1852, Benson organized on paper a firm called the Sandwich Island Steam Company to run ships among the islands, and Judd was named a director. Later, it became clear that this and one or two similar ventures (for example, Garet Ryckman's steamship line) were speculations gambling on annexation to the United States. Quite apart from his connection with Benson, Judd corresponded with a number of other people on the subject of annexation, among them the expansionist United

States Senator William Seward. Matters reached a peak just before Judd's removal, when, on behalf of Benson, he submitted to King Kauikeaouli an offer to buy the islands outright for five million dollars. Apparently, Judd had had possession of the offer since the summer of 1852, and it is significant that he waited to present it until the last days of his career as a Hawaiian cabinet minister.[109]

Judd's fairly spectacular reversal of fields cost him some friends among the chiefs, without causing the Committee of Thirteen to become reconciled to him. The Committee seems to have been determined to be rid of Judd, no matter what his views on annexation. It is uncertain whether the details of Judd's about-face were known to the Committee; it is uncertain, as well, whether the Thirteen were true annexationists or filibusterers.

The motives of the American-born extremists, in fact, were rather obscure. George Lathrop, a leading member of the Committee, showed nothing but contempt for the Hawaiian monarchy. To him, one Kamehameha was very like the next—"a nigger." Several of his fellow Committee members seem to have shared his racist opinions. Agreed upon this, they disagreed among themselves, or at least changed their collective mind a number of times, about the best disposition of the Hawaiian islands. On occasion, they appeared to advocate direct annexation by the United States, along orthodox Manifest Destiny lines. At other times, rumors emanating from their councils pointed to a filibuster accomplished by force, followed by the establishment of a revolutionary regime, and then, possibly, a sale at profit to the United States government.

The Committee, as has been noted, first became prominent at Honolulu when George Lathrop, Wesley Newcomb, and others emerged as leaders in the movement to have Judd dismissed from office. Soon, the names of these men were linked with rumors of filibusters. Overthrow of the monarchy by force was repugnant to many foreigners, including several who favored annexation to the United States. Accordingly, nineteen residents, mostly Americans, not connected with the Committee of Thirteen, but representing missionary, mercantile, and planter elements, signed a petition in support of annexation, which was laid before the Privy Council on August 24, 1853. The memorial was drawn up by Samuel N. Castle, a former missionary, with the silent help of United States Consul Elisha Allen. It was signed by Castle and his business partner Amos Cooke (founder of the Chiefs' Children's School); W.H. Rice (a missionary teacher at Punahou); three Honolulu doctors, Edward Hoffman, Seth Porter Ford, and B.F. Hardy; and thirteen businessmen, including Charles R. Bishop, Stephen Reynolds (a longtime annexationist), and Alexander Cartwright, one of the pioneers of baseball in

America and an enthusiastic participant in Honolulu's July 4 parades and dinners. Castle's petition was avowedly intended to forestall a filibuster, which was regarded as a strong probability, and to make the best of an impossible situation by hastening annexation. The Privy Council considered the memorial, and set it aside. On the same day, wrote United States Commissioner Luther Severance, a member of the Committee of Thirteen, D.P. Penhallow, sailed for California, carrying copies of petitions calling for Judd's removal. Penhallow hoped to gain support on the west coast for a filibuster, following which the conquered islands would be sold to the United States.[110] The dismissal of Judd, early in September, had the effect of settling somewhat the political climate at Honolulu. The Committee of Thirteen continued to meet and to plan the removal from office of Asher Bates and other protégés of Judd. For a time, however, no parades, speeches, or demonstrations disturbed the scene. The remaining months of 1853 passed more or less uneventfully, except for rumors about filibusters, all of which caused alarm before fading into insignificance.

Nonetheless, the American dream was by no means dead, as David Gregg, the newly-appointed United States Commissioner to Hawai'i, discovered on his way to the islands. At San Francisco, Gregg was buttonholed by annexationists. One of his first visitors in Honolulu was Gerrit Judd, who spoke no longer as a cabinet minister but as a convinced annexationist. Judd, in spite of his subversive views, had maintained close liaison with a few of the chiefs. He believed that opposition to the relinquishment of sovereignty centered only upon the two princes, Lot and Alexander. In Judd's opinion, Gregg would be able to negotiate a treaty of annexation if all the major ali'i were offered annuities.

Judd was not Gregg's only visitor. Gregg also talked at length with Wesley Newcomb and William Ladd of the Committee of Thirteen, who told Gregg that they contemplated peaceful agitation to compel the king to cede his sovereignty to America. Failing that, a revolutionary republic would be considered as an alternative. Two days later, Gregg met Garet Ryckman and Richard Bowlin, the former a San Francisco businessman investigating the feasibility of a steamship line, the latter a Honolulu attorney associated with Ryckman. The three men concurred in believing that the Committee of Thirteen was injudicious, and that it was widely criticized in the community. As for annexation independent of the Committee, it was agreed that the Hawaiian government might easily be induced to make an offer. Gregg was without instructions from Washington, and could not move openly, but at least the fears of the chiefs and the commoners should be kept "thoroughly excited" so that annexation might appear attractive by contrast with a filibuster.[111]

On January 9, the first annexation petition of 1854 reached the government. It was signed by fifty-six Honolulu foreigners, under the leadership of Gerrit Judd and Thomas Spencer (a Honolulu merchant who equaled Alexander Cartwright in demonstrative nationalism). A week later Ryckman told Gregg he had engaged Judd to buy a reef property in Honolulu harbor in preparation for the establishment of Ryckman's steamship line. According to Ryckman, Judd described himself as "poor" after a lifetime of government service and ready to earn his $10,000 commission. Within a day or so, Ryckman and his associates sailed for San Francisco, and Gregg's attention returned to the Committee of Thirteen.[112]

The attention of the Hawaiian government was also upon the Committee. King Kauikeaouli believed that his throne was in danger. At a cabinet meeting early in February, he authorized Foreign Minister Wyllie to ascertain, secretly, the terms upon which the United States might discuss annexing the islands. Wyllie was then, and remained thereafter, a strong opponent of any scheme to alienate sovereignty, but, at the king's behest, he conferred with David Gregg, who agreed to negotiate *ad referendum* while awaiting instructions from Washington.

More than six months passed before a treaty was ready for signature. Gregg found the Hawaiian way of conducting business dilatory and timid; the government found the pressure of events at Honolulu intolerable, preventing adequate reflection and the formulation of a consistent policy. One of the basic issues that emerged was the prospective status of native Hawaiians under American rule. British Consul-General Miller and French Consul-Commissioner Perrin, vociferous enemies of annexation, kept up a steady stream of public and private propaganda in the town about American race prejudice and lynch law. The two princes, Lot and Alexander, needed no second-hand warnings on this score: while in the United States in 1849–1850 with Gerrit Judd, they had suffered one or two indignities when they were mistaken for negroes. Both were intransigent foes of an American connection. In the end, a clause stipulating that Hawai'i enter the Union as a state was written into the unsigned treaty.[113]

Wyllie and Gregg began their secret negotiations early in February, 1854. At the same time, the Committee of Thirteen came to life again, posting handbills on the streets calling for a meeting. Gregg smelled treason against the Hawaiian monarchy, not surprisingly, since he had just talked to United States Consul Benjamin Angel, who had come from talking to George Lathrop, who asserted that the Committee now favored revolution rather than annexation. If Hawai'i entered the Union as a state, Lathrop said, then Hawaiians would become American citizens, and the Committee was against natives being treated like white men. To forestall this, the Committee was planning a coup for the summer of 1854, when there would be no American whalers in town, and no man-of-war at the islands. Five hundred stand of arms and two howitzers were to be imported, Californian filibusterers were to be enlisted, and King Kauikeaouli, Prince Alexander, and Governor Kekūanaō'a would be taken into custody and held until a new government was formed.[114]

Late in February, the Hawaiian Privy Council placed $5,000 at the disposal of the Secretary at War (the ubiquitous Wyllie). Thenceforth, natives drilled regularly at Honolulu. Lathrop was unimpressed. He had been watching, so he said, and thought sixteen good men could whip all the king's soldiers. Gregg, who was making little progress in his meetings with Wyllie, grew uneasy as he noticed the presence at Honolulu of a "Colonel" McDonald and a "General" O'Hinton from California, and as every vessel from the west coast brought down a few passengers, "able-bodied and hearty men, who have no business, but are in constant association with the 'Committee of Thirteen' and their adherents."[115]

Early in March, O'Hinton was heard to remark in Lathrop's store that a republic would be established in three weeks. Gregg concluded that Californians were being recruited gradually, in order to avoid all risk from the neutrality laws of the United States. At the first opportunity a blow would be struck.

The town was very tense, and for a few hours one night early in March, it seemed as if the time had come. A ship was seen standing off and on outside the harbor. Rumors ran about that it carried filibusterers, men who would land at a signal from their fellow conspirators ashore and put the natives' houses to the torch. The alarm was sounded, and troops took up defensive positions along the shore. In the morning, it was discovered that the ship was a trader, waiting for good weather to come inside. Everybody laughed, said Gregg, except the government, whose soldiers continued to drill six days a week.[116]

In mid-March, the orthodox annexationists made a bid for the support of Honolulu's natives. Over the noisy objections of the Committee of Thirteen (to which Miller and Perrin added their voices), a clerk in Richard Armstrong's Department of Public Instruction began to circulate a Hawaiian-language paper, the *Nūhou*, filled with articles favoring annexation. A meeting was called at Kawaiaha'o so that the natives might discuss matters. Prince Alexander spoke for moderation. King Kauikeaouli, he said, would never sign away his country without consulting his people; in the meantime, Hawaiians generally should be informed on the subject. The crowds of Hawaiians packed into the church found rational calm impossible. When John 'I'i spoke on behalf of independent sovereignty, they applauded him loudly; when Gerrit Judd spoke for annexation, they hissed him into silence. Judd could not let the matter rest. Later, he went to 'I'i's house, and so vehement did he become that 'I'i ordered him to leave.[117]

Soon afterward, the shrewd researches of Marshal William Parke brought to light a change in the filibusterers' schedule. They had decided to wait until the fall season, and to try then to enlist the aid of American sailors. Gregg believed he could see why. The revolutionaries were too few for an attempt in the near future; their necks might be in danger. "But when the whaling fleet is in port, it will be no hard matter to get 'Jack' into troubles with the police, and then persuade him that he is wronged..." Parke began to gather evidence against the Committee of Thirteen. He heard that they had signed a document pledging the establishment of a new government. He hoped to be able to get hold of the paper; having done that he would simply march the signatories to the fort and "leave consequences to take care of themselves."[118]

In the meantime, the leading members of the Committee and their adherents continued to be bumptious and obnoxious. The mysterious Colonel McDonald from California announced that he wanted to be appointed drillmaster of the native troops, so that when the revolution came he could deploy them to minimize bloodshed. He would "play a friendly part with the King, if he could get into his services, & quickly but effectually help to rid him of the cares of royalty."

Lathrop and his fellow-conspirator, the lawyer J.D. Blair, were no less offensive. They attended the king's birthday levee in mid-March, an act which David Gregg found sufficiently impertinent—they were planning the king's overthrow but accepting his hospitality at the same time. In conversation with Gregg, Lathrop found much to criticize at the levee: the supper was bad, the dancing was bad, everything was bad. The king did not know his own age, said Lathrop; Wyllie fixed the date of his birthday. No native, in fact, knew his own age, not even Bernice Bishop. Lathrop, for his part, could "never endure" being ruled by a king who was not white. Both Lathrop and Blair, Gregg observed, had much to say about "niggers."

Gregg had never been impressed by the leaders of the Committee. Blair he thought a poor lawyer, almost a simpleton, "wise in his own conceit however, and professing all the elements of a great man. He is for revolution and a Republic, in order to find a suitable theatre for his immense abilities!" Lathrop was a good physician, "no doubt," but he thought himself a statesman; the shoemaker, in Gregg's view, should stick to his last. And as for Wesley Newcomb, "he is tolerably learned in Conchology, but otherwise is not remarkably gifted with sense or discretion. A more violent, excitable little & unscrupulous partisan cannot be found on the face of the globe." The committee as a whole were "foolish conspirators, without anything but the desperation which pertained to

Kamehameha I *(HSA)*

Nāhiʻenaʻena *(BM)*

Kamehameha II *(HSA)*

Ka'ahumanu *(HSA)*

Kalanimoku *(HSA)*

Boki and Liliha *(HSA)*

Mataio Kekūanaōʻa, a prominent chief and governor of Oʻahu, with his daughter Victoria Kamāmalu. He was also father of Kamehameha IV and Kamehameha V *(BM)*

Queen Kalama, Kamehameha III,
Princess Victoria Kamāmalu,
Kamehameha IV, Kamehameha V *(BM)*

Kalākaua *(HSA)*

Queen Emma *(HSA)*

Hiram and Sybil Bingham *(HSA)*

Dr. Gerrit Parmele Judd and
Mrs. Laura Fish Judd *(HSA)*

Amos Cooke with daughter Mary Annis *(HMCS Library)*

Charles Reed Bishop and
Bernice P. Bishop *(BM)*

Don Francisco de Paula Marin *(HHS)*

Stephen Reynolds *(HHS)*

Robert Crichton Wyllie *(HSA)*

William Richards *(HSA)*

Early port of Honolulu, 1820s *(BM)*

This R.J. Baker photograph of a painting by an unknown artist shows a view of the king's palace on Beretania Street and the southeastern part of the town, May 26, 1826. *(HSA)*

STREET VIEW AT HONOLULU.

Early 1830s street view of Honolulu showing the protective stone walls on Fort Street. The foreigner in the cart is believed to be Levi Chamberlain. Engraving by A.T. Agate. *(BM)*

Honolulu's waterfront by Lauvergne, showing the harbor near the foot of Nuʻuanu Street, 1836. *(BM)*

This 1837 drawing by Louis-Jules Masselot, "Assembly of Chiefs in Conference," shows Halekauwila Palace in Honolulu, a one-room thatched government house located near Honolulu Fort that was used for executive and judicial meetings during the reign of Kamehameha III. The session in progress concurred the rights of French priests to practice Catholicism in Hawai'i. *(BM)*

In this 1837 engraving by French artist Louis-Jules Masselot, Queen Kīna'u and her retinue of mu'umu'u-clad ladies return from services at Kawaiaha'o Church. When she died just two years later in 1839, the Christian mission lost what Reverend Bingham described as "the kind, modest, firm, and sagacious patroness of the cause of reform at the islands." *(HSA)*

This oil painting by Paul Emmert shows the interior of Honolulu Fort with a group of soldiers presenting arms. With the construction of the Bethel police station and Oahu Prison, the Fort was demolished in 1857. *(HSA)*

Honolulu's famed pā'ū riders were Hawaiian women
in long skirts or pā'ū, 1850s. *(HSA)*

A view of Honolulu from the Catholic church tower
by Paul Emmert, 1850s. *(HHS)*

View of Honolulu from the steeple of Fort Street Church,
looking up Nuʻuanu Valley, 1850s. *(HMCS Library)*

Palace of King Kamehameha, III, 1854. *(BM)*

Looking southwest across Fort Street, Iwilei is far right of center,
by Emmert, 1854. *(HHS)*

Lithograph by George H. Burgess shows Queen Street,
now Fort Street, 1855. *(HSA)*

First photograph of Kawaiahaʻo Church, 1857. *(HMCS)*

Honolulu Harbor, circa 1857. *(unknown)*

Taverns along Hotel Street from Fort Street. *(BM)*

Photo source abbreviations: HSA, Hawai'i State Archives; BM, Bishop Museum;
HMCS Library, Hawaiian Mission Children's Society Library;
HHS, Hawaiian Historical Society

the character of Catiline & his Associates."[119]

All this time, Gregg and Wyllie had been carrying on their secret negotiations. At mid-year these ceased to be secret. Honolulu, in both official and private circles, was notorious for leakages of confidential matters; and Gregg found, late in May 1854, that Gerrit Judd knew all about the annexation treaty.

About the same time, British Consul-General Miller learned enough to know that something was afoot; by the end of the summer he too had the important facts in his hands. Gregg was now in difficulties, and, to add to his troubles, Honolulu's natives shied away from the idea of annexation as the Nebraska question, being argued bitterly throughout the United States, made its way into the Honolulu newspapers. Miller, who had always maintained that Americans were to a man racists and slaveowners, seized upon this as a means of intensifying his campaign against annexation. If the Hawaiians signed away their sovereignty, he said on innumerable occasions, they would be delivering themselves up to a country which practiced race hatred, slavery, vigilante-ism, and lynch law, which was filled with crime and corruption, and which had a congenital hatred of aristocracy.[120]

As July 4 approached, the opposed factions of Americanism, annexationist and filibusterer, fought for control of the anniversary celebrations. The committee on orations proposed J.D. Blair as speaker of the day, but the organizing meeting at large rejected the nomination. When the question was put to a vote, Blair was found to have only two supporters—George Lathrop, and A.J. McDuffie, the volunteer militiaman who had been Lathrop's associate in the early moves to oust Judd from the ministry in 1853. Instead of Blair, the meeting selected David Gregg to deliver the oration, and Stephen Reynolds to read the Declaration of Independence. Gregg thought these were good choices. In his opinion, if the people of Honolulu were given the idea that Blair represented American views, the prospects of annexation would have been killed then and there. Gregg and Wyllie had just placed a version of the treaty before Prince Alexander, who was considering some amendments. Public demonstrations, therefore, should be handled carefully.[121]

Gregg worked hard over his July 4 address. On the eve of the speech, he was pleased to find that he had a draft which read better than he had anticipated. He did not expect the British or French residents to like it, but he thought nonetheless that he was justified in trying to arouse a strong national feeling among American citizens at Honolulu. As he saw things, there had been too much subserviency to British arrogance; besides, he hoped to combat Miller's "insidious and unfair" prejudicing of Hawaiian minds on the subject of annexation.[122]

The July 4 procession was even more elaborate than usual, as Honolulu's Americans staged a splendidly symbolic parade:

> A car, decorated with evergreens, in which were seated thirty-two girls of American parentage, dressed in white, wreathed in flowers, each bearing the name of an American state on her sash, in large gold letters, was drawn by a power unseen. Next followed "Young America," a company of very young men in uniform, with another triumphal chariot, on which was placed a beautiful boy, the very personification of health, strength, and beauty. "Young Hawaii" was in tow, and represented by a boat gaily trimmed, in which were eight young native lads, fancifully dressed, and carelessly eating sugar cane.[123]

Gregg's oration, heard by a large crowd and reported fully in the press, altered the attitudes of the native population not at all. It did, however, goad Consul-General Miller to new heights of choler. The old Britisher had suffered a severe illness early in 1854, and soon he began, in the opinion of Wyllie (who had practiced medicine for some years before coming to Hawai'i), to show symptoms of softening of the brain.[124] This did not inhibit Miller from pressing the anti-annexationist cause. On the contrary, it gave his vehement utterances the obsessive urgency and sincerity of the slightly insane.

Gregg pushed on with his treaty negotiations, hoping to be able to lay a draft before the Hawaiian legislature in the session of 1854. Miller persisted with his opposition, arranging, among other things, for native members of the House of Representatives to bring forward motions opposing annexation. J.D. Blair and George Lathrop visited California at the end of July. Gerrit Judd went about town soliciting signatures in favor of annexation. John 'I'i and the high chief Pākī continued to be adamant against an American connection. Prince Alexander seemed to be wavering slightly. King Kauikeaouli, who had been for months in a state of drunkenness and ill-health, drank on. Yet another memorial reached the government from nineteen foreigners at Honolulu, men who had been depending for commercial reasons upon annexation, and who were dismayed at the slowness of the negotiations. At the beginning of September, disturbing rumors came once more out of California, and another mysterious military officer, this one named Colonel Wilkes, arrived at Honolulu. Wilkes stayed only a few days, but before leaving he remarked to David Gregg that the islands would soon have a government with which a treaty of annexation might be negotiated.[125]

At the customs house early in September, a box of pistols was discovered in some goods being landed. This was sufficient to bring out the native troops, who remained under arms all night. Such alarums and excursions were very frustrating to Gregg, who had drawn up a satisfactory treaty, approved, as he said, by the Hawaiian cabinet and the all-important Prince Alexander, but delayed because it was necessary that the king be consulted and the king could not be consulted because he was in a "peculiar condition." Gregg regarded the situation as serious. Subversion of the government was within the power of Honolulu's foreigners; an outbreak was likely at any moment. Placed as he was, Gregg was ready to accept a provisional transfer of sovereignty as soon as possible, in the expectation that Californians would then migrate to the islands in large numbers and make Hawai'i safe from Great Britain or France.[126]

The tension perceptible everywhere in Honolulu pushed Miller to new heights of eloquence. In a formal address to the king on September 18, he spoke of rumors of annexation coming from the United States, though not from the American government, and of alleged filibusters being prepared in California. Miller put no faith in the filibuster reports. He believed they were fabricated by annexationists, to frighten the Hawaiian king into abandoning his throne. Letters about cut-throats, thieves, robbers, and Frenchmen with designs on the kingdom were simply got up for the occasion; there was no truth in them. As for relinquishing sovereignty to the United States, Miller could see nothing in California that would make a good example for Honolulu or the islands generally. Taxes on property were outrageous at San Francisco, and yet the value of property was nullified by squatters. Americans talked a great deal about freedom, but not at all about slavery, squatting, filibusterism, and lynch law.[127]

After months of strain and uncertainty, the issue of annexation came to a head in November, 1854. On November 11, David Gregg, having observed for some weeks what he described as a threatening build-up of Californians at Honolulu, alerted Wyllie to the gravity of the situation. Dangerous men were in town, according to Gregg, armed with revolvers and other weapons. They would be joined by as many as three hundred residents, and more than three hundred other filibusterers were poised to leave California for the islands. Should the government resist, public and private property might be looted and the town set afire.

Gregg and Captain Dornin of USS *Portsmouth* (one of several foreign warships in port at the time) advised Wyllie on November 12 that an instant surrender of sovereignty to the United States was the only way to escape violence. The two Americans suggested that a deputation led by Gerrit Judd should be allowed to urge the wisdom of this course upon the king. Instead, Wyllie referred the warning to the Cabinet Council. It seemed clear that Wyllie considered Gregg and Dornin to be practicing polite blackmail. Wyllie had always been an opponent of annexation. Now he saw a chance to extricate himself and the government he served from an intolerable predicament. He wrote hasty notes to the representatives of France, Great Britain, and the United States— Perrin, Miller, and Gregg—asking for guarantees of protection should a filibuster be attempted. In the harbor were the *Portsmouth* and another American man-of-war. Also present, however, were the French *Artemise*, and the British *Trincomalee*. Gregg and Dornin had no option but to honor Wyllie's request. Having secured his tripartite guarantee, Wyllie returned enthusiastically to his favorite notion of a Hawaiian yeoman army. Quickly, he drummed up a local force, "infantry, artillery and outer island men available with short axes, cutlasses, swords and spears for close fighting." Clothed in military might, Wyllie halted all treaty negotiations, until "they could be honorably resumed, after every trace of coercion had been removed."[128]

Negotiations were never resumed. Honolulu remained in virtual suspended animation until December 8. On that day, the Cabinet Council met and composed a proclamation for signature by the king. It was announced that, in the face of threats to the kingdom, aid had been requested from Great Britain, France, and the United States. As a result, Hawaiian independence was "more firmly established than ever before."[129] The annexation issue, and attendant fears of filibusters, were diminished to nothing.

Honolulu's agitated official community, and its enemies both noisy and quiet, had supplied most of the actors in the unresolved drama, but perhaps more important than Gregg, Wyllie, Miller, Perrin, Judd, Lathrop, or J.D. Blair, were two men who, for months at a time in 1854, were not in Honolulu at all—Chief Justice William Lee and Prince Alexander Liholiho. Lee, from the beginning, had opposed annexation as strongly as had Wyllie. His strategy, however, was somewhat different from that of the Foreign Minister, and more subtle. During the prolonged negotiations between Gregg and Wyllie, Lee lingered on the outer islands, ostensibly occupied with legal business arising from his post as Chief Justice. All drafts of the treaty were sent to Lee. He was a conscious agent for procrastination, believing that, as long as there was a possibility of annexation, the United States would not permit a filibuster. At the same time, Lee advocated a statehood clause in the treaty, on the correct assumption that Hawai'i's demand for admission as a state of the Union would prove unpalatable to the government of the United States. Filibusters, then, would be impossible as long as the United States had a treaty in view; and the treaty would never be ratified by the United States as long as it contained a statehood clause. With any luck, the islands might emerge independent once more, and the future of the Hawaiian race would be secure at least for a time. Willingly associated with Lee in this devious plan was Prince Alexander, who absented himself deliberately from Honolulu more than once, knowing that no decision would be made without his consent, and therefore making his consent all but impossible to achieve. Wyllie, in the thick of things at Honolulu, was ready to allow Lee to shape the course of events at a distance and by indirection. In the end, Lee succeeded as completely as he could have wished.[130]

King Kauikeaouli had put his signature to the declaration of December 8 in an infirm, shaky, disconnected hand. It was probably the last time he signed an official paper. He died at Honolulu on December 15, 1854. Wyllie hastened to have his successor, Alexander Liholiho, proclaimed king as Kamehameha IV. Within an hour of Kauikeaouli's death, Governor Kekūanaō'a took a company of soldiers to the principal street corners of the town. While minute guns were fired on Punchbowl, the death of the old king and the accession of the new were announced. Together with Kauikeaouli, annexationism was dead. The Committee of Thirteen, too, lost its esprit de corps, and those of its members who remained at Honolulu began to reconstrue the history of their organization into a chronicle of serious-minded, well-intentioned, mild, orthodox American patriotism. Meanwhile, the young Kamehameha IV was creating a new focus of power in the government and a new style of life in the town; and cabinet members, foreign residents, and natives alike turned "with deference to the rising sun."[131]

CHAPTER 7

The New Society

In the reign of Alexander Liholiho, Kamehameha IV, Honolulu achieved for the first time something like style. Previously, social consensus had existed only in the city's rare periods of calm, disappearing without trace when crises (real or imagined) overtook the town. Now, by contrast, there emerged a conscious attention to ways of doing things in common which went beyond past experience. There became discernible, in fact, the beginnings of a concern for manners.

It would be misleading to exaggerate the importance and extent of this development. Courtesy by no means replaced bad temper as a prevailing note in the city. On occasion, however, politeness was added to the range of tonalities detectable in society, and for this reason alone the reign of Kamehameha IV would be worth marking as a period in the life of Honolulu, one which moreover failed to outlive the king.

Many circumstances contributed to the growth of new social attitudes. In the eighteen-thirties and forties, diplomatic issues had intruded all too often upon the local scene. Now, after fifteen troubled years ending in 1854, many old arguments were resolved or at least reduced to quiescence; and new problems of the first magnitude, though developing, were not yet sufficiently pressing to affect Honolulu roughly and directly. Of all diplomatic causes dating from earlier decades, only the matter of the French treaty continued in the later fifties to agitate the Hawaiian government disproportionately, and even this no longer threatened Honolulu's security. Wyllie and Perrin debated stormily still, but behind closed doors and without engaging the town. One local consequence of the diplomatic lull was that strenuous nationalism ceased to be urged incessantly by the foreigners of Honolulu. The town could begin to dispose itself more comfortably—less in emotional armed camps whose bounds were those of nationality than in pleasanter associations which, though based on nationality in many cases, could nevertheless find ways of coexisting, and which were fluid enough to give the town a semblance of the cosmopolitanism it had resisted thus far. Once again, this was not a definitive movement. National lines could, and sometimes did, reappear in all their old strictness. But at the very least it might be said that there occurred far fewer hostile infringements of that well-developed sense of territoriality which distinguished the nationality groups; and, further, there might be descried faint glimmerings of community feeling as opposed to, and superior to, the old and grudging agreements once accomplished after exhausting struggles by veto groups.

These developments were aided in part by a more sophisticated system of identifications working among the foreign residents of the town, many of whom had spent the better part of a lifetime at Honolulu and were coming to think of it as home for themselves and their families. If lines of demarcation remained clearly in evidence, at least their presence was noted more quietly and regarded more politely, with the consequence that occasions upon which the lines might be crossed safely became more numerous.[1]

The absence of important diplomatic issues in turn gave Hawai'i's royal court a chance to become what it should always have been—a place for the formal expression of good feeling. Since the mid-forties, court life had been regulated ostensibly by the Code of Etiquette of the Congress of Vienna, but there were unseemly breaches of protocol from time to time, as when foreign representatives noisily and forcibly demanded access to the king rather than being content to deal with his appointed ministers, or when the British Consul-General and the Hawaiian Attorney-General came to blows at a levee. Now, with the business of diplomacy becoming less a struggle and more a formality, court life could become at once more secure in its very existence and more elaborate in its arrangements, leading the United States Commissioner to remark that if any diplomat should die at Honolulu, it would be of a "fit of etiquette."

At the same time, changes in the composition of Honolulu's official community helped to open new social vistas. Since the end of the Great Revival, the town's New Englanders had been gradually losing their dominance in politics and in social life. With the accession of Alexander Liholiho, their displacement became an incontrovertible fact, manifesting itself in many ways. The exclusivists became the excluded.

The king himself lent support to this trend. He was, on coming to the throne at twenty, strongly anti-missionary. Gerrit Judd, former missionary and former cabinet minister, put it unkindly when he wrote some years later that Alexander Liholiho, "educated by the Mission, most of all things dislikes the Mission. Having been compelled to be good when a boy, he is determined not to be good as a man. Driven out by morning prayer meeting, Wednesday evening meeting, monthly concert, Sabbath school, long sermons, and daily exhortations, his heart is hardened to a degree unknown to the heathen. Naturally he chooses associates whose feelings and practices are in union with his own."[2]

There was far more complexity and sophistication in Alexander Liholiho's personality than Judd would acknowledge, and the king was moved by considerations more subtle than mere anti-Calvinist animus; but the royal fiat, in fact, did remove a number of mission-affiliated government officers in 1855, and death took more during the next few years. It was by no means a clean sweep: several Americans, among them some New Englanders, remained in office. New England leadership, however, was clearly at an end. In addition, the reign of Kamehameha IV coincided, almost exactly, with an administrative re-organization which greatly lessened the dependence of the Sandwich Island Mission on the American Board in Boston, and which culminated in the dissolution of the mission and the establishment of self-sustaining churches in the islands. Many former missionaries stayed on as pastors of native congregations, and their common voice made it possible still to refer to a "mission" group in the community. Many others, however, left the church to go into business, and in doing so they were led to make social concessions of a sort that would scarcely have been approved by Ladd & Co. in the forties, and certainly not by the mission fathers.[3]

No single group replaced the New Englanders as self-proclaimed leaders in government and town, and the varied origins of the new policy-makers encouraged compromises at the local level. Further, the admixture of Englishmen, Europeans, and non-puritan Americans in places of power and influence meant that Calvinist social practice ceased to be mandatory, commanded deference no longer, and became in the end positively unfashionable. Doctrinaire Protestants continued to fight to define the terms of polite behavior, but others at Honolulu came to value polish above simple, sober morality. The mission group, unyielding, found itself in time outnumbered and outmoded, its definitions now those of a passé minority rather than a powerful elite. Its members were faced with the choice of joining the dance of life at court or taking their leave. Most chose to depart. On rural O'ahu and in some districts of the outer islands, the old morality was preached still with unabated fervor, but in the generation which began with the accession of Alexander Liholiho, Honolulu ceased to belong, even formally, to the God of the Calvinists.

Forced onto the defensive, and confronted by opponents far more urbane, devious, disarming, and successful than those encountered in the early evangelical period, when right and wrong had seemed dramatically distinct, Honolulu's Protestants did not accept their dislocation quietly. Thenceforth, the times were perpetually out of joint for them, and the end of their term as handers-down of the social law opened a period in which they were identifiable primarily as disturbers of the social peace. In the failure of their protracted struggle against the liberal establishment could be seen the victory of a new social style.

Despite the government's best efforts, controversies reminiscent of the old days occasionally troubled Honolulu. In 1856, Honolulu Police Magistrate Jeremiah Evarts Chamberlain (son of the pioneer missionary Levi Chamberlain) wrongly ordered the whipping of George Bailey, an American seaman charged with attempted theft, but not properly convicted. United States Commissioner David Gregg took the matter to the highest diplomatic levels. Chamberlain resigned, and the Hawaiian government grudgingly paid compensation. Four years later, Gregg's successor, James Borden, waved a knife at Henry Whitney, editor of the *Pacific Commercial Advertiser,* in the course of investigations into the American consular hospital at Honolulu. At about the same time, French Commissioner Emile Perrin seized upon the testamentary bequest of a semi-literate Catholic foreigner, Jose Nadal, to create a teapot storm over the right of the Catholic Bishop of Honolulu to inherit under a will brought before the probate court. And when days were dull, the city's press reverted to the religious wrangling of earlier decades.[4]

Nevertheless, Alexander Liholiho's reign was marked by an essay at conscious elegance, as has been observed. The French language began to be heard in polite discourse, a circumstance unthinkable a generation before. The new photographic *cartes de visite* were much admired. Social functions were designated *à la française: levées, matinées, soirées, thés dansantes.* Invitations requested RSVPs. In this somewhat rarefied atmosphere, even the French Commissioner experienced some difficulty in arranging parties that were sufficient *soigné,* and derogatory comments circulated in the official community concerning the quality of his duty-free wines and brandies.

When contretemps did occur at the highest levels of society in Honolulu, they were *scandales* rather than diplomatic *causes* of the kind so familiar earlier. Three affairs in the reign of Alexander Liholiho were of particular importance. The first two, which provided a great deal of titillation for the community at large, demonstrated as well that the kingdom could manage its own affairs and those of foreigners much more firmly than had been the case in the forties and early fifties. The third involved the king himself, and brought in its train a social and religious re-alignment which contributed to Honolulu's strong drift away from American Protestantism.

The first of the affairs alternated between melodrama and bedroom farce. The chief actor was Chancellor Landais of the French Consulate at Honolulu, who had earned the reputation of a lady-killer. Throughout the early months of 1855, there had been rumors of liaisons with several ladies, young and not so young. Then, in May, it was asserted that he had been keeping assignations with the wife of one of the town's most successful American merchants. Natives working in kalo patches near Landais' house had observed the lady arriving and departing two or three times a week; so had some of the merchant's brethren among the Odd Fellows. There were private discussions in the official community about the best way of clearing up the matter, but nothing was done immediately. Gossip about this and other peccadilloes of Landais continued to flourish until the end of 1855.

One night at the turn of the year, French Commissioner Perrin was strolling about town. He happened to pass the Alakea Street home of the lady in question, where he saw Landais on the sidewalk blowing kisses to a figure in a window above. Perrin crossed to the other side of the street, but Landais caught him up and said that a French diplomat had come to a "pretty pass" when he "condescended to play the spy." Perrin replied that the French chancellor was "handsomely engaged," but that this was perhaps not very strange for a "Mulâtre Dominique." With that, Landais took his sword-cane to Perrin.

By chance, Marshal William Parke was passing. He intervened, but not before Perrin was bruised and bleeding. At Perrin's request, Landais was put in custody, and although Landais applied for a writ of habeas corpus, the Honolulu courts denied him, ruling that the affair was a matter for the French government, and that Perrin, being Landais' superior, was within his rights in seeking the temporary confinement of his subordinate.

Perrin and the local authorities agreed that no good purpose would be served by trying Landais for assault and battery at Honolulu, since a court case would only drag the compromised lady and her husband through the mud. Landais was duly sent back to France. With him went a sheaf of documents and the sword-cane in question (when Parke had seen it, the sword was hard to remove from its sheath, but Perrin apparently cleaned, sharpened, and oiled it before shipping it home). The American merchant left for the United States with his wife and family. Perrin alone remained in Honolulu, to spread the story that Landais some years before had committed incest with his daughter, that his wife had found out about it and deserted him, and that this was the reason why Landais had left France to come to Hawai'i in the first place.[5]

The second scandal of Alexander Liholiho's reign involved the Princess Victoria Kamāmalu, daughter of Kekūanaō'a, sister of Alexander Liholiho and Lot, heiress of Ka'ahumanu, ward of John 'Ī'ī, a product of the Chiefs' Children's School, and the intended bride of David Kalākaua. In mid-January, 1857, Prince Lot had entertained as a dinner guest at the palace the Honolulu auctioneer Marcus Monsarrat, British-born,

Hawaiian-naturalized, and a married man. Not long after Monsarrat had taken his departure, Lot, alerted by a servant, found him in Victoria's room with his clothing in some disarray. Lot told Monsarrat that if he remained in Honolulu it would be at the risk of his life. Monsarrat sailed for San Francisco on January 21; three days later the story became public and created a sensation in the town.

Though he was decidedly *persona non grata*, Monsarrat returned quietly to Honolulu in May. As soon as his presence was discovered, the king commanded him to leave forever. Monsarrat refused, declaring that he would never go voluntarily. Thereupon, the king ordered his arrest. Monsarrat was brought to the palace and confined overnight. Rumors reached Wyllie and others that some of the town's foreigners would attempt to rescue Monsarrat, but nothing happened. Early next morning, the prisoner was marched down to the harbor and set on board a ship which had been specially detained for the purpose. Monsarrat was to be banished for life on Alexander Liholiho's initiative and responsibility. Legalistic arguments might have been made against the king's course of action, but no one advanced them. The vindication of royal honor was all-important.[6]

According to David Gregg, Alexander Liholiho at one time had said that the befouler of his sister's reputation should have been shot down like a dog.[7] Within two years, however, the king, happy in his own domesticity, yielded to the pleas of Monsarrat's wife and reduced the term of Monsarrat's banishment from life to seven years.[8]

Just a few months after this royal gesture, the king shot and seriously wounded his own private secretary, Henry Neilson, in what he believed to be a defense of the virtue of his wife, Queen Emma.

Neilson, a young American of good family, had come to Honolulu in 1850. Quite quickly he joined the small circle of close personal friends gathered about the king and queen. In 1855, Neilson was made private secretary to the king with the rank of major. The relationship was more than official. Neilson was as much the king's drinking and travelling companion as anything else; and he shared with Charles Gordon Hopkins that extension of royal immunity which permitted bohemian members of the official group to take native mistresses.[9]

Alexander Liholiho, in 1859, was in his mid-twenties, a flashingly intelligent, charming, and handsome man, but less than robust, and given to occasional dark moods. He suffered frequent attacks of asthma, and for this and other reasons of general health he made it a habit to leave Honolulu as often as affairs of state allowed. Following the old royal practice, he travelled between islands with a convivial entourage. Many of his happiest months were spent in relaxation at places such as Kailua-Kona on Hawai'i and Lahaina on Maui, where his retinue occupied many houses in close proximity, indulging in a great deal of reciprocal visiting and entertaining.

In September, 1859, the king was at Lahaina, disporting himself with his friends in the seclusion of a cluster of grass huts and western houses which had been a playground of Hawaiian royalty for decades. The diversions available were mild enough, perhaps even boring. Somehow, within the close-knit group (just how has never been made clear), a suggestion arose that Neilson was trespassing on royal prerogative with Emma. The king, angry and mortified, took a small boat, loaded with liquor, out to sea for almost forty-eight hours, then came back at night, picked up a brace of pistols, walked to Neilson's house, found him on the verandah in his night-clothes ready to retire, and shot him in the chest at close range.

Within a day or two, Alexander Liholiho, stricken by conscience and alcoholic remorse, had established to his own satisfaction that Neilson and Emma were guiltless. This, of course, did not restore Neilson to health. The chest wound in itself was serious, but not immediately fatal; Neilson's general condition, however, was less than sound, and for the rest of his short life he remained an invalid, dying of consumption and related ailments in 1862. In the months following the shooting, the king was distraught. He prepared to abdicate, but was dissuaded by his advisers. His moods went up and down with the doctors' reports on Neilson, and his own health declined under the continual strain.[10] There was no question of legal expiation of guilt: formal proceedings were never discussed, much less initiated. Perhaps Alexander Liholiho could find solace in religion.

Here were the real origins of the Episcopal church in Honolulu. If the king were seeking religious consolation, it would not be to Congregationalism that he would turn. He had rejected long ago the spareness of New England Protestantism. By contrast, the Episcopal church was attractive, with its rich ritualism and general panoply, its hierarchical organization, and its close attachment to the monarchical polity of England. During his stay at London in the course of his world tour in 1849–1850, Alexander Liholiho had been greatly impressed, and when in 1856 he married Emma at Kawaiaha'o Church he directed the officiating minister, Richard Armstrong, to use the Church of England service.[11]

In 1859 the aging Robert Wyllie, too, was looking toward religion. At the time of the Neilson shooting, Wyllie was dangerously ill. He did not recover his health until early in 1860. He had thought himself close to death, and in these straits he had renewed his old enthusiasm for the Episcopal church, of which he had been a staunch advocate since his appointment to the Hawaiian cabinet.

By December, 1859, the king, with the support of his wife and of Wyllie, was ready to aid in setting up an Episcopal church at Honolulu. He offered to donate a site for the church, together with $1,000 a year to pay a clergyman. This was not to be considered as establishing the faith as the state religion of Hawai'i. The constitution of the kingdom placed all forms of worship on an equal footing, and thus no governmental appropriation could be made for the new church. But the king and queen, like other citizens, were free under this same constitutional provision to choose and to patronize any religious faith.[12]

The Hawaiian consul at London, Manley Hopkins (brother of Charles Gordon Hopkins), enlisted the help of prominent Anglican churchmen. An interested response led to the enlargement of the proposed mission from one headed by a simple clergyman to a bishopric. The Reverend Thomas Nettleship Staley was selected to fill the post. He arrived at Honolulu with his assistants in October, 1862.

The Episcopalian clergymen found themselves plunged directly into controversy. American Protestants at Honolulu had been watching the development of Anglican plans. In the beginning, when it had been assumed that the Anglican missionary would be a low church clergyman, there had been lukewarm approval. When it was learned that a bishopric was contemplated, and when it was further made known that Staley and others connected with the mission were in fact the highest of High Church Anglicans, calling themselves Reformed Catholics, coldness appeared in Protestant comments. For a decade, the work of Episcopalians at Honolulu was complicated greatly by unrelenting Calvinist opposition. The situation paralleled in many ways earlier quarrels over the Roman Catholic "invasion" of the islands.[13]

Alexander Liholiho and Emma, for their part, had awaited eagerly the despatch of Staley. The bishop was to have baptized their four-year-old son, Prince Albert, the apple of their eye and the darling of the native population. Since Kamehameha I, no reigning Hawaiian monarch had produced an heir who survived to maturity, and hopes for the perpetuation of the dynasty were thus locked up in the life of the young Haku o Hawai'i. Queen Victoria had consented to act as godmother by proxy for the little boy. A silver christening cup was sent to Honolulu in the care of the newly-appointed British Commissioner, William Webb Follett Synge.

Synge arrived at Honolulu in advance of Staley—on August 22, 1862, five days after the bishop and his party left Southampton on their voyage out. Synge found the Prince of Hawai'i fatally ill. Since birth, the little boy had been amazingly sturdy. He had travelled extensively with his parents, and be played vigorously and with good humor at all times. Just before Synge landed, however, a mysterious illness struck the prince: sunstroke, some thought, or "brain fever," as others said. The desperate efforts of the king's physicians were without avail. The prince was baptized hurriedly according to the rites of the Church of England (E.W. Clark of Kawaiaha'o performed the service). He died on August 27, leaving an anguished father and mother and a desolated Hawaiian community.[14]

Bishop Staley arrived to take up his work before the general grief had subsided. Emma was baptized within two weeks of his landing; and at the end of November, 1862, the royal couple were confirmed together as members of the newly-chartered Hawaiian Reformed Catholic Church. Wyllie followed them two days later, along with Attorney-General Charles Coffin Harris and Supreme Court Justice George M. Robertson. In December, David Kalākaua was confirmed. He took a seat on the first synod with Governor Kekūanaō'a.[15]

The first Reformed Catholic services were held in a small building at Nu'uanu and Kukui Streets, formerly used by Methodists. The site donated by Alexander Liholiho for a permanent building was on Emma Street, and there in 1867 a "pro-cathedral" was dedicated. The church's headquarters in Honolulu have been on that site ever since.

Within a few years of his arrival, Staley became a member of the Privy Council. There was also, at one time, a move to have him appointed President of the national Board of Education. The Reformed Catholics' own education program was quite energetic from the beginning, with boys' and girls' schools in Honolulu and elsewhere. Successor schools still exist today: 'Iolani School for boys, which grew out of St. Alban's College; and St. Andrew's Priory for girls, both at Honolulu.[16]

The tone of Staley's approach to religion continued to be offensive to Honolulu's Protestants. The bishop was quick to learn Hawaiian, and the king himself translated the Book of Common Prayer into the native language. As well as a good part of the official community, then, the Reformed Catholics hoped to attract natives, and services were held in English and Hawaiian. Native delight in theatricality was well met in the new church, with its chanted liturgy and rich vestments. Protestant natives could be found who ridiculed the whole business (one told his pastor that the bishop looked like a pupule—a crazy man—with an auction flag on his back); but in early competition with other denominations Staley did well. For quite a time, his church was crowded at each of three Sunday services.[17]

The social policy of the Reformed Catholics was very different from that of the Protestants. Temperance, so dear to Congregationalist hearts, was irrelevant to Staley. Sexual morality was taught with a less circumscribed view of what might be good for Hawaiians. As for the rest, Staley in his first months attended a hula at Waikīkī, and later became a leading advocate of the revival of native observances as part of the funeral rites of deceased ali'i.[18]

Such a combination of evident religious ritualism and apparent social retrogression was too much for the Protestants. They fought Staley as hard as they could from their position on the perimeter of official society, and were pleased to note that the Roman Catholics of the town also opposed the Reformed Catholics. During the reign of Alexander Liholiho and for a few years thereafter, Protestant agitation had little effect. When the king died on November 30, 1863, the palace grounds were filled with weeping natives, and while the body lay in state, memorial chants and dances were performed. Bishop Staley, in arranging the order of the funeral procession, relegated Protestant ministers to a place they found insulting. In consequence only one, E.W. Clark, attended the service, and he went, so he said, mostly because he wanted to see the Reformed Catholic church, which he had never visited. He reported that "nothing could be more popish" than the rites observed by Staley. Clark found the display of the bishop's crozier and "all the other flummery" to be "not a little disgusting."[19] The Protestants were humiliated further when, upon the death of Princess Victoria Kamāmalu in mid-1866, Staley assumed prerogatives which seemed perilously near to those of an established church. Henry Parker, the young pastor of Kawaiaha'o, conducted services at his meeting-house (Victoria Kamāmalu had been a member of his congregation), but Bishop Staley forbade Parker to pray at the graveside. Staley claimed the right to bury all members of the royal family, whether they were Reformed Catholics or not. He insisted that the royal cemetery in Nu'uanu was consecrated ground, and had been from the time of Alexander Liholiho's funeral. None but Reformed Catholics might officiate there.[20]

Sharp and hurtful definitions such as these rebounded finally upon the Reformed Catholic Church at Honolulu. Religious extremism of one kind had been injurious to the fortunes of the Congregationalists; now, at the other extreme, Staley began to experience difficulties. A lurking suspicion remained in the minds of many foreigners at Honolulu that the Reformed Catholics were tools of British policy, that a church-state alliance was formed by Alexander Liholiho (and continued by his brother-successor Lot Kamehameha) with a view to a close British connection. The journey of the widowed Queen Emma to England in the mid-sixties did much to strengthen these fears, and the *Advertiser* in particular played them up, beyond anything justified by facts. Thus, attacks upon the Reformed Catholics came not from American Protestants alone, but from the numerous American republicans in the town. Then too, the High Church tone of the bishop's Anglicanism offended many members of his own flock, who, as it, happened, were predominantly

Low Church. It was a very complex situation, but by the end of the sixties Staley had clearly worn out his welcome, even with Emma. While he was away on a visit to England, a large faction in his congregation petitioned to have him removed.

They did not agree with Staley on doctrine or practice, so they reported to the Society for the Propagation of the Gospel. Nor could they tolerate the ritualism of Staley's deputy, Thomas Harris. Staley faced an impossible state of affairs upon his return to the islands. He resigned in May, 1870. His final voyage to England was linked with a scheme to surrender the Episcopal Church at Honolulu to American control. This, as much as the temporary failure of the mission, angered the dowager queen Emma, who resented the idea that the church might be passed from hand to hand. "The incapacity of one man at its head," she wrote, "need not be a reason used to move its source or foundation...of course our late Bishop would do his uttermost to bring about such a change it would be just the thing to cover his own disgrace as it were of expulsion from his diocese he said as much to me two or three times during some threatening conversations before he left here..."[21]

Emma was more than ready to lay responsibility for the fiasco at Staley's door, and it may well be true that the bishop and his superiors in England misjudged matters. Had Staley been a Low Church-man, the new mission might have been able to take some sort of middle ground in the town's religious life. As it was, the Protestants and Catholics made things difficult for the fledgling church, and internal strife over forms of worship completed its roster of troubles.[22]

Honolulu's Episcopalian church survived, without the political and social standing it had enjoyed under the sponsorship of Alexander Liholiho and Emma. The town's Protestants were content with substantive victory. Their satisfaction, however, was limited virtually to this single instance. Church dogma and practice were not the only fields in which they tried to prevent change during the later fifties and the sixties. They were vigorous and acrimonious, but far less successful, in attempting to assert leadership in matters of moral concern such as the theater, social dancing, liquor, and prostitution.

The Protestant mission, from the beginning, had been stringent in its condemnation of the drama, regarding western theater as only slightly less corrupting than the Hawaiian hula. Not so much because of this as because of the inadequate resources of Honolulu's isolated white community, organized theater did not appear until 1834, when a group of young Americans (most of them Unitarians) founded the "Oahu Amateur Theatre." King Kauikeaouli, in the midst of his moral revolt, permitted the actors to use his grass palace for their first performance of "Raising the Wind," and even helped with the stage management. The Theatre moved later to the dining room of the well-known restaurant of Major Thomas Warren, where performances were given informally for several months. The mission kept up a steady proscriptive barrage, but the theater attracted good houses, which included natives as well as whites, indiscriminately seated.

In 1836, the "Friends of the Theatre" broached the subject of a permanent house for their company, but the king, by then allowing the Christian chiefess Kīna'u to make most decisions for him, would not give approval to a proposed subscription drive. The building was never constructed. Later in the thirties, most of the people associated with the group—the trader William Hinckley and his wife Charlotte; the anti-mission printer Stephen Mackintosh of the *Sandwich Island Gazette;* Charles Rand Smith and his wife Harriet—left Honolulu for one reason or another.[23]

A decade later, interest in theater was sufficient to bring into being the Oahu Thespian Association (whose members were mostly Americans and Englishmen). First performances were held on Maunakea Street, in a building large enough to seat seventy-five in boxes and two hundred in the pit. Petitions for a permanent site were received favorably by the king and the Privy Council. Gerrit Judd abstained from voting, but King Kauikeaouli and other important people in the community bought stock in a company formed to build and run a theater. Missionary protests achieved nothing. The "devil's playhouse," or Hale Diabolo, as the Protestants urged native Christians to call it, was attended reasonably well, and when the Royal Hawaiian Theatre was erected in 1848 at Hotel and Alakea Streets, audiences continued to be satisfactory.[24]

Thenceforth, Honolulu's theaters were never without royal patronage. Amateur performances were given particular encouragement in the late fifties by Alexander Liholiho and Emma, who sometimes took part in musical concerts and excerpts from opera.[25] Determinants of success in the theatrical world, in fact, were economic rather than moral or even social. One after another, the theatrical companies of the city encountered financial difficulties: the Thespians, the Royal Hawaiian Theatre, Foley's Varieties, and a number of independent managers.

Nonetheless, a great many famous actors and singers passed through Honolulu, especially in the late forties when both California and Australia were booming with gold rushes. Edwin Booth, early in his career, was at Honolulu for a month with a company of Shakespeareans. Booth was not yet a recognized star, and some of his daytime hours were spent with a bucket of poi and a brush, sticking posters on street corners. All the same, Honolulu saw his Hamlet before most of America did. Lola

Montez touched briefly at the port, en route to the Australian diggings and their showers of gold, but she could not find time to perform in Honolulu. In the wake of these and other celebrities came scores of second-rankers and unknowns, bringing with them snippets from Shakespeare, gems from opera, moralistic drama and farce, and a wide range of specialty acts—sword-swallowers, flame-eaters, living skeletons, Chinese tumblers, glass-blowers, trick riders, Swiss bell-ringers, jugglers, india-rubber men, magicians, mesmerists, and electro-magnetists. As always and everywhere, public taste was heavily in favor of frivolous entertainment, and the lot of the operatic soprano or the Shakespearean reader was not a happy one. The natives of Honolulu would break down fences to get to a circus, and minstrel shows almost always did well; but the tragedian Walter Montgomery committed suicide because his talents went unrewarded.[26]

By the sixties, all but the most intransigent in the mission community had conceded defeat on the question of theater. In fact, the flow of influence was in the other direction. The mission group had always been willing enough to allow church buildings to be used for "suitable" performances (for example, benefit concerts of sacred music by reputable singers for worthy causes). By mid-century, conditions were liberalized to include the use of churches for temperance dramas produced by Sunday-school associations; and church members were permitted to take part in concerts or tableaux-vivants staged in the town to raise money for church improvements. Partial rapprochement was assisted by the fact that Mary Cooke, daughter of the Chiefs' Children's School teachers and a graduate of Punahou, developed a voice of professional quality and went on to become an operatic singer in the United States, thus giving the mission community of Honolulu something of a vested interest in respectable though profane theater.[27]

In its own terms, drama was considerably less than mature at Honolulu. As late as the beginning of the reign of King Kalākaua in the seventies, there had not been a performance of a full-length serious play or opera by a cast consisting solely of professionals. Most touring companies were very small, and the aid of local amateurs was frequently enlisted. Then too, five acts of tragedy or of harrowing Italian opera on a hot tropical night would have exhausted the stamina of the average theatergoer. A typical bill offered a melange: perhaps the high spots of a Shakespearean play, a short farce, some singing, and one or two specialty acts.

Nonetheless, the theater at its height in Honolulu achieved a fair degree of social glitter. One indication of the decline of puritanism in the town was the linking of bohemian theatrical professionals and amateurs with socially prominent patrons. In the forties, it had been necessary on occasion to hire native policemen to keep order in the pit, and in the circle "gentlemen" used to sit in their shirtsleeves; but a generation later, a royal command performance was an event of a different nature. The Royal Hawaiian Theater on Alakea Street was a building incongruously like a New England meeting-house, set in a beautiful tropical garden where shimmering dragon-flies hovered and sailed in and out the windows (and where centipedes sometimes invaded the reserved seats). There, patrons could train their opera glasses at a range of less than fifty feet upon

> a really elegant audience; tickets ten shillings each, evening dresses, uniforms of every cut and color; chiefesses and ladies of every tinge in dresses of every color; flowers and jewels in profusion, satin playbills, fans going…Kanaka women in the garden below selling bananas and peanuts by the glare of gleaming torches on a sultry, tropical moonlight night…If a familiar air was struck upon the piano in the orchestra, the Kanakas lying in the grass under the garden fence took up the refrain and hummed it softly and sweetly; the music ceased, the play began, the listeners in the street, seeing no part of the stage— little, in fact, save the lamp-light streaming through the waving banana leaves—busied themselves with talk; they buzzed like swarming bees, they laughed like careless children, they echoed the applause of the spectators, and amused themselves mightily. Meanwhile the royal family was enjoying the play in the most natural and unpretentious fashion…Everybody in that house knew everybody else; a solitary stranger would have been at once discovered and scrutinized. It was like a social gathering, where, indeed, "carriages may be ordered at 10.30;" but most of the participants walked home.[28]

As with the theater, so with social dancing: from the beginning, the Protestant mission regarded it as immoral, like the hula. The course of subsequent events was similar. The white community in the twenties and early thirties was so small that the issue did not arise in public; but from the mid-thirties, with more whites—and especially white women— in town, and more visits by warships whose officers liked to dance, the question of acceptability became overt.

A test case arose quite soon. In 1836, a party was given for the British officers of Lord Edward Russell's *Actaeon* by Mrs. Little, the church-going widow of an American sea-captain (she later married William Hooper, a Ladd & Co. partner and acting United States consular agent). The guests drank brandy, played cards, and danced with her and with other Honolulu ladies. Peter Brinsmade, at that time still a mission supporter, Sunday-school teacher, and lay preacher at the Seamen's Chapel, remonstrated with Mrs. Little. She was unrepentant, holding that dancing had nothing to do with the state of her soul. She had danced at home on the American mainland and had been at the same time a member in good standing of her Protestant congregation, and she could not see that geography altered morality. When she was threatened with excision from the newly-formed Bethel Church unless she stopped dancing, she continued and was dismissed. Several other foreign women followed her lead, and the exhortations of Seamen's Chaplain John Diell did no good.[29]

This was a straw in the wind. The appetite of naval commanders for sophisticated entertainment persisted, and many people in town were ready to meet them more than halfway. Dancers, by 1839, were caught between two kinds of criticisms: visitors found that Honolulu's ladies could not waltz fast enough, and Protestant missionaries damned the ladies for daring to waltz at all. The first criticism was corrected by practice, the second was ignored. By 1840, official Honolulu was taking part. While the United States Exploring Expedition under Lieutenant Charles Wilkes was in town, Hannah Holmes gave an enormous lūʻau for the officers at her Nuʻuanu country house. Two hundred guests sat down to eat in the afternoon, and that night Governor Kekūanaōʻa and the mission-educated government adviser Timothy Haʻalilio watched as the company waltzed and formed sets for cotillions and reels.[30]

During the next few years (and for decades thereafter) shipboard balls were held almost every time a foreign man-of-war came to town, and often a foreign consul gave a dance in return at his home. When the socialite bachelor Robert Crichton Wyllie became Hawaiian Foreign Minister in 1844, the invasion moved a step closer to the center of society. Wyllie was a tireless dancer as well as a persuasive advocate of the idea that the monarchy should encourage the social graces. Less than eighteen months after his appointment, and in the face of strong mission criticism, there was dancing at the palace. Thenceforth, the mission was on the defensive. Courtesy dictated that royal and official invitations should be accepted; morality dictated that dancing could not be condoned. Commonly, missionaries attended dinners and departed before dancing began; and Wyllie (so one missionary complained) could hardly wait until they were out of the room. Former missionaries in government were caught fairly in the middle. Richard Armstrong found dancing at the palace "very objectionable." His colleague Gerrit Judd held out for some time, but finally allowed his eligible daughters to dance. The argument involved other young people as well. Precisely when Stephen Reynolds' dancing-school girls were making their debuts, the missionaries were convincing the king that the Chiefs' Children's School pupils should be kept away from official and private dancing parties.[31]

The missionary retreat became a rout in the fifties. Opponents of dancing had been able thus far to avoid royal balls and attend only *soirées*, but by 1851 dancing was beginning to encroach even upon minor social functions. During the next few years, most holidays were celebrated with dances in the evening, including some of the solemn national days which in the past had been marked by temperance feasts and early nights or periods of fasting and humiliation.

Alexander Liholiho's reign saw the triumph of dancing, and the sophisticated royal example led to private imitation. The pattern of formal official balls was repeated in the community at large. "Subscription assemblies" became part of the social season. Organizations such as lodges, fire companies, volunteer militia corps, and national clubs gave invitational balls, and private parties on a small scale came in large measure to stand or fall on the issue of dancing. Henry Whitney's *Pacific Commercial Advertiser* conceded this in 1856, saying that benevolent society meetings no longer seemed amusement enough. Older people, said the *Advertiser*, still opposed dancing. Some well-bred people omitted it from their parties for fear of giving offense; young people liked to dance, but they too feared offending. Thus, parties without dancing became "intolerable bores." Men stayed on the verandah talking about the weather, the rate of whalers' exchange, and the price of putty; women sat within discussing collars and hooped skirts, and all "got gratefully under weigh" when it was time to go home. In the same year, the *Advertiser* commented caustically on a holiday dance, not because there was a dance but because the invitation cards had been "poorly got up."[32]

There were problems associated with the dancing life, just as there had been with the infant theater in Honolulu. It was somewhat difficult, for example, to provide good music. Stephen Reynolds occasionally played the violin at his dancing school. At other times he engaged Black George Hyatt, the negro clarinetist, and whatever supporting musicians he could find around town—mostly faltering itinerants, drunken and unreliable. An embryonic royal band was assembled in the forties, but its existence and skills were less than secure. Ships' bands were often drafted into service on shore, and with the heavy incidence of dancing parties in the fifties one or two semi-professional "cotillion bands" were formed.

Still, in 1861, it proved hard to find adequate music for an important reception. It was Queen Victoria's birthday, a titled visitor was in town, and the anglophile Alexander Liholiho and his wife Emma attended a supper and ball for four hundred guests, organized by the British community. The young English merchant Theophilus Davies (later the founder of one of Honolulu's biggest business houses) was in charge of the music. He hired a French piccolo player, just off a warship, to put together a group. The evening was a disaster for Davies, though royalty and the English visitor were not visibly embarrassed. The piccolo prevailed over the violins in "God Save the King" (the current Hawaiian national anthem) and raced bars ahead in "Rule Britannia," during which the guests promenaded and made their bows. Davies fled outside, threw himself into a chair, and covered his face with a handkerchief. The first violinist followed him ("My God, Mr. Davies, I can't stay"). Davies went in again, removed the piccolo player, and left the two violins to finish the evening, The next day he got a note from the Frenchman: "Sir, I am surprised you have fall down all my orchestra. Here is my bill $60."[33]

Davies' mortification was a minor thing. Major social triumphs by far outweighed it in the town. One of the most lavish events of Alexander Liholiho's reign was a gigantic fancy dress ball given by Foreign Minister Wyllie in 1860 and attended by every prominent Honolulan outside the mission community (including the Catholic bishop, who of course came as himself). Special music for waltzes and quadrilles was composed by two resident German professionals, Herren Waldau and Hasslocher; the hall was decorated by the professional artist Paul Emmert, and the catering was by the French hotelier Victor Chancerel. Wyllie came as a Scottish highland chief, and so did the venerable Governor Kekūanaō'a. There was a Titania, an Undine, and a Beau Brummel; and Queen Emma herself came as Cybele—a very non-Protestant religious figure.[34]

Other signs of the times appeared. As early as 1850 necklines on evening gowns had descended very low; and propriety now permitted fan-play, whispered compliments over iced drinks, and midnight carriage rides after the dance. Courtship came to focus on the ballroom rather than the meeting-house. By the end of Alexander Liholiho's reign, holiday parties included children's cotillions. Young people grew up to dance at court and at the delightful evening parties held at Waikīkī for the entertainment of Honolulu socialites and of distinguished visitors such as the Duke of Edinburgh, who made an extended stay in Honolulu in the summer months of 1869.[35]

Just as theater had made its way into mission preserves, so did dancing. Punahou girls, confined to calisthenics in school, turned to dancing after graduation. The young New Englander J.B. Atherton, arriving with fine Protestant credentials to seek his fortune in Honolulu at the end of the fifties, was surprised to find that his letters of reference led him to families in which the young people danced. The apparent victory of frivolity was complete by the late sixties and early seventies. Queen Emma was present at the opening of a skating rink to watch the grand march, the lancers, and quadrilles—all on roller skates. Public balls were so crowded that two bands were needed and the gallopade became a positive danger. Temperance lodges sponsored temperance balls; the native members of Kawaiaha'o's choir organized mid-summer dances; and missionary offspring were seen "dancing themselves giddy" at weekend parties in the country.[36]

Among the most striking dancers in the reign of Alexander Liholiho and later kings were several young part-white and native girls of good family. The painful days of the first entry of Stephen Reynolds' girls into polite society were some years in the past, and those who succeeded them were fortunate enough to enjoy the ambience of a sophisticated court which had for its leader Queen Emma, herself part-white. Emma, far more than any queen before or after her (except perhaps the archetypal Ka'ahumanu), was a style-setter, and she chose to enhance her own considerable flair by surrounding herself with a bevy of young ladies-in-waiting, native, part-native, and white. During her reign and later, it would have been virtually impossible for a guest to wind his way through a court cotillion without encountering a non-white girl or two. Most visitors, and particularly naval officers, would not have preferred it otherwise. There were some very beautiful and sparkling girls at Emma's court, and they became favorite companions of visitors on picnics and horse rides. The social success of the young ladies was noticed approvingly in the *Polynesian,* whose editor, Charles Gordon Hopkins, was a bosom companion of Alexander Liholiho and Emma. Hopkins, an Englishman of bohemian tastes, was an outspoken critic of what he described as the lugubrious Anglo-Saxonism of most of Honolulu's Americans. His close friend Henry Neilson practiced what Hopkins preached. Neilson brought his native mistress to quadrille rehearsal parties, where she danced with the king and with Prince Lot.[37] The midwestern American David Gregg, recording this in his diary, found it a "significant fact" in Hawaiian morals. He remarked that in Europe it would seem strange for such a person to be the guest of royalty (all this proved, of course, was that Gregg knew very little about European court customs).[38]

Some remained at Honolulu who saw danger and not delight in even the most superficial mixing of the races. Opposition stemmed principally from the Protestant missionary group, many of whose members were at ease only in carefully delineated and institutionalized relationships with Hawaiians and part-whites—for example, as teachers, pastors, benevolent uplifters, but never as intimates or equals.[39] By the time of Alexander Liholiho and Emma, the mission could do little one way or another to affect the existence of interracialism at court. Downtown, however, there could be observed the recurrent spectacle of the races mingling in physical surroundings and circumstances which would have been regarded as sordid even had the issue of race not been present. Honolulu's middle and upper classes responded in a variety of ways to the flourishing waterfront demi-monde, almost all of whose denizens were native or part-white. Some citizens (principally those who had native mistresses) were permissive; a great many more pretended that the downtown area simply vanished after dark; and at the other end of the range of opinion was a quite strong punitive feeling, traceable to the Protestant community and its formal adherents.

The drawing of lines between polite and downtown society, of course, was not always a matter of race or morals alone, but rather of those two considerations together with class. Cultivated Hawaiians and part-whites, as much as pure whites, wanted to dissociate themselves from the lower reaches of that legally-branded area by the waterfront where mechanics, sailors, native artisans, and peddlers took their pleasure, where liquor was sold within the law to whites and outside the law to natives, and where women might be bought and sold, illegally but openly.

The lines were crossed from time to time. As in other port cities, respectable businessmen made money directly and indirectly from the demi-monde. Owners of downtown property, too, collected rents from enterprises of doubtful legality and morality (at one point Dr. T.C.B. Rooke accused Foreign Minister Wyllie, the city's most vocal urger of legislation to regulate prostitution, of allowing several small houses he owned to be used as brothels, and Rooke need not have stopped with Wyllie).[40] For the most part, however, tacit understandings born of expediency proved adequate to cover such situations. Some of the town's professional men and merchants even found it possible to divide their time between downtown dance halls and suburban drawing rooms. Nonetheless, outside the immediate royal circle (where a subtle kind of protective immunity seemed to operate), the members of polite society, and not Protestant society alone, found it unsettling to encounter at their dances and parties ladies from downtown, who had stepped outside the limits defined for them by custom.

It was unlikely that strict Protestants and prostitutes would ever meet socially. What did happen, all the same, was that young men of respectable if not puritan background, caught up in the social shift between non-dancing and dancing and unable to learn the new skills in "proper" circumstances, went to downtown dance halls and brought back not only techniques but attitudes. The *Advertiser*, conceding that the old version of polite society needed some enlivening, was upset by the implications of the new way: "If persons are to be tolerated in society who frequent such scenes, we shall soon cease to wonder at the effrontery with which on a recent public occasion, known prostitutes or cast-off mistresses, who by some chance had obtained admission, though we are informed that no tickets had been issued to them by the managers, were selected as partners by young men who would indignantly resent any imputation on their own respectability, and who danced with them under the very eyes of virtuous ladies, who perhaps had been their predecessors in the dance with these misguided youths."[41]

The downtown world of dance-houses, restaurants, taverns, and houses of assignation had arisen, like most of Honolulu, in response to the imperative needs of the whaling fleet. Within the legal area for liquor sales, inland as far as King Street and westward from Nu'uanu Street toward Nu'uanu stream, grew up a district of dilapidated native huts and tenements, tiny bar-rooms, coffee-shops, and run-down "boarding houses," all turning to the harbor for their opportunities and income. This part of town was not much frequented by polite Honolulans. As early as the mid-thirties, it had been well understood that the waterfront was no place for a lady, an impression confirmed year by year during every whaling season, even those unmarked by serious riots or depredations.

The lower classes—white "mechanics" and natives generally—found the crowds, the bright lights, and the gaminess very congenial. Night after night streets, shops, and bars were busy. As early as 1840, common seamen of the United States Exploring Expedition found native dancing partners downtown while their superiors waltzed at Hannah Holmes' lū'au in Nu'uanu. During the next fifteen years, there was a rapid importation of foreign dance forms. By the mid-fifties, the downtown world was able to celebrate Christmas and the Hawaiian Thanksgiving Day with an elegant supper, toasts to all and sundry, and "the most intricate quadrilles, foreign waltzes, mazurkas, redowas, etc." "The "Working-Man" who recorded this was amazed to find among the "humbler orders" of the native population so much "grace and elegance."[42]

What struck him as grace and elegance appeared to the official world as nothing more than swinishness. Chief Justice William Lee, in his annual report to the legislature in 1852, described the public dance halls of Honolulu as the great sources and indeed the primary cause of the vast amount of fornication and adultery that disgraced the city. He urged their suppression, predicting that otherwise the rising generation of Hawaiians, "from whom so much is expected, and for whom so much has been done, must irretrievably fail, and be consigned to infamy and shame."[43] Lee, a New Englander who had unbent sufficiently to attend formal dances, remained orthodox for the most part in his social views, supporting among other things quite harsh penalties for the offenses grouped under the moekolohe laws, on the unassailable ground that if exemplary punishments were good for New England they must be good for Honolulu.[44] Marshal William Parke carried out a campaign against the dance houses in 1853, under existing laws on common nuisance. It was then announced prematurely that, although some young men had opposed the purge, the dance houses were dead.[45]

That they were not dead was indicated unequivocally by their re-appearance during the fall whaling season of 1856. Bar-room hours had been extended till midnight,[46] and once again sailor and citizen alike might "pass the night in the 'mazy dance' with chaste Island maidens, or make appointments to 'meet me by moonlight alone.'" Opposition on the part of officialdom was not dead either. At the end of 1856, two well-known hotel-keepers, Joe Booth of the National Hotel and Joseph Dawson of Liberty Hall, were prosecuted under the common nuisance laws for allowing native women to assemble for "lewd purposes" at the dance-houses they ran in conjunction with their taverns.[47]

A conviction in the Honolulu police court was followed by an appeal to the Supreme Court. Booth's case was heard before a jury of foreigners chosen from a list supplied by the British Consul-General, a practice still sanctioned by treaty but not much used since the stormy days of the forties. The jury included Charles Gordon Hopkins, and also Marcus Monsarrat, who was soon to become notorious in a scandal involving Princess Victoria Kamāmalu. Booth was found not guilty by this "picked jury," in spite of a strong charge by Supreme Court Justice George Robertson. The acquittal produced a spate of shocked letters in the *Advertiser* and some hand wringing by the Hawaiian-language Protestant newspaper *Hae Hawaii*. One of the jurors wrote in reply a long letter to the *Polynesian*, explaining why he voted against convicting Booth. The prosecution's argument, he said, was that dancing with prostitutes corrupted public morals. His own view was that the words "strumpet" and "prostitute" connoted a class of women, socially degraded, who sold themselves for money—women entirely separated from the rest of society. In Honolulu and the rest of the kingdom, there was no such distinction. The dance-hall women "may be better looking, some more bold, some more mercenary than the general run of females throughout the islands, but it is a fact which we are all well aware of, that after singling out an insignificant fraction of the well educated and the well looked after, the remainder—the vast majority of native women—are all one class; one in habits, one in feeling, one in morals, one in their associations. There is no proscribed class as in other countries..." How, then, could the native women be prevented from gathering where they wished? They were the public; their morals were public morals. Could the whole female population be declared a nuisance? "It is much to be feared that there exists here some of the Anglo-Saxon race with the selfish, unsympathising, over-bearing natures, only too characteristic of it, who, in the anxiety to establish a *cordon sanitaire* around the pure morality of their own sons, or their own brothers, would hardly hesitate to return even this verdict." He himself could not support this idea; hence his not guilty vote.[48]

Booth and his fellow dance-hall proprietors opened their houses again after the trial. By then, the whaling season was almost over. The circus and the theater were closed for lack of business, and the dance-halls stayed open just long enough to prove their point.

Defeated in court, the moralists turned to executive means of putting down the nuisance. It was quite simple in the short run. Booth and others held retail spirit licenses issued by the government. In mid-1857, a clause was included in these, prohibiting the attachment of dance halls to premises used for the retailing of spirits. Booth and Joseph Dawson petitioned the government against this, but Prince Lot, heading the Department of the Interior at the time, ruled against them, and the triad of liquor, sex, and dancing was broken up for the time being.[49]

Was public morality served by the dispersal of the dance-hall women from their former haunts? Evidently not. In the fall of 1857 no dance hall opened—without a liquor connection, money could not be made. Neither was there, as it happened, a theater company or a circus in town during the first months of the fall whaling season. Yet convictions for offenses against morality, in a town offering no "immoral" amusements, increased rather than decreased for the fall months: 422 in 1855, 349 in 1856, and 513 in 1857.[50]

The tavern-keepers soon found ways of evading the license requirements. Dances were held in buildings close to but not owned by publicans, or were held by customers "privately" in halls rented by them rather than by a licensee. In 1864, the legislature passed a regulatory act, and there were more prosecutions following this, but the dance-house area retained its characteristic flavor until the end of the whaling era. A roving reporter on Nu'uanu Street in 1866 found whalemen, gaudy women, "nymphes du pave" awaiting customers in crowded coffee-shops, and at Booth's Corner a "fantastic babel" accompanying dancing to violins, piano, and castanets.[51]

Concurrently with the dance-hall affair, another case was producing acrimony between the Protestants and others whose definitions of public morality were less stringent. At the time when the Honolulu Sailors' Home was being planned as an adjunct to the Seamen's Bethel, its trustees memorialized the Privy Council, asking that no liquor licenses be granted in the block upon which the Bethel and the proposed Home were located. They further suggested that no licenses be awarded on the opposite sides of the streets bounding the block—King, Nu'uanu, Merchant, and Bethel. This area fell within margins previously designated by the legislature as open to licenses. An English tavern-keeper named John Maxey had already bought a lot on the corner of Nu'uanu and Merchant Streets, and, having been assured by the Minister of Interior that he would be granted a license, had spent $11,000 readying his new Royal Hotel for business. By the time Maxey applied for his license, however, the privy councillors had received the trustees' memorial. They decided that Maxey's license should be for one year only, not renewable.

At the end of the year, which was up in mid-1856, Maxey petitioned for a renewal, and the trustees of the Sailors' Home petitioned against it. Maxey pointed out that to deprive him of his license after only one year would be to ruin him. His hotel had been well run, without indecent dancing or other disturbances; furthermore, he said, no sailors from the Home came there—they would have been seen entering his place. Finally, there was another hotel on the other side of Nu'uanu Street not more than fifty feet from the proscribed block, and there were three more in the immediate vicinity. The privy councillors rescinded the decision limiting the period of Maxey's license, and informed him and the trustees that the Royal Hotel might remain open.

The trustees accused the Privy Council of bad faith. This set off a newspaper war. Henry Whitney's Protestant *Advertiser* claimed that Maxey was supported by Foreign Minister Wyllie, who was not only a notorious enemy of temperance but was also a shareholder in Maxey's hotel. Whitney alleged that Wyllie had railroaded the renewal of Maxey's license through a depleted Privy Council to further his own private interests. Wyllie, in fact, had written to his London bankers on behalf of Maxey to establish credit for him; and when Maxey went to England on business, Wyllie had taken delivery of goods consigned to Maxey at Honolulu. Wyllie denied, however, any financial connection with Maxey, saying he had acted out of friendship only, doing no more for Maxey than he had done for many others in the town (this was certainly true: Wyllie, independently wealthy, was prodigally generous with loans and gifts, most of which went unrepaid even in gratitude). Wyllie published relevant letters in the *Polynesian*, and threatened Whitney with a libel suit should the *Advertiser* continue to charge him with using his official position for personal ends. Whitney persisted. Wyllie put the matter in the hands of a lawyer for a time, but then let it drop, and the Maxey case faded from the papers.[52]

The Maxey affair was part of a larger struggle over the place of liquor in the community. Temperance followed much the same curve as did other moral crusades, rising and falling with the Protestants. King Kauikeaouli had signed the pledge in the early forties, and, although he broke it regularly, he made intermittent appeals for abstinence among his fellows. For some years in the forties, no liquor was served at official functions.

Liquor, imported and dispensed legally or illegally, had always been a part of low life downtown. It made its way into polite society at about the same time as dancing. Once more, Wyllie was its great champion. Protestant resistance was perhaps most methodical on this front. Honolulu's temperance societies were organized along the lines of those in New England. Even so, exhortation and example were nothing more than self-sustaining. Sunday-school children and Christian natives marched regularly in procession, waving temperance banners and singing cold-water hymns. Young men in the community formed groups such as the Dashaways (who promised to "dash away" liquor from their lips), and temperance societies of all kinds were given great publicity by the dry press—the *Advertiser* and the Hawaiian-language Protestant papers. Most of this, however, was mere preaching to the converted, and the converted did not necessarily remain convinced. During the forties, for instance, every surviving high chief who had become a church member was under censure or suspension at one time or another, many of them for offenses connected with drink. By the time of Alexander Liholiho, with Protestants unseated from the cabinet, much of white society pleasure-bent, and the chiefs' example to the natives in ruins, any Puritan hope for a community free of liquor was futile."

Even the compromise of a tightly-controlled liquor traffic proved impossible to accomplish. No matter how high the price of liquor licenses, competition was always keen, especially for retail licenses (interestingly, the retail liquor trade of Honolulu up to the seventies was overwhelmingly in the hands of Englishmen, the only major business that could be so categorized). Outside the law, smuggling was rife; and probably more liquor was made illegally in the islands than was brought in by importers at the customs house and by smugglers combined.

Since the early nineteenth century, natives had been making potent 'ōkolehao from the distillations of fermented and mashed kī-root. Many other alcoholic drinks were popular: "palm-tree gin," "swipes" made from potatoes, melons, pineapples, bananas, prickly pears, or molasses strainings, and so on. These were drunk throughout the islands. Most of the stills that supplied Honolulu were located in rural areas, although after mid-century one or two remained in operation in Mānoa valley, and at Hālawa, west of the city. To their list of local drinks, the natives of Honolulu added exotic tipples: brandied fruits and imported colognes. Such technical and aesthetic sophistication made it very clear that there was no way to stop Hawaiians from drinking. As late as the seventies, licensing laws excluded natives from legal access to alcohol in any form other than communion wine. The laws survived a test of their constitutionality, brought in 1862 by Joe Booth of the dance halls, but although the law was judged sound, it was unenforceable. Convictions for drunkenness among natives ranked near the top of criminal statistics in the capital and elsewhere. In 1860, Honolulu's native policemen ceased to be paid out of fines levied by the courts. Lacking direct incentive, they nevertheless arrested drunken natives by the hundreds each year. Liquor duties and liquor licenses between them were in many years the biggest direct money-earners for government, but those revenues were often matched dollar for dollar by the costs of running Honolulu's courts and prisons, whose business came in fair measure from crimes associated with liquor.[54]

Liquor, dancing, prostitution, the theater—to the Protestant community, all seemed infinitely seductive and therefore dangerous. Other Honolulans, not so rigid, also saw danger in parts of the new morality, not so much for the white community, whose members presumably could make moral judgments unassisted, as for the native community, which seemed to be on the verge of destroying itself. Ultimately, then, all social arguments broke upon one question: what was to be done with the Hawaiians? On all sides, concern mounted for the survival of the native race. When Alexander Liholiho came to the throne, the great smallpox epidemic was not long over. Depopulation was being accelerated even more by venereal diseases, present in the islands since the time of Captain Cook's expedition and now rampant in the record years of whaling. From 1851 to 1858, there was an excess of deaths over births in the kingdom of more than ten thousand.[55] Honolulu itself gained population, but only at the expense of all other districts of the kingdom. Victims of disease at the port were replaced by newcomers from rural areas. Whole valleys on the island of Hawai'i were emptied by death and migration (Hawai'i was particularly hard hit, the other islands to a lesser but still alarming extent). Predictions were made that the Hawaiian race would be extinct within a few generations.

Alexander Liholiho's first royal speech to his assembled legislators in 1855 made it clear how deeply worried he was about the fate of his people. The decrease of the population, he said, was a subject in comparison with which all others sank into insignificance. He and the elected representatives of the people shared a heavy responsibility. Neither God nor man would acquit them if they failed to act speedily on behalf of those who every day were dying. Hospitals, he believed, were an essential beginning.[56]

The legislature of 1855 moved to modernize laws for the organization and support of the Board of Health. At the same time, the Minister of the Interior was empowered to set up hospitals for natives on the major islands. Venereal disease was seen as the great "waster" of the Hawaiian population. Accordingly, an act was passed embodying an old idea of Wyllie's which aimed at preventing women from congregating at the ports during the whaling season, in the hope of limiting by this means the spread of disease from Honolulu and Lahaina to other districts.[57]

Four years passed before a hospital was opened at Honolulu. The government suffered acute financial embarrassment during the late fifties, and although successive legislatures voted money, in practice none could be spared. The interest of the king and queen remained strong, and the idea of private subscriptions to help finance the hospital probably originated with them. A plan was perfected in 1859. A hospital association should be formed; when it had raised $5,000, the government would deed it land of equal value.

On this basis, Alexander Liholiho himself canvassed the townspeople to obtain pledges of money. He was indefatigable. The newspapers remarked how often he was seen in earnest conversation on the streets, writing subscription promises in a memorandum book. By the end of April, 1859, he had $695 in hand and pledges for $13,530 more. In the next two months, the Queen's Hospital was named and incorporated, and trustees were chosen to bring hopes to fruition. From mid-1859 to early 1860, Dr. William Hillebrand, a resident German physician selected by the trustees, worked in a temporary building on King Street; in March, 1860, a lot was acquired at the corner of Beretania and Punchbowl Streets, and Hillebrand transferred his patients to an existing building there. Plans for a permanent structure were drawn by T.C. Heuck, another German, a "practical architect" who held various government offices during the sixties. Workmen broke ground in June, 1860, and the hospital was ready for patients by December, at a cost of almost $15,000, or $1,500 more than the original contract price.[58]

The two-story coral-stone building and its attendant structures rose from dusty, dry surroundings to the east of the town proper, in an area where Kawaiaha'o church and the royal palace were the only other major landmarks. Water was piped there from Pauoa valley in 1861, permitting the planting of lawns and shrubbery; and with that, the hospital grounds began to take on a physical character they retained for many years. Architect Heuck's plans pleased almost everybody; it would be in policy and administration that the hospital's success or failure lay. The usual internal problems were experienced—disagreements among trustees, difficulty in actually collecting pledged money, and so on. Of greater concern was the response of the Hawaiians. This, nobody could predict with any accuracy.

The hospital had been built to serve the native population.[59] Every trustee during the first years of operation was white, with two exceptions: Robert G. Davis, half-white son of Hannah Holmes, and David Kalākaua. The attending physician, William Hillebrand, was white (there were no western-trained native doctors in the kingdom), and the hospital itself was constructed on western lines, conceding nothing to traditional Hawaiian housing style. Doubts were expressed about the willingness of natives to submit themselves to western medicine, especially so soon after the tragic experience of the smallpox epidemic. Perhaps its frightful toll had reconciled Hawaiians to the use of white men's medicine; perhaps it had confirmed them in the old ways. No one could tell.

First indications were good. Admission was free for sick and indigent natives. When the temporary building on King Street was opened, notices in Hawaiian were posted about town, and natives came in considerable numbers to Ka Hale Maʻi o ka Wahine Aliʻi (the sick house of the lady chief—The Queen's Hospital). In the first five months there were 765 applications, and the beds were filled. The permanent hospital was also well-patronized, especially when measles came to Honolulu in 1861. The native population of the Kona district of Oʻahu in 1861 was about twelve and a half thousand. After almost two years, Hillebrand had treated 2,746 patients at the dispensary, and the hospital at its peak of occupancy housed 71 patients (its capacity was 124 beds). Thus, it might have been argued quite soundly that Queen's Hospital had proved its usefulness.[60]

The matter, in fact, was not quite so simple. Many natives came to Queen's Hospital, Hawaiianizing it somewhat in the process, as relatives who were visiting patients spread their mats on the floor and slept overnight in the wards. The *Polynesian* pointed out that it was impossible to impose strict rules and discipline upon the natives and still have them feel at ease; yet it was essential to have them feel at ease in order to keep them coming to the hospital. This was a reasonable accommodation that did little harm and promised more good. Nonetheless, many Hawaiians never lost their suspicion of white doctors. The memory was still strong of smallpox autopsies which violated the body, and the pull of the old medical kahuna was hard to resist.

Although Queen's Hospital was accepted by part of the native population, there was a persistence and even a recrudescence of native treatments. A small but steady incidence of deaths in the sixties and later could be traced to the ministrations of the kahuna. As many cases occurred in the Honolulu district as elsewhere (these were reported cases only: the actual state of kahuna practice must have been considerably more extensive than was known in the white community). Traces of ancient procedures showed above the surface of Honolulu's life at times, as when a bag drifted ashore at the Esplanade, containing a white pig, some 'awa, and other items used in casting spells. To this equipment, innovating kahuna added new elements, in imitation of western medicine, professional and amateur: draughts of gunpowder, quicklime applications, and phlebotomies performed with unorthodox instruments, such as lancets made of shards of broken glass.[62]

The government tried in several ways to extirpate kahuna-ism. It was hoped, for example, that the establishment of Queen's Hospital would help. Certainly, prosecutions in the criminal courts were less than successful. For every case brought to trial there might be dozens undiscovered, and even after conviction a kahuna often retained a hold over his followers.[63]

More promise was offered by the reverse process, that of training intelligent Hawaiians as western medical practitioners and orderlies. With the support of government, Gerrit Judd opened a medical school for natives at Honolulu in 1870, but shortages of money and of eligible candidates hampered progress. In the seventies, an interesting compromise was reached. The government selected Hawaiian medical kahuna of certain kinds (excluding, of course, adepts of the arts of medical sorcery), and licensed them to treat their own people in limited and well-defined circumstances. Thus, Queen's Hospital and kahuna-ism co-existed. In rural districts and on the outer islands, despite schemes for subsidiary hospitals, the presence of itinerant doctors supplied by the government, and, in serious cases, transfer of patients to Honolulu, kahuna-ism undoubtedly triumphed.[64]

Concurrently with the issuing of licenses to kahuna, an attempt was made to regulate the practice of white doctors. The Oahu Medical Association was formed in 1856, and in 1859-1860, legislation was passed stipulating that licenses to practice would be awarded only after examination of applicants by the Board of Health. Between 1860 and 1875, several quacks were exposed, and a number of practitioners were refused licenses because their homeopathic notions did not conform to the allopathic requirements of the Board of Health.[65]

Caught in the net were two Protestant missionaries, Dwight Baldwin of Lahaina and Lowell Smith of Honolulu. Baldwin had attended medical lectures before coming to the islands. Although he was always known as "Doctor," he had never taken a medical degree.

He arranged through the ABCFM in Boston to have Dartmouth College grant him an honorary degree, but the Hawaiian Board of Health did not accept this as evidence of competence.[66] Lowell Smith, pastor of Kaumakapili Church at Honolulu, had been treating natives since 1832 on the basis of a very sketchy medical knowledge. A great devotee of bleeding, he was described in 1859 by the *Polynesian* as a "well intentioned, but mischievous amateur in phlebotomy." Refused a license by the Board of Health in 1860, he continued to practice. He was fined in the Honolulu Police Court in 1863, when one of his Hawaiian patients died of lockjaw, following a phlebotomy.[67] Under circumstances that are not clear, he either obtained a license to practice, or dispensed medicines to natives under an existing law. Then, in the seventies, a succession of his native patients died, among them Z. Poli, a member of the House of Representatives. At an inquiry held by the Board of Health, qualified doctors testified that Smith was likely to have caused or hastened some of the deaths, by improper use of phlebotomies and administration of unsuitable medicines. Smith was ordered to cease attending natives, but apparently he did not comply: in 1876, another patient, a Hawaiian girl, died after he prescribed medicines for her which were dangerous, according to expert testimony. There was talk of prosecuting Smith, but in the end it was simply and strongly suggested that he stop practicing.[68] The whole episode is interesting, not only in terms of rising standards of medical practice, but also in terms of the falling prestige of the Protestant mission. Smith was regarded no longer as a selfless healer, but as a public menace.

Almost immediately after Queen's Hospital was opened, a basic question of policy arose, one which arrayed the white community along much the same lines as the dance hall case had done. The question was, indeed, in some ways an extension of the moral questions posed by the existence of dance-halls. Should prostitutes be admitted to Queen's Hospital for treatment? Prostitution meant disease, and both were rife, even after the passage of the act of 1855 designed to keep women away from the ports. What should be done? Moral obloquy had been tried, but it did not cure infections. Perhaps a system of licensing, inspection, and medical treatment would work. The issue was argued briskly in the period between 1855 and 1860, with the town split into familiar camps: permissive, regulatory, and prohibitive-punitive.[69]

Those in favor of licensing and inspection tended to dissociate questions of morality from questions of public health. Those against licensing argued that legal recognition implied legal approval of the institution of harlotry. They spoke at length about the wages of sin. Over strong Protestant opposition, the legislature of 1860 voted into law "An Act to Mitigate Evils and Disease Arising from Prostitution." The legislature's view was that experience had demonstrated the impossibility of stamping out prostitution. The public good therefore demanded that the traffic be regulated. Honolulu's prostitutes were ordered to register with the sheriff, on pain of imprisonment. Treatment for diseased women was to be provided without charge. Any registered prostitute found free of disease might have her name removed from the register on declaring her intention to give up prostitution.[70]

Where might prostitutes be inspected and housed for treatment? Queen's Hospital seemed to be the logical place. The Minister of the Interior and the hospital's trustees agreed toward the end of 1860 that the hospital should accommodate and treat prostitutes at the rate of forty-five cents per head per day, paid by the government. An instant objection was made by the ladies of Honolulu's Protestant community, thirty-four of whom inveighed against the proposal in a memorial directed to the trustees. The ladies interpreted the "Act to Mitigate" as having been passed to put "the mark of infamy on vice," thus making its votaries feel the "shame and disgrace" which were the due of such profligates in moral cities in other lands. This procedure in itself, the ladies claimed, would stimulate in the "young and ignorant nation of Hawaii" a love of character. No arrangements should be made which tended to "lessen the shame and ignominy which it is desirable should be attached to those who voluntarily and openly choose the path of vice." Prostitutes should be kept away from respectable people. Comfortable quarters at Queen's would only encourage them; a separate Magdalen hospital ought to be set up, where moral as well as medicinal influences could be brought to bear.[71]

The trustees' answer showed once more that moral initiative at Honolulu no longer rested with the Protestants. Governmental appointees on the board and those elected from among generous subscribers combined to agree that the hospital had been created for the benefit of the whole nation, and that no restrictions ought to be placed upon classes of patients or kinds of diseases. Even felons, said the trustees, were entitled to sympathy and care when they were ill; they should not be left to depend upon "a good Samaritan who might *not* pass near them to save them from physical destruction."[72]

The prostitutes were housed on the grounds at Queen's Hospital in an old building that had been standing when the government acquired the land. No official "moral influences" were brought to bear on them, although Protestant remonstrances continued unabated. The *Advertiser* took every opportunity to criticize the intent and working of the Act to Mitigate; so did the Protestant Hawaiian-language *Hokuloa*. The Oahu

Clerical Association added its condemnations, and a Hawaiian-language almanac printed at the mission press defined the Act to Mitigate as an act to "defend" or "encourage" prostitution.

The government's *Polynesian* took the opposite tack, and in the course of its defense of the act dealt quite harshly with the mission's achievement. At the time the Act was passed, observed the *Polynesian*, Protestant evangelists had been in the islands for forty years, and yet early registrations identified hundreds of prostitutes, no fewer than two-thirds of whom were married, or had been married, when their names were placed on the books. For the rest, the *Polynesian* relied upon statistics supplied by the sheriff of Honolulu and the inspecting physician. Before the passage of the Act, four of every seven patients at Queen's were syphilitic; within two years this proportion was down to two out of eight. The total number of prostitutes in Honolulu declined during the early sixties, and the proportion of diseased women was reduced markedly, from two out of three in 1860 to fourteen percent in 1864. It was less common than before to find prostitutes on the streets. Ships might even clear Honolulu harbor after a sojourn at the port with crews quite free from infection.[73]

One offshoot of wrangling over the treatment of prostitutes was that the Protestant church was less than enthusiastic in its support of Queen's Hospital. Clergymen themselves were not among the constant subscribers (contributors generally were spread among the Honolulu community: the cause crossed most factional lines). Even native Protestant congregations gave more to foreign missionary work than to the hospital. By the early seventies, most missionaries-turned-businessmen at Honolulu (people such as Samuel N. Castle, E.O. Hall, and Henry Dimond) were life members of Queen's Hospital, but elections to the board of trustees tended to pass them by.[74]

The Act to Mitigate worked well enough during its first few years, and then began to succumb to that devolution of energy and purposiveness so characteristic of Honolulu's administration. Sporadic attacks were made upon the Act in the legislature. Insufficient funds were voted. Some prostitutes refused to register or to subject themselves to inspection. Nonetheless, the conclusion of the officials charged with its execution was that the Act, despite weaknesses, had done some good. This seems unarguable. At the same time, prostitution in the late sixties and early seventies showed as lively a life as the dance halls. On Nu'uanu Street, and especially between King and Hotel Streets, city youths, sailors from the harbor, and "licensed women" thronged the tea and coffee shops where bargains were struck in the "infamous trade." Women turned out of bawdy houses on Maunakea Street and elsewhere simply moved to new lodgings close by. No civil law was strong enough to compete with the law of supply and demand; and Honolulu had a heavy surplus of males at all times, particularly during the shipping seasons.[75]

A new sophistication in the treatment of young criminals and also of the insane emerged in Honolulu during the sixties. A reformatory and an asylum were built, so that at least two special classes of deviants might be separated from the mass of prison inhabitants with whom they had shared accommodations previously. Both institutions were located on the west side of Honolulu, as was the prison.[76] Their placement confirmed moral and social divisions in the town. Respectability drained away in the lower reaches of Nu'uanu stream and was lost entirely where the waters flowed into the harbor. Society's outcasts were banished to the west. East of the downtown area, only the Magdalen ward of Queen's Hospital stood as a reminder of the persistent frailty of man and woman.

Provision for prostitutes, the insane, and the criminal population of Honolulu was about equivalent with that in most European countries and the United States. Hawai'i, naturally enough, made no striking innovations. Nonetheless, despite its insularity, the kingdom remained in reasonably close touch with current practice elsewhere. The city of Honolulu and the islands generally were fortunate to have the services of enlightened and well-read men such as Wyllie and Alexander Liholiho (in contrast with the benighted rulers and statesmen of many minor European countries). Then too, Honolulu usually had sufficient trained physicians to administer sensibly, if not exhaustively, any program financed by the legislature. At the same time, Honolulu, like most other cities, was less than sensitive about sanitary arrangements.[77]

Indifference to sanitation aside, it was the state of medical knowledge that determined the handling of disease. At mid-century, information was inadequate to ensure sound control, as the record showed in connection with smallpox and venereal infections; and so it proved when yet a third scourge appeared on a large scale in the early sixties—leprosy.

Its origins in the Hawaiian islands were obscure. Commonly, it was believed to have been introduced from China; hence the usual native name of ma'i Pākē, or "Chinese disease." Leprosy had been observed in Hawai'i as early as about 1830, but until the sixties its presence did not cause great concern. Late in the reign of Alexander Liholiho, matters became more serious. The government's smallpox vaccinator, making his rounds among the natives of O'ahu in 1861, found many with a disease resembling leprosy. In the same year, the Board of Health prepared lists of lepers on all islands. By mid-1863, Dr. William Hillebrand was faced with the problem of treating increasing numbers of native lepers at Queen's Hospital. He could do little beyond isolating those with "genuine Oriental leprosy" in a building on the hospital grounds. The disease spread rapidly. In 1864, the Board of Health recommended that Honolulu's lepers be brought together for examination.

At the turn of 1865, the legislature passed "An Act To Prevent the Spread of Leprosy," ordering the arrest, detention, and isolation of lepers. A receiving station was set up at Kaka'ako, an inspection hospital was built at Kalihi, west of Honolulu, and land on the island of Moloka'i was acquired for a permanent leper settlement. In mid-November, the first natives, sixty of them, reported to Kalihi hospital, where they were examined by the government-appointed physician, Edward Hoffman. Forty-three were diagnosed as lepers.[78]

To Honolulu thenceforth came lepers from all the islands, some more or less voluntarily though with dread, others under restraint. Once the presence of the disease was ascertained, isolation at Kalawao on Moloka'i was decreed. Beginning early in 1866, the twenty-foot government schooner *Warwick* and other vessels made regular trips to and from the leper settlement. By the early seventies, Kalawao housed several hundred patients in an anti-utopia where disease and dissolution, rather than a search for perfection, were the conditions of sequestered life.

Not until 1868 was the *Bacillus leprae* discovered by the Norwegian scientist Hansen. The paths along which leprosy was transmitted remained unknown. Medicines and prescriptions of every kind were used in a prolonged attempt to find a cure. Inquiries were made all over the world by the Hawaiian government, and, in the first ten years of the Kalihi hospital and the Moloka'i leprosarium, doctors came from many places to try their skills and their exclusive remedies at Honolulu— Mohabeer the Indian; Sang Ki and Akana, Chinese doctors; Kainokalani, a Hawaiian kahuna who was given permission to treat lepers at Kalihi but was removed for using incantations; Powell, Ostrom, and Kenedy, all Americans. Some treatments were palliative, none cured the disease.[79]

As with smallpox and syphilis, leprosy took more victims among natives than among white men at Honolulu and elsewhere.[80] Physical promiscuity among Hawaiians seemed to contemporaries to aid the spread of the disease: natives lived, ate, slept, and smoked pipes in common, and caught leprosy in common. White men, living separate from natives and also separate from each other to a large extent, were much more likely to escape the disease. Some members of the Anglo-Saxon community tended to see personal disaster in terms of moral judgment. The *Advertiser* of the early seventies concurred in the view propounded by many physicians of the time, that leprosy was associated with and was perhaps a form of venereal disease, and that it might well have been spread in 1853–1854 when the smallpox panic led to hurried vaccination without careful examination to see if donors of vaccine matter were free from syphilis. Besides, said the *Advertiser*, Hawaiians lived recklessly, without common prudence, vitiating the efforts of their doctors. So bestial were native appetites that it was difficult to summon on their behalf "that pity we are ready to feel for all unfortunates."[81]

Some diseased Hawaiians fled from Honolulu and other towns to live in caves or hidden valleys. Most famous of all fugitives was the Kaua'i leper Ko'olau, who, in the reign of Kalākaua, stood off the forces of the law with his rifle and his cunning, and was never taken. Violent resistance was encountered occasionally at Kalihi, as when the suspected leper Kimo Kamai (who denied having leprosy, claiming he merely had syphilis) fired shots at the examining physician George Trousseau, and then at Marshal William Parke, before he was overpowered and locked up. Later, Kamai escaped from the leper settlement on Moloka'i and came back to Honolulu, where he was captured and fitted with a ball and chain before being returned.[82] Ko'olau and Kamai were not the only ones to cry out against their fate. Generally, however, the resignation of the native lepers was striking, their cheerfulness even in doom remarkable. The self-sacrifice of the kōkua ("helpers," often wives or husbands, sometimes friends) who made the dreadful trip to Kalawao was a cause of amazement and incomprehension in the white community of Honolulu, whose members, until the era of Father Damien and even later, could scarcely bring themselves even to look upon a leper.

What was to be done with the Hawaiian? The question remained unanswered, for all its urgency, as the diseases of the fifties and sixties took their toll of native life. Sickness and death aside, the natives of Honolulu were faced with the subtler task of making their peace with urban life. By mid-century, the capriciousness of early adaptations had been succeeded by a more settled state, still fluid, but one in which could be identified accommodation, indifference, and resistance. The natives of the city found much to attract them in the white man's world, but by no means enough to encourage them to adopt it entirely.

One tendency was for western institutions to appear in applicative or imitative form in the Hawaiian and part-Hawaiian community of Honolulu. Among Protestants, this had been evident since the beginning. The major Honolulu churches, of course, had white ministers. Some small Hawaiian congregations in the district acquired native lay readers or even "licensed preachers" as time went by, but ordained ministers of Hawaiian descent were not common in the city as late as the seventies. Not until the twentieth century were the two most important pulpits, those at Kawaiaha'o and Kaumakapili, occupied by Hawaiians, though white ministers preached there in the native language. And of course no white congregation ever called a Hawaiian to serve it.

The situation in the Catholic community was somewhat different. There was no bifurcation along racial lines. It would hardly have been necessary in terms of administration, because the white Catholic community in Honolulu was very small. In general, too, the Catholic clergy at Honolulu and elsewhere in the islands were lenient in racial terms, demanding from their converts far less in the way of westernization than did their Protestant counterparts, expecting rather a Hawaiianization of Catholicism which their handful of white worshippers might condone. Very few Catholic missionaries of the first forty years or so spoke English as a first language, and Louis Maigret, Bishop from 1846 until his death in 1882, was French. This, as much as other considerations, kept the Catholic Church in Honolulu somewhat outside the mainstream of the city's development, but by the same token did not divorce it from the native community.[83]

Some governmental institutions serving Honolulu broke rather naturally in two, the better to serve a racially-mixed community. Others acquired internal flexibility. The jurisdictional limits of Honolulu's city police court dictated that it did the bulk of its business among natives (haoles were brought before the court as well as natives; most white offenders were sailors, not residents). Indispensable to the court's success was a magistrate who understood Hawaiian—and Hawaiians— well. From the time the courts opened in the forties until the seventies, all judges were white, with skill in the Hawaiian language ranging from excellent to very poor. There was only one exception: the half-white Robert G. Davis, son of Hannah Holmes and William Heath Davis, who was police magistrate for a time in the fifties. On the other hand, magistrates in Honolulu's district courts were invariably Hawaiians. In the supreme court, cases were heard by juries chosen according to the race of the principals or litigants. If both parties were foreigners, the jury was all foreign; if one were foreign and the other native, the jury was mixed; if both were natives, the jury was all native. White lawyers customarily served both white and native clients; Hawaiian or part-Hawaiian lawyers (most of whom were graduates of Lahainaluna School on Maui) served only natives. The supreme court, from the beginning, had one Hawaiian member, John 'I'i. He retained his seat until the sixties, largely ignorant of western law, but far more knowledgeable than his white colleagues in matters of Hawaiian custom and tradition, and therefore very useful. When he stepped down, he was succeeded by Robert Davis.

The quality of justice in the Hawaiian courts was mixed, as it would have been in a similar situation anywhere. Linguistic problems were great in cases concerning both natives and foreigners, and it was always difficult to find skilled interpreters (the shortage of intelligent bi-lingual people in government service is an indication of the obstacles confronting the educational system). It was just as hard to confine within strictly legal bounds the Hawaiian flair for story-telling and the Hawaiian enjoyment of conflict and drama. Native witnesses were often accused of perjury, and under at least one police magistrate in the sixties (the Englishman John Montgomery) there was a strong tendency to discount evidence offered by Hawaiians. A danger existed that judges and juries might arrive at verdicts conditioned by race, or that similar crimes would be weighed differently, depending upon the race of the criminal. There was, however, no racial segregation in jail.[84]

In the field of communications too, racial division was naturally apparent. The first newspapers in the islands had been Protestant missionary religious sheets printed in the Hawaiian language. As the foreign community grew, a need appeared for general-interest papers in English. From the late thirties onward, Honolulu was never without at least one English-language paper. Beginning in the forties, there was usually an opposition journal as well as a government organ; and in the fifties, the native-language press split along much the same lines (by then, of course, the Protestants were in opposition, and the New England propensity to publish and damn—in two languages—became even more extreme than when Protestants had controlled the government press). During the sixties and seventies, the declared circulations of native newspapers were three or four times greater than those of English-language papers. Hawaiian-language papers, however, were edited, published, and otherwise directed by white men as often as not. The degree to which they led or reflected native opinion cannot be ascertained very clearly.[85]

The post-office at Honolulu handled a very large interisland mail, and the building was always crowded with Hawaiians picking up and posting letters. So that white residents might do their postal business in comfort, a separate set of counters and boxes was marked off for Hawaiians.[86] It was the same with travel: on interisland schooners and steamers at mid-century, race meant class—"steerage" (actually deck-space) was for natives and cabins were for whites, even poor whites (an occasional white passenger objected to paying cabin class fares when Hawaiians far wealthier travelled steerage).[87]

Honolulu's business community was dominated by white men. If any second group was worth mentioning, it was not the Hawaiians but the Chinese. Scores of unskilled Hawaiians worked in retail and wholesale houses, manufactories, and other commercial enterprises. There were numbers of educated native clerks and skilled tradesmen: from the beginning of printing in Honolulu, for example, natives had been very competent compositors, press-men, and bookbinders. But native entrepreneurs outside the businesses of hawking and peddling and the running of small interisland craft were rare enough to merit special attention from the English-language press. A Hawaiian barber, tinsmith, signpainter, or cabinet-maker in business for himself was virtually one of a kind, and a native who owned a western business and employed other natives was even more singular. The Honolulu Chamber of Commerce in the fifties and sixties had no native members.[88]

In government service centering on Honolulu an obvious racial hierarchy obtained. In most departments, though not all, a white man held the top post (exceptions until mid-century were chiefs, not commoners: for example, Minister of the Interior Keoni Ana, Governor Kekūanaōʻa of Oʻahu and Postmaster David Kalākaua). Complex administration was almost a white monopoly at the customs-house, the government press, the public works bureau, and similar places. The only government establishment run mostly by Hawaiians and for Hawaiians was the produce market, where the Clerk was usually a native. In the generation after the institution of western government, the most responsible commoners in government were probably S.P. Kalama and W.L. Moehonua, Chief Clerks in the Interior Department for a time in the sixties and seventies. They handled correspondence in Hawaiian and English, and made low-level decisions on matters of roads and licenses. Moehonua became Minister of the Interior under Kalākaua.[89]

Separation was also the customary condition in the leading voluntary associations of the town. When, in the fifties, the city's fire department was organized, with volunteer companies subsidized by government, the first three companies came from the white community (predictably enough in terms of their property interest in the town). They were joined in 1861 by Engine Company No. 4, which was Hawaiian. As late as the seventies, no native had been chosen Chief Engineer for Honolulu, nor were there any Hawaiian district fire wardens in the town; but kings and princes patronized Engine Company No. 4, which was readily included in the good-natured rivalry that flourished between companies in matters of membership figures (Hawaiians liked the tax exemption that was a fireman's privilege), smartness (especially in the painting and decorating of engines), conviviality, hospitality, and professional speed and efficiency. All members turned out for firemen's funerals, regardless of race. Ceremonial observance of this kind was taken to have a real meaning, one which hopefully impressed Hawaiians "with the strong and salutary conviction that in the measure that Hawaiians assimilate themselves with the institutions and usages of civilization, they will be honored in life and death."[90]

Much the same sort of situation existed in the town's volunteer military companies. The standing armed forces of the government were almost wholly native, with white instructors. Most militiamen in the city were haoles, although one or two native companies were formed in the sixties, with organizational help from white men.[91]

Protestant church congregations, native and white, set up benevolent auxiliaries. The leaders were the haoles of Honolulu, who established Bible and Tract Societies, Strangers' Friend Societies, and so on. Their work was directed at natives, haoles, and at transient or immigrant foreigners. The benevolent offshoots of native congregations, strangely enough, leaned more to furthering overseas mission work than to the amelioration of local problems. About mid-century, the white Catholic community of Honolulu became large enough to underwrite similar enterprises, including financial support for Catholic sisters brought to the islands to do educational and charitable work. When, in the sixties, Episcopalianism came to the islands, yet a third group of charitable and benevolent societies was inaugurated.[92]

Freemasonry appeared at Honolulu in the late forties. It was a white man's preserve, except that Hawaiian kings (especially Alexander Liholiho, at the urging of Wyllie) became members of various orders, sometimes advancing to high degrees. The Good Templars, a temperance lodge of the late sixties admitting both men and women, developed separate branches for whites and for natives and part-Hawaiians. There was no immediate native equivalent of the several nationality-based social clubs and benevolent societies that emerged in Honolulu after mid-century. Nor was there anything in the native community resembling the Mechanics' Benefit Union.[93] Among the Hawaiians, kinship and locality ties provided a basis for social and protective functions. By the sixties, however, Hawaiian women under the leadership of female chiefs were forming benevolent and funeral associations.[94]

The imitation of western institutions by no means absorbed all the attention of Honolulu's Hawaiians. Much less did such activities serve even the public needs of the Hawaiian population, and what the private views of participating or non-participating natives were remains conjectural. For every western institution that was well-received, another was ignored or resented. This reaction, erratic in terms of the accepted configurations of western society, often produced juxtapositions that were surprising and dismaying to white men.

Enthusiastic, indeed over-enthusiastic, native participation in the western legal process, and simultaneous antipathy to western medicine were cases in point. Hawaiians even learned to commit suicide by hanging themselves, long before they learned to keep themselves alive by observing western medical rules. Another noticeable tendency among natives was that they took hold of some parts of the Protestant gospel and not others, so that a deacon at Kawaiaha'o or Kaumakapili might be famous for obeying or enforcing some commandments and not the rest (far more than New Englanders wanted Him to be, the Hawaiians' Protestant God was Love). Yet again, there was a determined and ingenious resistance by city natives against being counted and taxed. In the days of the kapu, the chiefs had maintained strict control of human and economic resources, but western government at mid-nineteenth century possessed no sanctions powerful enough to convince natives of their personal and financial obligations to society. From mid-century to the mid-seventies, in the first generation after censuses and tax assessments became facts of life in Honolulu, head counts and poll taxes were evaded by temporary migration to another part of the city or to a rural district, and taxes on animals were nullified by natives who killed and ate horses and dogs.[95]

Even when agents of western society did lay hands on Honolulu's natives, the Hawaiians seemed able to bend such occasions to their own style. Periodic work-days on the roads became a matter of communal jollification; men, women, and children sang and shouted together as they rolled rocks or carried logs. The same was true of chain-gang labor. At the waterfront, in Nu'uanu valley, or atop Punchbowl the convicts could be seen, dressed in prison trousers and shirts inscribed pa'ahao (prisoner), sauntering about during working hours, lying down, smoking, reading the government newspaper (free of charge), with their women ministering to their needs, and then packing up at three in the afternoon, to bathe and return to the prison.[96]

Indeed, among the natives of the town, the widest possible variety of response to urban life was observable, from utmost incomprehension to utmost sophistication. Once, late in the fifties, natives were terror-struck to hear that Honolulu's Odd Fellows were about to open a newly-built hall. For some reason, perhaps because in ancient times structures used for esoteric purposes were dedicated with human sacrifice, it was believed that the Mū (a dangerous denizen of the spirit world) was abroad and had captured a woman in Pauoa valley. A few years later, a native forger passed a bad check at Honolulu's only bank—as neat a manipulation of western symbols as can be imagined. At various points between these two extremes might be noted egg-sellers at the market fixing and maintaining their prices oblivious to the passage of time and the deterioration of their goods; horse-dealers on the waterfront setting their charges with a delicate awareness of what the traffic would stand; charcoal-makers in the valleys combining to inflate prices;

produce-peddlers tampering with weights and measures; and milk-men diluting their product to a mixture just on the acceptable side of translucency.[97]

Variety of response by natives might be explained in part by general reference to the nature of Hawaiian society before and after the coming of the white man. Without doubt, it is an over-simplification to view all Hawaiians of the kapu period as having been equally perceptive of the central truths and subtle nuances of their traditional life, or equally sensitive to its social controls. By the same token, it is less than sound to regard western culture as having affected in a consistent way all Hawaiians of later generations. The alien culture, lacking by nature even the consensual unity of traditional Hawaiian culture, presented itself in the Pacific in a particularly fragmented form. It was received in random rather than systematic fashion by natives liberated or deracinated in various ways from their past.

Customarily, a fundamental opposition has been posited between the kind of unconscious social and personal wholeness to be found in the simple human type of the villager, and the deep discontinuities within the *Teilmensch,* the divided urban man.[98] It is not necessary to talk in terms of ideal types to understand how at Honolulu, two generations after the abolition of the kapu, many different levels of creativity and inhibition had become noticeable in a shifting and floating native population, exposed in the city to new kinds of freedom and constraint.

Some differences might be attributed more specifically still to conflict between generations. By mid-century, the white community had become aware of the presence of a "new" Hawaiian, a type that seemed at once less attractive and less manageable than the old.[99] Among elderly natives in the town, traditional attitudes were, naturally, more common than among the young. Simple mission-Christian piety, too, characterized converts of the first twenty years of evangelism rather than those who joined the church later. As for Hawaiians born after the breaking of the kapu system and growing to maturity at mid-century, they tended to disregard social controls both old and new, and to show little respect for submerged tradition, established mission Christianity, or emergent western government.

The "new" Hawaiian showed neither the habitual deference of the traditionalist nor the acquired piety of the native Christian. He combined, in the opinion of the white community, the worst features of old and new. Native indolence persisted, and now it had the opportunity to grow and become all-consuming, because coercion by the ali'i no longer turned it to industry. Native child-rearing methods, allowing children maximum freedom before they took their place in a society closely governed by rank and custom, now produced ungovernable

young adults, as undisciplined infants grew up under a western constitution guaranteeing "liberty" and "equality" to all. Education for ancient
agricultural and technical skills seemed irrelevant to the new generation,
as kalo gave way in part to western foods, and as kapa was superseded
by western cloth. Young Hawaiians left their western schools perhaps
literate, but certainly undirected except in a very vague moral sense.[100]

For young men it was bad enough: no matter what their education or aptitude, clear limits were set on what they might accomplish
in business or government service. The case of the young women was
worse: much less even than white women could they expect to make
a useful life for themselves. At the same time, native girls could earn
a great deal of money from the sale of their bodies. This fundamental
dislocation of relations between the sexes in the Hawaiian community
completed a kind of circle—by mid-century, the family as an institution
was in considerable disarray, and appearances indicated that the next
generation might be in worse straits still.[101]

All these profound changes had done very little, apparently,
to affect the sociability and gregariousness of the town's Hawaiians.
It became customary to remark upon the great numbers of natives
constantly visible, constantly idle, and constantly unproductive: hordes
of little boys and girls swimming naked in the harbor; boat-boys asleep
under the wharves, when they were not pestering visitors, brawling
outside taverns, or silently stripping copper sheathing from ships' hulls
and jetty piles; grown men flying kites, playing marbles, or hilariously
enjoying a giant swing slung from a spar downtown; courthouse and
post-office loafers; market-place hangers-on; coffee-shop habitués who
jammed the downtown streets after dark in the whaling season; and
droves of flashily-dressed horseback riders who passed along the main
roads in clouds of dust and clamor.[102]

When the white community did manage to identify an individual Hawaiian amid the undifferentiated mass, it was rarely for
reasons regarded as commendable. Occasionally a native lawyer, politician, fireman, or church member, worthy in white men's eyes, would
die and be briefly remembered as "punctual," "exact," "temperate," or
"gentlemanly;" but most Hawaiians who came to white attention by
name were notable for deviations from settled norms of white behavior
and experience—engaging confidence men, kleptomaniacs, chronic
prison escapees, braggarts, victims of shipwrecks and other accidents,
murderers, madmen, or (among native women especially) sexual adventurers. For the rest, the Hawaiians were anonymous, each inseparable
from his fellows. This, in fact, was one complaint of the English-language
press—that Hawaiians were not named in western terms, and were thus
nameless and unnameable.[103]

At mid-century and later, then, in the white man's mind the huddled huts of Honolulu's natives still gave forth not individuals but masses. The waterfront gapers of early times were succeeded by the hula dancers of the twenties. They, in turn, were followed by the chanting school examinees, temperance marchers, and revival converts of the thirties, the downtown crowds of the whaling era, the smallpox victims of the fifties, and the aimless drifters of the sixties.

For the time being, it seemed as if Honolulu, acknowledged center of social decay, was irresistibly attractive to a generation of natives apparently passing from primitivism to decadence without assuming on the way the western attributes of civilized individuality and responsibility. Legal restrictions and limitations aimed at keeping the countryside free of vice led only to the depopulation of the countryside as a consequence of migration to the city. Despite the unceasing adjurations of the king, Prince Lot, Wyllie, and the editors of every newspaper, English and native, young Hawaiians scorned the yeoman life idealized by the native Agricultural Society and the simple health of the family kalo patch, diligently cultivated.

The great preference of the rising generation was for the city, where young women might earn great sums of money in season and spend it on the brightest of clothes, and where young men, with luck, might find an older relative who had clung to ingrained work habits. They would wear out his mats playing cards at home while he worked in his kalo patch, they would eat his fish and poi, they would sleep as long as they liked, and then, when the mood seized them, they would issue forth, splendidly dressed, to parade about the town.

The exemplar of the new style was a native porter in a wholesale and retail store, who, at the end of his week's work on Saturday afternoon, transformed himself into a dandy. His tall, shapely form was encased in a white linen suit, with a stand-up collar so high and stiff that he could not turn his head. Wearing a shiny beaver cocked to one side, gloves green, fawn, yellow, or white, with a rattan cane twirling in his hand, and a good cigar between his lips, he was the envy of his fellows of less cultivated tastes and an object of admiration among the native ladies. At least he worked for a living. Dozens like him in taste but not industry might be found in the congregation at Kaumakapili on Sundays, and scores and hundreds more neglected even the formality of church attendance, to ride about the country wearing yellow scarves, patronizing "the post-office and the Hawaiian-language papers, elocution and the district courts, singing schools, Hawaiian feasts, and hulas."[104]

In one way more than others, Honolulu's Hawaiians, like natives elsewhere in the islands, had not come properly to grips with the western world. They had not learned the worth of time expressed in western values. Influential Americans especially, but other westerners in town, too, were savers of time and money; Hawaiians were prodigal spenders of both assets. They were impulsive and ardent, plunging into enterprises that promised quick and brilliant returns of exciting experience, but they were notoriously unable to make prolonged efforts to benefit themselves and others; they had no capacity for self-denial, and in the end no "ambition," as the most severe of westerners remarked.[105]

Certainly they defeated attempts to encourage them to work regularly, hour by hour, day by day, week by week. On a more general level, they seemed simply uninterested in looking at the year as most westerners did: four quarters of a fiscal period, marked by two peaks and two depressions of commercial activity. Honolulu's Hawaiians, to be sure, responded heartily to the arrival of each whaling fleet, but their characteristic reaction was to make holiday. The whaling season offered them not an intensification of good business, but rather an end to dullness, in which for a time orthodoxy might be denied, more or less with impunity, in company with carousing foreigners.

As with the whaling season, so with shorter fiscal periods. The height of bustle in the haoles' commercial world came on "quarter day," when three-monthly accounts were settled by messengers hastening from office to office in the business district. By contrast, Hawaiians were happy when stores were closed in the evenings, happier at the end of the week, and happiest of all on holidays.

As late as the mid-sixties, Honolulu's Hawaiians had not been persuaded to use western names for the days of the week, even in Hawaiian transliteration (Monede, Tusede, and so on).[106] Despite four decades of western education, in the course of which the government and the Hawaiian-language newspapers had adopted the western calendar, natives clung stubbornly to the old names. This may be regarded as a superficial manifestation of a deeper unwillingness to relinquish old notions about time. The periods of the ancient era had been marked by kapu days and festivals, and these, far more than non-ritual days, bad represented periods of importance. The avidity with which natives in the city entered into ceremonial observances of all kinds would suggest that they had not abandoned altogether their ideas of time as divided between the profane, which was negligible, and the sacred, which was significant.

It is not contended that at mid-century the holidaying Hawaiians were realizing an abolition of profane time and a re-creation of sacred time as they had done, say, during the makahiki festivals of old, when, by the repetition of well-known ritual, they were able to renew the sources of their society's strength. The ancient wellsprings were drying up, and much of the natives' holiday activity was nothing but imitation of western ways. Nonetheless, the natives clearly thought of holidays as times when they could most fully "be themselves." Honolulu at work was reminiscent of New England in many respects; but on holidays the town was Hawaiian.

What the Hawaiians were at mid-century was, of course, a matter of some complexity, and this was demonstrated on holidays and other ceremonial occasions. For one thing, during the decades of contact with white men something of a change developed in relative emphasis accorded the personal crises of birth, marriage, and death. Native birth-rates were perilously low, the institution of marriage was insecure, and death-rates were tragically high. Funerals rather than naming or marriage feasts seem to have called forth the greatest expenditures of money and emotion.[107]

This was especially true when the death of a chief was mourned. By the same token, it was the death of a chief that produced the most striking ebullitions of traditionalism. At the peak of Protestant influence such outbursts were damped down considerably, but from the time of Alexander Liholiho they reappeared in force. Mark Twain happened to be at Honolulu when Princess Victoria Kamāmalu died in 1866, and his sharp eye was much taken by the scene at the palace: the weeks-long lying in state, the vigil by torchlight, the chanting, wailing, and dancing of grief-stricken natives clustered within the walled grounds.[108]

On less serious occasions, the Hawaiians of Honolulu found it easy to enjoy themselves, no matter whether the provenance of a celebration was Hawaiian or foreign. Since 1819, the death of Kamehameha I had been commemorated on a feast day every year. Birthdays, death days, and anniversaries of later kings, queens, princes and princesses were also noted. Added to these, as time went by, were foreign national days: for the Americans, July 4, which dated from the pre-missionary era, and (somewhat later) Washington's Birthday; for the British, Queen Victoria's Birthday; for the French, La Fête Napoléon. Such holidays affected the community in direct proportion to the number of resident nationals. Thus, July 4 was always the most explosive of holidays, and La Fête Napoléon was confined to flag-raising by consuls, private dinner parties, and dances.

Other designated holidays were connected with religion. The American Protestants abhorred over-indulgence. For a long time, they observed Christmas Day and Good Friday only at church; the leaven of other denominations was required to introduce the two days into the holiday calendar. Santa Claus and Christmas trees appeared at Honolulu during the fifties. Thanksgiving Day, New England-style, was made a Hawaiian holiday in the forties, and, by government order, was amalgamated with Christmas for some years. Social visiting on New Year's Day became popular after the decline of Protestantism. The Catholic Church at Honolulu celebrated a number of holy days, like Corpus Christi, without involving the rest of the town.

When Protestantism was at its height, strong pressure was exerted to keep holy even secular holidays. Under mission suasion in the forties, the government sometimes issued orders decreeing that holidays were kapu days, on which no riding, feasting, or even working should be permitted. As the social influence of Protestantism grew weaker, holidays more and more ceased to be closed and became open.

This was most noticeable on the specifically Hawaiian holidays, July 31 and November 28. On July 31, 1843, Admiral Richard Thomas had restored the sovereignty of the islands to Kamehameha III, and on November 28 of the same year Hawai'i's independence had been recognized by the major powers. Gargantuan feasting and frolic marked the anniversaries. For a few years in the forties, liquor and dancing were absent, but in the course of the liberalization of Honolulu's society they made their appearance among natives and whites on the two great days of the year as on less important occasions.

Although July 31 and November 28, as holidays, had been brought into existence by western intrusions, they were viewed as reaffirming in some vague way the integrity of old Hawai'i; and here, as at chiefs' funerals, the ancient arts might be seen. In the forties, and again in the sixties, Restoration Day programs included mock battles and spear-throwing exhibitions, together with hulas in the presence of official parties. The July holiday of 1847 was long remembered as the most spectacular commemoration of Restoration. Almost ten thousand people gathered at a lū'au in Nu'uanu valley and devoured 271 hogs, 482 calabashes of poi, 602 chickens, 3 oxen, 2 barrels of salt pork, 2 of beef, 3,125 salt fish, 1,820 fresh fish, 12-1/2 barrels of lū'au and cabbage, 2,245 coconuts, 4,000 heads of kalo, 180 squid, and other delicacies. In the afternoon, John 'I'i, childhood friend of Alexander Liholiho, counsellor of Kauikeaouli, and later Supreme Court Justice, demonstrated the parrying of spears. He faced twenty spearsmen without harm, and then, when all their weapons had been hurled, drove them from the field. Other athletes staged exhibitions of wrestling and of the lua, or bone-breaking technique. While the official party watched and ate, old women chanted endless meles in honor of the king and his ancestors, and that evening after most of the company had left, hula girls danced by torchlight.[109]

Over the span of several decades, the holiday calendar underwent some subtle changes. American enthusiasm for July 4, for example, waxed and waned with the coming and the passing of the Civil War. Toward the end of the sixties, Restoration Day, July 31, fell into desuetude as being a kind of affront to Great Britain, whose stock was high in the islands at the time. In 1871, July 31 was removed from the list of national holidays, but no matter about officialdom: common natives continued to celebrate it informally, with riding parties, picnics, drinking, hula-dancing, and general carousing.[110]

In the long perspective of Honolulu's history, the holiday-making of the Hawaiians was nothing but the first measure in a dance of death. Year by year the dancers were fewer as throughout the kingdom natives in great numbers succumbed to loathsome diseases. In the eighteen-seventies, by which time the survival of the Hawaiian people was in doubt and foreign influence had risen to unprecedented heights, racism of a very ugly kind appeared at Honolulu. Born of desperation on the part of natives and contemptuous arrogance on the part of haoles, it added to the exacerbations of a struggle in which Hawai'i ultimately lost its independence. The future course of events was hardly visible even to the acutest observers at the court of Alexander Liholiho, where the dance of life seemed to be at its most spirited. Just as the competing national groups of the town found ways to perform their advances and retreats with a modicum of finesse, so men of different races were able, for a brief period, to pass in complementary figures across the stage of the city.

CHAPTER 8

The New Economy

The flawed social elegance of Honolulu after mid-century found its counterpart in the physical arrangements of the city. Between the mid-fifties and the mid-seventies, the population rose from eleven thousand to almost fifteen thousand. New streets were added to the down-town area; homes and business buildings began to spread across the plains to the east and west of the harbor and to push farther toward the valleys. Expansion was virtually unplanned, as was to be expected in a mid-nineteenth century city lacking self-government. At any given moment the people of Honolulu were likely to be ruminating upon (though not necessarily correcting) the municipal errors of the past, and observing at the same time with the utmost complacency the commission of newer, greater blunders.

Civic carelessness gave the ground-plan of the city its shape; and the skyline, seen against the inland mountain ranges, was ragged. The era of thatch and adobe was coming to an end. More and more, Honolulu was emerging as a city of wood and stone;[1] but orthodox northern European and American building materials used in a new setting produced no innovations in design, except for the pleasant idea of adding a lānai or verandah to the bare front of a house. "Practical architects" and contractors in Honolulu—and most of their customers— were average men, with average imaginations and frontiersmen's tastes. Of the new public buildings, some were handsome, though imitative; most were quite undistinguished; none was consciously suited to a sub-tropical climate.[2] One or two small things saved the built-up part of Honolulu from complete aesthetic aridity and banality. Along the main roads, algarobas and other shade trees introduced in earlier decades were coming to maturity, lending a measure of relief to thoroughfares and house lots once exposed, hot and barren. The town's water supply, somewhat improved in the mid-fifties, brought touches of green to many places, and here and there ornamental fountains played.

Concurrently, however, the older sections of the city were becoming built up to the point of congestion. Well-to-do families in increasing numbers moved out of town. Nu'uanu, which had always been the choice of leading members of the official and mercantile communities, continued to be attractive. A newer resort for the fashionable developed at Waikīkī, which, after a half-century of comparative neglect, was returning to prominence as a locus of leisure.[3] There, overworked white men needing surcease from the city discovered the sun and the sea, whose value the less constrained Hawaiians had always appreciated.

This permanent removal from Honolulu proper was supplemented by a seasonal flight in the doldrum months of the summer, when business was slack and a burdensome heat settled over the city. Those who could afford it left for holiday homes in the valley, at the beach, across the Pali on windward O'ahu, or even on the outer islands. Others, forced to remain in town, made do with lesser expedients: a picnic, a horseback or carriage or omnibus ride along the one or two indifferent major roads leading out of the city, or perhaps a weekend "in the country."[4]

Close by, and regularly used, were a few breathing spaces. For a time in the sixties, it was modish to ride up to the Royal Hawaiian Agricultural Society's garden in Nu'uanu for a plate of fresh strawberries and a glass of white wine. Later, in the seventies, the Sunday concerts of the Royal Hawaiian Band at Emma Square or in the garden of the Hawaiian Hotel drew the social leaders of the city. They promenaded, smartly dressed, among crowds of natives and lower-class whites while bandmaster Heinrich Berger guided his uniformed Hawaiian musicians through Strauss waltzes, operatic arias by Donizetti and Rossini, and his own healthy German marches and polkas (to which he usually gave Hawaiian names). Between the east end of the town and the coconut groves and beaches of Waikīkī lay a broad plain, by no means green and fertile, but still open wide. There most holiday festivities were held. Ample space was available for the mandatory Saturday horseback riding of Honolulu's Hawaiians; and there, too, the sporting gentry of the town assembled, as they had done since early in the century, to race blooded horses.

It remained true that one of the best things about Honolulu as a place to live was that easy means of escape were at hand. God made the country, man the town, so William Cowper said, and the Honolulu newspapers were fond of quoting him. Nu'uanu and Waikīkī, to be sure, were pleasant enough examples of God's handiwork; but on the edges of town, where natural beauty needed man's help merely to survive, matters were less well ordered. For a long time, the government had intended to set aside part of the eastern plain as a public park dedicated to Admiral Richard Thomas, who had restored Hawaiian independence there in 1843. When rough boundaries were laid out in 1850 and house lots fronting on the open space were offered at auction, the wealthy rushed to bid and buy. But a quarter-century later, in the mid-seventies, Thomas Square was still undeveloped, a place of straggling trees and ill-defined tracks, and the government was considering renting the "park" to a man who wanted to raise jute.[5]

In the downtown area itself, where the municipal issue was not beauty but utility, public services lagged far behind growth. Financial difficulties, in fact, caused retrogression. At the beginning of the sixties, the government was so poor that general retrenchment was necessary. Local government in particular was affected. At Honolulu, sheriffs, marshals, policemen, and inferior judges were either dismissed or placed on reduced salaries; the governor's office, which carried out little work of importance anyway, did less and less. In one instance only—a premature attempt at the end of the fifties to introduce gas lighting—was innovation ahead of acute need in Honolulu; and this, naturally, was a private speculation financed by subscriptions, not a government-owned enterprise.[7]

Between the mid-fifties and the mid-seventies a million dollars was spent on public works. Given the state of the kingdom's finances, this was a great deal. Still more was needed—the rate of expenditure was insufficient—but no funds could be spared. The government found it hard to balance its budget even after taxes on real and personal property were imposed and tariffs were raised under a new Civil Code in 1859. Major public works projects from the fifties to the seventies could be contemplated only if governmental revenues were bolstered by loans. Even then, with deficit spending in vogue, money was short. The outer islands remained starved for funds;[8] the capital, enjoying first call on tax and loan revenues, continued to look shabby.[9]

Evidence of public penury was easy to find. The condition of Honolulu's streets reminded citizens every day of the inadequacy of works appropriations. Some gross irritants of earlier decades (rampaging bullocks and oozing cesspools) were less common, at least on the main thoroughfares; but even there litter, and mud and dust in season, continued to make travel unpleasant. Street lighting and numbering were introduced in the late sixties and early seventies on a small scale downtown. Elsewhere, and especially in the newer sections of town, conditions were worse. After mid-century, a useful local institution emerged to guide development at the neighborhood level: committees of property-owners might petition the government to have a street defined, and they were also allowed a voice in determining routes and setting compensation for condemned property.[10] Local initiative, of course, could take matters only so far, and as often as not the government for its part bestowed on streets nothing more than a name. For years after its formal designation,

Liliha Street, to the west of Nu'uanu stream, was interrupted in several places by the raised banks and swampy depressions of kalo patches. This was only one picturesque street nuisance among many in the environs of Honolulu.[11]

Outside the city, roads tended to dwindle to mere tracks within a very few miles. The newspapers were full of suggestions about the desirability of carriage paths east to Koko Head and west to 'Ewa, but nothing much could be done. In default of sustained government work, roads were marked simply by the passage of traffic. By the later fifties and early sixties, hardy men were taking carriages to the north and west coasts of O'ahu and back. A major effort of road-building was carried on in Nu'uanu valley, partly because a route over the Pali would open up the windward side of the island, partly (so the opposition press alleged) because many high-ranking government officials lived in Nu'uanu. In the mid-forties, Kamehameha III had been one of the first to ride a horse across the Pali and down the trail to the district of Ko'olau; but not until 1861 was a buggy driven over the same route (the pioneers were Gerrit Judd and Eli Corwin, the latter a pastor of Fort Street Church and a great enthusiast for better roads). In 1863 a horse-drawn vehicle made the trip in the other direction, from Ko'olau to Honolulu. For the most part, however, traffic over the Pali during the sixties and seventies was by horseback. The windward trail remained dangerous for heavy wheeled traffic.[12]

Within the Honolulu area as defined by streets, good or bad, there were other serious municipal deficiencies. Water supply, in particular, was a problem on more than one count. Nu'uanu stream, the town's biggest watercourse, had many uses. High up in the valley, waterfalls fed bathing pools. Carefully-engineered irrigation ditches took water from the main stream to the terraced kalo gardens of the natives. Cattle pastured in the valley came to wallow and drink at the stream; and farther down, along the last mile or so, the bath-houses of taverns abutted on the water, and washerwomen squatted on the banks to beat out clothes. Household needs before mid-century were generally supplied by back-yard wells, from which water was raised either by buckets or hand-pumps before the advent of windmills.[13]

The copious spring water of the Nu'uanu uplands was brought downtown in quantity for the first time in 1847, when the government laid a one-inch pipe from a kalo patch to a tank at the harbor-master's office on the waterfront, so that whaleships and merchantmen need no longer send watering parties with barrels inland to the tidal limit of Nu'uanu stream. In 1850, a four-inch pipe was laid from the King's Spring in Nu'uanu to the waterfront; thenceforth, a tap on the wharves was opened to ships for a small fee, and boats riding outside could be supplied from a water tanker licensed by the government. Five years later, in February, 1855, Honolulu residents were authorized to take water from the Nu'uanu pipe for $25 per annum. Petitions for water rights began to come in immediately, and very soon half-inch pipes were attached in many places, almost all at private expense. Pressure was poor, and as numerous branch pipes were added it became poorer. Those beyond the network paid a licensed water-carrier to make regular stops at their houses. In less than two years the system was overloaded and water was scarce throughout the city. It became necessary to refuse new petitions. Restrictions were placed upon the legal use of water. In the summer of 1857 fountains were outlawed, the sprinkling of dusty streets was forbidden, and a constable patrolled the town to see that taps and garden hoses were turned off at night.[14]

The continuing water shortage of the later fifties had many disturbing side-effects. Fire was always a danger in the downtown business area, with its closely-packed wooden buildings and thatch huts. Volunteer fire companies, however conscientious, could do little without an adequate water supply. The city, in fact, was ripe for disaster. By prolonged good fortune it escaped, at least until the final decades of the century, when huge conflagrations in 1886 and 1900 gutted large parts of the older town. In the meantime small fires were frequent, and in 1855, 1860, and 1877 there were major blazes, contained only with difficulty. The first of these produced expensive insurance claims. Honolulu's underwriters in a body refused thereafter to take the risk of insuring businesses housed in wooden fire-traps. Merchants hastened to petition the government for improvements in water and fire service. Public hydrants and storage tanks were supplemented by large reservoirs dug by businessmen on their city premises. Some took another way out, by investing in expensive fireproof buildings. The hazard remained great, nonetheless, and wariness on the part of insurance companies continued into the seventies.[15]

There seemed to be no shortage of water in Nu'uanu valley. The question, in the government's view, was simply one of getting it to town in sufficient quantity. In 1859 the legislature passed an act "to provide a further supply of water for the city of Honolulu." The Minister of the Interior was directed to borrow money on the security of future receipts from the sale of water rights. With these funds a new reservoir was to be built in the valley and new pipes were to be laid. The legislature of 1860 further authorized the Minister of the Interior to take possession of any land that might be needed for the new water-works. A quarter-million gallon reservoir was constructed below Kapena spring, which itself yielded about six hundred thousand gallons a day. A twelve-inch pipe was run down to the city; four-inch branch pipes were laid along intersecting streets; and a system of gates and stop-cocks made it possible to shut off small sections without closing the main pipe.[16]

By mid-1861 more than five hundred taps had been attached;[17] and within a few months, at the height of the summer, water was scarce in the city once again. Irritated comments greeted the re-imposition of water rationing. More important, there appeared for the first time a consideration of damage done to sources of water supply in Nuʻuanu valley by several decades of urban life.

Serious abuse of the Nuʻuanu uplands had begun as early as the mid-forties. Rights to water and land were matters of the greatest concern to Hawaiian chiefs and commoners in the old days, and, until the forties, the carefully-organized and laboriously-maintained traditional system had been kept reasonably intact under the close surveillance of the aliʻi and their konohikis. Conservation followed naturally: as long as the kalo gardens were in good condition, there was little danger of erosion or deforestation. By mid-century, however, this balance had been upset by legal, social, and economic innovations. After the land distribution, privately-owned holdings in Nuʻuanu changed hands rather rapidly. Old boundaries were altered, and traditional water rights became vested in individuals, causing disputes over access and distribution. Natives, no longer able to turn unquestioningly to their chiefs for decisions, tried to settle their affairs by discussion. White men applied to government; and commissioners of water rights and private ways busied themselves in Nuʻuanu (and elsewhere) for the remainder of the century.

With changes of ownership came changes in land usage. As kalo gardens were abandoned, their diligently-tended ditches were diverted or simply allowed to fall into disrepair. A conflict between the demands of the town and the needs of the remaining kalo growers was noticeable as early as 1856. In the early sixties, matters moved to a new stage. Many dispossessed kalo farmers had left the lower valley for the forests higher up, where they now earned their livings as wood-cutters and charcoal-makers. Their depredations in the forests were matched by those of goats, horses and cattle. Natural cover on the watershed disappeared steadily, and the process was accelerated by serious brush fires which in 1866 burned hundreds of acres in Kalihi, Nuʻuanu, and Pauoa valleys.[18] As long as ecological anarchy existed in Nuʻuanu, very little good could come of improvements in the capacity of reservoirs or extensions of the city's system of reticulation. A long-time resident of Nuʻuanu, J.H. Wood, put the case clearly and vigorously:

> The Nuuanu Stream—like all rapid, mountain streams varies much in its volume, often showing ten to fifty times more water than on the day previous It is tap'd by Auwai's [ditches]...

all the way from near its sea level to near its source, rendering the Valley a net-work of streams, conducting water to Kalo land culti- vated at present mostly near the Nuuanu Road:—a party having cleaned his Loi's [kalo-patches] & wishing to fill them up, or to soften the grass-grown beds of some he wishes to cultivate,— or wanting more water for his mill, animals, or other purpose, goes to the source of supply above—be it river or Auwai, dams the main stream—takes the water where he wants it for the time, & where it runs until another wanting it, helps himself likewise, turning it in another direction.

Now, if 5—50—or 500 men help themselves to water from its source, not one of the number would ever think of going to its source to shut it off when they had enough, or when their neighbor was entitled to it, but leave it to the man next entitled to it to look after his own interest, & so on, each for himself, but no one for his neighbor, or the public; if a smart shower happens, (they are frequent in this Valley) the River rises, dams turn the water into Auwai's—mains into latterals, and down it comes, overflowing & deluging all below,—sweeping everything away not fix'd beyond its power to remove—Such is the practice, & has been for years, Water Rights and Water Luna's [supervisors], notwithstanding.

If a scarcity of water in town prevails during a few months of the year, it is look'd after somewhat, & dealt out to some extent, by a system of Inn Gates on one or two of the prin- ciple Auwai's; but even that does not prevent frequent damage from carelessness or neglect, during the dryest months; and when water is abundant, as during the past year, every one appears to help himself, ad libitum—regardless of consequences...[19]

Wood wrote in 1875, when matters reached a critical stage. He and others for years past had been remarking that floods and freshets in the rainy months were becoming more common. Denuded hillsides gave up water as fast as it fell, and millions of gallons flowed quickly, uselessly, and sometimes dangerously to the sea. Lakes formed at street corners in Honolulu, houses leaked, adobe walls crumbled; and down Nu'uanu valley to the harbor, borne on rushing waters, came spars, abut- ments or even complete wooden bridges, big logs from timber-yards, flimsy bathing houses and laundries from the sides of the stream, occa- sional drowned livestock, and—most bizarre—coffins of natives buried in houseyards fronting on Nu'uanu stream. In the dry months, springs and minor streams formerly fed by soakage were reduced to nothing, and summer at Honolulu became a season of muddy water in short supply.[20]

As early as 1860, investigations were made to determine if the Nuʻuanu springs could be supplemented by water from the adjoining valleys—Pauoa, Makiki, and Mānoa. The expense was prohibitive. Nuʻuanu remained the sole source of supply. Debarred from exploiting other valleys, the government perforce turned conservationist in Nuʻuanu. Enabling laws dated from 1860, when the legislature had authorized the Minister of the Interior to acquire land needed for the planned water-works extensions of that year. This act and later amendments (passed in 1868 and 1874) were invoked in the seventies to gain control of major irrigation ditches such as the Pākī ʻAuwai and also of large tracts leased or owned by private individuals in vital areas of Nuʻuanu. The government at the same time began to plant trees on deforested land already in public hands. The new policy was inaugurated none too soon—the springs were dwindling to nothing. Already the town took some of its water from Nuʻuanu stream itself, and the social elite of the valley as well as the common people of the city faced the fact that, in the higher reaches of Nuʻuanu, the depleted stream passed through the large dairy farm of Mrs. William Hillebrand at Luakaha. In 1873 the government opened negotiations to buy her lease. Prolonged debate followed over the value of Luakaha, and Mrs. Hillebrand's claims were not the only ones which cost the government time and trouble in this respect.[21]

Salvation came from an unexpected quarter. In the eighties the first successful artesian wells in the Honolulu district were sunk; and it was soon discovered that below the easily-pierced capstone of most of leeward Oʻahu lay a marvelously pure, apparently inexhaustible supply of subterranean water.

Throughout the fifties and sixties the opposition press, most notably the *Pacific Commercial Advertiser,* subjected the government to criticism over the handling of public works appropriations. The soundness of projects was always in question after the fact. Then too, the *Advertiser* claimed continually that the ministry, especially in the sixties and early seventies, was corrupt in its awarding of contracts. By law, these were supposed to be open to public bid, but as often as not they were awarded in private and without advertisement to "favorites" of the government. Charges of conflict of interest, which had been levelled at Gerrit Judd in the forties and fifties, were now directed at the generation of politicians and civil servants who followed Judd in office.[22]

There may well have been private manipulation of public funds at Honolulu. Certainly, members of "the ring" so darkly referred to by the *Advertiser* appeared far better provided for in their private than in their public capacities. Expensive homes were common in the town, but it was the universal view that government buildings in the fifties and sixties were less than adequate.

In the middle forties, Kamehameha III had decided to make Honolulu rather than Lahaina the permanent seat of the monarchy. He took up residence at the east end of the city in a small, pleasant house which became known as 'Iolani Palace.[23] Governor Kekūanaō'a had built the house for his daughter, Princess Victoria Kamāmalu, but he gave it willingly to the king. High-ranking chiefs came to live nearby, and the general area of Pelekane took on the style of "the court end of town." The old "grass palaces" of earlier monarchs in downtown Honolulu were now things of the past. Nonetheless, more than a trace of traditional Hawaiian living arrangements lingered at 'Iolani. The king and his wife, for example, preferred not to live in the "palace" itself. Instead, small private apartments were built for them on the grounds.[24]

Three more kings lived at 'Iolani—Alexander Liholiho, Lot Kamehameha, and William Lunalilo—before the flamboyant David Kalākaua, soon after his accession in 1874, began to agitate for a new palace to match his royal eminence. Plans for a second palace actually dated from the mid-sixties, but one delay after another occurred over the site, the design, and the cost. By 1876, Kalākaua was disgusted with the old house: "The life of my noble wife and myself," he wrote, "is not so pleasant in this place, the houses are filthy and in poor condition, and it is only with great effort to hide the humiliation that we live here. And it would be well that the citizens feel humiliated also regarding this thing."[25] Construction of the second palace was begun on the grounds of the first 'Iolani in 1879 and was completed in 1883; the building still stands, a lavish monument to the last years of the monarchy.[26]

In the grounds of the first 'Iolani Palace stood a royal tomb, containing the coffins of every monarch since Kamehameha II as well as those of many high chiefs and a few distinguished foreigners. By the mid-sixties it had become crowded, and a new cemetery was prepared in Nu'uanu valley, with a chapel designed and built in simplified Gothic style by Theodore C. Heuck, architect of Queen's Hospital. After the funeral of Foreign Minister Wyllie in November, 1865, all the coffins, including Wyllie's, were taken from the palace grounds to the Nu'uanu cemetery, where today, a hundred years later, they remain.[27]

Kamehameha III's decision in the forties to make Honolulu his royal residence, and the later declaration of Honolulu as capital of the islands, raised the question of suitable accommodations for the various permanent agencies of government. At first, the major cabinet ministers occupied offices on Merchant Street in a coral building called Honolulu Hale (Honolulu House), owned by Kamehameha III and leased to the government. By 1850, Honolulu Hale was regarded as too small, too open to the public, and too far from the palace. Then, in 1853, a variety theater was built next to it, creating a fire hazard which threatened the safety of money in the Treasury and government documents housed in Honolulu Hale.[28] In February, 1854, most of the cabinet ministers moved to an adobe house on Hotel Street owned by Foreign Minister Wyllie and rented by him to the government. Here the ministers carried out their business for the rest of the fifties. By 1861, the house had come to the end of its useful life. A rainstorm undermined the foundations of Wyllie's own office, cracking the walls and producing "a scattering of redtape, sealing wax, cocked hats, and billets doux." No one was hurt, but clearly it was time for the government to move elsewhere. The next choice was the former French Hotel, located on a triangular lot at Fort, Hotel and Union Streets. The government maintained offices there until a new building was constructed in the early seventies not far from 'Iolani Palace.[29]

A large building near the waterfront called Mauna Kilika (mountain of silk) had been used in the early period of constitutional government variously as a legislative assembly-hall, a courthouse, an armory, a warehouse, and a public meeting-place. In the early fifties, it became more and more the domain of Governor Kekūanaō'a. The legislature met during the rest of the fifties and sixties in a new courthouse constructed not far from Honolulu's decaying fort; and then, after the new government building opposite 'Iolani Palace was finished in the seventies, legislators and judges moved there to occupy quarters under the same roof as cabinet ministers.

This new government building, Ali'iōlani Hale, was interesting in that the plans from which it was realized were originally submitted to the Hawaiian government by the Sydney architect Thomas Rowe in answer to a request for designs for a new 'Iolani Palace. When Rowe's plans arrived, together with those of another Sydney architect, discussions on the site and the cost of the new palace were in progress, but the government was ready to act on the question of a new office building. Rowe's plans were modified and used as the basis of a two-story concrete building erected on King Street opposite the palace grounds. Completed in 1874, Ali'iōlani Hale is still standing in 1965; it now serves as the State of Hawai'i's Judiciary Building.[30]

Of the million dollars spent on public works in the reigns of Kamehameha IV, Kamehameha V, and Lunalilo, about $120,000 was absorbed by Ali'iōlani Hale alone. Minor projects carried out during the same period included the royal cemetery in Nu'uanu, a new post-office building, a quarantine station, and the new prison, reformatory, and insane asylum mentioned earlier. These lesser projects together cost more than one hundred thousand dollars.

In the long run, by far the most expensive item in the public works budget was the maintenance and improvement of the harbor. The dredging of the shallows and the building of the Esplanade, begun in the fifties, were carried on even when all other schemes were halted for lack of funds. Work was stopped only once, when the treasury was almost empty in the early sixties. Concentration on the harbor was necessary so that Honolulu might enter the age of steam transportation with adequate basic equipment. Minor waterfront installations, largely the responsibility of government, were generally satisfactory—wharves, warehouses, markets, water-pipes and water-boats, lights, buoys, channel-markers and wig-wag telegraphs. The towing service offered by the governments tug *Pele* was good, and privately-owned shipyards were efficient. What was missing was reliable steam service.

After the last cumbersome side-wheeler of Garet Ryckman's ill-fated Hawaiian Steam Navigation Company was withdrawn in 1856, the archipelago was without steam transport, except for the tug *Pele*. Ryckman's speculative venture had been political as well as financial, and it had failed on both counts. The San Francisco syndicate had made heavy investments on the assumption that Hawai'i would soon fall into the hands of the United States. The annexation movement of 1854, however, came to nothing; and Ryckman, who had hoped to emerge as the holder of a lucrative monopoly, found himself instead deep in debt. From that time on, no foreign entrepreneur could be led to risk money on interisland steamers. Once again, then, Hawaiian-owned schooners carried passengers, livestock and general freight between the capital and the outer islands.

If steamers were to return to Hawaiian coastal waters, it would have to be at Hawaiian expense; and Ryckman's experience had shown that costs might be great. Income from passenger traffic alone could not keep a steamer's books balanced, and many Honolulu merchants who handled freight and livestock consignments also had financial interests in trading schooners. Enthusiasm for steamships continued lively, however. In 1856, the legislature took a leading position when it authorized the Minister of the Interior to spend up to $60,000 on the purchase or construction of an interisland steamer. Negotiations were soon begun, first in the United States and then in Great Britain, but the late fifties were a time of economic depression in the islands and elsewhere, and the plans were abandoned.

At last, in 1858, the government came to an agreement with the Honolulu mercantile firm of C.A. Williams & Co. A screw steamer for the interisland traffic was to be operated under the terms of a six-year monopoly held by a newly-constituted Hawaiian Steam Navigation Company. Charles Williams arranged in 1859 to have a ship built at Boston and New London. Her voyage out to the islands under sail and engine took 128 days. She arrived at Honolulu on June 28, 1860.[31]

Under the name of *Kilauea* (an occasionally active volcano on the island of Hawai'i), this 400-tonner gave fitful service for seventeen years. The experience was not altogether a happy one. Between 1860 and 1876, there was scarcely enough freight business to keep the steamer running. Successive combinations and companies, created at intervals to save the *Kilauea*, lost money and were dissolved one after the other. Ten major re-organizations and re-capitalizations were tried, as well as many shufflings of schedules and routes. Firms heavily involved included Janion, Green & Co.; Walker, Allen & Co.; and Hackfeld & Co. From the beginning, the government itself was an investor; late in the sixties a direct subsidy was granted, and for the last seven years of her active life the *Kilauea* was owned entirely by the government.[32] By the early seventies, virtually all that kept her in operation was the conviction of Kamehameha V and one or two of his cabinet ministers that the steamer should be regarded as part of the "road system" of the island kingdom—as, in fact, a major public improvement, a governmental responsibility.[33]

The islands, it seemed, could hardly support a steamer; neither could they quite do without one. Part of the trouble lay in competition. As has been mentioned, the freight-handling business was managed adequately by established commercial houses at Honolulu; and schooner-owners greeted the *Kilauea's* entry into the passenger trade by halving their own fares. Steamer accommodations, even in "cabin" class, were spartan, at best. Then too, the *Kilauea*, like her predecessors, proved unable to stay off the reefs of the outer islands. Within a few months of her arrival she ran aground at Lahaina. Later, in January, 1866, a navigating error put her over the reef at Kawaihae, Hawai'i; gales drove her ashore, and not until April could she be repaired, re-floated, and brought back to Honolulu. In 1871, she went on a reef on the island of Moloka'i. Minor mishaps were frequent. These, together with the endless mechanical adjustments needed to maintain the *Kilauea*, reduced the number of income-producing voyages she completed, and made her repair bills very high.[34] By 1868 the *Kilauea* was uninsurable. Only under the energetic management of Samuel G. Wilder in the early seventies did she keep at all consistently to her published schedules. Even then, she was withdrawn more than once to make special voyages for the government. Wilder could not get her to show a profit; much less could he prevent the steady deterioration of her hull and machinery. He urged again and again that she be replaced. Finally, in 1877, the government purchased the 592-ton *Likelike*, the first of several steamers which sailed between the islands in the last quarter of the century. Quite soon Wilder was able to buy the *Likelike* from the government. By then the sugar industry had begun to boom. Interisland traffic was up, and constantly rising; government support was no longer needed, and private enterprise could come into its own.[35]

If interisland steam transportation was a risky business, the trans-oceanic traffic was even more uncertain. For Hawaiian capitalists, barely able to keep one small steamer in service, a Honolulu-based line of ocean-going steamers was of course quite out of the question. Even American millionaires of the post-Civil War period could not stand alone in this field, and the earliest trans-Pacific lines were brought into existence with the aid of sizeable governmental subsidies. The kingdom of Hawai'i joined the United States, Great Britain, and the colonial governments of New Zealand and Australia in offering rights and privileges to several steamship lines during the sixties and seventies. Hawai'i stood to gain greatly, but the inducements its government could afford were small, and, as with the interisland line, results were mixed.

In the early and middle sixties, quite reliable sailing ships carried passengers, freight, and mail between Honolulu and San Francisco. These vessels continued to serve the islands while attempts were made to connect the west coast with Hawai'i by steam on a regular basis. In 1862, the Hawaiian legislature passed an act offering privileges and exemptions in Honolulu harbor to any line of trans-Pacific steamers, although at the same time it was acknowledged that Hawai'i could not supply much in the way of freight or passengers. The Pioneer Trans-Pacific Steam Company, which ran ships between San Francisco and Hong Kong for a short time in 1863, enquired about privileges at Honolulu; but not until 1865 was a regular United States-China run started, and even then Honolulu was not included as a stopping place.[36]

In 1865, the United States Congress passed an act to assist the establishment of a fast steam mail service between America and China, with scheduled stops at Hawai'i and Japan. The Pacific Mail Steamship Company was awarded a ten-year contract providing for monthly round trips, subsidized up to $500,000 a year. The company opened negotiations with the Hawaiian government for the use of harbor facilities at Honolulu, and there was an eager response in the islands. Despite this, it soon became clear that although the act of Congress stipulated a Honolulu stopover, Pacific Mail was against the idea. The islands were, after all, a long way from the shortest route to China, which ran far to the north along the great circle. In addition, some uncertainty persisted about the capacity of Honolulu harbor to accommodate the large steamers that were to be used. A company agent at Honolulu sounded the channel and found enough water—between 23 and 25-1/2 feet—and the Hawaiian government built a new steamboat wharf as part of the waterfront improvements that had been going on ever since the mid-fifties. The company's arguments of distance and expense prevailed, however; and Pacific Mail's first ship, the *Colorado*, which left San Francisco for China on January 1, 1867, was awaited in vain at Honolulu. Congress voted to remove the Honolulu stopover from the subsidized China mail service.[37]

Pacific Mail was reluctant to include Honolulu in its route; but another west coast line, the California Steam Navigation Company, was more than willing. Early in 1866, their steamer *Ajax* had sailed from San Francisco to Honolulu on the first of a series of voyages which, it was hoped, would encourage the Hawaiian government to award a subsidy. On its second voyage home, the *Ajax* carried fifty passengers and over a million pounds of sugar; but even this promising start did not secure the permanence of the run. At that time—April, 1866—the attention of the Hawaiian government was still upon Pacific Mail's China service, and the California Steam Navigation Company could neither persuade the cabinet to grant a subsidy, nor afford to keep the expensive *Ajax* on the Honolulu route.[38]

When a more or less permanent steamship connection was made between San Francisco and Honolulu, it was with the assistance of a subsidy from the United States government. After Pacific Mail had received permission to bypass Honolulu, Congress voted to support a monthly mail steamer service between the west coast and Hawai'i. The contract, carrying a $75,000 annual subsidy, went to the California, Oregon, and Mexico Steamship Company. The first ship of this line, the *Idaho*, docked at Honolulu on September 17, 1867. The company sought in addition a ten-year subsidy, but the Hawaiian cabinet found the demand unacceptable and proposed instead a bounty paid in installments over two years. Finally, the company agreed to carry Hawaiian mail free of charge in return for privileges and exemptions in Honolulu harbor. Patronage of the *Idaho* and its sister ship the *Montana* was not as heavy as had been expected. Steamer arrivals and departures drew crowds of spectators, but passengers apparently continued to travel on the fast sailing packets; and in 1869 the *Montana* was withdrawn, leaving the *Idaho* to make round trips every thirty-six days.[39]

In the spring of 1869 the California, Oregon, and Mexico Steamship Company changed its name to the North Pacific Transportation Company. The *Idaho* sailed between San Francisco and the islands under the new firm's flag; and at the same time the directors of the North Pacific line began thinking of a service that would link San Francisco and the Australasian colonies via Honolulu.

North Pacific Transportation was not alone. A British combination including the Cunard steamship interests did some preparatory work on a sea-and-land-line from Australia to England—by steamer to San Francisco, across the United States on the newly completed transcontinental railroad, and by steamer again across the Atlantic. Nothing came of this; but at the same time H.H. Hall of Sydney was in the process of organizing a Sydney-Auckland-Honolulu service. His two chartered ships, the *Wonga Wonga* and the *City of Melbourne,* formed the Californian, New Zealand, and Australian Line of Steam Packets, operating under subsidies from the governments of New Zealand, New South Wales, and (very briefly) Hawai'i. Hall's line, despite its title, did not in fact run as far as San Francisco. The *Wonga Wonga* and the *City of Melbourne* connected at Honolulu with the *Idaho* of the North Pacific Transportation Company, which took passengers, freight, and mail on the last leg of the trip.[40]

The first voyage of the *Wonga Wonga* brought her to Honolulu on April 19, 1870, twenty days out from Sydney. Almost exactly a year later, an American combination put ships into service on the Sydney-Honolulu run. While H.H. Hall in Sydney was arranging subsidies from the Australasian colonies, two groups had been attempting to do the same from an American base—first, Ben Holladay's North Pacific Transportation Company, whose *Idaho* already made subsidized voyages between San Francisco and Honolulu; and, second, William H. Webb, an important New York shipbuilder who was ready to extend his operations.

The American efforts were, to begin with, competitive. In 1871, however, cooperation replaced competition, and the Holladay-Webb groups joined forces to establish the United States, New Zealand, and Australia Mail Steamship Line, which, under Webb's control, took over the North Pacific Transportation Company's contract to carry mail between San Francisco and Honolulu. From April, 1871, the *Nevada* and the *Nebraska* of the new line ran between Honolulu and Sydney, and a smaller steamer, the *Moses Taylor,* carried mail, passengers, and freight between Honolulu and San Francisco. The entry of Webb's ships created competition for Hall between Sydney and Honolulu at the same time as it destroyed Hall's connection with Holladay's old North Pacific line between Honolulu and San Francisco. Hall could either fight or give in. He chose to fight. For some months his steamers covered the whole route between Sydney and San Francisco, but not even his subsidies could save him, and by the fall of 1871 he was beaten. He could do nothing but withdraw.[41]

Webb had managed to get subsidies from the Australasian colonies, and in April, 1872, after his new line had been in existence for a year, the Hawaiian government somewhat unwillingly made a short-term grant of money and privileges of the Hawaiian contract of the old

North Pacific Transportation Company, whose ships and mail contract he had bought in 1869. The government was ready to allow him these privileges, but several cabinet members opposed any extensions. Many arguments were raised against the Webb line. The steamers customarily arrived fully loaded from Australia and New Zealand, leaving no room for Hawaiian freight to be carried to the American mainland. If space happened to be available, the Webb line's Honolulu agents, Hackfeld & Co, took first priority. The trans-Pacific steamers were large; they occupied a great deal of wharf footage, and dust from their waterfront coal heaps blew over many of the other berths. Finally, without a United States government subsidy, the future of the line was doubtful.

For some months, the Hawaiian government paid the Webb line $1,000 for each voyage between Honolulu and Australia, but relations between the company and the government continued to be poor. Webb's agents, Hackfeld & Co, insisted that the new contract had not voided the old North Pacific arrangements, under which they had been permitted to store steamer goods free of charge in a shed on the waterfront. The government claimed Hackfeld & Co. abused this privilege by using the shed to store goods that were not intended for steamer transit. At one point, the government threatened to cancel the new contract with Webb unless the old one (with North Pacific) was surrendered. At the same time, on Webb's orders, the steamers had ceased to carry Hawaiian mail—Webb was holding out for a $25,000 annual subsidy from the government. Before these and other difficulties could be resolved, it became clear that the Webb line would fail. The United States Senate in February, 1873, rejected the last of several attempts to gain an American subsidy for the line; and three months later the last of Webb's ships, the *Nebraska,* sailed from Honolulu for San Francisco. Webb sold out to the Pacific Mail Steamship Company, the line which in 1866 had bypassed Honolulu on its China mail run.[42]

Pacific Mail took over the San Francisco-Honolulu mail run, patting into service the *Costa Rica,* The Hawaiian government offered the company every inducement short of an actual subsidy, reminding the directors in the course of correspondence that Honolulu harbor had been fitted with expensive wharves in the frustrated expectation that Pacific Mail's China ships would stop there in 1866. The *Costa Rica* made only a few trips to the islands, without a Hawaiian subsidy, before she was wrecked off San Francisco late in 1873.[43]

For a time, no trans-oceanic steam service linked Honolulu either with the west coast of the United States or with the Australasian colonies. Pacific Mail was slow to replace the *Costa Rica;* Webb had driven H.H. Hall from the South Pacific and then had failed to keep his own line running. Hall, with a new partner, formed the Australasian and American Mail

Steamship Company in 1873, subsidized once more by the Australasian colonies. His ships ran between Sydney and San Francisco via Honolulu. Though his company did not prosper, its successors maintained uninterrupted service between San Francisco, Honolulu, and Australasia.[44]

Occasional complaints about "terrapin service" notwithstanding, trans-oceanic steamers brought the islands within speedy reach of the American west coast and the Australasian colonies, thus meeting one of the kingdom's greatest needs. Ease of access also had its disadvantages, as Honolulu discovered when steamships brought smallpox with them twice in four years. Since earliest times, epidemic diseases—from the enigmatic "boo-hoo fever" to influenza, measles, and leprosy—had entered at the ports; and in the opening decades of the age of steam, trans-Pacific sailing packets continued to be carriers of disease. In 1868 and 1872, however, it was the speed of steamships that helped to reintroduce smallpox to Honolulu.

In December, 1868, the *Idaho* arrived from San Francisco, where smallpox was prevalent.[45] It was soon discovered that a passenger was diseased, and he was quarantined, but not before he had been allowed to visit the town. In the fifteen years since the great Honolulu epidemic of 1853, insular complacency had returned, to the point where existing regulations went unenforced and vaccination programs had lapsed. A meeting at Kawaiaha'o church (attended by natives and a few whites who identified themselves strongly with the Hawaiian viewpoint) called for the dismissal of the Board of Health. Port Physician Robert McKibbin, who had permitted the discharge of the *Idaho's* crew and the landing of passengers, handed in his resignation; but the cabinet upheld the Board. At the same time money was appropriated for a permanent quarantine station.

After some days, it became clear that the *Idaho* case was merely one of varioloid, a disease much less dangerous than smallpox proper; but for a few months there was a flurry of vaccinations, and rumors of smallpox spread through the town each time a steamer docked. Even after this alarm, inspection and quarantine were not uniformly enforced. Paradoxically, as the presumed danger diminished, the government was criticized for maintaining health standards so harsh as to inhibit the steamship company's performance of its contract. Restrictions were removed entirely in April, 1869, with the virtual disappearance of the disease in California.[46]

In May, 1872, the disease re-appeared, this time on the *Nebraska*, one of William Webb's trans-Pacific steamers. A sick passenger came ashore at Honolulu and died within a few hours. By the end of June, there were twenty-seven reported cases and seven deaths in the city.

Once again mass vaccinations were carried out, and stringent restrictions were imposed on interisland travel. Where did the blame lie? Port regulations provided that a ship's captain must present a certificate swearing to a clean bill of health aboard before he allowed passengers to land. The *Nebraska's* captain had done just that, and yet disease was clearly present. In July, the government moved to place an attachment on the *Nebraska*, with a view to obtaining damages from the Webb line. Webb's agents, Hackfeld & Co., posted bond so that their steamer could sail. Thenceforth, port physicians did not take the word of shipmasters, but carried out their own searches of newly-arrived vessels at a fee between $10 and $20, chargeable to the ships. Almost immediately Hackfeld & Co., on behalf of Webb, complained about this new "imposition." Callous impertinence on the part of men whose irresponsibility had brought about the death of eleven natives and cost the Hawaiian government thousands of dollars brought an enraged response. The government continued its inspections, and Port Physician George Trousseau went on boarding steamers in the outer harbor even though Webb's captains refused to slow down for him as he came alongside in his boat.[47]

Public policy could hardly be determined by catastrophe. Smallpox scarces were adventitious, and the fact that they developed on shipboard did not lessen the potential value of steamers in the islands' growth. At the same time as the government found itself fighting disease in the sixties and seventies, it was planning a great hotel to house the influx of travellers whose coming was seen as inevitable once regular steamship service was established. The tourist nimbus was beginning to form in the minds of some of Honolulu's businessmen; the Paradise of the Pacific was on the verge of becoming a conscious construct.

More immediately, the need for a first-class hotel in the city seemed self-evident. Even before the age of steam, hotel accommodations had sometimes been scarce at the height of the shipping season. Then too, the hotel was expected to serve as a social center for the town. By the late sixties, Honolulu was well into its post-missionary phase, and no serious objection was raised against the linking of hospitality with alcohol. Further, after decades of talk, the town was still without a good public hall. The government had never built one, and a private scheme to lease a downtown building on a subscription basis failed. Above all, boredom bred of isolation was a problem for Honolulans. In a city where the New England appetite for self-improvement had never been cultivated seriously outside the old missionary community, reading rooms and atheneums languished, debating societies had merely fitful lives, and moralizing lecturers starved. The only recourses of the convivial man were the social club, the lodge, the private musical society, or an occasional dance; and in a city whose haole population was less than two thousand, the same old faces turned up too often. A suitable common ground where Honolulu's fashionables could meet those of the outside world was a very appealing prospect.

Sporadic attempts were made in the late sixties to launch the hotel scheme. Money was pledged at public meetings, but no firm arrangements were completed until the end of 1870, when, with the strong approval of King Kamehameha V, the cabinet resolved to put Minister of the Interior Ferdinand Hutchison in charge of plans and Minister of Finance John Mott Smith in charge of raising money by selling bonds or stock.[48]

In a curious, informal arrogation of responsibility, Mott Smith and his close political friend Attorney-General C.C. Harris apparently took over the project altogether, leaving Hutchison without a real function. Mott Smith chose a site at the corner of Hotel and Alakea Streets, obtained the cabinet's approval for the purchase, bought the land in his name and that of Harris, and then issued subscription bonds. Plans called for a two-story concrete building, to cost not more than $50,000, Construction was started in May, 1871.[49]

Before the month was out, a storm of criticism broke. The *Advertiser* claimed that the great size of the hotel—forty bedrooms—was an invitation to instant bankruptcy. Then there was the strange financial arrangement Mott Smith had made. What was the nature of the combination in charge of building the hotel? What was the liability of subscribers to the government bonds? The bonds had been issued without the approval of the legislature; the hotel site appeared to be owned by Mott Smith and Harris rather than by the government itself. Was this really the case? A few weeks later, at the end of June, it became known that Mott Smith had been able to raise only a quarter of the money promised him by subscribers—less than $15,000 at interest rates between 3-1/2% and 5%—and suggestions were published in the government's *Hawaiian Gazette* that legal action might be necessary to force bondholders to pay the rest.[50]

By September, Mott Smith was telling the cabinet that he had spent $44,000 (very little of which had yet been collected from bondholders), and that another $25,000 at least would be needed to finish the job properly. At this point, Minister of the Interior Hutchison began to display considerable nervousness about the amount of money involved.[51] The legislature had not approved expenses. Would he be personally liable? Would the cabinet? Mott Smith attempted to quiet his colleague's fears by saying that the money being spent was the responsibility of subscribers, not of government. Shortly afterward, however, bondholders were informed that they would not be assessed any further. They were now to regard the money they had put up as a five-year loan to the government, interest-free. If the hotel made a profit in that period, they would share in the proceeds. (Did this, then, make the hotel a government-owned enterprise? No one seemed to know.) Construction costs continued to mount. The government looked on the bright side: the project was giving employment to a great many people. To be sure, remarked the *Advertiser,* but so had the building of the tower of Babel; doubtless many people had been employed there, and money had circulated freely, but the outcome of that enterprise was most unsatisfactory.[52]

By diverting to the hotel money previously appropriated for other purposes, and by borrowing more on personal responsibility, Mott Smith managed to provide contractor Christopher Lewers with enough cash to bring construction to a finish before the end of 1871. The Hawaiian Hotel had cost almost $120,000, as against the original estimate of $50,000. Mott Smith, reporting to the legislature of 1872, admitted that the figure was "larger" than anticipated, but thought it "not unreasonable." Some legislators disagreed with his reading, and a movement was begun to impeach the ministry for using public money unconstitutionally. A majority sustained Mott Smith and his colleagues.[53] It was known that the king favored the hotel scheme; and in the end the legislature voted to issue special bonds.

The grand opening of the hotel took place at the end of February, 1872. Allen Herbert had taken a five-year lease as soon as the building was completed.[54] He furnished it so lavishly that he exhausted his money before making arrangements to pay his license fees. The government accepted his note. Mott Smith was willing to wait and collect out of the profits.[55]

Prospects were good, so it seemed. The building was impressive—as it certainly should have been for $120,000—and it was pleasantly situated on wide lawns shaded by tamarinds and algarobas. Herbert was an experienced hotelier who set a good table. The Hawaiian Hotel quickly took its place as "the great resort" of Honolulu—"clubhouse, exchange, and drawing-room in one." The English traveller Isabella Bird found it a "perfection of a hotel...Its wide corridors and verandahs are lively with English and American naval uniforms, several planters' families are here for the season; and with health-seekers from California, resident boarders, whaling captains, tourists from the British Pacific Colonies, and a stream of townspeople always percolating through the corridors and verandahs, it seems as lively...as a place can be..."[56]

Lively or not, the hotel failed to prosper in its early years. Local patronage could not sustain it. Success would have to come with the foreign trade; but trans-oceanic steamships themselves were in great difficulties. In the mid-summer of 1873, the hotel was almost starving to death for lack of custom, and the hotel bonds issued in 1871 had slipped a long way below par. By late 1876, the government was able to pay off the "loan money" advanced by bondholders, and a tiny sum was distributed according to the profit-sharing agreement. But Allen Herbert found it impossible to go on under the terms of his old lease. His business was scarcely paying the rent; his bondsmen would not back him any further; bankruptcy stared him in the face, so he said. After prolonged negotiation, the government lowered the annual rent from more than $6,000 to $2,350, and Herbert took up the lease again. Some years passed before the hotel genuinely paid its way.[57]

Allen Herbert's problem was that the Hawaiian Hotel had to depend disproportionately upon the outside world for its existence. This was true of virtually every western enterprise in the islands, and it had been the case for decades. The age of the beachcomber was buried deep in the past: most white men in Hawaiʻi, consulting enlightened self-interest, now saw nothing but good in the increase of contact between the islands and the larger nations of the Pacific, especially the United States. Natives, whatever their own views of the haole, agreed perforce that there could be no return to the simple way of life their ancestors had enjoyed.

The growth of the port at Honolulu had spelled long ago the end of subsistence. After mid-century, the Hawaiian government emphasized the kingdom's dependence upon the port by pouring money into harbor improvements. Yet the more Hawaiʻi turned outward, the more sensitively its economy responded to pressures generated elsewhere.[58] Instability became chronic. Between the mid-forties and the mid-seventies at least one year in five was financially disastrous, for reasons beyond the control of Honolulu's merchants.

Beginning in 1847–1848, a temporary drop in the number of whalers visiting the islands caused a glut in local and imported merchandise, any many heavily-stocked businesses were saved only by the boom which accompanied the discovery of gold in California in 1848. At first the gold rush merely disrupted life. Hundreds of Honolulans, white and native, left for the diggings. Men thronged the office of the Governor of Oʻahu to apply for passports, and the *Polynesian* published lengthy departure lists.[59] The standard greeting on the streets was no longer "How do you do?" but "When are you off?" Impatient men bid at auction for places on ships, and within weeks the price of passage to the west coast rose to $100. Deck space, cabin, steerage, fore and aft—all were equally expensive and all were crammed, but no one complained: the only ones who did not pay the exorbitant rate were those unable to afford it. Crews as well as passengers disembarked at San Francisco, and captains found it hard to interest seamen in return voyages to the islands. Shipping schedules went awry. The gold-hungry at Honolulu, who could not bear to wait, formed syndicates and bought coastal schooners. Soon a "mosquito fleet" followed hazardously in the wake of fast packets bound for San Francisco. One man took his life in his hands and set off alone in a whaleboat. By the end of 1848, Honolulu looked almost like a ghost town. Its large floating population had vanished, after systematically stripping the stores of everything that might be useable or saleable at the gold-fields—everything from pickaxes and shovels to playing cards.[60]

As prices for goods and services rose to dizzy heights, those who had chosen to stay at Honolulu on fixed incomes found the cost of caution excessive. But Honolulu's businessmen, once they reconciled themselves to the sudden disappearance of debtors and got used to inflated demands from their remaining workmen, discovered to their delight that they could not help making money. Goods of all kinds, bought anywhere in the world, could be unloaded at a profit in San Francisco. At the diggings everything turned to gold, so it seemed.[61]

Under these circumstances restraint was difficult. Common-sense men who had refused to take a chance on the lottery of life in California took to gambling at home. Profits flowed to them from San Francisco; they used the money to speculate in real estate. In 1850, the Hawaiian government passed laws permitting aliens to buy land in fee-simple. Opportunity had never knocked so loudly. Many merchants went heavily into debt to purchase estates in Honolulu and elsewhere, betting in effect that the rush would never end. Some covered their bets mentally by reasoning that even if the gold gave out, America was committed to westward expansion and would not leave them stranded— the islands were certain to fall into the hands of the United States within a few years. In the short run, land-owners could supply the gold-fields with high-priced meat, vegetables, and sugar, and later their fee-simple titles would guarantee them wealth under the American flag. One way or another, the future was theirs.[62]

The reckoning came in 1851. By mid-year, San Francisco's surface gold was all but exhausted. The tides of trade and travel turned and set in the direction of Australia, where gold had been discovered by a man who learned his geology on the Sacramento River. Honolulu became something of a halfway house for prospectors sailing to renew their luck in the colonies. At the same time many former island residents, their Californian adventures over, came home to take up normal life again. But life was not normal. A sudden shrinking of the west-coast market and a simultaneous influx of unemployed men, most of them without money, created a severe depression.[63]

No part of the economy escaped. Maui potatoes, once figuratively worth their weight in gold, rotted in their casks. Waterfront warehouses were crammed with goods ordered in flush times from the American east coast or Europe and delivered in Honolulu months later, after the bubble burst. Tradesmen who had commanded high wages when their skills were scarce found themselves swamped by hungry competition. As for real-estate speculators—those who had used their new-bought lands to supply the California market and those who had aimed simply at holding property for profitable resale—they were trapped, unable to meet loan and mortgage payments.[64]

Paper fortunes were reduced to nothing overnight. The money and the confidence which had inspired Honolulans to name their town a city in 1850[65] disappeared so suddenly that by the end of 1851 hardly anyone could get cash for property. As 1852 opened, interest rates on loans went up to five per cent per month in some cases—when lenders could be found at all.[66] To make things worse, the whaling fleet of 1851 had a bad year. Although the whalers returned in great numbers in 1852, real estate prices at Honolulu fell into a prolonged slump from which they did not recover for more than a decade.

Many Honolulans looked toward the revival of whaling as necessary for the town's recovery after the depression of 1851. Before they became infatuated with gold, merchants had commonly remarked that no one could do business at Honolulu without the whalers. It was true. Seamen's wages and prostitutes' earnings, the sale of supplies, the transshipment of oil and bone from Hawai'i to the United States, speculation in bills of exchange, and profits on enterprise ranging from ship-chandleries to boarding-houses, had made whaling indispensable to the port. The gold rushes had ended this reliance, but now the gold was gone and the whalers had not yet returned. What if they ceased to come to Honolulu altogether? Might not the islands relapse into "primitive insignificance," as Robert Crichton Wyllie had predicted in 1844? The thought was unnerving. Well aware that New England whaling firms would send their ships where costs were lowest, the Hawaiian government had always tried to make Honolulu attractive to the industry by reducing charges and duties at every opportunity. This policy seemed all the more necessary now that San Francisco had become a full-fledged Pacific port city. Some economic amateurs even suggested that Honolulu should become a free port.[67] But whatever the government did, nothing could correct the basic instability of the whaling industry, and rewards were nowhere more uncertain than in the North Pacific and the Arctic.[68] Honolulu's merchants, disturbed by the gold rush debacle and wishing to return to the imagined security of an earlier period, forgot that they had always lived on the brink of disaster. As early as the eighteen-thirties, the slightest fall in the size of the whaling fleet, the average catch, or the price of oil and bone, had sent tremors through the counting-houses. Each season, as the first ships arrived from the north with advance news of the total catch, chances of profit and loss were hurriedly calculated along the waterfront. Unsteadiness was to be expected, and businessmen learned to live with it, contenting themselves with the thought that if they did badly on occasion at least the next year would be better. Whaling was actually most valuable to Honolulu between 1845 and 1855, despite the interruption caused by the gold rush. Fleets in the North Pacific and the Arctic were at their largest and prices for oil and bone were high.[69] But in the late fifties, when profits were desperately needed at Honolulu, the industry entered an irreversible decline.[70]

Actually, the first symptom had been evident for some time. As whaling grounds were exhausted one after another, ships went farther and farther afield, until at last the distant Arctic fisheries became the most important in the Pacific. Voyages as lengthy as four years were common in the fifties. In the beginning, this trend benefited rather than harmed the service industries of Honolulu, since whaling vessels which did not return to New England for several seasons were forced to make periodic stops at Honolulu to buy supplies and trans-ship cargoes. Islanders, of course, made money almost as readily from ships which had failed as from ships which had succeeded. Eventually, however, extended voyages proved so costly that owners' profit margins diminished, the number of ships in the fleet was reduced, and Honolulu's middlemen suffered together with the entrepreneurs of the home firms.

The two classes of businessmen did not relish their mutual plight. As early as 1853, New Englanders complained of the rapacity of Honolulu's merchants, accusing them of "fleecing and shaving" honest whaling captains.[71] Some New Bedford and New London firms began to send their own merchant ships to the islands, where agents distributed supplies and loaded return cargoes of oil and bone.[72] Thus, business was kept in the hands of the parent companies, and the "grasping" Honolulans were thwarted. Not all New Englanders followed this course. At Honolulu, locally-owned ship-chandleries and agencies for the trans-shipment of oil and bone continued to earn good money until the end of the whaling era. All the same, the issue was serious. The integrity of the city's businessmen had been impugned, and profits were threatened, because New England agents not only supplied company ships but also threw surplus goods speculatively on the open market at Honolulu.[73]

Indignant counter-attacks on the New Englanders appeared in the Honolulu press. As for allegations of sharp practice, these were dismissed as "unfounded in truth, and injurious in their effects."[74] Economic matters deserved and got detailed consideration. By the late fifties, Honolulans were convinced that the New Bedford and New London men had outsmarted themselves. In their zeal to bar the merchants of Honolulu completely from the profits of whaling, the New Englanders shipped items such as beef, flour, sugar, and molasses, all of which were produced in the islands and were for sale at Honolulu and Lahaina more cheaply than comparable goods shipped around the Horn or picked up on the west coast of America.[75] Then too, the practice of having large amounts of oil and bone transshipped from Honolulu to New England by merchantmen often led to flooded markets and poor prices on the east coast.[76]

Other unforeseen disadvantages arose. Whaling captains of earlier days, directly answerable to masters at home, had always been frugal in dealing with businessmen at Honolulu. Under the new system, agents handled all accounts. Freed from financial responsibility, the captains no longer "shaved the market," but ran up extravagant bills, to which owners had to add agents' commissions. By 1859, the New Bedford men were referring to bad management as one of the ills afflicting the industry. This was unreasonable, according to the *Polynesian*. Whaling captains were no less careful than they once had been. If anything, business had been handled more loosely at the peak of the whaling trade, but no one had complained then because whales were plentiful and profits were high. Only now, in hard times, did New England firms find fault with men who had served them well.[77]

While New Englanders were being criticized for attempting to build vertical monopolies in whaling, some Honolulans were trying to do the same. Beginning in 1851, locally-based whaleships sailed regularly, some to hunt in the North Pacific and the Arctic, others to comb the offshore waters of the islands. By the fall of 1858, nineteen whaleships were registered in Hawai'i, most of them under the control of Americans.[78] The fortunes of Honolulu's fleet matched those of the Pacific fleet at large. All were caught in a situation which no short-term expedient could improve. Local whaling survived on a small scale until 1880. As for the New Englanders, they kept harping on the "disproportionate" profits taken by the merchants of Honolulu, but at the same time they admitted grudgingly that perhaps business houses in the islands were not solely to blame for the distress of the whaling trade.[79]

Deeper forces were at work. In 1859, the success of the Drake oil well in Pennsylvania marked the opening of an era in which the oil products of whaling were driven off the market. At the same time, the growing industrialization of New England offered capitalists better and steadier returns than whaling.[80]

The Civil War all but broke the back of New England's whaling fleet. Owners sold many of their ships and converted others into merchantmen. The Union government bought a number and sank them to blockade the entrance of the harbor at Charleston, South Carolina, and other ports. Enough continued to sail the Pacific, however, to interest the Confederates. The raider *Shenandoah,* commanded by the famous Captain Waddell, pursued Union whalers and merchantmen as far north as the Arctic and as far west as Ascension Island, seizing cargoes and burning ships.

Many Hawaiian seamen aboard American vessels fell victim to Waddell and the *Shenandoah.* Abandoned at ports all around the North Pacific, they made their way home to Honolulu distressed and destitute. Eventually, the Hawaiian government declared the depredations of the *Shenandoah* a public disaster and voted money to meet the expenses of repatriation.[81]

Waddell overstepped himself in 1865 when he attacked the *Harvest,* which was not an American ship: she was owned by the Honolulu firm of Hackfeld & Co., she flew the Hawaiian flag, and she was manned by native seamen. Waddell encountered the *Harvest* at Ascension Island, ordered her crew ashore, and burned her to the waterline.[82]

Honolulu's businessmen lost money during the war because whaling and commerce were interrupted. The Hawaiian kingdom was neutral, but many American merchants at Honolulu were strongly pro-Union. They hated Waddell for what he had done to their pockets and to their pride. After the sinking of the *Harvest,* they encouraged the Hawaiian government to demand the seizure of the *Shenandoah* for piracy. Waddell himself was threatened with "the blubber room" if he ever showed his face in Honolulu.[83]

Before the animosity roused by Waddell and the *Shenandoah* had lost its sting, another disaster overtook the Pacific whaling fleet. In the fall of 1871, ice floes north of Bering Strait trapped thirty-three ships, including some of Hawaiian registry. The crews escaped, but vessels and cargoes had to be abandoned, and they were ground to pieces in the ice. Once again Honolulu was hard hit. Crowds clustered at photographers' windows to see pictures of the doomed fleet made from sketches drawn on the spot. Week after week, rescue ships brought seamen back to the islands. Four hundred Hawaiian sailors came ashore penniless and exhausted. Most were looked after by their families; the remainder signed on as plantation laborers. By the end of October, the city's American consulate hospital housed 541 foreigners, and another hundred officers and men were billeted in the town.

While they waited to be sent home the New Englanders sat about the streets, passing the time with songs:

Do your best for one another,
Making life a pleasant dream,
Help a worn and weary brother,
Pulling hard against the stream.[84]

Many preferred to help themselves. A few resorted to larceny; others sold to natives the clothes they had been given by the American consul. It was small recompense for lost livelihood. In all, the Arctic disaster cost Honolulu an estimated two hundred thousand dollars and the industry at large ten times as much.[85]

Each time the whalers betrayed Honolulu by their absence, voices were heard suggesting that the city and the kingdom would prosper more if wealth were taken from the soil rather than from the sea. Part of the argument was economic: if the islands could develop agricultural staples and find a market for them, the unreliability of the whalers would cease to be a problem. Occasionally, a moral component was added to economic strictures: the health of the nation would be better served if the people of the port abandoned their role as whoremasters to whalemen.[86]

The search for a staple took many forms. At one time or another in the nineteenth century silk, coffee, beef, wool, and dairy goods were produced in quantity, without solving the islands' economic problem. In the sixties, a cotton industry emerged; it failed quickly. At the same time, rice to some extent supplanted kalo as a wet crop around Honolulu and on the outer islands. The rice industry became permanent, at least for the rest of the nineteenth century, but it was not a sufficient earner of revenue.[87] The likeliest staple was sugar.

Sugar cane grew wild in the islands. Many attempts were made during the first half of the nineteenth century to turn it into a cash crop, but it took the California gold rush to make it profitable on a large scale. Techniques and equipment were rudimentary; the quality of Hawaiian sugar was very poor. Nonetheless, exports increased ten-fold between 1837 and 1841—from 4,200 to 420,000 pounds.[88] Exports fluctuated between three and six hundred thousand pounds a year during most of the eighteen-forties, and then the demand created by the gold rush pushed the figure as high as 750,238 pounds in 1850.[89]

Like most islanders in those dizzy days, the planters over-extended themselves. Land, machinery, and labor were expensive, but potential rewards were enormous. Scores of thousands of dollars, borrowed at perilous rates of interest, were poured into the plantations. When the Californian market collapsed in 1851 disaster followed immediately. "Times are hard here, money scarce, & property greatly depreciated," wrote Richard Armstrong. "Our planters are much discouraged, & Swinton, Gower, Munn, Torbert, Hubertson & Perry have failed!"[90]

The procession of bankruptcies, among planters and merchants alike was mournful in the extreme. All the same, the darkness was not entirely unrelieved. Most planters had failed for lack of experience and lack of working capital. Inexperience made them impetuous and wasteful, and when money dried up in 1851 they could not hold out. For that matter, no one in the islands was well versed in sugar-making, but at least a few planters had sufficient money to see them through the bad years of the early fifties.[91] Supreme Court Justice William Lee went into partnership in 1849 with Charles R. Bishop (who later founded Honolulu's first bank) and with Henry A. Peirce (former Honolulu merchant) to start the Līhu'e Plantation. Stephen Reynolds purchased a part interest in Hāli'imaile plantation on East Maui in the late forties, and became sole owner in the early fifties. Charles Brewer II and James Makee bought him out in 1855. Dr. Robert Wood had come into possession of Kōloa plantation on Kaua'i in 1847, after the failure of Ladd & Co. Two years later, he joined A.H. Spencer in buying the East Maui Plantation. Each of these enterprises was backed by enough capital to survive the depression, and the lessons learned from that setback made it less likely in turn that they would succumb if bad times came again.[92]

The depression shook many promoters and planters out of the business altogether. Not until 1856 did a long, slow recovery begin. In 1857 only five sugar plantations were at work. Late in the fifties, however, the end of whaling was in sight, and capital once tied up in service industries at the port was freed for re-investment. An expanding American market in California and Oregon made sugar attractive once more. By 1860, though commerce was still generally depressed at Honolulu, sugar prices were high, the number of plantations in the islands had risen to twelve, and all were busy.[93]

Most new plantations were set up on the outer islands. Agencies in Honolulu handled supplies and financing.[94] Planters of the forties and fifties had generally been "independent," and the complexities of administration had contributed to their downfall in the depression. At this stage of the industry's growth there was virtue in specialization of function, and there were advantages, too, in a continuing relationship between planter and agent. Hackfeld & Co. had inherited from Ladd & Co. the first agency, that of Kōloa Plantation, which dated from 1835. In the mid-fifties, the firm of C. Brewer withdrew its money from whaling and interested itself in plantation agencies. Castle & Cooke made the same move a few years later. On a somewhat smaller scale, others entered the agency business: the Chinese mercantile firms of Chung Hoon & Co., and Utai & Ahee; the English house of Janion, Green; the German firm of Melchers & Co.; George C. McLean; B.W. Field; and James M. Green.[95] Most adventurous of all was Walker, Allen & Co., an American firm, which by 1866 had connections with or direct financial interests in twelve plantations and mills.[96]

Walker, Allen's growth in the sixties was only slightly in advance of that of the industry at large. The Civil War, which crippled whaling, brought sugar to the forefront. The virtual disappearance of Louisiana sugar from the Northern market gave Hawai'i a chance to expand its sales in the United States; and even though the Union government raised tariffs during the war, prices climbed so high that island planters could make good profits. By 1866 there were thirty-two plantation and mill companies, compared with twelve in 1860. Less than a million and a half pounds was exported in 1860; in 1866 the figure was almost seventeen and three-quarter million pounds.[97]

The Hawaiian industry, under the direction of the agencies at Honolulu, was in a very buoyant state. But when the Civil War ended, it seemed as if the nightmarish year of 1851 had come again. The market on the American mainland contracted, prices dropped, and investments in Honolulu foundered. Walker, Allen & Co., the largest plantation agency, went spectacularly bankrupt. To finance the expansion for which its clients clamored, Walker, Allen had borrowed heavily from the San Francisco firm of Charles W. Brooks & Co., which itself needed wartime conditions to make profits. Peace killed prosperity, and Brooks & Co. closed its doors on October 8, 1866. In Honolulu Walker, Allen & Co. tried to stave off disaster. Reassuring notices were printed in the newspapers. Brooks & Co. sent a man to the islands to try to make arrangements for extended payments. The affairs of Walker, Allen were put in the hands of the banker Charles R. Bishop and an associate, under an amicable agreement in which all creditors were to be paid forty percent in ten months, the balance in twenty months. According to its own figures, Walker, Allen had liabilities of $600,000 ($300,000 was owed to Brooks & Co.) and assets of $700,000 (mainly debts owed by Hawaiian plantations to the Walker, Allen agency). It was doubtful if the firm could realize on its assets in time to pay its creditors. Still, the attempt had to be made: if the house fell, hundreds, even thousands of people in the islands might be ruined. The period of suspense was short. Just a week after creditors had consented to wait for their $300,000, a Honolulu ship-captain named Frank Molteno brought suit against Walker, Allen for recovery of a debt of $1,375. The judge was certain to find for Molteno. The decision would have set off a scramble in the law courts, and to forestall this, Walker, Allen declared bankruptcy on January 10, 1867.

The worst fears of the commercial community were realized. In the first nine months of 1867, eight plantations connected with Walker, Allen went under the hammer, many of them realizing no more than the amount of the mortgage. The Honolulu Sugar Refinery was closed until it could be re-financed. Walker, Allen owned a share of the *Kilauea;* her troubled career was interrupted, and several coastal schooners owned by the company were sold. Ultimately, creditors realized less than thirty cents on the dollar.[98]

The crisis had come precisely at a moment when Honolulu's merchants were struggling to find a permanent place for themselves in the sugar market at San Francisco after the war. At the heart of the matter were the twin problems of quality and quantity. When Hawaiian sugar was first produced in bulk, in the late thirties, it had been of poor grade and almost unsaleable. Technical advances in the fifties and early sixties brought it to a borderline in terms of quality.[99]

In the language of the business, most sugar sent from Honolulu to San Francisco before about 1863 was of low grade, below "No. 12, Dutch Standard." The San Francisco refiners used this low-grade sugar (and similar sugar from the Philippines and China) to produce white sugar. One by-product of the refining process was a large amount of yellow or "coffee" sugar, which was of "grocery grade," fit for sale to consumers. After 1863, increasing amounts of sugar came from Honolulu at No. 12, Dutch Standard, or above. Improvements, that is to say, had put more than half the Hawaiian sugar crop in "grocery grades," needing no further refining before sale. Hawaiian sugar was now in direct competition with the "coffee" sugar turned out by the San Francisco refineries.

At the end of the Civil War, planters and refiners alike found the business overcrowded. A danger existed that the peacetime market might be flooded. It was very much in the interest of the west coast refiners to control affairs. Early in 1865, Hawaiian planters were invited to subscribe to a proposal put before them by San Francisco & Pacific Refineries. The planters were asked to manufacture half or more of their sugar at grades lower than No. 12, Dutch Standard. This would ease immediate competition in the San Francisco market. In return, San Francisco & Pacific Refineries would import less raw sugar from the rest of the Pacific, and would pay Hawaiian producers for their low-grade sugar at a price fifteen percent above that listed in Manila.[100]

Essentially this was a quota system. Samuel N. Castle of Castle & Cooke, a former missionary whose Biblical background and business acumen gave his every utterance a magisterial, almost prophetic quality, supported the idea strongly, arguing that it was the only safe path back to prosperity. Most planters thought otherwise. They calculated that increasing demand on the mainland would take care of expanding production in the foreseeable future; thus Honolulu and Hawai'i would do best by continuing to manufacture high grades of sugar, even if the average price was a little lower than it had been in the war years.[101]

Castle was right; the others were wrong. When Hawaiian planters and their Honolulu agents refused to sign contracts, the San Francisco refiners placed heavy orders at Manila for raw sugar. This was made into high-grade sugar, which was sold in 1866 in competition with high-grade sugar from Hawai'i. The market was flooded; prices dropped; planters, agents, and refiners all suffered.[102]

Somewhat chastened by this experience, and sobered even more by the collapse of Walker, Allen & Co. in October, 1866, the men of the Hawaiian sugar industry listened more receptively in the early months of 1867 to Mr. R. Feuerstein of San Francisco & Pacific Refineries, when he arrived at Honolulu and re-opened the issue of contracts and quotas. Many arguments continued to be raised in favor of independence. Planters who owned their land might make profits at the low prices offered for low-grade sugar; those who had to meet mortgage payments needed the extra profits from high grades. The market at San Francisco appeared to be rising; why sign contracts at all? And if contracts must be signed, why with only one San Francisco house? Too many eggs would be in one basket. Against this, Samuel Castle and those who had been converted to his views spoke for safe and sane growing, milling, and marketing. Under the contract system, the buyer would come to the door; no longer would planters and agencies depend upon a capricious factor in San Francisco, thousands of miles away. True, contracts would mean a few changes in local business practice—for example, barrel-makers who had supplied kegs for high-grade sugar would be out of work, since low-grades could be shipped in bags; and quota limits might force one or two ships to withdraw from the San Francisco-Honolulu run. But the uncertainties of the free market had been demonstrated only yesterday. The sensible course was to sign. Some of the large planters took the lead, and Feuerstein was able to go back to San Francisco carrying contracts for more than half the crop of 1867.[103]

Most planters on contract did well. For that very reason, some were led to think they could do even better on the open market, and when Feuerstein returned to Honolulu in mid-1867 to negotiate contracts for the 1868 crop, the discussions of the previous year, pro and con, were heard once again. Feuerstein offered inducements: a general price increase, and a bonus of an additional eight or ten percent for those who guaranteed to sell all their crop to San Francisco & Pacific Refineries. By the end of September, 1867, most of the independents had capitulated, and Feuerstein's contracts for the season of 1868 covered a larger percentage than before of Hawai'i's output.[104]

The steadying influence of the contracts was felt once again in the San Francisco market, and prices responded favorably. As had happened before, this merely encouraged the planters and agents of Hawai'i to try their luck in the open field. Refinery contracts were abandoned midway through 1868, and thenceforth price levels were set by supply and demand. For the next few years, uncertainty ruled.

Hawaiian sugar, of course, entered the United States as a foreign product, and tariffs were added to its cost at San Francisco. Not long after the refinery contracts were terminated, the American consul at Honolulu uncovered a scheme to defraud his government's customs revenues. Hackfeld & Co. of Honolulu, in collusion with San Francisco & Pacific Refineries, were mixing charcoal into high-grade Hawaiian sugar. Analysis by governmental chemists at San Francisco showed it to be adulterated, and it passed through customs at a lower grade and thus at a lower tariff rate, to be refined to high grades again very inexpensively. The culprits were impenitent. The San Francisco refiner George Gordon said that he was doing nothing worse than importers who watered their whisky. Samuel Castle (a leading shareholder in the Honolulu Sugar Refinery) was unable to find an Old Testament text to support this view, but he agreed with Gordon: the sugar *was* low grade when it was examined; how it became low grade did not matter. The United States government saw things another way. Customs officials seized consignments of the adulterated sugar at San Francisco in September, 1868, and the refiners were taken to federal court, where the government put its case and won.[105]

Matters such as the scandal over adulterated sugar were nothing but froth and bubble on the agitated surface of Honolulu's commercial life. On a more serious level, the difficulties of the whaling and sugar industries caused continued concern. Even so, between the mid-fifties and the mid-seventies the value of domestic exports from Hawai'i increased from less than three hundred thousand dollars to a million and a half dollars. In 1869 a landmark was reached: for the first time exports exceeded imports in value. Two years later, in 1871, exports of domestic goods alone became worth more than imports, and with rare exceptions Hawai'i continued thereafter to have a favorable trade balance. Honolulu had ceased to be a city dependent principally upon the re-export trade, and had become the port of an economically productive hinterland.[106]

The transformation was brought about almost solely by the growth and consolidation of the sugar industry. Problems associated with capital, labor and a market were solved, and the solutions brought economic security to Honolulu and to the kingdom at large. In the mid-seventies the agency system of Honolulu, with the support of the bank of Bishop & Co. (founded in 1858), came to dominate the industry's finances.[107] Private and public organizations based on Honolulu directed the importation of labor for the plantations. Honolulu was the port of entry for laborers and the place to which they returned when their time on the plantations was up. Though most sugar cane was grown on the outer islands, Honolulu quickly acquired the largest alien enclave in the kingdom. Laborers came in at the port, sugar went out. The future of the capital would be determined by the state of the sugar market. As the great sounding-board of public opinion in the islands, Honolulu was the place where the commercial and political destiny of the kingdom was decided, and when after a quarter-century of effort the men of the capital achieved a working treaty of reciprocity with the United States in 1876, the rest of the islands followed Honolulu along the path that was to lead in the end to annexation by America.

The Royal Hawaiian Agricultural Society was founded at Honolulu in 1850 to discuss the labor shortage and other problems. At its organizing convention in August, the first propositions were made for the supplying of plantation labor and the replenishing of the native population of the islands. In preparation for the new era the Hawaiian legislature had passed An Act for the Government of Masters and Servants, and under its terms a shipload of Chinese "coolies" was brought to Honolulu in January, 1852, to be distributed among planters.[108]

These coolies were by no means the first Chinese to come to the islands. As early as 1794, Vancouver had seen a Chinese on Hawai'i; by the end of the eighteenth century a handful were scattered along the archipelago. Characteristically, they went into business for themselves. Honolulu had a Chinese peddler in 1823. In 1852, the year the first coolies arrived, 71 Chinese lived around Honolulu, and 31 of them were in trade of one sort or another.[109] The reputation of Chinese merchants generally was good, as was that of Chinese sugar planters and millers on the outer islands. Although their "customs" were regarded as either mysterious or laughable, and their doings were reported facetiously in the English-language press of Honolulu when they were mentioned at all, it was conceded that most Chinese businessmen were conscientious and industrious.[110] In the eighteen-fifties, the Chinese merchants of Honolulu started a volunteer fire company (after the haoles but before the Hawaiians); and in 1856, they gave a grand ball for the newly-married King Alexander Liholiho and Queen Emma. The hosts spent almost four thousand dollars on food and decorations, and they practiced quadrilles so that they could dance with their guests. Since the intricacies of directing a ball were "practically above the comprehension of a Chinaman," four white businessmen did the job, dressed in Mandarin costume complete with fans—"Weong Chong" Hoffman, "Chong Fong" Field, "Ming Ching" Reiners, and "Weong Kong" Waterman. The "celestial" evening was a great success.[111] The social position of the merchants was defined and guaranteed: commercial probity, decorum, deference, and an occasional happy ceremonial gesture would assure them of toleration in the town.

Coolies were not merchants, however. Within a year of the arrival of the first Chinese plantation workers in 1852, planters were invoking the penal clauses of the Masters and Servants Act, and recalcitrant coolies found themselves in the fort at Honolulu on bread and water for refusing to work. A few planters went further and whipped coolies, and one was shot in the leg by J.H. Wood of Nu'uanu Plantation.[112] Troublemakers among the Chinese were in a minority; most worked well. But when their five-year contracts were up in 1857 (just a few months after the Chinese merchants' ball), they left the plantations and settled in Honolulu, Complaints followed immediately. Unemployed coolies stole, gambled, fought, set fire to buildings, and made nuisances of themselves in general with their "filthy habits." In mid-1857, seventy white businessmen petitioned the government to invoke the vagrancy laws against unemployed Chinese found on the streets of Honolulu, and Marshal William Parke was directed to arrest offenders.[113]

Despite enforcement of the law, criminality continued. A brief pitch of hysteria was reached in August, 1858, when unfounded rumors came before the Privy Council that desperate Chinese were plotting to kill the king.[114] By the end of 1859, many white Honolulans had had enough. The *Pacific Commercial Advertiser* complained that nothing but "insecurity to life and property" resulted from the presence of the Chinese, who included "some of the vilest coolies that ever escaped hanging in their own countries. The thoughtless importation of coolies, a few years ago, because they were cheap labor, is now producing some lamentable fruit in the shape of burglary and murder."[115] The *Polynesian* agreed: "A murder one Sunday, an arson the next, by Coolie hands, is coming the Celestial rather strong upon the weak nerves of our community... In February next the last of the Coolie contracts expires, and we may then expect a still further increase of liberated laborers from the plantations of the other islands, to swell the crowd of Chinamen already prowling about Honolulu without any apparent means of livelihood. We fear that the next Legislature will be obliged to take their case under consideration, the constitution to the contrary notwithstanding."[116]

But what was the alternative? The native population of the islands continued to decline in the fifties and sixties; attempts to recruit plantation workers from the South Pacific failed almost completely; and it was generally conceded that imported European labor would be too expensive. At one time or another Malaysia, India, and Japan were considered as possible sources of supply. The first two yielded nothing; and the arrival of a single shipload of Japanese in 1868 was followed by an interval of almost twenty years.[117] Until 1876, the overwhelming majority of imported plantation laborers were Chinese.[118] By no means all returned home when their contracts expired,[119] and of those who stayed in the islands, a good many came to Honolulu.[120] The city therefore had to accommodate itself to their presence.

It was not easy. Even Chinese merchants such as Chung Hoon, Achuck, and Chulan, prosperous through their dealings in retail goods, sugar, and rice, and secure in the esteem of their fellow townspeople, admitted that their coolie countrymen were a problem. Plantation workers freed after their contracts expired were encouraged to take up rice-growing on old kalo patches behind Honolulu and elsewhere, and some did so.[121] Others found quiet, respectable work as clerks in stores or as domestic servants. The number of licensed Chinese traders and peddlers increased every year.[122] But so did the number of unemployed coolies in the town. Most Chinese businesses were housed in decaying buildings on the depressed lower blocks of Nu'uanu and Maunakea Streets, and in Chinatown the womanless coolies congregated to gamble, smoke opium, or simply pass the time.

In general, the coolies practiced a kind of self-segregation, confining their incursions upon the rest of the city to an occasional night-time burglary or chicken-theft. Accordingly, white Honolulans learned to regard the unassimilated Chinese in their midst with detachment, if not with complete calm. The police raided "gambling hells" behind Chinatown restaurants and stores with monotonous but reassuring regularity, and Chinese chain gangs at labor on the roads and the wharves became a familiar sight.

By the mid-sixties, however, matters had advanced to a new stage. The Planters' Society, formed at Honolulu in 1864 to succeed the moribund Royal Hawaiian Agricultural Society, made arrangements with the government's Bureau of Immigration to have more coolies brought in. More than six hundred arrived in 1865. Within a few years, Chinese men came to outnumber white men in the islands. Reports of violence on the plantations increased,[123] and every month more liberated coolies came to Honolulu's Chinatown.[124]

In July, 1866, Ahsee, a deranged domestic servant at the Nu'uanu home of former French consul Jules Dudoit, took a kitchen cleaver and hacked his employer to death. Murder was most uncommon in Honolulu (and in the rest of the kingdom, for that matter). From time to time natives killed natives, sailors killed sailors, Chinese killed Chinese, and white men killed Hawaiians and Chinese. Ahsee was the first Chinese to kill a white man. The government offered a reward of $500 for his capture, and the Chinese merchants of Honolulu matched the amount. With $1,000 at stake, most of the town's natives went hunting. Some coolies who worked for J.H. Wood at Nu'uanu Plantation caught Ahsee and claimed the reward. Wood took Ahsee to jail, followed by a crowd of natives and whites that grew to two thousand before the murderer was locked up.[125]

The *Advertiser* returned to the position it had taken earlier. Fears were expressed that the death of Dudoit was "only the beginning" of trouble with "unruly and desperate" coolies, many of whom had been "pirates and criminals" in China, and who were nothing but "cut-throats and murderers," ready to take a man's life on the slightest provocation.[126] The government's *Hawaiian Gazette* disagreed. An isolated murder meant nothing. Dudoit had provoked Ahsee repeatedly, and had been killed for it. But more than once, when white men on plantations had used violence, their coolies had remained calm. Legislation to keep Chinese off the streets of Honolulu at night was not needed; talk of vigilance committees was nothing less than hysterical.[127]

In fact, no crime wave followed the hanging of Ahsee in December, 1866. Until 1876, conditions at Honolulu remained much the same. The Chinese merchants continued to hold their good name; coolies whose labor contracts had expired left the plantations for the city; some made their way into the business class; most were swallowed up in Chinatown; an unregenerate minority broke the law and came to the attention of the white community. The first tentative moves to educate and Christianize the coolies were made by the Protestant churches and the Y.M.C.A., without great success.[128]

Despite some uneasiness among both whites and Hawaiians about the Chinese "invasion" of the islands, virtually no discriminatory legislation (other than a law banning the smoking of opium) was enacted before 1876. The Masters and Servants Act (amended from time to time), the vagrancy act, and the remainder of the penal code controlled the situation satisfactorily. Not until the eighties and nineties did the white men of Honolulu and the islands generally find it necessary to enact legislation openly intended to keep the Chinese—and especially the Chinese of Honolulu—"in their place."

Hawai'i had embarked upon the importation of labor at a time when the recruitment of plantation workers was under attack in many parts of the world. The British government was casting an anxious eye at "blackbirding" in the Pacific Ocean. Concurrently, the Congress of the United States passed an act in 1862 prohibiting American citizens from carrying on the "coolie trade" in American ships; and in January, 1867, resolutions were added to the act of 1862, describing the coolie trade as "inhuman, immoral, and abhorrent."[129]

Slavery proper was prohibited in the Hawaiian islands. Among the pioneers of constitutional government were several American Protestant missionaries, committed to the abolition of slavery in their homeland and determined to see that it did not spread to Hawai'i. The liberal Hawaiian constitution of 1852 and the conservative revision of 1864 both contained specific prohibitions of slavery. In the period between the making of these two constitutions, the Protestant mission had been virtually disbanded. Some of its former members, and some of their sons, went into the sugar business, taking on rather quickly the social and economic views of their fellow planters. Other former members of the missionary family who remained at Honolulu without a vested interest in sugar tended to equate coolie labor with slave labor.[130]

Conditions were generally better for Chinese in the Hawaiian islands than in California and many other places around the rim of the Pacific (including China).[131] Nonetheless, opponents of contract labor were numerous enough at Honolulu to make the fundamental morality of the system a public issue for many years. Plantation managers who had to make the system work lived mostly on the outer islands, but the capital was the home of the ideologues and the site of the liveliest encounters between exponents of different views.

Some people regarded the growth of Chinatown in Honolulu as a social evil, and they attacked the coolie trade as the cause of it all. Henry Whitney, editor of the *Pacific Commercial Advertiser*, apparently held this view for a time. He referred often to the disproportionate crime rate among the town's Chinese, and advocated harsh action against Chinese lawbreakers. But at the same time he recognized the sugar industry's need for labor. By the end of the sixties he had arrived at the view that free migration would meet the requirements of the planters, do away with the iniquities of the coolie trade, and bring a better type of worker to the islands. Contracts between worker and employer were necessary, he admitted, and China was the most likely place to place to find workers. But contracts should be made knowingly and voluntarily by laborers after they arrived at Honolulu, not before; and on no account should penal clauses be included.[132]

Even Whitney's less than absolute views were irksome to the planters. A group of sugar men met on Maui early in 1870 and resolved to do all they could to hinder the circulation of Whitney's *Advertiser* and his widely-circulated Hawaiian-language paper, the *Kuokoa*. Toward the end of 1870, Whitney sold the *Advertiser* to the firm of Black & Auld, and under its new proprietors the paper developed an editorial policy favorable to the planters. The *Kuokoa*, which Whitney retained, continued to attack the Masters and Servants Act.[133]

More intransigent than Whitney were young men such as Curtis Lyons (son of the celebrated evangelist Lorenzo Lyons), who harassed the government's Bureau of Immigration and the Planters' Society at every turn, criticizing vehemently the penal clauses of contracts and the practice of assigning contracts from employer to employer without the consent of employees. When the planters held a full-scale meeting at Honolulu in October, 1869, to discuss the future of contract labor, Lyons, Joseph Carter, Allen Judd, Sanford Dole, and C.C. Bennett of *Bennett's Own*, opposed the planters' spokesmen, who included Samuel Castle, Charles R. Bishop, Samuel Wilder, and Samuel Alexander. At a later meeting of "mechanics, working men and others," Lyons went further than the moderate majority when he proposed the abolition of the coolie trade in Hawai'i. Lyons was also on a committee chosen by a meeting of natives at Kaumakapili Church which advocated the suspension of the coolie trade in the interests of the survival of the Hawaiians.[134] When the government decided to go ahead with the importation of more coolies early in 1870, Lyons carried the fight against the penal clauses of contracts to the floor of the national legislature, where he led a movement to have the repugnant clauses repealed, Lyons' attempt failed,[135] just as all attempts to remove penal clauses completely were to fail until American law superseded Hawaiian law after the annexation of the islands at the end of the nineteenth century.

Honolulu's Chinese themselves came out against the contract labor system, belying by their actions the view that all was sweetness and light on the coolie ships and on the plantations. At the time of the public meetings of October, 1869, more than twenty Chinese merchants signed a letter which read in part: "We heartily oppose the introduction of coolies here under (the contract system). Some of the Chinese coolies are very bad men and criminals. We know our countrymen better than any one else; and we believe that a much better class of men for plantation and other kinds of work can be procured from China by some arrangement for the encouragement of free immigration."[136] With the tacit consent of the government, merchants such as Afong and Chulan brought in a few score free Chinese migrants thereafter.[137]

When the government resumed importation of coolies in 1870, some Chinese took direct action. In August, the ship *Solo* docked at Honolulu, carrying 168 coolies recruited by a government agent. Chinese from the town came to the wharves to warn their fellow-countrymen about contracts and rates of pay on the plantations. As a result, the new arrivals would not sign contracts. Hawaiian soldiers were finally sent to the waterfront to quiet the Chinese on the shore and on the ship.[138]

The concern of the Chinese for their countrymen extended beyond the Hawaiian labor system. Honolulu, as well as being the port where coolies recruited for island plantations disembarked, was also a port of call for coolie ships on the way to South America. The South American trade was virtually unregulated, and conditions aboard ship were often frightful. When the *Dolores Ugarte,* loaded with bonded workers for Callao, docked at Honolulu in August, 1870, forty-three men aboard were sick. They were brought ashore for treatment in Chinatown; the rest were kept in the holds under battened hatches. With the aid of Chinese merchants, the forty-three were dispersed and kept hidden until after the *Dolores Ugarte* sailed, despite the efforts of the ship's Honolulu agents and Hawaiian government officials to find them.[139]

These limited expressions of solidarity among the Chinese indicated the birth of a kind of community consciousness in Chinatown. Before 1876 its manifestations were slight. Increased anti-Chinese activity on the part of white men at Honolulu during the eighties and nineties led to a much more deliberate and formal organization among the Chinese of the city.[140]

Ever since the Californian gold rush had given impetus to the sugar industry and to the businesses which grew up at Honolulu to serve it, most white Honolulans had been convinced that the economic future of their city lay with the United States. Plantation capital might come from whatever source; plantation labor might be sought all over the Pacific; sugar would have to be sold in America. During the whaling era New England was closely tied to the islands; now San Francisco was of prime importance. East coast or west coast, it made no difference to Honolulu's Americans, virtually all of whom were enthusiastic about closer connections with their homeland. Foreign residents from other countries were less than wholehearted in their support of an American attachment; indeed, they were often quite openly opposed to anything of the kind. But no matter how strong their political animus, they could not deny the logic of the Americans' arguments. For good or ill, San Francisco dominated the sugar market, and sugar dominated the islands' economy.

As far as most Americans at Honolulu were concerned, economic premises led irresistibly to the conclusion that Hawai'i and the United States ought to formalize their already close ties. To many, the question was merely one of arrangements: would it be best for the United States to annex the islands, or would a treaty of reciprocity suffice? Some thought of reciprocity as a prelude to annexation; others thought a good commercial treaty might be a guarantee of the islands' continued independence. The matter was debated energetically at Honolulu.

If Hawai'i proposed, however, Washington disposed. Issues which seemed momentous at the national capital of the tiny kingdom were of much less consequence at the national capital of the great republic. Time after time during the fifties and sixties Honolulans took the initiative in negotiations; time after time their importunacies were brought to nothing by established American policies or by immediate circumstances on the American political and economic scene which did not favor closer involvement with Hawai'i.[141]

Annexationism as a policy supported by Americans at Honolulu reached a peak of influence in the early fifties. The movement lost impetus after the accession of Alexander Liholiho, Kamehameha IV, in 1855. Annexation was discussed as a marginal possibility thereafter, but not for another forty years could it be considered a realistic program. The idea of a reciprocity treaty had a much more consistent history. Formal approaches by Hawai'i were made several times in the fifties and sixties, but without success. The fact that so many efforts were made is an indication of the basic attractiveness of the idea, especially when it is considered that the climate of opinion at the royal court during the reigns of the brothers Alexander Liholiho and Lot Kamehameha was not altogether congenial to the United States. While American merchants and their supporters did their best to interest both the Hawaiian and the American governments in reciprocity,[142] conditions at Honolulu tended to cloud the issue.

The anglophilia of Alexander Liholiho, Kamehameha IV, was well-known: he had institutionalized it in the Episcopalian Church. A British connection lived on after his death in 1863. His widow, the dowager queen Emma, made a successful voyage to England in the mid-sixties, and the Episcopalian Bishop of Honolulu, Thomas Staley, went on a somewhat less happy journey to the United States.[143] Lot Kamehameha, who succeeded Alexander Liholiho with the title of Kamehameha V, was less a Christian of any kind than a latter-day Hawaiian nativist, so remote as to be considered unapproachable by most foreigners. He spent as little time as possible at court in Honolulu, preferring his kalo farm at Waikīkī, his "marine residences" there and at Hanauma Bay on eastern O'ahu, and his cattle ranch on Moloka'i. On taking control in 1864, he had presided over a conservative revision of the constitution, the outcome of which alienated many Americans of republican tendencies since it reduced the power of the House of Representatives almost to nothing.[144] King Lot's ministers included the devoted monarchist Robert Crichton Wyllie and the Frenchman Charles de Varigny, who cooperated with

British Commissioner William Webb Follett Synge in forming a counter-balance to the American interest at Honolulu. The cabinet, to be sure, contained Americans as well as anti-Americans, and the government's official policy was to support the idea of reciprocity, but it was hard to tell what the king himself really thought. Certainly some of America's consular and diplomatic representatives at Honolulu during the middle and later sixties (men not noted for their subtlety, as it happened) had trouble finding out.

One thing was obvious: King Lot did not respond well to pressure brought from outside, whatever its origin. This was demonstrated in mid-1867, while the Hawaiian government was considering the latest version of a reciprocity treaty. When United States Minister to Hawai'i Edward McCook returned from a trip to San Francisco in June, 1867, carrying a draft of the treaty he and Hawaiian Minister of Finance C. C. Harris had written, an American warship, USS *Lackawanna*, was in Honolulu harbor. This in itself was not unusual; since the end of the Civil War the United States had deployed a good many ships in the Pacific, and several of them, comprising the North Pacific Squadron, visited Honolulu in rotation. The *Lackawanna*, however, was a special case. She was assigned to the islands for an "indefinite" period. When McCook came back from San Francisco, she had been at Honolulu for more than three months, and the longer she stayed the less the Hawaiian government liked it.

The *Lackawanna* had been sent to Honolulu because a brief flare-up of bad feeling between Hawai'i and France seemed to threaten worse things to come. This reason for the *Lackawanna's* visit was never made convincingly clear to the Hawaiian government or the people of Honolulu.[146] It was believed that the United States wanted the islands under continuous surveillance because of the ill-health of King Lot. If he should die, a political crisis might follow, since he was the last of the Kamehamehas and no heir had been designated.

To King Lot, the *Lackawanna* may have looked like a bird of ill-omen. To the anti-Americans, she was an offensive intruder in Hawaiian domestic politics, the more so because her commander, Captain William Reynolds, was a loud and forceful advocate of American annexationism. Reynolds had lived in the islands during the middle fifties and early sixties. Then and later he was active in urging his country to take Hawai'i (at the height of the annexation crisis of 1853-1854, his wife made an embroidered silk American flag to be raised on Kaua'i). During Reynolds' stay as commander of the *Lackawanna*, he wrote many letters to Washington advocating annexation. His opinions were well known at Honolulu.[147]

All things considered, the Hawaiian government found it difficult to give Reynolds a cordial welcome. Reynolds himself was publicly polite. He held a shipboard ball, he took some of the chiefs on a pleasure cruise, he helped to put down an incipient mutiny on board a British merchant vessel in the harbor, and he entertained the native pastors of the Hawaiian Evangelical Association and their wives, who sang Hawaiian hymns set to "familiar patriotic airs;"[148] but still his presence was upsetting.

For almost a month after McCook's return from San Francisco, the *Lackawanna* and its egregious commander delayed Hawaiian ratification of the Harris-McCook treaty. The king had told McCook nothing would be done as long as the *Lackawanna* was in Hawaiian waters.[149] Then, on July 30, 1867, Reynolds received orders to sail to the westward and take possession of Middlebrook (Midway) Island. With the *Lackawanna* gone, King Lot called a special session of the legislature. The treaty was ratified on September 30.[150] Two days later, Reynolds was back.[151]

He stayed another eight months, despite Hawaiian efforts to have him replaced. In Washington, C.C. Harris, anxiously watching the progress of the reciprocity treaty, did not want to prejudice its chances by making strong objections to the *Lackawanna's* prolonged stay at Honolulu.[152] So the affair lingered on, with relations between Reynolds and the Hawaiian cabinet growing worse week by week, until the two parties virtually broke off communication with each other. When the *Lackawanna* went to Hawai'i in March, 1868, the Hawaiian government forbade her crew to go ashore at Hilo on liberty; and the next month, when the king arrived in Honolulu harbor after an interisland trip, the *Lackawanna* did not salute him.[153] Reynolds finally sailed from Honolulu on May 6, 1868, leaving instructions to his successor to have no dealings with Attorney-General Stephen Phillips or Minister of the Interior Ferdinand Hutchison.[154]

During the last months of Reynolds' stay, another enigmatic figure appeared at Honolulu. Zephaniah S. Spalding arrived in the islands in December, 1867, allegedly bearing dispatches from Washington for United States Minister to Hawai'i Edward McCook (whom he saw in San Francisco on his way out). Spalding remained at Honolulu, making quiet inquiries about the politics of the islands and writing letters to his father, an Ohio congressman, who passed them on to the State Department. Like Reynolds, Spalding was an outright annexationist; and like Reynolds, Spalding aroused the suspicion of the Hawaiian cabinet, whose members did not believe Spalding's story that he was hoping to start a cotton plantation in the islands. Attorney-General Stephen Phillips bribed a clerk from the *Lackawanna* to bring him confidential letters from the ship, including some by Spalding. The clerk was discovered, tried, and convicted;[156] but by then the Hawaiian government knew as much as it needed to know about Spalding—enough, certainly, to protest his appointment as acting vice-consul at Honolulu and acting chargé d'affaires in command of the American legation during Minister McCook's absence.[157] Late in 1868 Spalding was given a full commission as United States Consul at Honolulu, and the Hawaiian government was forced to suffer his presence until he was replaced in the fall of 1869.[158]

After all the alarums and excursions associated with Reynolds and Spalding, and after the seemingly endless negotiations at Washington, Hawai'i still had no reciprocity treaty. Thus, as the seventies opened, the plantation agencies at Honolulu continued to encounter problems in marketing their sugar. The planters and their commercial representatives had terminated their contracts with the San Francisco refineries in 1868 under the illusion that the United States would ratify the Harris-McCook treaty.[159] Time proved them wrong—the treaty finally failed in the Senate on June 1, 1870.[160] The immediate impulse of many at Honolulu was to abandon the reciprocity movement.[161]

But where to turn?—despite brave utterances, the islands were not self-sufficient and could not be made so. The Hawaiian legislature of 1870 passed acts encouraging local textile industries, and impromptu trades associations at Honolulu began talking in terms of protective tariffs;[162] these moves notwithstanding, sugar remained pre-eminent.

During the early seventies, something of a market was established in the British colonies of Australasia. Tentative and inconclusive overtures concerning possible reciprocity were made as early as 1867.[163] Using the steamship lines which linked Sydney and Auckland with Honolulu in 1870, the agencies began to ship sugar to ports other than San Francisco.[164] This trade reached its peak in 1873, when one-third of all Hawai'i's sugar went to Australasian (and Canadian) ports.[165] By the time the traffic got under way, however, the reciprocity movement and American annexationism at Honolulu had become active once more, and the dominance of the American market was quickly re-established. The threat of a Hawaiian connection with the British colonies was frequently referred to thereafter,[166] but it was a political shadow without economic substance.

In the midst of this period of economic and political indecision, King Lot, last of the Kamehamehas, died—on December 11, 1872, his fortieth birthday. Lot was famous for keeping his counsel about important questions, and he carried this habit to extremes in his last years, refusing again and again to name a successor. On his deathbed he was asked repeatedly to choose the next monarch. The names of several ali'i were suggested to him—William Charles Lunalilo, descended from a half-brother of Kamehameha I; the dowager queen Emma, widow of Kamehameha IV; Ruth Keʻelikolani, an old-style chiefess who was governess of Hawaiʻi; Bernice Pauahi Bishop, also a member of the Kamehameha dynasty; and David Kalākaua, an ambitious aristocrat of another family line. King Lot's personal preference seems to have been for Bernice Pauahi Bishop. She refused to consider taking the throne, and the king died with the matter unsettled.[167]

The cabinet ordered a special meeting of the legislature for January 8, 1873, at which, according to the constitution, a new king would be chosen. The popularity of William Lunalilo among the common people of Hawaiʻi was very great. His candidacy, which he declared on December 16, was greeted with acclamation. In addition, he was acceptable to the powerful American economic interests at Honolulu. Only one other aliʻi opposed him: David Kalākaua, whose "Skillful Genealogists" cast aspersions on Lunalilo's descent, and whose publicists urged native Hawaiians to beware the American influence behind Lunalilo's bid for the throne.[168]

In a popular vote on January 1, 1873. Lunalilo was supported almost unanimously. A week later the legislature met. Crowds of Lunalilo's supporters filled the chambers at the courthouse to watch as members of the assembly cast their signed ballots. With only one abstention (that of John Dominis, Governor of Oʻahu, Kalākaua's brother-in-law) Lunalilo was voted in as king.[169]

The foreign community had been more or less prepared for rioting by Lunalilo's partisans had not their favorite been chosen. British and American diplomats at Honolulu had called for warships; and USS *Benicia* was in port when the election was held.[170] In the wake of Lunalilo's triumph no violence occurred. The new king took the oath of office at Kawaiahaʻo Church on January 12, 1873, amid tremendous enthusiasm, and entered upon his duties the next day.

All but one of Lunalilo's cabinet ministers were Americans, and the portfolio of foreign affairs was held by the Honolulu banker Charles R. Bishop, a supporter of reciprocity. It was no surprise, then, when the subject of a treaty with the United States was raised once more early in 1873, especially since 1872 had been a bad year for Hawaiʻi's sugar industry. Droughts threatened the crop; even the expanding market in the British colonies did not reassure the planters; and in any case the steamship connection between Honolulu and Australasia was soon cut. For a brief period, indeed, it seemed as if the worrisome state of the economy might encourage annexationist thoughts among American residents.[171]

Something beyond simple reciprocity and short of annexation was suggested in January, 1873, by Henry Whitney, the Honolulu publisher whose opposition to the coolie system had so infuriated the sugar planters in 1870, His views on labor notwithstanding, Whitney, the Hawaiian-born son of American missionary parents, was a strong proponent of reciprocity. He now submitted to the new king a plan to lease Pearl Harbor to the American government for fifty years in return for the signing of a reciprocity treaty.[172]

Concurrently, two American military officers were at Honolulu, ostensibly on vacation, actually on business for their government, "ascertaining the defensive capabilities of the various ports and their commercial facilities..."[173] Major-General John M. Schofield and Brevet Brigadier-General B.S. Alexander agreed with earlier observers that Pearl Harbor, the largest natural harbor in the North Pacific, was potentially a port of the greatest strategic value.[174]

Neither Whitney's proposal to lease Pearl Harbor to the United States nor the inquiries of Schofield and Alexander were made public at the time; but the idea of adding an offer of naval facilities to a reciprocity treaty came into the open very soon. In mid-February, 1873, after a veil-attended meeting of the Honolulu Chamber of Commerce, a committee discussed the twin subjects of the cession of Pearl Harbor and a treaty of reciprocity,[175] and though their subsequent memorial to the Hawaiian cabinet did not mention Pearl Harbor specifically, United States Minister to Hawai'i Henry Peirce wrote home to Washington that he thought a proposal would be made. Peirce, himself an annexationist, believed that annexation would be opposed in Hawai'i, but that reciprocity plus a cession of Pearl Harbor would ultimately lead to annexation.[176]

Between February and June, 1873, private and official discussions made it clear that although most foreigners at Honolulu were against annexation, the Pearl Harbor question was very much alive; and when, early in June, United States Minister Peirce approached the Hawaiian government, memorials from planters and Honolulu businessmen encouraged the cabinet to make a firm offer to the United States.[177] As Foreign Minister Charles Bishop outlined it, Hawai'i wanted a reciprocity treaty based upon the 1867 Harris-McCook treaty, with the stipulation that Hawaiian sugar up to No. 16 Dutch Standard (as against the 1867 figure of No. 12) be admitted to the United States free of duty, and with the further understanding that Pearl Harbor might be ceded to the United States provided that agreement could be reached on conditions.[178]

Some months elapsed before Minister Peirce got word from Washington on the proposed treaty. The Grant administration was cool: a reciprocity measure was unlikely to succeed, and congressional opinion was against the acquisition of further territory. Even had Peirce been encouraged to go on with negotiations he could not have done so. The Hawaiian government had retreated from its offer to cede Pearl Harbor, under the pressure of native opinion, which erupted in unprecedented and quite startling fashion.

In 1873, the Hawaiians of Honolulu quite suddenly ceased to be mere political objects acted upon by others. They became instead a force in the making and changing of governmental policy. This was a somewhat surprising development, at least to white men who were accustomed to regard the native population as politically negligible. Hawaiians thus far had participated in western government mostly by being manipulated. It was true that the natives of the kingdom were literate in a formal sense, and from the first election by ballot in 1851 until 1876 their votes outnumbered those of white men many times over, even at Honolulu, where the proportion of haoles to Hawaiians was highest. Most legislatures had a majority of natives in the House of Representatives.[179] Yet if Hawaiians dominated debates, white men made the legislative and executive decisions that counted, so that mere weight of numbers went for nothing. Haoles were not willing to entrust real political power to common Hawaiians any more than they were willing to allow natives unrestricted access to liquor and other such symbols of the white man's capacity to indulge himself without losing self-control. Too much "freedom," like too much rum, was held to be dangerous for natives.

All the same, twenty-five years of political experience had taught urban Hawaiians at least the rudiments of the value of association and organization, and at Honolulu the natives were familiar with the use of such devices as the petition and the mass meeting, by which the sophistication of the haole might be partly offset. Organization, to be sure, might be put to the service of the white man, as when native Christians or governmental employees were marched to the polls en masse on election day to cast their marked ballots under the eyes of their superiors.[180] And native petitions and mass meetings did not produce much in the way of results.[181]

Still, in the right circumstances, urban Hawaiians might become formidable in politics. Such conditions developed during the sixties and early seventies over the all-embracing issue of Americanism versus nativism, upon which every resident of the capital, haole or Hawaiian, had an opinion. The fundamental divorce between American and native interests became more and more apparent with every passing year, and the issue was given poignancy by the inroads made upon the native population by leprosy, which reached a critical stage in 1873.

Of all haoles at Honolulu, Americans were by far the most numerous and by far the most strident in their declarations of allegiance to their home country. The Civil War had made them very demonstrative—Honolulu, the capital city of a neutral kingdom, was decked in bunting; women wrapped bandages for the gallant wounded lying in hospitals thousands of miles away; and every important battle was marked by torchlight parades, fireworks, flag-hoistings, speeches, champagne toasts, and patriotic singing. All this fervor was in support of the Union; most of Honolulu's Americans were connected in one way or another with New England or the middle states.[182] Distance from home did not inhibit feeling. Thomas Spencer, a Honolulu merchant who had moved to Hilo, Hawai'i, on the eve of the Civil War, organized a company of native militiamen ("Spencer's Invincibles") with the idea of taking them to the battlefront, and was reduced to tears when he was told that he would be violating Hawaiian neutrality if he did so.[183] Henry Whitney advertised Uncle Tom's Cabin and "Union Must Be Preserved" envelopes in patriotic colors at his bookstore; a visiting Southern lady rash enough to fly the Stars and Bars from her verandah had the flag pulled down and torn to shreds by her neighbor's daughter; and Lincoln did better in Honolulu's mock elections of 1860 and 1861 than be did in most states of the Union.[184]

What these transplanted readers of *Uncle Tom's Cabin* thought of the South's peculiar institution and its relation to life in Hawai'i is unclear. Abolitionism was still alive among some Honolulans with missionary connections,[185] and their spiritual heirs were men such as Curtis Lyons, Sanford Dole, and J.O. Carter, who unhesitatingly applied New England principle to Hawaiian practice in the debates over the contract labor system. Others who had invested in the sugar business saw no contradiction between the southern aspect of their livelihood and the northern aspect of their American ties. And in Honolulu as in most of the northern United States, there were strong Unionists who were strenuous racists. The archetypal American Alexander Cartwright, pioneer of baseball, organizer of July 4 parades, and leader of a Union fundraising drive in Honolulu, spoke publicly and habitually of "damned black kanakas" (and worse), by which he meant every Hawaiian from the royal family down. He even extended the epithet to include white men who paid the crown polite attention.[186]

At a time when extremism ruled the minds of many Americans and found expression in attitudes such as those of Cartwright, it was not surprising that Hawaiians at Honolulu came to connect Americanism with racism. After 1865, Civil War excitement faded away, but American agitation for a reciprocity treaty continued, and every so often annexationist talk was heard. By the later sixties many natives at Honolulu had convinced themselves that American residents were threatening the very existence of the Hawaiian kingdom and its people.

Charges of this kind began to be heard in political campaigns at Honolulu from the mid-sixties onward, and they overflowed during the election campaign of January, 1868, when a document entitled "Ka Makamae Hawaii" (The Loyal Hawaiian) appeared at Honolulu, couched in florid old-style language and signed "A Warning Voice," threatening dire results if the "American" party were returned to office. A vote for such foreigners was a vote for men who would high-handedly snatch the kingdom away; they had been conspiring for decades, and with the *Lackawanna* in port they were still conspiring, so the warning ran. To preserve the kingdom, natives must be elected.[187]

The *Pacific Commercial Advertiser*, organ of the "American" party, denied that Americans at Honolulu had anything more than a friendly interest in the fate of the kingdom, and turned to berate the government for raising the spectre of racial hatred and for practicing electoral fraud, intimidation, and general demagoguery in its appeal to race rather than reason. The *Advertiser* charged that Captain Mahuka of the Royal Household Troops threatened government tenants with loss of their lands if they voted for "American" candidates. And natives on the government payroll at Honolulu voted by strict orders. The Household Troops, wrote a contributor to the *Advertiser*, "did not vote as they usually carry their muskets, one one way, another the other, but they voted as one man and all one way, holding their ballots over their heads...This was a detachment of the Light Guards. Next came a body of the Blackguards..."[188]

The inflamed atmosphere at Honolulu did not clear between 1868 and the end of the reign of Kamehameha V in December, 1872. The election of King William Lunalilo, darling of the Hawaiians and ostensible friend of Americans, gave hope that difficulties might be papered over, but when the city's natives heard of the immediate re-opening of negotiations for reciprocity and the added danger of the cession of Pearl Harbor, the capital was brought to a higher pitch of restlessness than ever before.

Hawaiians and their white friends (including those who found native animus useful in promoting anti-Americanism) began to meet on the streets or at Kawaiaha'o and Kaumakapili to vent their bitterness. Discussions on Pearl Harbor soon became jeremiads on the state of the nation. The voices were many. A suggestion that King William Lunalilo might go to the United States to speak for the treaty brought fearful memories of that earlier Hawaiian king who had gone to a foreign country and never returned. A brilliant opportunist, the maverick American Walter Murray Gibson, moved to Honolulu and began his rise in national politics with the publication of a bilingual newspaper, *Nūhou;* dedicated, so he said, solely to the defeat of the Pearl Harbor cession.[189] A handful of western-educated natives and half-whites drew on the combined

American and Hawaiian oratorical traditions to advance their various causes (among them were Henry Thompson, a part-Hawaiian lawyer who had gone to school at Punahou, and David Malo, nephew of the Hawaiian scholar, an erratic but gifted stump speaker at home in both languages). Some young Hawaiians pushed for the revival of the observance of Restoration Day, July 31, the holiday most closely associated with ancient Hawai'i. Supporters of reciprocity and the harbor cession were castigated: at a meeting at Kaumakapili, resolutions were passed urging that Samuel N. Castle and his family be expelled from the kingdom. Hard-headed merchants such as Castle had given careful consideration to the effect of reciprocity and the means necessary to achieve a treaty. The natives of Honolulu did not have to be analytical; it was enough for them to know that the life of the land was in danger. Their feelings were perhaps best stated poetically, in the traditional manner:

> I am a messenger sent to you;
> I ascend the mountain heights;
> I descend into the deep vales;
> I sweep o'er the stormy main.
> The burning heat of day does not stay me.
> I am the comrade of the winds,
> And the companion of the rain;
> I am a shield against the cold
> And darkness cannot dwell with me.
> I am a messenger forbidding you
> To give away Puuloa [Pearl Harbor],
> Be not deceived by the merchants,
> They are only enticing you,
> Making fair their faces, they are evil within;
> Truly desiring annexation,
> Greatly desiring their own good;
> They have no thought of good for you,
> A presuming set only are they,
> A proud and haughty set,
> Ever soliciting, at the same time flattering,
> Desiring that you should all die,
> That the kingdom may become theirs.[190]

Not for the first time in the history of Honolulu, political crisis overwhelmed the nation's ruler. King William Lunalilo, whose American cabinet ministers had with much difficulty persuaded him to endorse the Pearl Harbor cession, found himself inundated by hostile petitions and resolutions from the natives who had so joyfully voted him into office a few months before. Lunalilo's health had never been strong. He was tubercular, and chronic drinking debilitated him further. By the late summer of 1873 his personal and political resources were almost exhausted, and he withdrew from the disturbed city to his beach house at Waikīkī. But serenity was nowhere to be found. As if the reciprocity question was not enough, a mutiny broke out among the Royal Household Troops, and the city was reduced to a state of utter confusion for a week.[191]

The trouble began on the night of Saturday, September 6, when the Household Troops' Hungarian drillmaster, Captain Joseph Jajczay, making his rounds, discovered that four native guards posted at the treasury had left to go carousing downtown. Jajczay found them near the Commercial Hotel and took them back to 'Iolani Barracks on Palace Walk opposite the royal residence, where they were locked up in a room with four other delinquent enlisted men.[192] Next morning, while Jajczay was away at church, the eight prisoners broke down their door with a ball and chain and took off their irons. When Jajczay returned to lock them up again they would not obey him. The martinet drillmaster hit one with the flat of his sabre, whereupon the prisoners knocked him to the ground. Jajczay left the barracks in great agitation. Governor of O'ahu John Dominis and Adjutant-General Charles Judd were summoned. On their orders, a reluctant handful of enlisted men made a halfhearted effort to seize the prisoners. Judd stepped forward, the enlisted men stepped back, and the prisoners knocked Judd down.[193] Eight native soldiers had thus defied their adjutant-general, their drillmaster, and the Governor of O'ahu, all white men. No native officer or non-commissioned officer had intervened. Judd and Dominis departed, and nothing further was done that day to halt the mutiny. Late on Sunday night or early on Monday morning, the mutineers crossed the street and brought back from the palace grounds three six-pounder cannon. By the time Judd and Dominis returned on Monday afternoon the cannon were in place, covering the courtyard of the barracks, and the number of mutineers had grown to about forty.[194] Fourteen loyalists left the barracks, but the remainder were defiant, telling Judd and Dominis they would not obey orders until Jajczay was dismissed. Oddly enough, the mutineers continued to mount guard in the regular way at the treasury and the prison.[195]

Knowing that the mutineers needed powder for their cannon, the government assigned police constables and militiamen to the armory in down-town Honolulu and the powder magazine on Punchbowl. Alexander McDuff, a white policeman, disarmed a reconnaissance party from the barracks which had come looking for powder at the magazine. McDuff, however, was shorthanded, and could not spare men to march the mutineers to jail, so he let them go.[196]

On Tuesday, the aliʻi David Kalākaua, an honorary colonel in the Hawaiian army, went with Colonel J. M. Kapena and a retired army captain named Mahuka to the barracks, where the mutineers stated their simple complaints: there was not enough food and there was too much discipline.[197] Meanwhile, King Lunalilo, lying seriously ill at Waikīkī, had signed an order commanding the Household Troops to return to their duties. Governor Dominis was authorized to carry out the order by force if necessary; any soldiers disobeying would be dismissed.[198] Dominis read the order at the barracks at about two o'clock on Tuesday afternoon. The entire Royal Hawaiian Band and about a dozen soldiers left the ranks of the mutineers, but the rest refused either to return to duty or to be discharged. They wanted Jajczay dismissed, and Judd too.[199] Military discipline had clearly collapsed completely. The mutineers paid no more attention to civil authority. Warrants were sworn out at Honolulu police court for their arrest, but the men in the barracks declined to be taken into custody by Marshal William Parke.

Now that two days had gone by, the government was ready at last to take more active steps. Certainly something had to be done. The active mutineers numbered less than thirty, but they were obstreperous, and they had cannon as well as ammunition they had smuggled into the barracks. White families living nearby had evacuated their houses, and the surrounding streets were crowded with natives, who shouted disparagement of all haoles and applauded as orators harangued them. On Tuesday afternoon, militiamen of the Honolulu Rifles (mostly haoles with a few half-whites) and the Hawaiian Cavalry (including some natives) were marched through the streets and placed in position at the barracks.[200] The town's Superintendent of Water Works, an elderly retired sea captain, was sent to disconnect a pipe supplying the barracks. It took him an hour to dig his way to the cock, and when he reached it he found his wrench was too small. In the meantime soldiers from the barracks came out to a storehouse and got buckets, which they filled and took inside.[201]

This was impudent enough, but after all very few militiamen had answered the call to duty. There were less than two dozen of the Honolulu Rifles on the Palace Walk side of the barracks, posted (as they were painfully aware) against a stone wall only thirty or forty yards from the mouths of the mutineers' cannon; and on the Beretania Street side the native members of the Hawaiian Cavalry were joining the mutineers in a fish and poi supper.[202] All through the day the barracks, outside and in, had been packed with native men and women. The red-shirted soldiers, some of them drunk, fired their chassepot rifles into the air and laughingly went through mock motions of loading and firing the cannon. On the barracks wall, a soldier in an old three-cornered hat stood gesturing rudely and singing an improvised song in the style of the old Hawaiian meles.[203]

That night the Rifles and the Cavalry were withdrawn, much to the relief of the native and half-white members, who could see no point in fighting their countrymen, and to the greater relief of most of the haole militiamen,[204] whose military experience before then had been confined to marching, mock maneuvers, inaccurate target-shooting, weekend bivouacs at Waikīkī, and dress-uniform banquets with their ladies' auxiliaries. Once the militiamen were gone, the mutineers crossed again to 'Iolani Palace and carried back more ammunition and powder; friends brought food; and a native policeman attached a hose to a tap in the king's stables and filled the soldiers' water buckets for them.[205]

The militia's watch was not renewed on Wednesday morning (though the mutineers continued to guard the treasury and the prison as usual). In the hope that reason might prevail if the king could talk to the rebels, a delegation of three was given safe conduct to visit the royal residence at Waikīkī. King William Lunalilo offered the mutineers clemency if they would obey orders. That night they stacked arms, but would not leave the barracks. On Thursday, some remained inside making ammunition while a second delegation went to confer with the king. At the same time a squad chosen from within the barracks marched up to Punchbowl under the orders of Governor Dominis to honor a Russian warship in the harbor by firing a salute for the birthday of Czar Alexander. The saluting squad stole powder from each charge and took it back to the barracks. On Thursday night, more natives joined the rebels inside the walls, bringing the number to sixty or seventy.[206]

Early on Friday morning a letter written by the king was delivered to the mutineers. It reiterated the offer of clemency if the soldiers would retire peacefully from the barracks. The rebel leaders set conditions: the Secretary at War must countersign the king's letter; the letter must be printed in the Honolulu papers; the loyalist soldiers who had deserted the barracks must bring their equipment back; and all warrants for arrest of the mutineers must be destroyed. One after another the conditions were met; and at about half past ten the mutineers moved out, taking with them uniforms and other belongings left by the loyalists.[207]

Within the short space of six days the government had been embarrassed, then humiliated, then held to ransom. By noon on Friday the barracks was empty, and the king, as commander-in-chief of the armed forces, signed an order disbanding the Household Troops.[208] Clearly it was in the government's best interests to forget that the mutiny had ever happened. The loyalists were allowed to draw pay for the month of September; the mutineers were given dishonorable discharges and forbidden to work as policemen or prison guards, but none were prosecuted; the chassepot rifles were dismantled and locked away in the barracks; an augmented police force took over guard duties in the town; and a foreigner was put in charge of the powder magazine.[209] Only the ragged remnant of the denuded loyalists, roaming the streets and begging for food and clothing, reminded people of the uprising.[210]

The mutineers had insisted from the beginning that their only purpose was to get rid of Jajczay and Judd, the unfeeling drillmaster and the irritating adjutant-general. The Royal Household Troops would be perfectly happy, so they said, to serve under Hawaiian officers. Apprehensive white men, gauging the mood of the natives who swarmed about the barracks, were afraid that the city was on the brink of racial war.[211] In this delicate situation the leaders of the kingdom did everything possible to see that no violence occurred. Governor John Dominis, in particular, leaned over backwards in his efforts to avoid trouble. But were Dominis' motives unmixed? As it happened, he belonged to a faction in the town which was not displeased at the embarrassment of Lunalilo and his cabinet. Dominis was married to the Hawaiian chiefess Lydia Kamaka'eha, sister of David Kalākaua. Lunalilo, of course, had thwarted Kalākaua's bid for the throne in the royal election of January, 1873. Then too, Dominis had been Adjutant-General of the Household Troops under Kamehameha V. He lost the post when the newly-crowned Lunalilo, drunkenly celebrating his accession, suddenly removed Dominis in the course of a sweeping set of new appointments suggested to him by his American advisers, among them Attorney-General Allen Judd, brother of Charles Judd, who was made Adjutant-General.[212] More than one person thought Dominis was playing a double game during the mutiny, with his vague orders and his frequent comings and goings between the barracks and the town; and more still accused Kalākaua of making political capital out of the affair.[213] Kalākaua had been adding to the general feeling of unease in Honolulu by forming and training a private military company of "Young Hawaiians." Its members, estimated at anything between eighty and four hundred in number, played no part at all in the mutiny, but it was believed that when King William Lunalilo died, as it seemed he soon must, Kalākaua would try once again for the throne.[214]

The mutiny was over, but the deeply controversial reciprocity treaty and the Pearl Harbor cession remained before the city and the government. Lunalilo's cabinet continued to urge him on, and less than three weeks after the last rebellious soldier left the barracks, Chief Justice Elisha Allen was commissioned minister plenipotentiary to negotiate a treaty with the United States.[215] For the next six weeks Lunalilo tried to make up his mind on the cession of Pearl Harbor. After several half-commitments he finally announced on November 14 that he could not give it his hearty support and that it should therefore be withdrawn from consideration.[216]

Immediately he had done this, the king left Honolulu for Kailua on the island of Hawai'i in the hope of regaining his health. By then, however, he was hopelessly ill. Since the mutiny, his advisers had been discussing the problem of the succession—like King Lot, Lunalilo was a bachelor, and like Lot, he had steadily refused to name a successor.[217] Uncertainty about the future mounted as the steamer *Kilauea* took the king's physicians back and forth between Kailua and Honolulu. Dr. George Trousseau examined Lunalilo at Kailua on January 16, 1874. He was convinced the king could live only a few more days. Lunalilo was brought back to Honolulu, where the most careful of nursing kept him alive until his birthday, January 31. He died at about half past eight on the evening of February 2, 1874.[218]

CHAPTER 9

Sugar is King

Lunalilo founded no dynasty; his body lies alone in its tomb at Kawaiaha'o Church. He was an elected king; of necessity, an election would decide the next occupant of the Hawaiian throne. Lunalilo's passing had been predicted by native augurs and haole physicians alike,[1] and long before his death two ali'i—David Kalākaua and the dowager queen Emma—began to make preparations for the contest.

The unanimous royal election of 1873 had shown that while Lunalilo was alive no one wanted Kalākaua to be king. As Lunalilo's health grew worse, the likelihood that Kalākaua would succeed him grew stronger, and Honolulans turned their attention to this prospect. Queen Emma's strictures against Kalākaua were orthodox: he was nothing but a pretentiously arrogant usurper, despite what his genealogists said.

Her own descent was admirable, and she was convinced that Lunalilo would name her.[2] But the critical months went by, Lunalilo said nothing definite, and by saying nothing he strengthened Kalākaua's chances. Genealogical squabbles among the Hawaiians concerned haoles very little. For their own reasons, however, many foreigners in the city anticipated with some alarm the time when Kalākaua might be king. Emma hated Kalākaua because he was of inferior descent, not worthy to be called king of Hawai'i (and, of course, because he stood in her way); haoles distrusted him because he seemed altogether too kingly, unresponsive to foreign interests. Kalākaua was suspected of being the author or at least the instigator of the inflammatory campaign document of 1868, "Ka Makamae Hawaii;" his enigmatic role in the barracks mutiny of 1873 had reinforced the idea that he was a hater of haoles; now he was busy among the natives of the city, authenticating his bloodlines, inveighing against foreigners, and training his "Young Hawaiians." Was this company of soldiers chosen from among Kalākaua's tenants and adherents just a political machine, or might it be a revolutionary force? No one could tell. Perhaps Kalākaua did not intend to put the question of the kingship to an election; perhaps he would seize the throne.[3]

No matter how the question was decided, and no matter who was successful, Americans at Honolulu were sure their interests would suffer. Emma and Kalākaua hated each other; either one might use violence in victory or defeat, and violence might become racial war. Emma was strongly pro-British; Kalākaua was strongly pro-Hawaiian, an apparent racial enemy of Americans. Neither seemed to realize the pressing urgency of the reciprocity treaty. In the months before Lunalilo died matters seemed to be getting out of hand, and the barracks mutiny of September showed Honolulu's haoles just how helpless they were once the eddies and ripples of native sentiment became a steady anti-foreign stream. Between September and December, the Americans came to find some comfort in the idea that if Kalākaua were elected, at least the pro-British Emma would not be.[4] Kalākaua's victory was expected but not certain, and everything else was uncertain, so warships were called for. On the day of Lunalilo's death, USS *Portsmouth,* USS *Tuscarora,* and HMS *Tenedos* were at anchor in Honolulu harbor.

If the foreigners of the town were more or less reconciled by February, 1874, to Kalākaua's success, Emma and her partisans were not. Emma, in fact, had already drafted a victory speech.[5] Her followers were gathering regularly at her country house in Nu'uanu, making plans for election day. The formal decision would be made in the national legislature, by the appointed nobles and the elected representatives voting as one body, but in the meantime public opinion might be swayed by demonstrations. To add to the complexities of the situation, the regular biennial election for the house of representatives happened to fall due on February 2, 1874, precisely at the time when Lunalilo lay dying. The Emma-ites took advantage of this to hold a straw vote on the monarchy among the people of Honolulu. Not surprisingly, they reported that Emma had won handsomely. On February 4, the day after Lunalilo's death, a meeting convened at Kawaiaha'o to pass resolutions of condolence. This done, resolutions in support of Kalākaua were introduced. The Emma-ites howled them down—Kalākaua's unseemly haste was offensive, with Lunalilo dead less than twenty-four hours (though apparently they considered their own straw vote in good taste).[6] On Friday, February 6, after Emma's people had distributed printed handbills in town, a disturbance occurred when it was found that a partisan of Kalākaua had added his own written comment to a poster on Henry Whitney's new bulletin board: "Aole makou makemake e ike i ka palekoki e hookomo ana i ka lolowawae—We do not wish to see the petticoat putting on breeches." Curtis Lyons, who was something of an Emma-ite and something of a gentleman, smashed the glass and scratched out the offending words, and within minutes a crowd gathered and rival orators were at work (one of them, the ubiquitous David Malo, took advantage of the occasion to castigate some drunken sailors as foreign disturbers).[7] Three days later, so Marshal William Parke reported, Queen Emma was campaigning vigorously at her house, promising "if elected to take no salary repeal the house tax roads tax and any other tax they want and the great unwashed are whooping and yelling."[8] The next day, February 10, rumors circulated in the town that if Emma were elected she would free all prisoners at the jail. Marshal Parke ordered that no prisoners be released on election day.[9]

So the time went by until February 12, when the legislature was scheduled to meet. In January, when it had become clear that Lunalilo would die almost at the time of the biennial elections, a point of some importance had arisen: the legislature of 1872 was still technically in existence—should its members cast the ballot for the new monarch, or should members of the 1874 legislature (which normally would not meet until April) be the ones to vote? After conflicting opinions were heard, the cabinet council decided that the right to vote rested with the 1874 legislature.[10]

Since February 2, the new members, most of them natives and part-whites, had been arriving at Honolulu. On the great day— Thursday, February 12—they met in the legislative chambers at the courthouse.[11] Emma's followers marched down from the valley to the sound of a fife-and-drum band and surrounded the courthouse while speakers for both parties, standing on high platforms, shouted above the noise. Inside, before packed galleries, the legislators cast their votes one by one. Kalākaua's supporters had been given ballots decorated with a printed heart, and these were clearly visible as they were presented. At about two in the afternoon the balloting came to an end, the "exquisite dignity" of the occasion marred, according to Curtis Lyons, only by the last voter, a member from Kaua'i, who was too drunk to see where he should deposit his vote. At a quarter to three the ballots were counted— 39 for Kalākaua, 6 for Emma.

As soon as the news reached the crowd outside a riot erupted. The Emma-ites seized rocks, tree branches, trellises, pieces of wood from a carriage they wrecked, and fought their way into the courthouse to get at the native legislators who had voted for Kalākaua. Marshal Parke had brought eighty Hawaiian policemen to control the crowds, but once the riot started they took off their badges and fought according to their private convictions. Parke, Sanford Dole, C.C. Harris, J.O. Carter and other haoles tried in vain to quiet the uproar. Major William Moehonua, a staunch supporter of Kalākaua, was badly wounded, as were several others, and one representative was thrown from a window; he died of his injuries. Parke stood in front of his own office door with a pistol, holding off intruders. He saved his records, but he was lucky. "The courthouse is a perfect wreck," he wrote later, "not a window sash table chair or bench is left Hartwells Widemanns and Montgomerys and Atty Generals rooms are gutted not a book or paper but what was torn into shreds..."[12]

The Hawaiian government was all but helpless. Parke's policemen had disappeared in the crowd; the standing army had been dissolved after the barracks mutiny of 1873; the city's militia companies were somewhat stronger than previously, but all the new members were white, and it would have been risky to turn them and their unwilling part-white companions upon a rioting native crowd. On board the American and British warships in the harbor were sailors and marines by the hundred. Kalākaua, Charles R. Bishop, and Governor John Dominis asked United States Minister Henry Peirce to order an armed force to land. Peirce and the senior American naval officer, Commander Belknap of the *Tuscarora*, had been expecting this.[13] One hundred and fifty men came ashore from the *Tuscarora* and the *Portsmouth*. They were joined by seventy or eighty men from the British warship *Tenedos*. The Americans cleared the courthouse and posted guards there, at the armory, the treasury, the prison, and the station house. The Britishers marched to Emma's house, drove off her supporters and returned to mount guard at the palace and the barracks. By evening some of the rioters had been arrested. The town was quiet that night, except for a few gunshots and the sound of windows being smashed at representatives' homes by Emma-ites still at large.

When it was all over, the Emma-ites had accomplished nothing. Kalākaua took the oath of office on the morning of February 13, and was recognized as king by the diplomatic corps. Emma had already been urged to accept her defeat,[14] and finally she rather grudgingly made a statement for publication, acknowledging the legality of the election, forswearing violence, and offering support to Kalākaua.[15] The American and British forces stayed on the streets until February 20 without encountering any resistance.

To westerners, Emma's defeat might have appeared conclusive. Her campaign for the throne had actually been very clumsy. Despite her insistence on the primacy of rank, few Hawaiians of any importance supported her (whether from conviction, or because Kalākaua paid more for support, is not clear).[16] But if Emma did not have followers enough to win the throne she had enough to embarrass the government, as the courthouse riot showed; and even after fifty rioters were tried and forty were jailed, some of the Emma-ites continued to meet at their patron's house.

Kalākaua was nervous about Emma's intentions. After one very strained meeting, the two avoided each other. The king seemed secure on the throne. Officially recognized as monarch of Hawai'i, he had founded a new dynasty by naming his brother as his successor.[18] He made a triumphal procession to all the major islands and was greeted by enthusiastic and affectionate crowds when he came back to Honolulu. The re-organized Hawaiian standing army guarded him faithfully.[19] Still, he feared Emma and she feared him.[20] One of Emma's supporters thought it necessary to warn her against eating food prepared at public receptions.[21] When the legislature of 1874 was prorogued in August, crowds gathered again at Emma's house, and Marshal Parke put extra policemen on duty in the city in case the Emma-ites made good their threat to assault the representatives.[22] Kalākaua ordered some dissidents arrested for using "seditious language;"[23] and when, a little later, a petition was circulated in the city claiming that Lunalilo had named Emma his successor in a verbal "will," and that Kalākaua was elected by fraud, the author, a Hawaiian named J.P. Zephyrin Kaho'ali'i, was tried for treason and convicted.[24]

Until the day of the royal election in February, 1874, Emma had placed her hopes for the throne in the hands of an Episcopalian Christian Divine Providence. After her defeat she turned to less Victorian sources of solace and inspiration. Her loyal cousin, the minor chief Peter Young Ka'eo, confined to the leprosarium on Moloka'i, had come to know two kahuna very well, and his letters to Emma throughout 1874 were full of information about encouraging omens—propitious dreams and signs in the heavens.[25] Emma, who in 1873 rebuked Peter for his interest in kahuna-ism, went so far in the next two years as to be ready, by the end of 1875, to combine Christianity and kahuna-ism. On the advice of an old woman, she was to

pray that God would please place me on the Hawaiian Throne, and on coming Monday at noon, December 20th, we should have a little feast. A young lamb should be eaten with it at noon, and three drops of its heart's blood with three drops of its gaul should be mixed in a glass of brandy, which I am to drink before eating at noon. This represents the heart's blood of the natives and the [gall is to represent the moving of the times], and on that day the heavens will be cloudless and some wonderful sign will happen...She says that the tree with all its roots, branches, etc., will be cut off, meaning the D.K.s [Kalakaua's dynasty] will all die off...they are all going to die soon and Queen Emma will reign supreme, living to a good old age over these Islands.[26]

It was in Emma's interests to conceal these machinations from Kalākaua and his party. Perhaps she did, perhaps not; in any event, Kalākaua continued as late as 1877 to be afraid of death by assassination, and Emma herself apparently lived in fear of her life at times.[27]

Very few haoles in the city knew or cared about the quiet war of nerves going on between Kalākaua and Emma. Almost as soon as the election riot was over, the Americans of Honolulu turned again to their great preoccupation in local, national, and international affairs: the immediate and long-term security of their property. Late in February, 1874, eighty merchants and other residents petitioned Minister Henry Peirce to ask for assistance, and, upon Peirce's recommendation, the United States Navy assigned the warships *Tuscarora, Benicia, Lackawanna, Portsmouth,* and *Pensacola* to visit Honolulu in rotation.[28]

Distrust of Kalākaua was still strong among haoles in general and Americans in particular. He was untried as a king, and his record in the year before the royal election led white men to believe he might be a troublemaker. United States Minister Peirce, writing not long before the election, predicted that if Kalākaua were elected a reign of "Saturnalia" would commence, causing "the sun of national prosperity to set in clouds of darkness."[29] Peirce, after almost forty years of experience in Hawaiian affairs, regarded Hawaiians as mild and amiable "to a certain degree." Beyond that they were "human tigers," fit for any kind of violence.[30]

The record, of course, showed otherwise. White men were as safe at Honolulu as anywhere in the world. In fact, when violence threatened in the town, it was usually instigated by haoles, not natives; and Hawaiians faced with violence habitually forbore to respond in kind. To be sure, feeling against foreigners in the city was strong, and growing stronger—not surprisingly, among a native people dispossessed to a large extent of land and life. Yet, in the critical years of 1873 and 1874, the barracks mutiny had come and gone with not a shot fired in earnest; and the rioters at the courthouse, unarmed to begin with, had solicitously set aside white men encountered in their pursuit of legislators, and had dispersed within minutes after armed forces were landed from the ships in the harbor. The trials of the rioters went ahead quietly, as they would have done in any western country; native juries correctly found native rioters guilty. W.L. Green, a wealthy English merchant who became Kalākaua's foreign minister, wrote more sensibly and temperately of the Hawaiians than did Henry Peirce. Green thought that despite the momentary outbreak at the courthouse, Hawaiians deserved their reputation as a law-abiding people. Indeed, the courthouse rioters might have been doing nothing more than following the recent example of election rioters in England, where people might have been expected to know better.[31]

As for King Kalākaua himself, he had chosen for his dynastic symbol the noonday sun, and he had no intention of allowing the sun of national prosperity to set in clouds of darkness, despite Peirce's gloomy prediction. If the Americans of the city had bothered to think back, they might have recalled that Kalākaua had said often enough before he became king that he was not against foreigners, that there was room in the kingdom for all, and that his prime concern was for the nation's survival and prosperity. He was not the first aspirant for power to state a belief in mutually contradictory principles. He had always been against the cession of Pearl Harbor, but almost from the day he took office he favored a reciprocity treaty.

Among members of the house of representatives elected in 1874 were several who wanted to see white men out of politics altogether, and proposals were made to reduce the salary of representatives to the point where only natives could afford to serve;[32] but at the executive level Kalākaua and his cabinet set about finding the best way to reconcile the economic interests of the businessmen of Honolulu and their planter allies on the outer islands with the policy of the United States government. In a conversation with Charles Alfred Castle (a supporter of reciprocity) late in December, 1873, Kalākaua had said he thought Lunalilo and his cabinet ministers had handled the Pearl River cession very badly: they should have allowed it to be defeated either by the American government or the Hawaiian government. By their inept withdrawal of the offer in November, 1873, they had simply made "weather cocks" out of themselves, and had all but insulted the United States, the best friend and the neighbor of the Hawaiian kingdom.[33] How might matters be ordered better?

Not long after Kalākaua became king, United States Secretary of State Hamilton Fish advised Henry Peirce that both houses of congress were currently against a Hawaiian reciprocity treaty. Despite this, Kalākaua and his ministers worked to forward negotiations.[34] Late in June, a petition supporting reciprocity came to the king, signed by planters and businessmen in great number. The names of the signatories showed that reciprocity could scarcely be considered any longer as nothing but an American conspiracy of some sort. Among those convinced that "serious disaster" would overtake the islands without a commercial treaty were Theophilus Davies, Henry Waterhouse, and A. S. Cleghorn, all British by background; the German firms of Hackfeld & Co., Bolles & Co., and F.A. Schaefer & Co.; and the Chinese houses of Afong & Achuck and Chulan & Co.[35]

In August, 1874, King Kalākaua decided that he himself would make a trip to the United States, partly for pleasure and partly to bring his royal influence to bear upon the question at Washington. The privy council approved his journey in September.[36] In October, the advance guard left—Elisha H. Allen and Henry A.P. Carter, special agents with the power to negotiate a treaty.[37] The royal party followed a month later on USS *Benicia*—Kalākaua, Governor Dominis, Colonel J.M. Kapena, and Minister Henry Peirce.

Kalākaua was the first reigning monarch of Hawai'i to leave the islands since Liholiho went to London to die in 1823–1824. At the waterfront, natives crowded around him, some crying, some chanting meles, some wanting simply to shake his hand or kiss him.[38] He was also the first reigning monarch of any country to visit the United States. His trip across country and his sojourn on the east coast aroused great interest, some of it serious, some less so, as when P.T. Barnum induced the king to visit the Hippodrome in New York to be looked at by the same crowds which delighted in animal acts and freak shows.[39]

At home in Honolulu, there was nothing to do but wait and mull over newspaper accounts of the king's reception at Washington. Kalākaua met President Grant on December 15, and was received by both houses of Congress on December 18. He attended a brilliant state ball in his honor that evening, and left for New York five days later. His eleven-day sojourn at Washington had been a great public success.[40]

Meanwhile, Elisha Allen and H.A.P. Carter were deep in discussion with Secretary of State Hamilton Fish, as they had been since November 18. During the first month of their talks, Allen and Carter were confronted with the same objections that had defeated reciprocity in the past—among them the arguments that Canadian reciprocity proposals had failed, and that the House of Representatives, regarding reciprocity treaties as revenue measures, was unwilling to allow the treaty-making function of the Senate to be extended thus far.[41]

King Kalākaua's visit no doubt did something to attract the attention of congressmen to the reciprocity negotiations; certainly Minister Peirce's unceasing advocacy had its effect on the Grant administration. When Carter presented a draft treaty on January 4, 1875, Fish agreed to show it to the cabinet next day. From then until the end of January, the negotiators argued not over the principle of reciprocity, but over the exact terminology which might be used in a treaty. A long list of articles to be exempted from duty was agreed upon readily; the most difficult question, and the one on which the efficacy of the treaty depended, was that of sugar. On January 30, a decision was reached which would admit a wide range of American products to Hawai'i duty-free, in return for the duty-free admission to the United States of all grades of Hawaiian sugar commonly referred to in the markets of San Francisco and Portland as "Sandwich Island sugar."

This was the state of affairs when Kalākaua arrived home in Honolulu on the morning of February 15, 1875. The marine telegraph on Diamond Head signalled the approach of USS *Pensacola*, with the royal standard flying; the signal guns on Punchbowl fired a salute; and crowds

flocked to the waterfront. Between ten and twelve thousand spectators lined the streets as Kalākaua rode to the palace beneath decorated
arches, reading "God Save The King," "Aloha Kalakaua," and "Hawaii-
America."[42]

The commercial clauses of the treaty were those of immediate
importance to the sugar interests of Honolulu, faced as they were with
"serious disaster." To the United States government, commercial considerations were important but secondary: indeed a case was made that
the Hawaiian reciprocity treaty would cost America money. The clause
that eventually secured continued discussion was Article IV, which to
some degree compensated the United States for the withdrawal of the
Pearl Harbor cession. Article IV bound the Hawaiian government not
to alienate any territory to foreign powers during the term of the treaty,
and not to allow to any nation other than America the privileges of reciprocity.[43] With Article IV readily conceded by the Hawaiian negotiators
as a condition of the treaty's success, the document was sent on its way
through the United States Senate, that graveyard of treaties.

On March 18, 1875, the required two-thirds vote was secured.
Three weeks later, the news reached Honolulu on the mail steamer
McGregor, which appeared off Diamond Head with its flags flying a
coded message of the treaty's success.[44] Kalākaua ratified the convention on April 18. Land values had already gone up about twenty-five
percent in the islands, despite the fact that the treaty still had to be ratified by President Grant and that enabling legislation in the House of
Representatives was necessary.[45] Henry Whitney, at that time publisher
of the *Hawaiian Gazette,* had no doubt things would be well: on the understanding that American newsprint would enter Hawai'i duty-free when
the treaty took effect, he lowered the annual subscription to the *Gazette*
from $6 to $5.[46]

Before the treaty reached the House of Representatives, the sugar
refiners of San Francisco mounted an attack upon it. The arguments of
the sixties were revived: the refiners feared that increased sugar production in Hawai'i would flood the west coast market, depress the refinery
business there, and cause nationwide distress in the American sugar
industry. The refiners' complaints were countered by the San Francisco
Chamber of Commerce, which predicted a general expansion of trade
between the west coast and Hawai'i, to the benefit of all.[47]

The version of the treaty ratified by Kalākaua was taken back
to Washington, where ratifications were exchanged on June 3. All that
remained now was for the House of Representatives to act; but nothing
happened for the rest of 1875. For one reason and another, the treaty did
not reach the floor of the House until January, 1876. Elisha Allen had
been sent to Washington again in November, 1875,[48] to do what he could

to speed matters along, but matters would not be speeded (later, Allen referred to these months as the most strenuous time of his life). When the House began to discuss the treaty, extended debates took place on topics already argued in the Senate. Week after week the mail ships came to Honolulu from San Francisco, reporting no progress. At last, on May 26, 1876, the bark *Mary Belle Roberts* arrived outside the harbor decked in bunting. She fired a twenty-one gun salute, and the news was brought ashore that the House had finished its deliberations on May 8.[49]

This was still not the end: the treaty had to go back to the Senate for its final concurrence in the House's implementation. The Hawaiian government made the necessary moves to see that the treaty would go into effect immediately the American government wound up its work. A proclamation by the king was issued on June 16 and published on June 21; an act admitting the stipulated American goods duty-free was passed in the Hawaiian legislature on July 18 and published on August 16.[50] All this time passed without an encouraging word from Washington, but the mood remained optimistic at Honolulu, at least as late as July 4, when the biggest celebration ever was held at Honolulu:[51] 1876 was the centennial year of the United States, and it was also the year of a great step forward in Hawaiian-American relations—or it would be, if only the Senate would hurry.

But last-minute attempts to stall the treaty were made by representatives of the Louisiana sugar industry, and as the mail ships brought little news—and bad news at that—the mood of Honolulu changed. Business was temporarily depressed; ships lay idle, unable to secure freight; the Hawaiian legislature, which had been in session since April 29, occupied its time with trivialities. Everybody was on the "ragged edge of uncertainty."[52] On August 23, the *Hawaiian Gazette* remarked that it seemed almost impossible that the senate would act before the close of the session. The waiting ended the very next day. The Pacific Mail Steamship *City of San Francisco* (commanded by Captain Waddell of *Shenandoah* fame) arrived with unofficial news that the treaty had finally been confirmed. As she came around Diamond Head dressed in a "rainbow of bunting," the word spread like wildfire in the town, and crowds gathered at the waterfront with "hearts too full for utterance."[53]

The silence was broken soon enough. The *Hawaiian Gazette* for August 30 carried the ecstatic headline: "Hurrah! For America and Hawaii! The Glorious News at Last! Hurrah! Our Luck Still 'Consistent!' Arrival of the PMSS City of San Francisco Bringing the News of the Passage of the Bill rendering operative the Treaty of Reciprocity!!! The Treaty goes into effect as soon as the bill is signed by the President! President Grant signed the bill on Tuesday of last week, August 15th.

Hip! Hip! Hurrah!!! With a Tiger."

Kalākaua and his ministers decided to delay any great public demonstrations until official word came from Washington. The next steamer to arrive, the *City of New York,* confirmed that President Grant had named September 9 as the day on which the treaty would go into effect. Kalākaua announced the date of the great occasion, and in the wake of an all-night torchlight procession and fireworks display Honolulu moved forward into a new era.[54]

Was the city ready? For twenty-five years the American merchants of Honolulu had been urging reciprocity. For a year, however, they had known the worst kind of uncertainty, and possible losses as well as benefits were discussed, especially by Englishmen whose British business connections were excluded from the treaty's provisions by Article IV. There might be a loss of revenue on the part of the Hawaiian kingdom—how would this be made up? Invoiced goods already in the city's warehouses would depreciate by ten percent as soon as the treaty went into effect. Not only Hawaiian sugar but Hawaiian rice would enter the United States duty-free—what would this do to the already inadequate labor force on the sugar plantations? Might not coolies desert sugar for rice cultivation? Ever since 1874 the Emma-ites had been developing an anti-reciprocity propaganda, and they did well in the 1876 elections, returning two out of four candidates in Honolulu and several elsewhere. In the legislature, just before the treaty went into effect, a small body of dissidents led by the anti-American Englishman Godfrey Rhodes mounted an inconclusive general attack on the whole idea of reciprocity.[55]

Whether or not these diversions had an influence, it seems that in the crucial weeks some of the town's businessmen were looking the wrong way. One of the passengers on the *City of San Francisco* was the west coast sugar refiner Claus Spreckels. Earlier an enemy of reciprocity, Spreckels had concluded by mid-1876 that the treaty would be passed. Taking the first available ship to the islands after news was telegraphed from Washington that the treaty was safe, Spreckels landed quietly at Honolulu and bought half the 1877 sugar crop of the islands before the price responded to the passage of the treaty.[56] Still, there was more than enough of everything to go around. The treaty would run for eight years. There seemed no reason why these should not be the fattest in Honolulu's history. In December, Peter Cushman Jones of C. Brewer & Co. struck a most satisfactory balance and wrote at the foot of the firm's account book: "So ends the year 1876, Praise God."[57]

Acknowledgments

I owe more than a conventional debt of gratitude to many people in Honolulu. First, those who gave me unstinted access to manuscript, book, and photograph collections, and arranged permission to read restricted materials: Miss Janet Bell and the staff of the Hawaiian room of the Sinclair Library, University of Hawai'i; Mrs. Kay Boyum, Mrs. Sophie Cluff, and Miss Albertine Loomis of the Mission-Historical Library, Honolulu; Miss Agnes Conrad and the staff of the Archives of Hawai'i; James Dunn of the survey room of the Hawai'i land office; Miss Margaret Titcomb and the staff of the library at the Bernice P. Bishop Museum, Honolulu. I thank Ernest Dodge of the Peabody Museum, Salem, Massachusetts, for permission to read the Journal of Stephen Reynolds. Several people generously allowed me to read work in progress: Jacob Adler and Charles H. Hunter of the University of Hawai'i; Richard Greer of Kamehameha Schools; Robert Horwitz of the Hawai'i Legislative Reference Bureau and Michigan State University; Robert Schmitt, statistician for the Hawai'i State Department of Planning and Economic Development; and Charles Peterson of Philadelphia. I have had the benefit of good ideas and good conversation from all these people. My good friends Dorothy Barrère of Bishop Museum; O. A. Bushnell of the University of Hawai'i; and Lawrence Windley of the Lahaina Restoration Foundation have given me wise and sympathetic criticism, and I have depended heavily on their expert knowledge.

It goes without saying that responsibility for errors of fact, lapses of style, and failures of intelligence rests solely with me.

Bibliography

This dissertation is based upon materials in the following Honolulu collections: the Archives of Hawai'i; the Mission-Historical Library (which houses the collections of the Hawaiian Mission Children's Society and the Hawaiian Historical Society); the Sinclair Library, University of Hawai'i; the library at the Bernice P. Bishop Museum; the Department of Land and Natural Resources; and the Honolulu Academy of Arts. Between them these collections contain virtually all available manuscript, printed, photographic, and artistic material that bears directly on the history of Honolulu in the nineteenth century, either in the original or in the form of copies made from originals housed elsewhere in the world.

In sheer bulk the material is formidable, but many gaps remain in the evidence. Reliable statistics of any kind are virtually nonexistent for the period before 1850, and estimates of quantities are therefore mostly impressionistic rather than exact. The directories published by C.C. Bennett in 1869 and 1873 are less than totally reliable. Again, sources on the life of the native community are all but intractable, despite a high literacy rate among the Hawaiians and despite the existence of a native-language press: Hawaiians simply did not have the New England habit of explaining or justifying themselves in print. Then too, the quantity and quality of independent comment on events varies greatly from period to period. Most of the early private manuscripts come from missionary families. Whatever their defects as source material, these journals and letters at least provide a record with some depth. There is no equivalent body of material for the later decades.

A description of those parts of holdings useful to the present study follows, institution by institution. These formal bibliographical categories give a listing of selected individual works.

ARCHIVES OF HAWAI'I

A general description of holdings is available in the Archives' mimeographed Department Manual. The staff has made a start on a systematic inventory, and the results so far are incorporated in the Department Manual. The list that follows draws on the Manual, using for consistency the order and titling adopted there. Note that this list contains *only* those materials directly useful in the preparation of the dissertation. Note also that since the publication of the standard secondary works of Kuykendall and Bradley, there has been some rearrangement and retitling of manuscripts in the Archives; citations in those works should now be checked against the Department Manual.

Attorney-General. Letters received, 1845–1876; outgoing letters, 1874–1876.

Cabinet Council and Ministerial Conferences, Cabinet Council Minute Books, 1846–1876; Ministerial Conferences, 1855–1863. See also FO & Ex folders marked "Cabinet Council" or "Privy and Cabinet Council," 1861–1865.

Census. 1843–1876. Very incomplete for early years—nothing more than summaries. For later years, an occasional list of names.

Collector General of Customs. Letters received, 1845–1876; outgoing letter books, 1846–1876; registry of Hawaiian ships, 1850–1852, 1866–1876; account books, 1852–1876.

Commissions. Royal commissions issued to office holders and consuls, 1852–1876. These names are listed in a separate card index of Office Holders.

Crown Lands, Agent and Commissioner. Accounts, 1862–1874; minutes, 1865–1873. Letters received are included in and indexed with Land Files (see below).

Finance, Minister of. Letters received and miscellaneous documents, 1839–1876; outgoing letter books, 1848–1869; account books, scattered.

Foreign Office And Executive (FO & Ex). Invaluable for Honolulu as the capital. As the Department Manual says, these are the most important records for the Kingdom of Hawai'i. All available correspondence of the kings, Ministers of Foreign Affairs, and Privy Council is here. The Manual continues: "There are a few records before 1840, but the bulk are later. It consists of letters and documents received and letter books and files returned by a few of the envoys and consuls. The records from 1790 to 1849 are filed chronologically; from 1850–1865, in large categories under each year...; 1866–1900, under each year by the official..." FO & Ex is fairly well indexed.

Governors of Islands. O'ahu. Outgoing letter books, 1855–1876 (mainly trivialities); letters received from Deputy Marshal, 1854–1876.

Harbor Master. Lists of ships entering and leaving the harbor; lists of native seamen shipped; pilots' records; lists of deserters. All incomplete. Filed here is the Journal of William Paty (see below, Manuscript Collections).

Health, Board of. Letters received, 1850–1876; outgoing letter books, 1865–1868 (many pages unreadable); Minutes of Board, 1858–1876.

Immigration and Naturalization. Passenger lists, 1843–1876; naturalization records, 1844–1876; denization records, 1846–1876 (all these are indexed but incomplete); Board of Immigration minutes, 1865–1876.

Interior Department. Letters received, 1828–1876; outgoing letter books, 1845–1876. The Department Manual says: "Letters prior to 1845 are primarily those of local residents and island governors to the King, and correspondence between the chiefs. Letters received are divided into four sections: 1) by subject [these are now listed in the inventory]; 2) undated but numbered documents; 3) letters filed by date; 4) documents concerning licenses. Letter books and some letters received are indexed." Just as FO & Ex is the most important file for the kingdom at large, so Interior Department is the most important for Honolulu as a locality. The Archives' Department Manual has a good account of the history of the Interior Department and its functions, as well as a quite detailed subject list.

Judiciary. Supreme Court letter books, 1847–1866; some letters received. O'ahu was the First Circuit; records of this court are still in the Judiciary Building, Honolulu. They include wills filed up to 1876. Important decisions of the Supreme Court were published from time to time under varying titles; the general designation is *Hawaiian Reports*, and the first five volumes contain most decisions important to the period before 1876.

Land File. The Department Manual says: "All of the letters of the Commissioners to Quiet Land Titles, and the records of the Minister of the Interior and the Board of Education dealing with land matters have been combined in this file. The records are fully indexed both by the names of the persons concerned and by the names of the lands, and the award numbers." The Mahele Book is also in AH. Recently, books of testimony heard by the Commissioners were lodged in AH and microfilmed. A great amount of raw material remains in the Department of Land and Natural Resources.

Legislative Records. Bills, resolutions, reports, petitions, minutes, journals, account books. A few records for 1840 and 1843. Journals for most sessions were printed in newspapers, sometimes in both English and Hawaiian. Laws were also published in the press, then collected in *Session Laws* (title varies). AH has drafts and printed copies of laws.

Marshal and Sheriffs. Marshal of the Kingdom: letters received, 1850–1876; outgoing letter books, 1873–1876.

Military Records. Army-Navy: letters received, 1844–1876; outgoing letter books, 1853–1876.

Palace Records. Kings' personal accounts and chamberlains' accounts, 1840–1876; guest books, 1855–1876.

Postmaster General. Letters received, 1868–1876; outgoing letter books, 1856–1876.

Prisons. Record of prisoners at the Fort, 1852–1876; daily record books, Oahu Prison, 1858–1876.

Privy Council. Minute books, 1846–1876. Correspondence and documents such as petitions and reports are filed in FO & Ex.

Public Instruction. Minutes of Board of Education, 1855–1876; outgoing letter books, 1847–1876; letters received, 1838–1876. The Department Manual says: "Separate files have been set up for essays by students, letters, and reports concerning Catholic schools (1846–1879), and documents on the industrial schools (1866–1876). Documents concerning land matters are part of the Land File." A few of the Public Instruction records have been indexed.

Public Works. Letters received, 1845–1876.

Tax Records. Record books of taxes collected, Oahu, 1855–1876.

Vital Statistics. Birth, marriage, and death records. Very incomplete in early period; mostly marriage record books of missionaries.

Cabinet ministers and others made periodic reports to the legislature. Drafts are often in relevant files at AH; and AH also has fairly complete runs of published reports. Reports were usually printed in full or at least excerpted in the press. Most useful were reports of Chief Justice; Minister of Finance; Minister of Foreign Affairs; Minister of Interior (see Department Manual for the many officials under his jurisdiction); Minister of Public Instruction; President of the Board of Education; President of the Bureau of Immigration.

The photograph, map, and plan files of AH were also used. These are quite well indexed.

AH has copies of records of the British Consulate, Honolulu, 1824–1876; and copies of Admiralty and Foreign Office records relating to Hawai'i. These copies are legible and quite reliable, but it is best to use the microfilm copies of this material from BPRO FO/58 at UH.

AH is the best place to find published government documents relating to Hawai'i. Session laws and Supreme Court decisions have been mentioned above; AH also has copies of civil and penal codes up to 1876, and collected speeches of Hawaiian kings. Special publications that proved useful included *Correspondence Relative to the Sandwich Islands...* (London, 1843); the several Hawaiian government pamphlets bound together as the *Charlton Land Claims*; and *Report of the Proceedings and Evidence in the Arbitration between the King and Government of the Hawaiian Islands and Messrs Ladd & Co....* (Honolulu, 1846). MS versions of most material in these publications are in AH, usually in FO & Ex.

MISSION-HISTORICAL LIBRARY
The manuscript and book collection of the Hawaiian Mission Children's Society is housed here, together with the collection of the Hawaiian Historical Society.
Not all of the HMCS manuscripts are catalogued. The core of the collection consists of: 1) ABCFM Letters: microfilm and xerox copies of letters, journals and reports of various kinds from members of the Sandwich Island Mission to the American Board of Commissioners for Foreign Missions at Boston (originals are in the Houghton Library, Harvard); 2) correspondence among members of the SIN, filed by name of author; 3) diaries and journals of missionaries, also filed by name; 4) letters of missionaries to relatives in the United States; 5) a few sizeable collections of family papers. The most useful of these materials are listed individually below, under Manuscripts. HMCS has printed material relating to the mission, including ABCFM instructions and reports, and SIM reports and minutes of general meetings. Also in HMCS is the ABCFM's *Missionary Herald* which often excerpted material in ABCFM Letters. HMCS has a good collection of early Hawaiian-language publications. The library's collection of voyages is listed in Bernice Judd, *Voyages to Hawaii Before 1860...*(Honolulu, 1929).
To a large extent the Hawaiian Historical Society library duplicates the printed materials in HMCS. Its manuscript collection is not particularly large, and as it happens very little of it was directly relevant to the dissertation. Exceptions are listed below, under Manuscripts. Naturally, HHS has complete runs of its own publications.

HMCS and HHS both have quite useful photograph collections.

SINCLAIR LIBRARY, UNIVERSITY OF Hawai'i
A recent publication, *Dictionary Catalog of the Hawaiian Collection University of Hawaii Library*, 4 vols. (Boston, 1963), indicates the extent of the University's Hawaiian collection. Printed material for the most part duplicates that in other collections in Honolulu. The University controls the Gregg Collection (see below, Manuscripts); also useful are some letters by William Hooper and Peter Brinsmade. The microfilm room has good collections of newspapers, together with diplomatic correspondence relating to Hawai'i: BPRO FO/58; USDS, Consular Letters, Honolulu; USDS,

Dispatches, Hawai'i. In the Hawaiian room itself are copies of important letters from the French National Archives.

BERNICE P. BISHOP MUSEUM LIBRARY

For a general guide to the library, see *Dictionary Catalog of the Bernice P. Bishop Museum*, 9 vols. (Boston, 1964). The library here, admirable for ethnography, was not greatly useful in this dissertation. Its major asset for these purposes is the R.J. Baker photograph collection, consisting of thousands of negatives and prints. The cream of the collection has been published by Baker in the following books: *Early Hawaiian Prints* (Honolulu, 1938); *Honolulu in 1853* (Honolulu, 1950; *Honolulu in 1870* (Honolulu, 1951); *Honolulu Then and Now* (Honolulu, 1941); *Sketches and Maps of Old Honolulu* (Honolulu, 1950). The Hawaiian Ethnographic Notes (generally known as HEN), a partial list of subjects discussed in Hawaiian-language newspapers, offered some leads. The library also has an index of ships' names prepared by George R. Carter.

DEPARTMENT OF LAND AND NATURAL RESOURCES

The survey room has working drawings, field notes, and maps from the nineteenth century, partially indexed. In the basement are raw materials relating to the land divisions. Testimony books and the Mahele Book, previously lodged here, are now in AH (see above).

HONOLULU ACADEMY OF ARTS

An excellent collection of originals and prints from the nineteenth century, and a useful photographic negative collection.

Manuscripts

ABCFM Letters (see above, Mission-Historical Library).

Alexander & Baldwin Collection. HMCS.

American Protestant Mission. AH, Private Collections.

Armstrong, Richard. Journal. HMCS.

Armstrong Papers. AH. Includes photostat copies of Armstrong–Chapman Papers, originals in Library of Congress.

Bingham Papers. HMCS.

Brinsmade Letters. UH.

Brinsmade Papers. AH.

Bryant & Sturgis Letterbooks. Originals in Baker Library, Harvard Graduate School of Business Administration. Copies of important documents in Kuykendall Collection, UH.

Chamberlain Papers. AH.

Chamberlain, Daniel. Journal. HMCS.

Chamberlain, Levi. Journal. HMCS.

Clark, E.W. Journal. HMCS.

Clark, E.W. Letter Books. HMCS.

Colcord, John. Journal. AH.
Cooke, Amos. Journal. HMCS.

Curtis Lyons Papers. AH.

Damon Papers. HMCS.

Davis Collection. Originals in California State Library. Extracts in Kuykendall Collection, UH.

Elisha Allen Papers. Originals in Library of Congress. Microfilm copy in UH.

Ely, Louisa Everest. Journal. HMCS.

Emma Collection. AH. The Archives' Department Manual says: "This collection is divided into three groups: 1) Archives, which has all the Queen Emma documents which were in the Archives on November 15, 1957. The source of this material is not known. 2) Flora Jones Collection, consisting of the letters written by Queen Emma to Flora Jones, and willed to the Archives by her daughter, Maude Jones. 3) Nylen-Altman Collection, consisting of the letters and documents purchased from Mr. Ray Nylen and Mr. Jack Altman in October, 1957." A complete list of material in the collection is available at AH.

Emma Taylor Papers. AH.

Forbes, Cochran. Journal. HMCS.

Gilman, Gorham. Journal. HHS.

Gregg Collection. AH. Diaries, Letter Books, and Letters Received. Housed at AH, but under control of UH, which has typescript copies. One volume of the Gregg Diary is in HHS, and one volume (late 1854) is missing. AH has complete list of material in the collection.

Hasslocher Papers. AH.

Heuck Papers. AH.

Hooper Papers. UH.

Hunnewell MSS. Originals in Houghton Library, Harvard. Copies of Honolulu letters in Kuykendall Collection, UH.
Josiah Marshall MSS. Originals in Houghton Library, Harvard. Copies of Honolulu letters in Kuykendall Collection, UH.

Kalanianaole Papers. AH. AH has list of contents.

Kuykendall Collection. UH. Contains copies of many letters and documents from repositories all over the world.

Loomis, Elisha. Journal. HMCS has most volumes, UH the remainder.

Loomis, Maria. Journal. HMCS. Two versions, collated in typescript with Elisha Loomis Journal.

Lyman, Chester Smith. Journal. HMCS.

Lyons, Curtis

Marin Collection. AH. AH has list of contents.

Marin, Don Francisco de Paula. Journal. AH. Original is lost. AH has excerpts in English translation.

Neilson Papers. Originals in possession of Nicholas Rutgers, Tahiti. Typescript copies in AH.

Parke Papers. AH.

Paty, William. Journal. AH.

Reynolds, Stephen. Journal. Original in Peabody Museum, Salem, Mass. Microfilm copy in HMCS.

Swan Papers. AH.

Tinker, Reuben. Journal. HMCS.

Turrill Collection. HHS. Most letters printed in HHS, *Annual Report*, 66 (Honolulu, 1958), pp. 27–92.

Whitney Papers. AH.

William Richards Papers. AH.

Wood Papers. AH.

Wyllie Papers. AH. Private letters of R.C. Wyllie.

Newspapers and Periodicals

A useful guide to newspapers is Charles H. Hunter's "A Checklist of Hawaiian Newspapers," mimeographed. An annotated copy is in UH. Collation and microfilming of basic nineteenth-century newspapers are being done at AH.

All the following papers were useful to a greater or lesser degree. All were published at Honolulu, except where indicated.

Annales de la Propagation de la Foi, 1836–1840. Lyon.

Ke Au Okoa, 1865–1873.

Bennett's Own, 1869–1870.

Daily Hawaiian Herald, 1866.

The Friend, (title varies) 1844–1876.

Hae Hawaii, 1856–1861.

Hawaiian Annual, (Title varies) 1875–1965. Invaluable for antiquarian information of all sorts, painstakingly gathered by the original editor, Thomas G. Thrum.

Hawaiian Gazette, 1865–1876.

Hawaiian Spectator, 1838–1839.

Hawaiian Times, 1870.

Honolulu Star-Bulletin, scattered use.

Honolulu Times, 1849–1851.

Islander, 1875.

Ke Kumu Hawaii, 1834–1839.
Maile Quarterly, 1868.

Missionary Herald, 1820–1840. Boston.

Ka Na'i Aupuni, 1906.

New Era and Weekly Argus, 1853–1855.

Ka Nu Hou, 1854.

Ka Nuhou Hawaii, 1873–1874.

Nuhou: The Hawaiian News, 1873.

Ka Nupepa Kuokoa, 1861–1876.

Pacific Commercial Advertiser, 1856–1876.

Polynesian, 1840–1841, 1844–1864.

Sandwich Island Gazette, 1836–1839.

Sandwich Island Mirror, 1839–1840.

Sandwich Island News, 1846–1849.

Saturday Press, 1882.

Weekly Argus, 1852–1853.

Unpublished Contemporary Accounts

"Answers By The Sandwich Island Missionaries To The Questions In The Circular Of March 15, 1833." HMCS.

Bishop, Charles. "Commercial Journal…Of Ship Rubys Voyage To NWt. Coast Of America And China, 1794–5–6." Original in Provincial Library and Archives, Victoria, B.C. Typescript in UH.

Boit, John. "The Journal Of A Voyage Round The Globe." Original in Massachusetts Historical Society Library. Photostat of Hawaiian entries in HMCS.

Colnett, James. "The Journal Of Captain James Colnett Aboard The Prince Of Wales And Princess Royal From 16. Oct. 1786 To 7. Nov. 1788." Original in British Public Record Office. Typescript in UH.

Davies, T.H . "Reminiscences." Typescript in HMCS.

Gilman, Gorham. "Honolulu–As It Is–1848." HHS.

_____."Journal Of A Tour On Oahu, 1848." HHS.

Ingraham, Joseph. "Hope's Track Among The Sandwich Isles." Original in Library of Congress. Photostat copy in HHS.

Jones, Thomas ap Catesby. "Report Of The Peacock's Cruise To The Sandwich, Society And Other Islands In The Pacific Ocean Performed In The Years 1826 And 1827." Original in National Archives. Photostat copy in Kuykendall Collection, UH.

Morineau, A. "Notice Sur Les Îles Sandwich, 1826–1829." Archives Nationales de France. Arch, des. Aff. Estr., S. 2., Vol. I, f. 61. Copy in Kuykendall Collection, UH.

Nott, Estrella. "Honolulu 1848." Typescript in HHS.

"Solid Men Of Boston In The Northwest." Original in Bancroft Library, University of California. Microfilm copy in UH.

United States. Navy Department. Office of Judge Advocate General. Court Martial Records, XXIII, 1830, No. 531. "Proceedings Of A Court Of Inquiry &c., In The Case Of Lieut. John Percival." Original in National Archives. Microfilm copy in UH.

Yates, Emma. "Reminiscences Of Honolulu." HHS.

Published Contemporary Accounts

Adams, Alexander. "Extracts From An Ancient Log." *Hawaiian Annual for 1906*, pp. 66–74.

Arago, Jacques Etienne Victor. *Narrative Of A Voyage Round The World In The "Uranie" And "Physicienne"...1817–1820.* 2 vols. London, 1823.

Atherton, Faxon Dean. *California Diary 1836–1839.* Ed. Doyce B. Nunis, Jr. San Francisco, 1964.

Barnard, Charles. *A Narrative Of The Sufferings And Adventures Of Capt. Charles Barnard...1812–1816.* New York, 1829.

[Bates, G.W.]. *Sandwich Island Notes.* New York, 1854.

Beechey, Frederick William. *Narrative Of A Voyage To The Pacific...1825–1828.* 2 vols. London, 1831.

Belcher, Edward. *Narrative Of A Voyage Round The World...1836–1842.* 2 vols. London, 1843.

Bennett, Frederick Debell. *Narrative Of A Whaling Voyage Round The Globe 1833–1836.* 2 vols. London, 1840.

[Bille, Steen]. *Steen Bille's Bericht Uber Die Reise Der Corvette Galathea Um Die Welt...1845–1847.* Tr. W von Rosen. 2 vols. Leipzig, 1852. Typescript translation of Hawaiian portion in HMCS.

Bingham, Hiram. *A Residence Of Twenty-One Years In The Sandwich Islands...* Hartford, 1847.

[Bishop], Isabella Bird. *Six Months Among The Pain Groves, Coral Reefs And Volcanoes Of The Sandwich Islands.* 5 ed. London, 1882.

[Bloxam, Andrew]. *Diary Of Andrew Bloxam.* Bernice P. Bishop Museum. *Special Publication*, 10. Honolulu, 1925.

Broughton, William. *A Voyage Of Discovery To The North Pacific Ocean...1795–1798.* London, 1804.

Campbell, Archibald. *A Voyage Around The World...1806–1812...* Edinburgh, 1816.

Chamisso, Adelbert von. *Werke.* Ed. Herman Tardel. 3 vols. Leipzig, n.d.

Choris, Louis. *Voyage Pittoresque Autour Du Monde...* Paris, 1822.

Cleveland, Richard J. *A Narrative Of Voyages And Commercial Enterprises.* 2 vols. Cambridge, 1842.

Colton, Walter. *Deck And Port.* New York, 1847.

Cook, James and James King. *A Voyage To The Pacific Ocean...1776–1780...* 3 vols. London, 1784.

Corney, Peter. *Voyages In The Northern Pacific...1813–1818...* Honolulu, 1896.

Cox, Ross. *Adventures On The Columbia River...* 2 vols. London, 1831.

Delano, Amasa. *A Narrative Of Voyages And Travels...* Boston, 1817.

Dibble, Sheldon. *History of the Sandwich Islands.* Lahainaluna, 1843.

Diell, John. "Sketch Of Honolulu, Oahu." *Hawaiian Spectator*, I, (April, 1838), pp. 83–94.

Dixon, George. *A Voyage Around The World...1785–1788...* London, 1789.

Duhaut-Cilly, A. *Voyage Autour Du Monde...1826–1829...* 2 vols. Paris, 1834–1835.

Dwight, Edwin Welles. *Memoirs Of Henry Obookiah...* New Haven, 1819.

Ellis, William. *Narrative Of A Tour Of Hawaii...* Honolulu, 1963.

_____. *Polynesian Researches...* 2 ed. 4 vols. London, 1831–1832.

Fragments: Family Record, House Of Judd. 6 vols. Honolulu, 1903–1935.

Franchere, Gabriel. *Narrative Of A Voyage To The Northwest Coast Of America...1811–1814...* New York, 1854.

de Freycinet, Louis. *Voyage Autour Du Monde...Sur...L'Uranie Et La Physiclenne...1817–1819...* 7 vols. Paris, 1823–1844.

Golovnin, Vasili. *Puteshestvie Vokrug Sveta... Na Voennom Schlupe Kamchatke... 1817–1819...* St. Petersburg, 1822. Typescript translation of Hawaiian portion in UH.

"Golovnin's Visit To Hawaii In 1818." *Friend*, LII (1896), pp. 50–53.

Gould, Rupert. "Bligh's Notes On Cook's Last Voyage." *Mariner's Mirror*, XIV, 4 (October, 1928), pp. 371–385.

[Graham, Maria]. *Voyage Of H.M.S. "Blonde To The Sandwich Islands...1824–1825...* London, 1826.

"Greatheed Manuscript." *Friend*, XIX (1862), pp. 42–43. Original is lost.

Hines, Gustavus. *A Voyage Round The World...* Buffalo, 1850.

Houston, Victor. "Chamisso In Hawaii." Hawaiian Historical Society. *Annual Report*, 48 (Honolulu, 1940), pp. 55–82.

Hunnewell, James. *Journal Of The Missionary Packet, Boston To Honolulu, 1826.* Charlestown, 1880.

_____. "Voyage In The Brig *Bordeaux Packet*, Boston To Honolulu, 1817..." Hawaiian Historical Society. *Papers*, 8. Honolulu, 1895.

Iselin, Isaac. *Journal Of A Trading Voyage Around The World, 1805–1808.* New York, n.d.

Jarves, James Jackson. *History Of The Sandwich Islands.* 3 ed. Honolulu, 1847.

"Ka Moolelo Hawaii." *Hawaiian Spectator*, II (April, 1839), pp. 58–77; 211–231; 334–340; 438–447.

Kotzebue, Otto von. *A New Voyage Round The World,...1823–1826*. 2 vols. London, 1830.

_____. *A Voyage Of Discovery...In The Years 1815–1818...in The Ship Rurick...* 3 vols. London, 1821.

Laplace, C.P.T. *Campagne De Circumnavigation De La Frégate L'Artemise...1837–1840.* 6 vols. Paris, 1841–1854.

Larkin Papers... Ed. George Peter Hammond. 10 vols. Berkeley, 19511964.

Lisiansky, Urey. *A Voyage Round The World...1803–1806...In The...Neva.* London, 1814.

Macrae, James. *With Lord Byron At The Sandwich Islands In 1825...* Ed. W.F. Wilson. Honolulu, 1922.

Martin, John. *An Account Of The Natives Of The Tonga Islands, In The South Pacific Ocean...* 2 vols. London, 1817.

Mathison, Gilbert Farquhar. *Narrative Of A Visit To...The Sandwich Islands,...1821–1822...* London, 1825.

Meares, John. *Voyages Made In The Years 1788 And 1789...* London, 1790.

Menzies, Archibald. *Hawaii Nei 128 Years Ago.* Honolulu, 1920.

Olmsted, Francis Allyn. *Incidents Of A Whaling Voyage...* New York, 1841.

Parke, William Cooper. *Personal Reminiscences Of William Cooper Parke, Marshal Of The Hawaiian Islands, From 1850 To 1884.* Cambridge, 1891.

Paulding, Hiram. *Journal Of A Cruise In The United States Schooner Dolphin...* New York, 1831.

du Petit-Thouars, Abel. *Voyage Autour Du Monde Sur La Vénus...1836–1839.* 4 vols. Paris, 18401843.

Portlock, Nathaniel. *A Voyage Around The World...1785–1788...* London, 1789.

Reynolds, J. N. *Voyage Of The Potomac...1831–1834...* New York, 1835.

Reynolds, Stephen. "Reminiscences Of Hawaiian Agriculture." Royal Hawaiian Agricultural Society. *Transactions*, I (1850), pp. 49–53.

_____. *The Voyage Of The New Hazard To The Northwest Coast Hawaii And China, 1810–1813...* Ed. F.W. Howay. Salem, 1938.

Ross, Alexander. *Adventures Of The First Settlers On The Oregon Or Columbia River...* London, 1849.

Ruschenberger, W.S.W. *Narrative Of A Voyage Round The World...18351837.* Philadelphia, 1838.

"The Second Interregnum: A Complete Resume Of Events From The Death To The Burial Of His Late Majesty Lunalilo." Honolulu, 1874.

Shaler, William. "Journal Of A Voyage Between China And the North-Western Coast Of America, Made In 1804." *American Register*, III (1808), pp. 137–185.

Simpson, Alexander. *The Sandwich Islands...* London, 1843.

Simpson, Sir George. *Narrative Of A Journey Round The World 1841–1842.* 2 vols. London, 1847.

_____. *An Overland Journey Round The World...1841–1842.* 2 vols. Philadelphia, 1847.

Staley, T.N. *Five Years Church Work In The Kingdom Of Hawaii.* London, 1868.

Stewart, C.S. *Private Journal Of A Residence At The Sandwich Islands...* 1822–1825. New York, 1828.

_____. *Visit To The South Seas...1829–1830...* 2 vols. New York, 1831.

Stoddard, Charles Warren. *The Island Of Tranquil Delights.* Boston, 1905.

Suppliment [sic] To The Sandwich Island Mirror. Honolulu, 1840.

Townsend, Ebenezer. *Extract From The Diary Of Ebenezer Townsend, Jr., Supercargo Of The Sealing Ship "Neptune" On Her Voyage To The South Pacific And Canton...* Hawaiian Historical Society. *Reprints*, 4. Honolulu, 1921.

Turnbull, John. *A Voyage Round The World...1800–1804...* 3 vols. London, 1805.

Twain, Mark [Samuel Clemens]. *Letters From The Sandwich Islands.* San Francisco, 1938.

[Tyerman, Daniel and George Bennet]. *Journal Of Voyages And Travels...1821–1829...* Revised American ed. 3 vols. Boston, 1832.

Vancouver, George. *A Voyage Of Discovery To The North Pacific Ocean...1790–1795...* 3 vols. London, 1798.

Warriner, Francis. *Cruise Of The...Potomac...1831–1834...* New York, 1835.

Wilkes, Charles. *Narrative Of The United States Exploring Expedition...18351842.* 5 vols. Philadelphia, 1845.

Woodbridge, W.C. *He Hoikehonua.* Honolulu, 1836.

Unpublished Secondary Works

Adler, Jacob. "Claus Spreckels, Sugar King Of Hawaii: Interaction Of An Entrepreneur With An Island Community." PhD. Columbia, 1959.

Brown, Thelma. "A History Of The Theater In Honolulu During The Reign Of Kamehameha V, 1863–1872." MA. Hawai'i, 1942.

Coller, Richard Walter. "Waikiki: A Study Of Invasion And Succession As Applied To A Tourist Area." MA. Hawai'i, 1952.

Daws, Alan Gavan. "Polynesian Religious Revivals: A Study With Background." MA. Hawai'i, 1960.

Forbes, David. Unpublished collection of source materials on the second Iolani Palace compiled for the 1965 session of the state legislature of Hawai'i. A copy is in AH.

Frowe, Margaret. "The History Of The Theatre During The Reign Of King Kalakaua, 1874–1891." MA. Hawai'i, 1937.

Glick, Clarence. "The Chinese Migrant In Hawaii: A Study In Accommodation." PhD. Chicago, 1938.

Greer, Richard A. "The Founding Of The Queen's Hospital." MS in possession of author.

_____. "In The Shadow Of Death—Smallpox Brushes The Neighbor Islands, 1853." MS in possession of author.

Jackson, Frances. "Koloa Plantation Under Ladd And Company, 1835–1845." MA. Hawai'i, 1958.

Kittelson, David James. "A Population Table Of Hawaii." MS, UH.

Odgers, G.A. "Education In Hawaii, 18201893." PhD. Stanford, 1935.

Peterson, Charles. "An Architectural History Of Honolulu." (A book in progress)

Taylor, John Lewis . "Waikiki: A Study In The Development Of A Tourist Community." PhD. Clark, 1953.

Published Secondary Works

1. Books and Pamphlets.
Alexander, Arthur C. *Koloa Plantation 1835–1935...* Honolulu, 1937.

Alexander, Mary Charlotte. *William Patterson Alexander In Kentucky, The Marquesas, Hawaii*. Honolulu, 1934.

Alexander, Mary Charlotte and Charlotte Peabody Dodge. *Punahou, 1844–1941*. Berkeley, 1941.

Amory, Cleveland. *The Last Resorts.* New York, 1952.

Anderson, Rufus. *History Of The Sandwich Islands Mission...* Boston, 1870.

Barth, Gunther Paul. *Bitter Strength: A History Of The Chinese In The United States 1850–1870.* Cambridge, 1964.

Bradley, Harold Whitman. *The American Frontier In Hawaii The Pioneers, 1789–1843.* Stanford, 1942.

Buck, Peter. *Arts And Crafts Of Hawaii.* Bernice P. Bishop Museum. *Special Publication,* 5. Honolulu, 1957.

Coman, Katharine. *The History Of Contract Labor In The Hawaiian Islands.* American Economic Association. *Publications,* Third Series, IV, 3 (August, 1903).

Cross, Whitney B. *The Burned-Over Distric:t The Social And Intellectual History Of Enthusiastic Religion In Western New York 1500–1850.* Ithaca, 1950.

Edmondson, Charles Howard. *The Ecology Of An Hawaiian Coral Reef.* Bernice P. Bishop Museum. *Bulletin,* 45. Honolulu, 1926.
Edwards, Jonathan. *...Works...* 8 vols. Worcester, Mass., 1808.

Elsbree, Oliver Wendell. *The Rise Of The Missionary Spirit In America., 1790–1815.* Williamsport, Pa., 1928.

Fornander, Abraham. *An Account Of The Polynesian Race...* 3 vols. London, 18781885.
_____. *Fornander Collection Of Antiquities...* 3 vols. Bernice P. Bishop Museum. *Memoirs,* IV–VI. Honolulu, 1917–1919.

Handy, E.S.C. *Cultural Revolution In Hawaii.* Honolulu, 1931.

_____. *The Hawaiian Planter.* Bernice P. Bishop Museum. *Bulletin,* 161. Honolulu, 1940.

Hobbs, Jean. *Hawaii A Pageant Of The Soil.* Stanford, 1935.

Huizinga, Johan. *Homo Ludens: A Study Of The Play-Element In Culture.* Boston, 1962.

Ii, John Papa. *Fragments Of Hawaiian History.* Honolulu, 1963.

Indices Of Awards Made By The Board Of Commissioners To Quiet Land Titles In The Hawaiian Islands. Honolulu, 1929.

Jenkins, J. T. *A History Of The Whale Fisheries.* London, 1921.

Judd, Bernice. *Voyages To Hawaii Before 1860...* Honolulu, 1929.

Judd, Gerrit P., IV. *Doctor Judd Hawaii's Friend.* Honolulu, 1960.

Judd, Laura Fish. *Honolulu...1828–1861.* Honolulu, 1928.

Kamakau, S.N. *Ka Po'e Kahiko.* Honolulu, 1964,

_____. *Ruling Chiefs Of Hawaii*. Honolulu, 1961.

Kent, Harold Winfield. *Charles Reed Bishop: Man Of Hawaii*. Palo Alto, 1965.

King, W.H.D. *Pictorial Maritime History Of Hawaii*. 5 vols. [n.p.] [n.d.].

Korn, Alfons. *The Victorian Visitors*. Honolulu, 1958.

Kuykendall, R.S. "Constitutions Of The Hawaiian Kingdom." Hawaiian Historical Society. *Papers*, 21. Honolulu, 1940.

_____. *The Hawaiian Kingdom*. 2 vols. Honolulu, 1938–1953.

Lydecker, Robert C., comp. *Roster Legislatures Of Hawaii 1841–1918*. Honolulu, 1918.

McAllister, J. Gilbert. *Archeology Of Oahu*. Bernice P. Bishop Museum. *Bulletin*, 104. Honolulu, 1933.

McLoughlin, William C. *Modern Revivalism: Charles Grandison Finney To Billy Graham*. New York, 1959.

Malo, David. *Hawaiian Antiquities*. Bernice P. Bishop Museum. *Special Publication*, 2, 2nd ed. Honolulu, 1951.

Meyer, Henry A., *et al*. *Hawai:i Its Stamps And Postal History*. New York, 1948.

Morgan, Theodore. *Hawaii: A Century Of Economic Change, 1778–1876*. Cambridge, 1948.

Mumford, Lewis. *The City In History*. New York, 1961.

Nelson, Larry A., *et al*. *Detailed Land Classification: Island Of Oahu*. University of Hawai'i Land Study Bureau. *Bulletin*, 3. Honolulu, 1963.

Pierce, Richard A. *Russia's Hawaiian Adventure 1815–1817*. Berkeley, 1965.

Restarick, Henry B. *Hawaii, 1778–1920, From The Viewpoint Of A Bishop…* Honolulu, 1924.

Richards, Mary Atherton. *The Chiefs' Children's School*. Honolulu, 1937.

Rock, Joseph F. *The Indigenous Trees Of The Hawaiian Islands*. Honolulu, 1913.

Smith, Bradford. *Yankees In Paradise: The New England Impact On Hawaii*. Philadelphia, 1956.

Starbuck, Alexander. *History Of The American Whale Fishery…To 1876*. Waltham, 1878.

Stearns, Harold T. *Geology Of The Hawaiian Islands*. Hawai'i Division of Hydrography. *Bulletin*, 8. Honolulu, 1946,

Stearns, Harold T. and K.N. Vaksvik. *Geology And Ground-Water Resources Of The*

Island Of Oahu, Hawaii. Hawai'i Division of Hydrography. *Bulletin*, 1. Honolulu, 1935.

Stearns, Norah D. *An Island Is Born.* Honolulu, 1935.

Sterling, Elspeth P. and Catherine C. Summers. *Sites Of Oahu.* 6 vols. in 1. Honolulu, 1963.

Stevens, Sylvester K. *American Expansion In Hawaii,* Harrisburg, 1945.

Stokes., J. F. G. "The Hawaiian King (Mo-i, Alii-aimoku, Alii-kapu)." Hawaiian Historical Society. *Papers*, 19. Honolulu, 1932.

Sullivan, Josephine. *A History Of C. Brewer And Company, Ltd.* Boston, 1926.

Thurston, Lorrin A. *Fundamental Law Of Hawaii.* Honolulu, 1904.

Tilton, Cecil G. *The History Of Banking In Hawaii.* Honolulu, 1927.

Tower, W.S. *History Of The American Whale Fishery.* Philadelphia, 1907.

Wentworth, Chester K. *Geology And Ground-Water Resources Of The Honolulu-Pearl Harbor Area, Oahu, Hawaii.* Honolulu, 1951.

Whipple, Henry B. *Lights And Shadows Of A Long Episcopate…* New York, 1899.

Wist, Benjamin 0. *A Century Of Public Education In Hawaii October 15, 1840 To October 15, 1940.* Honolulu, 1940.

Yzendoorn, Reginald. *History Of The Catholic Mission In Hawaii.* Honolulu, 1927.

Zimmerman, Elwood C. *Insects Of Hawaii.* Vol. I. Honolulu, 1948.

2. Articles.
Alexander, W.D. "Early Improvements In Honolulu Harbor." Hawaiian Historical Society, *Annual Report*, 15 (Honolulu, 1908), pp. 13–35.

_____. "The Oahu Charity School." Hawaiian Historical Society, *Annual Report*, 16 (Honolulu, 1908), pp. 20–38.

Blue, George Verne. "The Project For A French Settlement In The Hawaiian Islands, 1828–181i2." *Pacific Historical Review*, II (March, 1933), pp. 85–99.

Cartwright, Bruce. "Some Aliis Of The Migratory Period." Bernice P. Bishop Museum, *Occasional Papers*, X (Honolulu, 1933).

"Correspondence Relating To The Last Hours Of Kamehameha V." Hawaiian Historical Society, *Annual Report*, 6 (Honolulu, 1898), pp. 11–16.

Daws, Alan Gavan. "Evangelism In Hawaii: Titus Coan And The Great Revival Of 1837." Hawaiian Historical Society, *Annual Report*, 69 (Honolulu, 1960), pp. 20–34.

Elbert, Samuel H. "The Chief In Hawaiian Mythology." *Journal of American Folklore*, LXX (October–December, 1957), pp. 306–322.

Greer, Richard A. "Mutiny In The Royal Barracks." *Pacific Historical Review*, XXXI, 4 (November, 1962), pp. 349–358.

_____. "Oahu's Ordeal: The Smallpox Epidemic Of 1853." Parts 1, 2, *Hawaii Historical Review*, I, 12 (July, 1965), pp. 221–241; II, 1 (October, 1965), pp. 248–265.

"Honolulu's Share In The Pacific Whaling Industry Of By-Gone Days." *Hawaiian Annual for 1913*, pp. 47–68.

Howay, F. W. "Captain Henry Barber Of Barber's Point." Hawaiian Historical Society, *Annual Report*, 147 (Honolulu, 1938), pp. 39–49.
_____. "A List Of Trading Vessels In Maritime Fur Trade." Royal Society of Canada, *Transactions*, 3 ser., XXIV (1930), Sec. II, pp. 111–134; XXV (1931), Sec. II, pp. 117–149; XXVI (1932), Sec. II, pp. 43–86; XXVII (1933), Sec. II, pp. 119–147; XXVIII (1934), Sec. II, pp. 11–49.

_____. "The Ship *Pearl* In Hawaii In 1805 And 1806." Hawaiian Historical Society, *Annual Report*, 46 (Honolulu, 1938), pp. 27–38.

Hoyt, Helen P. "Theatre In Hawaii–1778–1840." Hawaiian Historical Society, *Annual Report*, 69 (Honolulu, 1961), pp. 7–18.

Kemble, John H. "Pioneer Hawaiian Steamers, 1852–1877." Hawaiian Historical Society, *Annual Report*, 53 (Honolulu, 1946), pp. 7–25.

Korn, Alfons and Mary Kawena Pukui. "News From Molokai: The Letters Of Peter Young Kaeo (Kekuaokalani) To Queen Emma, 1673–1876." *Pacific Historical Review*, XXXII, 1 (February, 1963), pp. 7–34.

Kuykendall, R.S. "Some Early Commercial Adventurers Of Hawaii." Hawaiian Historical Society, *Annual Report*, 37 (Honolulu, 1929), pp. 15–33.

Muir, Andrew F. "The Church In Hawaii, 1778–1862." *Historical Magazine of the Protestant Episcopal Church*, XVIII (1949), pp. 31–65.

_____. "Edmund Ibbotson (1831–1914): S.P.G. Missionary To Hawai'i, 1862–1866." *Historical Magazine of the Protestant Episcopal Church*, XIX (1950), pp. 214–241.

_____. "George Mason, Priest And Schoolmaster." *British Columbia Historical Quarterly*, XV (1951), pp. 47–70.

Peterson, Charles E. "The Iolani Palaces And The Barracks." Journal of the Society of Architectural Historians, XXII, 2 (May, 1963), pp. 91–103.

_____. "Pioneer Architects And Builders Of Honolulu." Hawaiian Historical Society, *Annual Report*, 72 (Honolulu, 19614), pp. 7–28.

Schmitt, Robert C. and Rose C. Strombel. "Marriage And Divorce In Hawaii Before 1870." *Hawaii Historical Review*, II, 2 (January, 1966), pp. 267–270.

_____. "Population Characteristics Of Hawaii, 1778–1850." *Hawaii Historical Review*, I, 11 (April, 1965), pp. 199–210.

_____. "Population Estimates And Censuses Of Hawaii, 1776–1850." *Hawaii Historical Review*, I, 8 (July, 1964), pp. 143154.

Stokes, J.F.G. "Dune Sepulture, Battle Mortality, And Kamehameha's Alleged Defeat On Kauai." Hawaiian Historical Society, *Annual Report*, 45 (Honolulu, 1937), pp. 30–46.

_____."Honolulu And Some New Speculative Phases Of Hawaiian History." Hawaiian Historical Society, *Annual Report*, 42 (Honolulu, 1934), pp. 40–102.

_____. "New Bases For Hawaiian Chronology." Hawaiian Historical Society, *Annual Report*, 41 (Honolulu, 1932), pp. 23–65.

Tate, Merze. "The Myth Of Hawaii's Swing Toward Australasia And Canada." *Pacific Historical Review*, XXXIII, 3 (August, 1964), pp. 273–294.

Webb, N.C. "The Abolition Of The Taboo System In Hawaii." *Journal of the Polynesian Society*, 74, 1 (March, 1965), pp. 21–39.

Endnotes

CHAPTER 1

[1] Southeastern O'ahu, the area enclosed by the Ko'olau range to the north and the Wai'anae range to the west, is about two hundred square miles in extent. Beyond Diamond Head, which lies to the east of Honolulu, the streams run less than four miles to the sea. Those which used to end in the swamps of Waikīkī (before twentieth-century land-reclamation projects) are not much longer. Nu'uanu stream behind Honolulu is about five miles long. To the west, several streams which have their sources in the Wai'anae uplands flow fifteen or twenty miles to the lochs of Pu'uloa (Pearl Harbor).

For geological information on the entire Hawaiian chain, see the introductory chapter of Elwood C. Zimmerman, *Insects of Hawaii* (Honolulu, 1948), I, 1–52; Harold T. Stearns, *Geology of the Hawaiian Islands*, Hawai'i Division of Hydrography, *Bulletin*, 8 (Honolulu, 1946). For detailed information on O'ahu, see Stearns and K. N. Vaksvik, *Geology and Ground-Water Resources of the Island of Oahu, Hawaii*, Hawai'i Division of Hydrography, *Bulletin*, 1 (Honolulu, 1935). For southeastern O'ahu, which includes the Honolulu area, see Chester K. Wentworth, *Geology and Ground-Water Resources of the Honolulu-Pearl Harbor Area, Oahu, Hawaii* (Honolulu, 1951). Larry A. Nelson *et. al. Detailed Land Classification: Island of Oahu* University of Hawai'i Land Study Bureau, *Bulletin*, 3 (Honolulu, 1963), has excellent aerial maps.

[2] Norah D. Stearns, *An Island Is Born* (Honolulu, 1935), p. 42; Charles Howard Edmondson, *The Ecology of an Hawaiian Coral Reef*, Bernice P. Bishop Museum, *Bulletin*, 45 (Honolulu, 1928), *passim*.

[3] For a discussion of Honolulu in the traditional period see J.F.G. Stokes, "Honolulu and Some New Speculative Phases of Hawaiian History," Hawaiian Historical Society, *Annual Report*, 42 (Honolulu, 1934), pp. 40–51. Stokes speculates that Honolulu was inhabited very early, but remarks that no traditional chronicler refers to it as an island capital, even in the limited sense that peripatetic chiefs could be said to have a capital. Within the traditional land district or ahupua'a of Honolulu, Stokes discovered, certain origin myths and legends were localized. Stokes took this to mean that early habitation was likely. Since he wrote, one or two of the examples he used have been found to be not authentic traditions but intrusions traceable to the native historian S.H. Kamakau, who wrote in the middle of the nineteenth century. Though there is evidence that the ahupua'a was well cultivated, it lacks traces of fishponds and heiau (temple) sites in great numbers, and Stokes concluded from this that it was not consistently inhabited by chiefs. He does not mention that lack of actual sites and information might reflect simply the diffi-

culty of recovering the past in what became the most heavily urbanized section of the islands. What is currently recoverable has been brought together in J. Gilbert McAllister, *Archeology of Oahu*, Bernice P. Bishop Museum, *Bulletin*, 104 (Honolulu, 1933); and Elspeth P. Sterling and Catherine C. Summers, *Sites of Oahu*, 6 vols. in 11 (Honolulu, 1963). The latter work omits Waikīkī and the area immediately around Honolulu harbor, which will be covered in a projected volume. Stokes goes on (pp. 51–61) to discuss the meaning of "Honolulu. He arrives at "sheltered bay," not far from the name of 'Fair Haven" given the harbor by its foreign discoverer.

[4] Abraham Fornander, *An Account of the Polynesian Race*, 3 vols. (London, 1878–1885), II, p. 89, says Waikīkī had been the seat of the O'ahu kings since Mā'ilikūkahi (15th C.) made his permanent residence there. It is not correct to talk of it as a capital—to repeat, the chiefs were great travelers. By the eighteenth century O'ahu's greatest luakini heiau (war temples) were at Waikīkī—'Apuakēhau, near the present site of the Royal Hawaiian Hotel, and Papa'ena'ena, below Diamond Head. Traditionally the oldest heiau on O'ahu was Waolani, in Nu'uanu behind Honolulu, dating from the time of Wākea, the legendary first inhabitant. 'Āpuakēhau was certainly in use by mid-seventeenth century, and may have been abandoned in favor of Papa'ena'ena in mid-eighteenth century. Fornander, *Polynesian Race* II, p. 276; *Fornander Collection of Antiquities*, Bernice P. Bishop Museum , Memoirs, IV–VI (Honolulu,1917–1919), VI, p. 285. The main references to these heiau are collected in McAllister, *Oahu*, pp. 71–77. McAllister mistakenly attributes some remarks on Papa'ena'ena to S.M. Kamakau. He followed earlier writers, who wrongly thought an account in a Hawaiian-language newspaper in mid-nineteenth century was by Kamakau. Actually it was by another native historian, John 'I'i. See 'I'i, *Fragments of Hawaiian History* (Honolulu, 1963), pp. 33–44, 51.

[5] Archibald Menzies, *Hawaii Nei 128 Years Ago* (Honolulu, 1920), pp. 23–24. Menzies was with George Vancouver.

[6] This count is based on genealogical tables in Fornander, *Polynesian Race*, I, p. 204; and *Fornander Antiquities*, VI, pp. 313–314. O'ahu's earliest radio-carbon date so far is 1004 plus or minus 180 years. This matches Fornander's date for Newalani. It is now known that Marquesan chiefs settled the Hawaiian islands, AD 750–AD 950. Tahitian chiefs, bringing a culture that became "Hawaiian," came later, perhaps early in the 12th century AD. Newalani was a Tahitian chief, probably one of the earliest. The question of migration and settlement is now under re-study, with finds being made in the South Pacific by Bishop Museum archeologists and others. In the meantime, Fornander's count is useful, and will be relied on here. Cf. Bruce Cartwright, "Some Aliis of the Migratory Period," Bernice P. Bishop Museum, *Occasional Papers*, X (Honolulu, 1933), p. 7.

[7] Available evidence suggests that kings of this sort appeared in the sixteenth and seventeenth centuries. J.F.G. Stokes, "The Hawaiian King (Mo-i, Alii-aimoku, Alii-kapu)," Hawaiian Historical Society, *Papers*, 19 (Honolulu, 1932), p. 25, gives these approximate dates: 1550 for royal incest, land distribution after conquest, and sacrifice of (deposed) kings; 1600 for land redistribution after king's death; 1675 *kapu-moe*, or prostration tabu. None of these dates can be linked immediately to O'ahu, except the last. Inferentially, development on all islands proceeded at much the same rate.

[8] For some aspects of the Hawaiians' methodical exploitation of their resources, see Peter Buck, *Arts and Crafts of Hawaii*, Bernice P. Bishop Museum, *Special Publication*,

Appendix: Chapter 1 Endnotes 355

45 (Honolulu, 1957); and E.S. Craighill Handy, *The Hawaiian Planter*, Bernice P. Bishop Museum, *Bulletin*, 161 (Honolulu, 1940), especially pp. 73–100, 155–156, 171, which deal with O'ahu. Joseph F. Rock, *The Indigenous Trees of the Hawaiian Islands* (Honolulu, 1913), lists botanical regions.

⁹ A literary abstraction of the qualities of the ideal chief-hero is in Samuel H. Elbert, "The Chief in Hawaiian Mythology," *Journal of American-Folklore*, LXX (October-December, 1957), pp. 306–322.

¹⁰ James Cook and James King, *A Voyage to the Pacific Ocean... 1776–1780...*, 3 vols. (London, 1784), II, pp. 190–191.

¹¹ J.F.G. Stokes, "New Bases for Hawaiian Chronology," Hawaiian Historical Society, *Annual Report*, 41 (Honolulu, 1932), p. 26, makes it clear that Peleiōhōlani was still alive in 1779.

¹² Fornander, *Polynesian Race*, II, p. 290.

¹³ S.M. Kamakau, *Ruling Chiefs of Hawaii* (Honolulu, 1961), pp. 128–141, gives Kahahana's story. Cf. Fornander, *Polynesian Race*, II, pp. 217–226, and *Fornander Antiquities*, VI, pp. 282–306.

¹⁴ McAllister, *Oahu*, pp. 95–96, brings together the literature on Kā'uwālua and discusses some variant stories.

¹⁵ Nathaniel Portlock, *A Voyage Around the World...1785–1788...* (London, 1789), pp. 69–75, 153–167; George Dixon, *A Voyage Around the World...1785–1788...* (London, 1789), pp. 52–53, 252–253.

¹⁶ Portlock, *Voyage*, pp. 161–163.

¹⁷ James Colnett, "The Journal of Captain James Colnett Aboard the Prince of Wales and Princess Royal from 16. Oct. 1786 to 7. Nov. 1788," MS in British Public Record Office, Admiralty 55, Series II, 146; typescript in UH.

¹⁸ John Meares, *Voyages Made in the Years 1788 and 1789...* (London, 1790), pp. 346–349.

¹⁹ For this stage of Kamehameha's career, see Ralph S. Kuykendall, *The Hawaiian Kingdom*, 2 vols. (Honolulu, 1938–1953), I, 35. Kuykendall tells the story of the conquests primarily from Kamehameha's side, and gives excellent general context for the battles involving O'ahu.

²⁰ Fornander, *Polynesian Race*, II, 239. Cf. Kamakau, *Ruling Chiefs*, p. 150. Maika stones, rounded and polished, were used in a favorite bowling game of the Hawaiian ali'i.

²¹ Kamakau, *Ruling Chiefs*, pp. 159, 167.

²² The battle, called Kepuwahaulaula (red-mouthed gun) was fought in April or May, 1791. Kuykendall, *Hawaiian Kingdom*, I, p. 37.

²³ It is unlikely that the dated circumstances of the discovery will ever be known exactly, unless new sources are uncovered. Brown's own logbooks do not seem to have survived, and the movements of his ships cannot be followed precisely. The

approximation above has been made possible only by the ingenious reconstruction in Stokes, "Honolulu," pp. 61 *ff.*

[24] Joseph Ingraham, "Hope's Track among The Sandwich Isles," MS, Library of Congress, copy in HHS. See especially entries for May 22–October 11–12, 1791.

[25] George Vancouver, *A Voyage of Discovery to the North Pacific Ocean...1790–1795...,* 3 vols. (London, 1798), I, p. 167.

[26] If Vancouver's informant was William Brown, as Stokes deduces, this would place Brown's knowledge of the harbor at mid-1792. Vancouver and Brown were at Nootka Sound together in the latter part of 1792. See Stokes, "Honolulu," pp. 71–72.

[27] Vancouver, *Voyage,* II, pp. 203–217. Brown was less than accurate about Honolulu's capacity. At the height of the whaling era sixty years later more than a hundred ships were able to crowd inside.

[28] Vancouver, *Voyage,* I, pp. 161–162; Menzies, *Hawaii Nei,* p. 23. The immediate result of Vancouver's negotiations was not the interisland peace he hoped for. On the contrary, Kamehameha asked him for arms. On Oʻahu, Kahekili's successor, his son Kalanikūpule, did not scruple to kill Brown and take his ships in 1795.

For their part, what did Brown and Vancouver hope to gain from the "cessions?" Stokes, whose "Honolulu." pp. 61–85, combines the utmost rigor about places and dates with the wildest extrapolation about motives, makes Brown the servant of London merchants seeking to dominate the northwest fur trade. In Stokes' reading, Vancouver was party to these plans, and he and Brown worked to bring all the Hawaiian islands under British protection. There is no doubt that the early years of the fur trade produced many such schemes; but Stokes predicates this venture merely upon what he calls "significant omissions" in the published journals of Vancouver. The supposition is not altogether wild—just unproved. And there are discrepancies even in the case Stokes presents. For one thing, if Brown and Vancouver made cession plans together in 1792 *after* Brown's harbor find, surely Brown would not have described the harbor, a major economic asset, so vaguely that Vancouver could not find it in March, 1793. Again, Stokes hypothesizes that Brown had instructed Kamohomoho to keep Honolulu harbor secret from other foreigners. Surely he would have exempted his cession-partner, Vancouver, from this injunction. Kohomoho would then have had no need to "mislead" Vancouver about Honolulu, as Stokes claims he did.

[29] Kamakau, *Ruling Chiefs,* p. 168.

[30] Fornander, *Polynesian Race,* II, p. 263.

[31] Fornander, *Polynesian Race* II, pp. 62–266; Kamakau, *Ruling Chiefs,* pp. 168–169.

[32] John Boit, "The Journal of a Voyage Round the Globe," October 16, 1795, MS in Massachusetts Historical Society Library, photostat of Hawaiian entries in HMCS. Cf. Amasa Delano, *A Narrative of Voyages and Travels...* (Boston, 1817), p. 400. Did Kendrick take part in the battle? Boit says he did, and that he ordered the salute. This would refute Stokes, who argues British influence alone in the politics of Oʻahu. Whatever the case, Kendrick's death was fairly clearly accidental. Sheldon Dibble, *History of the Sandwich Islands,* (Lahainaluna, 1843), pp. 67–71, says Kendrick was killed by "a wad" from the cannon.

[33] Fornander, *Polynesian Race* II, p. 266.

[34] This letter, dated January 14, 1795, is printed in *Diary of Andrew Bloxam*, Bernice P. Bishop Museum, *Special Publication*, 10 (Honolulu, 1925), pp. 93–94. Bloxam copied the letter from John Young in 1825. It does not go into much detail; we could wish for a good deal more from it and less from some other sources. Boit's Journal for October 16, 1795, gives a more elaborate version. Boit's informant was John Young. Charles Bishop, "Commercial Journal…of Ship Rubys Voyage to NWt. Coast of America and China, 1794–5–6," MS in Provincial Library and Archives, Victoria, B. C, typescript in UH, has an account dated September, 1795. The Greatheed Manuscript, written by an English clergyman sometime before 1800, has yet another version. The MS itself is lost, but parts were printed in *The Friend*, XIX (1862), pp. 42–43. Dibble, *Sandwich Islands*, pp. 67–71, drew on native sources, as did Kamakau, *Ruling Chiefs*, pp. 170–171, and Fornander, *Polynesian Race* II, pp. 266–268. Fornander also used Dibble. Kuykendall, *Hawaiian Kingdom*, I, p. 45, says he follows the Bloxam copy of Lamport and Bonallack's letter, and the Greatheed Manuscript. I cannot see why he favors Greatheed over Boit, who was in the islands less than a year after the event, or over Dibble, who used native sources unavailable to Greatheed, who wrote at a distance.

[35] Dibble and Kamakau say Lamport and Bonallack left some of Kalanikūpule's arms on Hawai'i.

[36] Documentation for this crucial battle is disappointing. Boit's Journal, October 16, 1795, describes it; and there is an account of doubtful usefulness in Bishop's Journal, February 28, 1796. The standard sources, Kamakau, *Ruling Chiefs*, p. 172, and Fornander, *Polynesian Race*, II, p. 348, have short accounts, as do Dibble, *Sandwich Islands* p. 71; James Jackson Jarves, *History of the Sandwich Islands*, 3rd ed (Honolulu, 1847), pp. 91–92; and Hiram Bingham, *A Residence of Twenty-One Years in the Sandwich Islands…* (Hartford, 1847), p. 47. Bingham has the story of Ka'iana's footprints. The Honolulu *Star-Bulletin*, June 6, 1953, reconstructs the battle, and has a good map. There are incidental mentions in published voyages which add nothing of interest. How many fought and died at Nu'uanu? William Broughton, at Honolulu early in 1796, recorded the figure of 300 Oahuans killed. Broughton, *A Voyage of Discovery to the North Pacific Ocean…1795–1798* (London, 1804), p. 41. "By 1854, the figure for deaths at was 3,000; by 1914, 10,000. See J. F. G. Stokes, Dune Sepulture, Battle Mortality, and Kamehameha's Alleged Defeat on Kauai," Hawaiian Historical Society, *Annual Report*, 45 (Honolulu, 1937), p. 38.

In connection with the tendency of battles to grow more fabulous with the passage of the years, there is a most interesting story about Nu'uanu in the native newspaper, *Ka Na'i Aupuni*, August 27, 1906. I thank Dorothy Barrere for bringing it to my attention. In this story, Kalanikūpule had guns behind a stone wall at Puiwa; the wall was blown to bits by Kamehameha's cannon. At the top of the Pali, Ka'iana had two embrasures dug for cannon; these badly damaged Kamehameha's army, but in the end the cannon were captured by men coming along the ridges from either side. The niches can still be seen; observers may make up their own minds about the possibility of getting cannon, however light, up the dreadfully steep slopes or along the razor-back ridges.

CHAPTER 2

[1] Kamakau, *Ruling Chiefs*, p. 182.

[2] Broughton, *Voyage*, pp. 41–45, 71, 73–74.

[3] Kamakau, *Ruling Chiefs*, p. 173.

[4] Kamakau, *Ruling Chiefs*, pp. 173–174.

[5] Kamakau, *Ruling Chiefs*, pp. 175–156; Kuykendall, *Hawaiian Kingdom*, I, pp. 51–54.

[6] Urey Lisiansky, *A Voyage Round the World...1803–1806* (London, 1814), p. 133, lists twenty-one schooners, some with cannon, some European-commanded, in addition to the war canoes. Cf. Kamakau, *Ruling Chiefs*, pp. 187–188.

[7] Kamakau, *Ruling Chiefs*, p. 188; Richard J. Cleveland, *A Narrative of Voyages and Commercial Enterprises*, 2 vols. (Cambridge, 1842), I, p. 232.

[8] Cleveland, *Voyages*, I, p. 230, has Kamehameha on Maui in June, 1803; Lisiansky, *Voyage* p. 133, gives the impression that by June, 1804, he had been on O'ahu for some months.

[9] Kamakau, *Ruling Chiefs*, pp. 188–189. As Kamakau has it, Hawaiian prophets were almost unerringly accurate, possibly because every major decision was attended with auguries, and Kamakau, writing in mid-nineteenth-century, could be selective in the re-telling.
    The Hawaiians called the disease mai 'ōku'u (with a meaning of squatting or crouching). It was probably cholera or typhoid, perhaps introduced by an American ship. In October, 1806, the *Port au Prince* was refused entry to Honolulu harbor with a sick man aboard because earlier en American ship had brought disease. John Martin, *An Account of the Natives of the Tonga Islands in the South Pacific Ocean*, 2 vols. (London, 1817), I, p. 40

[10] 'I'i, *Fragments*, pp. 33–38; [Daniel Tyerman and George Bennet], *Journal of Voyages and Travels...1821–1829...*, 3 vols., revised American ed. (Boston 1832), II, p. 49.

[11] Kamakau, *Ruling Chiefs*, p. 187.

[12] William Shaler, "Journal of a Voyage Between China and the North Western Coast of America, Made in 1804," *American Register*, III (1808), pp. 137–175; Isaac Iselin, *Journal of a Trading Voyage Around the World 1805–1808* (New York, n.d.), p. 78; Archibald Campbell, *A Voyage Around the World...1806–1812...* (Edinburgh, 1816), pp. 155–156; Delano, *Narrative of Voyages*, pp. 398–399.

[13] Kamakau, *Ruling Chiefs*, pp. 156–157.

[14] The date of Kaumuali'i's visit is fixed at late March or early April, 1810. See Kuykendall, *Hawaiian Kingdom*, I, p. 51, for the evidence. It was Nathan Winship, not his brother Jonathan as Kamakau thought, who brought Kaumuali'i to Honolulu. See "Solid Men of Boston in the Northwest," original MS in Bancroft Library, University of California, microfilm in UH. Records of the visit draw on native sources; as usual, versions differ widely. See "Ka Moolelo Hawaii," native history translated in *Hawaiian Spectator*, II (April, 1839), p. 226; Dibble, *Sandwich*

Islands, p. 73; Jarves, *Sandwich Islands*, p. 97; Kamakau, *Ruling Chiefs*, pp. 195–197; 'I'i, *Fragments*, pp. 81–83.

[15] Statement of Eliab Grimes in *Sandwich Island News*, February 24, 1847; Campbell, *Voyage*, p. 129.

[16] There is a suggestion that he did come back to O'ahu in 1814, but this is uncorroborated. See Kuykendall, *Hawaiian Kingdom*, I, p. 51.

[17] John Turnbull, *A Voyage Round the World...1800–1804...*, 3 vols. (London, 1805), II, pp. 64–65; Peter Corney, *Voyages in the Northern Pacific...1813–1818...* (Honolulu, 1896), pp. 84–90, 96; Charles Barnard, *A Narrative of the Sufferings and Adventures of Charles Barnard...1812–1816...* (New York, 1829), pp. 219–221; Iselin, *Journal*, p. 70; Ebenezer Townsend, *Extract From the Diary of Ebenezer Townsend, Jr., Supercargo of the Sealing Ship "Neptune" on her Voyage to the South Pacific and Canton...*, Hawaiian Historical Society, *Reprints*, 4 (Honolulu, 1921), p. 12; F.W. Howay, "Captain Henry Barber of Barber's Point," Hawaiian Historical Society, *Annual Reports*, 47 (Honolulu, 1938), pp. 42–45.

[18] There are many descriptions of Kamehameha the trader. Among the best dating from the O'ahu sojourn are Iselin, *Journal*, p 75; Alexander Ross, *Adventures of the First Settlers on the Oregon or Columbia River...* (London, 1849), pp. 35-43; Ross Cox, *Adventures on the Columbia River...*, 2 vols. (London, 1831), I, pp. 27–28; Gabriel Franchere, *Narrative of a Voyage to the Northwest Coast of America...1811–1814...* (New York, 1854), pp. 63–65; F.W. Howay, "The Ship *Pearl* in Hawaii in 1805 and 1806," Hawaiian Historical Society, *Annual Report*, 46 (Honolulu, 1938), p. 37.

[19] In addition to sources cited in the previous footnotes, see Campbell, *Voyage*, pp. 137, 199–201, 211–213. Stephen Reynolds, *The Voyage of the New Hazard to the Northwest Coast Hawaii and China, 1810–1813...*, ed. F.W. Howay (Salem, 1938), *passim.*, gives an excellent, unselfconscious account of trading as it looked to an ordinary sailor.

[20] Campbell, *Voyage*, pp. 193–194; 'I'i, *Fragments*, p. 87.

[21] Cox, *Columbia River*, I, pp. 52–53.

[22] Sixty was a high figure, according to Alexander Campbell. It varied greatly. Most came off American ships, but only one in three were Americans; the rest were English. Campbell, *Voyage*, p. 167. Cf. Franchere, *Voyage*, pp. 69–70.

[23] Campbell, *Voyage*, p. 167. Campbell (p. 146), credits William Stevenson with introducing distilling to the islands. 'I'i, *Fragments*, p. 85, mentions a man known only as Alexander.

[24] Campbell, *Voyage*, pp. 138–139; Townsend, *Diary*, August 26, 1798, p. 20.

[25] Cox, *Columbia River*, I, pp. 34–35, 39–40.

[26] Translated excerpts from Marin's Journal are in AH. The original is lost.

[27] Cox, *Columbia River*, I, pp. 31–41; Corney, *Voyages*, pp.116–117.

[28] 'I'i, *Fragments*, pp. 20, 61.

[29] 'I'i, *Fragments*, pp. 53, 87–88; Campbell, *Voyage*, pp. 212–213; Cox, *Columbia River*, I, pp. 64–65. Harold Whitman Bradley, *The American Frontier in Hawaii: The Pioneers,*

1789–1843 (Stanford, 1942), pp. 32–33, has several mentions of Hawaiians' general willingness to travel.

[30] Cox, *Columbia River*, I, 33.

[31] Campbell, *Voyage*, pp. 140–141, 199.

[32] Campbell, *Voyage*, pp. 166–167.

[33] 'I'i, *Fragments*, pp. 68–69; Kamakau, *Ruling Chiefs*, pp. 192–193; Campbell, *Voyage*, pp. 162–163.

[34] 'I'i, *Fragments*, pp. 70–76; Campbell, *Voyage*, pp. 179–180.

[35] Campbell, *Voyage*, pp. 207–208; 'I'i, *Fragments*, pp. 54–55, 66, 69.

[36] Cox, *Columbia River*, I, 36. These tattoos, together with gravestone epitaphs, were the first lasting written records left on O'ahu.

[37] Campbell, *Voyage*, p. 134.

[38] 'I'i, *Fragments*, pp. 59, 61. In general, 'I'i gives the best account of kapu in practice.

[39] Kamakau, *Ruling Chiefs*, p. 194, says Kamehameha feared rebellion by Ka'ahumanu; this was why he had Kanihonui killed. 'I'i, *Fragments*, pp. 50–51, writing from first-hand knowledge of events in the court, has another version; Kamehameha feared rebellion because Ka'ahumanu's wrath was aroused by the killing—she might in retaliation take the kingdom.

[40] Vancouver, *Voyage*, II, 210. Most authorities doubt that the three men shot at Waikīkī were really the murderers.

[41] Ii, *Fragments*, is full of references to the joint and separate education of the little boys.

[42] Kamakau, *Ruling Chiefs*, pp. 197–198.

[43] By far the best single description of this period of commerce is in Bradley, *American Frontier*, pp. 1–52, carefully researched, well-documented.

[44] Schäffer was ordered to recover the cargo of a Russian ship wrecked on Kaua'i, or get compensation from the Kaua'i king, Kaumuali'i. Baranov's instructions to Schäffer are translated in Richard A. Pierce, *Russia's Hawaiian Adventure 1815–1817* (Berkeley, 1965), pp. 41–44. Pierce's book supersedes the earlier accounts listed in his full bibliography, and clears up obscurities in standard works like Kuykendell, *Hawaiian Kingdom*, I, pp. 56–9, and Bradley, *American Frontier*, pp. 49–51. My general narrative is based for the most part on Pierce's introductory essay (pp. 1–33) and the documents he translates, especially Schäffer's Journal (pp. 157–218). I follow Pierce's dates and pagination in citing Schäffer, and also his spelling of names.

[45] Schäffer Journal, June 24, 1816, p. 177.

[46] Schäffer Journal, August 15, September 12, 24. 1816, pp. 181–182, 213.

[47] Otto von Kotzebue, *A Voyage of Discovery in the Years 1815–1818...in the Ship Rurik...*, 3 vols. (London, 1821), I, pp. 303–335. There is confusion about the buildings involved in these incidents at Honolulu. Kotzebue was told on Hawai'i that the Russians had profaned a sanctuary or "morai" at Honolulu. Later, one of his men attended a ceremony at a heiau "hastily" erected to take its place. Peter Corney, at Honolulu in February, 1817, later wrote that the Russians had begun to build a blockhouse in Honolulu and that Kamehameha sent men from Hawai'i to halt this and build a Hawaiian fort. Corney, *Voyages*, pp. 71–72. Schäffer does not mention putting up any buildings (Kamehameha had forbidden it, offering one of his storehouses instead), but, writing from Kaua'i, he records the destruction of the Russian "factories" (plural) in Honolulu. Perhaps the Russians had tried to occupy a *heiau* as well as the storehouse.

[48] Schäffer Journal, May 10, 1817, p. 201.

[49] Schäffer Journal, June 24–25, 1817, pp. 203–204.

[50] Schäffer Journal, July 4, 1817, p. 205.

[51] Schäffer Journal, July 7, 1817, pp. 206–210.

[53] All citations in the following section deal only with O'ahu. Other islands of course went through a similar experience. The formal abolition took place on Hawai'i.

[54] Dixon, *Voyage*, pp. 103–107.

[55] Campbell, *Voyage*, p. 171; 'I'i, *Fragments*, p. 101.

[56] Louis Choris, *Voyage Pittoresque Autour Du Monde...* (Paris, 1822), pp. 11–12 of Sandwich Islands section.

[57] Kotzebue, *Voyage*, I, p. 327. This applied as of November-December, 1816.

[58] Corney, *Voyages*, pp. 83–84. This was late in 1817. Note that Young, a "white chief," respected the kapu; he belonged to Kamehameha's own family by marriage.

[59] Iselin, *Journal*, pp. 69, 76.

[60] Campbell, *Voyage*, p. 188.

[61] Campbell, *Voyage*, p. 215. Fairly clearly, by this time women had learned that they need not fear the retribution of the gods, but only the temporal penalties exacted by the male ali'i on behalf of the gods.

[62] There was a parallel case: the availability of women. "Men are extremely jealous of their fellow-countrymen but they submit with good will their wives to the white men." Choris, *Voyage Pittoresque*, p. 9.

[63] Colnett Journal, January 15, 1788.

[64] Campbell, *Voyage*, pp. 92, 134.

[65] Cox, *Columbia River* I, p. 55. The head and shoulders were most sacred because a god might at any time come to "sit" there—the more so with Liholiho, since

he was of extremely high rank. See 'I'i, *Fragments,* pp. 99–100, for a chiefess who killed herself after offending against this sacredness.

⁶⁶ Kotzebue, *Voyage,* I, pp. 330–331; Victor Houston, "Chamisso in Hawaii," Hawaiian Historical Society, *Annual Report,* 48 (Honolulu, 1940), p. 67. Houston translated the Hawaiian section of Chamisso's account of the *Rurik* voyage from Adelbert von Chamisso, *Werke,* ed. Herman Tardel, 3 vols. (Leipzig, n.d.), III, pp. 158–181.

⁶⁷ Chamisso, *Werke,* III, 176–177; "Chamisso in Hawaii," pp. 68–69.

⁶⁸ "Primitive, or let us say, archaic ritual is…sacred play, indispensable for the well-being of the community, fecund of cosmic insight and social development but always play… an action accomplishing itself outside and above the necessities and seriousness of everyday life." Johan Huizinga, *Homo Ludens: A Study of the Play-Element in Culture,* paperback ed. (Boston, 1962), pp. 25–26.

⁶⁹ Corney, *Voyages,* pp. 87, 101–102. It is interesting that John 'I'i's retrospective accounts of kapu in operation contain no suggestion of levity. Neither do those of another reliable native writer, David Malo, in his *Hawaiian Antiquities,* Bernice P. Bishop Museum, *Special Publication,* 2, 2nd ed. (Honolulu, 1951), *passim.* What Chamisso and Corney saw occurred very close to the time of abolition, and away from the eye of Kamehameha.

⁷⁰ E.S.C. Handy, *Cultural Revolution in Hawaii* (Honolulu, 1931), p. 3.

⁷¹ Bingham, *Residence,* p. 163. For a revisionist view of this whole subject, see M.C. Webb, "The Abolition of the Taboo System in Hawaii," *Journal of the Polynesian Society,* 74, 1 (March, 1965), pp. 21–39.

CHAPTER 3

¹ Traditionally John Kendrick (the American killed at Honolulu harbor in 1794) is regarded as the pioneer of the sandalwood trade in the islands. Dibble, *Sandwich Islands,* p. 54; Jarves, *Sandwich Islands,* p. 80. The career of the Winships is followed in "Solid Men of Boston in the Northwest." By far the best treatment of the Hawaiian sandalwood era is in Bradley, *American Frontier,* pp. 53–120. Kuykendall, *Hawaiian Kingdom,* I, pp. 85–92, and Theodore Morgan, *Hawaii: A Century of Economic Change 1778–1676* (Cambridge, 1948), pp. 61–67, have shorter accounts.

² There are no good figures for Hawaiian sandalwood sold at Canton. American traders there made a total of about $400,000 from sandalwood between 1817 and 1821, and Bradley thinks it "reasonable to suppose that after 1816 the greater part of the wood…was of Hawaiian origin." *American Frontier,* p. 57.

³ Alexander Adams, "Extracts From An Ancient Log," *Hawaiian Annual for 1906,* p. 51; "Golovnin's Visit to Hawaii in 1818," *The Friend,* LII (1894), p. 52. This is a translation of the Hawaiian portion of Vasili Golovnin, *Puteshestvie Vokrug Sveta… Na Voennom Shlupe Kamchatke…1817, 1818, 1819…* (St. Petersburg, 1822). There is another translation in typescript in UH. In the early 1820s Liholiho raised charges considerably, to the point where captains came to prefer Lahaina on Maui as a port; in 1825 lowered charges brought traffic back. Bradley, *American Frontier,* p. 58, collects the evidence on this.

⁴ The best approach to Honolulu trade in its Pacific context is in F.W. Howay, "A List of Trading Vessels in Maritime Fur Trade," in several sections covering the years 1785–1825, in Royal Society of Canada, *Transactions*, 3rd ser., XXIV (1930), Sec. II, pp. 111–134; XXV (1931), Sec. II, pp. 117–149; XXVI (1932), Sec. II, pp. 43–86; XXVII (1933), Sec. II, 119–147; XXVIII (1934), Sec. II, pp. 11–49. For the Hawaiian islands themselves, see Bernice Judd, *Voyages to Hawaii Before 1860...* (Honolulu, 1929). This, admittedly not a complete list, is based on the good collection of voyages in HMCS. In Bernice P. Bishop Museum, Honolulu, is a card file of ships and personal names compiled by the late George R. Carter. Its usefulness is impaired by an obscure key and index system.

⁵ The Bryant & Sturgis Letterbooks are in Baker Library, Harvard Graduate School of Business Administration; copies of important documents are in Kuykendall Collection, UH. The Josiah Marshall MSS in Houghton Library, Harvard University, contain letters from Honolulu (copies in Kuykendall Collection, UH). Many of John Coffin Jones letters to Marshall & Wildes are reprinted in Massachusetts Historical Society, *Proceedings*, LIV (1920), pp. 29–47; his letters to the United States government are in USDS, Consular Letters, Honolulu, I.

⁶ The Hunnewell MSS are in Houghton Library, Harvard University, and copies of Honolulu letters are in Kuykendall Collection, UH. See also James Hunnewell, "Voyage in the Brig *Bordeaux Packet* Boston to Honolulu 1817...," Hawaiian Historical Society, *Papers*, 8 (Honolulu, 1895); James Hunnewell, *Journal of the Voyage of the Missionary Packet, Boston to Honolulu, 1826* (Charlestown, 1880); Josephine Sullivan, *History of C. Brewer and Company, Ltd.* (Boston, 1926).

⁷ SIM Journal, August 8, November 19, 20, 1520, January 5, 1821; Elisha Loomis Journal, August 8, November 20, 1820, January 4, 1821; Maria Loomis Journal, August 8, November 19, 20, 1820. All of these are MSS in HMCS, except part of the Elisha Loomis Journal, which is in UH. The Maria Loomis Journal is in two versions, one written day by day, the other at intervals for friends in the United States. The latter will be cited as the Maria Loomis Journal, Williams version. For a non-missionary comment on the ejections, see Memo of James Hunnewell for *Mercantile Journal*, February 14, 1840, Hunnewell MSS. There had been earlier moves to eject foreigners. James Hunnewell Journal, May 20, November 17, 20, 1818, Hunnewell MSS. Liholiho's fears of rebellion and his anti-haole feelings cropped up throughout his reign. J.C. Jones to Marshall & Wildes, November 16, 1822, January —, May 31, October 23, 24, 1823, Marshall MSS. In 1823, Marin and some others were temporarily dispossessed of property. Levi Chamberlain Journal, September 22, 1823, MS in HMCS. Banishment of haoles for specific crimes continued throughout the twenties.

⁸ The origins of the Hawaiian mission are, if anything, overdocumented. A few major works are cited here. For general background, see Oliver Wendell Elsbree, *The Rise of the Missionary Spirit in America 1790–1815* (Williamsport Pa., 1928). More immediately useful are Rufus Anderson, *History of the Sandwich Islands Mission...* (Boston, 1870); and Welles Dwight, *Memoirs of Henry Obookiah...* (New Haven, 1819). Bradford Smith, *Yankees in Paradise: The New England Impact on Hawaii* (Philadelphia, 1956), brings together a great deal of material in readable form.

⁹ The first days of the mission are covered in entries from March 30 to April 15 in SIM Journal, Elisha Loomis Journal, Maria Loomis Journal, all previously cited; Daniel Chamberlain Journal, MS in HMCS; Bingham, *Residence*, pp. 69–70, 81–92. The other major documentary sources for the mission are 1) internal correspondence of the SIM, and journals, filed by author at HMCS; 2) letters of SIM members to ABCFM,

MSS at Houghton Library, Harvard University, microfilm and xerox copies at HMCS. Letters and journals were frequently excerpted in the ABCFM organ, the *Missionary Herald*. Because the printed versions are often shortened and edited, I have in every case cited MS versions. In this mass of materials there is much duplication. I have cited only the fullest accounts, by people closest to events.

[10] Bingham, *Residence*, pp. 92–94.

[11] Levi Chamberlain Journal, November 13, 1826.

[12] Bingham, *Residence*, p. 96.

[13] *Instructions of the Prudential Committee of the American Board of Commissioners for Foreign Missions to the Sandwich Islands Mission* (Lahainaluna, 1838), p. 27; Bingham, *Residence*, p. 60.

[14] SIM Journal, May 8, 10, June 19, July 8, 28, August 24, September 15, 1820; Daniel Chamberlain Journal, June 19, 1820; Elisha Loomis Journal, May 10, June 19, 1820; Maria Loomis Journal, May 13, July 8, August 1, September 7, 16, 1820, and Williams version, July 10, September 16, 1820; Bingham, *Residence*, pp. 96–116.

[15] SIM Journal, March 23, 1821.

[16] The original memorial is in HMCS; copies are in SIM Journal, May 13, 1820; Bingham, *Residence*, p. 111.

[17] SIM Journal, May 10; 23, June 26, August 1, 4, September 14, 18, 24, 1820; Elisha Loomis Journal, May 12, 16, 23, 1820; Maria Loomis Journal, May 12, 13, 16, 23, June 23, September 14, 1820; Daniel Chamberlain Journal, June 29, 1820; Bingham, *Residence*, pp.105–107.

[18] The journals from September, 1820, refer constantly to work going forward around the mission: gardening, fencing, roofing and so on. Later a frame house and other western buildings were added, some of which still stand at Kawaiaha'o. "Mission Houses, Honolulu," a typescript in HMCS, collects all manuscript references to buildings, from 1820 through the early l850s.

[19] For evidences of good will on the part of the foreigners, see SIM Journal, May 5, 6, 12, 16, 30, 31, June 1, 8, 23, September 10, 26, 28, October 2, November 1, 2, 3, 1820, January 12, 1821; Maria Loomis Journal, May 5, 6, 16, 30, September 10, 26, October 2, 1820; Daniel Chamberlain Journal, June 23, 29, 1820.

[20] On Boki, see SIM Journal, July 9, 10, 12, September 14, 1820; Maria Loomis Journal, November 17, 1620; Daniel Chamberlain Journal, July 8, 1820; Bingham, *Residence*, p. 112. Thomas Hopu: Samuel Whitney to Samuel Worcester, July 20, 1820, ABCFM Letters. William Kanui: SIM Journal, July 22, 23, 1820; Elisha Loomis Journal, July 22, 23, August 6, 1820; Maria Loomis Journal, July 25, 1820; Daniel Chamberlain Journal, July 21, 22, 1820; Bingham to Tennooee, July 23, 1820, copy in HMCS; Unpublished Minutes of Prudential Committee of SIM, July 22, 1820, MS in HMCS. Sally Jackson: Maria Loomis Journal, September 4, 1820. Hannah Holmes: SIM Journal, October 8, November 5, December 23, 31, 1820; Elisha Loomis Journal, December 5, 1820; Maria Loomis Journal, November 29, 1820. Elisha Loomis' disappointment in preaching is in his Journal, August 6, 1820.

21 Bingham to Samuel Worcester, May 13, 1820, ABCFM Letters; SIM Journal, May 19, 20, July 8, 1820; Elisha Loomis Journal, May 20, July 8, 1820; Maria Loomis Journal, May 19, 20, 1820; Daniel Chamberlain Journal, June 19, July 8, 1820.

22 SIM Journal, October 21, 1820; Marin Journal, December 3, 4, 13, 14, 17, 1820.

23 Education of native children was very much on the mind of the missionaries, as the weight of journal entries shows. By 1825 the "boarding-house" idea had been abandoned as too expensive and unproductive. Mission mothers had come to fear, too, a reverse cultural flow in which their own children were contaminated by Hawaiians. They meant this in a moral sense, but it should, be noted that their promising pupil William Beals died of a venereal disease in 1824. Abraham Blatchely to Jeremiah Evarts, —15th, 1824, ABCFM Letters. On the general problem of dealing with natives, see SIM Journal, May 14, June 21, November 6, 27, December 27, 1820, February 13, March 3, April 7, May 7, June 29, August 2, 12, 1821; Elisha Loomis Journal, November 27, 1820, March 3, April 7, May 7, 9, 10, August 12, 1821, January 2, 30, February 6, 15, March 8, 19, 1822, October 9 December 7, 1824, April 4, December 19, 1825; Maria Loomis Journal, June 21, November 4, December 28, 1820 (and Williams version for same date), January 15, February 12, December 29, 1821, February 18, 1824; Daniel Chamberlain Journal, July 20, 1820; Levi Chamberlain Journal, August 16, 18, November 29, 1823, January 1, February 16, 18, September 28, 29, November 25, December 7, 1824, March 3, April 4, 30, May 23, August 15, December 19, 1825; Stephen Reynolds Journal, November 26, December 1, 1823, February 17, 18, November 24, 1824, MS of most volumes in Peabody Museum, Salem, microfilm in HMCS, two remaining MS volumes in HMCS.

24 SIM Journal, December 20, 1820, January 13, 114, 1821; Elisha Loomis Journal, September 2, 11, 1820, January 13, 114, 15, 1821; Maria Loomis Journal, January 15, 30, 1821, and Williams version September 16, 1820; Bingham, *Residence*, pp. 123–124.

25 Bingham, *Residence*, p. 126; SIM Journal, February 3, 4, 5, 6, 14, 1821; Elisha Loomis Journal, February 3, 14, 1821; Maria Loomis Journal, February 3, 14, 1821.

26 SIM Journal, February 18, 20, 25, 26, 27, March 4, 1821; Elisha Loomis Journal, February 7, 9, 14, 20, 22, 1821; Maria Loomis Journal, February 7, 14, 20, 22, 1821. SIM Journal, February 27, 1821, says the baby died of congenital venereal disease: "its feeble frame, infected with disease entailed upon it by vice, in common with many in this land of pollution, descends to the dust..."

27 SIM Journal, March 10, 11, 1821; Elisha Loomis Journal, March 10, 11, 1821; Bingham, *Residence*, pp. 128–129.

28 SIM Journal, February 22, 26, March 16, May 4, 1821; Elisha Loomis Journal, March 12, 1821. As with the hula, so with other things. Elisha Loomis, touring rural Oʻahu with William Beals in 1821, took it upon himself to destroy little Hawaiian wayside shrines for travelers wherever he found them. Later, he and others were to find them set up again. Elisha Loomis Journal, March 19, 20, 21, 1821.

29 Bingham *et al.* to Samuel Worcester, July 6, 1821, ABCFM Letters; SIM Journal, March 15, 17, April 3, 4, May 16, August 19, September 15, 16, 20, 1821; Elisha Loomis Journal, March 15, April 4, May 16, August 9, 19, September 15, 1821; Maria Loomis Journal, July 2, 3, 1821, January 27, 1822; Bingham, *Residence*, p, 132–133.

30 Bingham *et al.* to Prudential Committee, ABCFM, November 21, 1824, ABCFM Letters; SIM Journal, September 25, November 10, 1821; Elisha Loomis Journal, July 25, 30, August 1, 17, 18, October 23, 1821; Bingham, *Residence*, pp. 135, 147.

31 J.C. Jones to John Quincy Adams, December 31, 1821, USDS, Consular Letters, Honolulu, I; James Hunnewell to Blanchard, October 20, 1821, Hunnewell MSS; Jones to Marshall & Wildes, January 22, 1822, Marshall MSS. See also SIM Journal, January 4, 5, February 1, August 18, 1821; Elisha Loomis Journal, January 31, May 31, 1821; Maria Loomis Journal, January 4, 1821. A picul was 133-1/3 pounds.

32 Gilbert Farquhar Mathison, *Narrative of a Visit to the Sandwich Islands,...1821–1822...*, (London, 1825), p. 467.

33 Stephen Reynolds Journal, April 6–10, 20, May 1, 5, 6, June 9, 1825; SIM Journal, March 23, May 5, 1821. I have cited just a few of the dozens of journals' references to sandalwood.

34 J.C. Jones to Marshall & Wildes, October 5, November 20, December 23, 1821, January 22, August 10, November 9, 1822, October 23 1823, July 21, 1824, Marshall MSS; Bradley, *American Frontier*, pp. 62–68.

35 Jones to Marshall, December 23, 1821, Marshall MSS; SIM Journal, October 23, 1821.

36 SIM Journal, May 22, 24, 1821.

37 SIM Journal, January 1, 2, 21, March 24, May 22, 24, July 29, September 17, 29, October 2, 10, 24, November 6, 8, 1821; Elisha Loomis Journal, May 22, September 18, 20, 22, October 2, November 9, 18, 19, 1821; Maria Loomis Journal, April 29, 1821; Bingham, *Residence*, p. 134.

38 SIM Journal, October 10, 1821.

39 Marin Journal, November 26, December 1, 1822; Elisha Loomis Journal, March 18, 24, September 12, 13, 17, 18, 19, November 26, 1822.

40 Bingham, *Residence*, p. 180; Elisha Loomis Journal, September 2, 1821.

41 Tyerman and Bennet, *Voyages and Travels*, II, pp. 78–79.

42 Elisha Loomis Journal, March 1, 2, 1822; Maria Loomis Journal, March 1, 2, 5, 1822, and Williams version, March 5, 1822; Levi Chamberlain Journal, October 16, 1823; Bingham, *Residence*, pp. 158–159. Marin Journal refers often to Liholiho's drunkenness; finally it became easier for Marin to note the days when the king was sober.

43 Bingham *et al.* to Prudential Committee, ABCFM, November 25, 1821, ABCFM Letters; Liholiho to the American Board, March 18, 1823, ABCFM Letters; Elisha Loomis Journal, March 23, 1822; Maria Loomis Journal, September 1, 1822, February 3, 1823; Levi Chamberlain Journal, October 7, 1823; Bingham, *Residence*, p. 175; Tyerman and Bennet, *Voyages and Travels*, II, pp. 35, 44, 57–58; William Ellis, *Polynesian Researches...*, 2nd ed., 4 vols. (London, 1831), IV, p. 45.

44 For the chiefs' life, see SIM Journal, April 15, 1820; Elisha Loomis Journal, February 5, March 6, October 18, 1822; Maria Loomis Journal, February 17, 1821, February

22, 1822; Levi Chamberlain Journal, April 27, 28, May 5, 1823; Bingham, *Residence*, pp. 170, 180; Louisa Everest Ely Journal, April 29, May 14, 1823, MS in HMCS; Marin Journal, October 17, 1822; Mathison, *Narrative*, pp. 364–373; Tyerman and Bennet, *Voyages and Travels*, II, pp. 27, 40–41, 46, 83; C.S. Stewart, *Private Journal of a…Residence at the Sandwich Islands…* (New York, 1828), *passim*. Stewart was clearly fascinated by Hawaiian royalty. His descriptions are vivid and detailed.

[45] All the journals from August to December, 1821, have accounts of these happenings. The best version is in Bingham, *Residence*, pp. 138–151; he was an eye-witness of most of the events described. For the diplomacy of the Kaua'i visit, see Kuykendall, *Hawaiian Kingdom*, I, pp. 74–76; Bradley, *American Frontier*, p. 128.

[46] Levi Chamberlain Journal, January 2, March 31, 1824; Bingham, *Residence*, p. 213–214. "Handcarts" drawn by natives were used by chiefs and missionary ladies as late as the forties. Horses were available—why were humans used? We do not know, but my opinion is that some natives up to about mid-century were willing to perform menial work of this kind out of reverence for those with superior mana whether of a traditional or a Christian kind, Time brought changes, however. By the fifties and sixties, seemingly every Honolulu Hawaiian owned a horse, astride which he felt himself the equal of any man, and from which he could not be induced to descend to menial labor of any sort. See Chapter VII for a discussion of the "new Hawaiian."

[47] Smith, *Yankees in Paradise*, p. 98.

[48] Stewart, *Residence at Sandwich Islands*, pp. 109–113.

[49] Bingham, *Residence*, p. 178.

[50] William Ellis to George Burder, November 20, 1823, LMS; Bingham to Jeremiah Evarts, November 21, 1823, ABCFM Letters; Marin Journal, November 15, 19, 27, 1823; Stephen Reynolds Journal, November 11, 1823; Maria Loomis Journal, November 10, 11, 15, 27, 1823; Levi Chamberlain Journal, November 9, 11, 15, 19, 23, 1823.

[51] Kamakau, *Ruling Chiefs*, pp. 256–257. The "father" Kamāmalu refers to is Kamehameha. For the actual departure, see Maria Loomis Journal, November 23, 25, 27, 1823; Levi Chamberlain Journal, November 23, 25, 27, 1823; Bingham, *Residence*, pp. 203–204.

[52] Kamakau, *Ruling Chiefs*, pp. 256–257; Bingham, *Residence*, p. 204.

[53] Marin Journal, December 1, 21, 1823, April 10, 1824; Elisha Loomis to Jeremiah Evarts, December 31, 1823, ABCFM Letters; Bingham to Evarts, January 1, 1824, ABCFM Letters; Elisha Loomis Journal, January 2, 30, March 5, 7, 27, September 18, 1825; Levi Chamberlain Journal, December 21, 1823, April 13, 25, June 9, 27, July 11, August 8, 15, September 26, December 26, 1824, January 2, March 2, 4, 6, 7, 27, April 3, 10, May 15, September 4, 15, 18, 1825.

[54] Levi Chamberlain Journal, April 19, November 21, 1824, January 7, September 13, 1825; Chamberlain to Evarts, December 10, 1825, ABCFM Letters; Elisha Loomis Journal, November 15, 1825; Bingham, *Residence*, pp. 246–251. For the waterfront hula, see Stephen Reynolds Journal, June 15–24, 1824. Reynolds took a very cynical view of the accomplishments of the reform movement, seeing things in Honolulu that escaped the mission. See his Journal, May 2, 29, 30, 1825.

55 The British consul claimed that if Kalanimoku, seriously ill at the time, had died before the *Blonde* arrived, there would have been war; but he was merely projecting his own disturbances upon the Hawaiian scene. His personality is discussed later in this chapter. Richard Charlton to George Canning, June 10, 1825, FO 58/4.

56 Levi Chamberlain Journal, May 6, 1825; Elisha Loomis Journal, May 6, 1825; Bingham *et al* to Evarts, June 6, 1825, ABCFM Letters.

57 Stephen Reynolds Journal, May 6, 11, 1825; Levi Chamberlain Journal, May 6, 11, 1825; Bingham, *Residence*, pp. 264–271.

58 Maria Graham, comp., Voyage of H.M.S. *"Blonde" to the Sandwich Islands...1824–1825* (London, 1826), pp. 160–161. Other accounts of the *Blonde's* visit are in Andrew Bloxam, *Diary*, previously cited; and James Macrae, *With Lord Byron at the Sandwich Islands in 1825...*, ed. W.F. Wilson (Honolulu, 1922).

59 Bingham to George Burder, September 13, 1825, ABCFM Letters; Levi Chamberlain to Rufus Anderson, June 19, 1826, ABCFM Letters.

60 Chamberlain to Evarts, August 27, 1825, ABCFM Letters; Chamberlain Journal, August 6, 7, 1825; Elisha Loomis Journal, August 6, 7, 1825; Stephen Reynolds Journal, August 6, 7, 1825; Marin Journal, August 6, 7, 1825.

61 Stephen Reynolds Journal, April 26, 28, 29, May 2, August 26, 1825; Elisha Loomis Journal, April 28, 29, August 6, 1825; Chamberlain to Evarts, September 11, 1826, ABCFM Letters. Smith, *Yankees in Paradise, passim.*, follows the careers of the Holmes sisters in some detail.

62 An outstanding source of information for this society is the Stephen Reynolds Journal. Reynolds visited the islands as a common sailor ten years before the missionaries came and returned to live permanently in Honolulu in the early 1820s, first working for the American merchant William French, then going into business for himself. Reynolds saw and reported pungently on a great number of things quite outside the range of the mission vision. His social chronicle continues to the 1850s. In any given week he reports on most of the activities listed above.

63 Marin Journal, January 22, 1822, September 22, 23, 24, 26, 29, 30, October 2, 1823; Levi Chamberlain Journal, August 29, October 11, 1823; Elisha Loomis Journal, March 28, 1822, July 6, 1825; Maria Loomis Journal, Williams version, April 14, 1823; Stephen Reynolds Journal, June 6, 1825; Artemas Bishop to Evarts, June 1, 1825, ABCFM Letters; William Ellis to W.A. Hankey, October 30, 1823, LMS; Bradley, *American Frontier*, p. 80–82; Morgan, *Hawaii*, pp. 74–81. Marin, for a time, was the chiefs' intermediary in trade at Honolulu.

64 Elisha Loomis to Evarts, August 9, 1822, ABCFM Letters; William Ellis to Tyerman and Bennet, March 10, 1823, LMS; Levi Chamberlain to Evarts, October 15, 1823, January 9, 1824, May 7, August 27, 1825, ABCFM Letters; Bradley, *American Frontier*, pp. 8S–88; Morgan, *Hawaii*, pp. 98–99, 104–105.

65 Population estimates appear in: Mathison, *Narrative*, p. 448; Tyerman and Bennet, *Voyages and Travels*, II, 29; Joint Letter of SIM to ABCFM, March 20, 1823 ABCFM Letters; Macrae, *Byron*, p. 17; Ellis, *Polynesian Researches*, IV, pp. 17–18; Frederick William Beechey, *Narrative of a Voyage to the Pacific...1825–1828*, 2 vols. (London, 1831), I, p. 317. Beechey's description of the "regularity" of the town is rather more

flattering than that of other contemporary writers. The taverns whose signboards he remarked upon were precisely the sources of great irregularity.

[66] Daniel Chamberlain Journal, June 30, 1820; SIM Journal, May 11, 1820, December 19, 1821; Elisha Loomis Journal, February 23, 25, 1822, August 15, 22, 24, 1825; Levi Chamberlain Journal, September 22, October 24, 1825; Marin Journal, August 26, 28, 1821, September 1, October 26, November 11, 13, 1822, June 24, August 24, 1825; Stephen Reynolds Journal, April 18, 19, October 5, 1824, June 23, 25, 26, 27, 29, August 15, 21, 22, 23, 24, 27, 29, 31, September 3, 9, October 24, 25, 26, 1825; April 19, 20, 21, 22, 1826. Navarro returned to Hawai'i within a few months of his banishment. Reynolds Journal, December 1, 1825.

[67] Mathison, *Narrative*, p. 437.

[68] Levi Chamberlain Journal, October 1, 1823, November 17, 1824; Elisha Loomis Journal, November 17, 1824.

[69] Chamberlain to Evarts, August 27, 1825, ABCFM Letters.

[70] Bingham *et al.* to Evarts, June 6, 1825, ABCFM Letters; Bingham to Burder, September 12, 1825, LMS; Elisha Loomis Journal, June 6, July 6, October 1, 4, 1825; Levi Chamberlain Journal, June 6, 28, August 20, October 4, 1825.

[71] Marin Journal, October 19, 21, November 12, December 10, 11, 12, 13, 1825; Stephen Reynolds Journal, October 8, 20, 21, 28, December 10, 11, 12, 21, 1825; Elisha Loomis Journal, October 8, 11, 19, 25, 28, 29, November 6, 19, December 12, 1825; Levi Chamberlain Journal, October 7, 8, 11, 26, 29, November 12, December 12, 13, 22, 1825; Levi Chamberlain to Ellis, November 3, 1825, LMS; Levi Chamberlain to Evarts, December 10, 1825, ABCFM Letters.

[72] This account of the riot was compiled from: Elisha Loomis Journal, January 27, February 1, 22, 24, 26, 27, 28, March 1, 10, 13, April 3, 8, 9, May 11, 1826; Levi Chamberlain Journal, February 19, 22, 23, 26, 28, March 2, 11, 15, April 1, May 11, 1826; Stephen Reynolds Journal, January 14, 17, 18, 19, 21, February 14, 20, 21, 22, 23, 25, 26, March 17, 19, 20, 24, 29, 31, April 1, 3, May 10, 11, 1826; Levi Chamberlain to Evarts, February 7, September 11, 1826, February 22, 1827, April 10, 1828, August 13, 1829, ABCFM Letters. Also in ABCFM Letters is a translation of a letter by Boki, witnessed by David Malo and Kaniua, undated, but marked Received at the Rooms, April 18, 1829, detailing conversations between Percival and Boki. Bingham, *Residence*, pp. 283–289, carries the story to the courtmartial of Percival urged by the ABCFM and others. Percival was acquitted. The testimony is in United States, Navy Department, Office of Judge Advocate General, Court Martial Records, XXIII, 1830, No. 531, Proceedings of a Court of Inquiry &c., In the Case of Lieut. John Percival, original in National Archives, extracts in Kuykendall Collection, UH. It covers almost a thousand pages. Some witnesses said the kapu was effective; several others who had been in the islands at different times thought otherwise.

[73] Levi Chamberlain Journal, November 3, 13, 1826; Elisha Loomis Journal, November 13, 1826.

[74] For this and other abuse of the mission, see Jones to Marshall, May 5, 25, June 18, September 21, 1826; Jones to Wildes, July 20, 1827; Jones to Marshall, June 15, 1828, September 16, 1829, Marshall MSS.

[75] Levi Chamberlain to Evarts, September 11, 1826, ABCFM Letters; Elisha Loomis Journal, September 9, 14, 23, 25, 27, 30, October 2, December 15, 21, 1826; Levi Chamberlain Journal, September 5, November 11, 15, 1826.

[76] Otto von Kotzebue, *A New Voyage Round the World...1823–1826*, 2 vols. (London, 1830), II, pp. 228–229; Beechey, *Narrative*, II, pp. 101–105.

[77] Thomas ap Catesby, Jones, "Report of the Peacock's Cruise to the Sandwich, Society, and other Islands in the Pacific Ocean performed in the years 1826 and 1827," original in National Archives, copy in Kuykendall Collection, UH; Kuykendall, Hawaiian Kingdom I, pp. 98–99, 434–436; Bradley, *American Frontier*, pp. 106–117.

[78] Elisha Loomis Journal, October 8, 9, 11, 17, 19, 24, 25, November 14, December 8, 9, 14, 23, 1826; Levi Chamberlain Journal, September 28, October 26, 27, November 1, 14, 22, December 8, 14, 1826; Stephen Reynolds Journal, June 9, July 2, 29, August 1, 23, October 14, 17, 23, 27. November 1, 21, December 8, 1826. The mission's printed circular, dated October 3, 1826, together with an undated response signed by J.C. Jones and 12 others, and a further letter from Jones and others dated December 6, 1826, are in AH, Private Collections, American Protestant Mission.

[79] Beechey, *Narrative*, II, p. 107; Levi Chamberlain Journal, February 9, 12, 1827.

[80] Richards to Evarts, March 31, 1827, ABCFM Letters.

[81] Levi Chamberlain Journal, February 13, 1827.

[82] Levi Chamberlain Journal, May 19, 23, 1827.

[83] For the origins of the mission, see George Verne Blue, "The Project for a French Settlement in the Islands, 1828–1842," *Pacific Historical Review*, II (March, 1933), p. 85 *ff*. Documentation for the Catholics in Hawai'i is not as full for the Protestant mission. The Honolulu archives of the Catholic Church are not open to non-Catholics; I have not had access to them. The official history is by Reginald Yzendoorn, *History of the Catholic Mission in Hawaii* (Honolulu, 1927). The Catholic counterpart of the *Missionary Herald* is *Annales de la Propagation de la Foi*. The Honolulu Protestants and their fellows elsewhere in the islands had a great deal to say about the Catholics, in manuscript and in print, most of it polemic. The first commercial newspaper in Honolulu, the *Sandwich Island Gazette* (late 1830s) and its successor, the *Sandwich Island Mirror*, were pro-Catholic, anti-Protestant. They published frequent pieces about religious history in the islands. For immediate references to the establishment of the French mission, see Levi Chamberlain Journal, July 17, 23, 1827; Stephen Reynolds Journal, July 17, 30, December 25, 1827, May 17, September 14, 1828; Chamberlain to Anderson, September 14, 1827, ABCFM Letters; Bingham to Evarts, June 29, 1827, Bingham to Anderson, May 15, 1839, ABCFM Letters. Bradley, *American Frontier*, pp. 184–188, and Kuykendall, Hawaiian Kingdom, I, pp. 139–141 have good short accounts of the early years.

[84] Stephen Reynolds Journal, August 4, October 25, November 19, 26, 1827; Levi Chamberlain Journal, August 15, 16, October 23, 25, 26, 27, November 1, 2, 3, 5, 8, 12, 13, 14, 15, 19, 25, 26, 27, 28, 29, 1827; Hoapili to Ka'ahumanu, October 24, 1827, AH, FO & Ex, copies in ABCFM Letters and Bingham, *Residence*, pp. 314–315; Levi Chamberlain to Evarts, September 14, November 1, 1827, ABCFM Letters; Levi Chamberlain to Samuel Ruggles, December 1, 1827, HMCS; Levi Chamberlain

to Samuel Whitney and Samuel Ruggles, December 17, 1827, HMCS; William Richards to Anderson, December 6, 1827, ABCFM Letters.

[85] Stephen Reynolds Journal, December 8, 11, 14, 1827; Levi Chamberlain Journal, December 1, 7. 8, 14, 1827; Richards to Anderson, December 6, 1827, ABCFM Letters; [Bingham] to —, December 15, 1827, ABCFM Letters.

[86] By far the best among several mission biographies by descendants is Gerrit P. Judd VI, *Doctor Judd: Hawaii's Friend* (Honolulu, 1960).

[87] Stephen Reynolds Journal, July 13, 1828.

[88] The description of the hotel is by Kamakau, *Ruling Chiefs*, p. 276. For the political situation, see Stephen Reynolds Journal, April 1, 8, 18, 21, 1829; Levi Chamberlain Journal, April 4, 1829; E.W. Clark Journal, April 19, 1829, MS, HMCS: 'I'i, *Fragments*, pp. 154–155; Bingham, *Residence*, p. 342.

[89] Bingham, *Residence*, p. 343.

[90] Levi Chamberlain Journal, April 23, May 2, 3, 9, 10, 24, 1829.

[91] Levi Chamberlain Journal, June 9, 1829.

[92] Elisha Loomis Journal, June 28, 1824; Stephen Reynolds Journal, January 10, April 2, 1828, June 9, 11, 1829; Levi Chamberlain Journal, August 2, December 8, 18, 19, 25, 26, 1828; William C.B. Finch to Kauikeaouli and the Chiefs, November 3, 1829, AH, FO & Ex; C.S. Stewart, *A Visit to the South Seas...1829–30...*, 2 vols. (New York, 1831), I, pp. 192–202.

[93] Levi Chamberlain Journal, July 3 1829; Bingham, *Residence*, pp. 343–346.

[94] Stephen Reynolds Journal, July 4, August 9, 1829; Levi Chamberlain Journal, August 8, 10, September 3, 1829; Kamakau, *Ruling Chiefs*, p. 291. The edict on marriage is in AH, Laws, September, 1829.

[95] AH; FO & Ex, October 5, 1829, has a folder of documents on the cow case. See also Stephen Reynolds Journal, October 7, 8, 10, 1829; Levi Chamberlain Journal, October 5, 7, 9, 1829; Bingham, *Residence*, pp. 351–352. Charlton denied having used violence toward the Hawaiian: Charlton to Aberdeen, November 28, 1829, FO 58/5; but the evidence the other way is too strong. For the constitutional importance of the cow case, see Kuykendall, *Hawaiian Kingdom*, I, p. 129.

[96] Southard to Kamehameha III, January 20, 1829, AH, FO & Ex; Finch to Kauikeaouli, November 18, 1829, AH, FO & Ex; Stewart, *Visit to South Seas*, I, pp. 227–231.

[97] These figures are collected in Bradley, *American Frontier*, pp. 110–117.

[98] For Boki's plantation, see: Levi Chamberlain Journal, September 30, 1825, February 24, June 10, August 3 10, November 30, 1826, December 31, 1828, March 18, 1833; Levi Chamberlain to Elisha Loomis, November 29, 1830, HMCS; Stephen Reynolds Journal, June 4, August 9, September 17, 1826, March 2, July 4, 1827, November 17, December 3, 6, 8, 1828, February 2, 20, 21, 24, 25, 26, 28, March 4, 31, April 16, 24, 25, May 13, 26, June 8, 10, 11, 20, 22, July 21, 27, 1829, January 2, February 14, 1830; Bingham to Anderson, March 30, 1833, ABCFM letters. Reynolds wrote "Reminiscences of Hawaiian Agriculture," Royal Hawaiian Agricultural Society,

Transactions, I (1850), pp. 49–53; and he was almost certainly the author of the long letter by "Tatler" in *Sandwich Island Mirror*, March 15, 1840. See also Macrae, *Byron*, pp. 34–35; Hiram Paulding, *Journal of a Cruise in the United States Schooner Dolphin*... (New York, 1831), pp. 220–223; Beechey, Narrative, II, p. 100; Bradley, *American Frontier* pp. 242–243.

⁹⁹ R.S Kuykendall, "Some Early Commercial Adventurers of Hawaii," Hawaiian Historical Society, *Annual Report*, 37 (Honolulu, 1929), pp. 17–33, covers Boki's trading career quite well. See also Kamakau, *Ruling Chiefs*, p. 276.

¹⁰⁰ Kamakau, *Ruling Chiefs*, p. 294.

¹⁰¹ This account of Boki's expedition was compiled from: Stephen Reynolds Journal, December 1, 2, 3, 4, 7, 1829, July 11, August 9, 1830, June 22, 27, 1831, August 26, 1835; Levi Chamberlain Journal, June 7, July 11, August 3, 4, 7, 9, 1830, August 26, 1835 Reuben Tinker Journal, June 20, 28, 1831, MS in HMCS; Levi Chamberlain to Elisha Loomis, November 29, 1830, HMCS (has names of some Hawaiians who went with Boki); Levi Chamberlain to David Greene, August 26, 1834, ABCFM Letters; E.W, Clark to Secretary, ABCFM, September 20, 1830, HMCS; Jonathan Green to David Greene, July 17, 1830, ABCFM Letters; James Stephens to Kamehameha III, March 30, 1832, AH, FO & Ex; 'I'i, *Fragments*, pp. 155–157; Kamakau, *Ruling Chiefs*, p. 305; Bingham, *Residence*, pp. 361–362; *The Friend*, January 1, 1877.

Why did Boki take so many men to the New Hebrides? Richard Charlton reported to the Foreign Office that Boki was going to "take possession" of the islands. Charlton to Aberdeen, January 2, 1830, FO 58/5. A contract in AH, FO & Ex, November 30, 1829, signed by Boki and Kamehameha with Thomas Blakesly, talks about taking islands under protection. Boki himself, in sources cited above, made some mention of not being able to return to Hawai'i till "a certain chief" (Ka'ahumanu) was dead. Fairly clearly he had more on his mind than mere sandalwood.

What happened to him? No one knows; but in 1887 a man named Henry Poor, in Samoa on a mission for the Hawaiian monarchy, came across an old Hawaiian called John Kalama, who had been in Samoa for twenty years. In conversation, Kalama mentioned a man named "John Boki," and this led Poor to ask if Kalama had ever heard of the original Boki. Kalama remembered him faintly, and a few days later he brought an old Samoan to Poor. This man was called Kauikeaouli (the name of Kamehameha III). He said he had lived with an ali'i Hawai'i (a Hawaiian chief) named Boki, who was one of Kamehameha III's men, and who had landed at Saapalii on the Samoan island of Savaii with a ship and many Hawaiians, including his wife (Boki did not have Liliha with him). Boki had lived for years at Saapalii, but he and his companions were now all dead, though several sons of Boki were still living. Poor wrote to the Hawaiian government, asking for expenses to cover an investigation; but his mission was recalled shortly afterwards, and nothing was done. Henry F. Poor to J.S. Webb, March 20, 1887, AH, FO & Ex.

CHAPTER 4

[1] Stephen Reynolds Journal, January 22, February 9, 20, 21, 22, 23, March 2, 4, 5, 12, 15, 16, April 7, 21, 1831; Levi Chamberlain Journal, February. 20, 22, 23, 25, March 2, 3, 4, 5, 6, 7, 8, 11, 12, 15, 20, 1831; Bingham to Levi Chamberlain, January 19, February 17, 1831, HMCS; Artemas Bishop to Levi Chamberlain, March 10, 1831, HMCS; Levi Chamberlain to Samuel Ruggles, February 26 1831, HMCS; Levi Chamberlain to Jeremiah Evarts, December 5, 1831, ABCFM Letters; E. W. Clark to Jeremiah Evarts, September 14, 1831, ABCFM Letters; Gerrit Judd to --, September 26, 1831, HMCS; H. A. Peirce to James Hunnewell, January 30, 31, March 8, 1831, Hunnewell MSS.

[2] Kauikeaouli's proclamation of April 1, 1831, is in HMCS; AH, FO & Ex has a. copy.

[3] William French, Stephen Reynolds, H.A. Pierce, Richard Charlton, Eliab Grimes, T.C. B. Rooke, John Meek and others to Kauikeaouli, April 7, 1831, AH, FO & Ex.

[4] For the moral war, see Levi Chamberlain Journal, April 1, 2, 9, 13, 1.7, 18, May 3, 10, 1831; Stephen Reynolds Journal, April 1, 5, 6, 7, 8, 9, 13, 16, 17, 20, 21, 22, 27, 29, May 1, 7, 13, 14, 1831, Bingham to Jeremiah Evarts, November 23, 1831, ABCFM Letters; Levi Chamberlain to Jeremiah Evarts, April 20, December 5, 1831, ABCFM Letters; E. W. Clark to Rufus Anderson, April 20, 1831, ABCFM Letters; E. W. Clark to Jeremiah Evarts, September 14, 1831, ABCFM Letters; Bingham, *Residence* pp. 407–409.

[5] This account of the ejection has been compiled from: Levi Chamberlain Journal, March 4, July 7, August 8, 10, 1829, June 17, 18, July 29, 30, September 20, 21, 25, October 18, December 10, 25, 1830, January 3, February 12, April 2, September 8, December 12, 13, 24, 1831; Stephen Reynolds Journal, February 21, 23, August 9, December 25, 1829, January 4, 5, March 3, April 2, June 25, July 2, 14, December 23, 24, 1831; Hiram Bingham Journal, December 24, 1831, ABCFM Letters; Bingham *et al.* to Jeremiah Evarts, January 1, 1829, ABCFM Letters; Bingham to Jeremiah Evarts, September 8, November 23, 25, 1832, February 6, 1832, ABCFM letters; Levi Chamberlain to Elisha Loomis, November 29, 1830, HMCS; Levi Chamberlain to Rufus Anderson, February 6, 1832, ABCFM Letters; E.W. Clark to Rufus Anderson, November 10, 1830, ABCFM Letters; Richard Charlton to Aberdeen, December 20, 1831, FO 58/6; Bingham, *Residence*, pp. 415-422. Kauikeaouli's order for the priests to leave the country, January 6, 1831, is in AH, FO & Ex, as is Sumner's *Waverly* commission, November 5, 1831. Yzendoorn, *Catholic Mission*, pp. 53–75, quotes unpublished manuscripts of Bachelot and Short and extracts from *Annales de la Propagation de la Foi*, in giving many details about persecutions unavailable elsewhere.

[6] Hiram Bingham Journal, December 7, 12, 13, 21, 24, 1831, ABCFM Letters; Levi Chamberlain Journal, June 1, 1829, November 5, 1831; Stephen Reynolds Journal, June 1, 1829, April 2, August 22, 1831; Bingham to Jeremiah Evarts, July 19, 1828, ABCFM Letters; Bingham to Levi Chamberlain, September 14, 1830, January 19, 1831, HMCS; Bingham to Rufus Anderson, February 16, 1832, ABCFM Letters; Bingham *et al.* to Rufus Anderson, June 23, 1832, ABCFM Letters; E.W. Clark to Rufus Anderson, March 30, 1833, ABCFM Letters; Samuel Whitney to David Greene, October 25, 1830, ABCFM Letters; *Minutes* of the General Meeting of the Sandwich Island Mission for 1830 and 1831, *passim.* Yzendoorn, *Catholic Mission*,

makes the strongest case possible for direct Protestant instigation of persecution and expulsion; he collects manuscript evidence on pp. 44–75.

7 On the foreign community see Stephen Reynolds Journal, February 15, 1829, January 1, 7, July 4, August 14, September 22, 23, 1831, April 20, 1832. On the general prosperity of the Protestant cause see Levi Chamberlain Journal, July 2, 1829, February 12, March 2, April 15, June 24, July 1, 1830, January 8, 9, 15, 19, 25, February 8, April 5, 6, 22, May 8, September 7, December 29, 30, 1831, February 10, March 15, June 10, October 2, 9, 1832; Cochran Forbes Journal, May 21, 1832, MS, HMCS; Bingham to --, December 13, 1831, ABCFM Letters; Bingham to US Secretary of Navy, March 11, 1832; copy in HMCS; Bingham to Rufus Anderson, October 2, 1832, Letters; H.A. Peirce to James Hunnewell, June 11, 1832, August 10, 1833, Hunnewell MSS; Bingham, *Residence*, pp. 365–368; Laura Fish Judd, *Honolulu...1828–1861* (Honolulu, 1928), p. 45.

8 Reuben Tinker Journal, July 19, 1831.

9 Levi Chamberlain Journal, June 4, 5, 7, 8, 1832; Cochran Forbes Journal, June 8, 1832; Stephen Reynolds Journal, June 4, , 7, 23, 1832; Bingham to Rufus Anderson, June 5, 1832, ABCFM Letters; H. A. Peirce to James Hunnewell, June 11, 1832, Hunnewell MSS; Bingham, *Residence*, p. 433.

10 Kuykendall, *Hawaiian Kingdom*, I, p. 134, cites the proclamation of July 5, 1832, signed by Kīna'u and Kauikeaouli. He says Kīna'u was regent as well as kuhina nui.

11 Richard Charlton to Aberdeen, November 28, 1829, FO 58/5; Stephen Reynolds Journal, May 6, 7, 27, 30, July 29, 31, August 1, 11, 12, September 10, 11, 12, 13, 14, 17, 1829, May 10, 1830.

12 Levi Chamberlain Journal, October 21, December 31, 1831, January 1, 2, 4, 6, 12, 15, 17, 1832; Stephen Reynolds Journal, July 11, 16, October 12, November 16, December 31, 1831, January 1, May 1, 22, 30, 1832; Bingham to Jeremiah Evarts, February 6, 1832, ABCFM Letters; Chamberlain to Jeremiah Evarts, February 6, 1832, ABCFM Letters; Levi Chamberlain to Samuel Ruggles, February 7, 1832, HMCS.

13 Levi Chamberlain to Henry Hill, August 7, 1832, ABCFM Letters; Levi Chamberlain Journal, August 15, 1832; Mary Charlotte Alexander, *William Patterson Alexander in Kentucky, the Marquesas, Hawaii* (Honolulu, 1934), p. 85; Judd, *Honolulu*, p. 40. The general circumstances of Downes' visit are in J.N. Reynolds, *Voyage of the Potomac...1831–1834...* (New York, 1835); and Francis Warriner, *Cruise of the... Potomac... 1831–1834...*(New York, 1835).

14 Judd, *Honolulu*, p. 41; Bingham, *Residence*, p. 447; Kamakau, *Ruling Chiefs* p. 335. From the beginning of February, 1833, for almost eighteen months, the journals of Levi Chamberlain and Stephen Reynolds contain a day-by-day, sometimes hour-by-hour account of the doings of the king and the Hulumanu. They are by far the best sources; others merely repeat from a distance what these two saw first-hand or reported immediately. I have not thought it necessary to give repeated citations from these two sources; dates are given in the text from time to time. I have also made use of the following summary letters: Levi Chamberlain to Rufus Anderson, March 26, 1833, ABCFM Letters, and rough draft in HMCS; Bingham to Rufus Anderson, August 16, 1833, ABCFM Letters; Richard Charlton to

Palmerston, October 12, 1833, FO 58/7; B.W. Clark to Rufus Anderson, September 28, 1833, ABCFM Letters, and draft in HMCS; John Emerson to Rufus Anderson, November 2, 1833, ABCFM Letters; H.A. Peirce to James Hunnewell, October 4, 1833, Hunnewell. MSS.

[15] Bingham to Rufus Anderson, March 20–April 9, 1833, ABCFM Letters; H.A. Peirce to James Hunnewell, April 8, 1833, Hunnewell MSS.

[16] For the constitutional significance of March 15, 1833, see Kuykendall, *Hawaiian Kingdom I*, pp. 135–136.

[17] Direct citation of journals is resumed with these greatly important events. Levi Chamberlain Journal, March 27, 29, June 11, July 22, 1834; Stephen Reynolds Journal, June 8, 10, July 22, August 12, 1834; Alonzo Chapin to Samuel Ruggles, September 30, 1834, HMCS; Cochran Forbes to Lorenzo Lyons, September 31, 1834, HMCS; William to Rufus Anderson, October 15, 1834, ABCFM Letters.

[18] Kuykendall, *Hawaiian Kingdom*, I, pp. 136–137; and Bradley, *American Frontier*, pp. 275–276, collect the literature on the constitutional significance of 1835.

[19] Richard Armstrong to Rufus Anderson, October 22, 1832, ABCFM Letters; Bingham to Rufus Anderson, March 20–April 9 1833, ABCFM Letters; Bingham to James Hunnewell, April 2, 1833, Hunnewell MSS.

[20] *Minutes* of the General Meeting of the Sandwich Island Mission, 1835, p. 22.

[21] Bingham, Residence pp. 478–479, contains two petitions to the king on the liquor question, one from the Honolulu natives, the other from some sea-captains. AH, FO & Ex, has another captains' petition, dated November 30, 1835. For the progress toward abstinence, see Bingham *et al.* to ABCFM, July 7, 1836, ABCFM Letters; Richard Charlton to Palmerston, November 23, 1836, FO 58/8; Hawaiian Spectator, I (July, 1838), pp. 335–336, (October, 1838), pp. 389–390; and AH, Laws, March 13, 15, 20, 25, August 21, 1838, for the decrees of Kauikeaouli.

The whole question of temperance and the Sandwich Island Mission is an interesting one, not generally understood. It has been assumed that the Protestants were total abstinence men from the start. This is not so. There are many references to beer, porter, cider, wine and spirits in their journals through the twenties. They used them for medicinal, celebratory, and restorative purposes. They accepted them as gifts from foreigners; they themselves brewed beer. Elisha Loomis Journal, June 23, 1820, January 8, 1821, November 19, 20, 1824; Maria Loomis Journal, June 23, August 21, 1820; Daniel Chamberlain Journal, June 19, 1820; Levi Chamberlain Journal, December 13, 1822, January 10, 1823, June 8, 9, 1827; Levi Chamberlain to Jeremiah Evarts, October 15, 1823, ABCFM Letters; Levi Chamberlain to Samuel Ruggles, February 24, 1827, HMCS; Joseph Goodrich to Jeremiah Evarts, July 14, 1828, ABCFM Letters; Alonzo Chapin to Levi Chamberlain, October 31, 1834, HMCS.

About 1830 the mission decided that, for Hawaiians, total abstinence was the only sensible policy, and that missionaries should set an example. Here *temperance* became *abstinence*. The increased insistence on this through the thirties reflects the mainland United States emphasis over the same period. Even so, not all Sandwich Island missionaries were total abstainers, nor did some think it necessary to refuse alcohol to guests, or to refuse to attend functions where liquor was served. On this issue a sharp argument developed. See two remarkable letters by Hiram Bingham to Dwight Baldwin, dated January 15, and March --, 1838, HMCS, in which the reputedly arid Bingham takes a much more accommodating line than Baldwin. Generally, missionaries arriving in the thirties and forties were more stringent than those of the early contingents, again reflecting developments in America. Some even wanted to replace communion wine with non-intoxicants in the native churches.

22 Stephen Reynolds Journal, October 2, December 5, 1836; Levi Chamberlain Journal, November 12, 1836; Bingham to Rufus Anderson., August 8, 1835, ABCFM Letters; J.N. Reynolds, *Voyage of the Potomac...1834–1831...* (New York, 1835), pp. 418–419; Yzendoorn, *Catholic Mission* pp. 76–85, 88, 95–96; W. S. W. Ruschenberger, *Narrative of a Voyage Round the World* 1835–1837 (Philadelphia, 1838), p. 457; *Annales de la Propagation de la Foi*, (November, 1836), 189–191; Kamehameha III to Walsh, December 5, 1836, AH, FO & Ex.

23 The re-arrival of Bachelot and Short and the *Clementine* episode are very heavily documented. Levi Chamberlain and Stephen Reynolds Journals follow events day by day, from April 17 to July 22; Amos Cooke Journal, MS, HMCS does so too. There is a long account in John Colcord Journal, MS, AH. AH, FO & Ex, 1837, is virtually monopolized by the Catholic question—there are documents to and from all the principals, the most important of which are at May 21, 22, 23, 31, June 14, July 10, 17, 21, October 14–13, 23, November 2, 8, 10, December 18, 1837. Copies of some of these are in USDS, Consular Letters, Honolulu, I, December 2, 1837. Yzendoorn, *Catholic Mission*, pp. 98–112, devotes a whole chapter to the affair, using unpublished Catholic sources. Short accounts are in Edward Belcher, *Narrative of a Voyage Round the World...1836–1842...*, 2 vols. (London, 1843), I, pp. 52–55; Abel du Petit-Thouars, *Voyage Autour du Monde...1836–1839*, 4 vols. in 2 (Paris, 1840–1843), I, pp. 327–329; Bingham, *Residence*, pp. 505–514.

24 Stephen Reynolds Journal, August 4, 7, 1835; H. A. Peirce to James Hunnewell, August 6, 1837, Hunnewell MSS; Gerrit Judd to --, October 7, 1838, ABCFM Letters.

25 Elliot to Ka'ahumanu II (Kīna'u), September 29, October 1, 1838, and Ka'ahumanu II to Elliot, October 1, 1838, AH, FO & Ex.

26 Stephen Reynolds Journal, October 30, 1837; Levi Chamberlain Journal, November 1, 1837; *Sandwich Island Gazette*, January 12, 1839; *Kumu Hawaii*, January 16, 1839; Yzendoorn, *Catholic Mission*, p. 126.

27 *Sandwich Island Gazette* June 22, 1839; Yzendoorn, *Catholic Mission*, p. 128.

28 Stephen Reynolds Journal, June 25, 26, 1839; S.N. Castle to Anderson, September 16, 1839, ABCFM Letters; Yzendoorn, *Catholic Mission* pp. 131–132; Bingham, *Residence*, p. 535.

29 *Sandwich Island Gazette*, July 6, 1839.

30 Stewart, *Residence at Sandwich Islands* and *Visit to South Sea*, previously cited. See also Levi Chamberlain Journal, May 5, 1833, February 19, June 1, December 7, 1834; Bingham to Rufus Anderson, March 20, 1833, ABCFM Letters; Levi Chamberlain to Rufus Anderson, March 26, 1833, ABCFM Letters; William Richards to Rufus Anderson, December 7, 1832, ABCFM Letters; E.W. Clark to Rufus Anderson, March 30, 1833, ABCFM Letters; Gerrit Judd to Rufus Anderson., October 23, 1833, ABCFM Letters; Lorrin Andrews to Rufus Anderson, December 21, 1834, ABCFM Letters.

³¹ ABCFM, *Annual Report* 1838, 1839, *passim*. For an excellent treatment of the thirties in mission history, see Bradley, *American Frontier*, pp. 334–391, which gives good context for the happenings in Honolulu. It is particularly thorough on educational developments, the most important of which took place on Maui.

³² The best way into this complex subject is through William G. McLoughlin, *Modern Revivalism Charles Grandison Finney to Billy Graham* (New York, 1959); and Whitney B. Cross, *The Burned-Over Districts: The Social and Intellectual History of Enthusiastic Religion in Western York 1800–1850* (Ithaca, 1950). Alan Gavan Daws, "Polynesian Religious Revivals: A Study With Background," unpublished M. A. thesis, traces the transplanting of evangelistic ideas and techniques to the Hawaiian islands.

³³ Bingham, *Residence*, pp. 442–443.

³⁴ Lowell Smith to Rufus Anderson, November 20, 1837, September 3, 1838, January 3, 1840, ABCFM Letters; Bingham to Rufus Anderson, March 3, April 26, July 30, 1838, April 19, 1839, ABCFM Letters; Richard Armstrong to George Junkin, August 9, 1840, October 12, 1841, Richard Armstrong to Rufus Anderson, September 23, 1841, ABCFM Letters.

³⁵ Bingham, *Residence* p. 521; Jonathan Edwards, ... *Works...*, 8 vols. (Worcester, Mass., 1808), III, 18–21, 44.

Alan Gavan Daws, "Evangelism in Hawaii: Titus Coan and the Great Revival of 1837" Hawaiian Historical Society, Annual Report 69 (Honolulu, 19605, 20–31, goes into some detail on the relationships between Coan and the conservatives; and Daws, "Polynesian Religious Revivals," discusses the mechanisms of conversion identifiable in the Hawaiian awakening. Figures on conversions and admissions are collected in Rufus Anderson, *History of the Sandwich Islands Mission*, pp. 144–167. Station Reports from all islands for 1838–1839, MSS, HMCS, give good summaries of attitudes and accomplishments.

³⁶ The events of 1839 leading up to the visit of *L'Artemise* produced a spate of writing. This account has been assembled from Stephen Reynolds Journal, July 9–August 16, 1839; Levi Chamberlain Journal, July 10–August 15, 1839; Amos Cooke Journal, July 10–August 15, 1839; Bingham to Rufus Anderson, May 15, 1839, ABCFM Letters (a long account of Catholicism to the eve of the Laplace incident); William Richards to Rufus Anderson, August 29, 1839, ABCFM Letters; Peter Brinsmade to U.S. Secretary of State Forsyth, July 17, 1839, USDS, Consular Letters, Honolulu, I (containing the correspondence with the mission and the residents); Samuel Castle to Rufus Anderson, September 16, 1839, ABCFM Letters; *Sandwich Island Gazette* July 13, 20, 27, 1839; *Hawaiian Spectator* (July., October, 1839). AH, FO & Ex, has several folders of documents, filed under the relevant dates, including copies of the Laplace manifesto and the treaty of commerce and friendship, and a manuscript "History of the French War-Ship Artemise." Laplace's version of events is in his *Campagne de Circumnavigation de la Frégate L'Artemise...1837–1840*, 5 vols. (Paris, 1841–1854), V, 428–497, 531–542. The Honolulu Catholic version is in Yzendoorn, *Catholic Mission*, pp. 134–140. A Protestant version is in Bingham, *Residence*, pp. 536–551. See also Jarves, *Sandwich Islands*, pp. 162–166. There were long retrospective accounts in *Suppliment [sic] to the Sandwich Island Mirror* January 15, 1840; and in the "Historical Summary" by Robert Crichton Wyllie in Hawaii, Kingdom, Minister of Foreign Relations, *Report*, 1851, Appendix pp. 299–307.

37 Bingham's a plea for peace is in Bingham to Rufus Anderson, August 5, 1835, ABCFM Letters. For other self-estimates, see Bingham to Anderson, March 20, 1833, ABCFM Letters; and Bingham to Duncan Finlayson, January 24, 1834, HMCS. Armstrong's evaluation is in Richard Armstrong to Reuben Chapman, September 27, 1842, Armstrong Chapman Papers, MSS, Library of Congress, photostat copy in AH. See also Stephen Reynolds Journal, September 16, 1831. There are many descriptions of Kawaiaha'o church. Bingham's own is in *Residence*, pp. 571–574; and there is a most interesting Hawaiian document, detailing the allotment of labor among the Honolulu natives, in AH, FO & Ex, Interior Department, Miscellaneous, Awards and Surveys of Lands, O'ahu-Honolulu, August 1, 1838, An explicit statement concerning Kauikeaouli's governmental administration, and how the church was built.

CHAPTER 5

1 The general implications of constitutional government are well discussed in Kuykendall, *Hawaiian Kingdom*, I, pp. 153–169; and Bradley, *American Frontier*, pp. 319–333. See also Kuykendall, "Constitutions of the Hawaiian Kingdom," Hawaiian Historical Society, Papers, 21 (Honolulu, 1940). The 1840 constitution was succeeded in 1852 by an extremely liberal constitution, American-influenced.

2 The workings of the governor's office may be followed in part in the Governor's Letter Books, MS, AH, which record day-by-day transactions of a minor sort without giving much insight into the relations of the office with the rest of the government.

3 A Notice Respecting The Officers of the City of Honolulu, O'ahu, June 10, 1840, AH, FO & Ex; Lorrin A. Thurston, *Fundamental Law of Hawaii* (Honolulu, 1904), pp. 34–35.

4 For Waialua as a community, see *Polynesian*, August 25, 1849. Chapter VI of the present study mentions a resurgence of community feeling there in 1853. Largely responsible was the Protestant missionary J.S. Emerson, an economic and political activist rather than a narrow evangelist.

5 *Polynesian*, January 10, 1846, April 29, May 20, 1848; *Sandwich Island News*, June 8, 1848. Wylie's preoccupation with community may be traced to his family connections with minor Scottish lairds. Later, in the 1860s, when he became a plantation owner on Kaua'i, he attempted to set up a model community with himself as benevolent lord and master.

6 Wyllie to William Lee, May 28, 1850, AH, F0 & Ex, Local Officials; AH, Privy Council Records, III, 803, 505, VIA, 182a, VII, 203; *Polynesian*, August 30, September 14, October 26, 1850, March 1, 8, 1851, July 7, 1855; AH, Cabinet Council Minutes, December 5, 1850; AH, Journal of House of Representatives, April 28, May 12, 19, 25, 1852; Chief Justice, *Report*, 1854, pp. 12–13; AH, FO & Ex, Constitutional Convention, January 1, 1855; Wyllie to Elisha Allen, November 7, 1856, AH, FO & Ex. In the Henry Whitney Papers, MSS in AH, there is an undated petition to the legislature to incorporate the city and confer on it a charter. The subject and the names of the signatories indicate that it must have been prepared in 1850, but I have been unable to find that it was ever submitted to government.

7   The best single published source on this and all other periods in Hawaiian land history is Jean Hobbs, *Hawaii: A Pageant of the Soil* (Stanford, 193S). For innumerable case histories documenting the passage of land into white men's hands under the old dispensation, the various manuscript volumes compiled at the time of the great land divisions of the 1840s are invaluable. There are three general classifications: Registers, Testimony, and Awards, running in all to thousands of pages, often with survey maps. Each classification has two sub-categories, Native and Foreign. The great majority of foreigners holding land in the old days were around Honolulu, and their experiences are recorded for the most part in the early MS volumes. Thus, Foreign Register, I–III, and Foreign Testimony, I–III, are especially rich in information. There is an enormous reference work which should be consulted first if a single individual or piece of Property is of interest. *Indices of Awards Made by the Board of Commissioners to Quiet Land Titles in the Hawaiian Islands* (Honolulu, 1929), compiled by the office of the Commissioner of Public Lands of the Territory of Hawai'i, breaks down all land transactions of the mid-century into several cross-referenced categories which lead back to the MS material. It also has an excellent short introduction to the early land system. The MS volumes themselves have recently been placed in AH, where they have been microfilmed.

8   Ruschenberger, *Voyage Around the World*, p. 488; *Polynesian*, May 22, 1841.

9   Kennedy to Kamehameha III, October 7, 1836, AH, FO & Ex; *Sandwich Island Gazette*, October 1, 1836; Stephen Reynolds to James Hunnewell, November 14, 1836, January 1, 1837, Hunnewell MSS.

10 Kamehameha III to William IV, November 16, 1836, AH, FO & Ex; Benjamin Parker to David Greene, November 14, 1836, ABCFM Letters; Levi Chamberlain Journal, November 15, 1836; Kuykendall, *Hawaiian Kingdom*, I, p. 148.

11 Du Petit-Thouars to Kamehameha III, July 15, 1837, AH, FO & Ex; Lorrin Andrews to Robert Crichton Wyllie, —, AH, FO & Ex (this contains a copy of the treaty); Bingham, *Residence*, p. 511; Bradley, *American Frontier*, p. 292.

12 H. A. Peirce to James Hunnewell, August 6, 1837, Hunnewell MSS; "Ordinance for the cities of the islands," January 8, 1838, AH, Laws.

13 Proclamation of May 31, 1841, AH, FO & Ex; Stephen Reynolds Journal, June 18, 20, 24, 26, July 12, 14, 1841; Dudoit to Governor of O'ahu, June 25, 26, July 12, 1841, AH, FO & Ex; Kuykendall, *Hawaiian Kingdom*, I, p. 276. For a typical case argued between US Consul Brinsmade and the Hawaiian government in 1845, see several letter copies in AH, FO Letter Book, VI, 1 *ff*.

14 The most convenient way to comprehend the organization of the Board and the principles governing its activities is to consult the collected documents printed in *Indices of Awards Made by the Board of Commissioners* (previously cited), pp. 1–82.

15 *Indices of Awards Made by the Board of Commissioners*, pp. 1–12.

16 C. Brewer & Co.'s Fort Street lot was typical. First white owner was John Gowan, a chief's linguist. With chiefs' approval, it passed to James Hunnewell (1826), Henry A. Peirce (1830), 30, and the firm of C. Brewer (1843). The lot, like most others, lacked definition, and changed shape as roads, streets and lanes were made and straightened. Foreign Register, II, 56 *ff*., Claim 576; Foreign Testimony, II, 7 *ff*., Claim 576; Awards, III, 23, Claim 576.

[17] Foreign Testimony, II, 149 *ff.*, Claims 801–803; III, 102–103, 277, Claim 803.

[18] Foreign Testimony, II, 349 *ff.*, Claims 817–821.

[19] Reynolds was very generous with his time not only to Hannah Holmes but to other Honolulu half-whites. He was a great amateur of the law, and quite well-read. Stephen Reynolds Journal, March 25, 1841, September 17, December 2, 1843, July 15, 1845, April 13, 1846. For Judd and the Davises, see R.G. Davis to W.H. Davis, December 22, 1843, Davis Collection, MSS, California State Library.

[20] *Indices of Awards Made by the Board of Commissioners* lists Honolulu claimants by name, and refers to manuscript volumes and pages where testimony may be found.

[21] Land transactions of Protestant missionaries are compiled in Hobbs, *Hawaii: Pageant*, pp. 157 *ff.*

[22] Foreign Testimony, I, 43, Claim 32, II, 401–402, 428, Claims 85 and 273, III, 278, Claims 785 and 4452.

[23] Foreign Testimony, I, pp. 13–14, Claim 8.

[24] Bingham to Jeremiah Evarts, November 25, 1831, ABCFM Letters.

[25] Stephen Reynolds Journal, September 17, 1837, January 29, 30, 31, February 1, 2, 6, 8, 1838; *Kumu Hawaii*, January 31, 1838.

[26] AH, Privy Council Record, III, pp. 799–80. The 29 street, lane, and place names are listed here, but there is no accompanying map. See also *Hawaiian Annual for 1906*, p. 108.

[27] The increasing incidence of property cases readily becomes apparent in the legal columns of the *Polynesian*. Honolulu's natives as well as foreigners were actively litigious, and the native lawyer as a social type begins to appear in numbers about 1850.

[28] This account has been compiled from the raw information in *Indices of Awards Made by the Board of Commissioners*

[29] *Indices of Awards Made by the Board of Commissioners*, p. 45.

[30] *Friend*, July 1, 1844. Kuykendall, *Hawaiian Kingdom* I, 307; and Morgan, *Hawaii*, pp. 78–79, have statistical tables based on readily available figures. They admit doubts about completeness. I share those doubts, having checked their sources; but in the absence of other information, these figures must be used.

[31] Morgan, *Hawaii*, pp. 80–81.

[32] "Honolulu's Share in the Pacific Whaling Industry of By-Gone Days," *Hawaiian Annual for 1913*, pp. 47 *ff.*; Minister of Finance, *Biennial Report*, 1858, pp. 4–5.

[33] Sullivan, *C. Brewer*, p. 29; Bradley, *American Frontier*, p. 236.

[34] This is an incomplete listing. See *Polynesian*, October 17, 1840, for more detail. Incomparably the best description of the Honolulu business community in this

period is Bradley, *American Frontier*, pp. 211–270, a lengthy treatment of connections with all parts of the world and developments within the town. Bradley has worked as close to the sources as is possible and has devoted much more space to the subject than I can.

[35] I have been very greatly helped in my understanding of Lahaina history by Lawrence Windley, researcher for the Lahaina Restoration Foundation. He is working as close to the facts in Lahaina as Richard Greer is in Honolulu; that is to say, closer than anyone else. Windley has a yard-by-yard and month-by-month knowledge of his subject, and also knows at first-hand a great deal about the waters and shores of the Hawaiian islands. He has been able to save me from several errors of fact and interpretation in the section that follows, which now draws heavily on conversations with him and material from his notes. He and I agree that more work in MS sources might produce a better picture of Lahaina whaling arrivals, particularly if figures were arranged according to seasons rather than by calendar years, as is the case with all collected figures thus far published. In the meantime we must use what is available.

[36] Malo's remarks were printed in translation in the *Sandwich Island News*, March 10, 1847.

[37] *Sandwich Island News*, March 10, April 7, June 23, 1847.

[38] Kuykendall, *Hawaiian Kingdom*, I, p. 305.

[39] Wyllie to C.W. Wheat, December 2, 1855, AH, FO & Ex, Miscellaneous Foreign.

[40] The fate of Wyllie's preventive bills can be followed in the Journal of the House of Representatives for 1850, 1852, 1853, 1854, and 1855. He wrote dozens of letters on the subject, typical of which are: Wyllie to Armstrong, March 6, 1854, AH, FO Letter Book, XV, 199–200; Wyllie to William Martin, July 18, 1854., AH, FO Letter Book, XVIII, 120–121; Wylie to G.N. Robertson, April 2, 1855, AH, FO Letter Book, XX, —. For another viewpoint see Dwight Baldwin to Wyllie, July 7, 1854, AH, FO & Ex. Miscellaneous Local. Prostitution claimed public attention again in the late fifties at the time of the opening of Queen's Hospital in Honolulu. See Chapter VII.

[41] Almost every voyager mentions this towing arrangement; so does Stephen Reynolds Journal, particularly the years 1838–1842, when he was an active pilot in the harbor.

[42] For a typical complaint, see *Sandwich Island News*, September 9, 1846. This subject arose frequently in the Honolulu newspapers, especially with the growth of San Francisco at the end of the forties and the threat of competition from its well-equipped port.

[43] AH, Privy Council Record, IV, pp. 23–25; LeBorgne, Baillie and Lee to Kekūanaō'a, July 1, 1847, AH, FO & Ex; Minister of Interior, *Report*, 1848, p. 6; W.D. Alexander, "Early Improvements in Honolulu Harbor," Hawaiian Historical Society, *Annual Report*, 15 (Honolulu, 1908), p. 15.

[44] For a general discussion of these developments, see Kuykendall, *Hawaiian Kingdom*, II, pp. 1–32.

[45] Alexander, "Early Improvements," pp. 21–22; *Polynesian*, February 4, 1854.

[46] AH, FO & Ex, Privy Council Petitions, May 23, November 19, 1853, and Privy Council Reports, December 19, 1853; Journal of House of Representatives, July 5, 1854; *Polynesian*, July 8, 1854.

[47] Wyllie to Henry Peirce, June 26, 1857, AH, FO Letter Book, XXVI, p. 128.

[48] Alexander, "Early Improvements," brings together many of the documents relating to Kalama's claim. The disposition may be followed conveniently in AH, Privy Council Record, VIII, for 1851, especially at pp. 159, 279–283. There is a heavy correspondence in AH, Interior Department Letter Book, VI; and in AH, FO & Ex early in 1854.

[49] Lee's negotiations may be followed in AH, FO & Ex, Lee Mission.

[50] The harbor improvements were followed with great interest by the Honolulu press. Almost every week there were comments and letters about progress. On the failure of the dredger, see Wyllie to Elisha Allen, October 6, 1856, AH, FO Letter Book, XXIV, p. 99, enclosing an experts' report. Alexander, "Early Improvements," p. 26, makes a good summary statement.

During the fifties there were various proposals for drydocks and marine railways at Honolulu, none of which came to anything. In the same period there were minor improvements in things like water supply to the wharves, buoys, lights, and a wig-wag telegraph to signal ship arrivals off Diamond Head.

[51] A great deal of detailed information on interisland ships is in *Hawaiian Annual* in various issues, especially those for 1889, 1890, 1891, 1894, 1904, 1926, 1931, and 1932. Kuykendall, *Hawaiian Kingdom*, II, pp. 3–7, has a good short account.

[52] *Pacific Commercial Advertiser*, August 4, 1859; *Polynesian*, August 16, 1851. The papers carried regular notices of sailing times.

[53] Almost every resident took an interisland trip at one time or another, and some of the most vivid writing in the MS literature is on this subject. For a visitor's version, see [G.W. Bates], *Sandwich Island Notes* (New York, 1854), pp. 252–254.

[54] *Polynesian*, January 22, February 26, 1853. For some idea of the incidence of wrecks and mishaps, see the articles in *Hawaiian Annual* previously cited; and for a representative period, see *Pacific Commercial Advertiser,* February 12, 1857, April 1, September 30, November, 11, 1858; *Polynesian*, March 27, April 3, August 14, 1858, July 9, 1859.

[55] Stephen Reynolds Journal, May 22, 25, 27, 1846. Not everything under the sun was new: prostitutes stayed aboard longest.

[56] *Polynesian*, April 3, August 7, October 23, 1852, January 29, 1853.

[57] Kuykendall, *Hawaiian Kingdom*, II, p. 16.

[58] Honolulu press regularly carried advertisements for all San Francisco sailings.

[59] Kuykendall, *Hawaiian Kingdom*, II, pp. 17–18.

[60] For a general discussion of the early period, see John H. Kemble, "Pioneer Hawaiian Steamers," Hawaiian Historical Society, *Annual Report*, 53 (Honolulu, 1946), pp. 7–25.

61 *Polynesian*, April 2, 1853.

62 *Friend*, September 1, 1844; *Polynesian*, November 11, 1848, February 15, 1851.

63 Howard's proposal is in AH, Interior Department Letters, 1851; the ordinance granting privileges is filed there at July 25, 1851. See also AH, Privy Council Record, VIB, pp. 402, 405; *Polynesian*, August 2, 1851.

64 *Polynesian*, January 31, 1852.

65 Richard Bowlin to William Lee, June 23, July 8, 1853; Wyllie to Bowlin, August 10, 1853; Bowlin to Wyllie, September 26, 1853, all in AH, FO & Ex; AH, Privy Council Record, VII, pp. 245, 217, 255, VIII, pp. 25, 41, 43, 67; Ryckman *et al.* to Privy Council, AH, Privy Council Petitions, November 14, 1853; published *Laws* of 1854 legislative session, pp. 8–11.

66 Stephen Reynolds Journal, December 7, 10, 1853; *Polynesian*, December 10, 17, 24, 1853, January 7, 28, April 1, 1854.

67 *Polynesian*, February 25, 1854.

68 *Polynesian*, April 29, June 24, July 8, September 2, 1854.

69 Kuykendall, *Hawaiian Kingdom*, II, p. 13.

70 Gregg to Marcy, April 25, 1856, USDS, Dispatches, *Hawaii*, VI. Ryckman claimed to have lost $100,000 on the speculation, and he tried to recoup some of this by billing Gregg for the use of the *Sea Bird* to bring Prince Alexander Liholiho from Hawai'i to Honolulu at the height of the 1854 annexation excitement. There is a correspondence on this in the Gregg Letter Books for 1855, MSS in AH, in the course of which Ryckman raised his claims as high as $450,000. See also *Polynesian*, March 22, 1856; and several letters between Wylie and Ryckman in April-June, 1855, in AH, FO & Ex, Miscellaneous Foreign.

71 Kuykendall, *Hawaiian Kingdom*, II, p. 15.

72 *Polynesian*, October 9, 1858.

73 *Polynesian*, January 22, 1848, listed voyage tines from major world ports. For a characteristic complaint, see *Sandwich Island Gazette*, March 18, 1837.

74 Charles Bishop to James Milledge, May 23, 1873, AH, FO Letter Book, LII, pp 216–217.

75 Henry A. Meyer *et al., Hawaii: Its Stamps and Postal History* (New York, 1948) is exhaustive on this and related topics.

76 AH, Privy Council Record, VIB, p. 443; Meyer, *Hawaii Stamps*, pp. 18–20, 97.

77 The published *Reports* of the Minister of the Interior give year-by-year growth figures.

78 *Polynesian*, October 14, 1854, November 29, 1856.

79 Meyer, *Hawaii Stamps, passim.*

80 Foreign Testimony, III, 307, Claim 3122.

81 John Colcord Journal; Stephen Reynolds Journal, May 21, 1837; Diell to Hunnewell, May 29, 1837, Hunnewell MSS. The best account of Diell's accomplishment is in Bradley, *American Frontier*, pp. 377–381.

82 A biography of Damon, written by his grand-daughter Ethel Moseley Damon, will be published shortly, based for the most part on the Damon Papers, MSS in HMCS, and material in Damon's monthly newspaper, *The Friend.* I have been able to see the work in MS and galley proof, and the following account of Damon draws from this source, and from perusal of the Damon Papers and *The Friend.*

83 AH, Privy Council Record, IV, p. 418.

84 Convictions may be followed in the published Reports of the Chief Justice, beginning in 1852. There is a large MS and periodical literature on sailor crime and misadventure. The following sources are selected to give an idea of the range of the subject: Documents in AH, FO & Ex, May 21–22, 1846; Wyllie to Captain Howison, May 25, 1846, AH, FO Letter Book, V, pp. 167–168; Testimony in AH, FO & Ex, August 21, 1846; AH, Privy Council Record, III, p. 163; William Miller to Wylie, July 2, 1850, AH, FO & Ex; Stephen Reynolds Journal, October 20, 21, 1851; *Polynesian,* April 9, November 26, 1853, December 9, l854, May 16, November 21, 1857; *Pacific Commercial Advertiser*, December 4, 1856.

85 Proclamation of Kekūanaō'a, November 18, 1842, AH, FO & Ex; Ezra Smith and others to Kekūanaō'a, November 22, 1842, AH, FO & Ex, and other petitions filed there; Articles of Agreement between Kekūanaō'aand J. Hayward, June 26, 1846, AH, FO & Ex; Stephen Reynolds Journal. October 29, November 17, 18, 1842.

86 US Consul Alfred Caldwell eventually had to bar Hawaiian lawyers from his office. They continued to loiter outside. Caldwell to W.H. Seward, December 18, 1861, USDS, Consular Letters, Honolulu, VIII. The area of dispute over control of seamen was large, and the MS literature reflects this. Typical cases are discussed in: Wyllie to Jules Dudoit, April 22, 1816, AH, FO & Ex; Wyllie to Captain Glynn, November 30, 1849, AH, FO Letter Book, XIa, p. 442; H. Holdsworth to Minister of Interior, September 5, 1855, AH, Interior Department; David Gregg to Wyllie, December 1, 1857, AH, FO & Ex, US Commissioner; Thomas Dryer to Wyllie, December 26, 1861, AH, FO & Ex, US Commissioner; *Polynesian*, October 29, 1853, February 11, 1854, November 7, 1857, April 17, 1858.

87 John Diell, "Sketch of Honolulu, Oahu," *Hawaiian Spectator*, I, p. 2 (April, 1838), p. 86; Wyllie to J. A. Forbes, December 2, 1844, AH, British Consulate, Letters To Secretary of State and Others, ProConsul Wyllie, 1844; Wyllie to Anthony Barclay, May 28, 1846, AH, FO & Ex; Miller to Aberdeen, December 31, 1845, copy in AH, FO & Ex; Miller to Secretary of Admiralty, December 31, 1845, AH, British Consulate, Letter Book, Admiralty; Miller to Addington, February 16, 1846, FO 58/44; Alexander Abell to John 'I'i, February 24, 1846, AH, FO & Ex; Miller to Captain Collinson, December 21, 1850, AH, British Consulate, Letter Book, General Correspondence.

88 *Hawaiian Reports*, I, pp. 262–263.

89 The best sources on this subject are of course not the consuls, whose dispatches are unrevealing. US Commissioner David Gregg, however, had much to say,

publicly and privately, about Angel and others. David Gregg Diary, MS, AH, May 15, July 8, September 7, 1854, February 13, 14, 23, March 31, April 14, 16, 21, October 2, 13, December 9, 1855, June 24, September 26, October 24, November 25, 1857; Gregg to Marcy, April 13, June 18, 1855, October 17, November 10, 1856, USDS, Dispatches, Hawai'i, VI–VII; Gregg to Lewis Cass, October 30, 1857, Gregg Letter Books. See also Lewis Cass to James Borden, May 19, 1859, copy in AH, FO & Ex. US Commissioner; Borden to Wylie, March 21, 1861, AH, FO & Ex, US Commissioner.

[90] William C. Parke, *Personal Reminiscences of William Cooper Parke Marshal of the Hawaiian Islands From 1850 to 1884* (Cambridge 1891), pp. 9–18. For good detail on prison conditions, see The White Slaves in Woahoo Fort to [T. C. B. Rooke], August 24, 1835, AH, Emma Collection, T.C.B. Rooke, Miscellaneous Letters and Documents; Prisoners to G.P. Judd, June 27, 1846, AH, Interior Department, Miscellaneous; AH, Privy Council Record, IV, pp. 328–334; Report on Disorders Complained of By French Consul, January 11, 1848, AH, FO & Ex; Minister of Interior, *Report*, 1848, p. 6; Lorrin Andrews to G.P. Judd, January 8, 1847, MI, FO & Ex; Marshal's Report, April 1, 1847, AH, Attorney-General, Miscellaneous; AH, Privy Council Record, IV, pp. 362–384.

[91] For various road problems and attempted solutions, see List of Subscribers to Nu'uanu Road, December 24, 1840, AH, FO & Ex; Proclamation of Kekūanaō'a, February 15, 1841, AH, FO & Ex; R.W. Wood and others to Kekūanaō'a, January 4, 1843, AH, FO & Ex; Notice of Kekūanaō'a, November 24, 1846, AH, FO & Ex; Stephen Reynolds Journal, April 8, 9, 22, 30, 1835, July 22, 1840, January 19, 1841, April 11, 1847; *Polynesian*, January 2, 1841, October 26, 1844, March 22, June 28, 1845, November 28, 1846, January 8, 1848, October 5, 1850, February 7, 1852, September 15, October 13, 1855. Street improvements year by year can be followed in published *Reports* of the Minister of the Interior.

[92] The best single place to begin a study of public morality and related legislation is in the published *Reports* of the Chief Justice. Statistics of crime were usually included. These figures present a very erratic picture. By reference to the periodical press, it can be seen that variations were related to waves of activity or inactivity among the police rather than to any great change in the incidence of acts regarded as criminal. No matter how the figures are viewed, Honolulu as compared with the rest of the kingdom provided a disproportionate number of cases of drunkenness and fornication, among both foreigners and natives.

[93] For a general picture of Hawaiian education, see Benjamin O. Wist, *A Century Of Public Education In Hawaii, October 15, 1840 To October 15, 1940* (Honolulu, 1940); and G.A. Odgers, "Education in Hawaii, 1820–1893," unpublished Ph.D. thesis, Stanford, 1935. Both are administrative rather than social in emphasis. Kuykendall, *Hawaiian Kingdom*, I, pp. 317–367, has a short account of the period to 1834. The published *Reports* of the Minister of Public Instruction are useful, though infuriatingly inconsistent in statistical matters.

[94] For a sampling of missionary attitudes to the problems of raising children in the islands, see the Unpublished Minutes of the Prudential Committee of the Sandwich Island Mission. See also the following in ABCFM Letters: Bingham to Jeremiah Evarts, October 15, 1828; Levi Chamberlain to Anderson, October 16, 1832; William Richards to Anderson, December 7, 1832; Mrs. Thurston to Mrs. Goodell, October 16, 1829, October 23, 1834; Reuben Tinker to Anderson, December 1, 1836. See also the letters in HMCS: Bingham to Samuel Ruggles, January 8, 1834; Joseph

Goodrich to Bingham, December 11, 1835; Martha Goodrich to Nancy Barnes, May 15, 1833; Juliette Cooke to Mother and Friends, July 4, 1848. In the Baldwin file, HMCS, is a 57-article set of instructions made out by Dwight Baldwin to his children concerning behavior in America.

[95] Mary Charlotte Alexander and Charlotte Peabody Dodge, *Punahou, 1841–1941* (Berkeley, 1941), pp. 53–71. This is the official history, based on documents in HMCS. It is quite well done, with copious quotations from MS materials, and my account follows it for the most part.

[96] Alexander and Dodge, *Punahou*, pp. 71–98.

[97] Alexander and Dodge, *Punahou*, p. 230.

[98] Alexander and Dodge, *Punahou*, pp. 117–134.

[99] Throughout the fifties, the two principal Honolulu newspapers, the *Polynesian* (government-oriented but editorially independent) and the *Pacific Commercial Advertiser* (published by a missionary's son, Henry Whitney) fought a running battle over the existence, purpose, usefulness, exclusiveness, and ambitiousness of Punahou and O'ahu College. The *Polynesian* generally argued that government should not support an exclusivist school. Whitney took the stand that the good of O'ahu College was the good of the nation.

[100] *Pacific Commercial Advertiser*, January 28, 1858, January 1, 1859; Alexander and Dodge, *Punahou*, pp. 177–224.

[101] *Polynesian*, August 28, 1858.

[102] HMCS has genealogical charts of mission families.

[103] Alexander and Dodge, *Punahou*, pp. 288–289.

[104] Their first pupils included Moses Kekūāiwa, 9, son of Governor Kekūanaō'aand the kuhina nui Kīna'u, adopted by Kaikio'ewa, and presumptive Governor of Kaua'i; Lot Kamehameha, 8, brother of Moses, adopted by Hoapili, and presumptive Governor of Maui; Alexander Liholiho, 5, brother of Moses and Lot, adopted by King Kauikeaouli, and heir apparent to the throne; Bernice Pauahi, 7, daughter of the Honolulu chiefs Konia and Pākī, adopted by Kīna'u; and William Charles Lunalilo, 4, sons of Charles Kana'ina and Kekāuluohi, the successor of Kīna'u.

Others joined the school, bringing total enrollment to 16. Every Hawaiian monarch after Kauikeaouli (Kamehameha III) was a student there in early life. Alexander Liholiho became Kamehameha IV (1851–1863), and his wife Emma was a fellow-student. Lot became Kamehameha V (1863–1872). Lot remained single. On his death the throne was vacant. The monarchy became elective. William Lunalilo was chosen to reign (1873–1874). On his early death, yet another former pupil of the Chiefs' Children's School was elected king—David Kalākaua, son of Paakea and Keohokalole, adopted by Haaheo. After Kalākaua's death in 1891, his sister Lydia Kamaka'eha came to the throne as Queen Lili'uokalani, last monarch of Hawai'i.

For biographical information on the students, see Mary Atherton Richards, *The Chiefs' Children's School* (Honolulu, 1937). This volume, published on the centenary of the Cookes' arrival at Honolulu, consists of extracts from their journals and letters. It gives a quite full account of most happenings at the school, but there are some miscopyings and a good many errors in dating. I have in almost every case cited not the book but the MS sources.

[105] Cooke Journal, May 6–9, 1840; Juliette Cooke to Sister, April 5, 1840, HMCS; Stephen Reynolds Journal, May 16, 1840.

[106] Juliette Cooke to Sister, January 12, February 1, April 5, 1840, HMCS; Juliette Cooke to Mother, April 11, 1840, HMCS; Juliette Cooke to Brother, May 16, 1840, HMCS; Amos Cooke Journal, May 28, 1810, July 21, 1841, March 3, 1842; Juliette Cooke to Friends, May 9, July 4, 1844, HMCS.

[107] Amos Cooke Journal, August 13, 1839.

[108] Juliette Cooke to Mother, November 5, 1844, HMCS; Amos Cooke to David Greene, March 22, 1845, HMCS.

[109] Richards, *Chiefs' Children's School*, passim.

[110] Walter Colton, *Deck and Port* (New York, 1847), p. 337.

[111] Amos Cooke to A.F. Waller, April 8, 1843, MS in Oregon Historical Society Library, copy in HMCS; Amos Cooke Journal, March 20, 1842, October 30, 1843; Amos Cooke to Aunt Sally, March 30, 1846, HMCS.

[112] Moses' letters and other details are in Amos Cooke Journal, September 5–22, 1845; they were printed in Hawaiian Historical Society, *Annual Report*, 30 (Honolulu, 1921). The disposition of the case is in AH, Privy Council Record, I, p. 51 For continued misdeeds of the young chiefs, see Amos Cooke Journal for the rest of 1845, especially September 26, December 5; and Amos Cooke to Charles Montague, December 15, 1845, HMCS. For Steen Bille's visit, see *Steen Bille's Bericht Uber Die Reise Der Corvette Galathea Um Die Welt…1845–1847*, tr. W. v. Rosen, 2 vols. (Leipzig, 1852). In HMCS is a typescript English translation of the Hawaiian portion. At pp. 43 *ff.* of the typescript is the conversation with Moses.

[113] Amos Cooke Journal follows the cases of Moses, the queen, and Abigail day by day from December 26, 1846, to February 14, 1847. A copy of Moses' confession is there. See also AH, Privy Council Record, II, pp. 304–306. Kekūanaō'a's notice appeared in the *Polynesian* for some time.

[114] The courtship and marriage may be followed in John R. Jasper to Amos Cooke, July 23, August —, 1847, HMCS; AH, Privy Council Record, IV, p. 29; Amos Cooke Journal, July 23, 27, September 3, 1847; Juliette Cooke to Sister, August 28, 1847, HMCS; Juliette Cooke to Mother, November 6, 1847, HMCS; Levi Chamberlain Journal, September 2, 1847; Stephen Reynolds Journal, September 2, 1847.

[115] Amos Cooke Journal, September 21, 1844, December 8, 1847, December 31, 1848; Juliette Cooke to Mother, August 25, 1844, HMCS; Juliette Cooke to Aunt and Mother, March 12, 1845, HMCS; Amos Cooke to Mother, March 19, 1846, HMCS; Estrella Mott, "Honolulu 1848," typescript, HHS.

[116] Juliette Cooke to Mother, November 27, 1848, HMCS; Amos Cooke Journal, November 24, December 18, 1848.

[117] AH, Privy Council Record, III, pp. 121, 19–196 Amos Cooke Journal, October 2, 7, December 8, 1848, January 8, 1849.

[118] The courtship and marriage may be followed in Amos Cooke Journal, March 14, 30, August 30, September 1, 4, 6, 15, November 1, 14, 16, December 10, 1849, March 28, May 25, 30, 1850; Amos Cooke to Fanny Montague, September 18, 1847, February 25, 1850, HMCS. See also Harold Winfield Kent, *Charles Reed Bishop, Man of Hawaii* (Palo Alto, 1965), pp. 22–32.

[119] The school, renamed the Royal School in 1846, became a select school for white and half-caste children, and later flourished for several years as a competitor of Punahou, as previously noted.

[120] Amos Cooke to Rufus Anderson, February 22, 1850, ABCFM Letters.

[121] Emma Yates, "Reminiscences of Honolulu," MS, HHS.

[122] The "Monsarrat case" will be discussed in a later chapter.

[123] David Gregg Diary, August 11, 1854; Amos Cooke Journal, August 12, 23, September 23, 1854, February 5, 1855; *Saturday Press*, October 14, 1882.

[124] David Gregg Diary, August 11, 1854; AH, Privy Council Record, III, pp. 394–396; Amos Cooke to Fanny Montague, February 25, 1850, HMCS; Amos Cooke Journal, March 12, 1855; William Lee to Joel Turrill, December 29, 1850, Turrill Collection, MSS, HHS. Many letters from the Turrill Collection are printed in Hawaiian Historical Society, *Annual Report*, 66 (Honolulu, 1958), pp. 27–92.

[125] W.D. Alexander, "The Oahu Charity School," Hawaiian Historical Society, *Annual Report*, 16 (Honolulu, 1908), 20–38, gives a general view of the school. Bradley, *American Frontier*, pp. 382–386, has a good, short, very well documented summary of its first decade.

[126] Like most other matters that required mission members to search their souls the Johnstone case produced a great deal of writing. Among the letters of Levi Chamberlain, in HMCS, is a file titled Correspondence in Reference to Mr. Johnstone's Building. See also Chamberlain to Rufus Anderson, December 3, 1833, ABCFM Letters; Stephen Reynolds Journal, June 12, 13, 1834, June 7–11, 16, 17, 19, 23, 26, 1835; Jonathan Green to David Greene, June 22, 1835, ABCFM Letters; Chamberlain to Anderson, August 3, 1835, ABCFM Letters; Reuben Tinker and Jonathan Spaulding to Johnstone, August 3, 1835, ABCFM Letters; Johnstone to Anderson, August 4, 1835, ABCFM Letters; Bingham to Anderson, August 5, 1835, ABCFM Letters.

[127] Stephen Reynolds Journal, January 13, 20, July 30, August 4, 1833; Levi Chamberlain Journal, May 9, July 30, August 2, 9, 1833; Henry A. Peirce to Bingham, March 15, 1833, ABCFM Letters.

[128] Judd to Anderson, October 23, 1833, August 3, 1835, ABCFM Letters; Bingham to Anderson, August 5, 1835, ABCFM Letters.

[129] *Sandwich Island Gazette*, April 29, 1837; *Sandwich Island Mirror*, December 15, 1839, January 15, February 15, 1840.

[130] Stephen Reynolds to T.O. Larkin, June 27, 1844, Larkin Papers, MSS in Bancroft Library, University of California, copies of some documents in Kuykendall

Collection. The papers have been published: see George Peter Hammond, ed., *The Larkin Papers...*, 8 vols. (Berkeley, 1951—). See also Stephen Reynolds Journal, January 20, 21, 22, 24, February 2, 1844; *Polynesian*, August 24, 1844.

[131] *Polynesian*, April 10, 1841.

[132] Minister of Public Instruction, *Report*, 1851, p. 16; Laws 1851, pp. 84–86; *Polynesian*, January 4, June 7, December 27, 1851, January 3, 1852 (committee elections were held in January of each year and reported in the press); Kuykendall, *Hawaiian Kingdom* I, pp. 363–364.

[133] Stephen Reynolds Journal, January 16, 1846, September 18, 21, 1848, January 30, 1849; *Polynesian*, December 5, 1846, February 27, 1847; *Sandwich Island News*, February 24, 1847.

[134] Stephen Reynolds Journal, November 26, 1845, February 28, March 21, July 4, 11, 1849, September 29, 1854.

[135] Stephen Reynolds Journal, May 29, 1844, June 9, 10, 20, 22, 23, September 25, October 17, 1846, August 7, 1851. Brinsmade's cordiality emerged precisely at the time when he was falling out with the mission dominated, non-dancing Hawaiian government over Ladd & Co.'s business affairs. He was drifting away from the New England version of correct society. The mission itself, of course, was colder by far to the dancing school than to the OCS. The ultimate victory of dancing is discussed in Chapter VII.

[136] Stephen Reynolds Journal, April 1, 5, August 25, 1846, July 9, 1847, May 2, 1848, January 16, October 19, 1849, January 11, 20, 1850, May 5, 1854. Reynolds' journal over a long period of time shows the locus of sharpest racial feeling to be with these women: Mrs. Peter Corney and her daughters, Mrs. John Dominis, Mrs. Charles Brewer, and Mrs. Jules Dudoit. The last was the wife of the ex-French consular agent; the others were Americans, wives or widows of fairly well-off merchants and sea-captains who set a social tone among the town's non-mission elite.

[137] Stephen Reynolds Journal, October 28, 1844, April 13, May 28, November 23, 25, December 17, 18, 22, 1846, July 5, 6, l847, January 16, 17, 20, June 6, 7, 1849.

[138] Stephen Reynolds Journal, September 20, 22, 1840, October 7, 1842, April 22, 1843, June 16, 17, 20 August 3, 1844, January 3, 4, 5, 13, 22, 1846, July 28, November 26, December 1, 6, 7, 11, 17, 1848, January 7, 9, 1850, November 8, 1851; *Polynesian* January 6, 1848.

CHAPTER 6

[1] The grant was made with the consent of Ka'ahumanu, who in 1826 was regent for the boy king Kauikeaouli. In making over the land to the British Consulate, the Hawaiian chiefs expressed their gratitude for sympathy shown by the British government upon the death of King Liholiho in London in 1824. The land was to be used for official purposes by the incumbent consul.

[2] AH, FO & Ex, December 9, 1826, has several copies of the lease; I have been unable to find the original. Presumably, it remained in Charlton's possession.

An immense tangle of documentation grew up over Charlton's claim. Several printed pamphlets of the Hawaiian and British governments are bound together in AH under the title of *Charlton Land Claims*. These draw on the following MS sources: AH, FO & Ex; AH, FO Letter Books; FO 58; AH, Letter Books of Pro-Consul Wyllie, 1814; AH, Privy Council Record; AH, Cabinet Council Record. Partisan summaries of events appear in the lengthy Statement of Facts Relating to the Claim for Land, in Honolulu, by Richard Charlton..., FO Letter Book, VIII, pp. 312 *ff.*, and in *Sandwich Island News*, March 3, 1847.

3   Interview between Charlton, Kekāuluohi and Kekūanaō'a, April 16, 1840; Charlton to Kamehameha III, April 18, June 29, 1840; Kamehameha III to Charlton, June 30, 1840; all in AH, FO & Ex.

4   Kekūanaō'a to Charlton, January 16, 1841, AH, FO & Ex; Document in AH, FO & Ex, August 18, 1841; Charlton to Kekūanaō'a, August 20, 1841, AH, FO & Ex; Kekūanaō'ato Charlton, February 7, 1842, AH, FO & Ex; Stephen Reynolds Journal, August 4, September 15, 1840, August 19, 1841.

5   George Pelly and others to Charlton, February 19, 1841, AH, FO & Ex (copy); Kekūanaō'a to Charlton, February 22, 1841, AH, FO & Ex; Kekūanaō'a to Pelly and others, February—, 1841, AH, FO & Ex; Charlton to Kekūanaō'a, March 5, 1841, AH, FO & Ex; Juliette Cooke to her sister, March 1, 1841, HMCS; Amos Cooke Journal, March 8, 1841; Levi Chamberlain Journal, March 8, 1841; *Polynesian*, March 13, 20, 1841.

6   Charlton to the Captain or Commander of any of Her Britannic Majesty's Ships arriving at the Sandwich Islands, September 26, 1842, copy in AH, FO & Ex; Charlton to Kamehameha III, September 26, 1842, AH, FO & Ex.

7   The best short treatment of Simpson is in Bradley, *American Frontier*, pp. 410–411, 422–424. See also Simpson's own *The Sandwich Islands...* (London, 1843), *passim*.

8   Many documents relating to Pelly vs. Charlton were printed in the British government's *Correspondence Relative to the Sandwich Islands...* (London, 1843). The case can be followed in the same general sources in AH as listed for the Charlton land claims. For Simpson's first days as "consul," see Stephen Reynolds Journal, September 27, October 1, 8, 10, 11, 1842. The diplomatic literature on the circumstances of the Paulet visit is collected in Kuykendall, *Hawaiian Kingdom*. I, pp. 206–213; and Bradley, *American Frontier*, pp. 426–427.

9   Stephen Reynolds Journal, February 11, 12, 13, 14, 1843; William Paty Journal, MS, AH, February 11, 13, 1843; Levi Chamberlain Journal, February 11, 13, 1843.

10   William Paty Journal, February 18, 1843.

11   Events from Paulet's arrival to the cession are covered day by day in the journals of William Paty, Amos Cooke, Levi Chamberlain and Stephen Reynolds. Paulet's successive demands are recorded in British Commission Letter Book in AH. Simpson's reports to the British government are in FO 58. Hawaiian government responses are in AH, FO & Ex (see especially folder marked Dispute With Paulet). A good resume account from an indignantly partisan American viewpoint is Gorham Gilman, "Honolulu As It Is," MS, HHS.

12   See sources cited in footnote 11; also Judd, *Honolulu*, p. 94.

[13] For more detail, see Kuykendall, *Hawaiian Kingdom*, I, pp. 216–217.

[14] William Paty Journal, February 25, 1843; Gilman, "Honolulu–1848;" Stephen Reynolds Journal, February 25, 1843; Richards, *Chiefs' Children's School*, p. 169.

[15] Judd to the Commissioners in Europe, February 27, 1843, AH, British Commission; Judd to Paulet, February 27, 1843, AH, British Commission. Marshall described his mission in *Harper's Magazine*, LXVII (1883), pp. 511–520. See also Judd, *Honolulu*, p. 95; William Paty Journal, March 11, 1843; Stephen Reynolds Journal, March 11, 1843. Judd's relations with the Paulet regime are well covered in Judd, *Doctor Judd*, pp. 114–125.

[16] The proceedings of the commission are arranged chronologically in AH, FO & Ex, British Commission. Copies of correspondence are in British Commission Letter Book, AH. See also Stephen Reynolds Journal, March 2, 3, 4, April 27, May 1, 1843; Amos Cooke Journal, April 28, 1843.

[17] Judd's quarrel with Paulet appears in AH, FO & Ex, British Commission, documents for May 1–11. See especially Judd's journal filed there; and also the letter of Kamehameha III to Judd, June 12, 1843. See also *Fragments: Family Record, House of Judd*, 6 vols. (Honolulu, 1903–1935), I, p. 19, 21, II, pp. 165, 173; Judd to David Greene, August 20, 1844, January 25, 1845, ABCFM Letters: Judd, *Doctor Judd*, pp. 121–123.

[18] Paulet to Kamehameha III, July 18, 1843, AH, FO & Ex, British Commission; Gorham Gilman Journal, MS, HHS, July 7, 1843; Stephen Reynolds Journal, May 24, July 11, 12, 13, 14, 19, 1843.

[19] Thomas to Kekūanaō'a, July 26, 1843, AH, FO & Ex, British Commission; Stephen Reynolds Journal, July 26, 27, 28, 29, 1843; Levi Chamberlain Journal, July 26, 27, 28, 1843.

[20] Restoration documents are collected in AH, FO & Ex, British Commission, July 31, 1843. See also Gorham Gilman Journal, July 31, 1843; Levi Chamberlain Journal, July 31, 1843; Stephen Reynolds Journal, July 31, 1843; Judd to William Richards, August 1, 1843, AH, FO & Ex; *Friend*. August 1, 1843, for eyewitness accounts of the celebrations.

[21] Day-by-day accounts of the festivities of August 1–10 are in the journals of Gorham Gilman, Stephen Reynolds, Levi Chamberlain, Amos Cooke, and William Paty. The restoration hymn is in AH, FO & Ex, British Commission, July, 1843; and in MS, HHS.

[22] Levi Chamberlain Journal, August 10, 16, 19, 25, 1843; Stephen Reynolds Journal, August 10, 11, 12, 14, 16, 18, 22, 23, 25, 26, September 25, 1843; Aberdeen to Timothy Ha'alilio and William Richards, November 15, 1843, AH, FO & Ex, British Commission; Addington to Secretary of the Admiralty, November 21, 1843, FO 58/19; Canning to Herbert, June 13, 1844, FO 58/32; *Friend*, March 1, 1844; Judd to Wyllie, September 4, 1844; Wyllie to Judd, September 4, 1844, both in AH, FO & Ex; *Polynesian*, August 17, September 7, 1844. On Paulet and the laundryman, see Wyllie to Judd, October 7, 1814, AH, FO & Ex; and several letters in AH, FO & Ex, British Consulate, October, 1844.

[23] Aberdeen to Ha'alilio and Richards, September 12, 1843, AH, FO & Ex; Addington to Ha'alilio and Richards, September 30, 1843, AH, FO & Ex; Richards and Ha'alilio

to Kamehameha III, September 30, 1843, AH, FO & Ex; Ha'alilio and Richards to Aberdeen, October 7, 1843, FO 58/18; Aberdeen to Richards, March 13, May 8, 1844, AH, FO & Ex. A full account of negotiations is in Kuykendall, *Hawaiian Kingdom*, I, pp. 221–226.

²⁴ This account has been compiled from the hundreds of pages of testimony collected in the printed *Charlton Land Claims* pamphlets, MS versions of which are, as previously noted, in AH, FO & Ex, throughout the forties. See especially Judd to Richards, Ha'alilio and Simpson, May 4, 1844, AH, FO & Ex. A very useful annotated map is at p. 75 of the *Investigation...of Land Claimed by Richard Charlton...* (Honolulu, 1846), bound with the Charlton Land Claims. See also Stephen Reynolds Journal, March 30, 1844.

²⁵ Stephen Reynolds Journal, May 31, 1844; Amos Cooke Journal, May 30, 1844.

²⁶ Many documents are printed in a Hawaiian government pamphlet, *Pelly vs. Charlton* (Honolulu, 1845). MS versions are in AH. See especially A Protest by Charlton, June 13; 1844, AH, FO & EX; Judd to Sir George Simpson, June 22, 1844, AH, FO Letter Book, II, pp. 2–3; William Miller to George Pelly, June 20, 1844, AH, FO & Ex, British Consulate, Letter Book, General Correspondence, IV; Wyllie to J. Bidwell, September 5, 1844, AH, Letter Books of Pro-Consul Wyllie, To FO, I; Wyllie to George Pelly, AH, FO Letter Book, V, pp. 252–261. See also Stephen Reynolds Journal, June 6, 7, 18, 19, 20, 21, 1844; *Polynesian*, June 15, 22, 1844.

²⁷ Wyllie to Anthony Barclay, December 2, 18145, AH, FO & Ex: Stephen Reynolds Journal, February 18, 1846.

²⁸ To document this fully it would be necessary to cite literally hundreds of letters and depositions in AH. The *Charlton Land Claims* Pamphlets offer a beginning. For the surpassing triviality of the Beretania affair, see Wyllie to Anthony Barclay, September 28, 1846, AH, FO Letter Book, XI, p. 164 ff.; Judd to Wyllie, April 12, 26, 1847, AH, FO & Ex; Judd to Miller, April 15, 1847, AH, FO & Ex; and many other letters in FO & Ex for April, 1847. For the settlement of Victoria Kamāmalu's claim, see Keoni Ana to John 'I'i and Kekūanaō'a, August 17, 1847, AH, Interior Department Letter Book, II, Part 1, pp. 110–111.

²⁹ Documentation for the French-Greenway case matches that of Charlton's land claim in bulk and impenetrability. The Hawaiian government published a lengthy pamphlet in 1847. MS documents fill an entire file drawer in AH, and hundreds more letters are in AH, FO & Ex. Useful summary accounts are in Wyllie to Maguire Jardine & Co., October 20, 1845, AH, FO Letter Book, IX, p. 196 ff.; William French to the British Commission, May 22, 1843, AH, FO & Ex, British Commission. The *Polynesian* followed the case closely throughout the forties; so did Stephen Reynolds, who was heavily involved, and who recorded affairs in his journal.

³⁰ Statements of William Baker, Jr., and J. F. B. Marshall, February 14, 1843, AH, FO & Ex.

³¹ Copies of documents on Greenway's sanity are in AH, FO Letter Book, I, p. 47 ff. See also *Polynesian*, May 18, 1844; Stephen Reynolds Journal, January 16, February 16, May 9, 1844; William Paty Journal, April 5, 1844.

³² *Sandwich Island News*, September 23, 1846; *Polynesian*, March 20, 1847.

33 Documents on Greenway vs. Charlton are in AH, FO & Ex, November 1–10, 1846, and January 18, 1848.

34 *Polynesian.* December 6, 1841, February 21, 1852.

35 Material on Ladd & Co. was published in *Report of the Proceedings* and *Evidence in the Arbitration Between the King and Government of the Hawaiian Islands and Messrs. Ladd & Co....* (Honolulu, 1846). All major MS sources in AH, and journals and letters of the forties contain numbers of documents. *The Sandwich Island News* was established partly to present Ladd & Co.'s version of events as against the official version in the *Polynesian.* A good summary account is in the lengthy Plain Facts in the suit of Messrs. Ladd and Co. against the Hawaiian Government for $378,000, AH, FO & Ex, January 15, 1847. The standard secondary sources have short discussions of the case.

36 Hunnewell to Levi Chamberlain, December 15, 1832, HMCS; Peirce to Hunnewell, May 6, August 10, 16, October 4, December 1, 1833, January 26, May 6, 1834, Hunnewell MSS; Levi Chamberlain Journal, July 27, 1833.

37 Stephen Reynolds Journal, July 27, 29, August 8, November 23, 1833, March 8, October 15, 30, December 11, 12, 1834, March 26, April 6, 1835, October 28, 1836; Levi Chamberlain Journal, November 13, 1833, February 17, October 2, 1834, September 23, 1835; Chamberlain to Rufus Anderson, October 9, 1834, ABCFM Letters; Brinsmade to Mrs. Peter Brinsmade, November 23, 1836, Brinsmade Papers, MSS, AH; John Diell to James Hunnewell, May 29, 1837, Hunnewell MSS.

38 The Kōloa lease is printed in *Ladd Arbitration*, appendix, pp. 15–16. The William Hooper Papers, MSS in UH, describe the first years of operation. Drawing heavily on the Hooper papers are Frances Jackson, "Koloa Plantation Under Ladd And Company, 1835–1845," unpublished M.A. thesis, UH, 1958; and Arthur C. Alexander, *Koloa Plantation, 1835–1935...* (Honolulu, 1937).

39 Kuykendall, *Hawaiian Kingdom*, I, p. 178.

40 Stephen Reynolds Journal, October 26, 1835; Brinsmade to Mrs. Peter Brinsmade, January—, October 13, 1837, Brinsmade Papers. It developed later (in 1851) that Ladd & Co. in 1840 sold a half-interest in Kōloa to a New York business man. This did not inhibit them, as will be shown, from selling the *whole* plantation to another group later in the forties. Private Journal of Luther Severance, cited in Kuykendall, *Hawaiian Kingdom*, I, p. 182.

41 This contract was evidently kept secret even from the chiefs. The agreement is in AH, FO & Ex, November 24, 1841.

42 Brinsmade's European dealings may be followed in his letters to Ladd & Co. in 1842, MS in UH, especially those of April 28, May 15, July 25, 30, 1842. A draft agreement of the Belgian Contract is in AH, FO & Ex, British Commission, 1843. Kuykendall, *Hawaiian Kingdom*, I, pp. 252–253, has a good short account of this period.

43 *Ladd Arbitration*, appendix, pp. 33–40.

44 Brinsmade to Ladd & Co., February 27, September 14, 1844, February 3, 1845, Brinsmade Letters; Anthony Ten Eyck to James Buchanan, December 20, 1847, USDS, Dispatches, Hawai'i, II; Stephen Reynolds Journal, January—, 1844.

45 Richards to Brinsmade, May 4, 1844, AH, FO & ᴇx; see also Brinsmade's letters to Ladd & Co., previously cited.

46 Juliette Cooke to Sister, October 30, 1844, HMCS; Levi Chamberlain Journal, November 1, 1844; Stephen Reynolds Journal, November 1, 1844; William Richards to C. Hompesch, AH, FO & Ex, July 18, 1846. AH, Interior Department Letter Book, I, has a heavy correspondence with Ladd & Co.

47 Stephen Reynolds Journal, April 12, 15, 25, May 2, 12, 13, 1845; Judd to Sir George Simpson, April 2, 1845, AH, FO Letter Book, IX, p. 4; Wyllie to Simpson, April 10, 1845, AH, FO Letter Book, IX, pp. 5 *ff.*; Plain Facts in the suit of Messrs. Ladd and Co., AH, FO & Ex, January 15, 1847.

48 Protest of William Ladd, August 15, 1845, AH, FO & Ex; Wyllie to Anthony Barclay, November 1, 1845, AH, FO Letter Book, IX, p. 210; Protest of Ladd & Co., AH, Interior Department Letter Book, I, p. 3.

49 Stephen Reynolds Journal, April 16, 17, 30, May 6, 18, 1846; Wyllie to United States Secretary of State, May 6, 1846, AH, FO Letter Book, XI, 12; Extracts from the Proceedings of May 6, 1846, AH, FO & Ex; Wyllie to Anthony Barclay, May 30, 1846, AH, FO & Ex; Gorham Gilman to—, May 5, 1846, HHS; *Sandwich Island News*, September 23, 1846, May 5, 1847; John Ricord to Kamehameha III, January 15, 1854, AH, FO & Ex, Miscellaneous Foreign.

50 Kuykendall, *Hawaiian Kingdom*, I, p. 255.

51 AH, Privy Council Record, V, pp. 185, 199, 215, 216.

52 Ladd Arbitration, pp. 538–541.

53 AH, Cabinet Council Minutes, November 11, 20, 21, 1846, January 4, 13, 28, 29, March 17, 18, April 2, 7, 8, 10, 1847; documents in AH, FO & Ex, January 15, April 7, May 22, 1847; AH, Privy Council Record, II, pp. 123–199, 221, 229–235, 249, 259–291, 363; Stephen Reynolds Journal, November 21, 1846, February 3, 4, May 5, 11, 13, 14, 22, July 12, 1847; *Sandwich Island News*, May 5, June 2, 9, 1847; John Ricord to Kamehameha III, January 15, 1854, AH, FO & Ex, Miscellaneous Foreign.

54 Wyllie to Anthony Barclay, December 25, 1847, AH, FO Letter Book, XIII, pp. 153 *ff.*; James Jackson Jarves to Wyllie, August 15, 1848, AH, FO & ᴇx; William Ladd to Wyllie, February 10, 1851, AH, FO Letter Book, XIIIa, Part 3, p. 1160 *ff.*; Luther Severance to Wyllie, March 3, 1851, AH, FO & Ex, US Commissioner; Emile Perrin to Wyllie, April 25, 1851, AH, FO Letter Book, XIIIa, Part 3, p. 1268; Judd to Wyllie, December 29, 1851, AH; FO & Ex, Local Officials; Wyllie to Severance, June 3, 1853, AH, FO Letter Book, XVI, p. 165; David Gregg to Wyllie, April 18, 1854, AH, FO & Ex, US Commissioner; Wyllie to Gregg, May 22, 1854, AH, FO & Ex, US Commissioner; William Lee to Joel Turrill, December 29, 1850, Turrill Collection.

55 AH, Cabinet Council Minutes, May 29, 1856; L. Kamehameha to Paulo Kanoa, February 21, 1857, AH, Interior Department Letter Book, VI, p. 447; Wyllie to Brinsmade, March 27, 1857, AH, FO Letter Book, XXVI, pp. 77–78.

56 For the Wiley case, see these documents in AH, FO & Ex: Testimony Heard Before a Magistrate at the Fort, August 23, 1844; William Hooper to Kekūanaō'a, August 27, 1844; Kekūanaō'a to Hooper, August 28, 1844; Hooper to Kekūanaō'a, August 28, 1844; George Brown to Judd, August 30, 1844;. Judd to Brown, September 14,

1844; Brown to Judd; September 16, 1844. See also Wyllie to Brown, July 8, 1845, AH, FO Letter Book, VIII, pp. 68–142; *Polynesian*, May 26, 1849.

[57] Documents on the *Juno* riot are collected in AH, FO & Ex, September 30, 1846. See also *Polynesian*, October 3, 17, 1846; *Sandwich Island News*, September 30, October 14, 1846; AH, Cabinet Council Minutes, October 5, 1846; AH, Privy Council Record, II, p. 107, IV, p. 57; William Miller to Wyllie, August 28, 1847, AH, FO & Ex; Wyllie to Anthony Barclay, September 25, 1847, AH, FO Letter Book, XIII, pp. 107 *ff*.

For other sailor riots of the decade see *Polynesian*, February 15, 1845, November 14, 1846, July 21, August 4, September 15, October 6, 1849; Wyllie to Patrice Dillon, July 18, 1849, AH, FO Letter Book, XIIIa, Part 2, p. 749; Captain Eden to Wyllie, July 31, 1849, AH, FO & Ex; William Lee and Asher Bates to Kamehameha III, September 12, 1850, AH, FO & Ex; Kekūanaō'a to High Sheriff William Parke, December 21, 1850, AH, Interior Department Letter Book, V, Part 2, p. 442.

[58] For a sampling of anti-Judd opinion, see Amos Cooke Journal, May 14, 1842, February 2, May 29, 1843; Stephen Reynolds Journal, May 20, 22, July 16, 1842; E.W. Clark to Levi Chamberlain, October 17, 1844, HMCS; Elias Bond to Chamberlain, March 14, 1843, HMCS; Clarissa Armstrong to Reuben Chapman, November—, 1843, Armstrong-Chapman Papers; Lowell Smith to Rufus Anderson, March 10, November 15, 1843, November 28, 1846, ABCFM Letters; Alexander Simpson to E. Baron, November 1, 1842, AH, British Consulate Letter Book, Admiralty.

[59] This administrative intimacy is made clear in lengthy statements by the two chiefs in AH, Privy Council Record, V, pp. 269–273, 320–331.

[60] Stephen Reynolds Journal, December 13, 1845.

[61] The Brewer case may be followed in the following documents in AH, FO & Ex: Judd to H.A. Peirce, January 1, 1845; George Brown to Judd, February 20, 1845; Statements of C. Brewer and J.F.B. Marshall, February 26, 1845; George Brown to Judd, March 7, 1845, Judd to Brown, March 8, 1845; Depositions at the Palace, March 14–25, 1845; Declaration of Judd, September 1, 1845; Wyllie to Secretary of State, Peru, March 31, 1846. See also Wyllie to R.C. Janion, June 9, 1846, AH, FO Letter Book, V, p. 201; Stephen Reynolds Journal, December 2, 28, 1844, August 7, 21, 1845; Levi Chamberlain Journal, December 10, 26, 1844; *Sandwich Island News*, April 21, 1847.

[62] Order in Council, December, 1845, AH, FO & Ex; Robert Wyllie to Sir G.F. Seymour, October 10, 1845, AH, FO & Ex; Wyllie to George Pelly, April 23, 1847, AH, FO Letter Book, XIa, p. 112–113; Jules Dudoit to Wyllie, September 6, 1848, Wyllie Papers, MSS, AH; AH, Privy Council Record, II, p. 2, 349; George Brown to Secretary of State, July 1, 1844, USDS, Dispatches, Hawai'i, I; William Hooper to Secretary of State, March 11, 1845, USDS, Consular Letters, Honolulu, II; Brown to James Buchanan, September 1, 1845, USDS, Dispatches, Hawai'i, III; William Miller to Aberdeen, November 1, 1845, FO 58/36; Miller to G. Addington, March 18, 1851, FO 58/70; *Polynesian*, October 27, November 15, 1845. .

[63] Why did Robertson bring the impeachment? He certainly believed he had a case, as the number and detail of the charges showed. His animus against Judd personally and officially was dreadfully bitter, to the point where he could accuse Judd of being "unmatched" in selfishness, vindictiveness, arrogance, hardheartedness, partiality, and vile hypocrisy. Nothing else in Robertson's long and useful career in the Hawaiian government service bears any relation to the tone of the

impeachment speeches. Curiously, all the MS literature on the subject simply takes the impeachment as a given fact. I have not found anything to indicate why Robertson moved when he did, or whether he was directly backed by any of the other anti-Judd people in Honolulu, though an impressive number turned out to support Robertson's testimony. Robertson's opening speech and other documents concerning the administration of the impeachment appear in AH, FO & Ex, Sundry Documents Relating to Impeachment Charges Brought Against G.P. Judd by G. M. Robertson (several folders). The testimony takes up the entire volume of AH, Privy Council Record, V.

[64] The manuscripts stolen from the *News* office are in AH, FO & Ex, Privy Council of Emergency, Palace, December 27, 1848. There are penciled marginal comments about authorship. In the same folder are many documents containing testimony on the affair. Other testimony is collected in AH, FO & Ex, December, 1848. Judd's own account is there in Mr. Judd's Declaration to the Privy Council of the 9th December; the other side of the case is presented in Ten Eyck to Wyllie, December 8. More testimony is spread over scores of pages in AH, Privy Council Record, III, including a long statement by Peacock the printer, at pp. 177–194. For Ten Eyck's interdiction, see Wyllie to Ten Eyck, December 14, 1848, AH, FO Letter Book, XIIIa, Part 1, p. 428.

[65] Keoni Ana to Kamehameha III, December 10, 1848, AH, Interior Department, Letters, Miscellaneous; Richard Armstrong to Kamehameha III, December 11, 1848, AH, FO & Ex; Ten Eyck to Wyllie, December 8, 1848, AH, FO & Ex (with Judd's remark about chasing foxes); Wyllie to Armstrong, December 2, 1848, AH, FO Letter Book, X, p. 282.

[66] Wyllie to Patrice Dillon, February 4, 1849, AH, FO Letter Book, XIIIa, Part 2, p. 562; William Lee to Wyllie, December 9, 1848, AH, FO & Ex; Asher Bates to Lee, December 11, 1848, AH, FO & Ex; AH, Privy Council Record, III, pp. 251, 451.

[67] Impeachment testimony fills AH, Privy Council Record, V; there is a draft of the commissioners' decision for Judd in Wyllie, Pākī, ʻIʻi, Armstrong and Hopkins to Kamehameha III, April 23, 1849, AH, FO & Ex.

[68] The MS sources on Dillon's prolonged quarrels with the Hawaiian government are brought together in Kuykendall, *Hawaiian Kingdom*, I, pp. 388–392. The problem occupied most of Wyllie's waking hours, as the weight of material in AH, FO & Ex, 1848 and 1849, demonstrates.

[69] Wyllie to de Tromelin, June 24, 1848, AH, FO Letter Book, XIa, p. 289; *Polynesian*, July 1, 1848; Judd to Wyllie, August 6, 1849, AH, FO & Ex; Wyllie to de Tromelin, July 14, 1849, AH, FO Letter Book, XIII, pp. 569–570; Wyllie to de Tromelin, August 13, 1849, AH, FO Letter Book, XIa, pp. 383–384.

[70] The Wyllie–de Tromelin correspondence may be followed day by day in five folders in AH, FO & Ex, Correspondence between Minister of Foreign Affairs and Admiral de Tromelin in Relation to the Troubles Existing Between Hawaiʻi and France, August 17 to September 14, 1849. Other letters are in AH, FO Letter Book, XIa, p. 380 *ff.*

[71] This account of the de Tromelin incident draws on the following sources: Kamehameha III to Kekūanaōʻa, August 24, 1849, AH, Interior Department Letter Book, V, Part 1, p. 351; AH, Privy Council Record, III, pp. 317–350; Joel Turrill to Wyllie, August 25, 1849, AH, FO & Ex; Commission of Gerrit Judd and William

Lee, August 27, 1849, AH, FO & Ex; Wyllie to Dillon, August 27, 30, 1849, AH, FO Letter Book, XIIIa, Part 2, pp. 735–736; List of War Materials and Equipment of the Fort of Honolulu…Destroyed by the…French Battleships, September 1, 1849, AH, Interior Department Letter Book, V, Part 1, 354–355; Wyllie to Judd, September 10, 1849, AH, FO Letter Book, XIII, p. 611; Amos Cooke Journal, August 14–September 1, 1849; Stephen Reynolds Journal, August 22–September 6, 1849; Richard Armstrong Journal, August 25–September 5, 1849, HMCS; Clarissa Armstrong to Reuben Chapman, September 5–October 20, 1849, Armstrong–Chapman Papers; *Polynesian*, September 8, 15, November 10, 1849; *Saturday Press*, February 11, 18, 1882; Judd, *Honolulu*, pp. 145, 149. The diplomatic outcome is in Kuykendall, *Hawaiian Kingdom*, I, pp. 393–395.

[72] For Judd's diplomatic mission, see Kuykendall, *Hawaiian Kingdom*, I, pp. 395–399; Judd, *Doctor Judd*, pp. 164–191.

[73] The negotiations of Wyllie and Perrin are in MS form in AH, FO & Ex; they cover more than 300 printed pages in an appendix to Minister of Foreign Relations, *Report*, 1851. For the involvement of Miller, Severance and Gardner, see Miller to Palmerston, March 18, 27, 1851, FO 58/70; Wyllie to Miller, March 13, 1851, AH, FO & Ex; Severance to Daniel Webster, March 11–21, 31, 1851, USDS, Dispatches, Hawai'i, IV; AH, Privy Record, VI, pp. 310–312; Richard Armstrong to Reuben Chapman, March 29, 1851, Armstrong-Chapman Papers. See also AH, FO & Ex, United States Commissioner, March 31, 1851. Kuykendall, *Hawaiian Kingdom*. I, pp. 400–405, has a good account.

[74] "Observer," *Polynesian*, September 15, 1849. Cf. Robert Wyllie to Elisha Allen, September 21, 1857, AH, FO Letter Book, XLVII, 37.

[75] Miller to Addington, September 2, 1847, FO 58/56; Anthony Ten Eyck to—, December 3, 1849, USDS, Dispatches, Hawai'i, II; AH, Privy Council Record, VI, pp. 68, 280; Draft of An Act to Improve the Fortifications and Anchorage of the Harbor of Honolulu, 1850, AH, Public Works, Miscellaneous, 1848–1852; Wyllie to Miller, January 8, 1850, AH, FO Letter Book, XIIIa, Part 2, pp. 771–772; *Polynesian*, January 12, February 2, 1850.

[76] H. N. Crabb to Wyllie, November 7, 1850, AH, FO & Ex, Local Miscellaneous; Wyllie to Crabb, November 8, 1850, AH, FO Letter Book, XIa, p. 496; *Polynesian*, November 16, 1850; AH, Privy Council Record, VIb, pp. 400, 415, 481, 483, 485, 493–497, 503, 509–513; Wyllie to S. N. Castle, August 6, 1851, AH, FO Letter Book, XIa, p. 539.

[77] Document in AH, FO Letter Book, XIIIa, Part 3, pp. 1410–1411; Wyllie to Luther Severance, November 21, 1851, AH, FO Letter Book, XIIIa, Part 3, p. 1407; Wyllie to Thomas Eldredge, December 5, 1851, AH, FO Letter Book, XIII, 1403; Wyllie to William Lee, November 5, 1851, and succeeding letters in AH, FO & Ex, Local Officials; Elisha Allen to Daniel Webster, October 4, 1851, USDS, Consular Letters, Honolulu, V; Richard Armstrong Journal, November 5, 1851; *Polynesian*, November 8, 15, 22, December 6, 1851; Stephen Reynolds Journal, November 15, 17, 21, December 2, 1851.

[78] The Brannan episode may be followed in Wyllie to Kamehameha III, November 20, 1851, AH, FO Letter Book, XIIIa, Part 3, p. 1415 *ff.*; Wyllie to Charles Gordon Hopkins, November 20, 1851, AH, FO Letter Book, XV, pp. 82–83; Mr. Tanner's Declaration, a Printed Declaration on Oath, in AH, British Consulate Letter

Book, FO, II, January 1850 to December 1853; Wyllie to Captain Wallesby, HMS *Daedalus*, December 8, 1851, AH, FO Letter Book, XIa, p. 554; Wyllie to William Howard, December 15, 1851, AH, FO Letter Book, XIa, pp. 567 *ff.*; Kekūanaō'a to Kamehameha III, December 5, 8, 1841, AH, Interior Department Letter Book, V, Part 2, pp. 568, 569–570; AH, Privy Council Record, VIb, pp. 521, 574; Theophilus Metcalf to Peter Treadway, December 19, 1851, AH, Public Works, Miscellaneous; Stephen Reynolds Journal, March 4, 15, 18, 1852; *Polynesian*, January 17, 31, March 6, 13, 20, 27, April 24, July 10, 1852; Parke, *Reminiscences*, pp. 27–31. Also useful are the following letters in the Turrill Collection: Charles R. Bishop to Turrill, December 16, 1851, March 20, May 8, 1852, January 14, October 17, 1853.

Were the *Game Cock* men real filibusterers? A fellow-passenger on the *Golden Rule*, which took them back to California, thought not. He heard that Brannan's men were supposed to have been followed to the islands by a set of "real desperadoes," from whose efforts the *Game Cock* men were to "reap the rewards." They were, however, entirely ignorant of the true state of affairs at the islands. Henry I. Heap(?) to Wyllie, January 16, 1852, AH, FO & Ex, Miscellaneous Foreign. Cf. Charles R. Bishop to Joel Turrill, December 16, 1851, May 8, 1852, Turrill Collection. The deflating return of the *Game Cock* expedition quieted filibuster feeling in California for a time. Brannan's men reported unfavorably on settling in the islands, even under a revolutionary government. C.E. Hitchcock to Wyllie, January 1, 1852, AH, FO & Ex, Miscellaneous Foreign.

79 Wyllie to Captain Gardner, December 9, 1851, March 12, 27, 29, 1852, AH, FO Letter Book, XIa, pp.559–594; AH, Privy Council Record, VIb, pp.621–625, 633; *Polynesian*, March 20, April 3, July 24, November 20, 1852.

80 Observers estimated the number of sailors at two to three thousand. The figure may have been much higher. On November 20, 1852, 131 whalers and 18 merchantmen were in the harbor—a record number. Between thirty and fifty men were aboard each ship. The total would thus be between forty-five hundred and seventy-five hundred. To this might be added a few hundred beached seamen and deserters.

81 This account of the 1852 riot has been compiled from the following sources: AH, Privy Council Record, VIb, pp.767–769, VII, pp.7, 11, 19, 33; Alexander Liholiho to Wyllie, November 10, 1852, AH, FO Letter Book, XVI, 115; Wyllie to A.J. McDuffie and others, November 22, 1852, AH, FO Letter Book, XVII, p. 17; Wyllie to Deming Jarves, November 30, 1852, AH, FO Letter Book, XVIII, pp. 7 *ff.*; Circular of United States Commissioner Luther Severance, November 12, 1852, printed copy in AH, FO & Ex, US Commissioner, May–December, 1852; W.C. Parke to Kekūanaō'a, November 15, 1852, AH, FO & Ex, Privy Council Petitions; Kekūanaō'a to A.J. McDuffie, December 13, 1852, AH, Interior Department Letter Book, V, Part 2, p. 729; Kekūanaō'a to Hāpuku, AH, Interior Department Letter Book, V, Part 2, p. 728; Miller to Malmesbury, November 20, 1852, AH, British Consulate Letter Book, II, January, 1850–December, 1853; Miller to Wyllie, Wednesday, 9 pm, —, AH, FO & Ex, British Consul General; Richard Armstrong to W.N. Armstrong, October 17–November 28, 1852, Armstrong–Chapman Papers; Charles Judd to W.N. Armstrong, December 2, 1852, Armstrong-Chapman Papers; Stephen Reynolds Journal, November 10, 11, December 18, 1852; Amos Cooke Journal, November 11, 12, 1852; *Polynesian*, November 13, 20, 27, December 25, 1852, January 22, May 28, 1853; Parke, *Reminiscences*, pp. 35–44. Jailer George Sherman, the cause of it all, was found guilty of manslaughter at the January, 1853, term of the Supreme Court. *Hawaiian Reports*, I, pp. 150–151. On the anniversary of the riots a year later disturbances were threatened again. Marshal Parke made preparations to guard the town and the consuls were alerted, but the day passed peacefully. Parke to

King and Council, October 31, 1853, AH, FO & Ex, Local Officials; Wyllie to Emile Perrin, November 1, 1853, AH, FO Letter Book, XVI, p. 189; Wyllie to Severance, November 1, 1853, AH, FO & Ex, US Commissioner.

[82] *Polynesian*, February 12, 19, 26, March 5, 1853.

[83] Richard Greer, "Oahu's Ordeal: The Smallpox Epidemic of 1853," Part I, *Hawaii Historical Review*, I, 12 (July, 1965), pp. 223–224. Greer's article is the most exhaustive so far on the 1853 epidemic. I thank him for allowing me to see the work in MS form prior to its serial publication. O. A. Bushnell, Professor of Microbiology at the University of Hawai'i, has saved me from errors of fact and interpretation in this as in other sections of my work.

[84] *Polynesian*, April 2, 1853.

[85] Smallpox Epidemic, Original Minutes of the Commission Appointed to Take Evidence on All Claims Against the Government of Services Rendered during the Prevalence of the Smallpox and to Report to the Legislature of 1856, January 18, 1856, AH, FO & Ex; *Polynesian*, May 14, 21, August 6, 20, 1853; Parke, *Reminiscences*, p. 52.

[86] *Polynesian*, May 14, July 30, August 6, 13, 20, 1853; Judd, *Honolulu*, p. 174; Parke, *Reminiscences*, p. 57. Greer, "Oahu's Ordeal," pp. 225–226, discusses the problem at some length.

[87] Smallpox Epidemic, Smallpox Claims Commission Minutes, January 28, 1856, AH, FO & Ex; Luther Severance to US Secretary of State Marcy, June 24, 1853, USDS, Dispatches, Hawai'i, IV; *Laws*, 1853, p. 77; AH, Privy Council Record, VII, p. 189; Judd to Dwight Baldwin, May 23, 1853, HMCS; *Polynesian*, June 4, 1853.

[88] Statistics were published weekly throughout the epidemic in the form of Royal Health Commissioners' reports in the *Polynesian*. These figures have been collected in Greer, "Oahu's Ordeal," It should be noted that these are *reported* figures only. There were certainly many unreported cases; how many will never be known. In 1850 the census had shown a population of 14,484 in the Kona district of O'ahu, centering on Honolulu. The 1853 census, taken at the end of the year when the epidemic had run its course, gave a figure of 11, 355, for the same area—a population loss of 3,129 for the three-year period. The 1853 census also gave a figure for 1853's births and deaths in the First District (which extended from Maunalua, east of Honolulu, to Moanalua on the west—about fourteen miles): 3,759 deaths, about 2,800 of them attributed to the smallpox, as against 191 births. Richard Armstrong, Minister of Public Instruction, was in charge of the census. He reported to the 1854 legislature an estimated total number of smallpox deaths for all islands of between five and six thousand, leaving a total population in all islands of 73,137, including 2,118 foreigners. The census figures and Armstrong's report are in AH; a convenient way to enter the subject is through articles in *Polynesian*, January 7, February 25, April 15, 1854; and *New Era and Weekly Argus*, January 12, 1854.

[89] AH, Privy Council Record, VII, p. 203; William Hillebrand to T.C.B. Rooke, June 14, 1853; E. Bond to Board of Health, June 24, 1853; Edward Hoffman to Health Commissioners, August 10, 1853; A. Bishop to W.C. Parke, August 11, 1853, all in AH, Board of Health; Amos Cooke Journal, June 17, 24, 28, 1853; *Polynesian*, June 11, 25, July 30, 1853; Luther Severance to William Marcy, July 9, 1853, USDS, Dispatches, Hawai'i, IV.

90 AH, Privy Council Record, VII, p. 211; *Polynesian*, June 11, 1853; Luther Severance to William Marcy, July 2, 9, 1853, USDS, Dispatches, Hawai'i, IV.

91 Gorham Gilman to Judd, Rooke, and Parke, June 24, 1853, AH, FO & Ex, Smallpox Epidemic; J.S. Emerson to Rooke, July 6, 1853, AH, Board of Health (filed with this is a draft of the Waialua regulations, framed at a meeting convened by the district judge and dated July 4, 1853); Benjamin Pitman to Hardy, July 11, 1853, AH, Board of Health; William Lee to Royal Commissioners of Health, August 15, 1853, AH, Board of Health; *Polynesian*, July 9, 23, August 6, 1853.

The course of the epidemic on the outer islands is followed in Richard Greer's companion piece to his paper on the Honolulu area. This is "In The Shadow of Death—Smallpox Brushes the Neighbor Islands, 1853," MS in possession of author. About 450 died on Kaua'i, Maui, and Hawai'i. Isolation, lucky experience with vaccine, and stringent quarantine saved Ni'ihau, Moloka'i, and Lāna'i.

92 W.J. Hillebrand, Letter from Government Hospital, October 16, 1853, AH, Board of Health; Theophilus Metcalf to Peter Treadway, June 13, 1853, AH, Public Works, Miscellaneous; S.C. Damon to Commissioners of Health, July 26, 1853, AH, Board of Health; A. Bishop to Rufus Anderson, July 6, 1853, ABCFM Letters; Smallpox Epidemic, Smallpox Claims Commission Minutes, January 21, 1856, AH, FO & Ex.

93 *Polynesian*, July 16, 1853.

94 *Polynesian*. July 23, 1853, contains reports of the successive meetings. Cf. *Weekly Argus*, July 21, 1853.

95 The petitions are in AH, FO & Ex, Removal Letters.

96 The Privy Council Committee Report is filed in AH, FO & Ex, Against Removal, August 15, 1853. A sampling of the charges against Judd and Armstrong may be found in *Weekly Argus*, July 20, August 7, 1853; *Polynesian*, July 23, 30, August 20, 27, 1853.

97 *Polynesian*. August 20, 1853.

98 The progress of the Judd–Armstrong case may be followed day by day in AH, Privy Council Record, VII, pp. 241–291. At pages 268b–c are the crucial proceedings of August 17, at which the 5/4 vote was recorded against the ministers. These were excised from the record and reinserted subsequently, under circumstances outlined in a note enclosed there. Cf. William Miller's Memorandum of Recent Occurrences at Honolulu, AH, British Consulate, Letter Book, FO, II. Statements in self-defense by Judd and Armstrong are filed in AH, FO & Ex, Against Removal.

For the new cabinet, see AH, Privy Council Record, VII, pp. 271, 291; AH, Cabinet Council Minutes, September 5, 1853; Richard Armstrong Journal, September 5, 1843.

99 *Polynesian*, September 10, 17, October 1, 1854; *Weekly Argus*, September 14, 1853.

100 Greer, "Oahu's Ordeal," brings together the MS sources on the claims.

101 This becomes clear when it is considered that Richard Armstrong survived the purge, even though he was linked with Judd in charges of negligence. See Richard Armstrong Journal, September 5, 1853; Amos Cooke Journal, September 5, 9, 1853;

H.N. Crabb to Peter Treadway, September 23, 1853, Parke Papers, MSS, AH; David Gregg to William Marcy, January 21, February 6, 1854, USDS, Dispatches, Hawai'i, V.

[102] See Judd's reply to petitions against him in AH, FO & Ex, Against Removal.

[103] C.R. Bishop to Joel Turrill, October 9, 16, 1851, Turrill Collection; F. L. Hanks to Turrill, August 14, 1853, Turrill Collection; Richard Armstrong Journal, July 20, 1853; AH, Privy Council Record, VII, pp. 31, 67; George Lathrop to King in Council, November 19, 1852, AH, FO & Ex, Privy Council Petitions; AH, FO & Ex, Reports to Privy Council, December 16, 1852; AH, Journal of House of Representatives, 1853, pp. 442, 482; *Polynesian*, May 28, 1853; Judd, *Doctor Judd*, pp. 199–200.

[104] Judd to Dwight Baldwin, February 24, 1853, HMCS; Amos Cooke Journal, May 21, 1853; Charles Judd to W.N. Armstrong, June 26, 1853, Armstrong–Chapman Papers.

[105] Judd, *Doctor Judd*, pp. 199–200, discusses these affairs briefly.

[106] Wyllie to John Ricord, August 30, 1853, AH, FO & Ex, Miscellaneous Foreign; Severance to E. Hammond, August 24, 1853, USDS, Dispatches, Hawai'i, V.

Just as it proved impossible for Judd to enforce existing legislation on liquor, so did it prove impossible to prevent the smuggling of liquor into the kingdom. And just as Judd found official and private life inseparable, so did the smuggling of liquor invade his family's life. An apocryphal story was often told around town that Judd, the vigilant enemy of smugglers, was standing at the waterfront one day watching a ship unload cargo, unaware that some of the barrels contained, in addition to the goods listed on the manifest, carefully-concealed small kegs and bottles of liquor. In 1852, apocrypha became truth. The ship *Charles* brought to Honolulu two hundred barrels of beef consigned to Aaron B. Howe, who was to have married Judd's daughter Nellie at the year's end. In the course of unloading, a barrel was dropped and broken, revealing a cask of brandy packed inside. Customs Collector C. R. Bishop impounded the cargo. The captain of the *Charles* denied involvement, and Howe, publicly a temperance man, produced some (un-postmarked) letters clearing himself. But he had other consignments of beef on the way. Some days later, he was found dying in the house he occupied close to the Judds, and no sooner had the family begun to mourn his passing and the desolation into which it plunged the nineteen-year-old Nellie, than it was discovered that Howe had poisoned himself with strychnine. Richard Armstrong to W.N. Armstrong, October 17, 1852, Armstrong–Chapman Papers; *Polynesian*, November 13, 20, 1852; William Lee to Joel Turrill, January 15, 1853, Turrill Collection; and, for a different version, Judd, *Doctor Judd*. p. 232.

[107] Wyllie to Judd, July 14, 1853, AH, FO & Ex, Local Officials; Wyllie to Ricord, August 30, 1853, AH, FO & Ex, Miscellaneous Foreign.

[108] Judd, *Doctor Judd*, p. 212.

[109] The MS references to Judd's relations with Benson are brought together in Judd, *Doctor Judd*, pp. 208–209.

[110] A copy of the petition is in AH, FO & Ex, British Consulate, 1853. See also Severance to Marcy, August 25, 1853, USDS, Dispatches, Hawai'i, IV; S.N. Castle to Anderson, August 16, September 10, 1843, ABCFM Letters.

[111] David Gregg Diary, January 4, 6, 7, 1854.

[112] The Judd-Spencer petition is in AH, FO & Ex, Privy Council Petitions, January 9, 1854. See also AH, Privy Council Record, VIII, p. 77; William Miller to Addington, January 14, 21, 1854, FO 58/76; David Gregg Diary, January 13, 14, 16, 1854.

[113] The king's order is in AH, FO & Ex, February 6, 1854. Gregg's side of the negotiations may be followed in his Diary; his letters to Wyllie in AH, FO & Ex, US Commissioner; and his official dispatches to Marcy in USDS, Dispatches, Hawai'i, V. Wyllie's letters are in drafts and copies in AH, FO & Ex; and in FO Letter Books.

[114] David Gregg Diary, February 11, 13, 21, 1854, Gregg to Marcy, February 11, 1854, USDS, Dispatches, Hawai'i, V.

[115] AH, Privy Council Record, VIII, p. 121; AH, Cabinet Council Minutes,

March 4, 1854; David Gregg Diary, February 21, March 1, 4, 6, 1854; Gregg to Marcy, March 4, 1854, USDS, Dispatches, Hawai'i, V.

[116] Gregg to Marcy, March 4, 1854, USDS, Dispatches, Hawai'i, V; David Gregg Diary, March 6, 1854.

[117] Richard Armstrong Journal, March 11, 1854; Amos Cooke Journal, March 15, 17, 1854; Stephen Reynolds Journal, March 15, 22, 1854; David Gregg Diary, March 11, 22, 1854; Gregg to Marcy, March 14, 15, 1854, USDS, Dispatches, Hawai'i, V; Miller to Wodehouse, March 14, 1854, FO 58/79. The *Nūhou* continued to be published for some months.

[118] David Gregg Diary, March 30, April 3, 1854; Gregg to Marcy, March 30, April 13, 1854, USDS, Dispatches, Hawai'i, V. Parke never did "get hold of the paper."

[119] David Gregg Diary, March 2, 18, 21, 22, April 27, 1854. See also Gregg to Marcy, July 24, 1855, USDS, Dispatches, VI, in which Lathrop, at the July 4 dinner of that year, would not drink a toast to the new king Alexander Liholiho, Kamehameha IV, thinking it unbecoming to Americans to "drink to any nigger, even though he wore a crown." I have been quite unable to locate the source of Lathrop's racism. I have not been able to trace his origins beyond the unhelpful information that his family lived in New Jersey.

[120] David Gregg Diary, April 25, May 20, 1854; Gregg to Marcy, June 6, 1854, USDS, Dispatches, Hawai'i, V; Kuykendall, *Hawaiian Kingdom*, I; p. 423.

[121] David Gregg Diary, June 9, 10, 11, 12, 17, 1854.

[122] David Gregg Diary, July 3, 1854.

[123] Judd, *Honolulu*, p. 181.

[124] Wyllie to Barclay, October 12, 1854, AH, FO Letter Book, XVIII, p. 150. Wyllie commented frequently thereafter on the decline of Miller's health.

[125] AH, Cabinet Council Minutes, August 24, 1854; David Gregg Diary, July 7, 15, August 1, September 2, 7, 1854; Gregg to Marcy, July 13, 26, August 8, 1854, USDS, Dispatches, Hawai'i, V; Wyllie to Joseph Jardine, July 31, 1854, AH, FO Letter Book, XVIII, 178–179; Wyllie to William Lee, September 7, 1854, AH, FO & Ex,

Local Officials; Wyllie to Kamehameha IV, February 13, 1862, AH, FO & Ex, Local Officials, King's Book; Miller to E. Hammond, August 21, October 6, November 15, 1854. FO 58/79; *Polynesian*, September 2, 9, 1854.

[126] Gregg to Marcy, September 7 (misdated August 7), 1854, USDS, Dispatches, Hawai'i, V.

[127] There are several copies of Miller's Verbal Address in AH, FO & Ex; British Consul General, September 18, 1854; also filed there are some very interesting comments in Wyllie's hand.

[128] Events of the crucial November days may be followed in: "Wyllie to Kekuanaoa, November 11, 17, 1854, AH, FO & Ex; Wyllie to William Lee, November 15, 1854, AH, FO & Ex; Wyllie to Gregg, November 13, 1854, AH, FO Letter Book, XVI, p. 294; Gregg to Wyllie, November 23, 1854, AH, FO & Ex, US Commissioner; Wyllie to Dornin, November 27, 1854, AH, FO Letter Book, XVII, pp. 85 *ff.*; Wyllie to Charles St. Julian, November 16, 1854, AH, FO Letter Book, XVIII, p. 195; Miner to Clarendon, November 17, 1854, FO 58/79; Miller to E. Hammond, December 2, 1854, FO 58/79; Gregg to Marcy, November 30, 1854, USDS, Dispatches, Hawai'i, V; Wyllie to John Ricord, December 1, 1854, AH, FO & Ex, Miscellaneous Local. For retrospective comment, see documents in AH, FO & Ex, US Commissioner, January 20, 23, 24, 25, 26, 1855; Wyllie to Jules Remy, January 31, 1856, AH, FO & Ex, Local Officials; Richard Armstrong to Wyllie, March 11, 1858, AH, FO & Ex, Local Officials.

[129] The proclamation is in AH, FO & Ex, Local Officials, December 8, 1854. It was published in *Polynesian*, December 9, 1854, and remained there in the official notices column for some months.

[130] This revisionist view of Lee's role in the treaty negotiations of 1854, and the new perspective it gives to events in Honolulu, comes from Charles H. Hunter's work on the Hawaiian statehood movement. Professor Hunter's argument is circumstantial (none of Lee's private papers seem to have survived, though some of his correspondence with Wyllie is in AH), but in extended form it offers by far the best reading of a complex situation. For some indications of Lee's importance, overlooked in published works, see these documents in AH: the order of Kamehameha III to Wyllie to negotiate with Gregg, FO & Ex, February 6, 1854, Hawaiian and English versions by Lee; Lee to Wyllie, February 11, August 29, 1854, FO & Ex; Cabinet Council Minutes (Separate), July 17, September 12, 1854; Wyllie to John Ricord, May 30, 1857, FO & Ex, Miscellaneous Foreign. See also David Gregg Diary, February 12, June 16, 20, 1854.

[131] David Gregg Diary, January 21, 29, 1858; Gregg to Marcy, January 24, USDS Dispatches, Hawai'i, VI. George Lathrop, J.D. Blair, and Wesley Newcomb all left Honolulu before the end of the fifties.

The proclamation of Kauikeaouli's death is in AH, Privy Council Record, VIII, p. 323; the succession proclamation is at p. 325.

CHAPTER 7

[1] Three *Polynesian* editorials illustrate neatly this change and its limits. The first, on January 20, 1849, remarked that Honolulu, being small, was noted for private feuding over public questions, "Every new division into which our little society breaks itself, reduces by so much the extent of the views of each petty clique, because the first operation is to wall in, for the purpose of preventing egress, although the same barrier almost as often serves to hinder ingress also, so clumsily is it thrown up in most circumstances." The second, on June 28, 1856, remarked that the foreign community of Honolulu was very settled, content to live in the present, rather than looking to the past or the future as the focus of life. Just like the pandanus tree, said the *Polynesian*, man put down roots, and Honolulu's foreigners of the fifties were able to marry, educate their families, and enjoy a full social life in the town, so that "people now-a-days surround themselves with comforts and build up institutions that were not dreamed of a score of years ago, and taking root in the soil to which they have transplanted themselves, and without in the first place having intended anything of the kind, by the dove-tailing of events, become… 'permanencies.'" The third, on August 22, 1863, talked about Honolulu society as still basically "analytic," with numerous subdivisions and constellations, occasionally "interlacing." Further change might come as young locally-born people, without the stigmata of foreign origin, grew up to take their place in society.

[2] Judd to Rufus Anderson, May 1, 1861, in *Judd Fragments*, II, pp. 207–208. Judd wrote at a time when the king was hard at work helping to introduce the Episcopalian religion to Honolulu. Judd's remarks might have had some point before the king's marriage and before the Neilson shooting, but by 1861 they were grossly unfair.

[3] Amos Cooke, abandoning missionary work in favor of a business career, tried hard to reconcile the old and the new. "The Lord seems to be allowing such things to take place that the islands may gradually pass into other hands. This is trying but we cannot help it. It is what we have been contending against for years, but the Lord is showing us that His thoughts are not our thoughts, neither are His ways our ways. The will of the Lord be done…Honolulu never looked so green and pleasant as now and the trees increase very rapidly. Our large plain of sand is now covered with vegetation and is laid out into lots. I am proposing, ere long, to purchase some of them as I am about to become a citizen of the kingdom." Amos Cooke Journal, June 3, 1851.

[4] These affairs may be followed best in correspondence with the United States Commissioner and the French Commissioner for the relevant years, in AH, FO & Ex. The important point is that in each case the Hawaiian government was able to hold its stated positions against the foreign diplomats.

[5] The best single source on the Landais affair is the David Gregg Diary. Gregg, calling Honolulu a "scandal-ridden town," obsessed with "stories and suspicions," recorded scandals, stories, and suspicions fully. See entries for April 8, May 17, 20, 22, 30, August 16, December 31, 1855, January 2, 20, 21, 22, 23, November 27, 1856. See also AH, Ministerial Conferences, January 1, 1856; AH, Privy Council Record, X, p. 5; *Hawaiian Reports*, I, pp. 353 *ff.*; Perrin to Wyllie, January 1, 1856, AH, FO & Ex, French Commissioner; Wyllie to Parke, January 2, 1856, AH, FO & Ex, Local Officials; Statement of Marshal Parke, January 4, 1856, AH, FO & Ex, Local Officials. There are many letters on the case in AH, FO Letter Books, XIX, XX, XXI. The tiny French diplomatic and consular community continued to have

internal troubles for some years. No one could get along with Perrin, for one thing. No other dispute, however, involved the town at large.

6   The David Gregg Diary again is a good source. See entries for January 24–28, May 20, 21, 1857. AH, FO & Ex, has copies of the major documents concerning Monsarrat's arrest and banishment, filed at May, 1857. See also Gregg to B.F. Hardy, February 2, 1857, and Gregg to D.A. Ogden, July 25, 1857, both in Gregg Letter Book, 1857; Wyllie to Baron de Thierry, June 2, 1857, AH, FO Letter Book, XXVI, 114. Wyllie regarded Victoria as simple, goodhearted, and unsuspecting, the victim of what he described as a well-meant but totally mistaken education. In his mind, Victoria should not have had the education of an ordinary female schoolgirl or chorister, but should have been brought up to know her dignity as a princess. Had this happened, he said, an auctioneer would never have been able to find access to her person. Her fall was thus the fruit of the "ascetical fanatical" missionary spirit.

7   David Gregg Diary, January 27, 1857.

8   A proclamation appeared in the papers to this effect. See *Pacific Commercial Advertiser*, May 20, 1859.

9   For an interesting comment on the social position of Neilson and Hopkins, see David Gregg Diary, June 26, 1856.

10   Neilson's own letters from the time of his arrival in the islands to the shooting are in typescript copies in AH. There are many letters bearing on the case in the Emma Collection, MSS, AH. See also David Gregg Diary. The Honolulu newspapers never carried an open account, although brief references were published, understandable only to people who knew beforehand the matter at issue. After the immediate consternation, the press carried notices of the king's trips to and from Lahaina to see Neilson. In AH, FO & Ex, Local Officials, from September 17, 1859, to the end of the year, is a long series of letters between Wyllie, Alexander Liholiho, and some others. See also AH, Ministerial Conferences; and AH, Cabinet Council Minutes, for the same period. US Commissioner Borden showed some disposition to make a diplomatic case out of the shooting of Neilson, who was American-born but a naturalized Hawaiian. Wyllie stopped that immediately— another instance in which the Hawaiian government showed ability to contain crisis. Borden to Wyllie, September 21, 1859, and Wyllie to Borden, September 23, 1859, both in AH, FO & Ex, United States Commissioner.

Who incited the king? The evidence is incomplete and rather confusing, but the most likely suspect is Gorham Gilman, a New Englander and longtime resident of Lahaina, once very close to the monarchy but later a sour and strong opponent. The king was at Gilman's place not long before he set out to sea; and after the shooting Gilman was very energetic in trying to get Neilson to make statements for the papers. All this should be regarded as circumstantial and speculative, however.

11   Useful information of various kinds on the Episcopal mission may be found in T.N. Staley, *Five Years' Church Work in the Kingdom of Hawaii* (London, 1868); Henry B. Restarick, *Hawaii, 1778–1920, From the Viewpoint of a Bishop...* (Honolulu, 1924); Henry B. Whipple, *Lights and Shadows of a Long Episcopate...* (New York, 1899); and these articles by Andrew F. Muir: "The Church in Hawaii, 1778–1862," *Historical Magazine of the Protestant Episcopal Church*, XVIII (1949), pp. 31–65; "Edmund Ibbotson (1831–1914): S.P.G. Missionary to Hawai'i, 1862–1866," *Historical Magazine of the Protestant Episcopal Church*, XIX (1950), pp. 214–241; "*George Mason, Priest and*

Schoolmaster," *British Columbia Historical Quarterly*, XV (1951), pp. 47–70. The best short account of the origins and early years is in Kuykendall, *Hawaiian Kingdom*, II, pp. 86–99, which uses available documents well.

12 Wyllie to Manley Hopkins, December 5, 1859, AH, FO Letter Book, XXXIII, pp. 21–22. Thereafter, Wyllie's letters addressed to Hopkins in London, and Hopkins' replies, which are in AH, FO & Ex, Hawaiian Officials Abroad, contain great amounts of information.

13 E.W. Clark, pastor of Kawaiaha'o at the time, apparently felt particularly threatened. His letters are among the most strongly anti-Episcopalian. See letters to Rufus Anderson, October 30, 1861, November 8, 12, 1862, December 8, 1863, in E.W. Clark Letter Books, MSS, HMCS. Supporters of the new project criticized the exclusive spirit of the Protestants, and could even find humor in a situation the Protestants regarded as serious, "I suppose Judd and Corwin [pastor of Fort Street Congregational church for foreigners]…look upon this new establishment in the same light that Hopkins [Charles Gordon Hopkins, who had herds of cattle] viewed a rival butcher's shop, & they doubtless think that their fold is sufficient for all the sheep in this neighborhood," William Webster to Alexander, April 16, 1861, Kalanianaole Papers, MSS, AH. See also Kamehameha IV to Webster, September, 1861, Emma Collection. The *Pacific Commercial Advertiser* attacked Staley from the moment of his arrival; the *Polynesian* and later the *Hawaiian Gazette* defended him. A pastoral address by Staley on New Year's Day, 1865, produced a newspaper war for months afterward in which W.D. Alexander, a missionary son, engaged Staley. Both sides published lengthy pamphlets.

14 Wyllie's correspondence in AH, FO Letter Books for that period; the weekly newspapers; and the numerous expressions of grief that came from community organizations (filed in AH, FO & Ex; give indications of the great sorrow that was felt.

15 These events may be followed in the *Polynesian* for November and December, 1862. A draft of the charter is in AH, Interior Department, Miscellaneous, Charters, October 30, 1862; and the grant is in AH, Privy Council Record, XI, p. 95.

16 Kuykendall, *Hawaiian Kingdom*, II, p. 97, has a good short account of the founding of churches and schools.

17 Wyllie to Bishop of Oxford, November 14, 1862, AH, FO Letter Book, XLII, p. 145; E.W. Clark to Rufus Anderson, November 8, 1862, E.W. Clark Letter Books; Dwight Baldwin to Amos Cooke, October 30, 1862, HMCS; *Polynesian*, November 15, 1862, July 18, December 26, 1863.

18 E.W. Clark to Rufus Anderson, November 8, 1862, HMCS; Mark Twain, *Letters from the Sandwich Islands* (San Francisco, 1938), pp. 115–116.

19 E.W. Clark to Rufus Anderson, February 12, 1864, E.W. Clark Letter Books. See also Wyllie to M. Desnoyers, February 1, 1864, AH, FO Letter Book, XL, 411; *Pacific Commercial Advertiser*, February 4, 1864.

20 Gerrit Judd to Henry Hill, July 3, 1866, ABCFM Letters; *Pacific Commercial Advertiser*, July 7, 1866.

21 Emma to Kamehameha V, April 7, 1871, Emma Collection (Nylen-Altman). Some indication of the issues may be gleaned from: Thomas Harris to Secretary of SPG, April 27, 1869, HHS; Daniel Smith and others to Secretary of SPG, March 13, 1869,

copy in Emma Collection (Nylen-Altman), Miscellaneous Documents; Gerrit Judd to Rufus Anderson, March 23, 1869, ABCFM Letters; C.C. Harris to Manley Hopkins, December 26, 1870, AH, FO Letter Book, L, pp. 521 *ff.*; *Pacific Commercial Advertiser*, April 17, July 10, 1869, January 1, 1870, May 20, 1871, March 16, August 3, 1872.

[22] All in all the religious sector was perhaps the most troubled in the life of the community. In Alexander Liholiho's reign a tiny Methodist church came into existence and died away, victim of internecine strife. Mormon missionaries clashed with government officials over the right to preach and the right to perform marriages (the authorities were reluctant to stretch the constitution's religious freedom clauses to include the Mormons). And Fort Street Congregational Church, serving foreigners (including several ex-missionaries), was beset by arguments which resulted in a rapid turnover of pastors. None of these circumstances reached beyond the congregations into the community at large, and so they are merely noted here without amplification.

[23] This early period is very well covered in an interesting and amusing article: Helen P. Hoyt, "Theatre in Hawaii—1778–1840," Hawaiian Historical Society, *Annual Report*, 69 (Honolulu, 1961), pp. 7–18, which has a good bibliography.

[24] AH, Privy Council Record, IV, p. 73; G.M. Robertson to Stephen Reynolds, October 25, 1847, AH, Interior Department Letter Book, II, Part 1, pp. 160–161; Stephen Reynolds Journal, September 11, October 28, November 8, 1847; *Polynesian*, September 11, 1847. *Hawaiian Annual for 1881* has a good short account of the 1848 season, taken mainly from the *Polynesian* and the *Sandwich Island News*.

[25] By 1856 Gerrit Judd had capitulated and gone over to the enemy, to become treasurer of the Hawaiian Theatre Company. Wyllie Papers, Hawaiian Theatre Company, 1848–1856, Minutes, February 1, 1856.

[26] The *Polynesian* gave the drama a good press, especially under the editorship of the theatrically-inclined Charles Gordon Hopkins, an Englishman who was a stockholder in the Royal Hawaiian Theatre and who had played several parts on the Honolulu stage. The seasons and successes may be very well followed in the newspapers.

[27] The liberalizing process may be observed in the Protestant-dominated *Pacific Commercial Advertiser*, May 20, 1858, December 3, 1863, November 17, 1866, April 6, 20, September 28, October 5, November 2, 30, December 14, 1867, November 19, 1870, October 21, 1871.

[28] Charles Warren Stoddard, *The Island of Tranquil Delights* (Boston, 1905), pp. 197–200. Stoddard records here the impressions of the English actor Charles Mathews (hence the ticket price in shillings rather than dollars). Stoddard goes into great detail on the theater of his time in Honolulu, and is probably the most evocative single source. Newspapers have been used as the principal source for two UH MA theses: Thelma Brown, "A History of the Theater in Honolulu During the Reign of Kamehameha V, 1863–1872," (1942); and Margaret Frowe, "The History of the Theatre during the Reign of King Kalākaua, 1874–1891," (1937). Both theses have useful bibliographies.

[29] Peter Brinsmade to his wife, November 23, 1836, Brinsmade Papers. By the end of

the thirties, Mrs. Little had quite broken with the mission world, and was entertaining the free-living John Coffin Jones and his Spanish wife. C. McDonald to
Levi Chamberlain, December 12, 1838, HMCS.

30 Faxon Dean Atherton, *California Diary, 1836–1839*, ed. Doyce B. Nunis, Jr. (San
Francisco, 1964), p. 122; *Sandwich Island Gazette*, May 4, 1839; *Polynesian*, November
28, 1840.

31 Wyllie to John Young, March 5, 1846, AH, FO & Ex; Wyllie to Steen Bille, October
28, 1846, AH, FO Letter Book, V; AH, Cabinet Council Minutes, March 3, 1846;
Amos Cooke Journal, March 11, 1846; Richard Armstrong Journal, March 17, 1851;
Stephen Reynolds Journal, June 19, 1840, May 12, 1842, February 27, 1843, October
29, November 21, 25, 1845, March 5, 17, 1846, January 14, 1852; Mott, "Honolulu
1848;" *Polynesian*. April 17, 24, 1841, February 13, August 28, October 16, 23, 1858;
Sandwich Island News, September 23, 1846, April 20, 27, 1848; *Pacific Commercial
Advertiser*, April 3, August 14, 1862.

32 *Pacific Commercial Advertiser*, November 20, December 4, 1856. For the spread of
dancing in the town see Stephen Reynolds Journal, June 15, 27, 1849; David Gregg
Diary, January 19, 1854, February 9, 1857; Amos Cooke Journal, May 2, 1848, April
14, 1853; *Polynesian*, June 23, 1849, July 26, August 2, 1851, November 26, 1853,
June 3, 10, July 8, 1854, December 20, 1856, July 10, 1858, June 11, 18, 1859, February
4, 25, March 17, May 19, 1860, May 2, 1863; *Pacific Commercial Advertiser*. June 2, 16,
23, 30, 1859, March 22, 1860.

33 T.H. Davies, "Reminiscences," typescript, HMCS; Alfons Korn, *The Victorian
Visitors* (Honolulu, 1958), pp. 163–165.

34 *Polynesian*, July 7, December 1, 1860.

35 Stephen Reynolds Journal, July 25, 1850; Yates, "Reminiscences;" *Pacific Commercial
Advertiser*, March 26, April 2, July 9, 1864, July 8, 1865, July 24, 31, August 7, 1869;
Hawaiian Gazette, July 8, 1865. Wyllie spent days of official time in 1864 arranging
a children's fancy dress ball at which he proposed to appear as "Bobbie Wyllie" in
his Highland chief's costume. AH, FO Letter Book, XLV, pp. 1–12.

36 J.B. Atherton to Sisters, January 3, 1859, HMCS; Charles Alfred Castle to Wife;
July 21, 1873, HMCS; *Pacific Commercial Advertiser*, August 3, 1867, July 1, 22,
November 18, December 16, 1871, April 6, July 6, 1872; *Bennett's Own*, December 7,
1869, January 11, 1870.

37 David Gregg Diary, December 29, 1856.

38 See David Gregg Diary, March 17, 18, 1859; and *Polynesian*, April 17, May 1, 1858,
August 6, 1859, for other comments on half-whites in society.

39 This is a very complex subject, worth much more space than I can devote to it
here. Hawaiians, of course, were far from being the only people at Honolulu who
failed to measure up to New England standards, but the subject of social relations
with natives had an edge missing from discussion of other groups. To begin with,
Hawaiians found it very difficult to become ordained Protestant ministers before
the rise of an independent native church in the 1860s. It was even more difficult
for Hawaiians to enter the personal world of the missionaries: if there was a close
friendship between a missionary and a Hawaiian, it has escaped me (I should

perhaps exclude the rather special relation of Bingham and Judd to the high chiefs, and confine the question to petty chiefs and commoners). It was almost impossible to conceive of a missionary or a missionary son marrying a Hawaiian or part-white. Of all generally classifiable white groups in Honolulu from mid-century to the mid-seventies, the mission families were by far the least likely to marry away from their native American region, their religion, their class, and their race (see genealogical charts in HMCS, and tombstones in the missionary section of the cemetery at Kawaiahaʻo). Samuel Chenery Damon, the Seamen's Chaplain, preached a broad racial tolerance verging on equalitarianism, but he was regarded as eccentric on this point, and not by missionaries alone. Most mission people would have endorsed the remarks of young Charles Judd, son of Gerrit: no native wife for him, however well-born; he wanted good New England stock. By the time the plantation era was well under way, young men of missionary descent together with other owners and managers were ready to exercise the traditional rights of landed classes among their workers, but that is peripheral to considerations at hand here.

[40] T.C.B. Rooke to Chas. W. Vincent, September 26, 1854, AH, FO . Ex, Miscellaneous Local.

[41] *Pacific Commercial Advertiser*, November 20, 1856.

[42] *Polynesian*, October 10, 1840, December 27, 1856.

[43] Chief Justice, *Report*, 1852, p. 112.

[44] Chief Justice, *Report*, 1854, pp. 9–10.

[45] *Polynesian*, March 26, 1853.

[46] AH, Privy Council Record, X, p. 112; S. Spencer to Messrs. Booth and others, December 30, 1856, AH, Interior Department Letter Book, VI, p. 436.

[47] *Pacific Commercial Advertiser*, November 13, December 4, 1856.

[48] *Polynesian*, January 17, 1857. The dance-hall case took up a great deal of space in the major newspapers in December, 1856, and January–February, 1857. Hardly an issue of the *Polynesian*, the *Pacific Commercial Advertiser*, or the *Hae Hawaii* appeared without extensive comment, letters, or published correspondence.

[49] AH, Privy Council Record, X, 152; AH, Cabinet Council Minutes, August 26, 1857; copy of letter (unsigned but obviously from Minister of Interior) to J. Booth and J. Dawson, August 14, 1857, AH, Interior Department Letter Book, VII, 8a.

[50] *Polynesian*, November 21, 1857.

[51] *Daily Hawaiian Herald*, October 30, 1866. For a sampling of dance-hall issues in the sixties and seventies, see *Pacific Commercial Advertiser*, September 10, 1863, January 14, 21, 1865; *Hawaiian Gazette*, January 21, 28, 1865 (with the text of the 1864 regulatory act and comments on it), April 15, 1865 (a prosecution under the act); AH, Interior Department Letter Book, XII, pp. 6–7; W.C. Parke to E. Bond, December 18, 1876, AH, Marshal's Letter Book.

[52] In the manner of the dance-hall case, the Maxey affair took up a disproportionate amount of newspaper space. It may be followed in the *Polynesian* and *Pacific Commercial Advertiser* between August and December, 1856. Some of the official

correspondence was printed. There are copies of many angry letters from Wyllie to Whitney in AH, FO Letter Book, XXIX. The following documents in AH are helpful: Memorial to the King in Council from the Trustees of the Sailors' Home Society, May 21, 1855, FO & Ex, Miscellaneous Local; Ministerial Conferences, [May?] 1855; Petition of John Maxey, Privy Council Petitions, August 5, 1856; Privy Council Record, X, 80, pp. 90–92; Lot Kamehameha to S.N. Castle, August 8, 1856, Interior Department Letter Book, VI, pp. 395–396; Wyllie to Elisha Allen, August 9, 1856, FO Letter Book, XXIV, pp. 52 *ff.* Wyllie suggests here that one reason Maxey's license was extended was that the government, short of money, owed Gerrit Judd $1,000 from a long-standing case. The money had just come due; Maxey's license fee would be $1,000; it could be used to pay Judd.

53 For a sampling of the rise and fall of temperance societies, see *Pacific Commercial Advertiser*, July 17, 1856, November 24, 1859, February 6, 13, 27, March 1, 1862, November 5, 1864, February 25, June 17, 1865, February 16, March 2, 16, 23, 30, April 6, July 6, 1867, February 26, April 23, 1870; *Polynesian*, July 9, 23, August 13, September 24, October 1, 1859, June 16, July 14, 1860, January 24, 1861; *Hawaiian Gazette*, February 25, June 17, September 2, 9, 1865. My impression is that the Protestant churches kept up a fairly steady temperance campaign, but that most organizations formed in the white community of the town had active lives of only a year or two before sinking into stagnation, to re-form or re-organize a year or so later.

54 The most convenient way to begin a study of the liquor question is in the successive annual reports of the Minister of the Interior, the Minister of Finance, and the Chief Justice. The chronic question of allowing natives to drink may be followed in the Journals of successive legislatures and in the press, where it occupied a disproportionate amount of space—the *Advertiser* was against, the *Polynesian* in the middle of the road. Joe Booth's test case decision is in *Hawaiian Reports*, II, p. 616 *ff.*; and comment is in the press for November–December, 1862. From the fifties, it was legal to make wine. In 1864–1865, acts were passed permitting legal brewing of beer and distillation of spirits under license at Honolulu. None of these enterprises produced quality products; all were economic failures. Up through the seventies, Honolulu was the only place in the kingdom where liquor could be sold legally (another instance of the attempt to isolate vice), but contemporary comment and court reports make it clear that the illegal liquor traffic among whites and natives was brisk everywhere, from Lahaina and other port towns to the remotest countryside. For illustrative comment, see *Polynesian*, May 27, July 1, 1854, December 1, 1855, December 25, 1858, January 13, May 14, December 17, 1859, February 18, March 24, 1860, August 23, 1862; *Hawaiian Gazette*. January 21, 1865.

55 *Pacific Commercial Advertiser*, July 15, 1858.

56 *Speeches of His Majesty Kamehameha IV…* (Honolulu, 1861), pp. 12–16.

57 *Laws*, 1855, pp. 12–13, 20, 36–38.

58 This early period is well covered in a long paper by Richard Greer, "The Founding of the Queen's Hospital," MS in possession of the author. Greer takes the administrative story through the first years of operation. T.C. Heuck's plans are copied in a scrapbook, in Heuck Papers, MSS, AH. Also filed there are many of Heuck's letters in German to his family describing the enterprise.

[59] Limited provision was made for distressed foreigners, and for consular hospital patients. For the white population at large, private accommodations were more or less adequate.

[60] Hillebrand's successive reports may be found in AH, Board of Health. Greer, "Queen's Hospital," collects many figures.

[61] *Polynesian*, April 18, 1863.

[62] For some indication of the extent of kahuna-ism, see Stephen Reynolds Journal, January 24, 1847; Pai'ea to Antoinette Swan, September 15, 1858, Swan Papers, MSS, AH; Wyllie to Rufus Anderson, April 16, 1863, AH, FO Letter Book, XXXVII, 265; A. Doiron to F.W. Hutchison, June 26, 1872, AH, Board of Health; W.C. Parke to W.L, Lane, October 17, 1874, AH, Marshal's Letter Book; Yates, "Reminiscences;" *Hawaiian Reports*, III, p. 391; *Polynesian*, May 9, 1863; *Pacific Commercial Advertiser*, January 28, March 4, April 8, July 15, 1865, July 13, August 24, 1867, August 20, November 19, 1870, March 18, May 6, June 10, 24, July 1, 1871, January 6, February 3, 1872; *Hawaiian Gazette*, February 18, April 8, July 15, 1865; *Daily Hawaiian Herald*, September 6, 1866; *Friend*, February, 1894.

[63] A female kahuna called Waahia was convicted in police court at Honolulu. Appealing to the supreme court, she brought to the hearing many of her female followers dressed in expensive silks; and, upon conviction, she prophesied that the prison walls would collapse if she were sent to jail. The walls did not collapse, but neither did the faith of her followers. *Pacific Commercial Advertiser*, March 2, 9, April 6, October 12, 1872.

[64] On the battle between western medicine and kahuna-ism see H.K. Kapākūhaili to Ali'ioholani, June 1, 1859, AH, Interior Department Letters, Miscellaneous; Kamehameha V to Queen Emma, February 28, 1866, Emma Collection (Nylen-Altman); A. Unna to C.T. Gulick, September 3, 1872, AH, Board of Health. On the attempt to train natives, see *Pacific Commercial Advertiser*, January 7, 1864, July 15, 22, 1865, July 15, August 12, 1871; Report by Gerrit Judd, November, 1871, AH, Interior Department; AH, Cabinet Council Minutes, April 22, 1872; AH, Board of Health Minutes, March 1, 1873. On the licensing of kahuna, see Journal of House of Representatives for June 23, 1868; *Hawaiian Gazette*, February 24, 1869; J.O. Dominis and others to F.W. Hutchison, March 3, 1870, AH, Board of Health; C.T. Gulick to Charles Judd, October 28, 1874, AH, Interior Department Letter Book, XII; AH, Board of Health, Certificate for Lapa'au License, 1874–1878, which has a list of practicing Hawaiian kahuna.

[65] AH, Privy Council Petitions, May 19, 1856, January, 1859; AH, Privy Council Record, XI, p 9; AH, Board of Health Minutes, February 24, 1866; Susan E. Barry to F. W. Hutchison, January 31, 1867, AH, Interior Department Letter Book, X, 450 *ff.*; *Hawaiian Reports*, III, p. 462; J. Brown to W. Moehonua, August 20, 1875, AH, Board of Health.

[66] Baldwin to Rufus Anderson, December 17, 1861, HMCS; Baldwin to W. Hillebrand, February 3, 1863, AH, Board of Health; R. McKibbin to Baldwin, May 13, 1863, AH, Board of Health; AH, Board of Health Minutes, May 12, 1863.

[67] *Polynesian*, February 12, 1859; Lowell Smith to Board of Health, August 22, 1859, AH, Board of Health; AH, Board of Health Minutes, January 30, 1860; *Polynesian*, November 8, 15, 1862; *Pacific Commercial Advertiser*, November 13, 20, 1862; David Dayton to C.T. Gulick, September 8, 1875, AH, Board of Health.

68 AH, Board of Health Minutes, September 8, 1874, September 8, 9, 15, 1875, March 7, 1876; Lowell Smith to Minister of Interior, September 2, 1875, AH, Board of Health; Petition in favor of Lowell Smith, September 15, 1875, AH, Board of Health; C.T. Gulick to Smith, September 15, 1875; Statement by Dr. Shipley to Board of Health, March 7, 1876, AH, Board of Health; Statement of Attorney-General W.R. Castle to Board of Health, March 20, 1876, AH, Board of Health.

69 Wyllie was one of the strongest proponents of licensing. The mission group generally was against licensing. The following letters in AH give the issues clearly: Wyllie to G.M. Robertson, March 7, 1855, FO Letter Book, XX, p. 163 *ff.*; Wyllie to Henry Hill, May 3, 1855, FO Letter Book, XX, p. 73; Wyllie to C. W. Wheat, December 2, 1855, FO Letter Book, XXII, pp. 90a–91; Armstrong to Wyllie, March 11, 1858, FO & Ex, Local Officials. See also Laws, 1855, pp. 2–3; *Polynesian*, May 26, 1855, March 1, 1856, January 24, 1857, January 16, 1858, September 10, 1859.

70 *Laws*, 1860, p. 35; AH, Cabinet Council Minutes, September 18, 1860; David Gregg to J.W. Austin, September 20, 1860, AH, Interior Department Letter Book, VII, p. 288; Austin to Gregg, October 8, 1860, AH, Interior Department, Miscellaneous, Hospital; S. Spencer to Austin, October 22, 1860, AH, Interior Department Letter Book, VII, p. 305; *Polynesian*, January 28, February 11, 25, April 21, August 4, 18, 25, September 11, 29, November 17, December 8, 29, 1860; *Pacific Commercial Advertiser*. August 23, 30, September 6, 1860.

71 The arguments against admission are set out in an undated MS entitled To the Committee on the Memorial of Ladies of Honolulu to the Trustees of the Queen's Hospital, Kalanianaole Papers. Kamehameha IV's Reign, 1860–1861.

72 The trustees' deliberations and response are printed in *Polynesian*, December 29, 1860.

73 For the newspaper war, see *Pacific Commercial Advertiser*, January 31, February 14, March 7, 28, 1861, February 20, March 27, 1862; *Polynesian*, January 12, 26, February 2, 9, 22, March 2, 9, 23, July 6, 1861, February 15, March 8, 1862, January 16, 1864.

74 *Polynesian*, December 22, 1860, December 28, 1861, March 8, April 5, 1862, June 27, August 15, 1863, January 2, 1864; *Pacific Commercial Advertiser*. January 2, 1862. Lists of life members were compiled from time to time and may be found scattered through AH, Board of Health.

75 *Pacific Commercial Advertiser*, August 17, 1867. Officials reported quarterly; their reports may be found in AH, Board of Health. Marshal William Parke gave a resume in 1868 of the workings of the Act to that point: since October 3, 1860, 888 prostitutes had registered in Honolulu. In March, 1868, 234 remained on the register. Of these, 29 were 14–16 years of age; 114 were 16–20; 85 were 20–30; and 6 over 30. One hundred had been born on Hawai'i, 60 on Maui, 15 on Moloka'i, 55 on O'ahu, 2 on Kaua'i, and 2 on Lāna'i. One hundred and thirteen were married, 107 single, 11 widowed, and 3 divorced. Parke to Board of Health, March 13, 1868, AH, Board of Health, March–April, 1868. Attempts were made in almost every legislature during the sixties and seventies to repeal the Act. Most pressure was generated by native members from rural districts, under Protestant persuasion— or so the defenders of the Act alleged. English and Hawaiian-language papers worried the question endlessly, from fixed positions: no change of opinion was visible from the late fifties to the mid-seventies. Useful illustrative comment nay be found in the successive reports of the Minister of the Interior, and in these

documents in AH: Board of Health Minutes, September 3, 1862, January 25, 1867, August 20, 1874; Robert McKibbin to F.W. Hutchison, March 31, 1870, Board of Health; W.L. Moehonua, April 26, 1875, Interior Department Letter Book, XII, pp. 698–699; and in these letters in Marshal's Letter Book: W.C. Parke to J.H. Brown, August 24, 1874; Parke to Attorney-General, April 15, 1874; Parke to Moehonua, April 17, 1876.

[76] For an illustration of the treatment of the insane before the asylum was established, see Report on the Case of John Mitchiner, September 14, 1857, AH, FO & Ex, Local Officials; W.C. Parke to Lot Kamehameha, September 14, 1857, AH, Interior Department, Miscellaneous, Prisons; S. Spencer to Wyllie, September 15, 1857, AH, Interior Department Letter Book, VII, p. 22. For the asylum in planning and operational stage, see Chief Justice, *Biennial Report*, 1862, p. 3; *Polynesian*, June 7, 21, 1862, January 31, October 10, 1863; *Hawaiian Gazette*. August 11, November 24, 1866.

For similar information on the reformatory or "industrial school," see *Reports* of the President of the Board of Education from 1866 on; and *Polynesian*, December 14, 1861; *Hawaiian Gazette*, February 11, March 18, April 29, 1865; *Pacific Commercial Advertiser*, January 28, 1865, November 30, December 7, 14, 1867, May 7, November 12, 1870, January 14, 1871, April 6, 1872. By the early 1870s, some reformatory boys were being indentured to plantation owners to "learn the sugar trade."

[77] Lewis Mumford, the unexcelled master of the study of cities in history, has remarked on this peculiar propensity of humans to surround themselves with garbage. "For thousands of years city dwellers put up with defective, often quite vile, sanitary arrangements, wallowing in rubbish and filth they certainly had the power to remove, for the occasional task of removal could hardly have been more loathsome than walking and breathing in the constant presence of such ordure. If anyone had sufficient explanation of this indifference to dirt and odor that are repulsive to many animals, even pigs, who take pains to keep themselves and their lairs clean, one might also have a clue to the slow and fitful nature of technological improvement itself, in the five millennia that followed the birth of the city." *The City in History* (New York, 1961), p. 75. His remarks apply as well to Honolulu as to any other city.

[78] For the early years, see: *Pacific Commercial Advertiser*, October 24, 1861; undated list of lepers in AH, Board of Health, 1861; *Polynesian*, April 18, 1863; G.M. Robertson to Dr. Wetmore and others, January 19, 1864, AH, Interior Department Letter Book, VII, p. 506; AH, Cabinet Council Minutes, September 14, 1864; AH, Board of Health Minutes, February 10, 1864, January 31, February 2, March 11, 14, April 3, June 10, July 6, 18, September 20, November 3, 1865; *Laws*, 1864–1865, pp. 62–64; *Hawaiian Gazette*, November 18, 1865. Kuykendall, *Hawaiian Kingdom II*, pp. 72–75, has a good short account.

[79] Causes and treatments are discussed in: *Pacific Commercial Advertiser*. May 22, 1869, August 17, 1872; AH, Board of Health Minutes, June 28, August 5, 1873, August 1, 20, 1874; W.P. Powell to W.L. Green, June 13, 23, August 26, 1874, AH, Board of Health; Akana to W. Moehonua, April 21, 1875, AH, Board of Health; T. W. Everett to Moehonua, August 3, 1875, AH, Board of Health; J. Wodehouse to W.L. Green, December 21, 1874, AH, FO & Ex, British Commissioner.

Mohabeer was charged with malpractice not long before Lowell Smith was; and, over the strong protests of the British Commissioner, he was convicted and set to work on a chain gang. AH, Board of Health, many documents filed at August, 1874; AH, Board of Health Minutes, October 9, December 22, 1874;

Manley Hopkins to W.L. Green, January 23, 1875, AH, FO & Ex, Consul General at London; J. Wodehouse to W.L. Green, September 15, 1875, AH, FO & Ex, British Commissioner.

80 It has been pointed out to me by Professor O.A. Bushnell that more white men contracted leprosy than appear in government statistics. Natives were seen and treated by government physicians; whites went to private physicians. Whites were able to buy their freedom from banishment to Kalawao.

81 The moralist view was developed in: *Pacific Commercial Advertiser*, April 10, 17, 1869, April 22, May 20, June 24, July 1, 8, 29, 1871, July 20, August 17, October 19, 1872.

82 AH, Board of Health Minutes, May 1, 1869, February 8, March 1, April 21, 1873, July 29, 1875; W.C. Parke to A.F. Judd, April 4, 1873, AH, Marshal's Letter Book; W.C. Parke to S.W. Wilcox, April 4, 1873, AH, Marshal's Letter Book; AH, Cabinet Council Minutes, April 8, 1873.

83 Yzendoorn, *Catholic Mission*, pp. 186–222.

84 These remarks are based upon a reading of court calendars and legal reports in the Honolulu press from the mid-forties to the mid-seventies. The papers gave very full coverage to a wide range of cases, in all jurisdictions. Editorial comment and contributed letters on legal subjects were plentiful. A history of the bar in Honolulu and Hawai'i generally would be well worth writing and reading.

85 No systematic treatment of Honolulu's press exists. Professor Charles H. Hunter of the University of Hawai'i has prepared a typescript checklist of journals in various depositories. Some work has been done toward collation and microfilming of complete or near-complete runs. A full-scale study of the Hawaiian-language press is badly needed. It might throw some light on the infinite number of obscurities which limit current understanding of the native community. Ideally, an anthropologist with a taste for documentary work should attempt the task.

86 *Polynesian*, August 7, 1858; *Pacific Commercial Advertiser*, July 29, 1858.

87 *Pacific Commercial Advertiser*, January 15, 1863. Hawaiian chiefs always traveled cabin class.

88 These generalizations come from a perusal of the classified advertisement columns of the English and Hawaiian-language newspapers, as well as the government license books in which were recorded payments of fees necessary for permission to carry on business, and the books of the tax assessors of the Kona district of O'ahu, dating from the mid-fifties. License and tax books are in MS form in AH. They are in incomplete runs, making it very difficult to do quantitative studies with any accuracy.

89 This is mostly deductive work. Complete civil lists do not exist. Those available in AH give information only about the top levels of government and administration; and Hawaiians rarely appear there. Documents in AH emanating from government rarely show Hawaiian signatures.

90 *Polynesian*, December 21, 1861. For a sampling of fire company membership and activity, see *Polynesian*, February 16, April 6, June 8, 22, 1861; *Pacific Commercial Advertiser*, May 7, 1864, November 4, 1865, May 4, 1867, February 5, 1870; *Hawaiian*

Gazette, October 8, 1865, January 22, June 3, 1869, February 10, 1869. The race question aside, fire companies represented the mechanic classes of Honolulu rather than polite society, just as they tended to do on the American mainland and in Australia at the same time. There were occasional caustic remarks by firemen in the press to the effect that, when fires occurred, the gentlemen whose property was being saved stood around sipping whisky while honest working-men toiled at the pumps, hoses, hooks and ladders. See *Polynesian,* January 5, 1861.

91 For membership and activity, see AH, Privy Council Record, X, p. 176, XII, p. 23; AH, Cabinet Council Minutes, February 26, 1862, August 24, 1866, January 12, February 11, 1869; Wyllie to H. Kahanawai, March 11, 1862, AH, FO Letter Book, XLI, pp. 23–24; Wyllie to G.M. Robertson, March 21, 1862, AH, FO Letter Book, XLI, pp. 37–38; *Polynesian,* February 21, 1857, March 6, May 12, June 12, 1858, November 30, December 21, 1861, January 4, June 28, 1862; *Pacific Commercial Advertiser,* May 13, 1858, March 27, 1862; *Hawaiian Gazette,* November 4, 1865, September 4, 1867.

92 The affairs of benevolent societies may be followed in the periodical press. The Protestant groups held their annual meetings about mid-year; and from the sixties on, a New Year directory of Honolulu institutions of this sort was published in the papers.

93 The New Year directories in the newspapers give the best consecutive record of the existence of secular benevolent organizations.

94 *Pacific Commercial Advertiser,* September 3, 1864, February 2, March 2, 1867.

95 *Pacific Commercial Advertiser,* November 12, 1857, August 5, 1858, August 4, 1859, March 25, 1871; Polynesian, August 21, 1858.

96 *Pacific Commercial Advertiser,* March 20, 1862, August 31, September 28, 1867.

97 For a sampling of Hawaiian artifice, see: *Polynesian,* June 12, 1847, July 30, August 21, 1859, September 10, 1859, March 10, 1860; *Pacific Commercial Advertiser,* September 1, 1859, November 23, 1867.

98 This idea is stated elegantly in the early chapters of Mumford, *The City in History.*

99 White approval of the "emancipated" chiefs and courtiers was not extended to include their counterparts among the commoners.

100 For representative comment on the "new" Hawaiian from the forties to the seventies, see Mr. Wyllie's Answers to Questions Put By Dudoit, April 22, 1846, AH, FO & Ex; Minister of Interior, *Biennial Report,* 1857, pp. 11–13; Maria Patton Chamberlain to Isabella, July 10, 1858, HMCS; *Polynesian,* March 8, 15, May 24, 1856, February 4, 1860, March 2, May 25, 1861, September 12, 1863; *Pacific Commercial Advertiser,* February 2, 1860, January 27, 1872; *Nūhou,* March 10, 17, 1874.

101 On the question of changes in marriage and divorce, Robert C. Schmitt has written an interesting short paper, "Marriage and Divorce in Hawaii Before 1870," bringing together legal provisions as they evolved. I thank him and Richard Greer for the chance to see the MS, which will be published in the *Hawaii Historical Review.*

102 *Polynesian,* March 8, 1856, May 8, 1858; *Pacific Commercial Advertiser.* December 4, 1869, August 20, 1870, March 25, 1871, January 20, 1872; *Hawaiian Gazette,* October 2, 1867.

[103] Even a casual inspection of Hawaiian individual names shows that they were striking and memorable far beyond anything in the European or American tradition. Though complaint was made about lack of individuality, what it really concerned was a western difficulty in relating names to kinship groups, particularly in the courts, where issues of property might depend on correct rendering of Hawaiian names in testimony and on documents. Then, too, by mid-century some natives had abandoned their single Hawaiian polysyllabic name for a single "Christian" name—Jim or George or a Hawaiian equivalent—Kimo or Keoki. In this circumstance, the complaint about unidentifiability had some point. See *Polynesian*, September 17, 1859; *Pacific Commercial Advertiser*. September 13, 1860.

[104] For the dandy, see *Polynesian*, May 9, 1863. Even this spectacular native was not identified by the reporter. For the unemployed, see *Pacific Commercial Advertiser*, June 10, 1871, January 6, 1872.

[105] *Pacific Commercial Advertiser*, January 20, 1872. A wide range of opinion existed on the question of whether these characteristics were congenital or acquired. In certain circumstances natives worked "steadily" and "well," but these circumstances were evidently not typical. Majority opinion was as stated above.

[106] *Pacific Commercial Advertiser*, December 22, 1866.

[107] *Pacific Commercial Advertiser*, November 6, 1856, January 5, 1860, April 13, 1867; *Nūhou*, April 14, 1874.

[108] Twain, *Letters from the Sandwich Islands*, pp. 99–128. Interestingly, curiosity-seeking haoles behaved so badly at the palace that all whites were barred from the grounds until the last day of mourning, so Twain found.

[109] *Polynesian*, August 7, 1847.

[110] Some impression of the style and evolution of holidays may be gained from: *Sandwich Island News*, December 2, 1847, March 23, 1848; *Polynesian*, August 10, 1844, December 25, 1847, July 6, August 3, 1850, December 27, 1851, November 20, December 4, 25, 1852, May 27, 1854, December 20, 1856, May 22, August 7, 1858, July 5, August 9, December 27, 1862, July 25, August 1, 1863; *Pacific Commercial Advertiser*, May 24, 1860, June 29, 1861, July 10, 1862, November 5, 1864, April 15, May 27, July 22, August 5, 1865, December 1, 1866, July 6, October 5, 1867, January 2, July 31, 1869, December 3, 1870, June 10, July 1, 8, August 5, December 2, 30, 1871, March 30, 1872; *Hawaiian Gazette*, July 8, 22, August 5, 1865, January 5, November 27, December 25, 1867. See also Hipa to Emma and others, January 14, 1871, Emma Collection (Nylen-Altman); AH, Cabinet Council Minutes, January 17, 1873; *Hawaiian Annual for 1922*, 58–61; *Saturday Press*, October 29, 1881.

CHAPTER 8

[1] *Hawaiian Annual for 1917*, 153.

[2] In such matters, of course, Honolulu was little different from comparable towns on the American mainland. For a good introduction to the subject, see Charles E. Peterson, "Pioneer Architects and Builders of Honolulu," Hawaiian Historical

Society, *Annual Report*, 72 (Honolulu, 1964), pp. 7–28.

[3] The Hawaiian Hotel opened a branch at Waikīkī in 1875, but the beach did not really begin to come into its own until the 1880s and 1890s, by which time Honolulu publicists were referring to Waikīkī as the "Newport" or "Long Branch" of the islands. The analogy was absurd, as travelers discovered. Waikīkī was the show-place of Hawai'i, but its amenities were primitive in the extreme by comparison with those of the celebrated watering places on the east coast of the United States. Cf. Cleveland Amory, *The Last Resorts* (New York, 1952). Two unpublished theses deal with Waikīkī in the nineteenth and twentieth centuries: Richard Walter Coller, "Waikīkī; A Study of Invasion and Succession as Applied to a Tourist Area," MA, Hawai'i, 1952; and John Lewis Taylor, "Waikīkī: A Study in the Development of a Tourist Community," PhD, Clark, 1953. Both are strong on ecological theory and weak on history, particularly of the nineteenth century.

[4] For the omnibus experiment, see *Pacific Commercial Advertiser*, February 29, March 7, 21, November 21, 1868.

[5] C.T. Gulick to C.C. Coleman, October 7, 1876, AH, Interior Department Letter Book, XIII. For a sampling of policy statements and comment on the use of open spaces around Honolulu, see Gorham Gilman, "Journal of a Tour on Oahu, 1848," MS, HHS; Gilman, "Honolulu–1848," AH, Privy Council Record, III, pp. 437, 561, IIIb, p. 635, XII, p. 87; Charles Alfred Castle to his wife, September 28, October 23, December 12, 1873, HMCS; AH, Cabinet Council Minutes, April 9, 1875; C.T. Gulick to A.S. Cleghorn, August 31, 1875, AH, Interior Department Letter Book, XIII, p. 67; *Polynesian*, August 4, 1849, January 9, 1858, July 2, 9, October 8, 1859, June 30, 1860; *Pacific Commercial Advertiser*, August 20, 1857, August 5, 1858, August 25, September 1, October 8, 1859, March 28, 1861, March 5, 1864, September 16, 1865, May 26, 1866, January 12, July 20, 1867, July 22, 1871, June 8, 1872, September 27, 1873; *Hawaiian Gazette*, July 1, 1865, October 30, 1867, February 26, 1868, *July 14, 1875; Hawaiian Annual for 1910*, pp. 139–141.

[6] Policy discussions on retrenchment as it affected Honolulu's government are in AH, FO & Ex, Local Officials, several documents filed at July–August, 1861. See also documents at AH, FO & Ex, Privy and Cabinet Councils, March 13, 1862. For comments on the effect of retrenchment, see *Pacific Commercial Advertiser*, December 12, 1861; *Polynesian*, May 10, 1862.

[7] For the establishment and failure of the gasworks, see AH, FO & Ex, Privy Council Petitions, July 22, 1858; AH, Privy Council Record, X, p. 244, XI, p. 13; C.R. Goodwin to Wyllie, September 15, 1858, AH, FO & Ex, Hawaiian Officials Abroad; W.H. Tiffany to Lot Kamehameha, January 26, 1859, AH, Interior Department Letters, Miscellaneous; Wyllie to Goodwin, November 30, 1859, AH, FO & Ex, Hawaiian Officials Abroad; *Pacific Commercial Advertiser*, July 26, October 4, 11, 1860, May 23, 1861, A new firm was established in 1866–1867 to try again. *Hawaiian Gazette*, January 12, 1867.

[8] See, for example, *Pacific Commercial Advertiser*, September 8, 1859.

[9] The best place to begin a study of public works finances and accomplishments is in the periodic reports to the legislature of the Minister of the Interior and the Minister of Finance. The Honolulu press, both official and opposition, commented volumi-nously every time a new project was announced, or an old one was completed or abandoned.

[10] For some cases of the committee system at work, see AH, Interior Department, Miscellaneous, Roads, Oʻahu, August 15, 1860, June 29, 1871, January 24, 1877; AH, Interior Department, Miscellaneous, Royal Hawaiian Agricultural Society, October 2, 31, December 8, 1866; H.A. Widemann to W. Kaumahi and others, September 18, 1865, AH, Interior Department Letter Book, VII, pp. 617-1/2; Notice of F.W. Hutchison, October 2, 1866, AH, Interior Department Letter Book, VIII, p. 22; Widemann to G.H. Luce, November 3, 1866, AH, Interior Department Letter Book, VIII, p. 24; Notice of F.W. Hutchison, January 8, 1870, AH, Interior Department Letter Book, X, p. 101; C.T. Gulick to W.H. Thompson and others, February 16, 1871, AH, Interior Department Letter Book, X, p. 386. The committee system operated under Section 184 of the 1859 Civil Code.

[11] *Pacific Commercial Advertiser*, September 25, 1856, May 9, 1861, January 26, 1867, January 6, 1872; *Hawaiian Gazette*, July 22, 1865.

[12] *Polynesian*, October 4, 1856, November 19, 1859; *Pacific Commercial Advertiser*. October 2, 1856, September 12, 1861, March 27, April 10, 1862, May 14, 1863.

[13] According to John Colcord Journal, windmills were introduced to Honolulu by Captain Eliab Grimes. No date is given, but by the forties there were "four or five," so Colcord said.

[14] For these and other developments in the water system, see: AH, Journal of Internal Improvements, 1847–1848, September 20, 1847; AH, Privy Council Record, III, pp. 486–488, 577, 671, IX, pp. 69, 111, 133; AH, Ministerial Conferences, 1855–1856, *passim.*; S. Spencer to H. Holdsworth, May 22, 1855, AH, Interior Department Letter Book, VI, p. 296; A.P. Everett and others to Minister of War, September 19, 1855, AH, Public Works, Miscellaneous; C.H. Lewers and others to Wyllie, January 21, 1856, AH, Public Works, Miscellaneous; *Polynesian*, May 18, June 1, 1850, June 16, August 18, 1855, May 24, 1856, July 18, 23, 25, 1857, August 8, September 5, 1857; *Hawaiian Annual for 1923*, pp. 47–53.

[15] The preceding summary was drawn from; H. Swinton to Superintendent of Public Works, January 25, 1856, AH, Public Works, Miscellaneous; D. Weston to Wyllie, June 24, 1856, AH, Public Works, Miscellaneous; W.E. Cuttrell and others to Lot Kamehameha, September 15, 1857, AH, Interior Department, Miscellaneous, Water, Oʻahu; Theo. H. Davies and others to E.O. Hall, October 24, 1873, AH, Interior Department, Miscellaneous, Water, Oʻahu; John Kakina and others to W. Moehonua, May 27, 1875, AH, Interior Department, Miscellaneous, Roads, Oʻahu, Honolulu; Minister of Interior, *Report*, 1852, p. 8; *Polynesian*, August 21, 1852, September 19, November 14, 1857; *Hawaiian Annual for 1906*, pp. 55–62.

[16] The planning and building of the new water-works may be followed in: Wm. Webster to Lot Kamehameha, August 11, 1859, AH, Public Works, Miscellaneous; Janion, Green to Lot Kamehameha, December 1, 1859, AH, Public Works, Miscellaneous; Agreement of January 24, 1860, AH, Interior Department Letters, Miscellaneous; Minister of Interior to J. B. Webster, January 27, 1860, AH, Interior Department Letter Book, VII, p. 248; S. Spencer to Wyllie, January 30, 1860, AH, FO & Ex, Local Officials; Wm. Webster to Lot Kamehameha, September 10, 1861, AH, Interior Department Letters, Miscellaneous; Minister of Interior, *Report*. 1860, p. 6; Minister of Finance, *Report*, 1860, p. 2; *Polynesian*, April 23, 1859, January 28, May 12, 17, August 25, 1860; *Pacific Commercial Advertiser*, November 29, 1860, January 31, May 16, 1861.

[17] Honolulu Water Works Summary, July 1, 1861, AH, Interior Department, Miscellaneous.

[18] *Pacific Commercial Advertiser*, September 29, October 6, 1866; *Hawaiian Gazette*, September 29, 1866.

[19] J.H. Wood to W.L. Moehonua, January 16, 1875, AH, Interior Department, Miscellaneous, Roads, O'ahu.

[20] For a sampling of typical issues in the period of changing land use and conse-quent difficulty in Nu'uanu valley, see Kekūanaō'a to C.C. Harris, July 22, 1851, AH, Interior Department Letter Book, V, Part 2, p. 491; J.H. Wood to F.W. Hutchison, October 21, 1869, AH, Interior Department, Miscellaneous, Water Works, Honolulu, Luakaha Water Claims; AH, Cabinet Council Minutes, January 2, 12, 1869; Minister of Finance, *Report*, 1870, pp. 14–15; Charles Alfred Castle to his wife, September 22, 24, 29, October 6, November 5, 1873, HMCS; *Polynesian*, May 9, 1863; *Pacific Commercial Advertiser*, August 28, 1856, September 29, 1866, January 19, October 12, 1867, June 18, 25, September 10, 1870, August 30, September 20, 27, 1873; *Hawaiian Gazette*, September 22, 1866, February 13, 1867; *Nūhou*, August 22, 1873.

[21] The progress of the Luakaha claims may be followed in AH, Interior Department, Miscellaneous, Water Works, Honolulu Luakaha Water Claims, containing the Hillebrand case and several others. For other governmental activity in the late sixties and early seventies, including the growth of conservationist sentiment, see AH, Cabinet Council Minutes, January 13, 1865, October 1, 22, 1873, December 24, 1874, November 30, 1875, April 18, November 9, 21, 1876; Māmala and others to Minister of Interior, December 10, 1875, AH, Interior Department, Miscellaneous, Water, O'ahu; E.O. Hall to A.S. Hartwell, July 29, 1873, AH, Interior Department Letter Book, XII, p. 309; E.O. Hall to Palau, October 18, 1873, AH, Interior Department Letter Book, XII, p. 374; W. Green to Hawaiian Consul at Melbourne, September 21, 1874, AH, FO Letter Book, LII, 838; C.T. Gulick to A.S. Hartwell, October 19, 1876, AH, Interior Department Letter Book, XIII; *Hawaiian Gazette*, March 4, 1865, February 24, 1869; *Pacific Commercial Advertiser*, February 4, June 17, 1865, October 5, 12, 1867, August 26, 1871, March 16, 1872.

[22] A dispassionate inquiry shows some substance to the allegations. It is true without doubt that many contracts, large and small, were awarded without public adver-tisement. The government's *Hawaiian Gazette* handled the charges sophistically by saying that the government did not call for sealed tenders on works contracts because it wanted the "best workmen;" like private citizens, it reserved the right to choose them itself. If a man were competent, and had the confidence of the Ministers and the public too, the *Gazette* could not see what difference it made how he was chosen to do the work. Who were the beneficiaries of the govern-ment's closed policy? Theodore C. Heuck for one—for a time in the sixties, when his architectural and contracting business was at its height, he was also head of the Public Works Bureau, and was therefore in the happy position of being able to award himself contracts. Other names which crop up in this connection are those of Supreme Court Justice H.A. Widemann (who in 1867 was able to save Heuck from coming to trial on a charge of having knowingly received large amounts of whalebone stolen from ships in the harbor), Police Magistrate John Montgomery, and Attorney-General C.C. Harris. Heuck's Honolulu was far from being Tweed's New York, but *mutatis mutandis* there was a similarity in tone. See D. Foster & Co. to Robert Stirling, June 26, 1868, AH, Public Works, Miscellaneous; Gilbert

Waller and others to Minister of Interior, June 21, 1871, AH, Interior Department Letters, Miscellaneous; *Pacific Commercial Advertiser*, January 10, 1861, June 17, 24, September 2, 1865, November 3, 1866, July 31, August 7, December 4, 11, 1869, April 15, June 10, 1871, April 13, 1872; *Hawaiian Gazette*, August 26, 1865. Eventually, in 1873, a first move was made to restrain government officers from doing business on the side. Charles Alfred Castle to his wife, August 11, 1873, HMCS.

[23] For a convenient account of the circumstances, see *Hawaiian Annual for 1906*. pp. 75–78. See also Charles E. Peterson, "The Iolani Palaces and the Barracks," *Journal of the Society of Architectural Historians*, XXII, 2 (May, 1963), pp. 91–92.

[24] There are many descriptions of the first 'Iolani Palace. Among the best are those in *Polynesian*, November 9, 1844; Journal of Chester Smith Lyman, MS, HMCS, May 15, 1846; Judd, *Honolulu*, pp. 130–131; Bates, *Sandwich Island Notes*, p. 36. Cf. Foreign Testimony, I, 12, Claim 3, p. 39, Claim 31, II, p. 30 *ff.*, Claim 250.

[25] Kalākaua to W. Moehonua, March 24, 1876, AH, Interior Department, Miscellaneous, Prisons.

[26] For the planning of the second palace, see the reports of the Minister of Finance from 1866 on, which summarize a great deal of documentary material in AH, and at the same time give cost figures. The best way to begin a systematic study of the second palace is in the unpublished collection of source materials compiled by David Forbes for the 1965 session of the state legislature of Hawai'i. A copy is in AH. Peterson, "The Iolani Palaces and the Barracks," pp. 95–103, has a good account of the planning and building, Peterson quotes extensively from source materials in AH, and the article has several interesting photographs.

[27] AH, Privy Council Record, XI, pp. 141–143, 161; AH, Cabinet Council Minutes, January 29, 1864; C.S. Kittredge to Curtis Lyons, June 20–28, 1855, Curtis Lyons Papers, MSS, AH; *Pacific Commercial Advertiser*, December 17, 1863; *Hawaiian Gazette*, June 17; October 14, November 4, 1865 (this issue contained a list of coffins and their arrangement in the mausoleum).

[28] For Honolulu Hale, see *Sandwich Island Gazette*, July 30, 1836; Foreign Testimony, III, p. 434; Gilman, "Honolulu–1848;" AH, Cabinet Council Minutes, March 3, 1846, October 1, 1853; AH, Privy Council Record, II, p. 423, III, p. 687, 747, 819, VI, p. 70, 126–128, VII p. 327, VIII, p. 79, 113; AH, FO & Ex, Privy Council Reports, December 19, 1853; AH, FO & Ex, Reports of Trustees to Settle the King's Debts, Folder 7, Document 13, October 31, 1853; Wyllie to the Committee on Government Offices, October 31, 1853, AH, FO & Ex, Local Officials; *Polynesian*, February 18, 25, 1854.

[29] For the offices of the period before 1871, see Wyllie to Lot Kamehameha, January 9, 1858, AH, FO Letter Book, XLVII, p. 92 *ff.*; *Pacific Commercial Advertiser*, March 14, 1861, March 20, July 10, 1862; *Polynesian*, July 12, 1862.

[30] For Ali'iōlani Hale, see: AH, Cabinet Council Minutes, November 28, 1870, January 10, March 20, October 5, 1871; Minister of Finance, *Reports*, 1868–1872. There are many letters in AH, Interior Department Letter Book, XI, and in AH, 'Iolani Palace File. See also *Friend*, March, 1872; *Pacific Commercial Advertiser*, October 15, 1870, January 27, February 17, 1872, June 6, 1874.

[31] For general information on the new steamer, see *Hawaiian Annual for 1889*, pp. 73–77; Kemble, "Pioneer Hawaiian Steamers, 1852–1877," pp. 15–27; Kuykendall,

Hawaiian Kingdom, II, pp. 164–168; W.H.D. King, *Pictorial Maritime History of Hawaii*, 5 vols. (n.p.,n.d.), V, p. 133.

[32] For easy reference to company re-organizations, see Kuykendall, *Hawaiian Kingdom*, II, pp. 164–168.

[33] AH, Cabinet Council Minutes, February 28, March 1, 16, 1870.

[34] For a time in 1862–1865, the 80-ton schooner *Annie Laurie*, converted to steam by Honolulu shipwrights, supplemented the *Kilauea's* runs between the islands.

[35] The shifting fortunes of the *Kilauea* may be followed in the published reports of the Minister of Finance between 1860 and 1876. Policy discussions are in AH, Cabinet Council Minutes, September 26, November 3, 1860, February 26, May 7, 1862, September 5, 1863, January 11, 14, September 14, 19, 27, 1864, July 7, 1865, November 14, 1867, February 18, May 7, 1869, March 1, 16, 1870, April 17, December 24, 29, 1874, April 9, 22, September 1, 1875, December 27, 1876. See also the following letters and documents, selected from scores in AH, Interior Department, Miscellaneous, Shipping: Janion, Green to Lot Kamehameha, May 5, 8, 9, 10, October 13, 1862; Janion, Green to G.M. Robertson, January 12, 1864; W.L. Green to C.G. Hopkins, September 3, 1864; Janion, Green to Hopkins, September 19, 1864, January 19, July 5, 1865; Wm. Berrill and others to J.C. Pfluger, February 6, 1866; Janion, Green to F.W. Hutchison, March 19, 1866, May 30, 1867; Bishop & Co. to W.L. Green, January 15, 1868; Estimates of S.G. Wilder, March 28, 31, 1874; Wilder to W. Moehonua, December 26, 1874, May 4, 1875; Archibald McIntyre and others to Wilder, November 1, 1875; Balance sheet by Wilder, March 31, 1876. There are many letters in AH, Interior Department Letter Books, VII, VIII; and in AH, FO Letter Books, XL, XLI. The classified advertisement columns of the *Polynesian, Pacific Commercial Advertiser*, and *Hawaiian Gazette* supply information about changing schedules and routes; and editorial and letters columns comment on the quality of service.

[36] AH, Cabinet Council Minutes, February 14, 1863; C.G. Hopkins to J. Meek, September 15, 1864, AH, Interior Department Letter Book, VII, pp. 551–552; *Polynesian*, July 19, August 2, 1862, January 24, 31, August 20, 1864.

[37] For the Pacific Mail affair, see: AH, Cabinet Council Minutes, September 20, 1866, February 19, 1867; F.W. Hutchison to Captain Baby, October 2, 1866, AH, Interior Department, Miscellaneous, Shipping; Hutchison to Allan McLane, April 1, 29, 1867, AH, Interior Department Letter Book, VIII, pp. 96, 117–118; McLane to Minister of Interior, June 1, 1867, AH, Interior Department, Miscellaneous, Shipping; *Pacific Commercial Advertiser*, March 4, May 6, June 24, September 16, October 28, December 2, 1865, January 6, 1866, February 2, April 6, 13, 1867; *Hawaiian Gazette*, September 29, 1866.

[38] AH, Cabinet Council Minutes, February 3, 1866; *Hawaiian Gazette*, January 27, February 3, 1866; *Pacific Commercial Advertiser*, January 27, February 3, 10, 17, March 3, 24, April 7, May 12, 1866.

[39] For the California, Oregon, and Mexico Steamship Company, see: F.W. Hutchison to C. de Varigny, September 7, 1867, AH, Interior Department Letter Book, VIII, p. 173; R. Feuerstein to Hutchison, September 6, 1867, AH, Interior Department, Miscellaneous, Shipping; Hutchison to J. Bellman, November 1, 1867, AH, Interior Department Letter Book, VIII, pp. 199–200; Ben Holladay to Hutchison, March

31, 1868, AH, Interior Department, Miscellaneous, Shipping, and other documents filed here for 1868, including a contract dated August 10, 1868; Hutchison to Holladay, April 2, 1868, AH, Interior Department Letter Book, VIII, p. 250; AH, Privy Council Record, XI, 277; Minister of Finance, *Report*, 1868, pp. 4–5, See also documents in AH, FO & Ex, Consul at San Francisco, 1867, and US Minister, 1867. *Pacific Commercial Advertiser*, September 21, 1867, recorded the arrival of the Idaho, and on March 6, 1869, the withdrawal of the *Montana*. Press coverage was quite full between these dates.

[40] For the Australian connection, see: Collie, Stewart & Co. to F.W. Hutchison, October 19, 1869, AH, Interior Department, Miscellaneous, Shipping; Hutchison to Collie, Stewart, October 20, 1869, AH, Interior Department Letter Book, X, p. 57; Hutchison to J.C. Pfluger, November 27, 1869, AH, Interior Department Letter Book, X, p. 79; AH, Cabinet Council Minutes, March 16, April 23, 1870; Minister of Finance, *Report*, 1870, pp. 20–21; C.C. Harris to S.F. Odell, April 20, 1870, AH, FO Letter Book, L, p. 185 *ff.*; and several letters in AH, FO & Ex, Miscellaneous Foreign, 1870, See also *Pacific Commercial Advertiser*, October 23, 1869, February 5, 19, 26, March 5, April 23, 1870; *Hawaiian Gazette*, March 16, April 27, 1870.

[41] For the competition between Hall and Webb, see: W. Webb to Minister of Foreign Affairs, August 25, 1870, AH, FO Letter Book, Correspondence Received, I, p. 267; C.C. Karris to Webb, September 24, 1870, AH, FO Letter Book, L, pp. 401–402; Harris to H.H. Hall, October 25, 1870, AH, FO Letter Book, L, p. 443; Hall to Harris, November 29, 1870, AH, FO Letter Book, Correspondence Received, II, p. 69–71; F.W. Hutchison to W. Neilson, October 25, 1870, AH, Interior Department Letter Book, X, pp. 312–313; Webb to Harris, April 15, 1871, AH, FO & Ex, Miscellaneous Foreign; Robert Stirling to Hackfeld & Co., May 5, 1871, AH, Interior Department Letter Book, IX, p. 108; Ben Holladay to Harris, May 5, 1871, AH, FO Letter Book, Correspondence Received, II, pp. 264–265; Harris to Webb, May 17, 1871, AH, FO Letter Book, XLVIII, pp. 130–131; Hutchison to Hackfeld & Co., June 22, 1871, AH, Interior Department Letter Book, X, p. 490; Harris to H.W. Severance, August 1, 1871, AH, FO Letter Book, XLVIII, pp. 216–217; AH, Privy Council Record, XI, pp. 303, 309–311, 313, 321–325; AH, Cabinet Council Minutes, January 10, August 2, 1871; C. Brewer & Co. to Hutchison, October 21, 1871, AH, Interior Department, Miscellaneous, Shipping. The *Pacific Commercial Advertiser* throughout this period supported American interests, accusing the *Hawaiian Gazette* and the government of favoring the Hall line over the Webb line for anti-American political motives. There seems no reason to believe this was true.

[42] For the development of Webb's operation, see: AH, Cabinet Council Minutes, February 14, 22, March 26, December 18, 1872, February 7, March 4, 1873; Minister of Finance, *Report*, 1872, pp. 8–16; C.C. Harris to C. St. Julian, December 18, 1871, AH, FO Letter Book, XLVIII, p. 340 *ff.*; F.W. Hutchison to Julius Vogel, December 19, 1871, AH, Interior Department Letter Book, X, pp. 679–680; Harris to J. Cruikshank, March 13, 1872, AH, FO Letter Book, XLIX, p. 599; R. Stirling to A.S. Webster, March 17, 1872, AH, Interior Department Letter Book, IX, pp. 143–144; Hutchison to W. Webb, April 15, 1872, AH, Interior Department Letter Book, XII, p. 14; H.W. Severance to Hutchison, January 30, 1873, AH, FO & Ex, Consul at San Francisco; Hutchison to Hackfeld & Co., October 30, 1872, AH, Interior Department Letter Book, XII, p. 83; Hackfeld & Co. to Minister of Interior, February 5, 1873, AH, Interior Department, Miscellaneous, Postmaster General; E.O. Hall to Hackfeld & Co., February 7, 1873, AH, Interior Department Letter Book, XII, pp. 133–134; A. Webster to C. Bishop, April 9, 1873, AH, FO & Ex, Consul at Sydney; Bishop to J. Mitchell, April 10, 1873, AH, FO Letter Book, LII, pp. 164–165; E.O. Hall to Hackfeld

& Co., April 30, May 8, 1873, AH, Interior Department Letter Book, XII, pp. 205, 218; and these letters and documents in AH, Interior Department, Miscellaneous, Shipping: Collie, Stewart to Hutchison, February 15, 1871; Contract of April 16, 1871, with sketches of proposed wharf facilities; Hutchison to Hackfeld & Co., November 2, 1872; Hackfeld & Co. to Hall, April 30, 1873. In the Honolulu press hardly an issue went by without comment on the Webb line.

43 E.O. Hall to Thomas Russell, May 9, 1873, AH, Interior Department Letter Book, XII, pp. 219–221; Robert Stirling to Colonial Secretary, New South Wales, August 7, 1873, AH, FO & Ex, Miscellaneous Foreign; Hall to Hackfeld & Co., December 22, 1873, AH, Interior Department Letter Book, XII, pp. 420–421.

44 Draft contracts with the new Hall line are in AH, Interior Department, Miscellaneous, Shipping, at January, 1874. See also Manley Hopkins to C. Bishop, December 6, 1873, AH, FO & Ex, Consul General at London; E.O. Hall to Hackfeld & Co., January 13, 1874, AH, Interior Department Letter Book, XII, p. 446; H.W. Severance to W. Green, June 25, August 13, 15, September 30, 1875, AH, FO & Ex, Consul at San Francisco; A.P. Bacon to W. Moehonua, September 2, 1875, AH, Interior Department, Miscellaneous, Shipping; J.S. Walker to Bacon, October 22, 1875, AH, Interior Department, Miscellaneous, Shipping; AH, Cabinet Council Minutes, January 29, 1874; Minister of Finance, *Report*, 1874, pp. 4–5, *Report*, 1876, pp. 9–10.

45 A year earlier, she had brought measles: see correspondence in AH, Board of Health, for November, 1867.

46 For the *Idaho* case, see: AH, Board of Health Minutes, December 21, 24, 1868, January 1, 7, 8, 16, April 9, 1869; AH, Cabinet Council Minutes, December 30, 1868, January 2, 1867; AH, Privy Council Record, XI, p. 299; Dr. Buffum to Secretary of Board of Health, January 22, February 4, 1869, AH, Board of Health; and *Pacific Commercial Advertiser* and *Hawaiian Gazette*, January–April, 1869. *The Advertiser* was very critical of the government in this as in most matters.

47 For the 1872 case, see: Juliette Cooke to Sister, May 31, July 7, 1872, HMCS; AH, Board of Health Minutes, June 13, July 1, August 27, September 20, 1872; C.T. Gulick to S.H. Phillips, June 28, 1872, AH, Interior Department Letter Book, XII, p. 34; W. C. Parke to F.W. Hutchison, July 3, 1872, AH, Board of Health; Hutchison to Robert Stirling, October 2, 1872, AH, Interior Department Letter Book, XII, pp. 63–72; Smallpox Reports for 1872 in AH, Board of Health; and the Honolulu periodical press from late May to August, 1872.

48 AH, Cabinet Council Minutes, December 5, 1870.

49 AH, Cabinet Council Minutes, January 10, March 20, 1871; C.C. Harris to J. Mott Smith, March 22, 1871, AH, TO Letter Book, L, p. 691; *Pacific Commercial Advertiser*, May 13, 1871.

50 The *Gazette* and the *Advertiser* followed the progress of the hotel closely. Editorial comments and letters appeared in almost every issue. See especially *Pacific Commercial Advertiser*, May 27, June 24, 1871. See also AH, Cabinet Council Minutes, August 18, 1874

51 AH, Cabinet Council Minutes, September 27, 1871.

52 *Pacific Commercial Advertiser*, September 30, October 7, 1871.

[53] Minister of Finance, *Report*, 1872, pp. 6–7; *Pacific Commercial Advertiser*, May 18, June 22, September 7, 1872; *Hawaiian Gazette*, April 30, 1872.

[54] Herbert came to Honolulu from San Francisco, where he had managed big hotels for several years. *Hawaiian Gazette*, November 29, 1871.

[55] Herbert's lease is in AH, Interior Department, Flat File. See also AH, Cabinet Council Minutes, February 22, 1872.

[56] Isabella Bird [Bishop], *Six Months Among The Palm Groves, Coral Reefs, And Volcanoes Of The Sandwich Islands*, 5th ed. (London, 1882), pp. 23–24.

[57] For the business affairs of the hotel, see: AH, Cabinet Council Minutes, December 27, 1876; Charles Alfred Castle to his wife, June 10, July 5, August 15, 1873, HMCS; Allen Herbert to Castle, April 13, 1874, AH, Interior Department, Miscellaneous, Hawaiian Hotel; Report of Mott Smith, May 13, 1878, AH, Interior Department, Miscellaneous, Hawaiian Hotel. There are several letters in AH, Attorney-General Letter Book, for March and April, 1876.

[58] For the record of a typical business relationship between Honolulu and the American mainland, see AH, Private Collections, Daniel C. Waterman, Business Letters Received, 1854–1856.

[59] For the course of emigration, see AH, Governor's Letter Books; AH, Interior Department Letter Book, V, Part 1; and the *Polynesian's* weekly and quarterly statements. The departure rate was naturally highest in the months just after discovery; by mid-1849 passenger traffic was back to something like normal.

[60] Each issue of Honolulu's weeklies published after the discovery contained fresh stories of the impact of gold upon Honolulu. Characteristic accounts are in: *Sandwich Island News*, August 17, 1848; *Polynesian*, August 26, September 23, 30, 1848, March 31, 1849. The gossip column of "Jingle" in the *Polynesian* is interesting for the hectic months of late 1848.

[61] *Polynesian*, October 14, 1848, described the streets as a "moving panorama" of boxes, bales and bundles being shipped to California. Theodore C. Heuck arrived at Honolulu in February, 1850, to find the businessmen making "astounding" profits. Theodore C. Heuck to T.G. Heuck, February 17, 1850, Heuck Papers. Numbers of merchant ships visiting Honolulu went from 90 in 1848, to 180 in 1849, 469 in 1850, and 446 in 1851. Morgan, *Hawaii*, pp, 154–155.

[62] The ardent American nationalist George Lathrop (who became a leading member of the Committee of Thirteen) thought along these lines. He had gone into the sugar business in 1850. At the very end of the boom, he tried to interest Sam Brannan and other "filibusterers" in forming a partnership. Brannan independently bought several pieces of land in Honolulu during his short stay. Charles R. Bishop to Joel Turrill, December 16, 1851, Turrill Collection.

[63] The economic collapse may be followed in the *Polynesian*, On February 1, 1841, the paper considered opportunities for young people to be greater than ever before at Honolulu; on June 21, business was described as dull and markets overcrowded; by August 23, $300,000–1,00,000 of local produce was waiting in vain for ships to pick it up. With the temporary increase of population, food and lodging went up in price briefly, going against the general depression for a few months.

⁶⁴ W.P. Alexander to William Alexander, December 1, 1851, Alexander & Baldwin Collection, MSS, HMCS; William Miller to Richard Charlton, October 20, 1851, AH, British Consulate, Letter Book, General Correspondence; Richard Armstrong to C.S. Lyman, September 11, 1851, HMCS; Charles R. Bishop to Joel Turrill, October 9, 1851, Turrill Collection; R.C. Wyllie to Charles St. Julian, July 23, 1851, AH, FO Letter Book, XIa, p. 537.

⁶⁵ See, for example, the optimistic editorial in *Polynesian,* September 20, 1850.

⁶⁶ William Lee to Joel Turrill, October 11, 1851, March 24, 1852, Turrill Collection.

⁶⁷ The successive *Reports* of the Minister of Finance give the best picture of changing views on tariffs and the like.

⁶⁸ Morgan, *Hawaii*, p. 140.

⁶⁹ Morgan, *Hawaii*, pp. 140–141.

⁷⁰ For Hawai'i's experience in relation to the whaling industry as a whole, see the standard works: Alexander Starbuck, *History of the American Whale Fishery...to 1876* (Waltham, 1878); W.S. Tower, *History of the American Whale Fishery* (Philadelphia, 1907); J.T. Jenkins, *A History of the Whale Fisheries* (London, 1921).

⁷¹ *Polynesian*, May 21, 1853.

⁷² For the beginning of the system, see *Polynesian*, August 30, 1851.

⁷³ *Polynesian*, January 8, 1859.

⁷⁴ *Polynesian*, May 21, 1853.

⁷⁵ *Polynesian*, November 11, 1858, January 1, 1859; *Pacific Commercial Advertiser*, December 23, 1858.

⁷⁶ *Pacific Commercial Advertiser*, June 23, July 28, 1859; *Polynesian*, July 9, 1859.

⁷⁷ *Polynesian*, January 1, March 5, 1859. It is worth noting that even though 1858 and 1859 were good years for the Arctic fleet, the complaints continued unabated.

⁷⁸ *Hawaiian Annual for 1913*, p. 47 *ff.*; Kuykendall, *Hawaiian Kingdom*, II, p. 139; Morgan, *Hawai'i*, p. 146. See also the *Reports* of the Minister of the Interior and the Minister of Finance throughout the fifties and sixties. The newspapers generally encouraged the home industry, estimating that one Honolulu whaleship was worth four New England ships to the city. See, for example, *Polynesian*, February 6, 13, 27, 1858; *Pacific Commercial Advertiser*, February 25, 1858.

⁷⁹ *Polynesian*, August 27, 1859, May 30, 1863.

⁸⁰ Morgan, *Hawaii*, pp. 142–144, has an interesting discussion.

⁸¹ AH, Privy Council Record, XI, 253; C.E. Hitchcock to R.C. Wyllie, August 7, 1865, AH, FO & Ex, Hawaiian Officials Abroad.

⁸² AH, FO & Ex, has files on the Brig *Harvest* in 1864 and 1865. See also a heavy correspondence in AH, FO Letter Book, XLVIII. Between August and November, 1865,

426 Honolulu—The First Century

the Honolulu newspapers commented on the case. For the arrival of the abandoned seamen at Honolulu, see *Hawaiian Gazette*, November 25, 1865.

[83] See correspondence in AH, FO & Ex, Hawaiian Officials Abroad, November-
December, 1865. The government pressed the *Harvest* case for several years without
success.

Ten years after the war, Waddell was in command of the steamer *City of San Francisco*,
owned by the Pacific Mail Steamship Company, which ran a service between San
Francisco and Hawai'i for a time in the seventies. Waddell's employers transferred him to a run which did not take him between the west coast and the islands
because they feared that he might be arrested if he came ashore at Honolulu. In
January, 1876, the Hawaiian government, on the verge of completing a valuable
commercial treaty with the United States, and anxious not to offend the American
government, passed a resolution assuring Waddell that he could visit Honolulu
without fear of prosecution. AH, Cabinet Council Minutes, January 5, 1876; A.P.
Bacon to Hackfeld & Co., December 3, 1875, AH, FO & Ex, Miscellaneous Foreign;
H. Severance to W. Green, January 26, 1876, AH, FO & Ex, Consul General at San
Francisco. Ironically, the Honolulu agent for the Pacific Mail Steamship Company
was Hackfeld & Co., former owner of the *Harvest*.

[84] *Pacific Commercial Advertiser*, October 28, 1871.

[85] The Arctic disaster and its effects on Honolulu are described in the *Hawaiian Gazette*
and the *Pacific Commercial Advertiser* for October–November, 1871, especially the
Advertiser's special edition of October 28. See also W.C. Parke to F.W. Hutchison,
October 25, 1871, AH, Interior Department, Miscellaneous, Shipping, Hawaiian
Seamen; several letters in AH, FO & Ex, Miscellaneous Local, 1871; Minister of
Finance, *Biennial Report*, 1872, p. 5.

[86] For representative comment along these lines, see *Polynesian*, December 12, 1857;
Pacific Commercial Advertiser, February 10, 1859; *Hawaiian Gazette*, August 19,
1865.

[87] I have chosen not to go into these minor agricultural ventures in detail. Most
were abortive; most centered on the outer islands; all have been well covered
in published works. See Bradley, American *Frontier*, pp. 240–250; Kuykendall,
Hawaiian Kingdom, I, pp. 170–185, 313–327, II, pp. 149–162; Morgan, *Hawaii*, pp.
159-172.

[88] The latter figure was actually for 20 months from January, 1840 to August, 1841.
Polynesian, September 4, 1841.

[89] Kuykendall, *Hawaiian Kingdom*, I, p. 315.

[90] Richard Armstrong to W.N. Armstrong, January 14, 1852, Armstrong–Chapman
Papers. See also Charles R. Bishop to Joel Turrill, October 9, 1851, Turrill
Collection.

[91] Some of the more "substantial" planters were also able to get loans at 12% from the
government. AH, Privy Council Record, VIb, pp. 548, 552 *ff*.

[92] See Kuykendall, *Hawaiian Kingdom*, I, pp. 324–325, for more detail.

⁹³ *Pacific Commercial Advertiser*, August 30, 1860. For a sampling of comments indicating rising confidence in sugar, see *Pacific Commercial Advertiser*. November 25,
1858, March 17, 1859; *Polynesian*, April 16, 1859.

⁹⁴ Oʻahu had a handful of plantations. Closest to Honolulu was that of J.H. Wood in
Nuʻuanu. He acted as his own agent. The J.H. Wood Papers, MSS, AH, give a good
picture of the running of a plantation.

⁹⁵ The growth of the system is reflected in classified advertisements in the Honolulu
papers, from which this information is taken. For a summary, statement on C.
Brewer, see Sullivan, *C. Brewer*, pp. 111–113, 123.

⁹⁶ *Pacific Commercial Advertiser*, August 25, 1866.

⁹⁷ *Pacific Commercial Advertiser*, January 19, 1867.

⁹⁸ For Walker, Allen's bankruptcy, see *Pacific Commercial Advertiser* and *Hawaiian
Gazette* from October, 1866, to October, 1867. Progress reports of creditors' meetings and sales of property appeared frequently, especially during January–May,
1867.

⁹⁹ For improvements in growing and manufacturing, see Morgan, *Hawaii*, pp. 181–
185; Kuykendall, *Hawaiian Kingdom*, I, p. 326, II, pp. 145–146. As far as Honolulu
itself was concerned, the most important man in this process was David M. Weston,
whose adaptation of the centrifugal principle in sugar-drying was a great success.
Weston also started the Honolulu Iron Works (1853), which came to specialize in
the making and repair of sugar machinery.

¹⁰⁰ *Hawaiian Gazette*, June 24, 1865; *Pacific Commercial Advertiser*, July 1, 1865.

¹⁰¹ See *Hawaiian Gazette* and *Pacific Commercial Advertiser*, July–September, 1865, for
arguments on both sides.

¹⁰² *Pacific Commercial Advertiser*, August 18, 1866; *Hawaiian Gazette*, August 18, 1866.

¹⁰³ *Pacific Commercial Advertiser*, February 23, March 2, April 6, 1867; *Hawaiian Gazette*,
February 27, March 6, 27, 1867.

¹⁰⁴ *Hawaiian Gazette*, August 28, September 18, 25, 1867; *Pacific Commercial Advertiser*,
August 31, September 21, 1867.

¹⁰⁵ For the adulteration scandal, see Z. Spalding to William Seward, August 26, 1868,
USDS, Consular Letters, Honolulu, XI, and following letters. The United States
federal court decision was published in *Hawaiian Gazette*, March 2, 1870. For
comment on the case see *Hawaiian Gazette*, September 30, October 14, 1868; *Pacific
Commercial Advertiser*, January 1, 29, February 19, March 5, 12, 26, 1870.

¹⁰⁶ Morgan, *Hawaii*, pp. 195–196; Kuykendall, *Hawaiian Kingdom*, II, p. 63.

¹⁰⁷ By 1876, four of the "Big Five" firms which were to dominate the agency business
in the twentieth century were already established at Honolulu. C. Brewer & Co,
had developed out of James Hunnewell's retail store of the 1820s. The British partnerships of Starkey, Janion, and Janion, Green, ultimately became Theo. Davies &
Co. The German Henry Hackfeld came to Honolulu in 1849; his firm, Hackfeld
& Co, became American Factors after the First World War. Castle & Cooke was

founded in 1841 by two former American Protestant missionaries. The only one of the "Big Five" which originated outside Honolulu was Alexander & Baldwin, a Maui plantation partnership between two missionary sons. Castle & Cooke did their agency work until 1894, when Alexander & Baldwin opened their own office at Honolulu. For the Bishop Bank, see Cecil G. Tilton, *The History of Banking in Hawaii* (Honolulu, 1927), pp. 26–59; Kent, *Charles Reed Bishop*, pp. 42–47.

[108] Others followed. In the years 1852–1864, 704 Chinese were imported under the auspices of the Agricultural Society. President of the Bureau of Immigration, *Report*, 1886, pp. 266–271. A note on the use of the word "coolie:" in the Pacific labor trade, it sometimes referred to men kidnapped or forced into service. At other times, the meaning was broader, including any bonded or indentured or contract laborer. The second meaning was the one current in Hawai'i. Cf. Gunther Paul Barth, *Bitter Strength; A History of the Chinese in the United States, 1850-1870* (Cambridge, 1964), pp. 50-52.

[109] For a brief account of Chinese in the islands up to mid-century, see Clarence Glick, "The Chinese Migrant in Hawaii: A Study in Accommodation," unpublished Ph.D. thesis (Chicago, 1938), pp. 5–7. Glick's thesis is the only full-length study of the Chinese in Hawai'i.

[110] For a typical comment, see Gilman, "Honolulu–1848."

[111] *Pacific Commercial Advertiser*, November 20, 1856, contains the comment about Chinese social ineptitude. Other accounts of the ball are in *Polynesian*, November 15, 1856, David Gregg Diary, November 9, 10, 13, 1856; Gregg to John Forsythe, November 16, 1856, Gregg Letter Books; Theodore C. Heuck to Albertine, December 7, 1856, Heuck Papers.

[112] *Polynesian*, October 9, 1852, January 1, 8, 15, 1853; *Hawaiian Reports*, I, pp. 85-87.

[113] AH, Privy Council Petitions, March 5, 1857; AH, Privy Council Record, X, pp. 130–138; S. Spencer to W. Parke, June 4, 1857, AH, Interior Department Letter Book, VI, 489; Chief Justice, *Report*, 1857, p. 13; *Polynesian*, March 2, June 13, December 12, 1857; *Pacific Commercial Advertiser*, January 28, 1858. It is very clear from the tone of comment that Chinese vagrants upset white Honolulans much more than Hawaiian vagrants did.

[114] AH, Privy Council Record, X, p. 256.

[115] *Pacific Commercial Advertiser*, November 26, 1859.

[116] *Polynesian*, December 3, 1859.

[117] The best single account of discussion and action on the problem of migration is in Kuykendall, *Hawaiian Kingdom*, II, Ch. VI.

[118] Between 1852 and 1876, 3,908 Chinese were imported, compared with 148 Japanese and 223 South Sea Islanders. President of the Bureau of Immigration, *Report*, 1886, pp. 266–271.

[119] *Hawaiian Gazette*, September 2, 1868, said "very few" went back immediately to China.

[120] Between 1853 and 1872, about a third of all Chinese in the islands lived at Honolulu. The Chinese population of Honolulu rose from 124 in 1853 to 632 in 1872, and 1,299 in 1878. Glick, "The Chinese Migrant," p. 170.

[121] *Polynesian*, June 20, 27, 1857; Glick, "The Chinese Migrant," pp. 58–75.

[122] Glick, "The Chinese Migrant," pp. 85–87, 98.

[123] See, for example, J.S. Low to P. Kanoa, November 15, 1865, AH, Interior Department Letters, Miscellaneous; *Hawaiian Gazette*, December 23, 1865.

[124] *Pacific Commercial Advertiser*, February 10, 1866.

[125] *Pacific Commercial Advertiser*, July 21, 28, August 4, 1866; *Hawaiian Gazette*, July 21, 28, August 4, 1866.

[126] *Pacific Commercial Advertiser*, July 28, 1866.

[127] *Hawaiian Gazette*, August 4, 1866. Census figures put attitudes in proportion: in 1566, Honolulu had 13,521 inhabitants. Four out of five were native Hawaiians; more than seven out of eight had some Hawaiian blood. "Other foreigners," mostly haoles, numbered 1,851, and there were only 370 Chinese: 357 men and 13 women. In all the islands there were 1,206 Chinese, in a total population of about 63,000.

[128] Glick, "The Chinese Migrant," pp. 124–125.

[129] The American Minister to Hawai'i published the text of the 1867 resolutions and an abstract of the 1862 act in the *Hawaiian Gazette* and the *Pacific Commercial Advertiser* for some weeks beginning early in September, 1868.

[130] The division of the Protestant missionaries and their offspring on this question is interesting. Amos Cooke, co-founder of Castle & Cooke, had been an ardent abolitionist in the forties. He had since retired from business, but his partner, Samuel N. Castle, emerged in the sixties as the great voice of property-holding conservatism in the sugar industry. Supporting him were S.G. Wilder (son-in-law of Gerrit Judd) and Samuel T. Alexander (son of missionary W. P. Alexander) who founded with Henry P. Baldwin (son of Dwight Baldwin) the sugar house of Alexander & Baldwin. Charles Judd, son of Gerrit, was for the contract system; Allen Judd, Charles' brother, was against it on moral grounds. Other energetic opponents of the contract system were missionary sons Curtis J. Lyons, Sanford Ballard Dole, and Luther H. Gulick. In every case listed above, economic interest or lack of it conditioned the stand taken on contract labor. Members of the missionary family, of course, were not the only ones involved in the argument.

[131] See Katharine Coman, *The History of Contract Labor in the Hawaiian Islands*, American Economic Association, *Publications*, Third Series, IV, p. 3 (August, 1903).

[132] Typical statements by Whitney are in *Pacific Commercial Advertiser*. March 27, June 12, 1869, September 3, 1870.

[133] *Pacific Commercial Advertiser*, September 3, 24, October 1, 1870, October 12, 1872. *Bennett's Own*, a short-lived weekly which argued that the contract system was producing a nation of capitalists and paupers by driving the mechanic classes out of existence suspended publication almost at the same time as Whitney sold the *Advertiser*.

[134] The various meetings are reported in *Pacific Commercial Advertiser*, October 16, 23, 30, November 6, 1869; and in *Hawaiian Gazette* and *Kuokoa* for the same period.

[135] Debates in the legislature were printed in *Hawaiian Gazette* and *Pacific Commercial Advertiser*, May–July, 1870.

[136] *Pacific Commercial Advertiser*, November 6, 1869.

[137] See, for example, *Pacific Commercial Advertiser*, August 13, 1870.

[138] *Pacific Commercial Advertiser*, August 6, 13, 1870.

[139] *Pacific Commercial Advertiser*, September 3, 1870. Conflicting comment on the *Dolores Ugarte* case appeared in the *Advertiser* and the *Hawaiian Gazette* throughout September.

[140] The later period is discussed at length in Glick, "The Chinese Migrant," *passim*.

[141] The most complete published version of the diplomacy of the reciprocity and annexation movements to 1876 is in Sylvester K. Stevens, *American Expansion in Hawaii* (Harrisburg, 1945), pp. 46–140. A shorter version is in Kuykendall, *Hawaiian Kingdom*, II, *passim*, and III, early chapters. Between them, these authors have fairly well exhausted the subject from a diplomatic point of view. Their findings are set forth in heavily-documented form in the works cited above. I have very little to add. My account simply concentrates as much as possible on events in Honolulu, with enough general background to make happenings intelligible.

[142] See, for example, the petition printed in *Hawaiian Gazette*, October 14, 1868.

[143] See Chapter VII above.

[144] A full account of the significance of the constitutional changes is in Kuykendall, *Hawaiian Kingdom*, II, pp. 127–134.

[145] Kuykendall, *Hawaiian Kingdom*, II, pp. 207–208, 213–214, collects evidence on the background of the *Lackawanna* visit.

[146] See, for example, first mentions of the projected visit in *Pacific Commercial Advertiser*, June 2, 16, 1866.

[147] For a typical anti-Reynolds attitude see R. Wyllie to Sir John Bowring, May 19, 1861, AH, FO Letter Book, XXXVIII, p. 11 *ff*.

[148] *Pacific Commercial Advertiser*, February 9, April 20, May 11, June 15, 29, 1867. Henry Whitney of the *Advertiser* was flirting with annexationism at this point, and he made every effort to see that Reynolds was presented in a good light.

[149] McCook to Seward, July 23, August 5, 1867, USDS, Dispatches, Hawai'i, XII. See also several letters in AH, FO & Ex, Consul-General at New York, 1867.

[150] AH, Cabinet Council Minutes, September 30, 1867.

[151] *Hawaiian Gazette*, October 7, 1867.

[152] See letters in AH, FO & Ex, C.C. Harris Mission to Washington; AH, Cabinet Council Minutes, December 9, 1867.

[153] Frequent comments on the cold atmosphere may be found in *Pacific Commercial Advertiser* and *Hawaiian Gazette* for March–April, 1868. For the Hilo incident, see AH, Cabinet Council Minutes, March 2, 1868; F. Hutchison to R. Lyman, March 2, 1868, and following letters in AH, Interior Department Letter Book, VIII, pp. 236–249; Lyman to Hutchison, March 26, April 13, 1868, AH, Interior Department Letters, Miscellaneous.

[154] *Pacific Commercial Advertiser*, May 9, 1868.

[155] For the background of the visit, see Kuykendall, *Hawaiian Kingdom*, II, pp. 216–217. Spalding's letters to his father, December 10, 1867, January 15, March 29, April 14, 1868, are in USDS, Dispatches, Hawai'i, XII.

[156] This, at least, was Spalding's story; see Spalding to his father, March 29, 1868, USDS, Dispatches, Hawai'i, XII.

[157] By then, a list of American agents, published at Washington, had reached the islands. *Pacific Commercial Advertiser*, August 15, 1868. See also several letters in AH, FO & Ex, US Minister, 1868.

[158] Kuykendall, *Hawaiian Kingdom*, II, p. 217.

[159] *Hawaiian Gazette*, May 28, 1869.

[160] News of the failure was printed in *Pacific Commercial Advertiser*, July 2, 1870.

[161] *Pacific Commercial Advertiser*, November 19, 1870.

[162] Tariffs and the growth of local industry were discussed at the public meetings of late 1869 called to evaluate the contract labor system. See *Bennett's Own*, October 19, 1869; *Pacific Commercial Advertiser*, November 20, 27, December 11, 1869, January 1, 8, 1870.

[163] C. de Varigny to Manley Hopkins, December 5, 1867, AH, FO & Ex, Consul-General at London.

[164] *Pacific Commercial Advertiser*, April 16, June 25, July 2, 30, 1870.

[165] Merze Tate, "The Myth of Hawaii's Swing Toward Australasia and Canada," *Pacific Historical Review*, XXXIII, 3 (August, 1964), p. 281, has a convenient table prepared from Hawaiian customhouse statistics, showing comparative exports to American and British ports up to 1882.

[166] People at Honolulu were not above exploiting it for their own benefit. In 1874, when the expansionist New Zealand premier, Julius Vogel, was talking in terms of a British "Grand Dominion" in the Pacific, the Honolulu papers carried stories of the arrival of a New Zealand government agent to talk over reciprocity and loans. Tate, "The Myth of Hawaii's Swing Toward Australasia and Canada," pp. 275–278, shows that this was a fabrication, which nonetheless led the United States Minister to Hawai'i to write to Washington in some urgency. Nothing came of it, of course.

167 "Correspondence Relating To The Last Hours of Kamehameha V," *Hawaiian Historical Society, Annual Report,* 6 (Honolulu, 1898), pp. 11–16; AH, Cabinet Council Minutes, January 7, 1873; Kuykendall, *Hawaiian Kingdom,* II, pp. 239–242.

168 The election campaign was followed closely in *Pacific Commercial Advertiser* and *Hawaiian Gazette* during the last half of December, 1872.

169 For a good eyewitness account of the legislative vote and the inauguration, see Queen Emma to Eugen Hasslocher, January 17; 1873, Hasslocher Papers, MSS, AH.

170 *Pacific Commercial Advertiser,* January 11, 1873.

171 Theophilus Davies to Granville, February 11, 1873, FO 58/136; C.R. Bishop to Manley Hopkins, April 30, 1873, AH, FO Letter Book, LII, p. 184.

172 *Hawaiian Gazette,* February 22, 1873.

173 W. Belknap to J.M. Schofield, June 4, 1872, USDS, Miscellaneous Letters.

174 See Kuykendall, *Hawaiian Kingdom,* II, pp. 247–249.

175 *Pacific Commercial Advertiser,* February 15, 1873.

176 Peirce to Hamilton Fish, February 10, 28, 1873, USDS, Dispatches, Hawai'i, XV.

177 *Pacific Commercial Advertiser,* March 1, 1873; *Hawaiian Gazette,* July 9, 1873; AH, Cabinet Council Minutes, May 13, June 9, 1873.

178 Bishop to Peirce, July 7, 1873, AH, FO Letter Book, LII, —.

179 Robert C. Lydecker, comp., *Roster Legislatures of Hawaii, 1841-1918* (Honolulu, 1918), *passim.*

180 See, for example, *Polynesian,* January 24, 1852, January 11, 1862; *Pacific Commercial Advertiser,* January 9, 1862, February 8, 15, 22, 29, 1868.

181 As, for example, those in favor of Gerrit Judd in 1853, in favor of legalizing liquor sales to natives in 1862, and against the coolie system in 1869–1870.

182 Henry Whitney's *Pacific Commercial Advertiser* was ardently pro-Union. The *Polynesian,* semi-official organ of the neutral kingdom, was neutral in tone, but was frequently blackguarded as a "secessionist rag" by the overwrought Whitney.

183 Spencer to Abraham Lincoln, July 8, 1861, USDS, Miscellaneous Letters; R. Wyllie to Kamehameha IV, December 1, 1861, AH, FO & Ex, December 1, 1861; Wyllie to Spencer, December 27, 1861, AH, FO Letter Book, XXXVII, pp. 88–89. For a good account of Spencer's life, see *Hawaiian Annual for 1924.* pp. 117–125.

184 For these happenings, see *Polynesian,* November 10, 1860, June 29, 1861; *Pacific Commercial Advertiser,* September 26, 1861. The mock elections were held at the same time as those in the United States—November, 1860, and November, 1864, and were reported in detail in the Honolulu papers, with comment before and after.

[185] See, for example, R. Wyllie to C.W. Wheat, December 2, 1855, AH, FO & Ex, Miscellaneous Foreign. The family of Richard Armstrong was particularly active: Samuel Chapman Armstrong fought with the Union Army, rising to the rank of general; and Jennie Armstrong worked for the Freedmen's Bureau after the war. Several other missionary sons enlisted in the Union forces, some for definably abolitionist reasons.

[186] David Gregg, a midwesterner who found the Hawaiian monarchy congenial and eventually accepted a post in the cabinet, noted with scorn and indignation the racism of Cartwright and others during the late fifties. David Gregg Diary, June 3, September 12, 1857, January 7, 1858, January 18, 1859.

[187] "Ka Makamae Hawaii" was published in an English translation in *Hawaiian Gazette*, February 19, 1868. In December, 1867 and January, 1868, the government's Hawaiian-language paper *Au Okoa* ran a series of letters signed "A True Hawaiian" expressing much the same sentiments.

At the same time, a native prophet named Kaona appeared on Hawai'i, preaching the end of the world and the second coining of Christ. His millenarianism had distinct anti-haole overtones, and when a white sheriff and posse tried to remove the Kaona-ites from the land where they had gathered to await Christ's coming, the sheriff was killed. A short account of the affair is in Kuykendall, *Hawaiian Kingdom*, II, pp. 105–106. Kuykendall wrote before the nature of such cults was widely understood. Kaona's movement deserves fuller study in relation to others of its kind elsewhere in the Pacific.

[188] *Pacific Commercial Advertiser*, February 21, 1868. Charges and counter-charges were made in the *Advertiser* and the *Hawaiian Gazette*, the *Kuokoa* and the *Au Okoa* throughout December, 1867, and January–February, 1868. See also *Maile Quarterly*, January, 1868.

[189] Gibson's *Nūhou* is the best single source for the substance and quality of Hawaiian feeling at Honolulu in 1873–1874. The remarks in this paragraph are drawn from *Nūhou* over that period. As with other Hawaiian-language papers, it is hard to tell whether *Nūhou* reflected native opinion or distorted it. I have gone on the assumption that Gibson knew what was in the minds of Hawaiians, Certainly his later political career suggests that he and the Hawaiians had some sort of affinity.

[190] This Hawaiian mele was translated in *Nūhou*, November 18, 1873.

[191] Extended accounts of the day-by-day course of the mutiny appeared in *Pacific Commercial Advertiser*, September 13, 1873; *Hawaiian Gazette*, September 10, 17, 1873; *Nūhou*, September 9, 12, 16, 19, 1873. These accounts agree in the main; they differ only on inconsequential matters. They will not be cited repeatedly here. Kuykendall, *Hawaiian Kingdom*, II, pp. 259–261, describes the uprising briefly, and there is an excellent detailed treatment in Richard A. Greer, "Mutiny In The Royal Barracks," *Pacific Historical Review*, XXXI, 4 (November, 1962), pp. 349–358. Greer cites newspapers and documents in AH exhaustively. Events described but not footnoted in my account may be readily checked in Greer's article or in the newspapers. My citations are limited to manuscript sources, with emphasis on those not available to Kuykendall and Greer.

[192] C.A. Castle to his wife, September 6–28, 1873, HMCS, entry for September 7. Cited hereafter as Castle's letter, with date.

[193] Castle's letter, entry for September 7; Kaleleonālani (Queen Emma) to Dearest Coz (Peter Young Ka'eo), September 10, 1873, Emma Collection (Nylen-Altman); Theodore C. Heuck to My Beloved Ones, September 10, 1873, Heuck Papers.

[194] Castle's letter, entry for September 10.

[196] Castle's letter, entry for September 10.

[197] Kalākaua to J.O. Dominis, September 9, 1873. AH, FO & Ex, Army and Navy.

[198] Lunalilo to J.O. Dominis, September 9, 1873. AH, FO & Ex, Army and Navy; Dominis to C.R. Bishop, September 10, 1873, AH, FO & Ex, Army and Navy.

[199] C.R. Bishop to W.C. Parke, September 12, 1873, Parke Papers.

[200] The best account of the role of the militia is in Castle's letter, entry for September 10. Castle was an officer in the Honolulu Rifles. As the letter makes clear, Greer, "Mutiny In The Royal Barracks," p. 353, is in error when he says the volunteer companies had no native members. See also my discussion of the militia in Chapter VII above.

[201] Castle's letter, entry for September 10.

[202] Castle's letter, entry for September 10.

[203] Theodore C. Heuck to My Beloved Ones, September 10, 1873, Heuck Papers.

[204] Castle's letter, entry for September 10.

[205] Castle's letter, entry for September 10.

[206] C.R. Bishop to J.O. Dominis, September 10, 1873, AH, FO & Ex, Army and Navy; Castle's letter, entry for September 14.

[207] *Pacific Commercial Advertiser*, September 13, 1873; *Hawaiian Gazette*, September 17, 1873.

[208] Lunalilo's order, dated September 12, 1873, is in AH, FO & Ex, Army and Navy.

[209] AH, Cabinet Council Minutes, September 12, 13, October 1, 1873; C.R. Bishop to W.C. Parke, September 12, 1873; A.F. Judd to D. Dayton, September 12, 1873; Judd to Parke, September 12, 1873, all in Parke Papers; Parke to L. Severance, September 13, 1873, AH, Marshal's Letter Book; Parke to W.O. Smith, September 15, 1873, AH, Marshal's Letter Book,

[210] Castle's letter, entry for September 14.

[211] Theodore C. Heuck to My Beloved Ones, September 10, 1873, Heuck Papers; Castle's letter, entries for September 20, 22.

[212] Queen Emma to Eugen Hasslocher, February 17, 1873, Hasslocher Papers; Theophilus Davies to Granville, February 11, 1873, FO 58/136.

[213] Queen Emma to Peter Young, September 10, 1873, Emma Collection (Nylen-Altman); Castle's letter, entry for September 27.

[214] Queen Emma to Peter Young Ka'eo, August 26, September 5, 1873, Emma Collection (Nylen-Altman); Charles Alfred Castle to his wife, September 2, 1873, HMCS; Henry Peirce to Hamilton Fish, September 2, 1873, USDS, Dispatches, Hawai'i, XV. Cf. Theophilus Davies to Granville, August 26, September 13, 1873, FO 58/136.

[215] AH, Cabinet Council Minutes, September 29, 1873.

[216] AH, Cabinet Council Minutes, November 14, 1873.

[217] See especially AH, Cabinet Council Minutes, September 16–17, 1873, January 20, 1874.

[218] G. Trousseau to A.F. Judd, February 11, 1874, AH, Cabinet Council Minutes.

CHAPTER 9

1   Peter Young Ka'eo to Emma, August 8, 1873, Emma Collection (Nylen-Altman); Kekelaokalani to Emma, November 23, 1873, Emma Collection (Nylen-Altman); Theophilus Davies to Granville, November 12, 1873, FO 58/136; Charles Alfred Castle to his wife, November 13, 16, 1873, HMCS.

2   Emma to Peter Young Ka'eo, September 2, 20, 26, 1873, Emma Collection (Nylen-Altman); Emma to Lucy [Peabody], January 19, 1874, Emma Collection (Archives) Correspondence, 1867–1884. There was even some talk in the town that Lunalilo would marry Emma. *Nūhou*, January 6, 1874; Charles Alfred Castle to his wife, January 7, 1874, HMCS.

3   For a sampling of anti-Kalākaua comment, see Henry Peirce to Hamilton Fish, May 26, September 2, November 11, December 18, 1873, USDS, Dispatches, Hawai'i, XV; Theophilus Davies to Granville, August 26, November 7, 1873, FO 58/136; Charles Alfred Castle to his wife, November 13, 1873, HMCS.

4   Henry Peirce to Hamilton Fish, February 7, 1874, USDS, Dispatches, Hawai'i, XVI.

5   The MS speech is in Emma Collection (Nylen-Altman), Documents Concerning 1874 Election, which also contains drafts of slogans and election posters.

6   Theodore C. Heuck to My Beloved Ones, February 12–22, 1874. Heuck Papers; Curtis Lyons to Dear Folks, February 14, 1874, Lyons Papers, AH.

7   Curtis Lyons letter cited above.

8   Parke to T.W. Everett, February 9 [?], 1874, AH, Marshal's Letter Book.

9   Parke to Jailor Fyfe, February 10, 1874, AH, Marshal's Letter Book.

10 C.R. Bishop to R.H. Stanley, January 29, 1874, AH, FO Letter Book, LII, pp. 522–523; AH, Cabinet Council Minutes, January 20, 29, February 2, 1874.

11 For the events of February 12, see Theodore C. Heuck to My Beloved Ones, February 12–22, 1874, Heuck Papers; Curtis Lyons to Dear Folks, February 14, 1874, Lyons Papers; J. Wodehouse to Granville, February 20, 1874, FO 58/143; Maria Patton Chamberlain to M.J. and Bella, February 12, 1874, Chamberlain Papers, AH; Emma Taylor, "Old Hawaii In Retrospect," typescript in Emma Taylor Papers, AH; W.C. Parke to T.W. Everett, February 14, 1874, AH, Marshal's Letter Book; Parke to L. Severance, February 16, 1874, AH, Marshal's Letter Book. Newspaper accounts are collected in "The Second Interregnum: A Complete Resume of Events From The Death To The Burial Of His Late Majesty Lunalilo" (Honolulu, 1874), which also contains texts of official notices and campaign documents. This pamphlet is in a scrapbook in Heuck Papers.

12 Parke to L. Severance, February 16, 1874, AH, Marshal's Letter Book. See also AH, Interior Department, Miscellaneous, Claims For Reimbursement, Riot of 1874. From then on the legislature was to meet at Ali'iōlani Hale.

13 Peirce to Hamilton Fish, February 7, 1874, USDS, Dispatches, Hawai'i, XVI.

14 C.R. Bishop to Emma [n.d., but from other evidence February 12, 1874], Emma Collection (Archives), 1867–1884; Theodore C. Heuck to My Beloved Ones, February 12–22, 1874, Heuck Papers.

15 A draft of the statement, later published, is in Emma Collection (Nylen-Altman). See also a document by W.L. Green, addressed to Committee of Privy Council on the February 12 riots, undated, filed in AH, FO & Ex, Privy Council Documents, ND.

16 See Curtis Lyons to Dear Folks, February 14, 1874, Lyons Papers; William Parke to T.W. Everett, February 9 [?], 1874, AH, Marshal's Letter Book; Parke to S.H. Phillips, February 23, 1874, AH, Marshal's Letter Book; Document of W.L. Green to Privy Council Committee on February 12 riots, AH, Privy Council Documents, ND. During her campaign, Emma had said she was rich and needed no salary; but by mid-March her disappointed creditors were claiming about $27,000 from her. Parke to Everett, March 19, 1874, AH, Marshal's Letter Book.

17 A.S. Hartwell to Emma, April 20, 1874, Emma Collection (Nylen-Altman); Charles Alfred Castle to his wife, April 15, 1874, HMCS.

18 AH, Cabinet Council Minutes, February 14, 1874; C.R. Bishop to all diplomats and consuls, February 14, 1874, AH, FO Letter Book, LII, p. 557.

19 W.L. Green to A.S. Hartwell, February 20, 1874, AH, FO Letter Book, LIII, p. 567; AH, Cabinet Council Minutes, February 21, 26, 1874; AH, Privy Council Record, XII, p. 39.

20 Theodore C. Heuck to My Beloved Ones, February 12–22, 1874, Heuck Papers.

21 J. K. Naone to Emma, April 16, 1874, Emma Collection (Nylen-Altman).

22 Parke to D. Dayton and S.G. Wilder, August 6, 1874, AH, Marshal's Letter Book.

23 Juliette Cooke to Sister, August 7, 1874, HMCS.

24 For the Zephyrin case, the first treason trial since the introduction of constitutional government, see J.P. Zephyrin to Emma, February 2, 1874, Emma Collection (Nylen-

Altman); Henry Peirce to Hamilton Fish, September 10, 1874, USDS, Dispatches, Hawai'i, XVI. Zephyrin wanted France to intervene, for reasons obscure. See French Commissioner Ballieu to Kalākaua, October 12, 1874, AH, FO & Ex, French Commissioner. Zephyrin's death sentence was commuted to ten years.

25 Alfons L. Korn and Mary Kawena Pukui, "News From Molokai: The Letters of Peter Young Ka'eo (Kekuaokalani) to Queen Emma, 1873–1876," *Pacific Historical Review*, XXXII, 1 (February, 1963), pp. 7–34, is based on the Emma Collection (Nylen-Altman).

26 Emma to Peter Young Ka'eo, December 16, 1875, Emma Collection (Nylen-Altman). I follow the translation and explanation in Korn and Pukui, "News From Molokai," 29.

27 Peter Young Ka'eo to Emma, April 3, 1874, Emma Collection (Nylen-Altman); Emma to Peter Young Ka'eo, February 5, 1876, Emma Collection (Nylen-Altman); Henry Peirce to Hamilton Fish, August 10, 16, 1876, USDS, Dispatches, Hawai'i, XVII. Document in AH, Attorney-General Miscellaneous Letters, September 30, 1876; Kalākaua to William Parke, May 31, 1877, Parke Papers. This last letter lists the names of nine men believed by Kalākaua to be conspiring to take his life. "All these men live at Queen Dowager Emmas, and all have firearms."

28 Peirce to Hamilton Fish, February 17, March 3, 1874, USDS, Dispatches, Hawai'i, XVI.

29 Peirce to Hamilton Fish, December 18, 1873, USDS, Dispatches, Hawai'i, XV. Cf. Charles Alfred Castle to his wife, November 13, 16, 17, 1873, HMCS.

30 Peirce to Fish, March 3, 1874, USDS, Dispatches, Hawai'i, XVI.

31 Green to Edward Reeve, April 8, 1874, AH, FO Letter Book, LII, p. 637. Cf. *Nūhou*, March 10, 1874.

32 William Parke to W.O. Smith, May 16, 22, 1874, AH, Marshal's Letter Book.

33 Charles Alfred Castle to his wife, December 20, 1873, HMCS.

34 See Kalākaua's speech at the opening of the 1874 legislature, in Lydecker, *Roster Legislatures*, p. 129.

35 *Pacific Commercial Advertiser*, June 27, 1874.

36 AH, Privy Council Record, XII, p. 93.

37 *Pacific Commercial Advertiser*, October 24, 1874. For their reports, see AH, FO & Ex, Envoy to Washington, 1874, 1875, 1876.

38 *Hawaiian Gazette*, November 18, 1874; *Pacific Commercial Advertiser*, November 21, 1874.

39 Kalākaua's American journey was followed in detail by the Honolulu papers, November–December, 1874, and January, 1875.

40 *Hawaiian Gazette*, January 6, 13, 20, 1875.

[41] Both Allen and Carter had heavy investments in sugar at the islands. For their negotiations with Fish, see AH, FO & Ex, Envoy to Washington, 1875, 1876; and Stevens, *American Expansion*, pp. 120 *ff*.

[42] *Hawaiian Gazette*, February 17, 1875.

[43] A quarter-century later, the United States Senate Committee on Foreign Relations made the relation between economics and politics clear: "The Hawaiian treaty was negotiated for the purpose of securing political control over those islands, making them industrially and commercially a part of the United States and preventing any other great power from acquiring a foothold there which might be adverse to the welfare and safety of our Pacific coast in time of war. *Senate Reports*, 53 Cong. 2 sess., Appendix No. 227. Cf. Stevens, *American Expansion*, pp. 125–130.

[44] *Hawaiian Gazette*, April 14, 1875.

[45] AH, Cabinet Council Minutes, April 9, 1875.

[46] *Hawaiian Gazette*, April 14, 1875.

[47] The San Francisco memorials were printed in *Hawaiian Gazette*, March 24, 1875. The refiners were brought into line later in 1875 when they agreed to drop opposition to the treaty in return for contracts with Honolulu sugar agencies.

[48] See documents in AH, FO & Ex, Envoy to Washington; and Elisha Allen Papers, MSS, Library of Congress, microfilm copy in UH.

[49] *Pacific Commercial Advertiser*, May 27, 1876; *Hawaiian Gazette*, May 31, 1876.

[50] For a sarcastic comment on ministerial ineptitude in handling these details, see *Pacific Commercial Advertiser*, June 24, 1876.

[51] *Hawaiian Gazette*, July 5, 1876; *Pacific Commercial Advertiser*, July 8, 1876.

[52] *Hawaiian Gazette*, July 26, 1876; *Pacific Commercial Advertiser*, July 29, 1876.

[53] *Hawaiian Gazette*, August 30, 1876; *Pacific Commercial Advertiser*, August 26, 1876.

[54] *Hawaiian Gazette*, September 20, 27, 1876; *Pacific Commercial Advertiser*; September 16, 23, 1876.

[55] For a sampling of this kind of comment, see *Hawaiian Gazette*, May 26, July 26, 1875. January 5, June 7 (supplement), 21, August 30, 1876. Cf. Emma to Peter Young Ka'eo, February 4, 1876, Emma Collection (Nylen-Altman).

[56] *Hawaiian Gazette*, September 13, 1876; *Pacific Commercial Advertiser*, August 26, September 26, 1876. See also Jacob Adler, "Claus Spreckels, Sugar King Of Hawaii: Interaction Of An Entrepreneur With An Island Community," unpublished Ph.D. thesis (Columbia, 1959). Ch. 1. Adler's thesis will shortly be published in revised form by the University of Hawai'i press.

[57] Sullivan, *C. Brewer*, p. 142.

Index

Prince Alexander, 194, 204, 213, 215, 216, 217, 218, 219, 383
Prince Lee Boo, 9, 11, 12
Prince Lot, 167, 202, 224, 237, 241, 261
Prince of Wales, 7, 355
Pūlaholaho, 162, 163, 166, 172, 173, 174, 176, 185
Puna, 103
Punchbowl, 1, 40, 85, 88, 95, 169, 170, 219, 245, 258, 315, 317, 327
Pupuka, 6
Pu'uloa, 2, 9, 10, 15, 21, 95, 353
Pu'uowaina, 1, 40, 45

Q
Queen Charlotte, 6
Queen Victoria, 166, 169, 227, 235, 263

R
Rees, Lewis, 117
Reiners, "Ming Ching," 299
Reynolds, Stephen, 64, 67, 69, 71, 74, 75, 76, 79, 80, 87, 89, 92, 93, 96, 98, 99, 106, 107, 117, 118, 121, 154, 155, 156, 170, 173, 174, 175, 176, 180, 181, 210, 215, 234, 235, 237, 293, 331, 359, 365, 366, 367, 368, 369, 370, 371, 372, 373, 374, 375, 376, 377, 378, 379, 380, 381, 382, 383, 384, 385, 387, 388, 389, 390, 391, 392, 393, 394, 395, 397, 398, 402, 407, 408, 411
Reynolds, William, 306
Rhodes, Godfrey, 330
Rice, W.H., 210
Richards, William, 58, 64, 72, 75, 92, 101, 106, 107, 115, 150, 161, 172, 177, 178, 179, 182, 208, 371, 376, 377, 385, 391, 394
Ricord, John, 115, 176, 181, 185, 187, 188, 208, 394, 401, 403
Riho-riho, 54
Rives, Jean, 38, 39, 74
Robertson, George N., 206, 207, 240, 381
Robinson, James, 106
Rooke, T.C.B., 86, 95, 198, 238, 385, 399,
409
"Rosebank," 190
Rotuma, 82
Rowe, Thomas, 275
Ruddacks, James, 184
Rurik, 27, 30, 31, 361, 362
Russell, Edward, 113, 233
Russia, 26, 27, 28, 29, 31
Ryckman, Garet W., 131

S
Sacramento River, 287
San Blas, Mexico, 164
sandalwood, 17, 25, 26, 27, 36, 37, 45, 47, 48, 51, 60, 65, 68, 69, 70, 80, 81, 82, 117, 119, 368, 372, 378
San Francisco, 126, 129, 130, 131, 132, 134, 193, 194, 195, 197, 198, 211, 212, 217, 225, 276, 278, 279, 280, 281, 282, 286, 287, 288, 294, 295, 296, 297, 304, 306, 307, 308, 327, 328, 329, 330, 381, 382, 406, 408, 422, 423, 424, 426, 438
S. B. Wheeler, 131
Schäfferthal, 27
Schäffer, Georg Anton, 26
Schofield, John M., 310
Sérieuse, 191, 192
Serriere, Dr., 81
Severance, Luther, 192, 195, 207, 211, 393, 394, 397, 398, 399, 400
Seward, William, 210, 427
Shenandoah, 291, 329
Sherman, George, 195, 398
Short, Patrick, 88, 89, 100
Simpson, Alexander, 164, 165, 166, 168, 174, 175, 395
Simpson, George, 163, 392, 394
Sistare, 62
Skinner, Henry, 174, 175, 176
Smith, Charles Rand, 231
Smith, J. Mott, 202, 423
Smith, Lowell, 102, 104, 200, 247, 248, 377, 395, 411, 412, 413
Smith, Marcia, 145
Snibbs, Governor B.F., 148

About the Author

GAVAN DAWS has written twelve books, published worldwide, in a life that has taken him back and forth between the United States and Australia, with stints in Europe and Asia. He first came to Hawai'i in 1958. His books about the islands include *Shoal of Time; Holy Man: Father Damien of Molokai; and Land and Power in Hawaii.* He has been named a Distinguished Living Historian by the Hawaiian Historical Society, and is the recipient of the Hawai'i Award for Literature. The University of Hawai'i has named him a Distinguished Alumnus, and he was the first recipient of the Regents' Award for Excellence in Teaching. He has been a Senior Fellow at the Center for Cultural and Technical Interchange between East and West. Beyond Hawai'i, he has been awarded grants from, among others, the National Endowment for the Arts, the National Endowment for the Humanities, the American Philosophical Society, and the Australian Film Commission. His documentary films about the Pacific have won awards internationally. For fifteen years, he headed historical research on the Pacific and Southeast Asia at the Institute for Advanced Studies, Australian National University. During that time he was elected a fellow of the Academy of Humanities in Australia, and he served on the UNESCO Commission on the Scientific and Cultural History of Humankind. He and his wife live in Honolulu.